D1068595

Authorized Self-Study Guide
Cisco IP Telephony (CIPT)
Second Edition

Jeremy D. Cioara, CCIE No. 11727

Cisco Press

800 East 96th Street
Indianapolis, IN 46240 USA

Cisco IP Telephony (CIPT) (Authorized Self-Study Guide), Second Edition

Jeremy D. Cioara, CCIE No. 11727

Published by:
Cisco Press
800 East 96th Street
Indianapolis, IN 46240 USA

Printed in the United States of America 1 2 3 4 5 6 7 8 9 0

First Printing October 2006

Library of Congress Cataloging-in-Publication Number: 2006926698

ISBN: 1-58705-261-x

Warning and Disclaimer

This book is designed to provide information about the Cisco Unified CallManager 4.x platform as it relates to Cisco CIPT certification exam 642-444. Every effort has been made to make this book as complete and as accurate as possible, but no warranty or fitness is implied.

The information is provided on an "as is" basis. The authors, Cisco Press, and Cisco Systems, Inc., shall have neither liability nor responsibility to any person or entity with respect to any loss or damages arising from the information contained in this book or from the use of the discs or programs that may accompany it.

The opinions expressed in this book belong to the author and are not necessarily those of Cisco Systems, Inc.

The Cisco Press self-study book series is as described, intended for self-study. It has not been designed for use in a classroom environment. Only Cisco Learning Partners displaying the following logos are authorized providers of Cisco curriculum. If you are using this book within the classroom of a training company that does not carry one of these logos, then you are not preparing with a Cisco trained and authorized provider. For information on Cisco Learning Partners please visit:www.cisco.com/go/authorizedtraining. To provide Cisco with any information about what you may believe is unauthorized use of Cisco trademarks or copyrighted training material, please visit: http://www.cisco.com/logo/infringement.html.

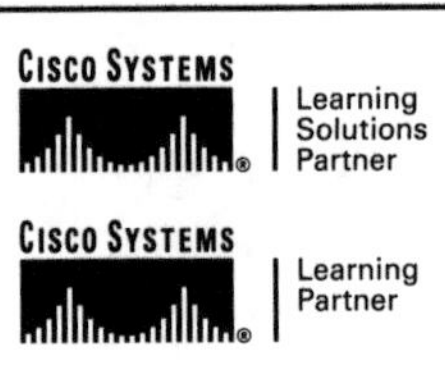

Corporate and Government Sales

Cisco Press offers excellent discounts on this book when ordered in quantity for bulk purchases or special sales. For more information, please contact: **U.S. Corporate and Government Sales** 1-800-382-3419 corpsales@pearsontechgroup.com

For sales outside of the U.S. please contact: **International Sales** 1-317-581-3793 international@pearsontechgroup.com

Trademark Acknowledgments

All terms mentioned in this book that are known to be trademarks or service marks have been appropriately capitalized. Cisco Press or Cisco Systems, Inc., cannot attest to the accuracy of this information. Use of a term in this book should not be regarded as affecting the validity of any trademark or service mark.

Feedback Information

At Cisco Press, our goal is to create in-depth technical books of the highest quality and value. Each book is crafted with care and precision, undergoing rigorous development that involves the unique expertise of members from the professional technical community.

Readers' feedback is a natural continuation of this process. If you have any comments regarding how we could improve the quality of this book, or otherwise alter it to better suit your needs, you can contact us through e-mail at feedback@ciscopress.com. Please make sure to include the book title and ISBN in your message.

We greatly appreciate your assistance.

Publisher: Paul Boger

Cisco Representative: Anthony Wolfenden

Cisco Press Program Manager: Jeff Brady

Executive Editor: Brett Bartow

Production Manager: Patrick Kanouse

Development Editor: Andrew Cupp

Project Editor: Mandie Frank

Copy Editor: Karen Annett

Technical Editors: Michael Coffin, Dennis Hartmann, Larry Roberts, Kevin Wallace

Publishing Coordinator: Vanessa Evans

Cover and Book Designer: Louisa Adair

Composition: Mark Shirar

Indexer: Brad Herriman

Corporate Headquarters
Cisco Systems, Inc.
170 West Tasman Drive
San Jose, CA 95134-1706
USA
www.cisco.com
Tel: 408 526-4000
800 553-NETS (6387)
Fax: 408 526-4100

European Headquarters
Cisco Systems International BV
Haarlerbergpark
Haarlerbergweg 13-19
1101 CH Amsterdam
The Netherlands
www-europe.cisco.com
Tel: 31 0 20 357 1000
Fax: 31 0 20 357 1100

Americas Headquarters
Cisco Systems, Inc.
170 West Tasman Drive
San Jose, CA 95134-1706
USA
www.cisco.com
Tel: 408 526-7660
Fax: 408 527-0883

Asia Pacific Headquarters
Cisco Systems, Inc.
Capital Tower
168 Robinson Road
#22-01 to #29-01
Singapore 068912
www.cisco.com
Tel: +65 6317 7777
Fax: +65 6317 7799

Cisco Systems has more than 200 offices in the following countries and regions. Addresses, phone numbers, and fax numbers are listed on the **Cisco.com Web site at www.cisco.com/go/offices.**

Argentina • Australia • Austria • Belgium • Brazil • Bulgaria • Canada • Chile • China PRC • Colombia • Costa Rica • Croatia • Czech Republic Denmark • Dubai, UAE • Finland • France • Germany • Greece • Hong Kong SAR • Hungary • India • Indonesia • Ireland • Israel • Italy Japan • Korea • Luxembourg • Malaysia • Mexico • The Netherlands • New Zealand • Norway • Peru • Philippines • Poland • Portugal Puerto Rico • Romania • Russia • Saudi Arabia • Scotland • Singapore • Slovakia • Slovenia • South Africa • Spain • Sweden Switzerland • Taiwan • Thailand • Turkey • Ukraine • United Kingdom • United States • Venezuela • Vietnam • Zimbabwe

Printed in the USA

About the Author

Jeremy D. Cioara, CCIE No. 11727, CCVP, MCSE, CNE, is the owner of AdTEC Networks and works as a network consultant, instructor, and author. He has been working in network technologies for more than a decade and has deployed networks worldwide. His current consulting work focuses on network and voice-over-IP (VoIP) implementations. Jeremy has written many books on Cisco network technology but has a true passion for educating individuals both in the classroom and through e-learning environments. Jeremy currently lives with his wife in Phoenix, AZ.

About the Technical Reviewers

Michael Coffin, CCIE No. 9789, is a technical marketing engineer at Cisco Systems and currently focuses his time on Cisco Mobility products. He began his career at Cisco in the Cisco Technical Assistance Center, where he worked on troubleshooting large service provider core networks. Then moved into the Cisco IP Communications Business Unit as a CallManager escalation engineer. Mike has contributed to several design guides and white papers, worked on supporting many large Cisco IP Telephony deployments, and often provides internal and external training around the world. Mike holds CCIE certifications in Routing & Switching, Service Provider, and Voice.

Dennis Hartmann, CCIE No. 15651, CCVP, CCIP, CCNP, MCSE, is a consultant for White Pine Communications. He has been a technical instructor teaching Cisco classes for Global Knowledge and providing network architecture work for customers. He teaches all of the classes associated with the CCVP certification, as well as all classes associated with the CCNP, CCIP, and optical specialist certifications.

Kevin Wallace, CCIE No. 7945, CCSI, CCVP, CCNP, CCDP, MCSE 4, CNE 4/5, is a full-time instructor for Thomson NETg. With 17 years of Cisco internetworking experience, Kevin has been a network design specialist for The Walt Disney World Resort and a network manager for Eastern Kentucky University. Kevin holds a bachelor of science degree in electrical engineering from the University of Kentucky. Among Kevin's publication credits are *Cisco Voice over IP (CVoice) Authorized Self-Study Guide,* Second Edition*; Voice over IP First-Step; CCDA/CCDP Flash Cards and Exam Practice Pack* (coauthored with Anthony Sequeira); *CCIE Routing and Switching Flash Cards and Exam Practice Pack* (coauthored with Anthony Sequeira); and *Cisco IP Telephony Flash Cards and Exam Practice Pack*, all of which are available from Cisco Press. Additionally, Kevin authored the *Cisco Enterprise Voice over Data Design* (EVoDD) 3.3 course, was a contributing author for the *Cisco IP Telephony Troubleshooting* (IPTT) 2.0 course, and has written for *Packet* magazine from Cisco Systems. Kevin also holds the IP Telephony Design Specialist, IP Telephony Operations Specialist, and IP Telephony Support Specialist CQS certifications.

Dedications

First and foremost, I'd like to thank Jesus Christ who continues to bless me in every way and keeps me from killing myself by doing something stupid. You will always be at the core of everything I do. Second, to my darling wife, Susan: Thank you for your support through all these projects that keep me glued to a computer screen through all hours of the day and night. You are a more wonderful companion than I could have ever hoped for. I love you! To the cricket chirping in the room right now: I hate you. If I ever find you, I'm going to feed you to my fish and dance merrily around the room as they eat you slowly. To my cat, Snuggles: Thanks for being soft. To the dog, Buttercup: I have nothing to say to you at this time, but at least I've acknowledged your existence. To all my readers: Be warned; this is what happens to you after months of writing hundreds of pages.

Acknowledgments

I'd like to give special recognition to Kevin Wallace, Larry Roberts, Michael Coffin, and Dennis Hartman for providing their expert technical knowledge in editing the book. As usual, they're not afraid to tell you when you're wrong.

A big "thank you" goes out to the production team for this book. Brett Bartow and Andrew Cupp have been incredibly professional and a pleasure to work with. I couldn't have asked for a finer team.

Contents at a Glance

Contents

Icons Used in This Book

Command Syntax Conventions

The conventions used to present command syntax in this book are the same conventions used in the IOS Command Reference. The Command Reference describes these conventions as follows:

- **Boldface** indicates commands and keywords that are entered literally as shown. In actual configuration examples and output (not general command syntax), boldface indicates commands that are manually input by the user (such as a **show** command).
- *Italic* indicates arguments for which you supply actual values.
- Vertical bars (|) separate alternative, mutually exclusive elements.
- Square brackets [ ] indicate optional elements.
- Braces { } indicate a required choice.
- Braces within brackets [{ }] indicate a required choice within an optional element.

Foreword

Cisco IP Telephony (CIPT), Second Edition is an excellent self-study resource for the CCVP CIPT exam. Whether you are studying to become CCVP certified or are simply seeking to gain a better understanding of VoIP and PSTN components and technologies, you will benefit from the information presented in this book.

Cisco Press Self-Study Guide titles are designed to help educate, develop, and grow the community of Cisco networking professionals. As an early-stage exam preparation product, this book presents a detailed and comprehensive introduction to the technologies used to install, configure, and support Cisco CallManager 4.1 in a Cisco network, including such features as security and video. Developed in conjunction with the Cisco certifications team, Cisco Press books are the only self-study books authorized by Cisco Systems.

Most networking professionals use a variety of learning methods to gain necessary skills. Cisco Press self-study titles are a prime source of content for some individuals and can also serve as an excellent supplement to other forms of learning. Training classes, whether delivered in a classroom or on the Internet, are a great way to quickly acquire new understanding. Hands-on practice is essential for anyone seeking to build, or hone, new skills. Authorized Cisco training classes, labs, and simulations are available exclusively from Cisco Learning Solutions Partners worldwide. Please visit http://www.cisco.com/go/training to learn more about Cisco Learning Solutions Partners.

I hope and expect that you'll find this guide to be an essential part of your exam preparation and a valuable addition to your personal library.

Don Field
Director, Certifications
Cisco Systems, Inc.
August 2006

Introduction

Professional certifications have been an important part of the computing industry for many years and will continue to become more important. Many reasons exist for these certifications, but the most popularly cited reason is that of credibility. All other considerations held equal, the certified employee/consultant/job candidate is considered more valuable than one who is not.

Goals and Methods

The most important and somewhat obvious goal of this book is to help you pass the Cisco IP Telephony (CIPT) exam (642-444). In fact, if the primary objective of this book was different, then the book's title would be misleading; however, the methods used in this book to help you pass the CCVP Cisco IP Telephony exam are designed to also make you much more knowledgeable about how to do your job. Although this book has more than enough questions to help you prepare for the actual exam, the method in which they are used is not to simply make you memorize as many questions and answers as you possibly can.

One key methodology used in this book is to help you discover the exam topics that you need to review in more depth, to help you fully understand and remember those details, and to help you prove to yourself that you have retained your knowledge of those topics. So, this book does not try to help you pass by memorization, but helps you truly learn and understand the topics. The Cisco IP Telephony exam is just one of the foundation topics in the CCVP certification and the knowledge contained within is vitally important to consider yourself a truly skilled voice engineer or specialist. This book would do you a disservice if it didn't attempt to help you learn the material.

Who Should Read This Book?

This book is not designed to be a general networking topics book, although it can be used for that purpose. This book is intended to tremendously increase your chances of passing the CCVP Cisco IP Telephony exam. Although you will achieve other objectives from using this book, the book is written with one goal in mind: to help you pass the exam.

The placement of CallManager in the CCVP series of exams is unique in that it could be one of the very first CCVP exams you take, or it could be one of the last. It stands as an isolated product in the CCVP series of exams. This means you could be getting into this book with an extensive knowledge of voice gateways, switches, and quality of service (from reading the CVOICE and/or QoS books) with a basic CCNA-level knowledge. Regardless, your learning curve will be the same; CallManager is configured differently, troubleshot uniquely, and managed distinctively from the rest of the voice network.

So why should you want to pass the CCVP Cisco IP Telephony exam? Because it is one of the milestones toward getting the CCVP certification; no small feat in itself. What would getting the

CCVP mean to you? A raise, a promotion, recognition? How about to enhance your résumé? To demonstrate that you are serious about continuing the learning process and that you are not content to rest on your laurels. To please your reseller-employer, who needs more certified employees for a higher discount from Cisco. Or one of many other reasons.

How This Book Is Organized

Although this book could be read from cover to cover, it is designed to be flexible and allow you to easily move between chapters and sections of chapters to cover just the material that you need more work with. If you do intend to read them all, the order in the book is an excellent sequence to use.

The chapters cover the following topics:

Chapter 1, "Introduction to Cisco Unified Communications and Cisco Unified CallManager"—This chapter provides an overview of the Cisco Unified Communications (AVVID) strategy, how the Cisco Unified CallManager product suite fits into the scheme, the interaction between CallManager and Cisco IP Phones, and the CallManager server platforms.

Chapter 2, "Cisco Unified CallManager Clustering and Deployment Options"—This chapter discusses the design strategies behind a Cisco CallManager cluster, cluster replication, and CallManager deployment models.

Chapter 3, "Cisco Unified CallManager Installation and Upgrades"—This chapter covers the requirements to perform a CallManager server installation, the CallManager installation and upgrade process, and postinstallation procedures.

Chapter 4, "Cisco IP Phones and Other User Devices"—This chapter examines the basic features of all Cisco IP Phones, the entry-level, midrange, and upper-end Cisco IP Phone models, the IP Phone startup process, and audio codec communication.

Chapter 5, "Configuring Cisco Unified CallManager to Support IP Phones"—This chapter examines the configuration of Cisco CallManager to support IP Phone registration and communication within a cluster, the creation of device pools, and manually or automatically registering Cisco IP Phones with the SQL Database.

Chapter 6, "Cisco IP Telephony Users"—This chapter covers the addition of IP telephony users to the CallManager LDAP database, associating users with devices, and allowing users to access the User Options web page to configure common features.

Chapter 7, "Cisco Bulk Administration Tool"—This chapter covers the features and components of the BAT application, the installation of BAT, and the configuration of BAT to apply bulk moves, adds, and changes to the Cisco CallManager cluster.

Chapter 8, "Cisco Catalyst Switches"—This chapter examines the functions that Catalyst switches perform in a Cisco IP telephony solution, the three options for powering Cisco IP Phones, the two types of power supplied by PoE switches, inline power configuration, dual VLAN configuration, and CoS configuration.

Chapter 9, "Configuring Cisco Gateways and Trunks"—This chapter discusses the role of the gateway in the IP telephony infrastructure, core gateway requirements, and gateway communication protocols; it also examines the configuration of analog and digital gateways, Cisco CallManager trunk configuration, and enabling the CallManager to use SIP capabilities.

Chapter 10, "Cisco Unified CallManager Route Plan Basics"—This chapter covers the fundamentals of the Cisco CallManager route plan, including the identification of the route plan building blocks, the configuration of route groups, route lists, and route patterns, and the design of a basic route plan.

Chapter 11, "Cisco Unified CallManager Advanced Route Plans"—This chapter covers the concepts and configurations behind route filters, digit discard instructions, transformation masks, translation patterns, and route plan reports.

Chapter 12, "Configuring Hunt Groups and Call Coverage"—This chapter examines the call distribution components and algorithms supported by CallManager; examines call hunting concepts; discusses the concepts and configurations of line groups, hunt lists, and hint pilots; and provides a scenario-based design discussion for hunting and forwarding calls.

Chapter 13, "Implementing Telephony Call Restrictions and Control"—This chapter discusses the concepts behind class of service as it relates to users of a phone system; it also covers the design and configuration of partitions, calling search spaces, and time-of-day routing.

Chapter 14, "Implementing Multiple-Site Deployments"—This chapter discusses why call admission control is important to maintain voice QoS across an IP WAN; describes the Cisco CallManager locations feature and how it provides the necessary call admission control for centralized call-processing environments; and explains the concepts and configurations behind locations, H.323 gatekeepers, and SRST.

Chapter 15, "Media Resources"—This chapter examines the necessary Cisco CallManager resources you should use as media resources, the configuration of conference bridges, media termination points, transcoders, and music on hold.

Chapter 16, "Configuring User Features, Part 1"—This chapter discusses the core Cisco IP Phone features supported by Cisco CallManager along with the enhanced IP Phone features configurable by an administrator; this chapter also examines the configuration of softkey templates, call park, call pickup, call back, barge, shared line appearances, and IP Phone services.

Chapter 17, "Configuring User Features, Part 2"—This chapter covers the configuration of the Cisco CallManager Extension Mobility service, FAC and CMC call accounting and restrictions, call display restrictions, malicious caller ID, and multilevel precedence and preemption.

Chapter 18, "Configuring Cisco Unified CallManager Attendant Console"—This chapter explains the functions and features of the Cisco CallManager Attendant Console application, and defines the key Attendant Console components and redundancy process. This chapter also covers the configuration of the Cisco CallManager server to support the Attendant Console and the client-side Attendant Console installation and configuration.

Chapter 19, "Configuring Cisco IP Manager Assistant"—This chapter covers the features of Cisco IPMA and the two modes of operation, the IPMA components, and the configuration of Cisco IPMA for shared-line mode installations.

Chapter 20, "Securing the Windows Operating System"—This chapter examines the security threats to the Windows operating system, the Cisco security and hotfix policy, the included enhanced security scripts, and the antivirus protection options for the CallManager server. This chapter also covers the suggested administrative password policy, the protection of the server from common exploits, the Cisco Security Agent, and the not-recommended security settings for the Cisco CallManager server.

Chapter 21, "Securing Cisco Unified CallManager Administration"—This chapter discusses the threats targeting remote Cisco CallManager Administration and other applications, the function of HTTPS in remote communication, the HTTP certificate operations, and the CallManager multilevel administration configuration.

Chapter 22, "Preventing Toll Fraud"—This chapter examines the vulnerability of legitimate devices to be used for fraudulent use in the IP telephony network, the use of partitions and calling search spaces to restrict call forwarding, the blocking of specific area codes, the configuration of CallManager to route calls based on time-of-day, the implementation of FAC to implement user authorization, and the restriction of conference call features to limit toll fraud.

Chapter 23, "Hardening the IP Phone"—This chapter covers the potential threats against IP Phones and the attack tools and methods a hacker can use, signed firmware images, CallManager IP Phone security techniques, and IP Phone authentication and encryption.

Chapter 24, "Understanding Cryptographic Fundamentals"—This chapter discusses the foundations of cryptography and the four cryptographic services, basic operation and uses for symmetric and asymmetric encryption algorithms, hashing, and digital signatures.

Chapter 25, "Understanding the Public Key Infrastructure"—This chapter examines the problem of secure, scalable distribution of public keys, the concepts behind a trusted introducer, certificates, CAs, certification paths, certificate enrollment, and certificate revocation.

Chapter 26, "Understanding Cisco IP Telephony Authentication and Encryption Fundamentals"—This chapter explains how file manipulation, tampering with call signaling, man-in-the-middle attacks, eavesdropping, and IP Phone theft can compromise a Cisco CallManager system. This chapter also discusses the authentication and encryption mechanisms supported by CallManager, the roll of CAPF, MICs, LSCs, CTLs, and the CTL Client. This chapter covers the processes and protocols used for signaling encryption and media encryption.

Chapter 27, "Configuring Cisco IP Telephony Authentication and Encryption"—This chapter examines the steps to configure a Cisco CallManager system for authentication and encryption, the activation of the CTL Provider and CAPF services, the installation of the CTL Client, and configuring the IP Phones for a hardened security structure.

Chapter 28, "Introducing IP Video Telephony"—This chapter covers the functions and components of the Cisco IP video telephony solution, the connection of a video call, H.323 versus SCCP video signaling, the two factors in determining the bandwidth requirement for video, and video call admission control.

Chapter 29, "Configuring Cisco VT Advantage"—This chapter discusses the features and function of the VT Advantage, placing and receiving calls with VT Advantage, configuring the Cisco CallManager to support video, and the VT Advantage client installation process.

Chapter 30, "Introducing Database Tools and Cisco Unified CallManager Serviceability"—This chapter examines the database structure and replication status of broken database connection, the services provided by CallManager Serviceability, the CallManager Control Center, the CallManager Service Activation window, and the various tools used to monitor Cisco CallManager listed by function.

Chapter 31, "Monitoring Performance"—This chapter defines performance objects, covers the Microsoft Event Viewer and Performance Monitor, and the Cisco Real-Time Monitoring Tool.

Chapter 32, "Configuring Alarms and Traces"—This chapter identifies the functions of the Cisco CallManager Alarm interface, and discusses the configuration of alarms and traces, the trace analysis process, and the Bulk Trace Analysis tool.

Chapter 33, "Configuring CAR"—This chapter discusses the usage, features, and operations of the CAR tool; the contents of CDR and CMR records; the three levels of CAR users and their reporting capabilities; the configuration of CAR system parameters, system schedule, and alerts; and the generation of user reports using CAR.

Chapter 34, "Using Additional Management and Monitoring Tools"—This chapter examines the use of SNMP, Syslog, and CiscoWorks ITEM in remotely managing and maintaining a Cisco CallManager system, the use of dependency records, the Password Changer tool, the Dialed Number Analyzer, and the Quality Reporting tool.

Finally, Appendix A, "Answers to Review Questions," contains the solutions to the review questions throughout the book.

Part I: Cisco CallManager Fundamentals

This chapter covers the following topics:

- An introduction to the Cisco Unified Communications strategy (formerly Cisco AVVID) and Cisco Unified CallManager technology
- An understanding of the placement of Cisco Unified CallManager in an IP telephony design
- The interaction between Cisco Unified CallManager and Cisco IP Phones
- Cisco Unified CallManager server platforms

CHAPTER 1

Introduction to Cisco Unified Communications and Cisco Unified CallManager

Although IP telephony might seem like the new, emerging technology in IT environments, it has actually been around for many years. As WAN and LAN data connections became more stable and the total amount of available bandwidth increased, legacy PBX vendors rushed to add IP processing functions to their chassis-based management systems. Cisco Systems also saw the writing on the wall and in 1999 unveiled both the Cisco 7900 series IP Phones and the Cisco Architecture for Voice, Video, and Integrated Data (AVVID) strategy for the future. This was also the year that Cisco announced Cisco Unified CallManager version 2.4.

A Cisco IP telephony deployment relies on Cisco Unified CallManager for its call-processing and call-routing functions. Understanding the role that Cisco Unified CallManager plays in a converged network from a system, software, and hardware perspective is necessary to successfully install and configure Cisco Unified CallManager. This chapter discusses Cisco Unified Communications and the Cisco Unified CallManager functions, hardware requirements, software requirements, and installation and upgrade information.

NOTE With the recent launch of the new Cisco Unified Communications portfolio, Cisco AVVID has become an obsolete term because it no longer accurately describes the breadth of Cisco's converged, unified communications offerings. This chapter still occasionally makes reference to Cisco AVVID in historical contexts, but for the most part uses the term Cisco Unified Communications. You might find them used interchangeably during this transition period.

NOTE Cisco has recently changed the name of the Cisco CallManager product to Cisco Unified CallManager to reflect the Cisco Unified Communications campaign. For brevity, this book mainly uses the shortened name of Cisco CallManager or just CallManager.

Cisco Unified Communications

When Microsoft announced their new .NET platform, there was a huge amount of confusion in the industry. Systems administrators did not know if they were to expect a new operating system, programming language, or company direction. The same effect happened when Cisco announced the Architecture for Voice, Video, and Integrated Data (AVVID), now known as Cisco Unified Communications. Network administrators did not understand if this was a new router type, IOS feature set, or marketing campaign. Cisco Unified Communications is not any of these things. Instead, it is a company strategy that provides the foundation for converged networks. The goal of Cisco Unified Communications is to create network equipment that has the capability to handle voice, video, and data traffic within a single network infrastructure.

Figure 1-1 shows the four standard layers of the Cisco Unified Communications voice infrastructure model: the infrastructure layer, which lays the foundation for network components; the call-processing layer, which maintains PBX-like functions; the applications layer, where applications that provide additional network functionality reside; and the client layer, where end-user devices reside.

Figure 1-1 *The Cisco Unified Communications Model for Voice Networks*

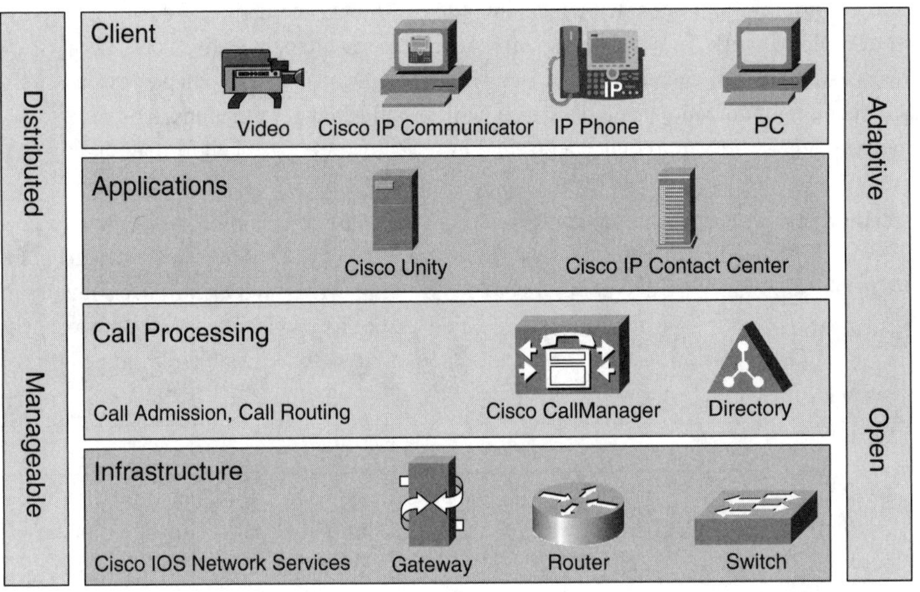

Each of the major areas of the Cisco Unified Communications architecture has a similar model focused around the technologies of voice, video, and data. The key points about the four standard layers of the voice model are as follows:

- **Infrastructure layer**—The infrastructure carries data between all network devices and applications and consists of routers, switches, and voice gateways.
- **Call-processing layer**—Call processing is physically independent of the infrastructure. Thus, a Cisco CallManager in Chicago can provide call control for a bearer channel in Phoenix.
- **Applications layer**—Applications are physically independent of call-processing functions and the physical voice-processing infrastructure; that is, they can reside anywhere within the network.
- **Client layer**—The client layer makes the voice applications available to the user, whether the end device is a Cisco IP Phone, a PC using a Cisco IP Communicator, or a PC delivering converged messaging.

At first, this might seem like just another model to commit to memory; however, understanding Cisco's design of this model allows you to make the most of your voice network. The OSI model creates a standard for communication across networks. In addition, it allows vendors to isolate network functionality and specialize in equipment working at a specific layer. Likewise, one of the huge benefits of using an IP telephony system over a PBX system is the open standards for protocols and equipment. A vendor could specialize and design devices that work only at the client layer of the Cisco Unified Communications voice model. These devices could use an open standard protocol to communicate with the Cisco CallManager at the applications layer.

NOTE Because of the flexibility of the Cisco IP telephony network, many organizations have created their own custom applications for the voice network. Cisco has made a Cisco CallManager Software Development Kit (SDK) freely available to aid in the process of creating custom Extensible Markup Language (XML) applications.

Understanding Cisco Unified CallManager

The vast majority of this CIPT book is focused on the core product that controls a Cisco IP telephony network: Cisco Unified CallManager. Cisco CallManager brings enterprise telephony features and functions to packet telephony devices. These devices include Cisco IP Phones, media-processing devices, voice over IP (VoIP) gateways, and multimedia applications. Additional data, voice, and video services, such as unified messaging, multimedia conferencing, collaborative contact centers, and interactive multimedia response systems, interact with the IP telephony solution through the Cisco CallManager application programming interface (API).

Cisco CallManager provides the following functions:

- **Call processing**—Call processing refers to the complete process of originating, routing, and terminating calls, including any statistical collection processes.
- **Signaling and device control**—Cisco CallManager sets up all of the signaling connections between call endpoints and directs devices such as phones, gateways, and conference bridges to establish and tear down streaming connections.
- **Dial plan administration**—The dial plan is a set of configurable rules that Cisco CallManager uses to determine call routing. Cisco CallManager provides the ability to create flexible dial plans for users.
- **Phone feature administration**—Cisco CallManager extends services such as hold, transfer, forward, conference, speed dial, last-number redial, Call Park, and other features to IP Phones and gateways.
- **Directory services**—Cisco Unified CallManager uses DC Directory as an embedded Lightweight Directory Access Protocol (LDAP) directory. This directory stores authentication and authorization information about users and is a standard feature of Cisco CallManager (it does not require any special configuration or installation). However, Cisco CallManager can also be integrated with a corporate directory such as the Netscape Directory Server or Microsoft Active Directory.
- **Programming interface to external applications**—Cisco CallManager provides a programming interface to external applications such as Cisco IP SoftPhone, Cisco IP Communicator, Cisco IP Interactive Voice Response (IVR), Cisco Personal Assistant, and Cisco CallManager Attendant Console.

Cisco Unified CallManager and IP Phone Interaction

Cisco CallManager provides the intelligence behind call-processing functions when integrated with Cisco IP Phones. These IP Phones are virtually a paperweight without the Cisco CallManager instructing them with what they should do. The Cisco CallManager uses the Skinny Client Control Protocol (SCCP, or Skinny) signaling protocol over IP to communicate with Cisco IP Phones for call setup and maintenance tasks. When the call is set up, Cisco IP Phones communicate directly using Real-Time Transport Protocol (RTP) to carry the audio.

> **TIP** Most Cisco 7900 IP Phones ship with a software image, allowing them to use the Skinny protocol to communicate with the Cisco CallManager. Cisco has also made a Session Initiation Protocol (SIP) image that allows Cisco IP Phones to be used with a third-party management system. Cisco CallManager does not support controlling the IP Phones using the SIP image as of Cisco CallManager 4.1. However, Cisco has added this support in the Cisco CallManager 5.0 release.

You can better understand how Cisco CallManager performs call processing and signaling functions by tracking a basic IP telephony call, as shown in Figure 1-2.

Figure 1-2 *Cisco CallManager Basic Call Processing and Signaling Capabilities*

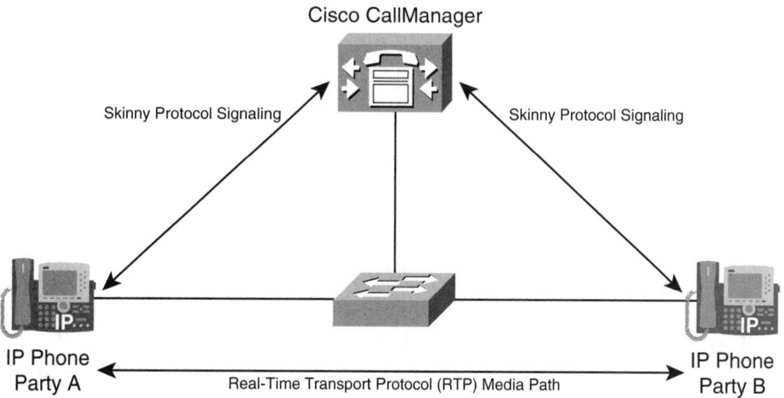

In Figure 1-2, Party A (left IP Phone) wants to call Party B (right IP Phone). Party A picks up the handset and dials the number of Party B. In this environment, dialed digits are sent to Cisco CallManager, the call-processing engine. Cisco CallManager finds the address and determines where to route the call.

Using the Skinny protocol, Cisco CallManager signals the calling party over IP to initiate a ring back, and Party A hears ringing. Cisco CallManager also signals the destination phone to initiate ringing.

When Party B picks up the telephone, the RTP media path opens between the two stations. Party A or Party B can now initiate a conversation. Because the IP Phones manage this RTP media path themselves, the Cisco CallManager is able to move out of the call-processing functions for this call. The IP Phones require no further communication with Cisco CallManager until either Party A or Party B invokes a feature, such as call transfer, call conferencing, or call termination. Even if the Cisco CallManager were to fail during the course of the call, the RTP stream would continue until one of the parties involved in the call decided to disconnect the call.

TIP The Skinny (SCCP) protocol uses TCP port 2000, whereas the RTP bearer stream uses dynamically negotiated even UDP port numbers in the range from 16,384 to 32,767.

The Components of Cisco Unified CallManager

Cisco CallManager installs using an image-based procedure. The image expands and deploys the following foundation operating system components:

- Windows 2000 Server
- Microsoft SQL Server 2000
- DC Directory
- Cisco IP Telephony Backup and Restore System (BARS)

Cisco CallManager server relies on Microsoft Windows 2000 for its operating system and Microsoft Structured Query Language (SQL) Server 2000 for its database (both provided by Cisco Systems). The operating system version that Cisco provides is called the Cisco IP Telephony Operating System. For example, Cisco CallManager 4.1(2) requires Cisco IP Telephony Operating System Version 2000.2.6 (or later) and the latest Cisco IP Telephony Server Operating System service release. The latest operating system updates and service releases can be obtained from Cisco using an authorized CCO login.

Cisco CallManager uses DC Directory as an embedded LDAP directory. This directory stores authentication and authorization information about users and is standard with Cisco CallManager (it does not require any special configuration or installation). Maintaining a user database for your IP telephony system is optional, as the phone system will work just fine without requiring users to log in to the system. However, if you want to deploy any of the advanced features such as Extension Mobility or the Cisco IP SoftPhone, user authentication is necessary. Authentication establishes the right of the user to access the system, whereas authorization identifies the telephony resources that a user is permitted to use, such as a specific telephone extension.

The Cisco Customer Directory Plugin allows you to integrate Cisco CallManager with one of the following enterprise directories:

- Microsoft Active Directory, available with Microsoft Windows 2000
- Microsoft Active Directory, available with Microsoft Windows 2003
- Netscape Directory Server, Versions 4.1 and 4.2
- Sun ONE Directory Server 5.x

The Cisco IP Telephony Backup and Restore System (BARS) can be used to back up Cisco CallManager. Cisco BARS is installed separately from Cisco CallManager.

Cisco Unified CallManager Servers

In the original 2.4 version of Cisco CallManager, you were able to install the software on any platform that you desired. By allowing this freedom, a level of hardware-based instability plagued the original versions of the Cisco CallManager software. To compete with the legacy PBX-based voice network, VoIP networks should maintain an uptime of 99.999 percent. To achieve this, Cisco now requires you to install Cisco CallManager on a server that meets Cisco configuration standards. For this reason, Cisco has collaborated with two server hardware manufacturers, Hewlett-Packard and IBM, to create Cisco Media Convergence Servers (MCSs). Cisco chose these platforms because they have proven their reliability in the industry over time. Table 1-1 provides the current hardware specifications for the Cisco CallManager MCSs at the time of this writing.

Table 1-1 *Cisco Media Convergence Server Platforms*

Platform	Space	Processor	CPU Equipped	CPU Maximum	Maximum Phones Per Server
MCS 7815-I1	Tower	Pentium 4 3060 MHz	1	1	300
MCS 7825-I1	1U Rack Mount	Pentium 4 3400 MHz	1	1	1000
MCS 7835-I1	2U Rack Mount	Nocona Xeon 3400 MHz	1	2	2500
MCS 7825-H1	2U Rack Mount	Nocona Xeon 3400 MHz	2	2	7500
MCS 7835-H1	2U Rack Mount	Pentium 4 3400 MHz	1	1	1000
MCS 7845-H1	2U Rack Mount	Nocona Xeon 3400 MHz	1	2	2500
MCS 7845-H1	2U Rack Mount	Nocona Xeon 3400 MHz	2	2	7500

All of these servers, with the exception of the 7815-I1, are rack-mountable and do not include a monitor, mouse, or keyboard. Cisco designed the Cisco MCS for local setup, rack mounting, and remote administration.

NOTE The higher-end Cisco servers (beginning with the MCS 7835-I1) also include redundant power supplies and hard disk configurations.

Summary

At the turn of the millennium, Cisco moved forward with a new company direction described in the acronym of AVVID: Architecture for Voice, Video, and Integrated Data. Under this new banner, all three methods of communication would collapse under a single network infrastructure. The evolved term to describe this converged, IP-based environment is now Cisco Unified Communications. Standing at the forefront of the voice technology is the Cisco CallManager, the Cisco call-processing system that controls and manages converged voice over data networks.

Cisco CallManager runs on a foundation of Windows 2000 and SQL 2000 and can integrate with many popular directory services for user authentication purposes. Ever since the 3.x versions of Cisco CallManager, Cisco restricted the hardware platforms capable of running Cisco CallManager to the MCS series. This ensures a consistent hardware platform to provide stable support for the critical voice services of an organization.

Review Questions

You can find the solutions to these questions in Appendix A, "Answers to Review Questions."

1. The Cisco Unified Communications strategy is primarily focused around what goal?
   a. to create a new line of routers and switches equipped with increased processor and memory resources to handle a converged network environment
   b. to design network equipment equipped with the hardware resources and software features to handle a converged network environment
   c. to allow voice, video, and data to flow smoothly across the Internet
   d. to upgrade WAN links between locations to a speed capable of handling increased network traffic
2. In which layer of the voice infrastructure model does the Cisco Unified CallManager reside?
   a. infrastructure layer
   b. call-processing layer
   c. applications layer
   d. client layer

3. Which of the following functions are performed by the Cisco CallManager server? (Choose three.)

   a. call processing
   b. directory services
   c. PBX integration and signaling
   d. cial plan administration
   e. RTP audio processing

4. Which of the following protocols does the Cisco CallManager use to communicate with Cisco IP Phones?

   a. H.323
   b. MGCP
   c. Skinny
   d. SIP

5. Which of the following functions is the Cisco CallManager responsible for when setting up a phone call between Cisco IP Phones? (Choose three.)

   a. receiving dialed digits
   b. initiating ring tones on dialed IP Phone
   c. streaming RTP audio between devices
   d. handling call-processing functions when the calling party presses the Hold button

6. Which of the following software components constitute the foundation operating system of Cisco CallManager? (Choose two.)

   a. Windows 2000
   b. Windows 2003
   c. SQL 2000
   d. Exchange 2000
   e. Solaris

7. If you decide not to integrate Cisco CallManager into your company LDAP-compliant directory, what built-in option does Cisco CallManager provide to store user information?

   a. DC Directory
   b. Active Directory
   c. LW Directory
   d. Cisco LM Directory

8. You have purchased a Cisco MCS 7825 server. What is the maximum number of Cisco IP Phones you will be able to support?
   a. 250
   b. 500
   c. 1000
   d. 2500
   e. 7500
9. Maintaining a user directory is essential to the day-to-day operation of the IP telephony network. (True/False)
10. Cisco IP Phones can use which of the following signaling protocols? (Choose two.)
    a. H.323
    b. Skinny
    c. SIP
    d. MGCP

This chapter covers the following topics:

- The concepts and design strategies behind a Cisco Unified CallManager cluster
- The types of replication that occur in a Cisco Unified CallManager cluster
- Properly designing the Cisco Unified CallManager cluster for redundancy
- The four Cisco Unified CallManager deployment models

CHAPTER 2

Cisco Unified CallManager Clustering and Deployment Options

Legacy PBX systems have quite the reputation for reliability. As a general track record, PBXs provide an uptime of 99.999 percent (known as the "five-nines" of reliability). This translates to an unbelievable 5.3 minutes of downtime per year! To match this standard of reliability, multiple Cisco CallManager servers are grouped into a cluster. Most administrators recognize the term "cluster" as an ability to allow multiple servers to act as one device, which is the type of clustering provided by Windows clustering services. The Cisco CallManager cluster operates quite differently.

After you understand the clustered relationship of Cisco CallManager, you can plan your deployment strategy using the four deployment models provided by Cisco CallManager. This chapter discusses the cluster relationship and deployment options provided by the Cisco CallManager and the options available to enterprises to deploy a highly available IP telephony network.

The Two Sides of the Cisco Unified CallManager Cluster

As a network administrator, you are accustomed to quite a bit of fiscal responsibility riding on your shoulders. Under the Cisco Unified Communications architecture, that responsibility has grown exponentially. Not only are you responsible for the operation of the data environment; you are now responsible for the company's voice network, which rides on top of this infrastructure. This voice network is critical to day-to-day business operations. Because of this, you should approach it just like any key network service: the more redundancy, the better.

A Cisco CallManager cluster is two or more servers grouped together to support a Cisco IP telephony network. The cluster relationship between Cisco CallManager servers provides redundancy and load balancing for the voice network. Cisco defines this cluster relationship in two ways: the SQL database structure and the intracluster run-time data.

The SQL Database Cluster

As discussed in Chapter 1, Cisco CallManager relies on Microsoft SQL 2000 as an information store for the data of the voice network. This data includes the phone extensions on the network, calling restrictions, route plan information, and so on. The database replication capability provided by Microsoft SQL Server makes clustering possible by allowing the same database to be on multiple machines. Database replication makes it appear as if a single machine is handling call processing along with other functions of the voice network and ensures that standby processors (Cisco CallManager servers) can seamlessly step in and fulfill the functions if the primary processor fails. This SQL database replication also ensures that all clustered Cisco CallManager servers have access to the same information.

You must have at least two Cisco CallManager servers to obtain this redundancy, and one of these servers must be a publisher database server. The publisher database server manages the only writable copy of the Microsoft SQL Server 2000 database. The subscriber database servers maintain read-only copies of the database. You can have only one publisher server and up to eight subscriber servers per cluster. It is these database servers that are able to actively participate in the call-processing functions of the Cisco voice network. This SQL limitation is also a key factor in determining the maximum size of a cluster, which is covered later in this chapter.

When you make changes to the Cisco CallManager configuration, these changes are made directly to the publisher server database. The publisher then replicates these changes to the subscriber servers. When the publisher server is offline, the Microsoft SQL Server 2000 database automatically locks, and thus prevents any database changes. The IP telephony network continues to operate, but you will not be able to add or configure any devices that are managed by Cisco CallManager. The only exception to this rule is the Call Detail Records (CDRs), which record information regarding the calls occurring within the cluster. When the publisher is down, the subscribers store CDRs until the publisher comes back online, and then the subscribers update the publisher with the CDRs.

In Cisco CallManager Release 3.3 and later, a single cluster is capable of handling approximately 30,000 Cisco IP Phones. This cluster limitation does not restrict the size of the voice over IP (VoIP) network. By creating additional clusters, you can increase the network size. However, the more clusters you create in a network, the more management the network requires to operate.

NOTE The 30,000 IP Phone maximum cluster size is only possible if you are using the MCS-7845 servers throughout your cluster deployment.

Intracluster Run-Time Data

The second communication method that defines the cluster relationship between Cisco CallManager servers is the intracluster run-time data, which is also called Intra-Cluster Communication Signaling (ICCS). This type of communication encompasses the "happenings" of the cluster. For example, when a new Cisco IP Phone connects to the network, it registers with its primary Cisco CallManager. That primary Cisco CallManager tells all the other servers in the cluster, "Hey everyone, a new phone just registered with me! I've given it the extension 4003." (IP address 10.5.5.1 in this example). All the other servers now know to send calls directed at extension 4003 to the Cisco CallManager at the IP address 10.5.5.1, which, in turn, makes the Cisco IP Phone ring.

After the initial phone registration, the Cisco IP Phone sends keepalive messages to the primary Cisco CallManager server every 30 seconds and sends a TCP connect message (which is technically a TCP three-way handshake) to its secondary Cisco CallManager server to ensure it is online and ready to accept a device failover, if necessary. When the Cisco IP Phone detects the failure of its TCP keepalive messages with the primary Cisco CallManager, the device attempts to register with a secondary Cisco CallManager server. The secondary Cisco CallManager server accepts the registration from the device and announces the new registration (using intracluster run-time data) to all of the Cisco CallManager servers in the cluster.

NOTE If the Cisco CallManager service is ever stopped manually (through the Services Windows 2000 Control Panel or a system shutdown), the Cisco CallManager server will clear all of its active TCP connections with the IP Phones. This causes them to failover immediately to their backup server rather than wait for the keepalive failure.

Cisco IP Phone registration is just one example of intracluster run-time data. You will discover many other types of intracluster communication as this book introduces new concepts in upcoming chapters.

Cluster Redundancy Designs

Because the IP telephony network is critical to business operation, you should never configure a single Cisco CallManager to support any organization. You should maintain at least two Cisco CallManager servers for the voice network to support the network should one server fail. Smaller organizations (240 users or less) might decide to use Cisco CallManager Express, which operates on an IOS-based router platform. The number of Cisco CallManager servers you use typically depends on the server platform you purchase and your cluster design strategy. Chapter 1, "Introduction to Cisco Unified Communications and Cisco Unified CallManager," discussed the server platforms and the number of phones that each server model supports. This section discusses the proper way to use those server platforms to build a Cisco CallManager cluster.

1:1 Redundancy Design

In a 1:1 Cisco CallManager redundancy deployment design, you can have a dedicated backup server for each primary server. This design guarantees that Cisco IP Phone registrations will never overwhelm the backup servers, even if multiple primary servers fail. However, the 1:1 redundancy design considerably limits the maximum cluster size and can be cost-intensive for the initial Cisco CallManager deployment.

Each cluster must also have a designated TFTP server. Depending on the number of devices that a server is supporting, you can combine this TFTP server functionality with the publisher or subscriber Cisco CallManager servers, or you can deploy the TFTP functionality on a separate, standalone server. The TFTP server is responsible for delivering IP Phone configuration files to each telephone, along with streamed media files, such as music on hold (MOH) and ring files; therefore, the TFTP server can experience a considerable network and processor load.

In the example shown in Figure 2-1, a Cisco 7835 Media Convergence Server (MCS) is used because each Cisco CallManager server installed on that platform supports a maximum of 2500 Cisco IP Phones.

Figure 2-1 *1:1 Server Redundancy Design*

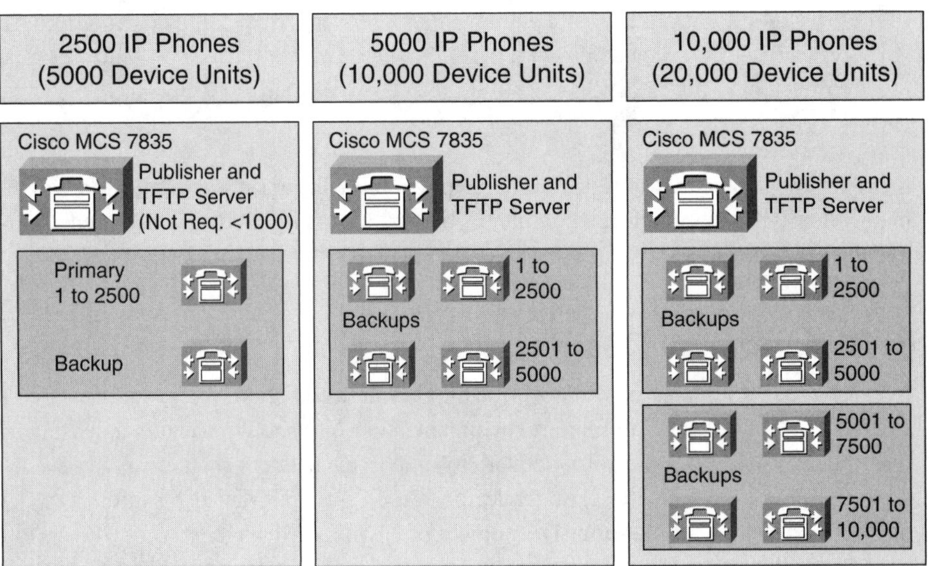

The shading in the figure divides up the functions performed within a cluster. The lighter shading (outside the Primary/Backup server area) represents the server that is not participating in call processing. This is the SQL publisher server, which is also acting as a TFTP server. In cluster environments with less than 1000 IP Phones, the SQL publisher can also participate in the call-processing functions. However, in clusters larger than 1000 devices, you should isolate the SQL publisher because it will be quite busy handling updates to the SQL database and TFTP requests.

The darker shaded box (containing the Primary/Backup servers) represents Cisco CallManager servers handling the call-processing functions (intracluster run-time data) of the cluster. In the example showing cluster design for 2500 IP Phones, a single Cisco CallManager is the primary server, with a secondary server acting as a dedicated backup. The primary or backup server can also serve as the Microsoft SQL publisher and the TFTP server in smaller IP telephony deployments.

TIP Be sure you understand how the two types of intracluster communication apply to the Cisco CallManager cluster design. The publisher and subscriber relationship relates to the SQL database replication. The Primary and Secondary server roles (shown in Figure 2-1 as Primary and Backup) relate to the intracluster run-time relationship and device registration. The Primary and Backup servers will be SQL subscribers if you isolate the SQL publisher from call-processing functions.

When you increase the number of IP Phones, you must increase the number of Cisco CallManager servers that are required to support the telephones. Some network engineers might consider the 1:1 redundancy design excessive because a well-designed network is unlikely to lose more than one primary server at a time. With the low possibility of server loss and the increased server cost, many network engineers elect to use a 2:1 redundancy design. However, other engineers choose to deploy the 1:1 redundancy to ensure maximum uptime of the IPT network. In addition, you can load-balance your IP Phones between the primary and backup servers in a 1:1 redundancy design. If any one server fails, only half of the phones must failover to the backup server (which provides a faster failover process).

2:1 Redundancy Design

In a 2:1 Cisco CallManager redundancy deployment design, you have a backup server shared between every two primary servers, as shown in Figure 2-2. Although this design offers some redundancy, there is the risk of overwhelming the backup server if multiple primary servers fail. In addition, upgrading the Cisco CallManager servers can cause a temporary loss of service because you must reboot the Cisco CallManager servers after the upgrade is complete.

NOTE Figure 2-2 assumes that each Cisco CallManager server can support a maximum of 2500 IP Phones.

Figure 2-2 *1:2 Server Redundancy Design*

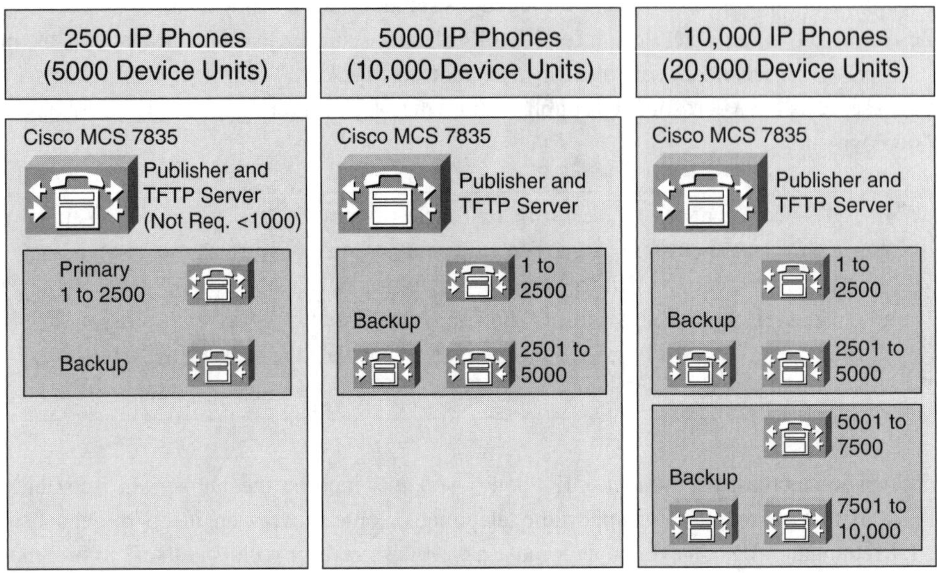

Network administrators use this 2:1 redundancy model in most IP telephony deployments because of the reduced server costs. If you are using a Cisco MCS 7835 (shown in the figure), that server is equipped with redundant, hot-swappable power supplies and hard drives. When you properly connect and configure these servers, it is unlikely that multiple primary servers will fail at the same time, which makes the 2:1 redundancy model a viable option for most businesses.

Because of tight budgets, some network administrators are forced into 3:1 and even 4:1 redundancy designs (three or four primary servers supported by a single backup server). Cisco does not support these designs because of the high risk involved.

TIP The Cisco CallManager architecture limits a cluster to nine servers (one publisher and eight subscribers) that have access to the SQL database. Only these servers can participate in call-processing functions. The redundancy model and server platform you choose has a huge impact on the total size of your Cisco CallManager cluster. Although it might be possible to create a cluster capable of supporting a tremendous amount of IP Phones by minimizing redundancy, Cisco TAC only supports a maximum cluster size of 30,000 IP Phones. If you reach this maximum cluster size, you will need to divide your network into multiple clusters.

Call-Processing Deployment Models

After you understand the concepts and design of a Cisco CallManager cluster, you can move on to the design of the organization IP telephony network. Cisco proposes four primary design models:

- Single-site deployment
- Multisite deployment with centralized call processing
- Multisite deployment with distributed call processing
- Clustering over the IP WAN

Single-Site Deployment

In a single-site deployment model, all Cisco CallManager servers, applications, and IP Phones are in the same physical location. A single Cisco CallManager cluster can support a maximum of 30,000 IP Phones. If you need to support more IP Phones at the site, you can implement multiple clusters within the single location and interconnect them through intercluster trunks (intercluster trunks are covered in Chapter 10, CallManager Route Plan Basics). Gateways that connect directly to the Public Switched Telephone Network (PSTN) handle external calls. If an IP WAN exists between sites, it is used to carry data traffic only; no telephony services are provided over the WAN. Figure 2-3 shows a typical network diagram of a single-site deployment.

Figure 2-3 *Single-Site Cisco CallManager Design*

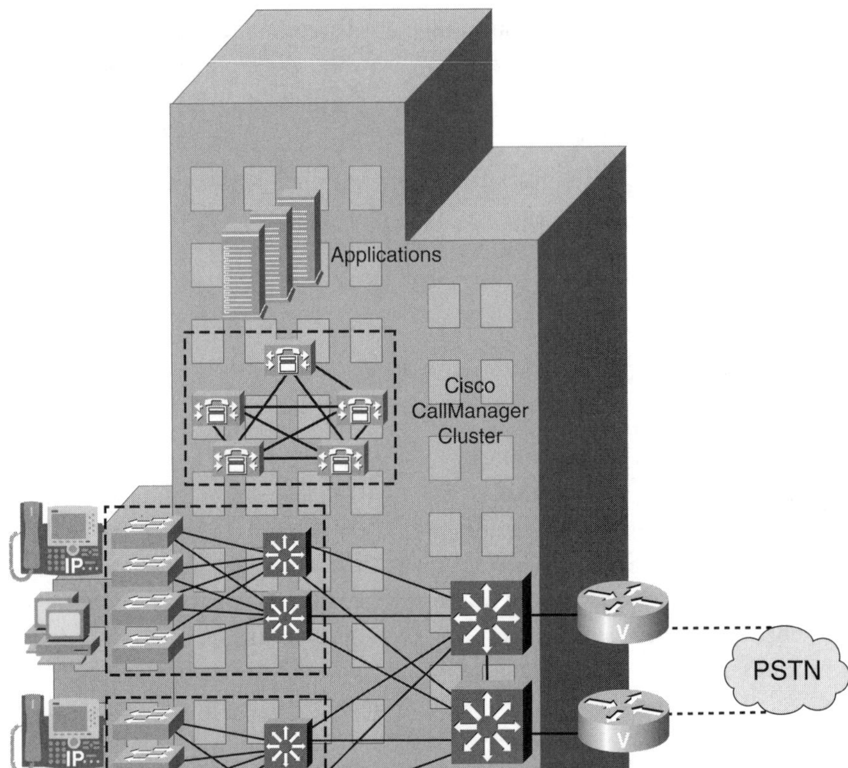

Use the following guidelines for single-site deployments:

- You must understand the current calling patterns within the enterprise. How and where are users making calls? How many calls are intersite or interbranch versus intrasite? If calling patterns dictate that most calls are intrasite, use the single-site model to deploy IP telephony and make use of the relatively inexpensive PSTN. This design also simplifies the dial plans and avoids provisioning dedicated bandwidth for voice in the IP WAN.
- The IP Phones should use the G.711 coder-decoder (codec). Because the call will stay in the LAN, G.711 is a simple and high-quality codec for deployment. It does not require dedicated Digital Signal Processor (DSP) resources for transcoding (which means converting between codec types, such as between G.711 and G.729), and older voice-mail systems might support only G.711. You can allocate these DSP resources to other functions, such as conferencing

and Media Termination Point (MTP). Although the 64 kbps per-call bandwidth that G.711 consumes is higher than that of other commonly used codecs, it is not a concern in this design because the call is not traversing the WAN, where bandwidth is generally limited.

- All off-net calls will be diverted to the PSTN or sent to the legacy PBX for call routing if the PSTN resources are being shared during migratory deployments.
- Use Media Gateway Control Protocol (MGCP) gateways for the PSTN if the network does not require H.323 functionality. Centralize the gateway dial plans by using H.323 gatekeepers when deploying multiple clusters, rather than using MGCP gateways. In addition, PSTN gateway redundancy should also be a consideration because a single gateway failure could affect the inbound and outbound PSTN calls for an entire corporation.
- Deploy the recommended network infrastructure for high-availability connectivity options for telephones (inline power), quality of service (QoS) mechanisms, and other services.
- Do not oversubscribe Cisco CallManager to scale larger installations. In earlier software releases, Cisco used various schemes to allow the capacity of a system to be calculated using device weights, busy hour call attempt (BHCA) multipliers, and dial plan weights. With Cisco CallManager Release 4.0, this scheme has been replaced by a capacity tool to allow for more accurate planning of the system. The capacity planning tool is currently available only to Cisco employees. If your system does not meet the guidelines found in the Cisco IP Telephony Solution Network Reference Design, or if you consider the system to be more complex and would like to verify the capacity, please contact your Cisco Systems engineer. The Cisco IP Telephony Solution Reference Network Design (SRND) is found at: http://www.cisco.com/univercd/cc/td/doc/solution/esm/ (or can be browsed to through http://www.cisco.com/go/srnd).

Multisite Deployment with Centralized Call Processing

Figure 2-4 illustrates the multisite centralized call-processing deployment model with a Cisco CallManager cluster at a central site and a connection to several remote sites through a QoS-enabled IP WAN. The remote sites rely on the centralized Cisco CallManager cluster to handle call processing. Applications such as voice mail and interactive voice response (IVR) systems usually reside at the central site, thus reducing the overall cost of ownership and centralizing administration and maintenance. However, centralizing these application servers is not a requirement.

Figure 2-4 *Multisite Deployment with Centralized Call Processing*

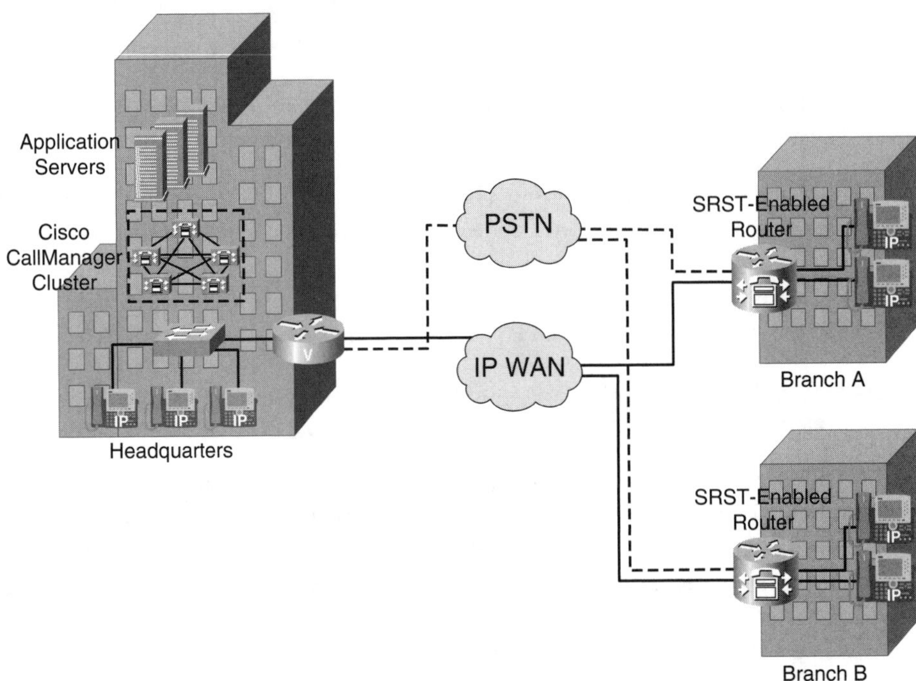

Routers that reside at WAN edges require QoS mechanisms, such as low latency queuing (LLQ) and traffic shaping, to protect voice traffic from data traffic across the WAN (where bandwidth is typically scarce).

To avoid oversubscribing the WAN links with voice traffic (thus causing deterioration of the quality of established calls), the network might need a call admission control scheme. With the introduction of Cisco CallManager Release 3.3, centralized call-processing models can take advantage of automated alternate routing (AAR) features. AAR allows Cisco CallManager to dynamically reroute a call over the PSTN if the call exceeds the WAN bandwidth.

NOTE AAR is a feature specific to centralized call-processing environments and is discussed in depth in Chapter 14, Implementing Multiple-Site Deployments.

You can provide PSTN access for the voice network through a variety of Cisco gateways. When the IP WAN is down, the users at remote branches can place their calls through the PSTN using the Cisco Survivable Remote Site Telephony (SRST) feature that is available for Cisco IOS gateways that can provide call processing during the outage.

Follow these best-practices guidelines when deploying a centralized call-processing model:

- Installations adopting the centralized call-processing deployment model are limited to hub-and-spoke topologies because the locations-based call admission control mechanism used in centralized call-processing deployments records only the available bandwidth in and out of each location.
- There is no limit to the number of IP Phones at each individual remote branch. However, the capability that is provided by the SRST feature in the branch router limits remote branches to 720 Cisco IP Phones using a 3845 router during failover. Smaller platforms have lower limits. SRST is covered in its entirety in Chapter 14, "Implementing Multiple-Site Deployments."
- Controlling WAN bandwidth utilization in a centralized call-processing deployment model is quite simple. Through the use of the Cisco CallManager Locations feature, the central Cisco CallManager cluster can decide if the remote-site call should use the WAN or PSTN for its connection.
- When communicating over the IP WAN, the G.729 compressed codec should be used to save considerable WAN bandwidth.

Multisite Deployment with Distributed Call Processing

A multisite distributed call-processing deployment has one or more call-processing agents at each site, and each site has its own Cisco CallManager cluster consisting of two or more servers. By separating these sites into different clusters, the Cisco CallManager servers do not share the SQL database and intracluster run-time data between sites. This requires some additional configuration because it will be necessary to trunk these sites together through an IP WAN. Figure 2-5 illustrates a typical multisite design using distributed call processing.

When deciding between a centralized or distributed call-processing model, you will usually base your decision on two factors: how many phones must you support at each site and what features does the company require to be available during failover. If you are using a smaller number of IP Phones and only require basic call-processing functionality, the centralized call-processing model might be most appropriate. If you are using a larger number of IP Phones or require more advanced features (such as call center applications), a distributed model might be more appropriate.

Figure 2-5 *Multisite Deployment with Distributed Call Processing*

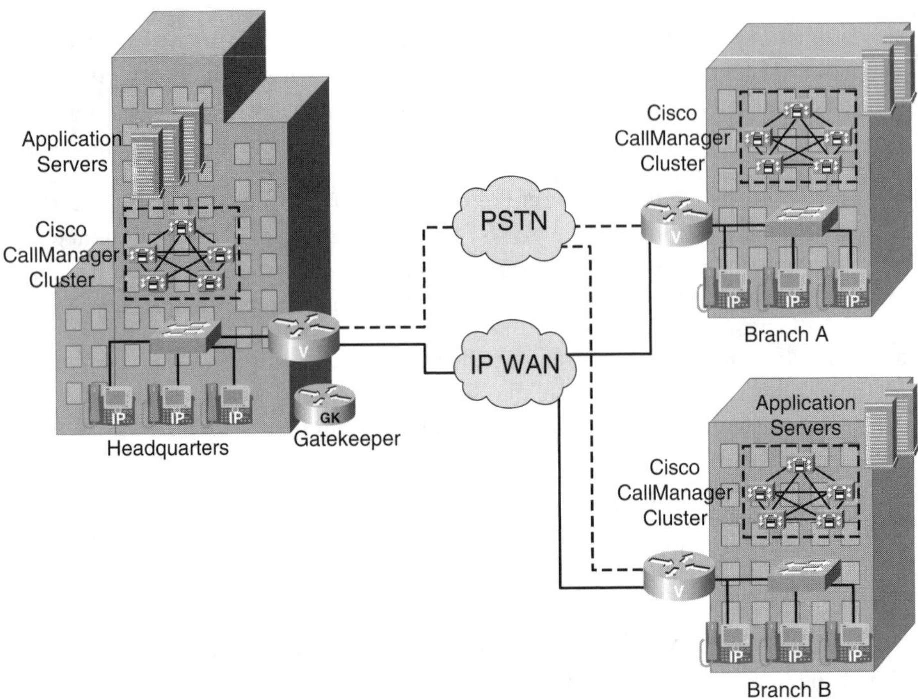

Depending on your network design, an individual site in the distributed call-processing design might consist of the following:

- A single site with its own call-processing agent, which can be a Cisco CallManager or a third-party call agent
- A centralized call-processing site (and all of its remote sites) that the network views as a single site for distributed call processing
- A legacy PBX with a VoIP gateway or a legacy PBX that is attached using a time-division multiplexing (TDM) interface to a VoIP gateway

The distributed call-processing model requires all sites to be connected through an IP WAN. Cisco considers a site connected only through the PSTN to be a standalone site.

Multisite distributed call processing allows each site to be completely self-contained. In the event of an IP WAN failure or insufficient bandwidth, the site does not lose call-processing service or functionality. Cisco CallManager simply sends all calls between the sites across the PSTN.

The main benefits of this deployment model are as follows:

- Cost savings when you are using the IP WAN for intersite calls. The IP Phones and voice gateways can compress calls using the G.729 codec, reducing the bandwidth required for the audio and increasing efficiency over the standard PSTN connections.
- Toll-bypass savings when you are using remote gateways to drop off into the PSTN (known as "tail end hop off," or TEHO). For example, if one of your sites is located in Arizona, all the other sites can forward calls across the IP WAN to obtain toll-bypass when calling a number in Arizona.
- No loss of functionality during an IP WAN failure.
- Scalability to hundreds of clusters.

The multisite WAN with distributed call-processing deployment model is a superset of the single-site and multisite WAN with centralized call-processing models. You should follow the best-practices guidelines mentioned previously for single-site and multisite deployments in addition to those listed here, which are specific to this deployment model.

The H.323 gatekeeper or Session Initiation Protocol (SIP) proxy servers are among the key elements in the multisite WAN with distributed call processing. Both provide centralized dial plan resolution, with the gatekeeper also providing call admission control.

A gatekeeper is an H.323 device that provides call admission control and centralized dial plan resolution. Otherwise, the network administrator at each of the sites must configure a full dial plan to reach all devices on the network. Additional gatekeeper guidelines include the following:

- Cisco recommends that you use backup gatekeeper support to provide a gatekeeper solution with high availability. It is also recommended that you use multiple gatekeepers to provide spatial redundancy within the network.
- Cisco recommends that you use a single WAN codec. This design makes capacity planning easy and does not require you to overprovision the IP WAN to allow for worst-case scenarios.

SIP proxy servers provide resolution of dialed numbers (also called E.164 numbers) as well as SIP uniform resource identifiers (URIs) to enable endpoints to place calls to each other. Cisco CallManager supports the use of E.164 numbers only.

The following best practices apply to the use of SIP proxies:

- Provide adequate redundancy for the SIP proxies.
- Ensure that the SIP proxies have the capacity for the call rate and number of calls required in the network.

For more detail on bandwidth capacity planning and call admission control for each deployment model, refer to the Cisco IP Telephony Solution Reference Network Design (SRND) for Cisco CallManager 4.0 at: http://www.cisco.com/univercd/cc/td/doc/solution/esm/iptele/index.htm.

Clustering over the IP WAN

Cisco supports Cisco CallManager clusters over a WAN, shown in Figure 2-6.

Figure 2-6 *Clustering over the IP WAN*

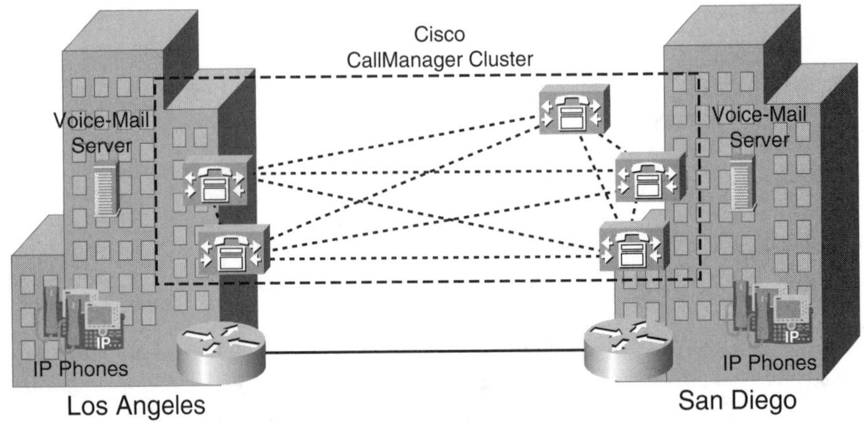

Although there are stringent requirements, this design offers the following advantages:

- Single point of administration for users for all sites within the cluster
- Feature transparency; features such as call transfers and conference calls work seamlessly using an internal dialing scheme
- Shared line appearances over a WAN connection, which allows multiple phones to share a line instance
- Extension mobility within the cluster, allowing users to log in to remote phones and have their phone profile follow them

This design is useful for customers who require more functionality at remote sites than the limited feature set that is offered by SRST. This network design also allows remote offices to support more Cisco IP Phones than SRST in the event that the connection to the primary Cisco CallManager is lost.

Although the distributed single-cluster call-processing model offers some significant advantages, it must adhere to these strict design guidelines:

- Two Cisco CallManager servers in a cluster must have a maximum round-trip delay of 40 ms between them. In comparison, high-quality voice guidelines dictate that one-way end-to-end delay should not exceed 150 ms. Because of this strict guideline, you can use this design only between closely connected, high-speed locations (Metropolitan Ethernet would be a good example of this connectivity type).
- For every 10,000 Busy Hour Call Attempts (BHCAs) within the cluster, you must support an additional 900 kbps of WAN bandwidth for intracluster run-time communication. The BHCA represents the number of call attempts made during the busiest hour of the day.
- Up to eight small sites are supported using the remote failover deployment model. Remote failover allows you to deploy the backup servers over the WAN. Using this deployment model, you can have up to eight sites with Cisco CallManager subscribers being backed up by Cisco CallManager subscribers at another site.
- SRST can function in this model but is not necessary to protect against Cisco CallManager failure. The telephones can failover across the WAN to other Cisco CallManager servers. This design may require significant additional bandwidth, depending on the number of telephones at each location.

NOTE If the WAN connection between sites fails, users will receive a fast busy signal for any intersite call. This might be confusing to users who are used to ringing followed by voice mail.

Summary

This chapter covered the key factors you must consider when you are initially designing a Cisco CallManager–based IP telephony deployment. The key to understanding your deployment options is first understanding the Cisco CallManager cluster relationship as defined by the Microsoft SQL replication and intracluster run-time data. The Cisco CallManager cluster provides redundancy and failover in an IP telephony environment. This redundancy can be implemented using the 1:1 server redundancy design, which offers the most redundancy available, or a 2:1 redundancy design, which balances the cost factors with overall redundancy. The chapter ended with a discussion of the four call-processing deployment models:

- Single-site deployment
- Multisite deployment with centralized call processing
- Multisite deployment with distributed call processing
- Clustering over the IP WAN

Review Questions

You can find the solutions to these questions in Appendix A, "Answers to Review Questions."

1. Which four of the following are IP telephony deployment models that are supported by Cisco? (Choose four.)

   a. a single site with one call-processing agent

   b. multiple sites with centralized call processing

   c. multiple sites each with its own call-processing agent

   d. a single cluster with distributed call processing

   e. multiple clusters with no call-processing agent

2. A 1:1 redundancy design offers _________.

   a. increased redundancy; however, the increased server cost is often prohibitive

   b. some redundancy; however, a server reboot is required after an upgrade

   c. maximum uptime; however, no more than a 20-ms round-trip delay can exist between servers

   d. high availability; however, you might overwhelm the backup servers

3. A single cluster that spans multiple sites can have which two benefits compared to a branch office in a multisite WAN with a centralized call-processing deployment? (Choose two.)

   a. completely self-contained individual sites

   b. WAN bandwidth cost savings

   c. a common dial plan across all sites

   d. more IP Phone features during failover

   e. scalability to hundreds of sites

4. Which two of the following enable the cluster to achieve redundancy? (Choose two.)

   a. Windows clustering

   b. database replication

   c. at least two servers

   d. directory access

5. When configuring the SQL database relationship between Cisco CallManager servers, how many publisher servers should you configure for the cluster?

   a. It depends on the server platform; you should have one publisher for each group of phones followed by a backup.

   b. You should have only one publisher server for the entire cluster.

c. You should have at least two publisher servers to provide database redundancy.

d. You must configure a publisher for each subscriber you install.

6. What is the maximum number of SQL subscribers that can exist in a Cisco CallManager cluster?

a. 3

b. 5

c. 8

d. 9

e. 12

7. To support a centralized, multisite Cisco CallManager design, what feature should be employed at the remote offices?

a. QoS

b. SRST

c. Classification

d. SQL database replication

8. When using a multisite, single-cluster Cisco CallManager design, it is not necessary to employ SRST features to support the IP Phones in the case of Cisco CallManager failure. (True/False)

9. When designing a distributed, multicluster Cisco CallManager design, what pieces of equipment might be necessary to ensure the IP telephony network maintains a consistent and centralized dial plan? (Choose two.)

a. H.323 gatekeeper

b. H.323 gateways

c. SIP proxy server

d. Cisco CallManager

10. What is the maximum Cisco CallManager cluster size Cisco will support using Cisco CallManager 4.x?

a. 7500 IP Phones

b. 10,000 IP Phones

c. 12,000 IP Phones

d. 15,000 IP Phones

e. 30,000 IP Phones

This chapter covers the following topics:

- The requirements to perform Cisco Unified CallManager server installation
- Cisco Unified CallManager installation process
- Cisco Unified CallManager postinstallation procedures
- Cisco Unified CallManager upgrade process

CHAPTER 3

Cisco Unified CallManager Installation and Upgrades

When Cisco first announced that the Cisco CallManager platform would use Microsoft Windows 2000 as a foundation operating system and Microsoft SQL 2000 as a database store, concern arose that the Cisco administrator would require a thorough understanding of these applications to successfully operate a Cisco IP telephony network. Although an understanding of these components can be useful for monitoring and troubleshooting purposes, it is not necessary for Cisco CallManager installation and setup. Cisco has done a fantastic job of "wizard-izing" and scripting the complete installation of both Windows 2000 and SQL 2000, hiding any complexity behind a friendly **Next** button.

The upgrade process of Cisco CallManager is not quite as friendly as a clean install; however, if you keep the potential pitfalls in mind, a Cisco CallManager upgrade can go quite smoothly. This chapter discusses both the clean install and upgrade process of Cisco CallManager.

Cisco Unified CallManager 4.x Clean Installation Process

A clean installation of Cisco CallManager has always been an extremely simple process. As you perform the Cisco CallManager installation, the automated setup process prompts you for the information that is necessary to build Windows 2000, Microsoft SQL Server 2000, and Cisco CallManager with a base configuration. The entire operating system installation process, excluding preinstallation tasks, takes approximately 25 to 45 minutes per server, depending on your server type. Installing Cisco CallManager, excluding pre- and postinstallation tasks, takes 45 to 90 minutes per server, depending on your server type.

Installation Disks

All Cisco MCSs and customer-provided servers that meet approved Cisco configuration standards ship with a blank hard drive. When you purchase a Cisco IP telephony application, you use the appropriate disks to install or upgrade the operating system and application:

- **Disk 1: Cisco IP Telephony Server Operating System Hardware Detection Disk**— Checks the server and displays an error message if it detects an unsupported server. After you boot the server using the Hardware Detection CD-ROM, the automated installation process prompts for the correct CD-ROMs to use based on the type of hardware platform detected.

- **Disk 2: Cisco IP Telephony Server Operating System Installation and Recovery Disk**— Installs the operating system. Use only one of the server-specific Cisco IP Telephony Server Operating System Installation and Recovery disks that come in your software kit. Depending on your platform, the Operating System disc could be CD-ROM or DVD-based. After the operating system installation, a prompt instructs you to insert the appropriate Cisco CallManager software disk into the drive.
- **Disk 3: Cisco CallManager 4.1 Software Disk**— This disk installs the Cisco CallManager application on the server.

You might also receive a Cisco IP Telephony Server Operating System Upgrade Disk. Use this disk to upgrade the operating system on existing (not new) servers in the cluster. You do not need to use this disk if you are performing a new operating system installation.

Installation Configuration Data

As mentioned previously, the installation process for Cisco CallManager is automated by a step-by-step wizard. You will initially boot off the Hardware Detection CD-ROM, which will walk you through a wizard prompting you for the basic configuration data to get the server running. The process erases all data on the server hard disk. During the installation, you are prompted for the following items:

- **New installation or server replacement**—Choose this option if you are installing the Cisco IP telephony application for the first time, overwriting an existing installation, or replacing a server. To replace the server, you must store the data to a network directory or tape device before the operating system installation. Choosing this setting erases all existing drives.
- **Cisco product key**—Cisco supplies a product key when you purchase a Cisco IP telephony product. The product key is based on a file encryption system that allows you to install only the components that you have purchased. It also prevents you from installing other supplied software for general use. The product key consists of alphabetical characters only.
- **Username and organization name**—The system will prompt you for a username and an organization name to register the software product that you are installing. Do not leave the field blank. You can enter letters, numbers, hyphens (-), and underscores (_).
- **Computer name**—The system will prompt you to assign a unique computer name, using 15 characters or fewer, to each Cisco CallManager server. The computer name can contain alphabetic and numeric characters, hyphens, and underscores, but it must begin with a letter of the alphabet. Follow your local naming conventions, if possible. If you want to change the computer name after the application installation, you must completely reinstall the operating system and the application.

- **Workgroup**—The system will also prompt you for a workgroup name. A workgroup consists of a collection of computers that share the same workgroup name. Computers in the same workgroup can more easily communicate with each other across the network. Ensure that this entry, which must also be 15 characters or fewer, follows the same naming conventions as the computer name.

- **Domain suffix**—When prompted, you must enter the Domain Name System (DNS) suffix in the format "mydomain.com" or "mycompany.mydomain.com." If you are not using DNS, use a fictitious domain suffix, such as fictitioussite.com.

- **TCP/IP properties**—You must assign an IP address, subnet mask, and default gateway when installing a Cisco CallManager server. Changing the Cisco CallManager IP address after you install the software can be a tedious process, so be sure to plan accordingly.

CAUTION It is strongly recommended that you choose static IP information, which ensures that the Cisco CallManager server obtains a fixed IP address. With this selection, Cisco IP Phones can register with Cisco CallManager when the telephones are plugged into the network. Using Dynamic Host Configuration Protocol (DHCP) can cause problems, including failure of the telephony system.

- **DNS**—You can identify a primary DNS server for this optional field. By default, the telephones will attempt to connect to Cisco CallManager using DNS. Therefore, you must verify that the DNS server contains a mapping of the IP address and the fully qualified domain name (FQDN) of the Cisco CallManager server. If you do not use DNS, use the server IP address, instead of a server name, to register the telephones with Cisco CallManager.

NOTE Before you begin installing multiple servers in a cluster, you must have a name resolution method in place, such as DNS, Windows Internet Naming Service (WINS), or local name resolution using a configured LMHOSTS file. If you use DNS, you must verify that the DNS server contains a mapping of the IP address and the hostname of the server that you are installing. This verification must take place before you begin the installation. If you use local name resolution, ensure that the LMHOSTS file is updated on the existing servers in the cluster before you begin the installation on the new subscriber server. You must add the same information to the LMHOSTS file on the new server during installation.

TIP Although it might seem tedious, Cisco considers the creation of LMHOST file IP address to hostname mappings on each Cisco CallManager server a better practice. Using DNS services introduces another point of failure for the voice network.

- **SNMP community string**—The Windows 2000 Simple Network Management Protocol (SNMP) agent provides security through the use of community names and authentication traps. Cisco sets the community rights to none for security reasons. If you want to use SNMP with this server, you must configure it.
- **Database server**—You must determine whether you will configure this server as a publisher database server or as a subscriber database server through a radio button selection during the Cisco CallManager installation. This selection is permanent. You must reinstall the Cisco CallManager server if you want to reassign the database server type at a later date.

NOTE You must install a Cisco CallManager publisher server before you can install any subscriber servers. When you are configuring a subscriber database server, ensure that the server that you are installing can connect to the publisher database server during the installation. This connection facilitates the copying of the publisher database to the local drive on the subscriber server. You must supply the name of the publisher database server and a username and password with administrator access rights on that server. The installation will be discontinued if, for any reason, the publisher server cannot be authenticated.

- **New password for the system administrator**—Cisco CallManager Releases 3.0 and later support password protection. A prompt at the end of the installation procedure will ask you to supply a new password for the system administrator.

NOTE For Cisco CallManager database replication, you must enter the same Administrator account password for the publisher and all of the subscribers in the cluster. The installation wizard will request this password.

Sample Configuration Data Worksheet

Table 3-1 shows the configuration information that you need to install the Cisco CallManager software on your server. You should complete all of the fields in the table, unless otherwise noted. You must gather this information for each Cisco CallManager server that you are installing in the cluster. Make copies of this table, and record your entries for each server in a separate table. Table 3-1 summarizes the data you should have available when you begin the installation.

Table 3-1 *Configuration Data for Cisco MCS*

Configuration	Data
Cisco product key	
Username	
Name of your organization	

Table 3-1 *Configuration Data for Cisco MCS (Continued)*

Configuration	**Data**
Computer name	
Workgroup	
Microsoft NT domain (optional)	
DNS domain suffix	
Current time zone, date, and time	
DHCP parameters	It is recommended that you program a fixed IP address in TCP/IP properties for the server instead of using DHCP.
TCP/IP properties (required if DHCP is not used): • IP address • Subnet mask • Default gateway	
DNS servers (optional): • Primary • Secondary WINS servers (optional): • Primary • Secondary • LMHOSTS file (optional)	
Database server (choose one): • Publisher • Subscriber If you are configuring a subscriber server, supply the username and password of the publishing database server: • Publisher username • *Publisher password*	
Backup (choose one or both): • Server • Target	
New Windows 2000 administrator password	

Postinstallation Procedures

After you complete the Cisco CallManager software installation, the installation wizard will prompt you to change all passwords used in the Cisco CallManager cluster. These passwords should be the same on all servers you install into the cluster. In addition, many supporting services are running on your server that you might be able to stop. The fewer services you have running on your server, the more server resources you will have available to support the IP telephony network. In addition, running more services on the Cisco CallManager server introduces more security vulnerabilities for the underlying Windows operating system. You should stop all of the following services on both the Publisher and Subscriber servers in your cluster and set them to manual-start status unless they are otherwise needed on the system:

- DHCP client
- Fax service
- FTP Publishing Service
- Smart Card (unless using security tokens)
- Smart Card Helper
- Computer browser
- Distributed File System
- License Logging Service

By default, the installation wizard configures all Subscribers with Internet Information Server (IIS) Services running. This allows you to make changes to the cluster by accessing the web interface on your subscriber servers. Even though you are accessing the web interface on the Subscriber server, the changes are actually being made on the Publisher server (because it has the only writable copy of the database). In addition, allowing the web services to run on all Subscriber servers introduces more security risk as there are now multiple points of access for the Cisco CallManager administration interface. Because of this, it is usually best to save the Subscriber resources by stopping the web services on all servers except the Publisher. You can accomplish this by stopping the following services:

- Microsoft Internet Information Server (IIS) Admin Service
- World Wide Web Publishing Service

You can stop all of these services through the Windows 2000 Services console. To open this console, click **Start > Programs > Administrative Tools > Services**. When the console opens, Windows lists all services in alphabetic order. Right-click on the service you want to disable and choose **Properties**. In the Properties window shown in Figure 3-1, use the drop-down box to select either a **Manual** startup or to **Disable** the service. These will take effect the next time you reboot the Cisco CallManager server. You can also choose to stop the service without restarting the server from this page.

> **TIP** Because Cisco CallManager requires these services to be active when upgrading to new Cisco CallManager versions, setting them to a state of Manual is suggested.

Figure 3-1 *Windows 2000 Service Properties*

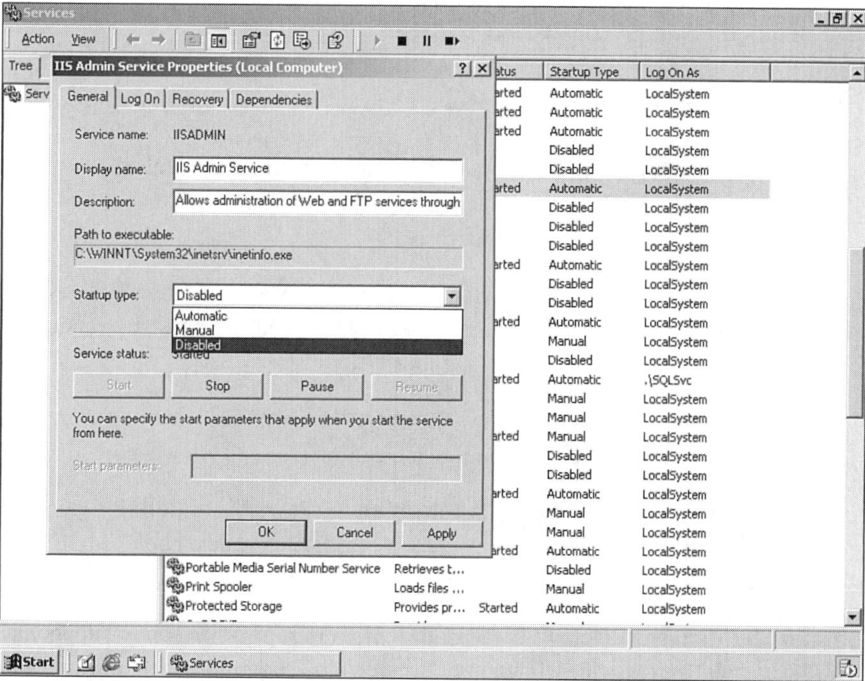

Activating Cisco Unified CallManager Services

If you are installing Cisco CallManager for the first time, all services that are required to run Cisco CallManager automatically install on the system; however, none of the services are activated at the completion of the installation (except for the Cisco Database Layer Monitor service). Cisco CallManager Serviceability provides a web-based Service Activation tool that is used to activate or deactivate multiple services and to select default services to activate.

It is recommended that you activate only the required components for each server in the cluster. Each component that you activate adds to the server load.

If you are upgrading Cisco CallManager, the services that you have already started on your system will start after the upgrade.

Each service performs specific functions for the IP telephony network. Some services might need to run on a single Cisco CallManager server in a cluster; other services might need to run on all of the Cisco CallManager servers in the cluster.

> **CAUTION** Be sure to activate at least the Cisco CallManager service before you apply any configuration to your Cisco CallManager server. Failure to do so can lead to unpredictable results, potentially leading to a server reinstall.

The following information briefly describes each available Cisco CallManager service:

- **Cisco CallManager Service**—Allows the server to participate in telephone registration, call processing, and other Cisco CallManager functions. Cisco CallManager Service is the core service of the Cisco CallManager platform.
- **Cisco TFTP**—Activates a TFTP server on Cisco CallManager. The TFTP service delivers Cisco IP Phone loads and configuration files to IP Phones, along with streamed media files, such as music on hold (MOH) and ring files.
- **Cisco Messaging Interface**—Allows Cisco CallManager to interface with a Simplified Message Desk Interface (SMDI)-compliant, external voice-mail system.
- **Cisco IP Voice Media Streaming Application**—Allows Cisco CallManager to act as a Media Termination Point (MTP), a conference bridge, a music on hold (MOH) server, and an annunciator. The voice network uses these media resources for feature functionality.
- **Cisco CTIManager**—Allows Cisco CallManager to support computer telephony integration (CTI) services and provides Telephony Application Programming Interface (TAPI) or Java Telephony Application Programming Interface (JTAPI) client support. Cisco CTIManager allows you to use applications such as Cisco IP SoftPhone.
- **Cisco Telephony Call Dispatcher**—Distributes calls to multiple telephone numbers (hunt groups). Cisco WebAttendant, Attendant Console, and Auto Attendant require Cisco Telephony Call Dispatcher (TCD).
- **Cisco MOH Audio Translator**—Allows Cisco CallManager to convert MP3 or WAV audio files into voice codec format used for MOH.
- **Cisco Real-Time Information Server (RIS) Data Collector**—Allows Cisco CallManager to write trace and alarm file information to a database, Microsoft Event Viewer, or alert an SNMP server.

- **Cisco Database Layer Monitor**—Monitors aspects of the Microsoft SQL 2000 database, as well as call detail records (CDRs).
- **Cisco CDR Insert**—Allows Cisco CallManager to write CDRs to the local database and replicates CDR files to the Microsoft SQL publisher at a configured interval.
- **Cisco CTL Provider**—Works with the Cisco Certificate Trust List (CTL) client to change the security mode for the cluster from nonsecure to secure (called mixed mode).
- **Cisco Extended Functions**—Provides support for some Cisco CallManager features, including Cisco Call Back and Quality Report Tool (QRT).
- **Cisco Serviceability Reporter**—Generates the following daily reports: Device Statistics, Server Statistics, Service Statistics, Call Activities, and Alert.
- **Cisco WebDialer**—Provides click-to-dial functionality by using a web page or a desktop application.
- **Cisco IP Manager Assistant**—Allows Cisco CallManager to support the Cisco IP Manager Assistant (IPMA), an application designed to allow a receptionist and manager to support special functionality between their phones.
- **Cisco CallManager Extension Mobility**—Allows Cisco CallManager to support extension mobility functions for roaming users. By using extension mobility features, you can assign users roaming phone profiles that activate when they log in to a phone. Works similarly to the roaming profiles in a Windows-based domain environment.
- **Cisco Certificate Authority Proxy Function**—Working in conjunction with the Cisco Certificate Authority Proxy Function (CAPF) application, the Cisco CAPF service can perform the following tasks, depending on your configuration:
  - — Issues locally significant certificates to supported Cisco IP Phone models
  - — Requests certificates from third-party certificate authorities on behalf of supported Cisco IP Phone models
  - — Upgrades existing certificates on the phones
  - — Retrieves phone certificates for troubleshooting
  - — Deletes locally significant certificates on the phone

You must activate the Cisco CallManager services from the Service Activation web interface rather than the Windows 2000 Services control panel. To access this interface, perform the following steps:

Step 1 Open Internet Explorer, and go to https://<CallManager_IP_Address>/ccmadmin. The <CallManager_IP_Address> is the IP address of the Cisco CallManager server that is running IIS web services. Enter the administrative username and password information.

Step 2 From the Application menu, choose **Cisco CallManager Serviceability**. The Cisco CallManager Serviceability interface appears.

Step 3 From the Tools menu, choose **Service Activation**. A window similar to the window shown in Figure 3-2 appears.

Figure 3-2 *Cisco CallManager Service Activation Interface*

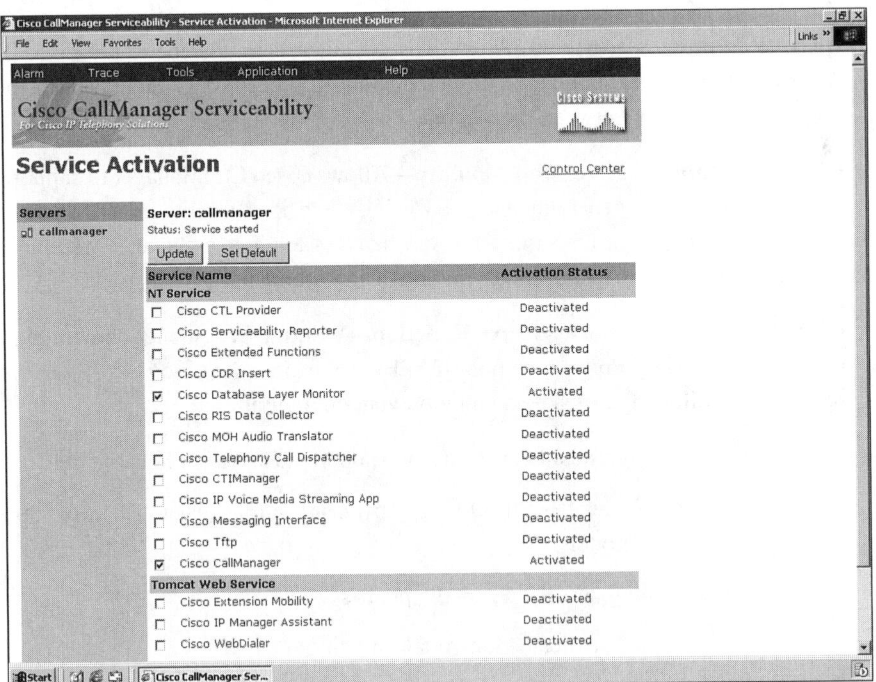

Step 4 Click the server that you want to configure from the Servers column. Next click the services that you want to activate, and click the **Update** button. (You will experience a slight delay.) The Service Activation window will refresh when the process is complete.

TIP The method shown is just one way to access the Cisco CallManager Serviceability pages. If you are working on the Cisco CallManager itself, you can get there quicker by using the Windows 2000 Start menu (**Start > Programs > Cisco CallManager > Cisco CallManager Serviceability**) or by accessing https://<CallManager-IP-Address>/CCMService.

CAUTION Remember to activate the Cisco CallManager services from the Service Activation web interface. Activating the services through the Windows 2000 Services console will produce unpredictable and unstable results.

When you click the **Set Default** button in the web interface, the Service Activation tool chooses the services required to run Cisco CallManager based on a single-server configuration. This is the bare minimum to have a working Cisco CallManager–based IP telephony network. Because Cisco highly advises against single-server installations, you will most likely use the **Set Default** button in a lab environment.

Upgrading Prior Cisco Unified CallManager Versions

Cisco supports the upgrade to Cisco CallManager 4.1 from Cisco CallManager Release 3.3(4), 3.3(5), 4.0(1), and 4.0(2a). You must first upgrades earlier versions to one of these releases before you can upgrade to version 4.1.

NOTE Cisco CallManager 4.1(3) is the most recent version available at the time of this writing. If you are upgrading to a more recent version, refer to the specific upgrade instructions provided in the documentation for the more recent Cisco CallManager version.

If your server runs a version of Cisco CallManager Release 3.2 or earlier, you must first upgrade every server in the cluster to the latest version of Cisco CallManager Release 3.3 before you can upgrade to a version of Cisco CallManager Release 4.1. This is because the database structure and storage system changes from versions prior to release 3.3. (Earlier versions use SQL 7.0 rather than SQL 2000.)

Before you perform any upgrade procedures, it is strongly recommended that you install the latest operating system upgrade and service release, SQL service releases and hotfixes, and Cisco CallManager service release for the versions that currently run in the cluster. Cisco provides the service release and corresponding "readme" documentation on Cisco.com. To obtain these documents, go to http://www.cisco.com/kobayashi/sw-center/sw-voice.shtml (CCO login is required).

> **NOTE** Cisco releases all service packs, hotfixes, and Windows operating system upgrades through the CCO website. Updates released by Microsoft should *never* be applied to the Cisco CallManager server as they can potentially cause the Cisco CallManager software to become unstable or to crash. Cisco guarantees that they will release any critical operating system patch within 24 hours of the Microsoft announcement. Noncritical patches are rolled up into a monthly update.

Cisco requires that you install Cisco IP Telephony Server Operating System Version 2000.2.6 (available from Cisco CCO) before you upgrade to Cisco CallManager Release 4.1.

> **CAUTION** Because the foundation operating system components might change, the upgrade procedure will many times require you to back up the database on the Publisher server, reimage Cisco CallManager completely (using the clean installation method discussed earlier in the chapter), and then restore the SQL data from backup. If your version of Cisco CallManager requires this, be absolutely sure to install the newer backup software on the Cisco CallManager you are upgrading before you initially back up the database. Many times, the backup software changes between the 3.x and 4.x versions of Cisco CallManager. Because of this, you will usually find the latest version of the backup software in the /backup folder on the first Cisco CallManager Installation CD-ROM. If you do not install the new backup software before performing the Cisco CallManager upgrade, your backup file (and SQL data) might be unreadable in the new Cisco CallManager version.

Because many of the Cisco CallManager servers are equipped with RAID 1 configurations (mirrored hard disks), a common upgrade strategy is as follows:

Step 1 Remove the mirrored hard disk from the production Cisco CallManager server.

Step 2 Boot a lab server using the mirrored hard disk.

Step 3 Perform the Cisco CallManager software upgrade on the mirrored hard disk.

Step 4 During a scheduled window of downtime, reboot the production server using the upgraded, mirrored drive.

Step 5 The hard drive running the older Cisco CallManager version will become the new, backup mirrored drive.

By using this upgrade process, you can reduce the amount of voice network downtime to the amount of time it takes to reboot the Cisco CallManager server on the upgraded drive.

> **CAUTION** The upgrade process described will cause a loss of any database changes performed from the time you have removed the mirrored drive until the time you reboot your Cisco CallManager server using the new version. Plan your upgrade windows accordingly.

Summary

This chapter covered the Cisco CallManager installation and upgrade process. When you purchase a Cisco MCS and Cisco CallManager software, you will receive a number of CDs (and even DVDs). Of those, you will only need three discs for the installation: the hardware detection CD, the operating system CD/DVD, and the Cisco CallManager installation CD/DVD. The installation itself is very automated and disk image-based. It requires very little knowledge of the foundation Windows 2000 operating system and SQL 2000 database store. After the installation completes, you should stop any unnecessary services running on your Cisco CallManager and start the Cisco CallManager services required for your network.

The upgrade process for Cisco CallManager varies wildly depending on the version of Cisco CallManager you are using. The process can be as simple as inserting the Cisco CallManager installation disk and following a step-by-step wizard or as complex as a complete reimage of all servers in the cluster. The key is to make sure that you have backed up all data from the SQL server with the newest version of the backup software available from the Cisco CallManager installation CD-ROM or the Cisco website.

Review Questions

You can find the solutions to these questions in Appendix A, "Answers to Review Questions."

1. Cisco CallManager uses which of these operating systems?

   a. Linux

   b. Windows NT

   c. Windows 2000

   d. Windows 2003

2. Why is it recommended that you stop IIS on the subscriber servers? (Choose two.)
   a. enhances server call processing and redundancy
   b. maximizes the number of devices in a cluster
   c. disables the use of remote terminal services
   d. helps prevent unauthorized access to the server
   e. makes more resources available for critical voice services
3. When you first install Cisco CallManager software, which CD-ROM should you use to boot the server to determine the correct CD-ROM to insert next?
   a. Cisco CallManager 4.0 Software Disk
   b. Cisco IP Telephony Server Operating System Hardware Detection Disk
   c. Cisco CallManager Installation, Upgrade, and Recovery Disk
   d. Cisco IP Telephony Server Backup and Restore Disk
   e. Cisco Extended Services and Locales Disk
4. If you are not using DNS, what must you configure to resolve server names for the Cisco CallManager installation process?
   a. DHCP
   b. backup server
   c. LMHOSTS file
   d. DNS reverse lookup
5. Which of the following represent Windows services that you are able to stop on both Publisher and Subscriber servers? (Choose three.)
   a. computer browser
   b. DHCP client
   c. database layer monitor
   d. CTL provider
   e. FTP Publishing Service
6. If you want to set up a Cisco CallManager as a single-server configuration in a lab environment, what button can you click on the Service Activation web page to start the necessary services?
   a. Single Server
   b. Lab
   c. Set Default
   d. Minimal Service

7. You have just completed the installation of a Cisco CallManager server, entered the new passwords for all accounts, and restarted. What is the next step you should take?

   a. Configure the Cisco CallManager server settings to send IP address information to the IP Phones rather than hostname.

   b. Activate the necessary services through the Service Activation web page.

   c. Upgrade the backup software to the latest version.

   d. Apply the latest operating system service pack from the Cisco website.

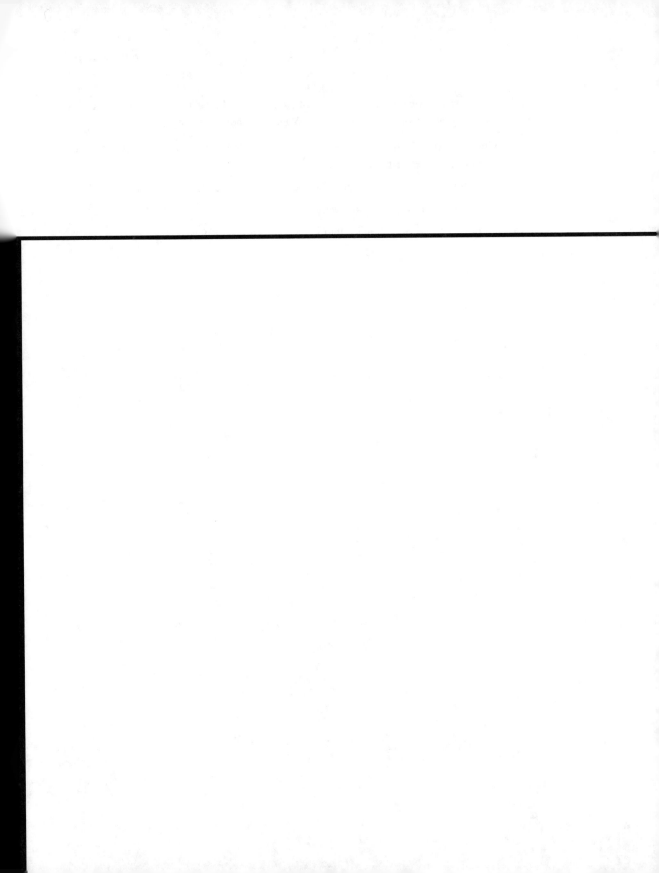

Part II: IPT Devices and Users

This chapter covers the following topics:

- The basic features of Cisco IP Phones
- The entry-level Cisco IP Phones and their features
- The midrange Cisco IP Phones and their features
- The upper-end Cisco IP Phones and their features
- The features and functions of additional Cisco IP telephony endpoints, including video endpoints, conference stations, expansion modules for Cisco IP Phones, PC-based Cisco IP Phones, and analog adapters
- The six steps of the Cisco IP Phone startup process in the correct order
- The two audio codecs that are supported by Cisco IP Phones

CHAPTER 4

Cisco IP Phones and Other User Devices

Thus far, you have focused on the Cisco Unified CallManager server as the management system of the Cisco IP telephony network. It is now time to focus on the devices that Cisco CallManager controls. An important task of implementing and supporting an IP telephony deployment is managing the end-user devices, or endpoints. You should be able to distinguish among the various Cisco IP telephony end-user devices that you might encounter during the course of deploying and administering a Cisco IP telephony network.

This chapter explains the various models of Cisco IP Phones and how they work within a Cisco IP telephony solution. You will learn the basic features of Cisco IP Phones, analog adapters, and conference stations; the IP Phone power-up and registration process; and the audio coders-decoders (codecs) that are supported by Cisco IP Phones.

Cisco IP Phones

To the user, the telephone is the most visible component of the voice communications network. Cisco IP Phones are next-generation, intelligent communication devices that deliver essential business communications. Fully programmable, the growing family of Cisco IP Phones provides the most frequently used business features.

The majority of Cisco IP Phones provide the following features:

- Display-based user interface
- Straightforward user customization
- Inline Power over Ethernet (PoE)
- Support for the G.711 and G.729 audio codecs

Each Cisco IP Phone provides toll-quality audio. Because it is an IP-based phone, you can install it in any location on a corporate local or wide-area IP network. Some corporations have even made the Cisco CallManager publicly available on the Internet (with appropriate firewall platforms in place), allowing Cisco IP Phones to register from any location that has an Internet connection.

Entry-Level Cisco IP Phones

Cisco has produced a number of low-cost, entry-level IP Phones for a variety of business functions. Depending on user requirements, these IP Phones may function well for employees or for use only in public areas, such as lobbies or break rooms. Figure 4-1 shows the four entry-level Cisco IP Phones available at the time of this writing.

Figure 4-1 *Entry-Level Cisco IP Phones*

Entry-level Cisco phones provide the following common features:

- Display-based user interface (except Cisco IP Phone 7902G)
- G.711 and G.729 codec
- Single line (directory number [DN])
- Cisco inline power, powered patch panel, or local power option support via a power cube (the same power supply as the Cisco IP Phone 7910, 7940, or 7960)
- Visual message waiting indicator (MWI)
- One-way speakerphone (no built-in microphone) and no headset port

The following list briefly describes the major features of each entry-level Cisco IP Phone:

- **Cisco IP Phone 7902G**—The Cisco IP Phone 7902G is a single-line, entry-level, no-display business phone with fixed feature keys that provide one-touch access to the redial, transfer, conference, and voice-mail access features. The following briefly describes the major features of the Cisco IP Phone 7902G:
  - — Fixed features: redial, transfer, conference, messages
  - — Hard Hold key
  - — Single 10-Mbps RJ-45 connection (no internal Ethernet switch)

> **NOTE** Even though it might appear from the figure that the Cisco IP Phone 7902G has an LCD display, Cisco has equipped this low-end IP Phone with a piece of paper for a user to label key buttons and phone numbers.

- **Cisco IP Phone 7905G and Cisco IP Phone 7912G**—The Cisco IP Phone 7905G provides single-line access and four interactive softkeys that guide a user through call features and functions via the pixel-based liquid crystal display (LCD). Use this IP Phone for employees who do not need a full-featured phone or for a common area such as a hallway, manufacturing floor, break room, reception space, or office cubicle. The Cisco IP Phone 7912G includes an integrated Ethernet switch that provides LAN connectivity to a collocated PC (allowing only a single cable drop to each location). The following briefly describes the major features of the Cisco IP Phone 7905G and Cisco 7912G:
  - — Pixel-based display (approximately five lines plus softkeys (on-screen feature buttons) and date, time, and menu title
  - — Hard Hold key
  - — Access to all standard IP Phone features through four physical buttons able to access multiple on-screen softkeys
  - — Support for limited Extensible Markup Language (XML) script processing
  - — Support for Cisco Skinny Client Control Protocol (SCCP), H.323 version 2 (Cisco 7905G only), and Session Initiation Protocol (SIP; compliant with RFC 2543)
- **Cisco IP Phone 7911G**—The Cisco IP Phone 7911G provides identical features as the Cisco 7912G with the following differences:
  - — Support for IEEE 802.3af and Cisco proprietary inline power standards
  - — Enhanced memory and XML application support similar to the Cisco IP Phone 7970
  - — Support for enhanced security features
- **Cisco IP Phone 7910G+SW**—The Cisco IP Phone 7910G+SW is for common-use areas that require only basic features, such as dialing out, accessing 911, and intercom calls. Locations that might benefit from these limited features include lobbies, break rooms, and hallways. The Cisco IP Phone 7910G+SW includes a two-port switch for use in applications where you require basic IP Phone functionality and a collocated PC. The following briefly describes the major features of the Cisco 7910G+SW:
  - — Ability to handle low-to-medium telephone usage
  - — Single line with call waiting
  - — Display area of 2 x 24 inches (5.08 x 60.96 cm)

— Cisco 10BASE-T/100BASE-T, two-port FastEthernet switch

— Basic features: line, hold, transfer, settings, messages, conference, forward, speed dial, redial

— Adjustable foot stand (flat to 60 degrees)

— Basic and optional wall mounting

> **NOTE** Cisco has positioned the Cisco IP Phone 7912G to replace the Cisco IP Phone 7910G+SW. The Cisco 7910+SW should reach End-of-Life (EOL) in January 2006.

Midrange and Upper-End Cisco IP Phones

Cisco designed the IP Phones 7940G, 7941G and 7941G-GE, 7960, 7961G and 7961G-GE, 7970G and 7971G-GE, and 7985G to meet the demand for a corporate-level, full-featured IP Phone for medium-to-high telephone use. Figure 4-2 shows the midrange and upper-end Cisco IP Phones available at the time of this writing.

Figure 4-2 *Midrange and Upper-End Cisco IP Phones*

Cisco IP Phone 7985G

A description of features that are common to all midrange and upper-end IP Phones follows:

- Multiline capability
- Large pixel-based displays, which allow for the inclusion of XML and future features
- Integrated two-port FastEthernet or Gigabit Ethernet switch
- Built-in headset connection and quality full-duplex speakerphone (does not come with a headset)
- Information key for "online" help with features
- A minimum of 24 user-adjustable ring tones
- Adjustable foot stand (flat to 60 degrees) for desktop use or appropriate kit included for wall mounting
- SCCP and SIP support
- XML service support
- An EIA/TIA-232 port for options, such as line expansion and security access

NOTE The 79XXG-GE IP Phone models offer features identical to the 79XXG models with the exception of the integrated two-port switch. The 79XXG-GE models have integrated, two-port 10/100/1000 switchports, whereas the 79XXG models have integrated, two-port 10/100 switchports.

Additional details of these phone models follow:

- **Cisco IP Phone 7941G and 7941G-GE**—The Cisco IP Phone 7941G and 7941G-GE is for medium traffic and has these features:
  - — Ideal for transaction workers who use cubicle phones
  - — Two lines and programmable feature buttons, and four interactive softkeys
  - — PoE compatible (Cisco prestandard PoE and IEEE 802.3af industry standard)
  - — Increased memory for advanced applications
  - — Higher resolution display
  - — Backlit screen and line keys
- **Cisco IP Phone 7961G and 7961G-GE**—The Cisco IP Phone 7961G and 7961G-GE is for high or busy telephone traffic and has these features:
  - — Ideal for professionals or managers

— Six lines and programmable feature buttons, and four interactive softkeys

— PoE compatible (Cisco prestandard PoE and IEEE 802.3af industry standard)

— Increased memory for advanced applications

— Higher resolution display

— Backlit screen and line keys

- **Cisco IP Phone 7970G**—The Cisco IP Phone 7970G is one of Cisco's current high-end devices featuring a high resolution, full-color display that can make a passerby look twice. It has the following features:

  — Ideal for executives, decision makers, and high-visibility areas of your organization

  — Eight lines and programmable feature buttons, and five interactive softkeys

  — Larger, color display with touch-screen capabilities

  — 3.5-mm stereo jack sockets for connection to PC-style speakers or headphones, and microphone

  — PoE compatible (Cisco prestandard PoE and IEEE 802.3af industry standard)

  — Advanced XML development platform for more dynamic applications

- **Cisco IP Phone 7971G-GE**—The Cisco IP Phone 7971G looks identical to the 7970G with the following differences:

  — Delivers Gigabit Ethernet bandwidth to the desktop with an integrated 10/100/1000 Mbps switch

  — "Feature identical" to the Cisco IP Phone 7970G

  — PoE compatible (IEEE 802.3af PoE only; does not support Cisco prestandard PoE)

- **Cisco IP Phone 7980G**—The Cisco 7980G harnesses next-generation video technology offering the following features:

  — Ideal for executives, decision makers, and high-visibility areas of your organization (such as conference rooms)

  — Provides a desktop video phone making instant, face-to-face communication possible using the H.264 video codec

  — Offers an integrated, two-port 10/100 Ethernet switch

  — Enables digital clarity video

— PoE compatible (IEEE 802.3af PoE only; does not support Cisco prestandard PoE)

> **TIP** Cisco has recently upgraded the 7940G and 7960G IP Phones to the 7941G and 7961G. The primary features Cisco added are the support for the IEEE 802.3af PoE standard, higher resolution and backlit display, multiple color line buttons (to support different line states), and advanced XML application support. All other features remain the same.

Additional Cisco IP Telephony Endpoints

Cisco provides a complete portfolio of IP endpoints to meet business needs for conferencing, wireless voice communications, PC-based voice calls, and connecting analog devices to the VoIP network. Figure 4-3 shows the additional IP telephony endpoints available at the time of this writing.

Figure 4-3 *Additional IP Telephony Endpoints*

Cisco VT Advantage

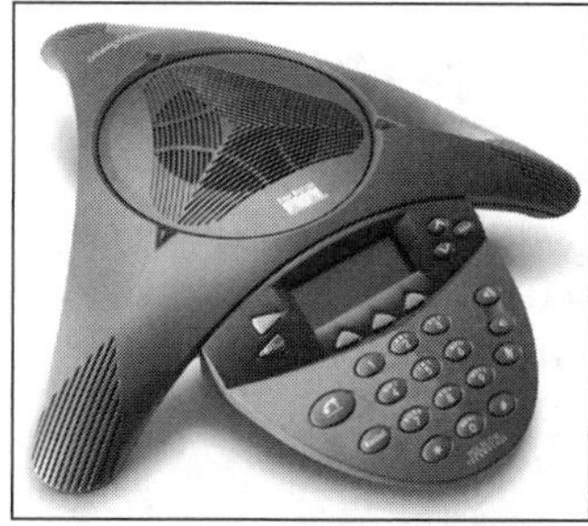

Cisco Conference Station 7936

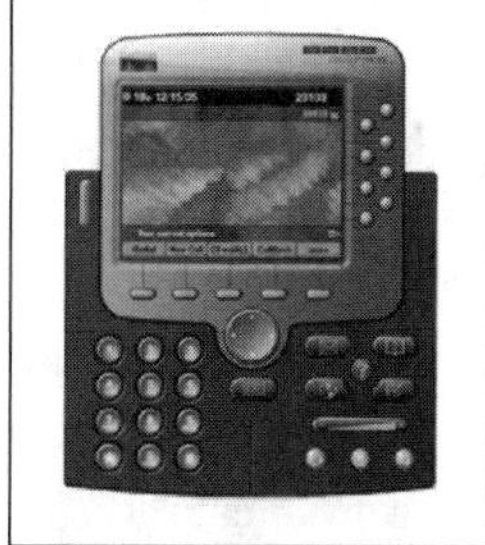

Cisco IP Communicator

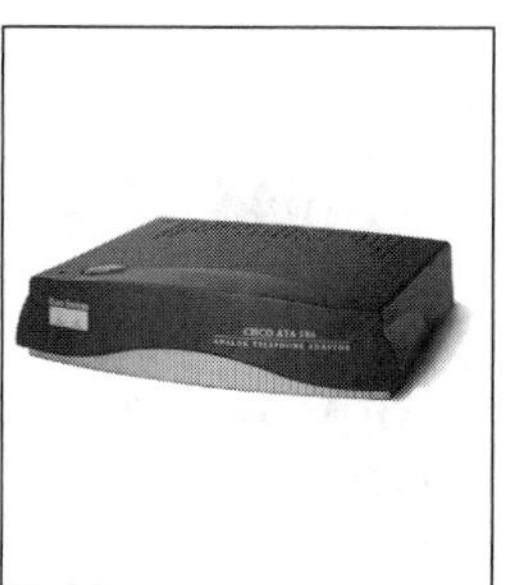

Cisco ATA 186 and 188

Cisco 7914 Expansion Module

Cisco Wireless IP Phone 7920

These products are as follows:

- **Cisco VT Advantage**—Cisco VT Advantage is a video telephony solution consisting of the Cisco VT Advantage software application and Cisco VT Camera, a video telephony Universal Serial Bus (USB) camera. With the Cisco VT Camera attached to a PC that is connected to the switch port of a Cisco IP Phone, users can place and receive video calls on their enterprise

IP telephony network. Users make calls from their Cisco IP Phones using familiar phone interfaces, but calls are enhanced with video on a PC, without requiring any extra button pushing or mouse clicking. When registered to Cisco CallManager, the Cisco VT Advantage–enabled IP Phone has the features and functionality of a full-featured IP videophone. System administrators can provision a Cisco IP Phone with Cisco VT Advantage as they would any other Cisco IP Phone, which can greatly simplify deployment and management.

- **Cisco IP Conference Station 7936**—The Cisco IP Conference Station 7936 is a full-featured, IP-based, full-duplex, hands-free conference phone for use on desktops, in offices, and in small-to-medium conference rooms. The Cisco IP Conference Station 7936 offers external microphone ports, optional external microphone kit, audio-tuned speaker grill, and a backlit LCD display. The optional microphone kit includes two microphones with 6-foot (1.8288-m) cords so that you can place the microphones across a 12-foot (3.6576-m) area, effectively expanding to a suggested conference room size of 20 x 30 feet (6.096 x 9.144 m). The backlit LCD display improves visibility in low-light conditions. The display font size is also adjustable for improved distant viewing. The Conference Station 7936 does not support inline power and requires an external power supply at this time.

- **Cisco IP Communicator**—The Cisco IP Communicator is a Microsoft Windows software–based application that delivers enhanced telephony support through personal computers. This application endows computers with the functionality of Cisco IP Phones and provides high-quality voice calls on the road, in the office, or from wherever users might have access to the corporate network. Cisco IP Communicator has an intuitive design, is easy to use, and delivers convenient access to a host of features, including eight lines and five softkeys. Cisco IP Communicator offers handset, headset, and high-quality speakerphone modes. The application appears as an on-screen Cisco 7970 IP Phone. Cisco plans to add video support to the IP Communicator by the time this publication reaches press.

- **Cisco Analog Telephone Adaptor (ATA) 186 and 188**—The Cisco ATA 186 and Cisco ATA 188 interface analog devices with your IP-based telephony network. These adapters are useful for customers who have existing analog devices, such as fax machines or telephones, that they do not want to replace after they have migrated to VoIP. The Cisco ATA 186 provides two voice ports, each with its own independent telephone number, and a single 10BASE-T Ethernet port for network connectivity. The Cisco ATA 188 provides two voice ports and two 10/100-Mbps Ethernet connections, which allows for network connectivity and the ability to collocate a network device with the analog voice equipment.

- **Cisco IP Phone 7914 Expansion Module**—The Cisco IP Phone 7914 Expansion Module extends the capabilities of the Cisco IP Phone 7960G, 7961G, 7970G, and 7971G-GE with additional buttons and an LCD display. The Cisco IP Phone 7914 helps administrative assistants and others who must monitor, manage, and cover the various status of a number of calls beyond the line capability of the standard Cisco IP Phone models. This expansion module enables you to add 14 buttons to the existing buttons of the Cisco IP Phone 7960G,

7961G, 7970G, and 7971G-GE, increasing the total number of line and speed dial buttons available. You can use up to two Cisco 7914 Expansion Modules on each of the Cisco IP Phones listed previously.

> **TIP** The 7914 Expansion Module cannot receive inline power and requires a local power supply. A single power supply can power both 7914 expansion modules attached to an IP Phone.

- **Cisco Wireless IP Phone 7920**—The Cisco Wireless IP Phone 7920 is an easy-to-use IEEE 802.11b wireless IP Phone that provides comprehensive voice communications in conjunction with Cisco CallManager and the Cisco Aironet 1200, 1100, 350, and 340 Series of Wi-Fi (IEEE 802.11b) access points and their related security standards (such as TKIP/MIC, WPA, LEAP, and so on). The Cisco Wireless IP Phone 7920 is designed for ease of use, with a pixel-based display to access calling features and two softkeys, support for up to six directory numbers, a four-way rocker switch, a Hold key, a Mute key, and a Menu key that allows quick access to information such as directories, call history, and phone settings. The phone also offers XML support on models with a recent firmware upgrade.

Table 4-1 provides a feature-by-feature comparison of the various Cisco IP Phone models. This table comes from "Cisco IP Telephony Solution Reference Network Design (SRND) for Cisco CallManager 4.0 and 4.1" (http://www.cisco.com/en/US/products/sw/voicesw/ps556/products_implementation_design_guide_book09186a00805fdb7b.html) and is printed with permission from Cisco Systems.

Table 4-1 *IP Phone Features*

Feature	7902G	7905G	7910G	7910 +SW	7912G	7920G	7935G, 7936G	7940G	7960G	7970G
Ethernet Connection	Y[1]	Y[1]	Y[1]	Y[2]	Y[2]	N	Y[3]	Y[2]	Y[2]	Y[2]
Ethernet Switch	N	N	N	Y	Y	N	N	Y	Y	Y
Cisco Power-Over-Ethernet (PoE)	Y	Y	Y	Y	Y	N	N	Y	Y	Y
IEEE 802.3af Power-Over-Ethernet (PoE)	N	N	N	N	N	N	N	N	N	Y
Localization	N	Y	N	N	Y	N	N	Y	Y	Y
Directory Number	1	1	1	1	1	6	1	2	6	8
Liquid Crystal Display	N	Y	Y	Y	Y	Y	Y	Y	Y	Y

continues

Table 4-1 *IP Phone Features (Continued)*

Feature	7902G	7905G	7910G	7910 +SW	7912G	7920G	7935G, 7936G	7940G	7960G	7970G
Caller ID	N	Y	Y	Y	Y	Y	Y	Y	Y	Y
Call Waiting	N	Y	Y	Y	Y	Y	Y	Y	Y	Y
Caller ID on Call Waiting	N	Y	Y	Y	Y	Y	Y	Y	Y	Y
Call Hold	Y	Y	Y	Y	Y	Y	Y	Y	Y	Y
Call Transfer	Y	Y	Y	Y	Y	Y	Y	Y	Y	Y
Call Forward	Y	Y	Y	Y	Y	Y	Y	Y	Y	Y
Auto-Answer	Y	Y	N	N	Y	Y	N	Y	Y	Y
Ad Hoc Conference	Y	Y	Y	Y	Y	Y	Y	Y	Y	Y
Meet-Me Conference	N	Y	Y	Y	Y	Y	Y	Y	Y	Y
Call Pickup	N	Y	Y	Y	Y	Y	Y	Y	Y	Y
Group Pickup	N	Y	Y	Y	Y	Y	Y	Y	Y	Y
Redial	Y[4]	Y[4]	Y[4]	Y[4]	Y[4]	Y	Y	Y	Y	Y
Speed Dial	Y	Y	Y	Y	Y	Y	N	Y	Y	Y
On-hook Dialing	N	Y	Y	Y	Y	Y	Y	Y	Y	Y
Voice Mail Access	Y	Y	Y	Y	Y	Y	N	Y	Y	Y
Message Waiting Indicator (MWI)	Y	Y	Y	Y	Y	Y	N	Y	Y	Y
Video call	N	N	N	N	N	N	N	Y	Y	Y
Survivable Remote Site Telephony (SRST) Support	Y	Y	Y	Y	Y	Y	Y	Y	Y	Y
Music on Hold (MoH)	Y	Y	Y	Y	Y	Y[5]	Y	Y	Y	Y
Speaker	N	Y[6]	Y[6]	Y[6]	Y[6]	N	Y	Y	Y	Y
Headset Jack	N	N	N	N	N	Y[7]	N	Y	Y	Y
Mute	N	N	Y	Y	N	Y	Y	Y	Y	Y

Table 4-1 *IP Phone Features (Continued)*

Feature	7902G	7905G	7910G	7910 +SW	7912G	7920G	7935G, 7936G	7940G	7960G	7970G
Multilevel Precedence and Preemption (MLPP)	Y	Y	Y	Y	Y	N	N	Y	Y	Y
Barge	N	N	N	N	N	N	N	Y	Y	Y
cBarge	N	Y	N	N	Y	N	N	Y	Y	N
Disable General Attribute Registration Protocol (GARP)	Y	Y	Y	Y	Y	N	N	Y	Y	Y
Signaling and Media Encryption	N	N	N	N	N	Y[8]	N	Y	Y	Y
Signaling Integrity	N	N	N	N	N	N	N	Y	Y	Y
Manufacturing-Installed Certificate (X.509v3)	N	N	N	N	N	N	N	N	N	Y
Field-Installed Certificate	N	N	N	N	N	N	N	Y	Y	N
Third-Party XML Service	N	Y	N	N	Y	N	N	Y	Y	Y
External Microphone and Speaker	N	N	N	N	N	N	N	N	N	Y
Dial Plan Mapping	N	N	N	N	N	N	N	N	N	N
Signaling Packet ToS Value Marking	0x60	0x68	0x68	0x68	0x60	0x68	0x68	0x60	0x60	0x60
Media Packet ToS Value Marking	0xB8	0xB8	0xB8	0xB8	0xB8	0xB8	0xB8	0xB8	0xB8	0xB8
Skinny Client Control Protocol (SCCP)	Y	Y	Y	Y	Y	Y	N	Y	Y	Y

continues

Table 4-1 *IP Phone Features (Continued)*

Feature	7902G	7905G	7910G	7910 +SW	7912G	7920G	7935G, 7936G	7940G	7960G	7970G
Session Initiation Protocol (SIP)	N	Y	N	N	Y	N	N	Y	Y	N
H.323	N	Y	N	N	N	N	Y	N	N	N
Media Gateway Control Protocol (MGCP)	N	N	N	N	N	N	N	Y	Y	N
G.711	Y	Y	Y	Y	Y	Y	Y	Y	Y	Y
G.723	N	Y	N	N	N	N	N	N	N	N
G.726	N	Y	N	N	N	N	N	N	N	N
G.729	Y	Y	Y	Y	Y	Y	Y	Y	Y	Y
Voice Activity Detection (VAD)	Y	Y	Y	Y	Y	Y	Y	Y	Y	Y
Comfort Noise Generation (CNG)	Y	Y	Y	Y	Y	Y	Y	Y	Y	Y

[1] One 10 Base-T

[2] Two 10/100 Base-T

[3] One 10/100 Base-T

[4] Last Number Redial

[5] Supports only unicast MoH

[6] One-way listen mode

[7] The only supported headset for the Cisco IP Phone 7920 is one with a 2.5 mm jack, available at http://www.cisco.getheadsets.com.

[8] Signaling and Media Encryption are available with Static WEP and LEAP security configurations.

IP Phone Startup Process

Figure 4-4 provides an overview of the startup process for a Cisco IP Phone if you are using a Cisco Catalyst switch that is capable of providing Cisco prestandard Power over Ethernet (PoE). Understanding the boot process of a Cisco IP Phone is critical to your abilities to troubleshoot an IP telephony network.

Figure 4-4 *Cisco IP Phone Startup Process*

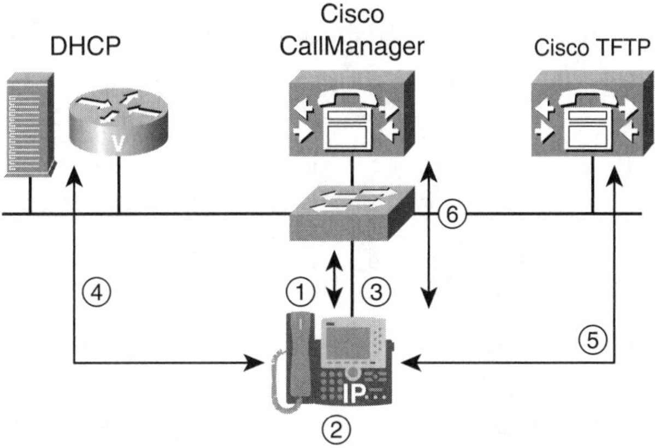

1. IP Phone obtains power from the switch
2. Phone loads stored image
3. Switch provides VLAN information to IP Phone
4. Phone sends DHCP request; receives IP information and TFTP server address
5. IP Phone gets configuration from TFTP server
6. IP Phone registers with Cisco CallManager server

The following list explains the normal boot process of a Cisco IP Phone:

Step 1 **Obtain power from the switch**—When a Cisco IP Phone is connected to a Cisco Catalyst switch model that is capable of providing inline power (called Power over Ethernet [PoE]), the switch automatically detects an unpowered phone and sends power down the Ethernet cable to the IP Phone. The details of how the switch detects an unpowered IP Phone and how it delivers power to the IP Phone are covered in Chapter 8, "Cisco Catalyst Switches."

Step 2 **Load the stored phone image**—The Cisco IP Phone has nonvolatile flash memory in which it stores firmware images and user-defined preferences. At startup, the phone runs a bootstrap loader that loads a phone image stored in flash memory. Using this image, the phone initializes its software and hardware.

Step 3 **Configure the VLAN**—After the IP Phone receives power and boots, the switch sends a Cisco Discovery Protocol version 2 (CDPv2) trigger packet to the IP Phone. CDP packets that are "triggered" do not need to wait for the default 60-second CDP hello interval. This CDPv2 packet provides the

IP Phone with voice VLAN information, if you have configured that feature (voice VLANs are also discussed in Chapter 8). The IP Phone will then tag all its traffic with the appropriate voice VLAN information.

Step 4 **Obtain the IP address and TFTP server address**—Next, the IP Phone broadcasts a request to a DHCP server. The DHCP server responds to the IP Phone with a minimum of an IP address, a subnet mask, the default gateway, and the IP address of the Cisco TFTP server.

> **TIP** A DHCP server can give a Cisco IP Phone the location of a TFTP server in two different ways:
>
> - **DHCP Option 66**—Gives the Cisco IP Phone the hostname of the TFTP server (requires DNS resolution)
> - **DHCP Option 150**—Gives the Cisco IP Phone the IP address of the TFTP server
>
> The DHCP administrator must add one or both of these options to the DHCP scope used for the Cisco IP Phones. If you cannot use the DHCP server to distribute this information, you must hard code the IP address of the TFTP server manually on each IP Phone. Cisco recommends using DHCP Option 150 because it allows you to configure the IP Phone to use multiple TFTP server addresses for redundancy.

Step 5 **Contact the TFTP server for configuration**—The IP Phone then contacts the Cisco TFTP server. The TFTP server has configuration files (.cnf file format or .cnf.xml) for telephony devices, which define parameters for connecting to Cisco CallManager. The TFTP server sends the configuration information for that IP Phone, which contains an ordered list of up to three Cisco CallManagers. In general, any time that you make a change in Cisco CallManager that requires a phone (device) to be reset, a change has been made to the configuration file of that phone. If a phone has an XML-compatible load, it requests an XMLDefault.cnf.xml configuration file; otherwise, it requests a .cnf file. If you have enabled auto-registration in Cisco CallManager, the phones access a default configuration file (sepdefault.cnf.xml) from the TFTP server. If you have manually entered the phones into the Cisco CallManager database, the phone accesses a .cnf.xml file that corresponds to its device name. The .cnf.xml file also contains the information that tells the phone which image load that it should be running. If this image load differs from the one that is currently loaded on the phone, the phone contacts the TFTP server to request the new image file, which is stored as a .bin or .sgn (secured load) file.

Step 6 **Register with Cisco CallManager**—After obtaining the file from the TFTP server, the phone attempts to make a TCP connection to a Cisco CallManager, starting with the highest-priority Cisco CallManager in its list. After the phone registers with the Cisco CallManager, it receives an extension number and becomes operational.

Cisco IP Phone Codec Support

Before a VoIP device is able to stream audio, the analog audio signal must be converted to a digitized format. This is accomplished by an audio codec, which digitizes the audio input at the transmitting end and converts the digital stream back to analog audio at the receiving end.

Because converted audio streams can consume a significant amount of bandwidth over slower WAN connections, many of the audio codecs also provide a level of compression, which can considerably reduce the bandwidth that they consume. However, different types of compression can cause degraded voice quality, which is why the different audio codecs offer different compression algorithms and quality levels.

The International Telecommunication Union Telecommunication Standardization Sector (ITU-T) standards committee specifies several standards (called recommendations) for audio codecs. Cisco IP Phones natively support two primary codecs: G.711 and G.729. The G.711 and G.729 codecs deliver relatively equal sound quality (both considered toll quality), with G.711 scoring slightly higher than G.729 in a mean opinion score (MOS) test, which is a rating of voice quality. Because of this similarity, some network administrators choose to operate an entirely G.729-based network, whereas others choose to implement G.729 over the WAN and G.711 on the LAN. A G.711 conversation consumes 64 Kbps of network bandwidth (not including packet header overhead), whereas a G.729 conversation consumes 8 Kbps of network bandwidth (not including packet header overhead).

Although this configuration is ideal for many network environments, you might eventually encounter a codec mismatch. A codec mismatch occurs when two devices cannot negotiate a common codec or when the network administrator has forbidden the use of their common codec, such as using G.711 over the WAN. Regardless of the cause, you now have a need for transcoding. Transcoding resources perform conversions between the audio codecs. These resources are often costly and can introduce significant delay and quality degradation into your IP telephony network. When designing a voice network, you should attempt to limit the amount of transcoding that takes place between devices.

Although it is not mentioned often, the Cisco 7900 IP Phone models support the Wideband codec. This is a Cisco proprietary codec that consumes four times the amount of bandwidth as the G.711 codec, using 256 kbps for the audio payload. The codec delivers extremely high-quality 16-bit audio that gives a clean, crisp sound to voice and music on hold.

Summary

This chapter covered IP Phones and other end devices in a Cisco IP telephony network. Although there are many similarities between the Cisco IP Phone models, there are also marked differences as you move through the ever-expanding line of IP Phone models. Each of these phones fit a niche in businesses worldwide. The entry-level Cisco IP Phones include the 7902G, 7905G, 7910G+SW, and 7912G. The midrange and upper-end Cisco IP Phones include the 7941G and 7941G-GE, 7961G and 7961G-GE, 7970G and 7971G-GE, and 7985. The additional IP telephony devices include the Cisco Conference Station 7936, Cisco IP Communicator, Cisco ATA 186 and 188, Cisco 7920 wireless phone, and Cisco 7914 Expansion Module.

Review Questions

You can find the solutions to these questions in Appendix A, "Answers to Review Questions."

1. Which of the following two codecs do current Cisco IP Phones support? (Choose two.)

   a. G.711

   b. G.723

   c. G.728

   d. G.729

2. Which of the following PoE standards does the Cisco IP Phone 7961G support? (Choose two.)

   a. Cisco Pre-Standard Inline Power

   b. 802.11af

   c. 802.11b

   d. 802.3af

3. Which of the following devices has a built-in Ethernet switch? (Choose three.)

   a. Cisco IP Phone 7905

   b. Cisco IP Phone 7912

   c. Cisco IP Phone 7970

   d. Cisco ATA 186

   e. Cisco ATA 188

4. Which of the following Cisco IP Phones provides video-processing capabilities without the VT Advantage software?

   a. Cisco 7970

   b. Cisco 7971

   c. Cisco 7980

   d. Cisco 7936

5. Place these steps in the order that an IP Phone must go through before it can register with Cisco CallManager.

   a. Obtain power.

   b. Get configuration from TFTP server.

   c. Load firmware image.

   d. Obtain VLAN information.

6. Which of the following options can you configure on a DHCP server to deliver the IP address of a TFTP server to a Cisco IP Phone?

   a. Option 6

   b. Option 66

   c. Option 150

   d. Option 170

7. Most Cisco IP Phones provide built-in ______ processing, which allows them to read data stored in this industry standard format.

   a. XML

   b. HTTP

   c. TXT

   d. SQL

8. What is the difference between the Cisco IP Phone 7960 and Cisco IP Phone 7961? (Choose two.)

   a. The 7961 provides a 10/100/1000 built-in switch, whereas the 7960 provides only a 10/100 built-in switch.

   b. The 7961 adds support for the VT Advantage.

   c. The 7961 supports six extensions, whereas the 7960 only supports four extensions.

   d. The 7961 supports both the Cisco prestandard and 802.3af inline power, whereas the 7960 supports only the Cisco prestandard.

9. A company wants to migrate to a VoIP network, but it has an expensive all-in-one voice-fax-copier device that it wants to connect to the VoIP network. Which device would you recommend?

   a. Cisco Conference Station 7936

   b. Cisco IP SoftPhone

   c. Cisco ATA 188

   d. Cisco 7905G

   e. Cisco 7914 Expansion Module

10. A firm wants to install a Cisco IP Phone in the lobby area. The IP telephony network runs only the G.729a codec. The IP Phone should support a single line and all standard features. An LCD display is not required because cost is a concern. Which IP Phone would best meet these requirements?

    a. Cisco IP Phone 7902G

    b. Cisco IP Phone 7905G

    c. Cisco IP Phone 7910G+SW

    d. Cisco IP Phone 7912G

This chapter covers the following topics:

- Configuring Cisco Unified CallManager to support Cisco IP Phone registration and communication within the cluster
- Required elements to create a device pool
- Applying required settings to a Cisco IP Phone through a device pool
- Manually and automatically registering Cisco IP Phones into the SQL database

CHAPTER **5**

Configuring Cisco Unified CallManager to Support IP Phones

After reading the previous chapter, you decided to purchase ten Cisco IP Phones, one of each model. You receive them in the mail, unwrap them (filling the air with the scent of fresh cellophane), and set them on the desk. Nothing happens. Now what? Now you must configure the Cisco CallManager to support the IP Phones. Without the Cisco CallManager, these devices are nothing more than expensive paperweights.

This chapter describes the Cisco CallManager configuration to support Cisco IP Phones. You will learn how to configure Cisco CallManager to manually and automatically add IP Phones and assign directory numbers (DNs). You will also learn how to configure device pools to provide a convenient way to define a set of common characteristics that can be assigned to devices, such as date or time zone, codec use, and other functionalities.

Configuring Intracluster IP Phone Communication

Unbelievably, you can have an entire Cisco IP telephony network deployed in a matter of seconds using the Cisco CallManager in its base configuration. However, setting up the voice network correctly can take a considerable amount of planning and configuration. Thankfully, this chapter shows you how to set up the network manually, and then shows you how to pull it off automatically in a matter of seconds.

Removing DNS Reliance

Chapter 4 discussed the boot process of a Cisco IP Phone. It is critical to understand that process to effectively troubleshoot the IP telephony network. Just to review, the following are three of the critical steps in the process:

1. Cisco IP Phone obtains an IP address from the DHCP server along with the IP address of the TFTP server.
2. The Cisco IP Phone contacts the TFTP server and downloads its configuration.
3. The Cisco IP Phone registers with the Cisco CallManager.

These steps (along with a few others) were presented in the preceding chapter. Now you might be wondering, "The Cisco IP Phone downloads its configuration from the TFTP server.

So…where does that configuration come from?" Great question! It comes from you. As you configure the Cisco CallManager, it will generate a configuration file that it places on the TFTP server for the IP Phone to download. In that configuration file will be a list of up to three Cisco CallManagers for the Cisco IP Phone to contact.

One of the most common problems that occur in the field is a Cisco IP Phone failing to register with the Cisco CallManager because it cannot resolve the Cisco CallManager's hostname to an IP address. This is because, by default, the Cisco CallManager puts a list of up to three Cisco CallManager hostnames the Cisco IP Phone can contact. If you have not configured the IP Phones for DNS name resolution (or the IP Phones cannot reach the DNS server), the phone registration will fail.

Because of this, changing the name of the selected server to the IP address of the server in the Cisco CallManager Administration window is the first step in configuring Cisco CallManager to support Cisco IP Phones.

NOTE Removing DNS reliance is considered a best-practice step in configuring Cisco CallManager. If you prefer, you can keep the Cisco CallManager hostnames in the configuration and still have a functional network.

Renaming the server to the IP address has the following benefits:

- It allows IP Phones and other devices to find Cisco CallManager on the network without having to query the Domain Name System (DNS) server to help resolve the server name to an IP address.
- It prevents the IP telephony network from failing if the IP Phones lose the connection to the DNS server.
- It decreases the time that is required when a device attempts to contact Cisco CallManager.

Complete these steps to eliminate DNS reliance:

Step 1 In Cisco CallManager Administration, choose **System > Server**. The Find and List Servers window appears. Click **Find** to display a list of available servers.

Step 2 Click a server name. The Server Configuration window appears.

Step 3 Remove the hostname and enter the IP address for the server in the Host Name/IP Address field. Click **Update**.

Step 4 Repeat Steps 1-3 for every Cisco CallManager in the cluster.

After the Cisco CallManager hostnames are changed to the appropriate IP addresses, the Cisco CallManager automatically updates the configuration file on the TFTP server, causing the IP Phones to contact the Cisco CallManagers via the IP address rather than the hostname. Figure 5-1 illustrates the Server Configuration screen.

> **NOTE** There are other places where server names must be changed to IP addresses to fully remove DNS resolution from the cluster. Most of these can be found in the **Service > Enterprise Parameters** options.

Figure 5-1 *Cisco CallManager Server Configuration Window*

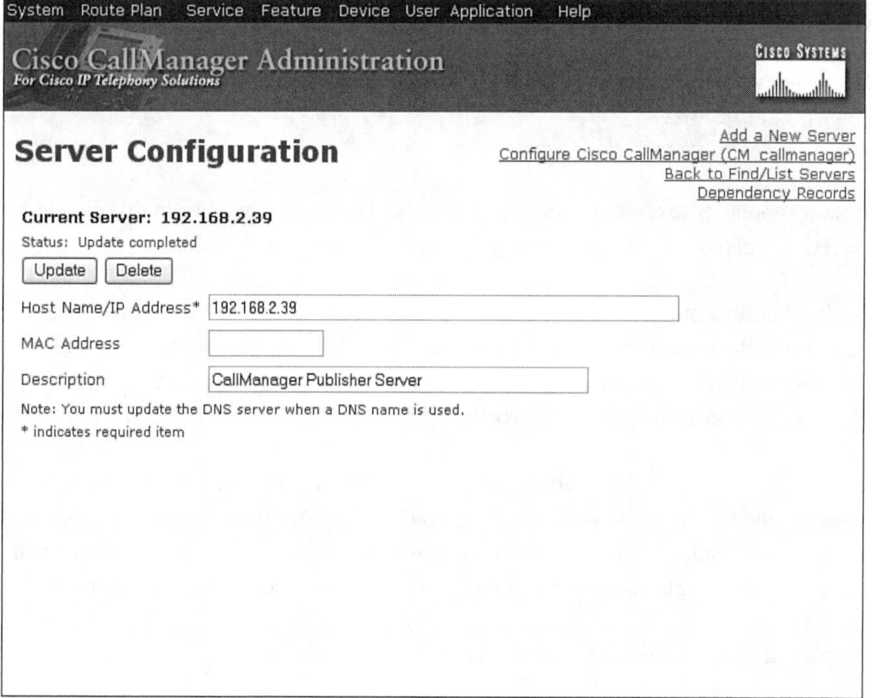

Configuring Device Pools

Device pools provide a convenient way to define a set of common characteristics that can be assigned to devices, such as IP Phones, instead of assigning individual characteristics to individual phones. Device pools enable you to simply assign the phone to the device pool so that the phone automatically inherits the common configuration items. You must configure the device pool for Cisco IP Phones before adding them to the network.

To create a new device pool, you must first create (or use default settings where applicable) the following minimal mandatory components:

- Cisco CallManager group
- Date/time group
- Region
- Softkey template
- Cisco Survivable Remote Site Telephony (SRST) reference

NOTE The SRST Reference field allows you to specify the IP address of the Cisco SRST router. Cisco SRST enables routers to provide call-handling support for Cisco IP Phones when they lose their connection to remote Cisco CallManager installations or when the WAN connection is down.

These components (except for the SRST reference) are covered later in this chapter. SRST is covered in Chapter 14, "Implementing Multiple-Site Deployments."

The device pool combines all of the individual configurations that you have created into a single entity. You will eventually assign this entity to individual devices, such as IP Phones. This process will configure these devices with most of the configuration elements that they need to operate efficiently in your IP telephony network.

For example, configuring 100 different Cisco IP Phones to use the Arizona time zone, the English language, and the classical-style music on hold (MOH) option is tedious. Instead, you can create a device pool, named "Arizona," that configures the correct time zone, language, and MOH, and you can make a single assignment of the Arizona device pool to each IP Phone.

Complete these steps to create the device pool:

Step 1 Choose **System > Device Pool**. The Find and List Device Pools window opens.

Step 2 Click the **Add a New Device Pool** link to open the Device Pool Configuration window shown in Figure 5-2. Choose, at a minimum, the **Cisco CallManager group**, **date/time group**, **region,** and **softkey template**.

NOTE It is a good practice to name your configuration components in Cisco CallManager to reflect their purpose. For example, you could name the Arizona Device Pool "Arizona_DP." You could name the Arizona Date and Time Group "Arizona_DT." This allows you to easily identify these items in the Cisco CallManager database.

Figure 5-2 *Cisco CallManager Device Pool Configuration Window*

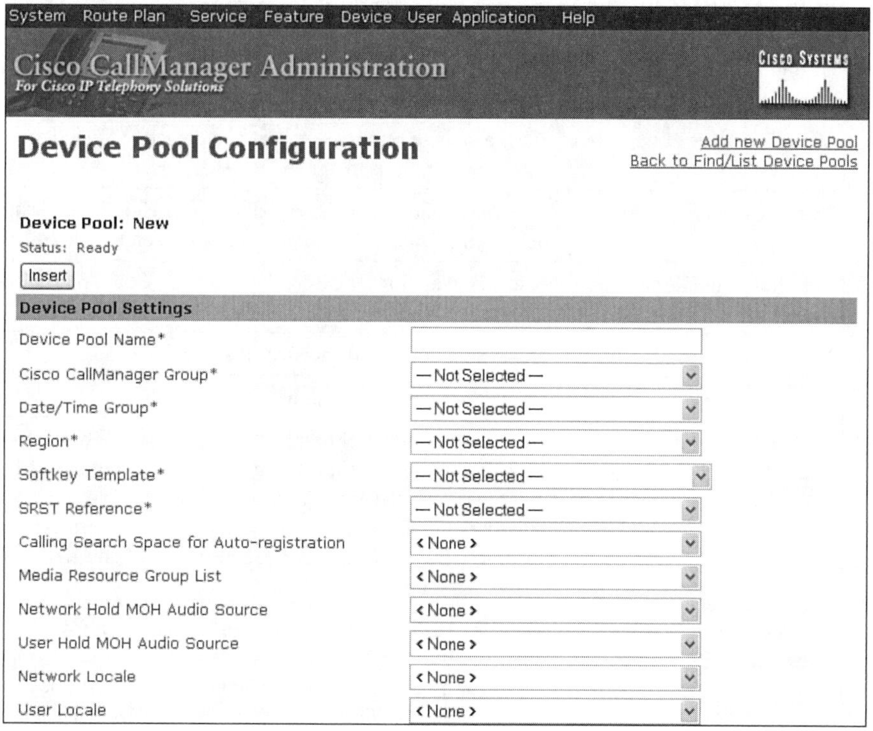

System Route Plan Service Feature Device User Application Help

Cisco CallManager Administration
For Cisco IP Telephony Solutions

Cisco Systems

Device Pool Configuration

Add new Device Pool
Back to Find/List Device Pools

Device Pool: New
Status: Ready
Insert

Device Pool Settings

Device Pool Name*	
Cisco CallManager Group*	— Not Selected —
Date/Time Group*	— Not Selected —
Region*	— Not Selected —
Softkey Template*	— Not Selected —
SRST Reference*	— Not Selected —
Calling Search Space for Auto-registration	< None >
Media Resource Group List	< None >
Network Hold MOH Audio Source	< None >
User Hold MOH Audio Source	< None >
Network Locale	< None >
User Locale	< None >

You can configure many options through a device pool. Some of these options are shown here; others are fully explained later in the book. Table 5-1 provides a quick reference for each of the configuration options in the device pool.

Table 5-1 *Cisco CallManager Device Pool Configuration Options*

Field	Description
Device Pool Name*	Describes a name for the device pool.
Cisco CallManager Group*	Selects a redundancy group for the device pool. This redundancy group can contain a maximum of three redundant Cisco CallManager servers.
Date/Time Group*	Assigns the correct time zone to the device.
Region*	Determines the coder-decoder (codec) selection used by the device, depending on the end location of the call.
Softkey Template*	Defines the type and order of the softkeys that are displayed on the liquid crystal display (LCD) of a Cisco IP Phone.
SRST Reference*	Configures SRST and selects the gateway that will support the device if the connection to the Cisco CallManager is lost.

continues

Table 5-1 *Cisco CallManager Device Pool Configuration Options (Continued)*

Field	Description
Calling Search Space for Auto-registration	Defines whom an IP Phone is able to call if it auto-registers with the Cisco CallManager.
Media Resource Group List	Assigns media resource support to a device for functions such as conferencing, transcoding, or MOH.
Network Hold MOH Audio Source	Selects the audio that Cisco CallManager should play when a user presses the Transfer or Conference button on the Cisco IP Phone.
User Hold MOH Audio Source	Selects the audio that Cisco CallManager should play when a user presses the Hold button on the Cisco IP Phone.
Network Locale	Defines the tones and cadences that the device uses.
User Locale	Defines the language that the device uses.
Connection Monitor Duration	Defines the amount of time that the IP Phone monitors its connection to Cisco CallManager before it unregisters from SRST and reregisters to Cisco CallManager. This is to ensure that the link is stable (not "flapping"). The default for the enterprise parameter specifies 120 seconds, which can be modified on a device-pool basis or left at the default value.
MLPP Precedence and Preemption Information	Manages Multilevel Precedence and Preemption (MLPP) settings: **MLPP Indication:** Specifies whether devices in the device pool that are capable of playing precedence tones will use the capability when the devices plan an MLPP precedence call **MLPP Preemption:** Specifies whether devices in the device pool that are capable of preempting calls in progress will use the capability when the devices plan an MLPP precedence call **MLPP Domain:** A hexadecimal value for the MLPP domain that is associated with the device pool

*Indicates a required field.

If you make changes to a device pool, you must reset the devices in that device pool before the changes will take effect.

You cannot delete a device pool that has been assigned to any device or one that is used for device defaults configuration. To find out which devices are using the device pool, click the **Dependency Records** link in the Device Pool Configuration window. If you try to delete a device pool that is in use, an error message is displayed. Before deleting a device pool that is currently in use, you must perform one of the following tasks:

- Update the devices to assign them to a different device pool.
- Delete the devices that are assigned to the device pool that you want to delete.

Individual components of a device pool are explored in the following subtopics.

Cisco Unified CallManager Group Configuration

A Cisco CallManager group specifies a prioritized list of Cisco CallManager servers for a Cisco IP Phone to register to, with a maximum of three in the list. The first Cisco CallManager in the list serves as the primary Cisco CallManager for devices that are assigned to that group. The other members of the group serve as the secondary and tertiary backups. Changes to the Cisco CallManager group affect the configuration file that is given to Cisco IP Phones by the TFTP server when they initially boot.

Complete these steps to configure a Cisco CallManager group:

Step 1 Choose **System > Cisco CallManager Group**. The default group that was created by Cisco CallManager during the installation appears.

Step 2 Choose **Add New Cisco CallManager Group** to create a new Cisco CallManager group.

Step 3 Move the "Available" Cisco CallManager servers to the "Selected" Cisco CallManagers using the left and right arrows to place them in the group. You can change the order of Cisco CallManager servers using the up and down arrows, which adjusts the priority of the Cisco CallManager servers where the top server will be the primary server of the group and the bottom server will be the tertiary server of the group.

In Figure 5-3, you can see the Cisco CallManager group called "Arizona" has three Cisco CallManager servers. You would assign the Cisco CallManager group to a device pool, and you then assign this device pool to the Cisco IP Phone. The IP Phone uses the Arizona Cisco CallManager as its primary Cisco CallManager, the California Cisco CallManager as its secondary, and the Michigan Cisco CallManager as its tertiary. Cisco CallManager Administration will present an error message if you attempt to add a fourth Cisco CallManager (for example, the EAST1A Cisco CallManager) to the list.

NOTE The **Auto-registration Cisco CallManager Group** check box (shown in Figure 5-3) dictates that all devices that auto-register will receive the current Cisco CallManager Group assignment. You can only designate a single Cisco CallManager Group as the auto-registration group. Auto-registration is covered thoroughly at the end of this chapter.

Figure 5-3 *Cisco CallManager Group Configuration Window*

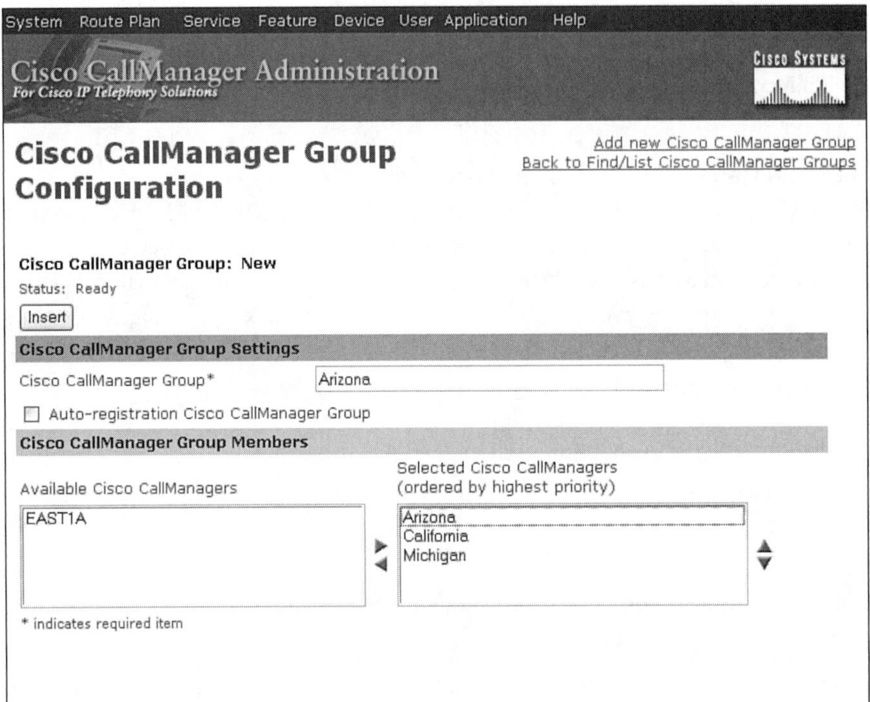

NOTE The sample Cisco CallManager group configuration is an example of clustering over the IP WAN because only Cisco CallManagers in the same cluster can be added to a Cisco CallManager group. More commonly, Cisco CallManager clustered servers reside in the same physical location. You can then configure Cisco CallManager groups based on the servers within your data center. For example, the server Arizona_SUB1 could be the primary, Arizona_SUB2 could be the secondary, and Arizona_PUB could be the tertiary server in a Cisco CallManager group.

Date/Time Group Configuration

Date/time groups define time zones for the various devices that are connected to Cisco CallManager. You can assign each device to only one device pool. As a result, the device has only one date/time group.

Cisco CallManager has a default date/time group called CMLocal. The CMLocal date/time group synchronizes to the active date and time of the operating system on the Cisco CallManager server. You can change the settings for CMLocal after installing Cisco CallManager.

NOTE All Subscriber Cisco CallManager servers in a cluster synchronize their time with the Publisher server through a Microsoft process known as W32TIME. Cisco highly recommends using the Microsoft NTP client on the Publisher server to synchronize its time with a more accurate source.

Complete these steps to configure the date/time group:

Step 1 Choose **System > Date/Time Group**. The default CMLocal group appears.

Step 2 Choose **Add a New Date/Time Group** to insert additional date/time groups as required.

Figure 5-4 illustrates the addition of a California date/time group.

Figure 5-4 *Cisco CallManager Date/Time Group Configuration Window*

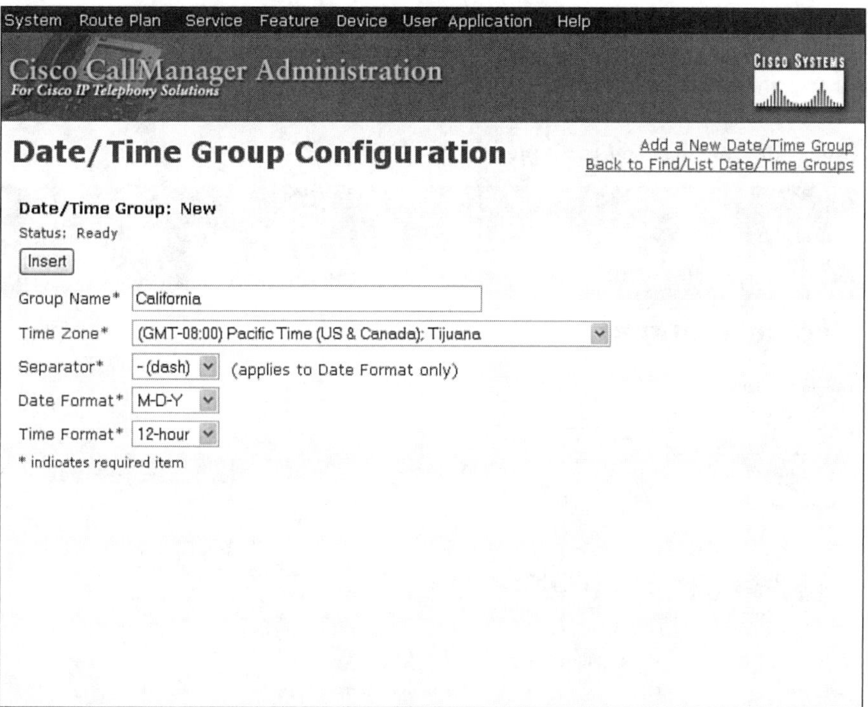

TIP For a worldwide distribution of Cisco IP Phones, you will want to create one named date/time group for each of the time zones where you have deployed Cisco IP Phones.

Region Configuration

The region is typically the most confusing item of the device pool configuration. When you create a region, you specify the audio codec that can be used for calls between devices (such as IP Phones) within that region and between that region and other regions. As of Cisco CallManager Release 4.0, you can also specify the video call bandwidth.

You can create regions to modify the codec selection for any reason; however, most network administrators create regions based on geographical areas. The default voice codec for all calls through Cisco CallManager is G.711. If you do not plan to use any other voice codec, you do not need to use regions. The system will use the default region.

For example, in Figure 5-5, there are four regions: Arizona, California, Default, and Michigan; the configuration of the Michigan region is displayed. If a device that is assigned to the Michigan region calls another device in the Michigan region, the devices use the G.711 codec. However, if a device assigned to the Michigan region calls a device that is assigned to the Arizona region, the devices use the G.729 codec. Cisco CallManager creates the Default region during the installation process. You can rename the Default region to a more logical name to avoid confusion, or you can ignore it and use only regions that you have created.

Figure 5-5 *Cisco CallManager Region Configuration*

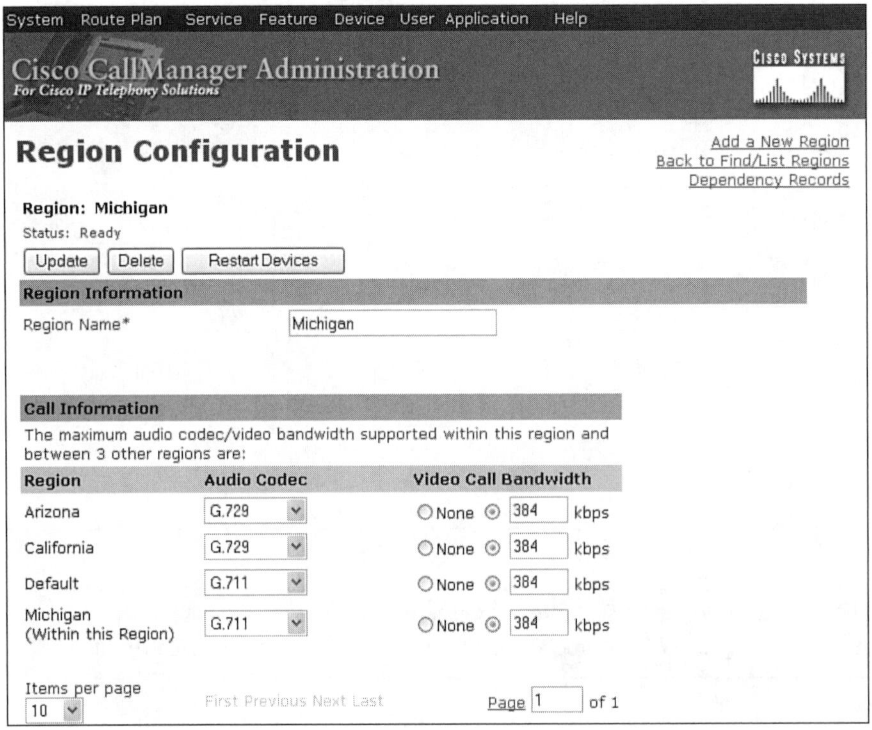

Complete these steps to configure a region:

Step 1 Choose **System > Region**. The default region that was created during the Cisco CallManager installation appears.

Step 2 Choose **Add a New Region** to configure the regions, and choose the codec and video bandwidth as appropriate between the regions. Click **Insert** to save your changes.

Softkey Template Configuration

The Softkey Template Configuration window allows the administrator to manage the on-screen softkeys that the Cisco IP Phones support (such as the Cisco IP Phone 7960 and 7940 models). Softkeys govern functionality such as Hold, Conference, Transfer, and so on. You can configure these softkeys with many Cisco CallManager functions and features. You can also use the softkey templates to restrict what features the user can access. For example, if you do not want the user to have the ability to initiate conference calls, you can just remove the conference button from their softkey template.

To access the Softkey Template Configuration window, open the Cisco CallManager Administration window and choose **Device > Device Settings > Softkey Templates**. Cisco CallManager comes with a few default softkey templates shown in Figure 5-6, which are discussed fully in future chapters. You cannot modify or delete these default templates; however, you can make copies of them for your own use by clicking the **Copy** icon located to the right of the template name.

Figure 5-6 *Cisco CallManager Softkey Template Configuration*

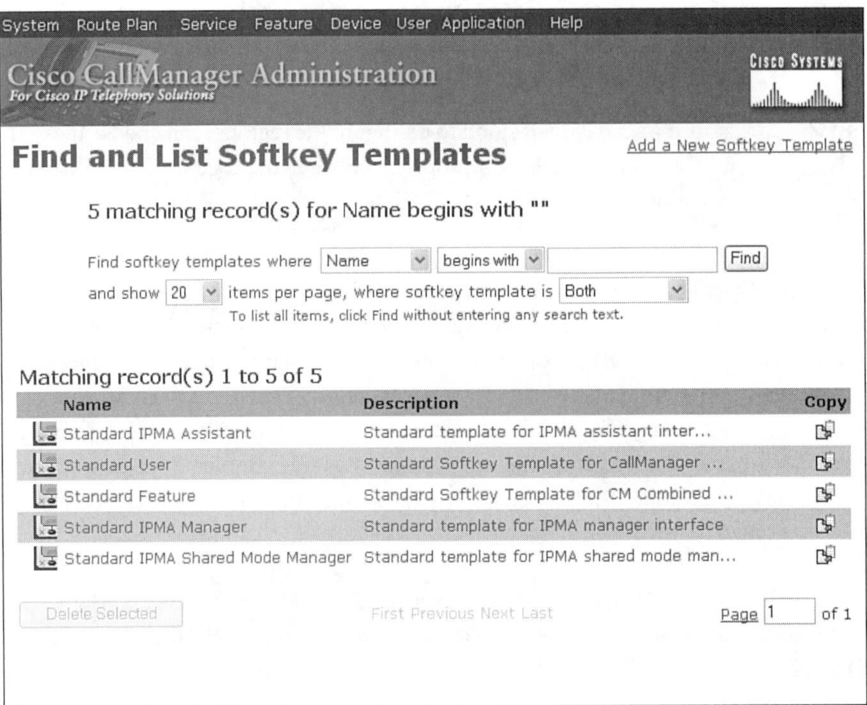

After you have made a copy of the softkey template you want to use, you can modify the softkeys available, and assign the template to a device pool. The full configuration of the softkey templates are covered in future chapters.

IP Phone Button Templates

Whereas softkey templates focus on modifying the features assigned to Cisco IP Phones, the IP Phone button template focuses on assigning line and speed dial buttons to the phone. Although Cisco CallManager does not require the IP Phone button templates for the device pool, it is good to have all the button templates you plan on using created before you begin to add IP Phones to the Cisco CallManager SQL database. Figure 5-7 shows the physical buttons affected on the Cisco 7961 IP Phone.

Figure 5-7 *Cisco 7961 IP Phone Softkey and Line Buttons*

You must assign at least one line per IP Phone; usually this line is button 1. Depending on the Cisco IP Phone model, you can assign additional lines.

Before adding any IP Phones to the system, create phone button templates with all of the possible combinations for all IP Phone models. An IP Phone model can have various combinations; for example, a Cisco IP Phone 7960 supports six lines and can use the following phone button template combinations:

- One line, five speed dial buttons
- Two lines, four speed dial buttons (default)
- Three lines, three speed dial buttons
- Four lines, two speed dial buttons
- Five lines, one speed dial button
- Six lines, no speed dial button

To create a phone button template from Cisco CallManager Administration, click **Device > Device Settings > Phone Button Template**. Click the **Find** button to see the default templates included with Cisco CallManager (shown in Figure 5-8).

> **TIP** There are additional methods to add speed dial capabilities to a Cisco IP Phone; you are not limited to just the phone button template buttons. These mechanisms are discussed in future chapters.

Figure 5-8 *Cisco CallManager Phone Button Template Configuration*

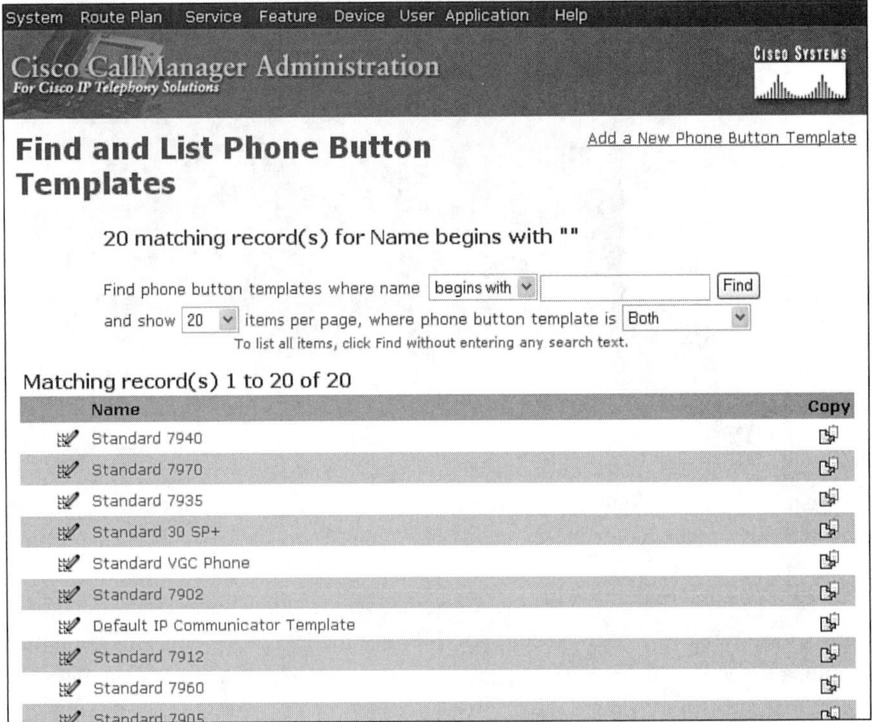

As with the softkey templates, you are unable to modify the default phone button templates. Rather, you can make copies of the default templates (by clicking on the Copy icon) and saving them under a unique name.

Create easily recognizable naming conventions for the phone button template. A suggested best practice is to use the model number of the Cisco IP Phone followed by the number of lines and speed dials. For example, a phone button template named "7960 1-5" would indicate a Cisco 7960 IP Phone with one line and five speed dial buttons.

Putting It All Together

The previous sections discussed creating the mandatory, minimum elements to assemble a device pool. After you have created all the individual elements you need, create device pools that group the common configuration elements together. For example, you might have the following device pool configuration:

- **Device Pool Name**: Arizona Phones
- **Cisco CallManager Group**: Arizona_CG (CCM_AZ Primary, CCM_CA Secondary)
- **Date/Time Group**: Arizona_DT (selects Arizona as the time zone)
- **Region Configuration**: Arizona_REG (selects G.711 for calls within Arizona, G.729 for calls elsewhere)
- **Softkey Template**: Standard User
- **SRST Reference**: Disable (the default, disables SRST)

You would then create additional device pools based on location, Cisco CallManager Groups, or other unique configurations. The final step is to assign the device pools to the Cisco IP Phones that will use them. As of yet, you have yet to add these IP Phones to the Cisco CallManager database.

IP Phone Configuration

The bulk of your initial Cisco CallManager configuration comes in adding Cisco IP Phones to the SQL database. After you add the phones to the database, you can manage and configure them through the Cisco CallManager interface. You can add the phones to the database using one of three methods:

- Manual entry
- Automatic registration
- The Bulk Administration Tool (BAT)

This chapter discusses the manual and automatic methods of adding IP Phones to the database. BAT is covered in Chapter 7, "Cisco Bulk Administration Tool."

Manual IP Phone and Directory Number Configuration

Manually adding new IP Phones to the network is often tedious, but it can constitute a large part of day-to-day voice network management. The Bulk Administration Tool (BAT) allows you to add a large number of IP Phones to the Cisco CallManager database at once, but BAT is not appropriate for adding or modifying a single IP Phone for a new employee.

Cisco CallManager uses the IP Phone MAC address to track the phone in the voice network. Cisco CallManager ties all IP Phone configuration settings to the IP Phone MAC address. Before you can perform any configuration on a Cisco IP Phone through Cisco CallManager, you must find the MAC address of that IP Phone. Use the following guidelines to locate a MAC address:

- You can find the MAC address in the text and Universal Product Code (UPC) form, which is imprinted on the shipping box for the IP Phone. Some administrators use bar code scanners to simplify the process of adding multiple IP Phones.
- You can also find the MAC address in the text and UPC form on the back of the IP Phone, on the middle sticker near the bottom.
- If you boot the IP Phone, you can press the Settings button on the face of the phone. Use the arrow keys to navigate, and choose **Network Configuration**. The MAC address will be displayed on line 3 of the network configuration.

You can continue the Cisco IP Phone configuration on the Cisco CallManager configuration after you have the MAC address of the IP Phone, as follows:

Step 1 In Cisco CallManager Administration, choose **Device > Phone** to open the Find and List Phones window.

Step 2 Choose **Add a New Phone** in the upper-right corner of the window.

Step 3 Choose the model of the IP Phone from the drop-down menu, and click **Next**.

Step 4 At a minimum, you must configure the **MAC Address, Device Pool**, and **Phone Button Template** fields; then click **Insert**.

Step 5 Cisco CallManager prompts you to add a DN for line 1; then click **OK**.

Step 6 When the Directory Number Configuration window appears, enter the DN of the IP Phone in the appropriate field, and click **Insert**.

Figures 5-9 and 5-10 illustrate the IP Phone and directory number configuration screens, respectively.

Figure 5-9 *Cisco CallManager IP Phone Configuration*

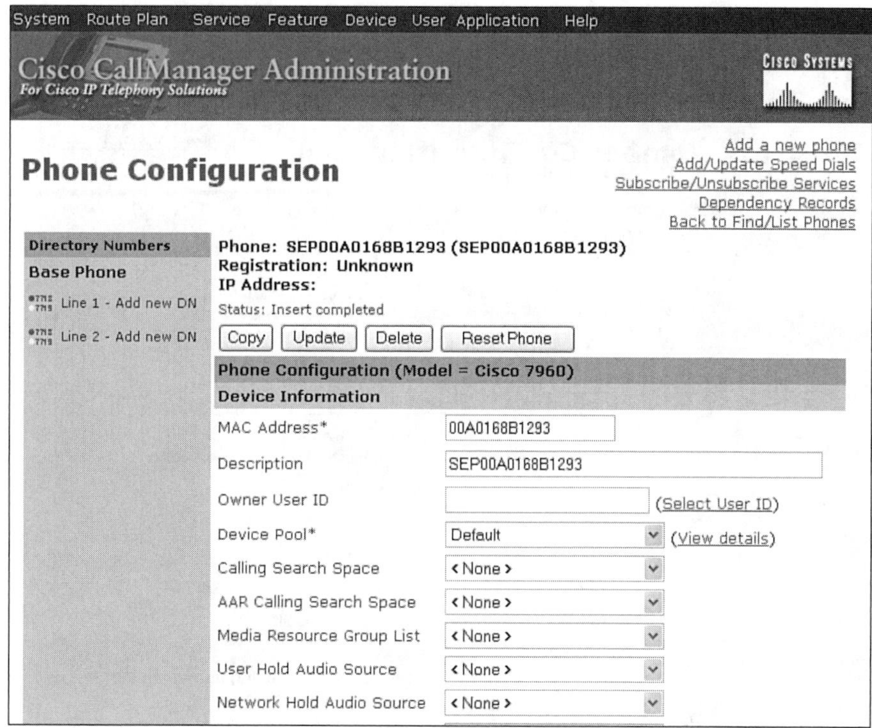

Figure 5-10 *Cisco CallManager Directory Number Configuration*

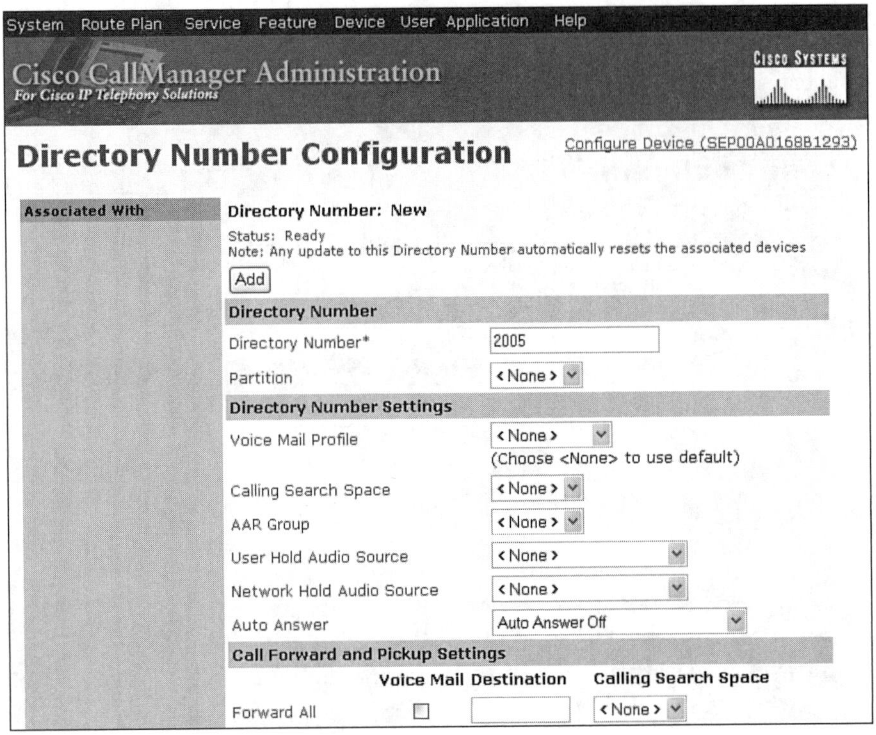

Automatic IP Phone Registration

Auto-registration allows Cisco CallManager to issue extension numbers to new IP Phones, which is similar to the way in which the Dynamic Host Control Protocol (DHCP) server issues IP addresses. When a new IP Phone boots and attempts to register with Cisco CallManager for the first time, Cisco CallManager issues an extension number from a configured range. After Cisco CallManager issues the extension, it records the extension number to the MAC address mapping in the SQL database.

Although auto-registration simplifies the process of deploying a new IP telephony network, it is an option that is available only in some new IP telephony deployments. Because administrators deploy most IP telephony networks as a migration from a PBX environment, users have existing telephone extensions. These existing telephone extensions typically map to Direct Inward Dial (DID) numbers from the Public Switched Telephone Network (PSTN) and cannot change. Therefore, these IP telephony deployments usually use manual configuration rather than auto-registration.

You should carefully evaluate auto-registration before implementing it because its use can pose a security risk to the network. Auto-registration allows anyone with physical access to the voice network to connect an IP Phone and use it, regardless of whether they are authorized. For this reason, many organizations, as part of their security policy, disable the use of auto-registration or use auto-registration in a secure staging environment for initial Cisco CallManager configuration.

Complete these steps to configure the Cisco CallManager server to support auto-registration:

Step 1 From Cisco CallManager Administration, choose **System > Cisco CallManager**.

Step 2 From the list of Cisco CallManager servers, select the server that you want to support auto-registration.

Step 3 Under the Auto-Registration Information Configuration section, enter the appropriate DN range in the Starting and Ending Directory Number fields.

Step 4 Ensure that the **Auto-registration Disabled on this Cisco CallManager** check box is unchecked.

Step 5 Click **Update** to save your changes.

Figure 5-11 shows the auto-registration configuration window.

Figure 5-11 *Cisco CallManager Auto-Registration Configuration*

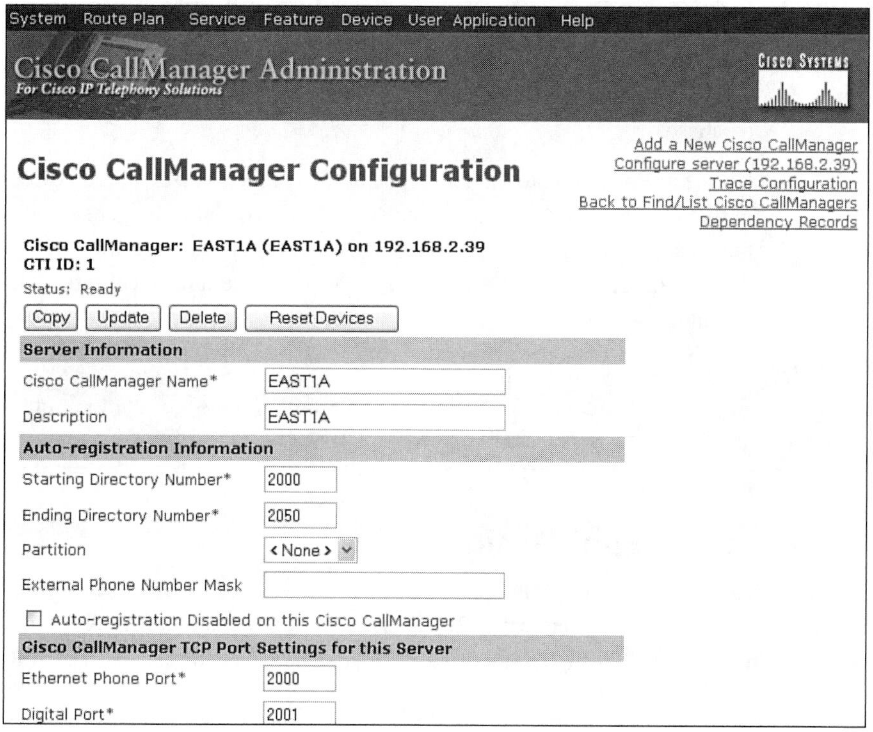

Installing Cisco CallManager automatically sets device defaults. You cannot create new device defaults or delete existing ones, but you can change the default settings. Use device defaults to set the default characteristics of each type of device that registers with a Cisco CallManager. The device defaults for a device type apply to all auto-registered devices of that type within a Cisco CallManager cluster. You can set the following device defaults for each device type to which they apply:

- **Device load**—Lists the firmware load that is used with a particular type of hardware device
- **Device pool**—Allows you to select the device pool that is associated with each type of device
- **Phone button template**—Indicates the phone button template that is used by each type of device

When a device auto-registers with a Cisco CallManager, it acquires the device default settings for its device type. After a device registers, you can update its configuration individually to change the device settings.

Complete these steps to update the device defaults:

Step 1 In Cisco CallManager Administration, choose **System > Device Defaults** to open the Device Defaults Configuration window.

Step 2 In the Device Defaults Configuration window, modify the appropriate settings for the device that you want to change.

Step 3 Click **Update** to save the changes in the Cisco CallManager configuration database.

Step 4 Click the **Reset** icon to the left of the device name to reset all the devices of that type and load the new defaults on all Cisco CallManager servers in the cluster. If you choose not to reset all devices of that type, only new devices that are added after you change the device defaults receive the latest defaults.

CAUTION Updating device load files and performing a phone reset can affect a large number of devices and cause significant WAN utilization as firmware files are sent to remote phones. Cisco recommends saving these large device resets for network off-hours.

Case Study: Device Pool Design

Scenario: You are designing the IP telephony network for Widgets, Inc. The company has two locations: a central site in Arizona with 1200 users and a remote site in Missouri with 20 users. These sites are connected through a fractional T1 CAS line supporting a speed of 768 Kbps. The company has deployed a centralized Cisco CallManager cluster of three servers: AZ_CCM1 (SQL Publisher), AZ_CCM2 (SQL Subscriber), and AZ_CCM3 (SQL Subscriber). You must configure the central Cisco CallManager cluster to support phones at both locations.

There is no better way to get a firm grasp on the concept of device pools than to put it in action. This scenario shows the perfect example of a centralized Cisco CallManager deployment where the remote site does not have enough phones to justify a multicluster configuration, nor does it have enough bandwidth to support running a cluster split over the IP WAN. In this scenario, the customer network will require two device pools to appropriately configure the devices. This is because the IP Phones reside in two different time zones and will need to use different codecs when communicating (G.711 uncompressed for the LAN and G.729 compressed for the WAN). Table 5-2 illustrates the configuration of the device pool elements.

Table 5-2 *Device Pool Elements*

Device Pool Element	Description
Cisco CallManager Group	Unless the network requires load balancing, the network will only require one Cisco CallManager group: • **Name**—Widget_CG — Primary CCM server—AZ_CCM3 — Secondary CCM server—AZ_CCM2 — Tertiary CCM server—AZ_CCM1 Notice that the SQL Publisher server (AZ_CCM1) is listed last. This is because you want to keep as much device registration and support load off the Publisher as possible.
Date/Time Group	This network requires two date/time groups to support the phones in differing locations: • **Name**—Widget_AZ_DT — **Time zone**—(GMT-07:00) Arizona — **Date format**—M-D-Y — **Time format**—12-hour • **Name**—Widget_MO_DT — **Time zone**—(GMT-06:00) Central time — **Date format**—M-D-Y — **Time format**—12-hour

continues

Table 5-2 *Device Pool Elements (Continued)*

Device Pool Element	Description
Region	Because the WAN has limited bandwidth available, it is necessary to configure two regions to select different codecs: • **Name**—Missouri_RG — **Audio Codec (within Missouri_RG)**—G.711 — **Audio Codec (to Arizona_RG)**—G.729 • **Name**—Arizona_RG — **Audio Codec (within Arizona_RG)**—G.711 — **Audio Codec (to Missouri_RG)**—G.729 Phones assigned to the Missouri_RG will now use a compressed codec when communicating with phones assigned to the Arizona_RG, and vice versa.
Softkey Template	Because Widgets, Inc., specified no special requirements for the users, they should be able to use the **Standard User** softkey template, which provides a basic set of functions to the IP Phones.
SRST Reference	Although the SRST reference is discussed in later chapters, this scenario requires you to create a SRST reference for the phones in Missouri. The SRST reference would allow the router in Missouri to support the IP Phones and provide basic PSTN calling if the connection to the centralized Cisco CallManager cluster were lost. In this case, we will assume you created a SRST reference called **Missouri_SRST** that pointed to the Missouri gateway IP address 10.5.1.1.

Now that the device pool elements are created, you can create the two device pools:

Device Pool 1

Name—Arizona_DP
Cisco CallManager Group—Widget_CG
Date/Time Group—Widget_AZ_DT
Region—Arizona_RG
Softkey Template—Standard User
SRST Reference—Disabled

Device Pool 2

> **Name**—Missouri_DP
> **Cisco CallManager Group**—Widget_CG
> **Date/Time Group**—Widget_MO_DT
> **Region**—Missouri_RG
> **Softkey Template**—Standard User
> **SRST Reference**—Missouri_SRST

All that is left is to assign the Cisco IP Phones in each location to the correct device pool.

Summary

This chapter covered the configuration of Cisco CallManager to support Cisco IP Phones. Starting off, the first configuration administrators typically attack is to change the Cisco CallManager server configuration to distribute server IP addresses to the IP Phones rather than to hostnames. This eliminates the IP Phone reliance on DNS. From there, you must configure device pools, allowing you to assign the correct configuration to the Cisco IP Phones. The required elements of the device pool were covered in this chapter. They are as follows:

- Cisco CallManager Group
- Date/Time Group
- Region
- Softkey Template
- SRST Reference (covered in later chapters)

After you have created these elements, you can group them together in one or more device pools and assign them to the devices.

The Cisco IP Phones can be added to the Cisco CallManager SQL database manually, automatically, or by using the Bulk Administration Tool. This chapter discussed the manual and auto-registration addition of IP Phones. Auto-registration allows the Cisco CallManager to assign phone extensions like DHCP addresses; however, this configuration is only good for a "green field" deployment where there are no preexisting phone extension assignments. Most of your day-to-day administration will consist of adding IP Phones manually to the Cisco CallManager configuration.

Review Questions

You can find the solutions to these questions in Appendix A, "Answers to Review Questions."

1. Which five settings are required to configure a device pool? (Choose five.)
   a. Media Resource Group List
   b. Cisco CallManager group
   c. date/time group
   d. region
   e. softkey template
   f. SRST reference
   g. phone template
   h. phone load
   i. device defaults
2. Which of the following combinations is a valid phone button template configuration for a Cisco IP Phone 7960?
   a. 0 lines, 6 speed dials
   b. 2 lines, 4 speed dials
   c. 6 lines, 1 speed dial
   d. 4 lines, 4 speed dials
3. Which navigation path would you use to configure Cisco CallManager to automatically register an IP Phone?
   a. **System > Server**
   b. **System > Cisco CallManager**
   c. **Service > Service Parameters**
   d. **Device > Phone**
   e. **System > Device Pool**
4. How does Cisco CallManager tie configuration information to the IP Phones in the Microsoft SQL database?
   a. IP address
   b. unique GUID
   c. hostname
   d. MAC address
   e. device pool ID

5. Which of the following device pool characteristics allows you to configure the codec the Cisco IP Phone will use when communicating with other devices?

   a. Region

   b. Softkey Template

   c. Compression

   d. Compression Group

6. By default, the IP Phones will receive a list of Cisco CallManager hostnames they can use to register from the TFTP server. How can you modify this so the IP Phone receives a list of Cisco CallManager IP addresses from the TFTP server?

   a. You must manually edit the IP Phone configuration files on the TFTP server, replacing hostnames with IP addresses.

   b. You must access the Cisco CallManager server configuration from **System > Server** and change the hostnames to IP addresses. The Cisco CallManager will automatically update the TFTP server.

   c. The IP Phones must use hostname resolution to communicate with the Cisco CallManager. Ensure DNS redundancy is in place.

   d. In the Cisco CallManager, access the **Service > Service Parameters** window and change the preferred resolution method to IP addresses rather than hostnames.

7. Which of the following device pool elements allows you to configure a redundant group of Cisco CallManager servers your IP Phone can use for registration?

   a. Cisco CallManager Servers

   b. CallManager List

   c. CallManager Gaggle

   d. CallManager Group

8. The Cisco CallManager has one date/time group by default. What is this date/time group?

   a. RegionalDT

   b. Pacific Time

   c. CMLocal

   d. CCMServerClock

9. You want to remove the Hold button from a user's IP Phone. Which device pool configuration item would you use to accomplish this?

  a. IP Phone Button Template

  b. Softkey Template

  c. Feature Restrictions

  d. Feature Template

10. What three locations can you use to find the MAC address of a Cisco IP Phone?

  a. You can find the MAC address in the UPC form, which is imprinted on the shipping box for the IP Phone.

  b. You can find the MAC address in the text and UPC form on the back of the IP Phone, on a sticker near the bottom.

  c. You can find the MAC address by pressing the Settings button on the face of the phone, using the arrow keys to navigate, and choosing Network Configuration.

  d. You can find the MAC address by telnetting to the IP address of the Cisco IP Phone and issuing the **show interface** command.

This chapter covers the following topics:

- Using Cisco CallManager Administration to add users and associate users with a device
- Logging in to the Cisco CallManager User Options web page and selecting a device to personalize
- Activating or subscribing typical user options from the User Options web pages, such as call forwarding, speed dial configuration, and CallManager services
- Creating personal address books in the Cisco CallManager User Options web page of stored names and numbers and assigning Fast Dial codes to personal address book entries to enable users to dial those codes in place of telephone numbers
- Describing how to change the way that the voice-message light on the handset works when a user receives a voice-mail message
- Describing how to change the language for the Cisco CallManager User Options web pages or telephone

CHAPTER 6

Cisco IP Telephony Users

After you have configured the Cisco CallManager to support the various Cisco IP Phones deployed around your network environment, your next logical step is to configure the IP telephony users. Configuring users for the voice network is not a mandatory step; however, it will ease your network administration load considerably because (with proper training) voice network users can configure their own IP Phones for common features such as speed dials and call forwarding without adding another support call to the help desk group. In addition, Cisco CallManager requires user configuration to support many of the advanced features, such as Cisco Auto Attendant, IP Manager Assistant (IPMA), and Extension Mobility, which are discussed in Chapters 17-19.

This chapter describes the Cisco CallManager configuration to support voice network users. You will learn how to add these users to the Cisco CallManager user database and assign these users access to their respective IP Phone. From there, the chapter discusses the process an end-user would go through to configure their phone through the Cisco CallManager user web pages.

Cisco CallManager User Database

Cisco CallManager stores most configuration information for the voice network in the underlying SQL 2000 database infrastructure. However, user information does not fall under this category; rather, the user information is stored in a separate database accessible through the Lightweight Directory Access Protocol (LDAP). LDAP is an industry standard protocol that allows applications to access and potentially modify information stored in the database. Cisco decided to keep the user database separate from the rest of the CallManager configuration because network administrators might want to harness their existing corporate directory (that is already filled with user information used to access the data network) for the voice network.

By default, Cisco CallManager uses an embedded LDAP directory that installs with the CallManager software image. This directory is called DC Directory. However, you can also choose to use your existing corporate directory as the CallManager user database. CallManager supports the following directory integrations as of version 3.3(3) and 4.0(1)sr2:

- Microsoft Active Directory 2000
- Microsoft Active Directory 2003

- Netscape Directory Server 4.x
- iPlanet/Sun Directory Server 4.1

Although integrating Cisco CallManager with the corporate directory provides tremendous advantages, there are equally tremendous caveats to this configuration:

- To integrate with a corporate directory, the network administrator must modify the schema of that directory. This is a networkwide change that affects all servers participating in the replication of the corporate directory and might cross political boundaries in the organization.
- The CallManager servers must be able to access the corporate directory servers at all times. Failure of this communication will result in authentication failures (and equipment inoperability) in the voice network.
- The additional read/write operations on the corporate directory will result in additional load for the servers maintaining this directory. An overlay of the voice network to your network infrastructure can potentially double the number of requests to the corporate directory servers.

NOTE Because the process of integrating the Cisco CallManager into an LDAP corporate directory differs greatly depending on the type of directory service you are using and its configuration, we will assume you are using the embedded DC Directory service for the remainder of this text. The Cisco website and CallManager SRND documentation provides detailed instructions if you are considering this integration.

The following CCO link also provides excellent information about Active Directory integration:

http://www.cisco.com/en/US/products/sw/voicesw/ps556/products_implementation_design_guide_chapter09186a0080447505.html#wp1043120

Cisco CallManager User Configuration

Regardless of the directory you use to store user information, the CallManager configuration remains the same. You can perform all user administration for Cisco CallManager from the same CallManager Administration web pages you have used thus far for the CallManager configuration.

Adding a User

Figure 6-1 shows an example of adding a user to the Cisco CallManager directory database by using Cisco CallManager Administration. To add a user in Cisco CallManager Administration, choose **User > Add a New User** from the CallManager CCMAdmin web pages.

Figure 6-1 *Cisco CallManager User Configuration Window*

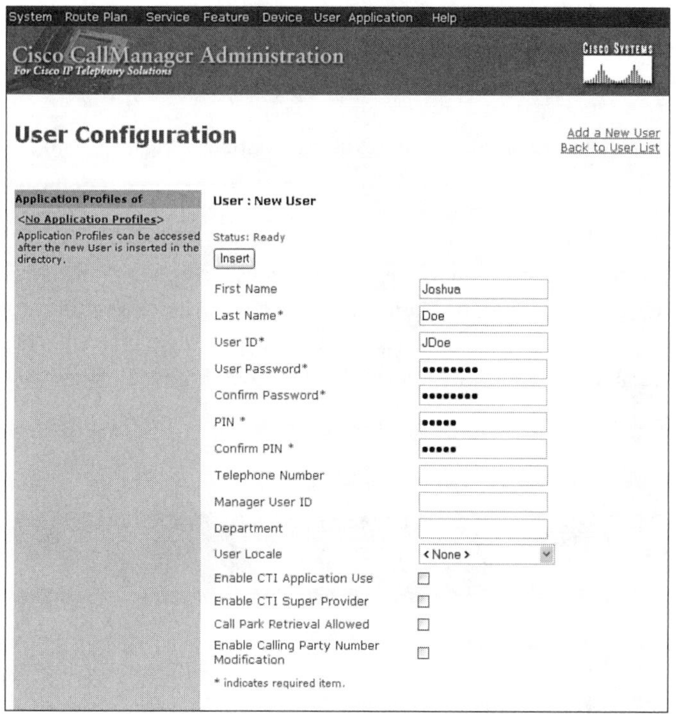

Before adding a user, gather the following user information:

- First name
- Last name
- User ID (username)
- Telephone number or DN
- Manager user ID (manager username)
- Department

If the user is going to access the Cisco SoftPhone application, Cisco Auto Attendant, or any other computer telephony integration (CTI) application, check the **Enable CTI Application Use** check box.

When you are first setting up a user, assign a simple password (at least four characters) and a personal identification number (PIN), which must be at least five digits, for the user to use on the initial login. The user can then change the initial password and PIN from the Cisco CallManager

User Options page. The Cisco CallManager uses the user password and PIN for different functions in the voice network. For example, the user can use their password to log in to the User Options web pages while they can use their PIN to access a phone using Extension Mobility (which is covered in Chapter 17, "Configuring User Features, Part 2").

After the directory information is added, you can associate the user with a device or devices.

Configuring Device Pools

After you have added a user, you can associate devices over which the user will have control. When users have control of an IP Phone, they can control certain settings for that phone, such as speed dialing and call forwarding. You can associate a user with many devices; however, only one of the devices can be the primary extension for that user. Figure 6-2 shows the Device Association window.

Figure 6-2 *Cisco CallManager Device Association Window*

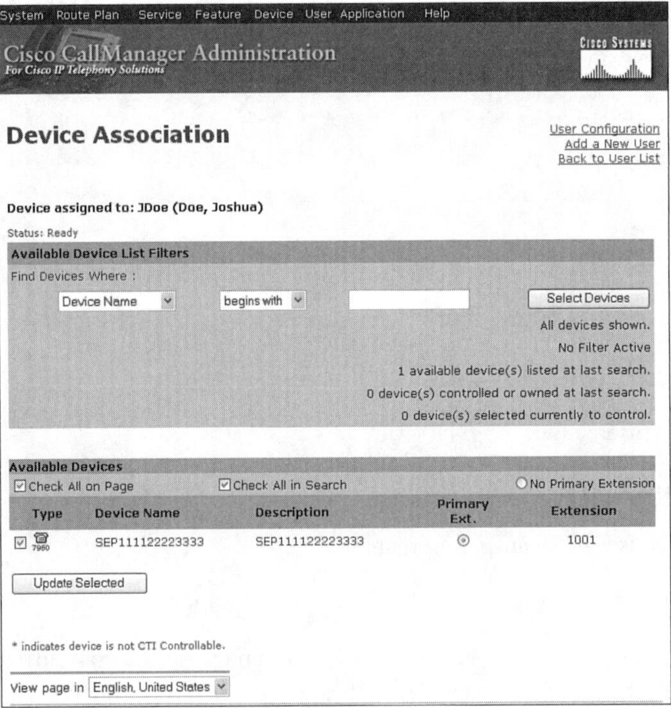

To assign devices to a user, access the User Configuration window for that user and then complete the following steps to assign the devices:

Step 1 In the Application Profiles pane on the User Configuration page, click **Device Association**.

Step 2 Limit the list of available devices by entering the search criteria in the Available Device List Filters section, if desired, and click **Select Devices**.

Step 3 Check the check box of one or more devices that you want to associate with the user. You can assign one primary extension from the devices to which the user is assigned by clicking the radio button in the Primary Ext. column for that device.

Step 4 When you have completed the assignment, click **Update Selected** to assign the devices to the user.

User Logon and Device Configuration

After you have added users to the LDAP database and associated them with the appropriate devices, those users will be able to log on to the CallManager User Options web page to configure their devices. Of course, before the users begin accessing these web pages, some training will be necessary. You might find it beneficial to create a step-by-step training manual for your organization that you can distribute to users or post on an intranet website describing each of the following sections.

TIP You can use the following sections in the book (which walk through the user configuration options) as a model when creating your organization user training manual.

CallManager User Options: Log On

To open the Cisco CallManager User Options web page, enter this URL:

https://<server_name>/ccmuser

The server name is the hostname or IP address of the Cisco CallManager server.

TIP It would be very beneficial to use a network policy, such as the Active Directory Group Policy options, to automatically add a desktop shortcut or Microsoft Internet Explorer favorite linked to the CCMUser web pages for all PCs in the network.

At the Cisco CallManager User Options page (shown in Figure 6-3), enter the correct username and password. If this is the first time that the user is logging on, the user should obtain the URL, username, and password from the administrator.

Figure 6-3 *Cisco CallManager User Options: Log On Window*

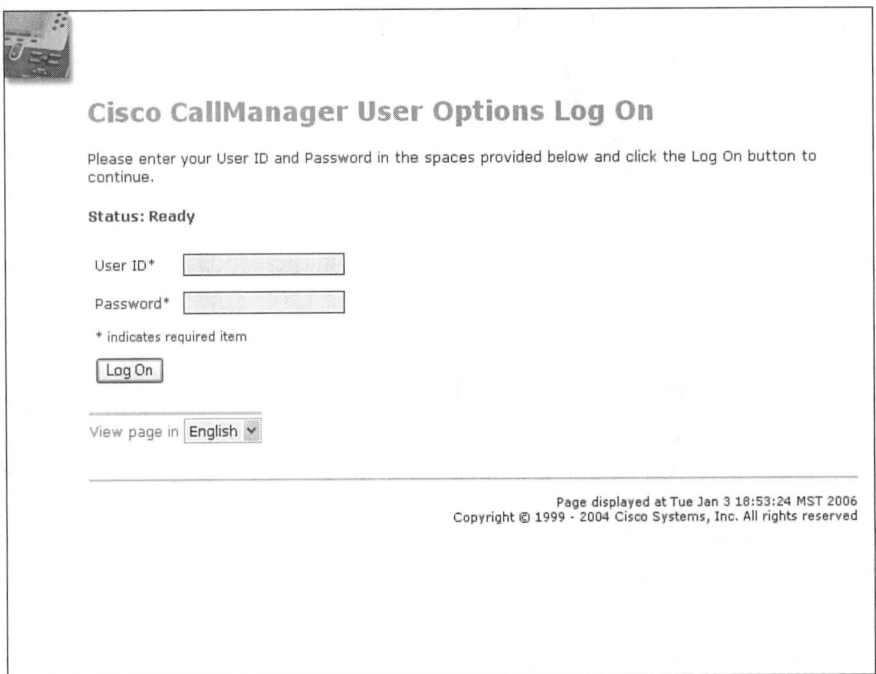

From any page within Cisco CallManager User Options web pages, a user can change the language of the page by choosing the language (locale) from the **View Page In** drop-down menu, if additional locales have been configured.

CallManager User Options: Welcome

After logging on, CallManager presents a user with the User Options welcome screen, shown in Figure 6-4. From there, the user can select an associated device to configure. The user can customize multiple associated devices by choosing more than one device.

Figure 6-4 *Cisco CallManager User Options: Welcome Screen*

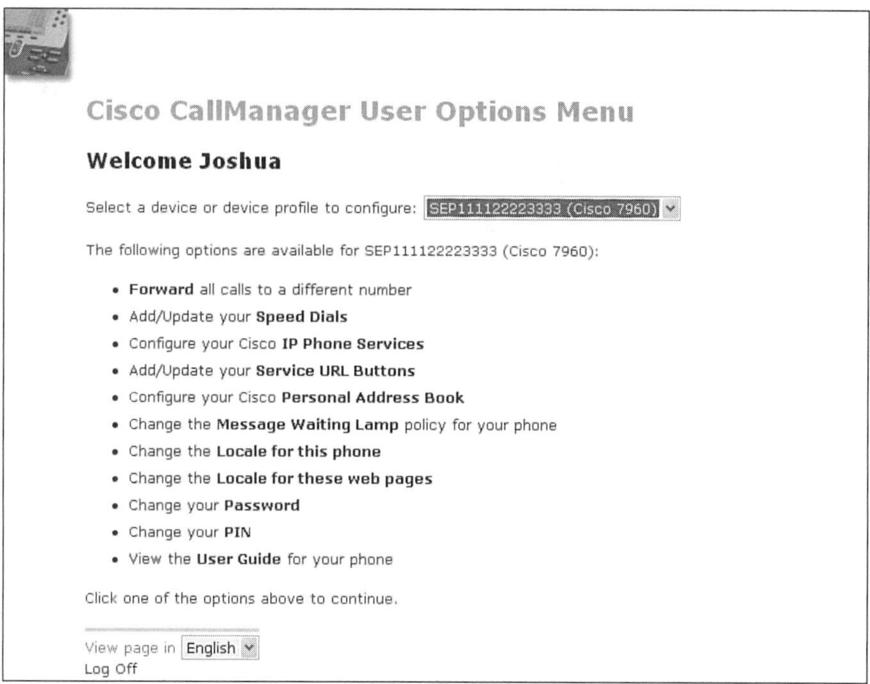

A web location allowing users to customize Cisco IP Phone settings, such as adding speed dials and forwarding calls means that users can be more productive in their work environment. For example, when a user is not going to be in the office to receive an important call, the user can access the Cisco CallManager User Options web page from home and forward calls from the Cisco IP Phone to a cellular telephone or any other DN.

CallManager User Options: Call Forwarding

Figure 6-5 shows the Forward Your Calls page. To display this page, click the **Forward All Calls to a Different Number** link in the User Options main menu.

Figure 6-5 *Cisco CallManager User Options: Call Forwarding Window*

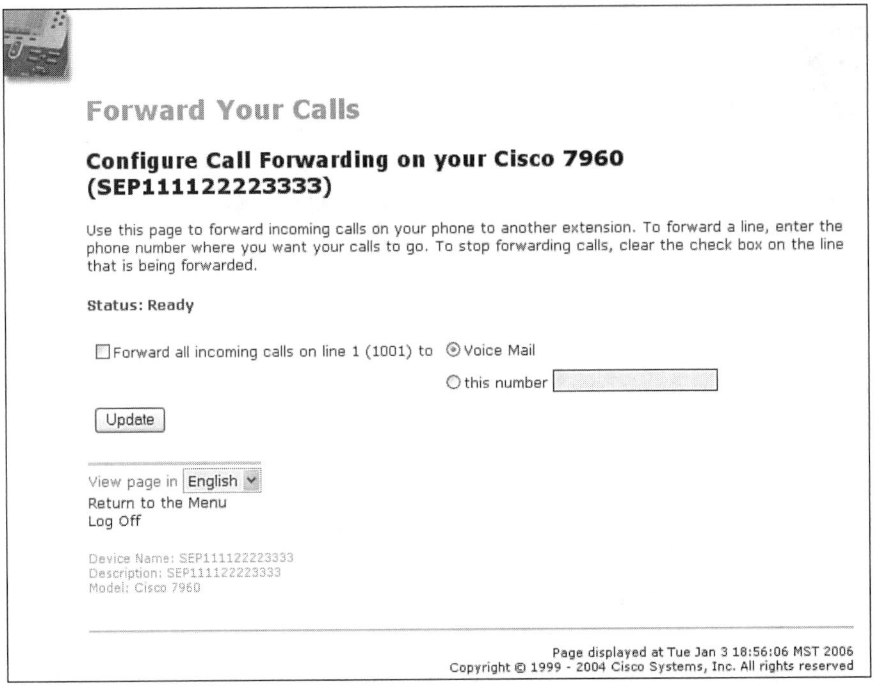

From here, this user can forward all incoming calls on line 1 of a device to either voice mail or another number.

If the user is forwarding calls to another number, the calling search space of the device using Call Forward All (CFA) will restrict which numbers will be valid. Also, if the number is forwarded off-net, the user must enter the number as if dialing from that telephone device. For example, a user who wants to work from home wants all calls to the office telephone to forward to the home number. If the user dials 92145550122 to call home from the office, the user must enter 92145550122 as the forwarding number.

CallManager User Options: Speed Dials

Figure 6-6 shows the Add/Update Your Speed Dials web page. To display this page, click the **Add/ Update Your Speed Dials** link in the User Options main menu.

Figure 6-6 *Cisco CallManager User Options: Speed Dials Window*

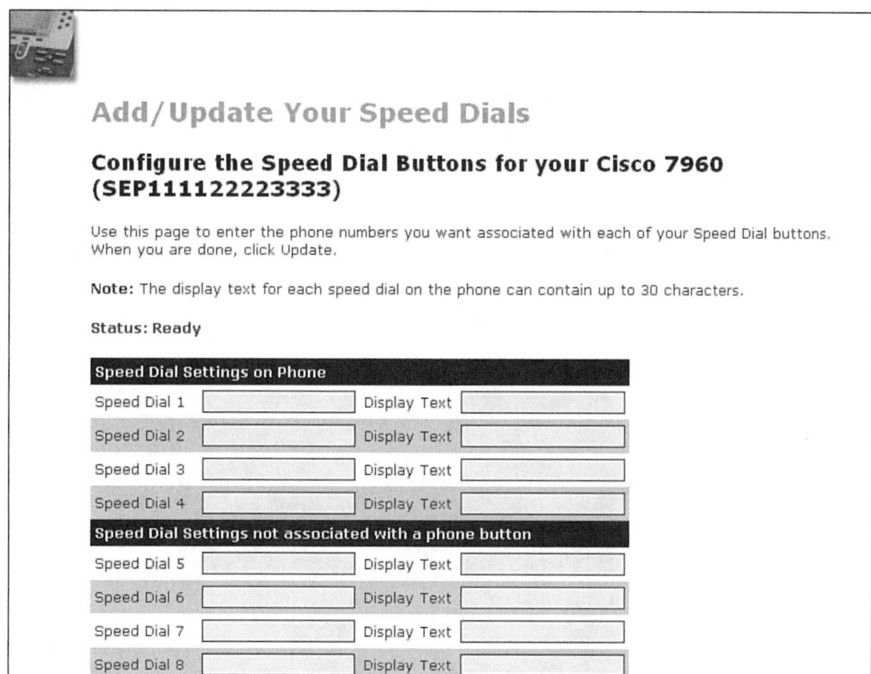

Depending on the device, the number of speed dials is limited based on settings in the phone button template. The user can enter a number and label for each available speed dial button. Buttons are available if the user is not using them for lines or services.

As you can see from Figure 6-6, the speed dial configuration window is divided into two sections: Speed Dial Settings on Phone and Speed Dial Settings not associated with a phone button. The settings on a phone represent the speed dials that correspond to a physical button on the IP Phone. For example, if the user is using a Cisco IP Phone 7960 with the default template, they will have two line buttons and four speed dial buttons. These four speed dial buttons represent the buttons programmable from the "Speed Dial Settings on Phone" section. The settings not associated with a phone button are accessed when the user first presses the **AbbrDial** softkey on their Cisco IP Phone then dials the corresponding number. For example, to access the speed dial listed in field 5 shown in Figure 6-6, the user would press **AbbrDial** on the phone, then press the **5** button on the numeric keypad. The user can also perform the reverse steps to activate the speed dial number (for example, dial 5 followed by pressing the **AbbrDial** softkey).

When programming speed dials, enter the number precisely as it is dialed from the device. If the number 9 must be dialed before the telephone number, the 9 must be part of the speed dial number that is entered. For example, if the telephone number is 4805550199 and the access code for an outside line is 9, the speed dial number must be entered as 94805550199.

> **TIP** In older versions of CallManager, the Cisco IP Phone required a restart to update speed dial configurations. Since CallManager version 3.3, a restart is no longer necessary.

CallManager User Options: IP Phone Services

Figure 6-7 shows the Subscribe/Unsubscribe IP Phone Services web page. To display this page, click the **Configure Your Cisco IP Phone Services** link in the User Options main menu.

Figure 6-7 *Cisco CallManager User Options: IP Phone Services Window*

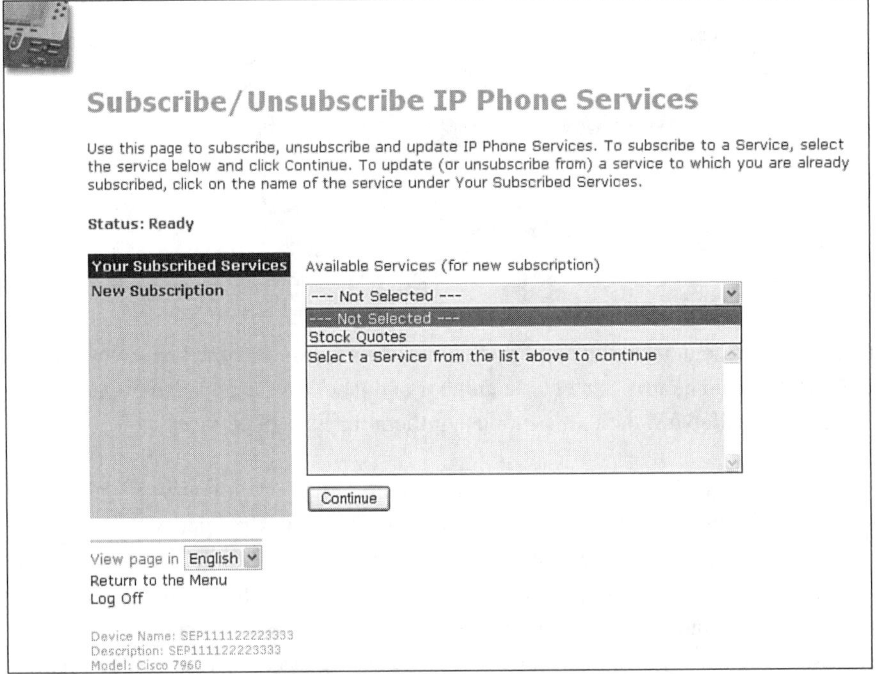

You can configure a number of IP Phone services for user subscription. For example, you could configure services that store telephone numbers, meeting room availability, traffic reports, and more. The user can then use the Subscribe/Unsubscribe IP Phone Services page in Cisco CallManager User Options to subscribe to or unsubscribe from any of the Cisco IP Phone Services that you have configured. IP Phone service configuration is covered in Chapter 16, "Configuring User Features, Part 1."

For example, if you have configured a service that looks up the stock price of a company, a user can subscribe to that service from the Subscribe/Unsubscribe IP Phone Services page in CallManager User Options. To view the stock price of a company, the user can press the **Services** button on a Cisco IP Phone 7970, 7960, or 7940 and view the stock price on the IP Phone liquid crystal display (LCD). You can also associate a service with one of the line/speed dial buttons to allow quick access to XML applications, such as a corporate directory or speed dial list.

CallManager User Options: Personal Address Book and Fast Dial

The Personal Address Book service allows a user to store names and numbers for people internal and external to the company. A user can also assign Fast Dial codes to Personal Address Book entries and dial those codes in place of phone numbers. With the Fast Dial service, users can assign one- or two-digit index numbers (from 1 to 99) for quick dialing from the Cisco IP Phone. Users can assign index numbers either to Personal Address Book entries or to directory entries that they add that do not correspond to address book entries.

The Personal Address Book and Fast Dial features are not available from the base Cisco IP Phone feature set. Rather, Cisco has implemented them as XML services. You must configure these services in the Cisco CallManager Service Configuration web interface before the CallManager will make them available for user subscription. Chapter 16 covers XML Service configuration.

Users can configure the Personal Address Book and Fast Dial features from the Personal Address Book page in Cisco CallManager User Options. After subscribing to these services, a user can access the Personal Address Book and Fast Dial codes from the Cisco IP Phone by pressing the **Services** button.

Figure 6-8 shows the Find/List Address Book Entries page. To display this page, choose the **Configure Your Cisco Personal Address Book** link in the User Options main menu. From the Find/List Address Book Entries page, users can add a new Personal Address Book entry, create or modify Fast Dial codes to reach address book entries, or search for address book entries by using either complete or partial strings.

Figure 6-8 *Cisco CallManager User Options: Address Book and Fast Dial Window*

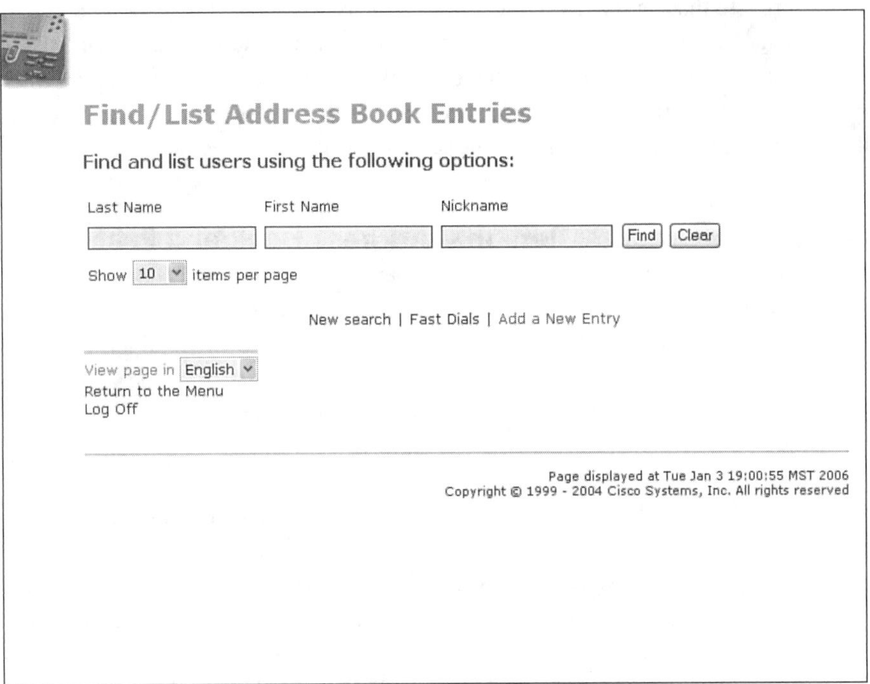

CallManager User Options: Message Waiting Lamp Policy

Figure 6-9 shows the Change Your Message Waiting Lamp Policy page. To display this page, click the **Change the Message Waiting Lamp Policy for Your Phone** link in the User Options main menu. From here, a user can set the message waiting lamp policy for their device. The mainline Cisco IP Phones have extremely noticeable message waiting lights (they have been called a "Beacon in the Night" by some). Because of this, there are five settings that the user can configure: Use System Policy, Light and Prompt, Prompt Only, Light Only, and None. The light configuration illuminates the external lamp on the phone. This can be seen from some distance (such as in a lighthouse from the ocean). The prompt configuration displays an envelope animation on the display screen of the phone. The default system policy is set to light the lamp and prompt the user.

Figure 6-9 *Cisco CallManager User Options: Message Waiting Lamp Policy Window*

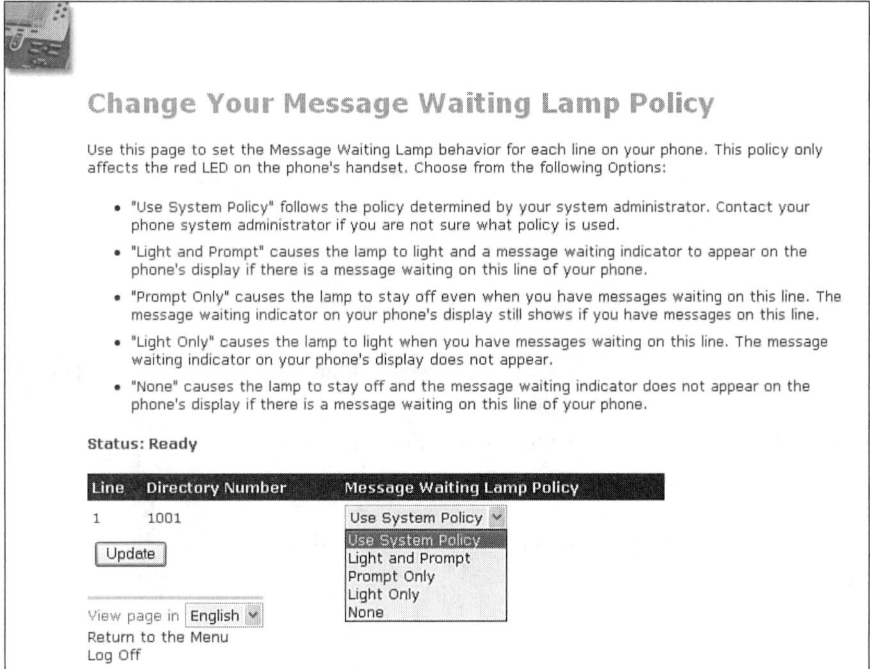

CallManager User Options: Locale Settings

Cisco CallManager allows users to select their preferred language settings for both the devices they are using and the user web pages they access. By default, the Cisco CallManager comes with only the English language selection. However, you can obtain additional languages from Cisco based on the location(s) of your users. Supported locales include the following:

- Chinese Simplified (China)
- Chinese Traditional (Taiwan)
- Danish (Denmark)
- Dutch (Netherlands)
- Finnish (Finland)
- French (France)
- German (Germany)
- Greek (Greece)
- Hungarian (Hungary)
- Italian (Italy)

- Japanese (Japan)
- Korean (Korea)
- Norwegian (Norway)
- Polish (Poland)
- Portuguese (Portugal)
- Russian (Russia)
- Spanish (Spain)
- Swedish (Sweden)

If a user locale is not selected, the systemwide locale is used.

Figure 6-10 shows the Select a User Locale for Your Phone page. To display the language selection pages, click the **Change the Locale for This Phone** or **Change the Locale for These Web Pages** link in the User Options main menu. These options allow the user to modify the language selection for the Cisco IP Phone or the web pages, respectively.

Figure 6-10 *Cisco CallManager User Options: Phone Locale Window*

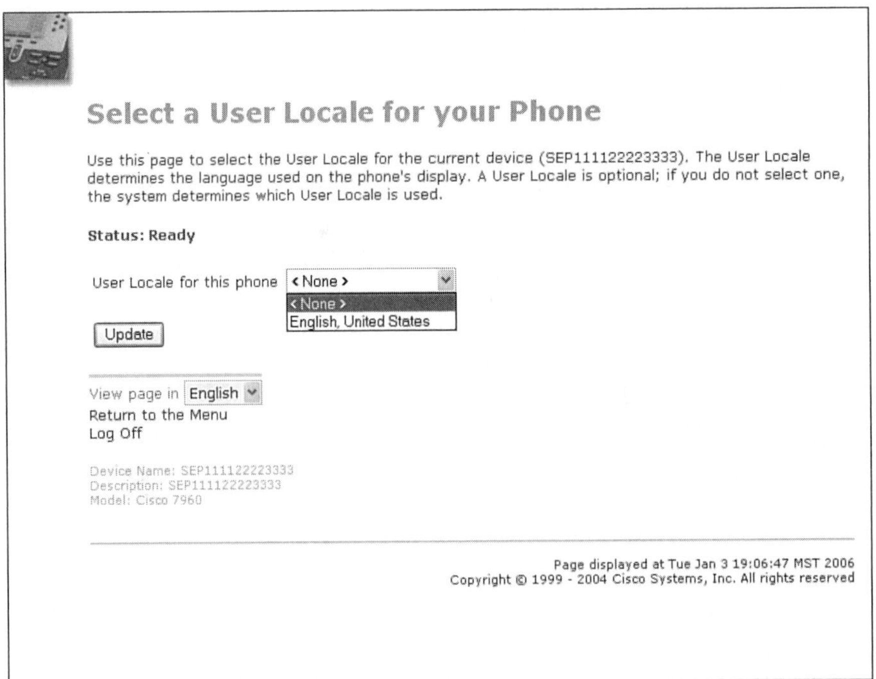

Summary

This chapter covered the configuration of the user database for the Cisco IP telephony network. Although a functional voice network does not require a user database, there are many applications you will be missing. In addition, adding a user database allows your users to configure many of the everyday options, such as call forwarding and speed dials, on their IP Phone through an easy-to-use web interface.

To support a user database, you must first decide whether you will use the integrated DC-Directory LDAP-compliant database that ships with CallManager or integrate the CallManager with one of the supported directory services that are already running for your data network environment. After making this decision, you can perform the user configuration and device association from the CCMAdmin web interface. After you have associated the user with one or more IP Phones, the user can access the CCMUser web interface (https://*<CCM IP Address>*/CCMUser) to manage the devices.

Review Questions

You can find the solutions to these questions in Appendix A, "Answers to Review Questions."

1. Which of the following URLs can you use to access the Cisco CallManager User web pages assuming the CallManager IP address is 10.1.1.1?

   a. https://10.1.1.1/CCMAdmin

   b. https://10.1.1.1/CCMUser

   c. https://10.1.1.1/CCM

   d. xml://10.1.1.1/CCMAdmin

   e. xml://10.1.1.1/CCMUser

   f. xml://10.1.1.1/CCM

2. The Cisco CallManager DC Directory is a/an _______-compliant database. (Choose the best answer.)

   a. SQL

   b. Oracle

   c. LDAP

   d. Standards

3. For the Cisco CallManager–based IP telephony network to function correctly, you must add users to an LDAP-compliant database. (True/False)

4. Which of the following fields are required to create a user who is able to use a Cisco Softphone application? (Choose five.)

   a. First Name

   b. Last Name

   c. User ID

   d. Password

   e. PIN Number

   f. Manager User ID

   g. Department

   h. Enable CTI Application Use

   i. SoftPhone Support Enabled

5. Before a user is able to configure a Cisco IP Phone through the CCMUser web pages, what must be true? (Choose two.)

   a. The user must have a valid user account.

   b. The user must have Java support enabled on their workstation.

   c. The user account must be associated with at least one Cisco IP Phone.

   d. The user must use a Windows-based operating system.

6. You receive a technical support call from a troubled user of the IP telephony network. The user has configured a personal address book through the CCMUser pages for their Cisco IP Phone 7960. They are unable to figure out how to access this personal address book from their Cisco IP Phone. What do you tell them?

   a. You can access the personal address book by pressing the **Directories** button on the Cisco IP Phone.

   b. You can only view the personal address book through the CCMUser web pages.

   c. You need to press the **PAB** softkey on your Cisco IP Phone.

   d. You must first subscribe to the personal address book service and can then access it by pressing the **Services** button on your IP Phone.

7. Which of the following is the default Message Waiting Lamp policy for the Cisco CallManager system configured on each Cisco IP Phone? (Choose the best answer.)

   a. Use System Policy

   b. Light and Prompt

   c. Light Only

   d. Prompt Only

8. By default, Cisco CallManager supports three language selections for users: English, Spanish, and French. (True/False)

9. A user can configure their IP Phone with up to _____ fast dial codes.

   a. 20

   b. 50

   c. 99

   d. 150

10. Which of the following options are available for a user who wants to forward their IP Phone using the CCMUser web pages? (Select all that apply.)

    a. Call Forward All

    b. Call Forward Busy

    c. Call Forward No Answer

    d. Call Forward Selected

This chapter covers the following topics:

- Identifying the major features and components of the BAT application
- Installing the BAT application on a Cisco CallManager publisher server
- Using the BAT Wizard to perform bulk configuration tasks
- Creating an IP Phone template to use with BAT
- Identifying the two ways to create CSV files for importing data into BAT
- Using the BAT Wizard to validate the IP Phone template and CSV file for errors prior to inserting the devices into the Cisco CallManager database
- Using the BAT wizard to insert the IP Phones into the Cisco CallManager database
- Describing how to use BAT to update IP Phone settings for a group of similar phones
- Describing the major requirements for proper installation of TAPS

CHAPTER 7

Cisco Bulk Administration Tool

Adding, updating, and deleting phones, users, and gateway ports are important functions in the day-to-day activities of a Cisco CallManager administrator. When you use Cisco CallManager Administration, each database transaction requires an individual manual operation. Manually adding and configuring large numbers of these entities can be time consuming and tedious. The Cisco Bulk Administration Tool (BAT) automates the process and achieves faster add, update, and delete operations so that the system administrator can focus on more business- and network-critical activities.

As a supplement to BAT, you can further ease the load of adding new phones to the network through the Tool for Auto-Registered Phones Support (TAPS). You can use TAPS in conjunction with BAT to update MAC addresses and download a predefined configuration for new phones after a user has walked through an automated process. This chapter discusses the design and implementation of both BAT and TAPS.

The Cisco Bulk Administration Tool

After you discover the Cisco BAT utility, it will quickly become your new best friend for most day-to-day administration of the IP telephony network. Although there will always be individual changes to the voice network, such as adding a phone extension or a new user, most of the changes you will perform will need to occur in bulk. For example, the accounting department needs different hold music or the department managers need specialized calling restrictions. You can attack these types of tasks one device at a time (which can quickly become tedious and time consuming) or with a few mouse button clicks using the Cisco BAT.

You can use BAT to work with the following types of devices and records:

- Add, update, and delete Cisco IP Phones
- Add, update, and delete users
- Add, update, and delete user device profiles
- Add, update, and delete Cisco IP Manager Assistant (IPMA) managers and assistants
- Add, update, and delete ports on a Cisco Catalyst 6000 FXS Analog Interface Module

- Add or delete Cisco VG200 analog gateways and ports
- Add or delete forced authorization codes
- Add or delete client matter codes
- Add or delete Call Pickup groups
- Update or delete locally significant certificates on Cisco IP Phones

BAT provides an optional application, TAPS, which retrieves the predefined configuration for auto-registered telephones. By using TAPS, CallManager no longer assigns auto-registered phones random extension numbers from the pool. Instead, after the user enters their extension number through an automated process, the TAPS system retrieves the complete configuration you have created for that user.

BAT Components

Every device includes a multitude of individual attributes, settings, and information fields that enable the device to function in the network and provide its telephony features. Many devices have the same attributes and settings in common, whereas other values, such as the directory number (DN), are unique to a user or to a device.

For bulk configuration transactions involving the Cisco CallManager database, the BAT process uses two components: a template for the device type that includes settings that devices have in common and a data file in comma-separated values (CSV) format that contains the unique values for configuring a new device or updating an existing record in the database. The CSV data file works in conjunction with the device template.

For instance, when you create a bulk transaction to import a group of Cisco IP Phones, you set up the CSV data file that contains the unique information for each phone, such as the DN and MAC address. In addition, you set up or choose the BAT template that contains the common settings for all phones in the transaction, such as a Cisco IP Phone 7960 template. By combining the unique settings defined in the CSV file with the common settings created in the IP Phone template, you have everything you need to import a group of IP Phones successfully.

CAUTION Because bulk transactions can affect Cisco CallManager performance and call processing, use BAT only during off-peak hours.

BAT Installation

BAT must be installed on the same server as the publisher database for Cisco CallManager. During BAT installation, the setup program stops the following services:

- Microsoft Internet Information Server (IIS) administration
- World Wide Web publishing
- FTP publishing

These services automatically restart when the installation is complete.

When BAT is installed, the Microsoft Excel file BAT.xlt file for the BAT spreadsheet is placed on the publisher database server at the following path: C:\CiscoWebs\BAT\ExcelTemplate\. You can use this file to generate the necessary CSV files used to import groups of devices into the Cisco CallManager SQL database.

> **NOTE** You must install BAT directly on the publisher server (either through the console directly or using a program such as VNC); do not use Windows Terminal Services.

These steps describe the BAT installation process:

Step 1 Using administrator privileges, log in to the system running the publisher database for Cisco CallManager.

Step 2 Choose **Application > Install Plugins** from the CallManager Administration web interface. The Install Plugins window is displayed, as shown in Figure 7-1.

Figure 7-1 *Cisco CallManager Plugins Installation Window*

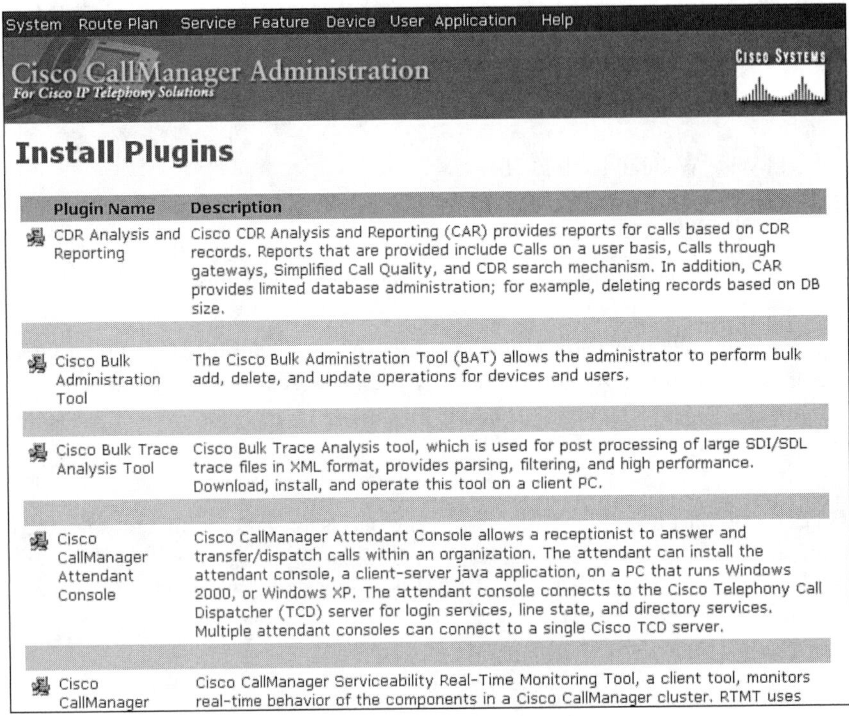

Step 3 Click the setup icon for the Cisco Bulk Administration Tool.

Step 4 A standard Windows dialog box appears. Determine whether to copy the BAT installation executable to the system or run it from the current location.

If an existing version of BAT is detected on the server, you are prompted to confirm the reinstallation or upgrade. To reinstall BAT or to upgrade from a previous version, click **OK**.

Step 5 The Welcome screen appears. Click **Next**, and the Current Settings window appears.

Step 6 Click **Next** to install to the default location C:\CiscoWebs\BAT\. BAT installs to C:\CiscoWebs\BAT\. You cannot change this path. The Start Copying Files window appears. The setup program begins copying files.

Step 7 The Setup Complete window appears. You have successfully installed BAT.

Step 8 To close setup, click **Finish**.

Step 9 After you have installed BAT, from Cisco CallManager Administration, choose **Application > BAT** to access BAT. If after you have installed BAT, BAT is not visible under the Application menu, refresh your browser.

Adding Cisco IP Phones Using BAT

BAT uses a multistep process to prepare the bulk configuration transaction. BAT Release 5.0(1) introduced a wizard to step you through bulk configurations. The BAT configuration process includes these tasks:

Step 1 Set up the template for data input. You can create BAT templates for the following types of device options:

- **Phones**—All Cisco IP Phone models and Cisco ATA 186, Cisco VGC phones, CTI ports, and H.323 clients
- **Gateways**—Cisco VG200 and ports for the Cisco Catalyst 6000 FXS Analog Interface Module
- **User device profiles**—Cisco IP Phone 7900 Series and Cisco SoftPhone

Step 2 Define a format for the CSV data file. You can use the BAT Excel spreadsheet or a text editor to create the CSV data file.

Step 3 Validate the data input files with the Cisco CallManager database. Cisco CallManager runs a validation routine that checks the CSV file and the template for errors against the publisher database.

Step 4 Insert the devices into the Cisco CallManager database.

Using BAT Wizard Step 1: Choosing Devices

From the Configure menu shown in Figure 7-2, you can access the wizard by choosing one of these devices or configuration options:

- Phones
- Users
- Managers/Assistants
- User Device Profiles
- Gateways
- Forced Authorization Codes
- Client Matter Codes

- Pickup Group
- TAPS (optional, when installed)

Figure 7-2 *Bulk Administration Tool Configure Menu*

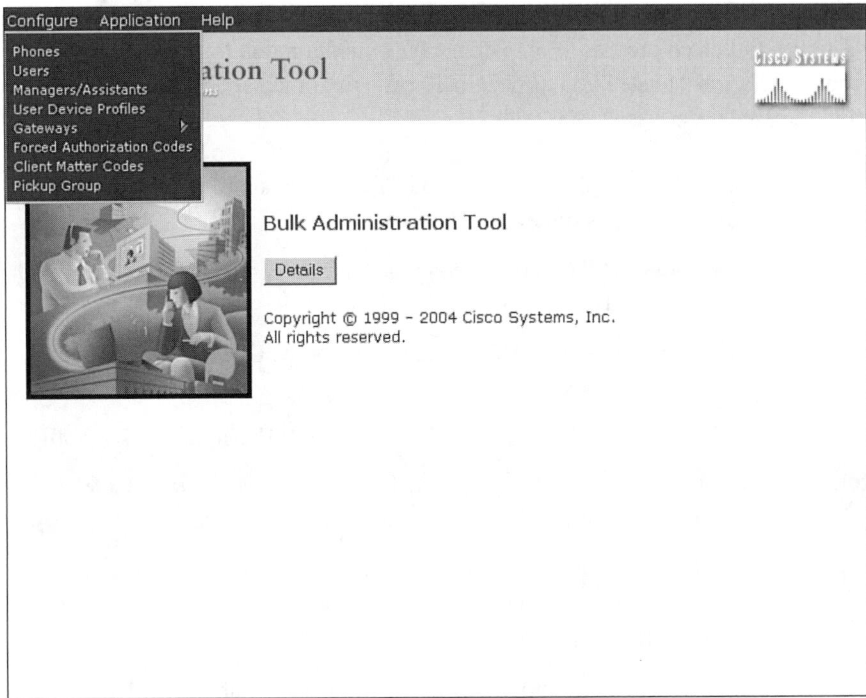

Using BAT Wizard Step 2: Device Specifics

After you choose a device or configuration option, the wizard displays a list of configuration tasks that are specific to that option. For example, when you choose Phones, the following list of tasks is displayed (shown in Figure 7-3):

- **Insert Phones**—Add new phones
- **Update Phones**—Locate and modify existing phones
- **Delete Phones**—Locate and delete phones
- **Export Phones**—Locate and export specific phone records or all phone records
- **Update Lines**—Locate and modify lines on existing phones
- **Add Lines**—Add new lines to existing phones

- **Reset/Restart Phones**—Locate and reset or restart phones
- **Insert Phones with Users**—Add new phones and users
- **Generate Phone Reports**—Generate customized reports for phones
- **CAPF Configuration**—Locate and modify or delete the digital certificates (called locally significant certificates [LSCs]) issued by the Cisco Authority Proxy Function (CAPF) server to IP Phones

Figure 7-3 *Bulk Administration Tool Wizard Phones Options Menu*

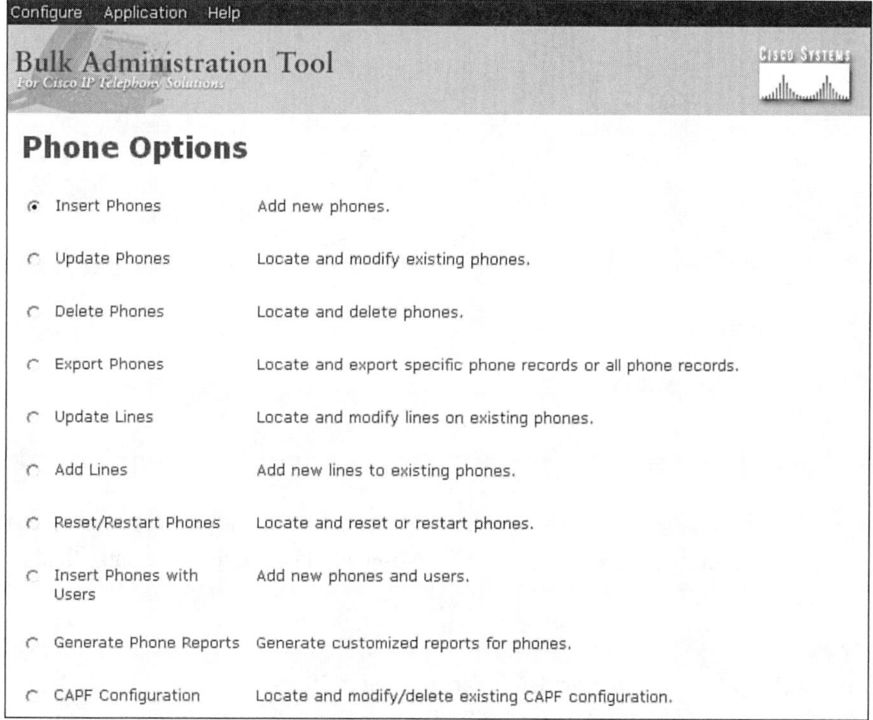

Using BAT Wizard Step 3: Proceed with Task

After you choose the configuration task, the wizard provides a list of steps that are specific to the task. For example, to guide you through the Insert Phones task (shown in Figure 7-4), the wizard displays the following steps:

Step 1 Add, view, or modify existing phone templates.

Step 2 Create the CSV data file.

Step 3 Validate phone records.

Step 4 Insert phones.

Figure 7-4 *Bulk Administration Tool Wizard Insert Phones Window*

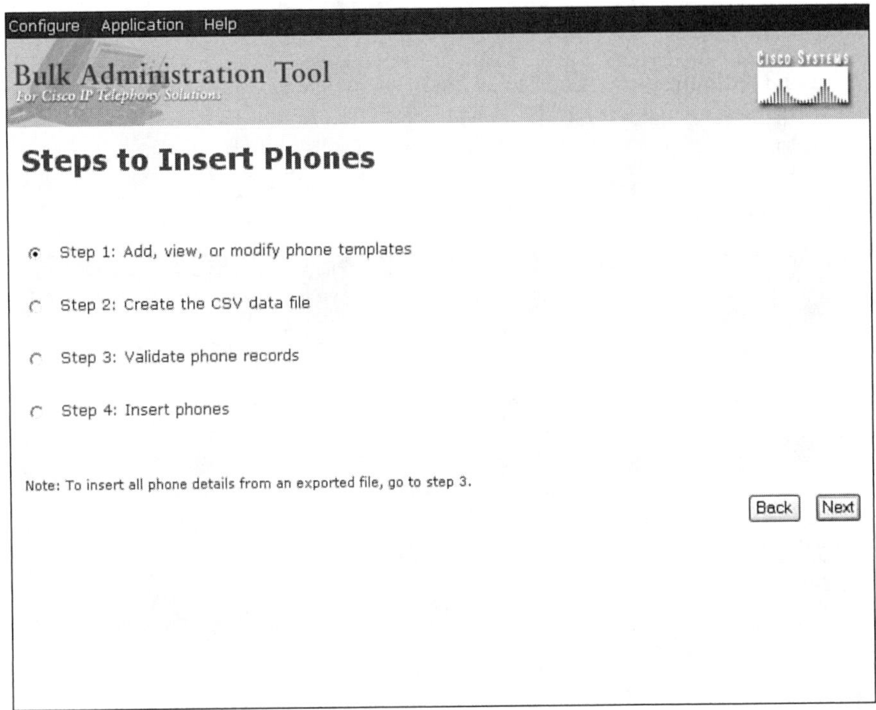

When you choose a step from the task list, you open a configuration window such as the Phone Template Configuration window. The configuration window provides the entry fields for defining a template.

Adding Phones Step 1: Configuring BAT Templates

The first task in creating the data for the BAT configuration process is to set up a template for the devices that you are configuring. You specify the type of phone or device that you want to add or modify, and then you create a BAT template that has features that are common to all the phones or devices in that bulk transaction.

Prior to creating the template, make sure that phone settings, such as device pool, location, calling search space, button template, and softkey templates, have already been configured in Cisco CallManager Administration. You cannot create new settings in BAT.

The first steps in configuring an IP Phone template are to give the phone template a unique name, and choose an IP Phone (device) type in the Phone Template Configuration window, as shown in

Figure 7-5. Choose the template that encompasses all of the IP Phones in the group. If you have multiple telephone types in a given group, you must create multiple templates.

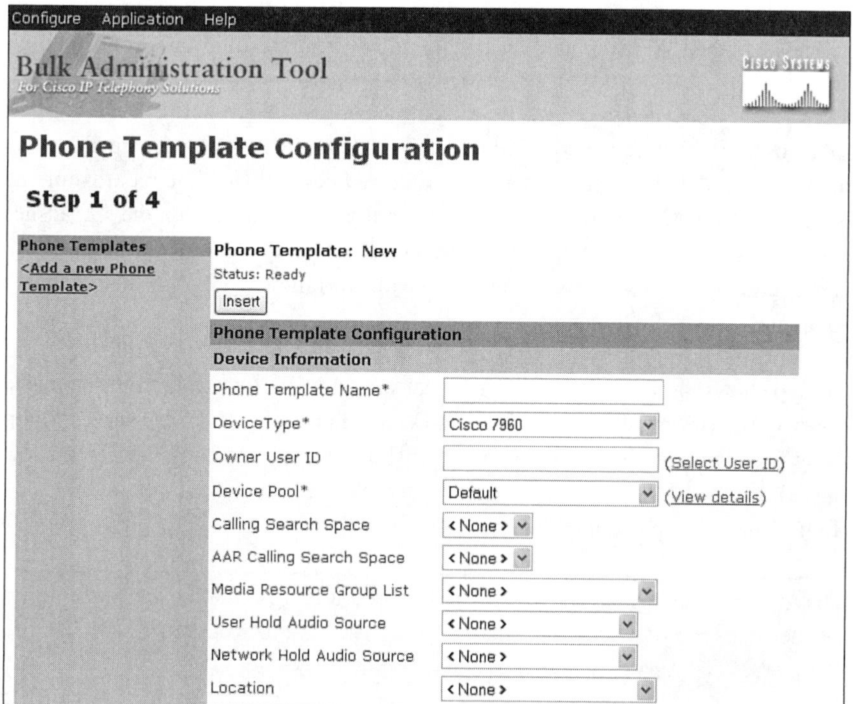

Figure 7-5 *Bulk Administration Tool Phone Template Configuration Window*

Next, assign the template to a device pool. After you have configured the initial template information, click **Insert** to add the template to the BAT utility.

After configuring the initial template settings, you can modify specific line configurations. From the initial template window, choose a line to configure, and a new configuration window appears. These general configuration settings can apply to multiple IP Phones, such as partitions, calling search spaces, and call waiting settings. BAT obtains line configurations that are specific to the user from the imported Microsoft Excel spreadsheet.

When you are adding a group of phones that have multiple lines, you can create a master phone template that provides multiple lines and the most common values for a specific phone model. You can use the master template to add phones that have differing numbers of lines, but do not exceed the number of lines in the master phone template. For example, you can create a master phone template for a Cisco IP Phone 7960 that has six lines. You can use this single template to add phones that have one line, two lines, or up to six lines (because the template provides the base configuration for up to six lines).

Adding Phones Step 2: Creating CSV Files

The CSV data file contains the unique settings and information for each individual device, such as its DN, MAC address, and description. Make sure that all phones and devices in a CSV data file are the same phone or device model and match the BAT template. The CSV data file can contain duplicates of some values from the BAT template. Values in the CSV data file override any values that were set in the BAT template. You can use the override feature for special configuration cases.

You can create CSV files in one of two ways: by using the Microsoft Excel spreadsheet BAT.xlt file or by using a text editor such as Microsoft Notepad. The BAT Excel spreadsheet simplifies the creation of CSV data files. You can add multiple devices and view the records for each device in a spreadsheet format. It allows you to customize the file format within the spreadsheet and provides validation and error checking automatically to help reduce configuration errors. Experienced BAT users who are comfortable with working in a CSV-formatted file can use a text editor to create a CSV data file.

Figure 7-6 shows the BAT.xlt Microsoft Excel spreadsheet. You can find this spreadsheet in the directory C:\CiscoWebs\BAT\ExcelTemplate\ on the publisher database server. You probably do not have Microsoft Excel running on the publisher, so you must copy the file to a local machine (using either a floppy disk or a mapped network drive). After you have copied the file, double-click **BAT.xlt**. When prompted, click **Enable Macros**.

> **TIP** After you have installed BAT, a BAT shared folder is created automatically on the publisher. This can provide easier access to the BAT files; to access the share, click **Start > Run** and type **\\\\<*CCM Server Name or IP Address*>\BAT.**

The BAT spreadsheet includes tabs along the bottom of the spreadsheet for access to the required data input fields for the various devices and user combinations in BAT. The CSV data file works in combination with the BAT template. For example, when you choose the **Phone** tab in the BAT spreadsheet, you can leave Location, Forward Busy Destination, or Call Pickup Group blank. The values from the BAT phone template are used for these fields; however, if you specify values for Forward Busy Destination or Call Pickup Group, those values override the values for these fields that were set in the BAT phone template.

Figure 7-6 *Bulk Administration Tool Excel Spreadsheet*

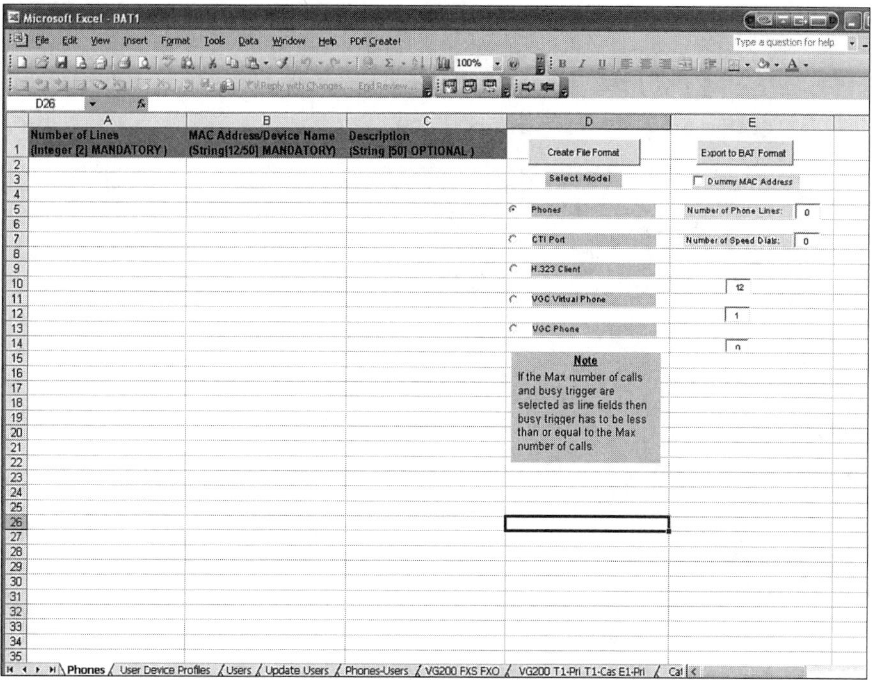

After entering the data into the BAT spreadsheet, click **Export to BAT Format** to create the CSV file. The format for CSV files is <tabname><timestamp>.txt. The system saves the file to C:\XLSDataFiles\ or to a folder of your choice. You must move the converted CSV file from the C:\XLSDataFiles\ folder on your local computer back to the publisher, where BAT can access the CSV file and place it in the appropriate folder under C:\BATFiles. (For example, you could save a phone CSV data file to the C:\BATFiles\Phones\Insert\ folder on the publisher database for Cisco CallManager.)

Using a text editor is the other way to create a CSV file. When using a text editor, follow these steps:

Step 1 Create the customized file format using the BAT File Format Configuration window shown in Figure 7-7. The file format specifies the order in which you enter values in the text file. This allows you to add attributes to the file format that are also in the BAT template, and override the template entry with a specific attribute for a device. For instance, you can choose the route partition attribute for your file format and enter different partitions for each phone in the CSV data file.

Figure 7-7 *Bulk Administration Tool CSV File Format*

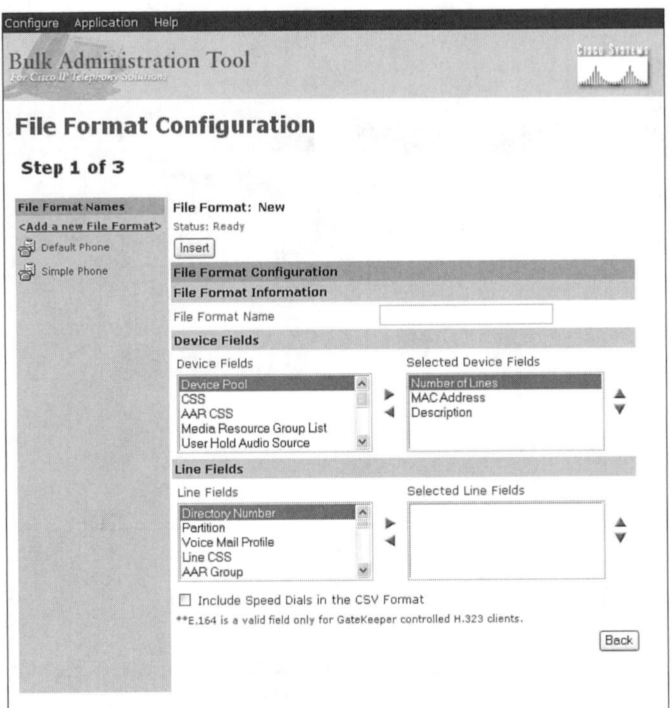

> Earlier versions of BAT supported only a default file format with a fixed and limited number of attributes and settings for each device and an All Details format that includes all attributes and settings for each device.

Step 2 Create the CSV data file using a basic text editor that follows the file format you defined in Step 1.

Step 3 Associate the file format with the CSV data file in Cisco BAT. You can associate only one file format with a CSV data file. Use the Add File Format window, shown in Figure 7-8, to choose the name of the CSV data file <CSVfilename>.txt from the **File Name** drop-down menu. Next, you choose your file format from the **File Format Name** drop-down menu. The data in the CSV data file must match the custom file format that you have chosen.

Figure 7-8 *Bulk Administration Tool CSV Format Association*

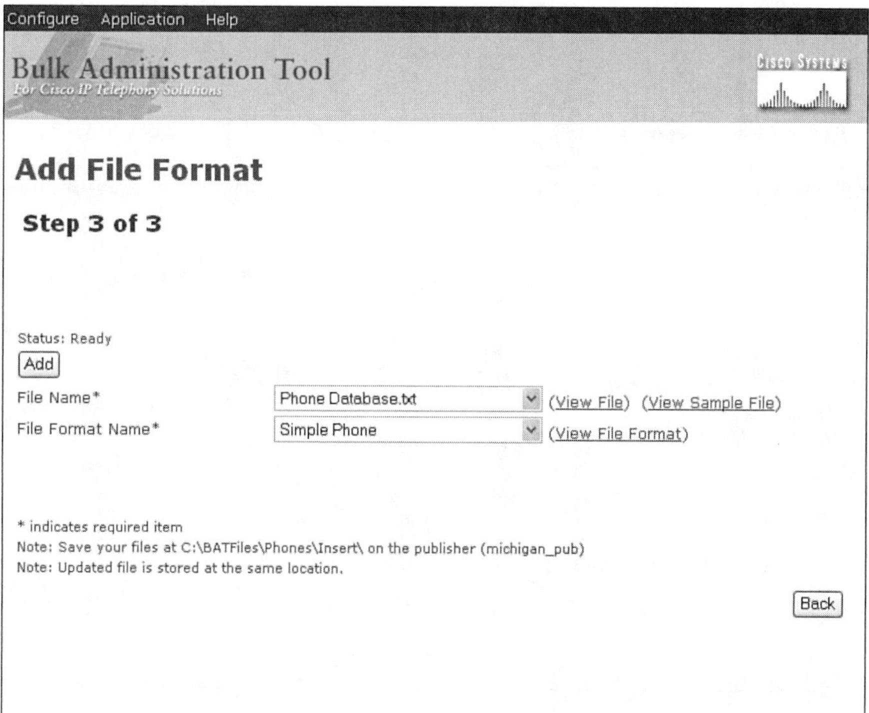

Adding Phones Step 3: Validating Phones

In the next task in the BAT wizard, you use the **Validate** option, shown in Figure 7-9, to validate the format of the text file you have chosen. In this task, you choose the name of the CSV data file and the BAT template for the device or the model when you have a CSV data file with all details. You have these options for how records are validated:

- **Specific Details**—For validating records that follow the default or custom file format
- **All Details**—For validating records from a file that was generated with the export utility by using the All Details option

Figure 7-9 *Bulk Administration Tool Validate Phones Window*

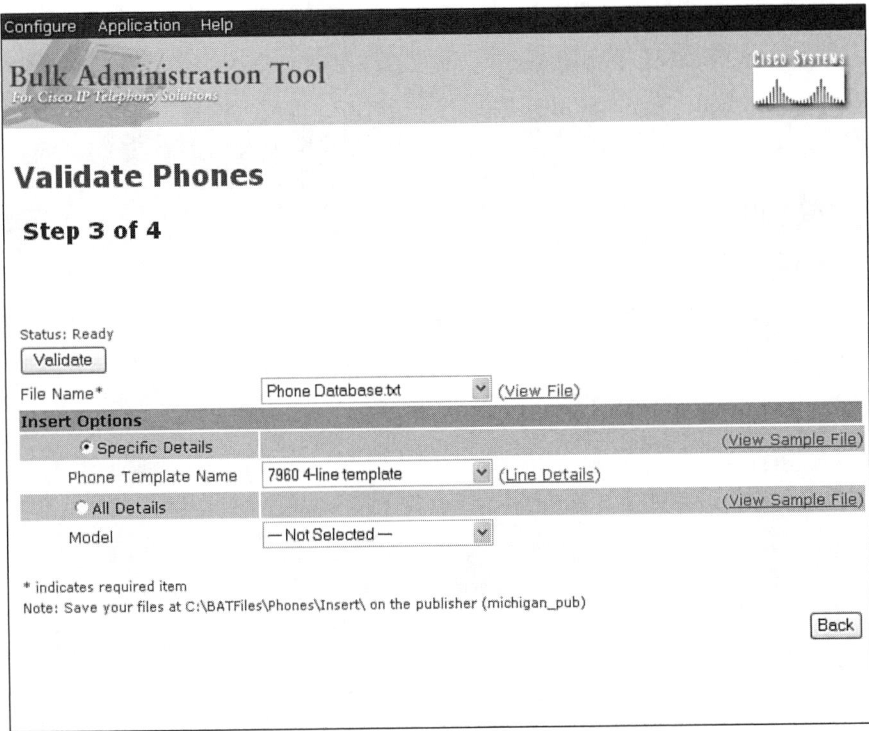

When you choose **Validate**, the system runs a validation routine to check for errors against the publisher database. These checks ensure the following:

- Fields, such as description, display text, and speed dial label, use valid characters.
- Cisco CallManager groups, device pools, partitions, and other referenced attributes are already configured.
- The number of lines that are configured on a device does not exceed the device template.

Validation does not check for the existence of a user or for mandatory or optional fields that are BAT-defined, such as the dummy MAC address.

Adding Phones Step 4: Inserting Phones

Inserting the device into the Cisco CallManager database is the last step in using BAT to perform bulk configurations, shown in Figure 7-10.

Figure 7-10 *Bulk Administration Tool Insert Phones Window*

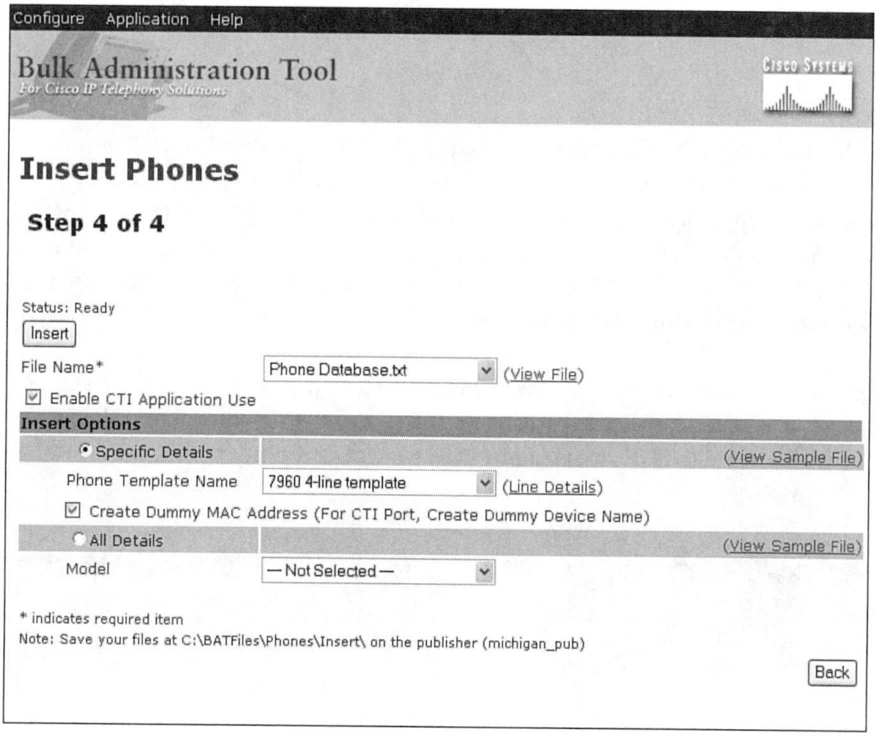

The following steps are involved in this procedure:

Step 1 In the File Name field, choose the CSV data file that you created for this specific bulk transaction.

Step 2 To enable the use of applications such as Cisco IP SoftPhone, check the **Enable CTI Application Use** check box (for CTI ports only).

NOTE CTI application use is not required for the Cisco IP Communicator.

Step 3 Choose the Insert option that corresponds to your CSV data file.

Step 4 In the **Phone Template Name** field, choose the BAT phone template that you created for this type of bulk transaction.

Step 5 If you did not enter individual MAC addresses in the CSV data file, check the **Create Dummy MAC Address** check box.

This field automatically generates dummy MAC addresses in the following format: *XXXXXXXXXXXX*, where *X* represents any 16-character, hexadecimal (0 to 9 and A to F) number. You can update the phones or devices later with the correct MAC address by manually entering this information into Cisco CallManager Administration or by using TAPS.

Step 6 Click **Insert** to insert the phone records.

Updating IP Phones Using BAT

In addition to using BAT for bulk device addition to the CallManager database, you can also use BAT to make bulk device updates to the system. This can be extremely useful when modifying a configuration for a large number of users. For example, a group of users might want to change their music on hold (MoH) to a new song. Rather than modifying the configuration of each phone individually, you can use BAT to make a bulk change to all phones based on unique match criteria (such as the department name or partition).

Figure 7-11 shows the Update Phones window. To update phone settings, such as changing or adding a device pool or calling search space for a group of similar phones, choose **Phones > Update Phones** in the BAT Configure window.

Figure 7-11 *Bulk Administration Tool Update Phones Window*

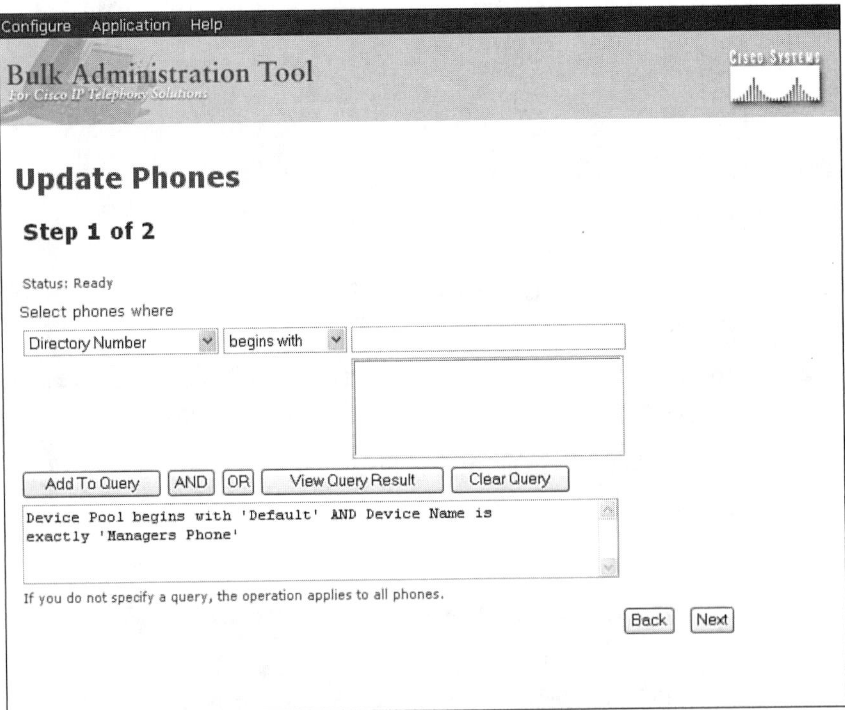

You can locate the existing phone records by using a query or a custom file containing the device names or DNs. You can query using any number of fields, such as the model, device name, DN, or description. You can also specify search criteria such as "begins with," "contains," or "is exactly."

Choose **View Query Result** to check that the query returns the information that you need. Choose **Clear Query** to remove the query items.

After you have defined the query or custom file to search for phones, follow this procedure to update the IP Phones or users to the Cisco CallManager database in bulk:

Step 1 Specify the values to be updated within Cisco CallManager, as shown in Figure 7-12.

Figure 7-12 *Bulk Administration Tool Update Phones Detail Window*

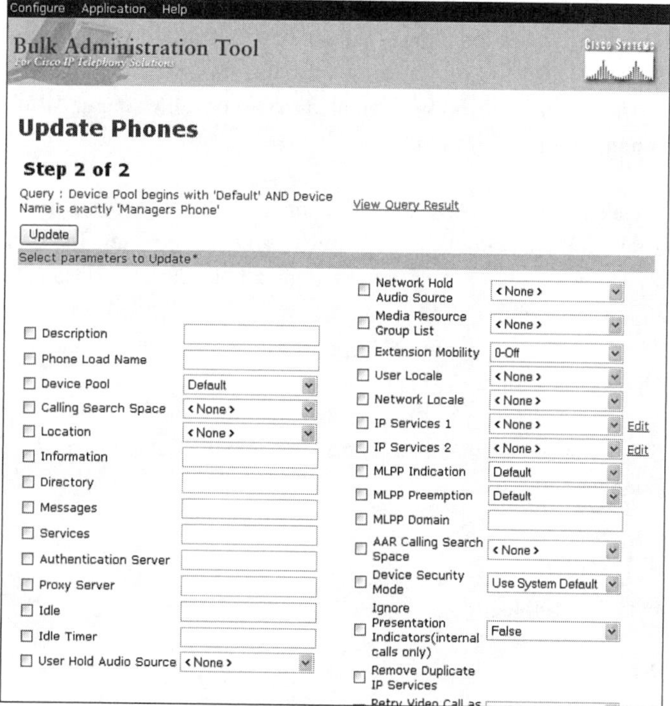

Step 2 Click **Update**.

Step 3 Reset or restart the IP Phones through Cisco CallManager.

To check the status of your insertion, read the status line, located above the **Insert** button.

If the status bar indicates a failure, click **View Latest Log File** to display a window that will help you to determine where the operation failed.

Using the Tool for Auto-Registered Phone Support

Use TAPS in conjunction with BAT to provide two features:

- Update MAC addresses and download predefined configuration for new phones
- Reload configuration for replacement phones

When new phones are added to Cisco CallManager, TAPS works in conjunction with BAT to update phones that were added to BAT using dummy MAC addresses. After BAT has been used to bulk-add the telephones with dummy MAC addresses to Cisco CallManager Administration, you can plug the telephones into the network. You or the user of the telephone can dial a TAPS directory number that causes the phone to download its configuration. At the same time, the telephone is updated in Cisco CallManager Administration with the correct MAC address. You must make sure that auto-registration is enabled in Cisco CallManager Administration (**System > Cisco CallManager**) for TAPS to function.

Prior to BAT Release 5.0(1), TAPS installation and uninstallation for Cisco CallManager was part of the BAT installation program. With BAT Release 5.0(1) and later, TAPS is installed separately. In addition, for TAPS to operate, you must also install the Cisco CallManager Extended Services CD (which ships with current CallManager 4.x versions or can be downloaded from Cisco CCO) or have purchased the Cisco Customer Response Application (CRA) server, which is typically used in call center environments.

During TAPS installation or reinstallation on the publisher database server, the setup program halts the following services:

- Microsoft IIS administration
- World Wide Web publishing
- FTP publishing

These services restart when the installation is finished.

You cannot use Windows Terminal Services to install TAPS. You must install TAPS directly from the Cisco CallManager publisher server and the CRA server (if you are using a CRA server).

> **NOTE** In earlier versions of CallManager (prior to 4.x), CRA servers were required to be separate from the CallManager server. In the 4.x versions, Cisco CRA services can reside on the same server as Cisco CallManager. Cisco CRA allows CallManager integration with outside applications.

These prerequisites apply to the TAPS installation for BAT:

- Make sure that the publisher database for Cisco CallManager is configured and running. The publisher database can reside on its own server or on the same server as Cisco CallManager.
- Before installing TAPS, ensure that the latest BAT release is installed on the publisher database server for Cisco CallManager.
- Have the IP address for the Cisco CallManager publisher server and the private phrase for the installation procedure.
- If you are not using the CallManager Extended Services CD, ensure that the Cisco CRA server is configured. The Cisco CRA application can reside on its own dedicated server or can be colocated on the same server as Cisco CallManager.
- Be sure to use the locale installer to create the country-specific TAPS prompts.
- Ensure that the Windows 2000 Services window is closed.

NOTE Because TAPS relies on advanced CallManager configuration concepts, many of the details in the steps pertaining to the TAPS installation and configuration, such as CTI ports and route points, move outside of the CIPT material. Detailed information about TAPS can be found in the Cisco CallManager Bulk Administration Guide available on the Cisco website.

Complete the following steps to install TAPS:

Step 1 Log in with administrator privileges to the system that is running the publisher database for Cisco CallManager (where you installed BAT).

Step 2 Access BAT.

Step 3 Choose **Applications > Install Plugins**.

Step 4 Double-click the TAPS setup icon.

Step 5 Determine whether to copy the TAPS installation executable to the system or run it from the current location.

Step 6 The Welcome window for the installation wizard opens. This installation program installs TAPS on the Cisco CallManager publisher server and the CRA applications server at the same time, if applications are colocated on the same server. Click **Next**.

NOTE When you are installing TAPS in a network with a dedicated CRA server, you must run the TAPS installation program again on the CRA server. Use CRA online help for assistance with installation and configuration.

Step 7 Enter the private phrase for the Cisco CallManager publisher server in the Installing Cisco CallManager Components window and click **Next**. The Installing TAPS on CCM window displays a progress bar that shows the status of the installation.

Step 8 The Installation Completed window is displayed when the installation ends. Click **Finish**.

After you have completed the TAPS installation, you must configure TAPS by adding a Computer Telephony Interface (CTI) route point, CTI ports, and users in Cisco CallManager Administration. One CTI route point and at least one CTI port are required for TAPS.

The following procedure describes how to configure TAPS in Cisco CallManager Administration:

> **NOTE** To use TAPS, verify that auto-registration is enabled in Cisco CallManager. Because TAPS can replace a DN, you can protect certain DNs from being overwritten by using the Secure TAPS option. Turning on Secure TAPS keeps a user from overwriting an extension that is already in use.

Step 1 Create a CTI route point and assign it a unique DN.

Step 2 Choose the **Call Forward Busy**, **Call Forward No Answer**, and **Call Forward on Failure** options for the operator number on the TAPS CTI route point.

Step 3 Create one or more CTI ports with consecutive DNs. You can create CTI ports in BAT or Cisco CallManager Administration.

Step 4 Create a user. The TAPS route point and ports should be in the Controlled Devices list of the user.

Step 5 Create an auto-registration partition or calling search space or both to prevent IP Phones that have auto-registered from dialing any DN other than the number that is assigned to the TAPS CTI route point. Restricting access to this DN ensures that users download the proper configuration information for their IP Phones.

> **NOTE** TAPS supports a maximum number of simultaneous sessions equal to the number of CTI ports that are configured for TAPS. For example, if you have configured five CTI ports, up to five users can dial into TAPS at the same time. The sixth caller cannot connect to TAPS.

Summary

This chapter discussed the Bulk Administration Tool (BAT) and the Tool for Auto-Registered Phone Support (TAPS) utilities from Cisco. These tools ease the administrative load of Cisco CallManager in a huge way by allowing you to make bulk adds, deletes, and changes to the devices in the CallManager database. By combining a Comma Separated Value (CSV) text file containing unique values with a template, you can insert devices (or users) in bulk into the CallManager system. In addition, you can use BAT to define a query matching multiple existing devices and perform a mass update to chance settings across your IP telephony network.

Cisco has provided TAPS to create a semiautomated system to add IP Phones to your network. Using TAPS, new IP Phones auto-register with the Cisco CallManager and receive a generic extension assignment. When you assign a user to an IP Phone, they dial the TAPS number and walk through an automated process in which they type in the extension number you have assigned them. TAPS then queries the data from your imported CSV file to find the specific settings that CallManager should apply to the IP Phone and sets it up with the correct extension and configuration settings.

Review Questions

You can find the solutions to these questions in Appendix A, "Answers to Review Questions."

1. Which of the following configurations can you add to the CallManager database in bulk using BAT? (Choose three.)
   a. Route Groups
   b. Route Patterns
   c. Users
   d. IP Phones
   e. Phone Templates
   f. Device Profiles
2. For TAPS to function correctly, what must you enable on at least one Cisco CallManager server?
   a. Voice Media Streaming Application service
   b. Auto-Registration
   c. Cisco IPCC
   d. All of the above

3. Which two pieces of information are required to perform a successful device import using BAT? (Choose two.)

   a. a tab-delimited text file
   b. a comma-separated text file
   c. a valid device template
   d. CallManager 4.x or later

4. When you install BAT, the installation process stores an Excel template on the hard drive of the CallManager server. Where is the file located?

   a. C:\Cisco\BAT
   b. C:\Program Files\Cisco\BAT
   c. C:\BAT
   d. C:\CiscoWebs\BAT\ExcelTemplate

5. On which CallManager server should you install the Cisco BAT utility?

   a. the Publisher server
   b. a Subscriber server participating in call processing
   c. a Subscriber server not participating in call processing
   d. a CallManager server not performing database replication

6. You have created an entry in a CSV file that defines an IP Phone with two lines. You combine this CSV file with a BAT device template that defines an IP Phone with six lines. What happens?

   a. The BAT utility inserts the IP Phone into the CallManager database with only the two lines defined in the CSV file.
   b. The BAT utility inserts the IP Phone into the CallManager database with the six lines defined in the device template.
   c. The BAT utility rejects the configuration and produces an HTTP 4xx error.
   d. The BAT utility prompts you for the configuration for the additional four lines.

7. You are using the BAT Excel template to define a CSV file for a bulk import. You notice a check box in the template that says "Create Dummy MAC Address." What does this check box accomplish?

   a. It assigns all IP Phones a MAC address of 0000.0000.0000 until the IP Phone auto-registers.
   b. It enters the IP Phones into the CallManager database without a MAC address.
   c. It generates random MAC addresses for the IP Phones until the administrator changes them.
   d. It is for use for updates only with the TAPS utility.

8. You want to perform a bulk update to change the music on hold setting for all Cisco IP Phones to a classic Frank Sinatra song. How do you specify the IP Phones to change in the BAT utility?

   a. by specifying a range of DNs

   b. through a query process

   c. using a drop-down menu

   d. by checking the **Select All** check box

9. What additional application does CallManager require to support TAPS?

   a. Microsoft Exchange 2000

   b. Customer Response Application

   c. SQL 2000

   d. additional phone ports

10. What two methods can you use to create CSV files? (Choose two.)

   a. the Microsoft Excel Template

   b. the CSV file generator downloadable from CCO

   c. the query utility included with BAT

   d. a text editor

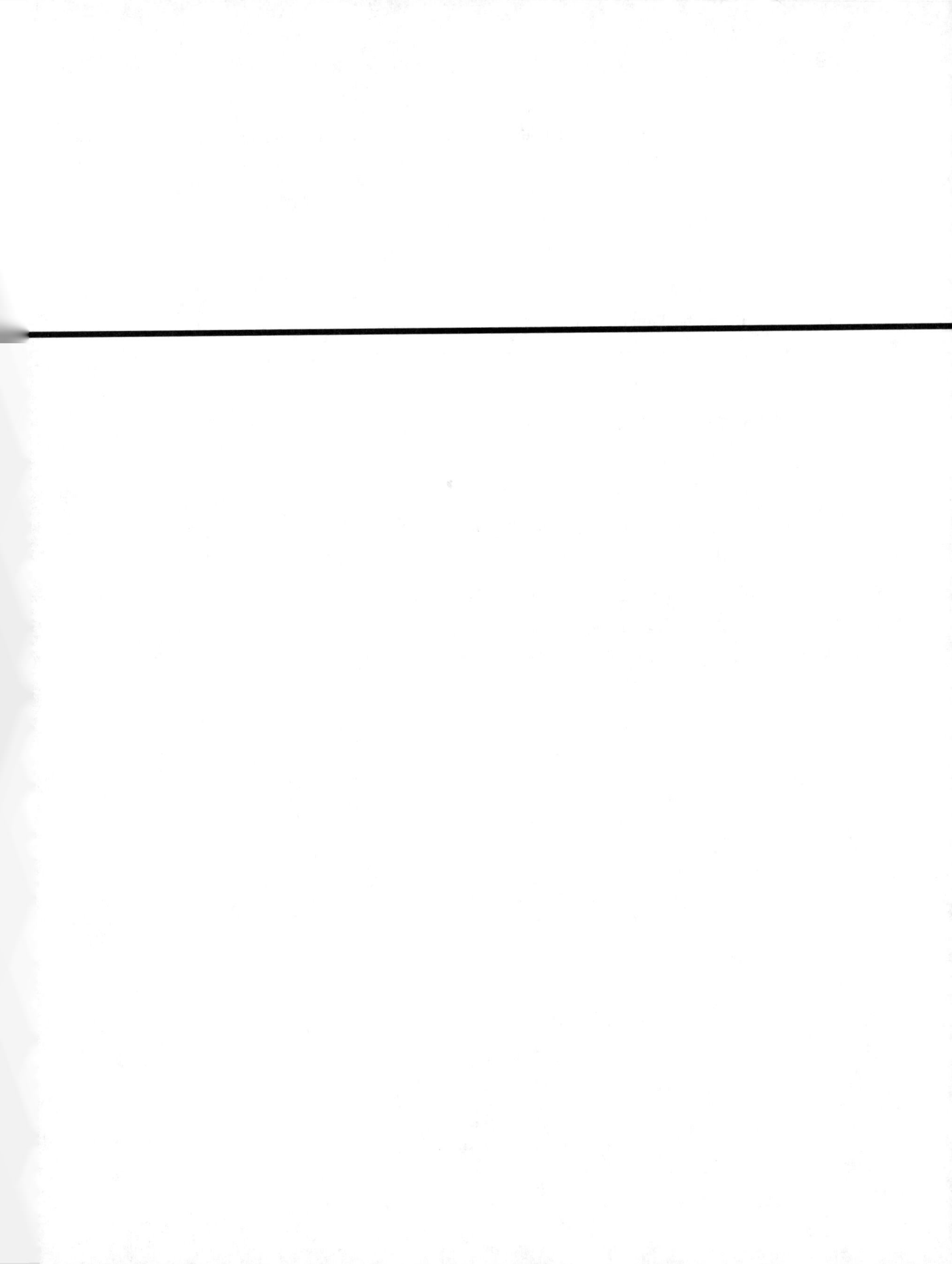

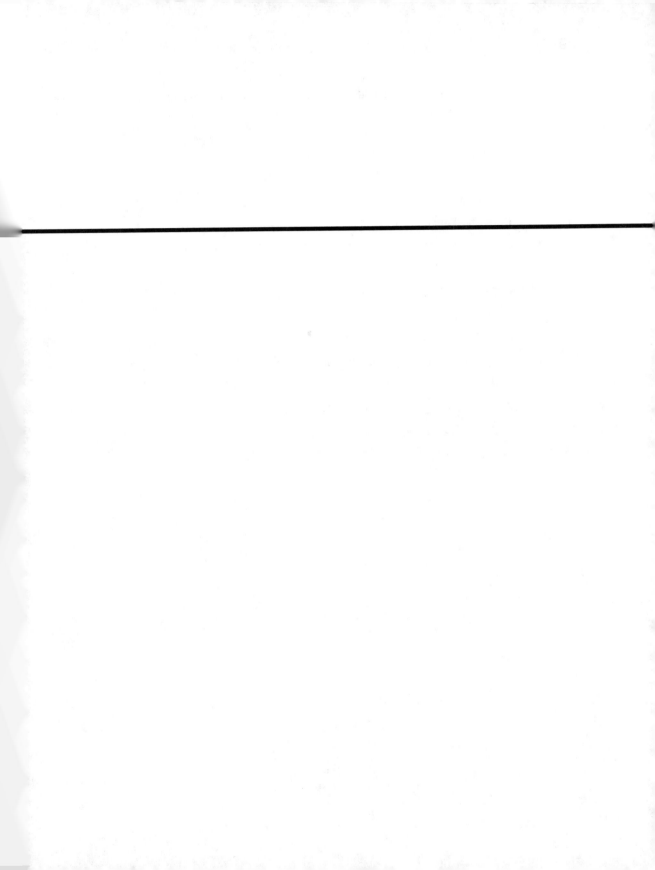

Part III: IPT Network Integration and Route Plan

This chapter covers the following topics:

- Identifying the functions that Cisco Catalyst switches perform in a Cisco IP telephony solution
- The three options for powering Cisco IP Phones
- The two types of PoE that Cisco Catalyst switches provide and the Cisco Catalyst switches that support PoE
- Identifying the commands to configure PoE on Cisco Catalyst switches
- Configuring dual VLANs on a single port on a Cisco Catalyst switch so that the IP Phones reside in a separate VLAN
- Configuring CoS on Cisco Catalyst switches so that voice traffic has priority over data traffic as it travels throughout the network

CHAPTER 8

Cisco Catalyst Switches

Deploying IP telephony requires planning how you will power the IP Phones and how the voice network traffic will mix with the data network while ensuring that the data traffic does not degrade the quality of the voice calls.

Cisco Catalyst switches provide three features that aid an IP telephony deployment: inline power, voice VLANs, and class of service (CoS). Using the Cisco Catalyst switch to power IP Phones can save on wiring costs and simplifies management. Enabling multiple VLANs in a single port and placing voice packets in one VLAN and data in another VLAN saves money by reducing the number of switch ports. Extending CoS to the IP Phone improves voice quality by ensuring that voice packets receive priority over data.

This lesson discusses the three major functions that Cisco Catalyst switches perform in an IP telephony network and describes how to configure a Cisco Catalyst switch to enable these functions.

Catalyst Switch Role in IP Telephony

Cisco voice-capable Catalyst switches can provide three primary features to assist you with your IP telephony deployment:

- **Inline power**—Inline power capabilities allow a Cisco Catalyst switch to send power through the Category 3 (or better) copper cabling to a Cisco IP Phone or other inline power-compatible devices (such as wireless access points) without the need for an external power supply. Inline power is also referred to as Power over Ethernet (PoE). Inline power was developed in 2000 by Cisco to support the emerging IP telephony solution and was later standardized by the IEEE as the 802.3af standard.

- **Auxiliary VLAN support**—Auxiliary VLAN support allows a switch to support multiple VLANs on a single access port. You can connect a PC to the back of the Cisco IP Phone because some Cisco IP Phones have built-in switches. Auxiliary VLANs allow you to place the IP Phone, and the devices that are attached through the IP Phone, on separate VLANs.

- **Class of service (CoS) marking**—CoS marking is data link layer (Layer 2) marking that is used to prioritize network traffic. Prioritizing voice traffic is critical in IP telephony networks. If voice traffic is not given priority, poor voice quality may result because voice frames wait in the switch queue behind large data frames. The switch can use existing CoS marking to prioritize network traffic and can also classify and mark traffic that it receives.

Powering the Cisco IP Phone

Most Cisco IP Phone models are capable of using the following three options for power:

- **PoE**—With PoE, the phone plugs into the data jack that connects to the switch, and the user PC in turn connects to the IP Phone. Power-sourcing equipment (PSE), such as Cisco Catalyst PoE-capable modular and fixed-configuration switches, insert power over the Ethernet cable to the powered device, for example, an IP Phone or 802.11 wireless access point.

- **Midspan power injection**—Because many switches do not support PoE, the powered device must support a midspan power source. This midspan device sits between the LAN switch and the powered device and inserts power on the Ethernet cable to the powered device. A technical difference between the midspan and inline power mechanism is that power is delivered on the spare pairs (pins 4, 5, 7, and 8). An example of midspan PSE is a Cisco Catalyst Inline Power Patch Panel.

- **Wall power**—Wall power needs a DC converter for connecting the IP Phone to a wall outlet.

NOTE You must order the wall power supply separately from the Cisco IP Phone. This can increase the cost of the end devices significantly. Before you decide to use wall power rather than PoE to power the Cisco IP Phones, be sure to verify the total cost of this decision.

Two Types of PoE Delivery

Cisco provides two types of inline power delivery: the Cisco original implementation and the IEEE 802.3af PoE standard. You can refer to both inline power types as PoE.

Because Cisco was the first to develop PoE, there was not an established PoE industry standard to which Cisco could conform. Because of this, the industry considers Cisco's original implementation PoE as prestandard and proprietary. Although Cisco will eventually discontinue this prestandard implementation, Cisco devices will continue to support it for many years to come. The Cisco prestandard PoE implementation supports the following features:

- Provides –48 V DC at up to 6.3 to 7.7 watts (W) per port over data pins 1, 2, 3, and 6.

- Supports most PoE-capable Cisco devices (IP Phones and wireless access points).

- Uses a Cisco proprietary method of determining whether an attached device requires power. Power is delivered only to devices that require power.

Since first developing PoE, Cisco has been driving the evolution of this technology toward standardization by working with the IEEE and member vendors to create a standards-based means of providing power from an Ethernet switch port. The IEEE 802.3af committee has ratified this capability. The IEEE 802.3af PoE standard supports the following features:

- Specifies –48 V DC at up to 15.4 W per port over data pins 1, 2, 3, and 6 or the spare pins 4, 5, 7, and 8 (a PSE can use one or the other, but not both).
- Enables a new range of Ethernet-powered devices that consume additional power.
- Standardizes the method of determining whether an attached device requires power. The PSE delivers power only to devices that require power. This type has several optional elements, such as power classification, where powered devices can optionally support a signature that defines the maximum power requirement. PSE that supports power classification reads this signature and budgets the correct amount of power per powered device, which will likely be significantly less than the maximum allowed power.

Without power classification, the switch reserves the full 15.4 W of power for every device. This behavior might result in oversubscription of the available power supplies so that some devices will not be powered even though there is sufficient power available.

Power classification defines these five classes:

0 (default)—15.4 W reserved
1—4 W
2—7 W
3—15.4 W
4—Reserved for future expansion

All Cisco IEEE 802.3af-compliant switches support power classification.

TIP The Cisco Power Calculator is an online tool that enables you to calculate the power supply requirements for a specific PoE configuration. The Cisco Power Calculator is available to registered Cisco.com users at www.cisco.com/go/poe.

PoE Device Detection

The Cisco prestandard PoE and industry standard IEEE 802.3af PoE have slightly different methods of detecting an inline power-capable device. Figure 8-1 illustrates how a Cisco prestandard Catalyst switch detects a Cisco IP Phone, wireless access point, or other inline power-capable device. When a switch port that is configured for inline power detects a connected device, the switch sends an Ethernet Fast Link Pulse (FLP) to the device. The Cisco powered device (IP Phone) loops the FLP back to the switch to indicate its inline power capability. The switch then delivers –48 V DC PoE (inline) power to the IP Phone or other inline power-capable endpoint.

Figure 8-1 *Cisco Prestandard PoE Device Detection*

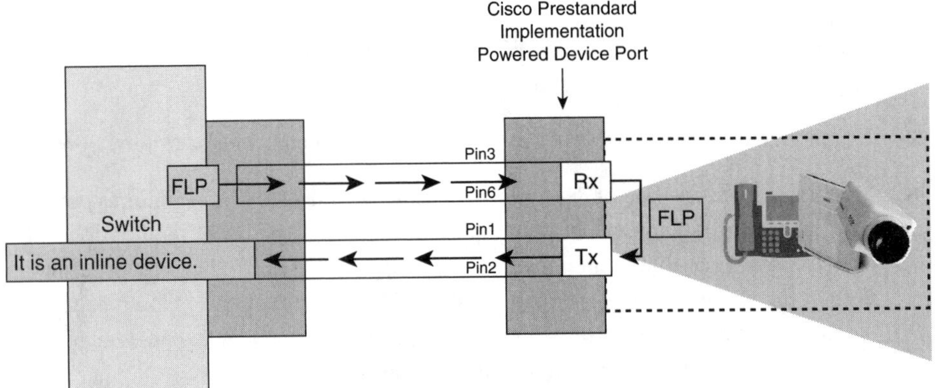

A Cisco Catalyst IEEE 802.3af-compliant switch detects a Cisco IP Phone, wireless access point, or other inline power-capable device through a very similar process. The PSE (Cisco Catalyst switch) detects a powered device by applying a voltage in the range of –2.8 V to –10 V on the cable and then looks for a 25K ohm signature resistor rather than using the Cisco proprietary FLP signal. Compliant powered devices must support this resistance method. If the appropriate resistance is found, the Cisco Catalyst switch delivers power.

Catalyst Family of PoE Switches

The Cisco Catalyst LAN switching portfolio is the industry-leading family of intelligent switching solutions delivering a robust range of security and quality of service (QoS) capabilities. The Cisco Catalyst switch portfolio allows organizations to enable new business applications and integrate new technologies such as wireless and IP telephony into their network infrastructure. Here are the switches in the Cisco Catalyst family:

- **Cisco Catalyst modular switching**—The Cisco Catalyst 6500 Series delivers a 96-port 10BASE-T/100BASE-T line card and 48-port 10BASE-T/100BASE-T and 10BASE-T/100BASE-T/1000BASE-T line cards. The Catalyst 6500 Series offers a modular PoE daughter card architecture for the 96-port card and the 48-port 10/100/1000 card. The Cisco Catalyst 4500 Series delivers 48-port 10/100 and 10/100/1000 line cards. All line cards support both IEEE 802.3af and Cisco prestandard inline power. The cards are compatible with any Cisco Catalyst 6500 or 4500 chassis and Supervisor Engine. The Cisco Catalyst modular chassis switches can deliver 15.4 W per port for all 48 ports on a module simultaneously.

- **Cisco Catalyst stackable switching**—The Cisco Catalyst 3750 Series offers 48- and 24-port Fast Ethernet switches that comply with IEEE 802.3af and Cisco prestandard PoE. The Cisco Catalyst 3560 Series offers 48- and 24-port Fast Ethernet switches that support both the industry standard and Cisco standard PoE.
- **Cisco EtherSwitch modules**—The Cisco 36- and 16-port 10/100 EtherSwitch modules for Cisco 2600 and 3700 Series routers offer branch office customers the option to integrate switching and routing in one platform. These modules can support Cisco prestandard PoE and provide straightforward configuration, easy deployment, and integrated management in a single platform. The Cisco 2600 Series requires a separate external PoE power supply; the Cisco 3700 Series integrates the power supply. Cisco has also released EtherSwitch modules for the newer Integrated Service Routers (ISRs). These new EtherSwitch modules support both the Cisco prestandard PoE and the IEEE 802.3af PoE.

Table 8-1 lists the Cisco Catalyst PoE options.

Table 8-1 *Catalyst Switch PoE Options*

PoE Option	Cisco Catalyst 6500	Cisco Catalyst 4500	Cisco Catalyst 3750	Cisco Catalyst 3560	Cisco EtherSwitch Module
PoE Configuration Options	48-, 96-port 10/100 or 48-port 10/100/1000	48-port 10/100 or 10/100/1000	24-, 48-port 10/100	24-, 48-port 10/100	16-, 36-port 10/100
IEEE 802.3af-Compliant	Yes	Yes	Yes	Yes	No (older series) Yes (ISRs)
Cisco Prestandard PoE	Yes	Yes	Yes	Yes	Yes

TIP The switches that are listed here also support multiple VLANs per port and QoS capabilities.

NOTE The pace of change in IP telephony is intense. By the time you are reading this text, Cisco will have most likely introduced multiple new product lines and switch models that support PoE and many other features. Always be sure to check the Cisco website for the latest product information.

Configuring PoE

By default, PoE is enabled on all Cisco devices that support the PoE feature. The default mode for PoE is auto, which means the switch will automatically detect if a device is PoE capable and supply power, if necessary. If you are using a switch that is running Cisco Catalyst Operating System software (CatOS), use the following syntax to modify the default PoE settings:

```
CatOS>(enable) set port inlinepower <mod/port> ?
    auto      Port inline power auto mode
    off       Port inline power off mode
```

The two modes are auto and off. In the off mode, the switch does not power up the port even if an unpowered phone is connected. In the auto mode, the switch powers up the port only if the switching module has discovered the phone. Examples of devices running Cisco CatOS include the Cisco Catalyst 6500, 4500, and 4000 Series.

> **TIP** It can be useful to turn PoE capabilities off on ports that you are sure will never use the feature. If the power supply your switch is equipped with is unable to extend power to all ports, you can specify ports that should receive power. Otherwise, the switch will allocate power to ports with lower port numbers until it exhausts the available power supply leaving the higher port numbers unpowered. The switch allocates power to ports configured with the "auto" setting regardless of whether the port is using the power.

If you are using a switch that is running Cisco IOS (NativeIOS), use the following syntax to modify the default PoE settings:

```
NativeIOS(config-if)# power inline [auto | never]
```

Use the **power inline** command on switches that are running native Cisco IOS software (examples include the Catalyst 6500, 4500, 3750, and 3560 switches). The powered device-discovery algorithm is operational in the auto mode. The powered device-discovery algorithm is disabled in the never mode. Other modes exist for allocating power, depending on the version of Cisco IOS, for example, the ability to allocate power on a per-port basis with the **allocation** *milliwatt* command.

> **NOTE** The Catalyst 6500 Series can run either Cisco Catalyst Operating System software or native Cisco IOS software if the switch Supervisor Engine has a Multilayer Switch Feature Card (MSFC). Otherwise, these switches can run only Cisco Catalyst software. The Cisco Catalyst 4500 and 4000 Series can also run Cisco Catalyst software or native Cisco IOS software, depending on the Supervisor Engine. Generally, late-edition Supervisor Engines run native Cisco IOS software; however, you should check the product documentation to determine the Supervisor Engine and the operating system that is supported on your specific model.

Verifying PoE

You can use the following command to display a view of the power allocated on Cisco Catalyst switches running the CatOS:

```
CatOS>(enable) show port inline power 7
Default Inline Power allocation per port: 10.000 Watts (0.23 Amps @42V)
Total inline power drawn by module 7: 75.60 Watts (1.80 Amps @42V)
Port    InlinePowered       PowerAllocated
        Admin    Oper    Detected   mWatt        mA @42V
----    -----    ----    --------   ---------    -----------
7/1     auto     off     no         0            0
7/2     auto     on      yes        6300         150
7/3     auto     on      yes        6300         150
7/4     auto     off     no         0            0
7/5     auto     off     no         0            0
7/6     auto     off     no         0            0
7/7     auto     off     no         0            0
```

You can use the following command to display a view of the power allocated on Cisco Catalyst switches running the NativeIOS:

```
NativeIOS#show power inline
Available:360(w)  Used:22(w)  Remaining:338(w)

Interface Admin  Oper       Power   Device              Class Max
--------- ------ ---------- ------- ------------------- ----- ----
Fa0/1     auto   off        0.0     n/a                 n/a   15.4
Fa0/2     auto   off        0.0     n/a                 n/a   15.4
Fa0/3     auto   off        0.0     n/a                 n/a   15.4
Fa0/4     auto   off        0.0     n/a                 n/a   15.4
Fa0/5     auto   off        0.0     n/a                 n/a   15.4
Fa0/6     auto   off        0.0     n/a                 n/a   15.4
Fa0/7     auto   off        0.0     n/a                 n/a   15.4
Fa0/8     auto   on         10.3    IP Phone 7970             15.4
Fa0/9     auto   off        0.0     n/a                 n/a   15.4
Fa0/10    auto   on         6.3     IP Phone 7960       n/a   15.4
Fa0/11    auto   off        0.0     n/a                 n/a   15.4
Fa0/12    auto   off        0.0     n/a                 n/a   15.4
Fa0/13    auto   off        0.0     n/a                 n/a   15.4
Fa0/14    auto   on         6.3     IP Phone 7960       n/a   15.4
```

Table 8-2 provides a brief description of the output.

Table 8-2 *Inline Power Output Descriptions*

Output		**Description**
Port		Identifies the port number on the module
Inline Powered	Admin	Identifies the port configuration from using the **set inlinepower** *mod/port* [**auto** | **off**] command
	Oper	Identifies whether the inline power is operational
Power Allocated	Detected	Identifies whether power is detected
	mWatt/Watts	Identifies the milliwatts (CatOS) or Watts (NativeIOS) supplied on a given port
	mA @42V	Identifies the milliamps at 42 V supplied on a given port (the actual voltage is –48 V)

Data and Voice VLANs

All data devices typically reside on data VLANs in the traditional switched scenario. You might need a separate voice VLAN when you combine the voice network into the data network. Although you can think of it as a voice VLAN, in the future, other types of nondata devices will reside in the voice VLAN.

> **NOTE** The Cisco Catalyst software (CatOS) refers to this new voice VLAN as the auxiliary VLAN for configuration purposes.

The placement of nondata devices (such as IP Phones) in a voice VLAN makes it easier for customers to automate the process of deploying IP Phones. IP Phones will boot and reside in the voice VLAN if you configure the switch to support them, just as data devices boot and reside in the access (data) VLAN. The IP Phone communicates with the switch via Cisco Discovery Protocol when it powers up. The switch provides the telephone with the appropriate VLAN ID.

> **NOTE** Although a voice VLAN is not required, it is encouraged by Cisco to isolate voice traffic for QoS and security purposes. It might also be impossible to put more devices on the existing data VLAN due to address space depletion in the data subnet DHCP scope, in which case, the voice VLAN becomes imperative.

Administrators can implement multiple VLANs on the same port by configuring trunk port. A tagging mechanism must exist to distinguish among VLANs on the same port. 802.1Q is the IEEE standard for tagging frames with a VLAN ID number. The IP Phone sends tagged 802.1Q frames. The PC sends untagged frames and the switch adds the access VLAN tag before forwarding toward the network. When the switch receives a frame from the network destined for the PC, it removes the access VLAN tag before forwarding the frame to the PC.

There are some advantages in implementing dual VLANs:

- This solution allows for scalability of the network from an addressing perspective. IP subnets usually have more than 50 percent (often more than 80 percent) of their IP addresses allocated. A separate VLAN (separate IP subnet) to carry the voice traffic allows you to introduce a large number of new devices, such as IP Phones, into the network without extensive modifications to the IP addressing scheme.
- This solution allows for the logical separation of data and voice traffic, which have different characteristics. This separation allows the network to handle these two traffic types individually.
- This solution allows you to connect two devices to the switch using only one physical port and one Ethernet cable between the wiring closet and the IP Phone or PC location.

Configuring and Verifying Dual VLANs Using the CatOS

Configure auxiliary VLAN ports in Cisco Catalyst software 5.5 and later using the **set port auxiliaryvlan** command to configure the auxiliary VLAN ports:

```
set port auxiliaryvlan [mod/port] {vlan | untagged | dot1p | none}
```

Table 8-3 provides a brief description of the syntax.

Table 8-3 **set port auxiliaryvlan** *Command Syntax Description*

Syntax	Description
[*mod/port*]	Number of the module and (optional) ports
vlan	Number of the VLAN; valid values are from 1 to 1000
untagged	Keyword to specify that the IP Phone 7960 sends untagged packets without 802.1p priority
dot1p	Keyword to specify that the IP Phone 7960 sends packets with 802.1p priority
none	Keyword to turn off auxiliary VLAN tagging

For example, if you want to configure a 6500 switch using the CatOS with a voice VLAN of 222 for all 48 ports on Module 7, you can use the command in Example 8-1.

Example 8-1 *Auxiliary VLAN configuration (CatOS)*

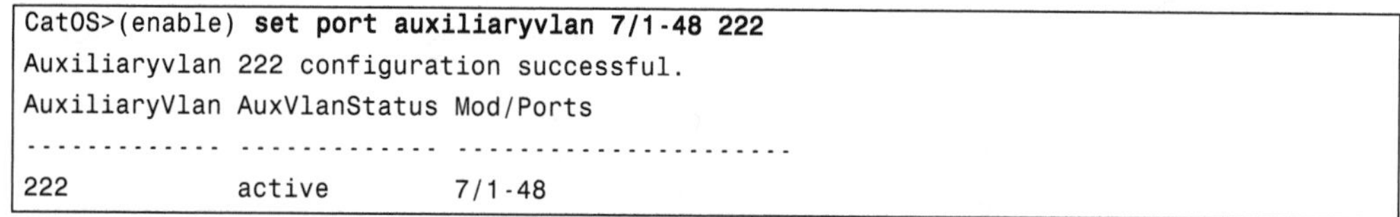

```
CatOS>(enable) set port auxiliaryvlan 7/1-48 222
Auxiliaryvlan 222 configuration successful.
AuxiliaryVlan AuxVlanStatus Mod/Ports
------------- ------------- ----------------------
222           active        7/1-48
```

You can check the status of the auxiliary VLAN on a port or module in one of two ways:

- Use the **show port auxiliaryvlan** *vlan-id* command to show the status of that auxiliary VLAN and the module and ports where it is active.
- Use the **show port** [*module*[*/port*]] command to show the module, port, and the auxiliary VLAN and the status of the port.

Configuring and Verifying Dual VLANs Using the NativeOS

Use the commands in Example 8-2 to configure voice and data VLANs on the single-port interface of a switch that is running native Cisco IOS software. These commands apply the same functionality as setting a port to use an auxiliary VLAN on a Cisco Catalyst switch that is running Cisco Catalyst software.

Example 8-2 *Voice VLAN configuration (NativeIOS)*

```
NativeIOS(config)#interface FastEthernet0/1
NativeIOS(config-if)#switchport mode access
NativeIOS(config-if)#switchport voice vlan 261
NativeIOS(config-if)#switchport access vlan 262
NativeIOS(config-if)#spanning-tree portfast
```

Table 8-4 provides a brief description of these commands.

Table 8-4 *Configuring Dual VLANs Using the NativeOS Command Descriptions*

Command	Description
switchport mode access	Configures the switchport to be an access (nontrunking) port.
switchport voice vlan *voice-VLAN_ID*	Configures the switchport with the voice VLAN (261 in this example) to be used for voice traffic. The range is 1 to 4094.
switchport access vlan *data_VLAN_ID*	Configures the interface as a static access port with the access VLAN ID (262 in this example); the range is 1 to 4094.
spanning-tree portfast	Causes a port to enter the spanning-tree forwarding state immediately, bypassing the listening and learning states. You can use PortFast on switch ports that are connected to a single workstation or server (as opposed to another switch or network device) to allow those devices to connect to the network immediately.

You can verify your voice VLAN configuration on the Cisco Catalyst switches that are running native Cisco IOS software by using the **show interfaces** *mod/port* **switchport** command, as displayed in Example 8-3.

Example 8-3 *Voice VLAN Verification (NativeIOS)*

```
NativeIOS#show interfaces fa0/4 switchport
Name: Fa0/4
Switchport: Enabled
Administrative Mode: static access
Operational Mode: static access
Administrative Trunking Encapsulation: negotiate
Operational Trunking Encapsulation: native
Negotiation of Trunking: Off
Access Mode VLAN: 262 (VLAN0262)
Trunking Native Mode VLAN: 1 (default)
Voice VLAN: 261 (VLAN0261)
<output truncated>
```

Configuring Class of Service

CoS is a data link layer marking that you can use to classify traffic as it passes through a switch. You should ensure that voice traffic has priority as it travels throughout your network because it is extremely sensitive to delay. Cisco IP Phones send all voice packets tagged with CoS 5 by default, which is the highest level of CoS that Cisco recommends for user traffic.

The multi-VLAN port also receives packets from the devices (PCs and workstations) that are connected to the PC port of the IP Phone. The attached device, if it is not in the native VLAN, can send packets with a CoS equal to or higher than the packets that are being sent by the IP Phone, which can cause severe voice quality problems on your IP telephony network. This can be done only if the device is *not* in the access VLAN or is sharing the same VLAN as the IP Phone.

Cisco Catalyst switches have the ability to extend the boundary of trust to the IP Phone. You can use the switch to instruct the IP Phone to accept the CoS value of frames that are arriving from connected devices (trust) and allow the CoS to remain unchanged. Alternatively, you can choose not to trust the attached device and set the CoS to 0 or set the CoS to a configured value that you determine.

The Cisco Catalyst switch uses Cisco Discovery Protocol to send this configuration information to the IP Phone. The switch sends an additional Cisco Discovery Protocol packet to the IP Phone whenever there is a change in the CoS configuration.

The switch uses its queues, which are available on a per-port basis, to buffer incoming and outgoing frames. The switch can use the CoS values to place the frames in the appropriate queues. Voice frames should be placed in the priority queue for minimal delay.

> **NOTE** Setting CoS markings represents one small piece of the big picture of QoS. For detailed information regarding QoS design and configuration, check out *Cisco QOS Exam Certification Guide, Second Edition* published by Cisco Press (ISBN: 1-58720-124-0) and the online Cisco QoS Solution Reference Network Design Guide (SRND) at http://www.cisco.com/go/srnd.

You can configure the switch with different QoS settings on a per-port basis. In the CatOS, use the **set port qos** [*mod/port*] **cos** command to set the default value for all packets that have arrived through an untrusted port. For example, the command **set port qos 3/1 cos 3** sets the CoS value to 3 on port 3/1. The *cos-value* specifies the CoS value for a port; valid values are from 0 to 7. Seven is the highest priority. The default is 0 (not trusted).

Use the **set port qos** [*mod/ports*] **trust-ext** {**trusted** | **untrusted**} command to either extend trust to the PC by specifying that all traffic received through the access port passes through the phone switch unchanged, or to not trust the port and change the CoS value to 0.

In the NativeIOS, use the **switchport priority extend** {**cos** *cos-value* | **trust**} interface configuration command to set a port priority for the incoming frames received by the IP Phone connected to the specified port. The *cos-value* is used to set the IP Phone port to override the priority received from the PC or the attached device. Valid values for the *cos-value* are from 0 to 7. Seven is the highest priority. The default is 0 (not trusted). Alternatively, the **trust** keyword causes the IP Phone port to trust the priority received from the PC or the attached device, that is, to not change the CoS value. Figure 8-2 provides a visual representation of the different CoS behaviors the IP Phone can support.

Figure 8-2 *Extending QoS to the IP Phone*

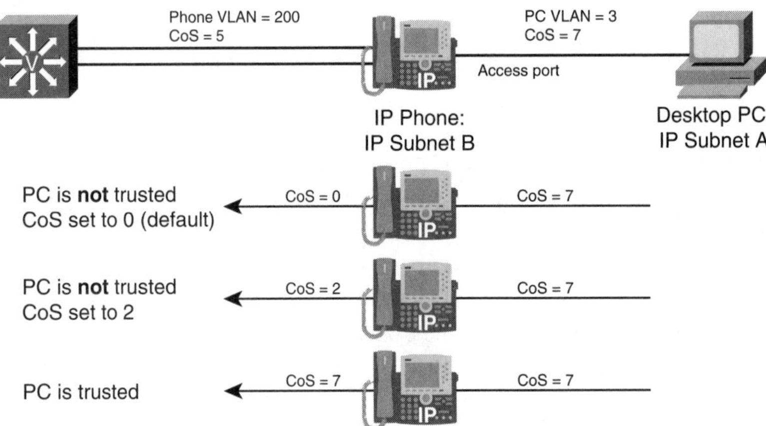

Summary

This chapter covered the role of the Catalyst switch platform in a Cisco IP telephony design. To support the new voice data traversing the network, Cisco has equipped their mainline switch platforms with three new capabilities:

- **The ability to support inline power**—Allows a Cisco Catalyst switch to send power through the Ethernet copper to a Cisco IP Phone or other inline power-compatible devices using either the Cisco prestandard PoE or the IEEE 802.3af industry standard PoE.
- **The ability to support auxiliary/voice VLANs**—Allows a Cisco Catalyst switch to support multiple VLANs on a single port to separate voice and data traffic.
- **The ability to support CoS/QoS capabilities**—Allows a Cisco Catalyst switch to mark voice and data traffic with CoS values that other equipment can use to prioritize network traffic.

These capabilities play a vital role in ensuring the voice network operates seamlessly with the highest possible quality and reliability.

Review Questions

You can find the solutions to these questions in Appendix A, "Answers to Review Questions."

1. Which command enables inline power on port 3 of module 2 of a Cisco Catalyst 6000 Series switch that is running Cisco Catalyst software?

   a. **power inline** in global configuration mode

   b. **power inline auto** in interface configuration mode

   c. set port inline power default

   d. set port inline power 3/2 802.3

   e. set port inline power 2/3 auto

2. Cisco Catalyst switches can provide which three functions in an IP telephony deployment? (Choose three.)

   a. Convert SCCP signaling packets from the IP Phone to MGCP.

   b. Power IP Phones through the same Ethernet cable that carries data.

   c. Enable the classification and prioritization of voice packets at Layer 2.

   d. Instruct the IP Phone to change the CoS of an incoming data frame.

   e. Determine available bandwidth before placing a call over the WAN.

3. What are three requirements for configuring dual VLANs on a single port that is attached to an IP Phone? (Choose three.)

   a. Configure the interface for access and voice VLANs.

   b. Tag the voice packets with a voice VLAN identifier.

   c. Extend the CoS boundary to the IP Phone.

   d. Ensure that the IP Phone has an internal switch.

   e. Ensure that the IP Phone is inline power-capable.

4. What three methods can you use to power all PoE-capable Cisco IP Phones?

   a. wall power

   b. solar power

   c. Cisco prestandard PoE

   d. IEEE 802.3af PoE

   e. Cisco Inline Power Patch Panel

5. Which of the following represent the industry standard PoE mechanism?

  a. 802.3

  b. 802.11

  c. 802.11b

  d. 802.3af

6. Which of the following commands will activate PoE on a Catalyst 3750 switch?

  a. **`set port inlinepower`** *`mod/port`* **`auto`**

  b. **`set port inlinepower`** *`mod/port`* **`on`**

  c. `power inline auto`

  d. `power inline on`

7. To support dual VLANs from a Catalyst 6500 running CatOS and a Cisco IP Phone, what should be configured? (Choose two.)

  a. an ISL trunk

  b. an 802.1Q trunk

  c. an auxiliary VLAN configuration

  d. a voice VLAN configuration

8. You are attempting to set up a dual VLAN configuration between a Cisco IP Phone and a CatOS-based 6500 switch. You enter the command **set port auxiliaryvlan 3/1 50** to place the IP Phone on the voice VLAN 50. What more must be done?

  a. Configure an 802.1Q trunk.

  b. Configure an ISL trunk.

  c. Enable PoE.

  d. Nothing more must be done.

9. By default, a Cisco IP Phone tags all voice packets with what CoS value?

  a. 1

  b. 3

  c. 5

  d. 7

10. How does the Cisco IP Phone mark traffic from an attached PC?

a. The Cisco IP Phone trusts the CoS marking coming from the attached PC.

b. The Cisco IP Phone does not trust the CoS marking and sets it to 0.

c. The Cisco IP Phone does not trust the CoS marking and sets it to 3.

d. The Cisco IP Phone does not support CoS markings for data traffic.

This chapter covers the following topics:

- Describing the role of the gateway in an IP telephony infrastructure
- Comparing analog and digital gateways with respect to interfaces and the types of telephony devices that they can connect
- Describing the core gateway requirements that a gateway must have to support an IP telephony network
- Describing the gateway communication protocols that Cisco CallManager supports
- Adding and configuring H.323, MGCP, and non-IOS MGCP gateways in Cisco CallManager and on the gateway to interface to the IP WAN and PSTN and support analog phones and faxes
- Choosing the appropriate trunk type to satisfy deployment requirements for call-control requirements and call routing
- Configuring non-gatekeeper-controlled trunks in Cisco CallManager Administration to enable calling to remote clusters across an IP WAN
- Describing the SIP signaling protocol and how it is implemented in Cisco CallManager
- Explaining how to create a SIP trunk and route calls to a SIP endpoint

CHAPTER 9

Configuring Cisco Gateways and Trunks

Voice gateways and trunks provide the bridge between an IP telephony network and the public switched telephone network (PSTN), and between Cisco CallManager clusters. This chapter prepares you for integrating Cisco gateways and trunks in a Cisco CallManager solution.

You will learn about analog and digital gateways, recommended gateway requirements, gateway protocols, the types of trunks that Cisco CallManager supports, and how to configure gateways, intercluster trunks, and Session Initiation Protocol (SIP) trunks.

Cisco Gateway Concepts

A gateway is a device that translates one type of signal into another type of signal. One type of gateway is the voice gateway. A voice gateway is a router or switch that converts IP voice packets to analog or digital signals that are understood by trunks or stations. Gateways are used in several situations, for example, connecting to a PSTN or PBX, or connecting individual devices such as an analog phone or fax.

NOTE This chapter provides an overview of the voice gateways that you can use with the Cisco CallManager system and describes their basic configuration. For more information on configuring voice gateways, refer to *Authorized Self-Study Guide: Cisco Voice over IP (CVOICE)*, Second Edition (ISBN: 1-58705-262-8) or *Cisco Voice Gateways and Gatekeepers* (ISBN: 1-58705-258-X) from Cisco Press.

Analog and Digital Gateways

There are two types of Cisco access gateways: analog and digital. At a high level, the difference between these two types of gateways is their capacity. Analog gateways (and analog connections) receive one line per port. This port could be a connection to the PSTN, an end device such as a fax machine, or a link to a PBX. Regardless of the connection, analog ports only permit one voice path per line. There are two categories of analog gateways:

- **Access analog station gateways**—Access analog station gateways connect Cisco CallManager to plain old telephone service (POTS) analog telephones, interactive voice response (IVR) systems, fax machines, and voice-mail systems. Station gateways provide Foreign eXchange Station (FXS) ports for connecting to analog devices such as telephones and faxes.
- **Access analog trunk gateways**—Access analog trunk gateways connect Cisco CallManager to PSTN central office (CO) or PBX trunks. Trunk gateways provide Foreign eXchange Office (FXO) ports for PSTN or PBX access and E&M (known by various names, primarily receive and transmit, or ear and mouth, or earth and magneto) ports for analog trunk connection to a legacy PBX. Analog Direct Inward Dial (DID) is also available for PSTN connectivity.

Depending on the cards you have installed into a gateway, it could fill both station (FXS) and trunk (FXO) roles.

On the flip side, digital gateways typically allow multiple calls per port. These gateways connect the Cisco CallManager to the PSTN or to a PBX via digital trunks, such as PRI common channel signaling (CCS), BRI, T1 channel-associated signaling (CAS), or E1. Digital T1 PRI trunks might also connect to certain legacy voice-mail systems. Regardless of the connection type, you will typically use a digital gateway to provide a high-capacity connection to an alternate network type.

Core Gateway Requirements

To support modern VoIP networks, your IP telephony gateways must meet these core feature requirements:

- **Dual tone multifrequency (DTMF) relay capabilities**—DTMF signaling tones, which contain the digits a user has dialed, must be processed. Gateways must separate DTMF digits from the voice stream and then send the signaling in voice over IP (VoIP) signaling protocols, such as H.323, Cisco IOS software Media Gateway Control Protocol (MGCP), SIP, and so on.
- **Supplementary services support**—These services are typically basic telephony functions, such as hold, transfer, and conferencing.
- **Cisco CallManager redundancy support**—Cisco CallManager clusters provide for Cisco CallManager redundancy. The gateways must support the ability to re-home to a secondary Cisco CallManager in the event of a primary Cisco CallManager failure, which differs from call survivability in the event of a Cisco CallManager or network failure.

- **Call survivability in Cisco CallManager**—The voice gateway preserves the Real-time Transport Protocol (RTP) bearer stream (the voice conversation) between two IP endpoints when the Cisco CallManager that the endpoint is registered to is no longer reachable.

Any IP telephony gateway that you select for an enterprise deployment should support these core requirements. In addition, every IP telephony implementation has its own site-specific feature requirements, such as analog or digital access, DID, and capacity requirements.

Gateway Communication Overview

For Cisco CallManager to reach other networks (including the PSTN), it must be able to communicate with the gateways connected to these networks. Cisco CallManager 4.x supports these three types of gateway communication protocols:

- **H.323**—H.323 uses a peer-to-peer model. You perform most of the configuration through Cisco IOS software on the voice gateway device. With the peer-to-peer model, Cisco CallManager does not have control over the gateway, which limits the Cisco CallManager feature support on H.323 gateways. For example, H.323 gateways do not support call survivability, and only devices that support H.323 version 2 (H.323v2) can take advantage of Cisco CallManager supplementary services, such as hold, transfer, and conference features. However, H.323 gateways support additional Cisco IOS features outside of Cisco CallManager that the other gateways do not, such as call admission control, fractional PRI support, FXO caller-id support, NFAS signaling, and Cisco Survivable Remote Site Telephony (SRST).

  Examples of Cisco gateway devices that support H.323 include the Cisco VG224 Analog Phone Gateway (FXS only), Cisco 2600, Cisco 2800, Cisco 3700, and Cisco 3800 devices.

- **MGCP**—MGCP uses a client/server model, with voice-routing intelligence that resides in a call agent (the Cisco CallManager). Because of its centralized architecture, MGCP simplifies the configuration of voice gateways (the gateway requires no advanced dial-peer configuration) and supports multiple (redundant) call agents in a network. MGCP gateways provide call survivability (the gateway maintains calls during failover and fallback). If the MGCP gateway loses contact with its Cisco CallManager, it falls back to using H.323 control to support basic call handling of FXS, FXO, T1 CAS, and T1 and E1 PRI interfaces. In addition, MGCP controlled gateways can support the Q Signaling (QSIG) protocol, which is used to communicate with many PBX systems.

  Examples of Cisco gateway devices that support MGCP are the Cisco VG224 (FXS only), Cisco 2600, Cisco 2800, Cisco 3700, and Cisco 3800 devices. Examples of non-IOS devices that support MGCP are the Cisco Catalyst 6000 WS-X6608-T1 and -E1.

- **SCCP**—Skinny Client Control Protocol (SCCP, or Skinny), is a client/server protocol that uses Cisco proprietary messages to communicate between IP devices and Cisco CallManager. The Cisco IP Phone is an example of a device that registers and communicates with Cisco CallManager as an SCCP client. During registration, a Cisco IP Phone receives its line and all other configurations from Cisco CallManager. After it registers, it is notified of new incoming calls and can make outgoing calls. SCCP is used for VoIP call signaling and enhanced features such as message waiting indication (MWI).

  Examples of Cisco devices that support SCCP are the Cisco VG224 Analog Phone Gateway (FXS only) and the Cisco VG248 Analog Phone Gateway. The Cisco VG224 gateway is 24-port gateway for analog phones, fax machines, modems, and speakerphones using Cisco CallManager or Cisco CallManager Express. The Cisco VG248 device is a 48-port gateway.

NOTE SIP can also be used as a gateway control protocol. Most Cisco IOS images that support H.323 and MGCP also support SIP. Cisco CallManager 4.x supports SIP trunks to connect CallManager to distributed SIP networks.

Most gateway devices support multiple gateway protocols. Selecting the protocol to use depends on site-specific requirements and your installed base of equipment. You might prefer MGCP to H.323 because of the simpler configuration of MGCP or its support for call survivability during a Cisco CallManager switchover from a primary to a secondary Cisco CallManager. In addition, you might prefer H.323 to MGCP because of the interface robustness of H.323 or the ability to use it with call admission control or SRST. The Cisco-recommended best practices direct corporations to use MGCP unless they have a specific reason to choose another protocol.

Configuring Access Gateways

To make the Cisco CallManager aware of the gateways it can use, you must add them to the configuration. You must add the gateways to the CallManager database based on the protocol the CallManager uses to communicate with the gateway. After you have added the gateway to the CallManager configuration, you can include it in your route plan design to allow your IP Phones to dial off the local network. The full route plan design and configuration is covered in Chapters 10-13.

NOTE This section focuses on configuring the CallManager to communicate with the gateway. You must have also configured the gateway to communicate with the CallManager and additional networks such as a PBX or the PSTN. Although this book presents brief configuration examples, the full gateway configuration is covered in depth in *Authorized Self-Study Guide: Cisco Voice over IP (CVOICE)*, Second Edition and *Cisco Voice Gateways and Gatekeepers*.

H.323 Gateway Configuration

Complete these steps to add an H.323 gateway to your CallManager configuration:

Step 1 Choose **Gateway** from the Device menu in the Cisco CallManager Administration window.

Step 2 Click the **Add a New Gateway** link and choose **H.323 Gateway** from the Gateway Type menu.

Step 3 Cisco CallManager automatically populates the **Device Protocol** field with H.225. Click **Next**.

Step 4 In the **Device Name** field shown in Figure 9-1, enter the IP address (recommended to remote DNS reliance) or hostname of the Cisco router that will be acting as the gateway.

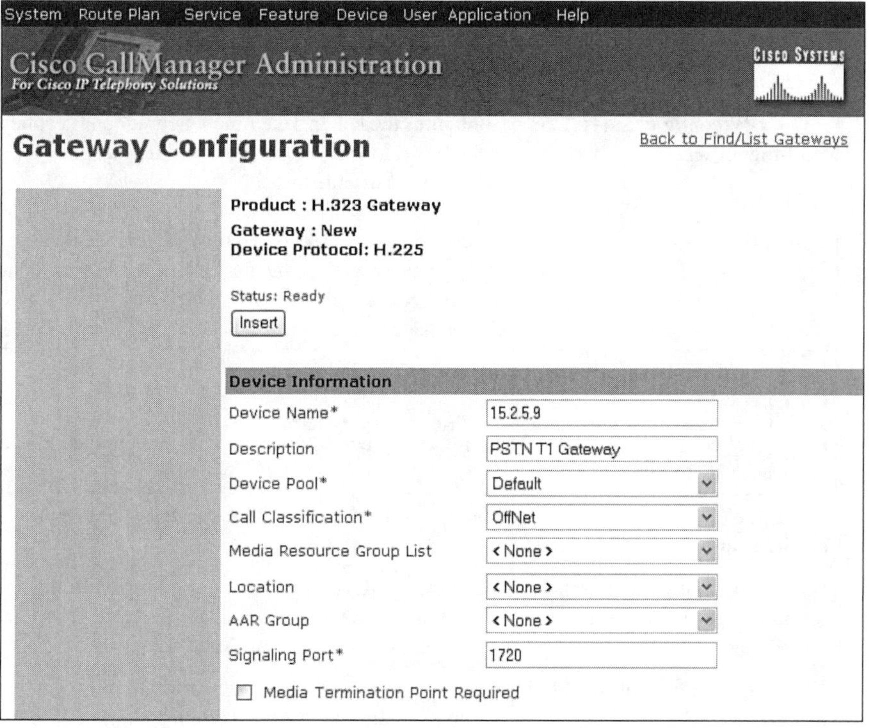

Figure 9-1 *CallManager H.323 Gateway Configuration*

Step 5 Assign the gateway to a device pool.

Step 6 Click **Insert** when finished.

TIP The prior configuration allows you to add an H.323 gateway to the CallManager configuration. However, many more configuration options are available. For information on all the settings available in the Gateway Configuration window, refer to the Cisco CallManager "Help for this Page" option (available from the CCMAdmin Help menu). This page provides a brief explanation for each configuration field available.

Because H.323 is a peer-to-peer protocol, you must configure most of the gateway configuration using Cisco IOS software on the gateway itself. Table 9-1 lists the Cisco IOS commands you can use to configure an H.323 voice gateway.

Table 9-1 *Cisco IOS Commands to Configure an H.323 Voice Gateway*

Command	Description
H323_GW(config)# **gateway**	Enables H.323 VoIP gateway functionality. After you enable the gateway, it attempts to discover a gatekeeper by using an H.323 gatekeeper request message.
H323_GW(config)# **voice class h323** *tag*	Creates an H.323 voice class that is used to configure a TCP timeout duration.
H323_GW(config-class)# **h225 tcp timeout** *seconds*	Configures the H.225 TCP timeout duration in seconds. Possible values are 0 to 30. The default is 15. If you specify 0, the H.225 TCP timer is disabled. When the duration (seconds) of the H.225 TCP is exceeded, the voice gateway will use the next ordered dial peer (controlled via the **preference** command), which points to a backup Cisco CallManager.
H323_GW(config)# **dial-peer voice** *tag* **voip**	Creates a VoIP dial peer.
H323_GW(config-dial-peer)# **voice class h323** *tag*	Assigns the previous created voice class to this dial peer.
H323_GW(config-dial-peer)# **destination-pattern** *dial-string*	Configures the dial string that this dial peer matches.
H323_GW(config-dial-peer)# **session target ipv4:***ccm-ip-address*	Identifies the IP address to route a call to when the destination pattern in the previous command is matched. The IP address is the address of the Cisco CallManager on an H.323 gateway.
H323_GW(config-dial-peer)# **preference** *0–10*	Assigns a preference to a dial peer when multiple dial peers contain the same destination pattern but different session targets. 0 is the highest, 10 is the lowest (used to configure Cisco CallManager redundancy on H.323 gateways).

Table 9-1 *Cisco IOS Commands to Configure an H.323 Voice Gateway (Continued)*

Command	Description
H323_GW(config-dial-peer)# **dtmf-relay h245-alphanumeric**	Configures the gateway to use out-of-band DTMF relay. DTMF relay sends DTMF tones across the signaling channel, instead of as part of the voice stream. DTMF relay is needed when you are using a low-bit-rate coder-decoder (codec) for voice compression, because the potential exists for DTMF signal loss or distortion.

Example 9-1 shows an H.323 gateway that has been configured for Cisco CallManager redundancy.

Example 9-1 *H.323 Gateway Configuration*

```
H323_GW(config)#!Creates VoIP dial-peer 101
H323_GW(config)#dial-peer voice 101 voip
H323_GW(config-dial-peer)#!Sends DTMF digits out-of-band
H323_GW(config-dial-peer)#dtmf-relay h245-alphanumeric
H323_GW(config-dial-peer)#!Matches all 4-digit extensions
H323_GW(config-dial-peer)#destination-pattern ....
H323_GW(config-dial-peer)#!Target address of Primary CallManager
H323_GW(config-dial-peer)#session target ipv4:10.1.1.101
H323_GW(config-dial-peer)#!Selects this as the preferred dial-peer
H323_GW(config-dial-peer)#preference 0
H323_GW(config)#!Creates VoIP dial-peer 102
H323_GW(config)#dial-peer voice 102 voip
H323_GW(config-dial-peer)#dtmf-relay h245-alphanumeric
H323_GW(config-dial-peer)#destination-pattern ....
H323_GW(config-dial-peer)#!Target address of Secondary CallManager
H323_GW(config-dial-peer)#session target ipv4:10.1.1.102
H323_GW(config-dial-peer)#!Selects this as the secondary dial-peer
H323_GW(config-dial-peer)#preference 1
```

Call Classification

The Call Classification feature, introduced in Cisco CallManager Release 4.1, provides the ability to configure gateways and trunks as on the network (OnNet) or off the network (OffNet) at the device or at the global level. As a result, a call through these devices is classified as either OnNet or OffNet. With these classifications, Cisco CallManager provides the ability to restrict OnNet-to-OffNet transfers and to drop an ad hoc conference when no OnNet parties remain in the conference. This field provides an OnNet or OffNet alerting tone when the call is classified as OnNet or OffNet, respectively.

The corresponding **Call Classification** field in the gateway and trunk configuration windows, shown in Figure 9-2, marks the corresponding devices as OnNet or OffNet or Use System Default.

The default Call Classification settings are **OnNet** for all IP Phones and intercluster trunks and **Use System Default** (which is OffNet) for other gateways.

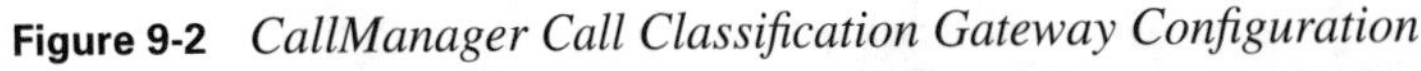

Figure 9-2 *CallManager Call Classification Gateway Configuration*

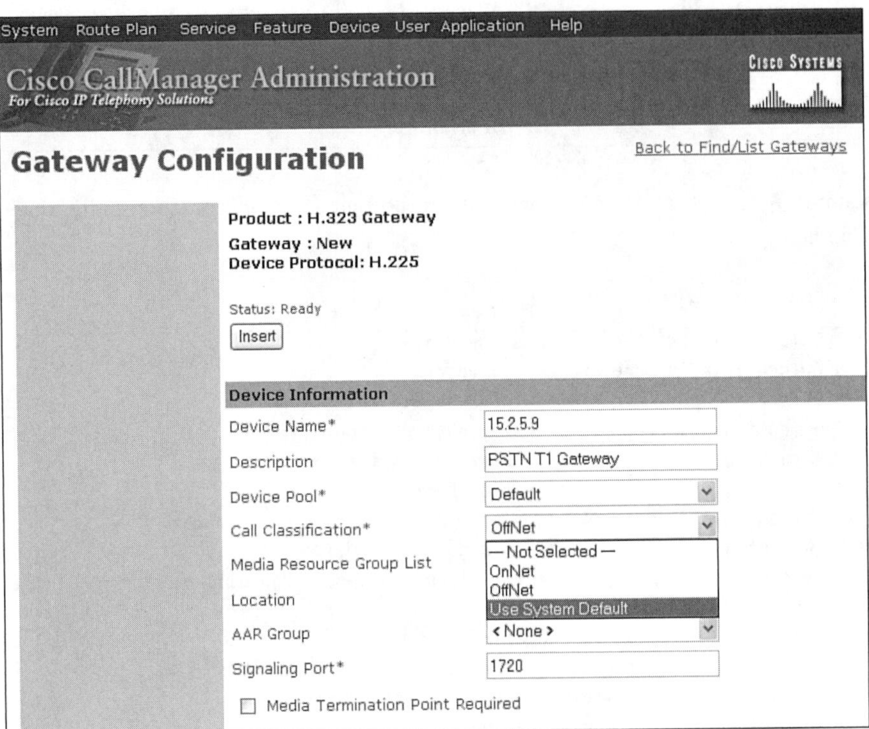

In Cisco CallManager 4.X releases, Cisco defined a new, global service parameter called Call Classification. The default value of this parameter is **OffNet**. When **Use System Default** is selected at the device level for a particular gateway or trunk, the value of the service parameter (defined using the **Service > Service Parameters > Cisco CallManager** menu option in CCMAdmin) is used to judge the device as OnNet or OffNet. Therefore, gateways are classified as external (OffNet) by default.

FXS ports and IP Phones are not configurable and are always treated as OnNet.

The parameters that determine whether a transfer is allowed or restricted are as follows:

- The Call Classification setting on the gateway or trunk.
- The Call Classification setting and **Allow Device Override** check box setting on the route pattern. If the **Allow Device Override** check box is checked, the Call Classification setting on the gateway or trunk takes precedence.
- The Service parameter Block OffNet to OffNet Transfer. When this parameter is set to **False**, the transfer is not restricted. When this parameter is set to **True** (the default) and the transfer is initiated between two OffNet parties, the transfer is blocked.

NOTE The ability to restrict external transfers and to drop an ad hoc conference when no OnNet parties remain on the call help to prevent toll fraud. Preventing toll fraud and many other IP telephony security considerations are covered in detail in Chapter 22, "Preventing Toll Fraud."

MGCP Gateway Configuration

Complete these steps to add an MGCP gateway to the CallManager configuration:

Step 1 Choose **Gateway** from the Device menu in the Cisco CallManager Administration window.

Step 2 Click the **Add a New Gateway** link and choose one of the various MGCP-capable devices from the **Gateway Type** menu.

NOTE Selecting a Cisco router by the actual model of router from the **Gateway Type** drop-down menu automatically chooses the MGCP protocol for communication.

Step 3 Cisco CallManager automatically populates the **Device Protocol** field with the MGCP protocol. Click **Next**.

Step 4 For the **Domain Name** field, shown in Figure 9-3, enter the unique hostname (or fully qualified domain name [FQDN]) of the Cisco device that will be acting as the gateway.

Figure 9-3 *CallManager MGCP Gateway Configuration*

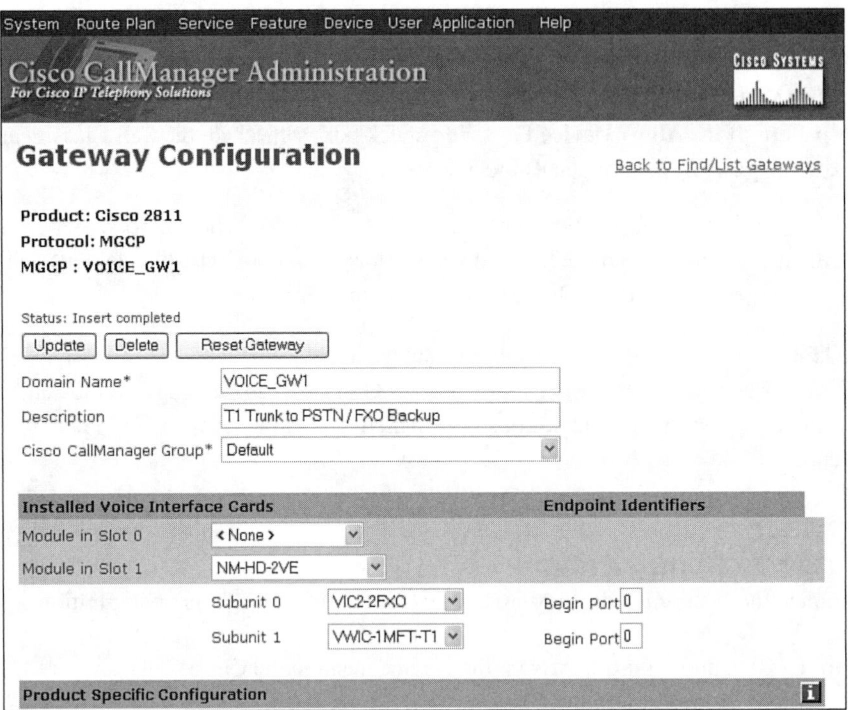

Step 5 Assign the gateway to a Cisco CallManager group for redundancy.

Step 6 Choose the type of network modules that are used in the MGCP gateway.

Step 7 Choose the type of voice interface cards (VICs) that are used in the subunit slots of the MGCP gateway.

Step 8 Click **Insert**.

Step 9 Click an endpoint identifier (for example, 1/0/0) to configure device protocol information and add ports for the installed types of VICs.

Table 9-2 lists the IOS commands to help configure endpoint identifiers for analog devices connected to the MGCP gateway.

Table 9-2 *Cisco IOS Commands to Configure an MGCP Voice Gateway*

Command	Description
Router(config)# **hostname MGCP_GW**	Assigns a unique name to the voice gateway so that the Cisco CallManager server can identify it. This name must be unique throughout the network.
MGCP_GW(config)# **mgcp**	Enables MGCP on the voice gateway.
MGCP_GW(config)# **mgcp call-agent** *ip-address*	Identifies the primary Cisco CallManager for the gateway.
MGCP_GW(config)# **ccm-manager mgcp**	Indicates to the gateway that the Cisco CallManager is using MGCP.
MGCP_GW(config)# **ccm-manager redundant-host** *ip-address1 ip-address2*	Specifies the secondary and tertiary Cisco CallManager servers that are used for Cisco CallManager redundancy.
MGCP_GW(config)# **ccm-manager switchback** {**graceful** | **immediate** | **schedule-time** *hh*:*mm* | **uptime-delay** *minutes*}	Specifies how the gateway behaves if the primary server becomes unavailable and later becomes available again. The keywords and arguments are as follows: • **graceful**—Completes all outstanding calls before returning the gateway to the control of the primary Cisco CallManager server. • **immediate**—Returns the gateway to the control of the primary Cisco CallManager server without delay, as soon as the network connection to the server is reestablished. • **schedule-time** *hh*:*mm*—Returns the gateway to the control of the primary Cisco CallManager server at the specified time, where *hh*:*mm* is the time according to a 24-hour clock. If the gateway reestablishes a network connection to the primary server after the configured time, the switchback occurs at the specified time on the following day. • **uptime-delay** *minutes*—Returns the gateway to the control of the primary Cisco CallManager server when the primary server runs for a specified number of minutes after a network connection is reestablished to the primary server. Valid values are from 1 to 1440 (from 1 minute to 24 hours).
MGCP_GW(config)# **mgcp dtmf-relay voip codec all mode out-of-band**	Configures the gateway to use out-of-band DTMF relay for all codecs. If this command is not configured, DTMF tones will not be regenerated correctly on remote endpoints.
MGCP_GW(config)# **dial-peer voice** *tag* **pots**	Creates a POTS dial peer.

continues

Table 9-2 *Cisco IOS Commands to Configure an MGCP Voice Gateway (Continued)*

Command	Description
MGCP_GW(config-dial-peer)# **application MGCPAPP**	Configures the dial peer to use the MGCP application. The **MGCPAPP** option is case sensitive in some Cisco IOS software releases. Unless you know that your version is not case sensitive, always issue this command in uppercase. You can check whether your version is case sensitive after you configure this command by looking at the output of the **show running-config** command.
MGCP_GW(config-if)# **isdn bind-l3 ccm-manager**	Places a PRI or BRI ISDN interface under CallManager control (known as backhauling the interface). This allows CallManager to control all L3 (network layer) communication of the PRI/BRI line. This command is entered under the interface configuration mode for the PRI/BRI connection.

Example 9-2 shows an MGCP gateway that has been configured for Cisco CallManager redundancy placing one FXS port under CallManager control.

Example 9-2 *MGCP Gateway Configuration Example*

```
Router(config)#!The hostname links the gateway in the CallManager configuration
Router(config)#hostname MGCP_GW
Router(config)#!enables the protocol
MGCP_GW(config)#mgcp
Router(config)#!Identifies the IP address of the primary CallManager
MGCP_GW(config)#mgcp call-agent 10.1.1.1
Router(config)#!Uses MGCP to communicate with the CallManager
MGCP_GW(config)#ccm-manager mgcp
Router(config)#!Identifies secondary CallManager
MGCP_GW(config)#ccm-manager redundant-host 10.1.1.2
Router(config)#!All DTMF digits sent out-of-band
MGCP_GW(config)#mgcp dtmf-relay voip codec all mode out-of-band
Router(config)#!Creates POTS dial-peer 101
MGCP_GW(config)#dial-peer voice 101 pots
Router(config-dial-peer)#!Selects the physical port the CallManager will control
MGCP_GW(config-dial-peer)#port 1/0/0
MGCP_GW(config-dial-peer)#!Places the port under CallManager control
MGCP_GW(config-dial-peer)#application MGCPAPP
```

Non-IOS MGCP Gateway Configuration

You can equip Cisco Catalyst 6500 series switches with a variety of modules, allowing them to act as a voice gateway. If the Catalyst 6500 is running the NativeIOS software image, you can perform the configuration as you would a typical Cisco gateway. However, the Cisco Catalyst 6500 can also function using the CatalystOS operating system. If you are operating in this type of environment, you will need to configure the CallManager to communicate with the 6500 as a Non-IOS MGCP Gateway. Complete the following steps to add a non-IOS MGCP gateway to Cisco CallManager:

Step 1 Choose **Gateway** from the Device menu in the Cisco CallManager Administration window.

Step 2 Click the **Add a New Gateway** link and choose one of the various non-IOS MGCP devices from the Gateway Type menu. If you have selected the Cisco Catalyst 6000 T1 or E1 VoIP Gateway module (WS-X6608), the **Device Protocol** field provides you with the option of specifying either digital access PRI or digital access T1. After you have made your selection, click **Next**.

Step 3 Add the MAC address to the **MAC Address** field.

Cisco CallManager associates with a non-IOS MGCP gateway (such as the Cisco Catalyst 6608 T1 or E1 blade) through the MAC address of the port. The **show port** *module* command from enable mode on the Cisco Catalyst 6000 is a quick way to identify and list the MAC addresses of each digital gateway port on the Voice T1/E1 and Services (WS-X6608) module:

```
Cat6000(enable)show port 3
Port     DHCP    MAC-Address       IP-Address      Subnet-Mask
-------- ------- ----------------- --------------- ---------------
 3/1     disable 00-30-b6-3e-8e-c4 172.16.10.121 255.255.255.0
 3/2     disable 00-30-b6-3e-8e-c5 172.16.20.122 255.255.255.0
 3/3     disable 00-30-b6-3e-8e-c6 172.16.30.123 255.255.255.0
 3/4     disable 00-30-b6-3e-8e-c7 172.16.40.124 255.255.255.0
 3/5     disable 00-30-b6-3e-8e-c8 172.16.1.125 255.255.255.0
 3/6     disable 00-30-b6-3e-8e-c9 172.16.1.126 255.255.255.0
 3/7     disable 00-30-b6-3e-8e-ca 172.16.1.127 255.255.255.0
 3/8     disable 00-30-b6-3e-8e-cb 172.16.1.128 255.255.255.0
```

To display detailed information about a specific port on the module, use the **show port** *mod/port* command.

Step 4 Assign the gateway to a device pool.

Step 5 Configure additional parameters as desired, and click the **Insert** button when finished.

Step 6 Repeat Steps 1 through 5 for each T1 or E1 port that you want to add as a gateway in Cisco CallManager administration.

After you add the gateway to the database, Cisco CallManager creates a configuration file in the cluster on the Cisco TFTP server, and this file is where the T1 or E1 port downloads its configuration details, which include an ordered list of Cisco CallManager servers.

On the gateway itself (Cisco Catalyst 6500 T1 or E1 port), it is recommended that you statically configure the IP address, subnet mask, default gateway, and TFTP server address of each T1 and E1 port that is used as a digital gateway. The TFTP server address should be the IP address of the Cisco CallManager to which you want the port to register and download its configuration file. The following command statically configures the following voice port settings: IP address, subnet mask, VLAN ID, TFTP server IP address, and default gateway:

```
Cat6000 (enable) set port voice in 3/1 dhcp disable 172.16.1.121 255.255.255.0
    vlan 1 tftp 172.16.1.5 gateway 172.16.1.1
```

NOTE When a port resets, the module has the ability to reset the adjoining port because all eight ports on the WS-X6608 module share the same XA processor. This reset process creates a domino effect, and all of the ports on the module reset, creating the following error message:

```
%SYS-4-MODHPRESET:Host process (860) mod_num/port_num got reset asynchronously
```

If you are not going to use a port, you should either disable the port or configure and register it to Cisco so that it does not continually perform an asynchronous reset.

When you have successfully placed an individual 6608 T1 port under CallManager MGCP control, you will see the following output:

```
AV-6509-1 (enable) show port 2/1

Port  Name                Status      Vlan       Duplex Speed Type
----- ------------------- ----------- ---------- ------ ----- -----------
 2/1                      notconnect 1             full 1.544 T1

Port     DHCP    MAC-Address       IP-Address       Subnet-Mask
-------- ------- ----------------- ---------------- ---------------
 2/1     disable 00-30-b6-3e-8e-c4 172.16.1.121     255.255.255.0

Port     Call-Manager(s)   DHCP-Server     TFTP-Server     Gateway
-------- ----------------- --------------- --------------- ---------------
 2/1     172.16.1.5        -               172.16.1.5      172.16.1.1

Port     DNS-Server(s)     Domain
-------- ----------------- -------------------------------------------------
 2/1     -                  -

Port     CallManagerState DSP-Type
-------- ---------------- --------
 2/1     registered       C549
```

Cisco Trunk Concepts

In addition to adding gateways to the CallManager configuration, trunks can also provide connectivity to outside devices. Trunks are seen by Cisco CallManager as logical links to other networks. These links have the ability to determine the location of an endpoint, but do *not* carry voice traffic. This underscores the major difference between trunks and gateways: Gateways can typically locate (or represent) an endpoint and carry the voice traffic to that endpoint; trunks only locate an endpoint. For example, you could create an intercluster trunk from your CallManager cluster containing 3XXX extensions to another CallManager cluster containing 4XXX extensions. When a user in your cluster (extension 3505) dials an extension in the other cluster (extension 4505), the local CallManager signals over the trunk to the remote CallManager. This signaling occurs to locate the IP address of extension 4505. After this IP address has been found, the audio path opens directly between the local extension 3505 and the remote extension 4505.

Your choices for configuring trunks in Cisco CallManager depend on whether the IP WAN uses gatekeepers to handle call routing and on the types of call-control protocols that are used in the call-processing environment.

Cisco CallManager Administration supports the following trunk types:

- **H.225 trunk gatekeeper-controlled**—Use an H.225 gatekeeper-controlled trunk for toll bypass or for integration with an existing H.323 environment. The H.225 gatekeeper-controlled trunk enables Cisco CallManager to communicate with Cisco CallManager clusters and other H.323 devices registered to the H.323 gatekeeper. The H.225 gatekeeper-controlled trunk is not recommended in a pure Cisco CallManager environment, but it is required in a mixed environment with Cisco CallManager and Cisco CallManager Express or another third-party H.323 gateway. The H.225 trunk attempts to discover the other H.323 device on a call-by-call basis. If it discovers a device that understands intercluster trunk protocol, it automatically uses that protocol. If it cannot discover the other device, Cisco CallManager uses the standard H.225 protocol. To use this method, choose **Device > Trunk** and choose **H.225 Trunk (Gatekeeper Controlled)**.

- **Intercluster trunk gatekeeper-controlled**—The intercluster gatekeeper-controlled trunk enables Cisco CallManager to communicate with other Cisco CallManager clusters registered to an H.323 gatekeeper. It is recommended that you use the intercluster gatekeeper-controlled trunk only in deployments based entirely on Cisco CallManager. To use this method, choose **Device > Trunk** and choose **Inter-Cluster Trunk (GateKeeper Controlled)** in Cisco CallManager Administration.

> **TIP** Because the intercluster trunk format is Cisco proprietary, Cisco recommends using H.225 gatekeeper trunks wherever possible. The gatekeeper-controlled intercluster trunk option remains for backward compatibility with early CallManager versions.

- **Intercluster trunk nongatekeeper-controlled**—In a distributed network that has no gatekeeper control, you must configure a separate intercluster trunk for each remote cluster that the local Cisco CallManager can call over the IP WAN. The intercluster trunks statically specify the IP addresses or hostnames of the remote devices. To use this method, choose **Device > Trunk** and choose **Inter-Cluster Trunk (Non-GateKeeper Controlled)** in Cisco CallManager Administration.

NOTE Intercluster trunks (nongatekeeper-controlled) between Cisco CallManager clusters are unidirectional. You must configure trunks to and from the cluster you are connecting for the trunks to operate.

- **SIP trunk**—Cisco CallManager Release 4.x supports a Session Initiation Protocol (SIP) trunk for interworking with a SIP network or gateways, but it currently does not allow SIP IP Phones to register directly with Cisco CallManager. To use this method, choose **Device > Trunk** and choose **SIP Trunk** in Cisco CallManager Administration.

Configuring Intercluster Trunks

Although the SQL 2000 database shared between CallManagers in your cluster provides a listing of all extensions that a user can dial within the cluster, you must manually add connections and route patterns to remote clusters before they can be reached. The connection type that acts as the road between CallManager clusters is the intercluster trunk. Depending on the size of your IP telephony network, you can create trunks directly between CallManager clusters or you can create trunks to connect to an H.323 gatekeeper.

NOTE You can create a network of enormous size using only intercluster trunks; however, because the trunks are a full-mesh configuration, it can become increasingly difficult to manage the larger your network gets. Intercluster trunks also lack the ability to perform call admission control, which could result in the WAN becoming swamped with VoIP traffic.

A gatekeeper provides call admission control by using the H.225 Registration, Admission, and Status (RAS) protocol message set that is used as a central point for call admission control, bandwidth allocation, and dial pattern resolution (call routing). The gatekeeper provides these services for communications between Cisco CallManager clusters and H.323 networks. Note that the voice path is between the endpoints; no RTP audio travels through the gatekeeper.

You can configure gatekeepers and trunks in Cisco CallManager Administration to function in either of the following ways:

- **Nongatekeeper-controlled trunks**—In this case, you explicitly configure a separate Intercluster Trunk for each remote device cluster that the local Cisco CallManager can call over the IP WAN, as shown in Figure 9-4. You also configure the necessary dial plan details to route calls to and from the various Intercluster Trunks. The Intercluster Trunks statically specify the IP addresses of the remote devices. To use this method, choose **Device > Trunk** and then choose **Inter-Cluster Trunk (Non-Gatekeeper Controlled)** in Cisco CallManager Administration.

Figure 9-4 *Nongatekeeper-Controlled Trunk Design*

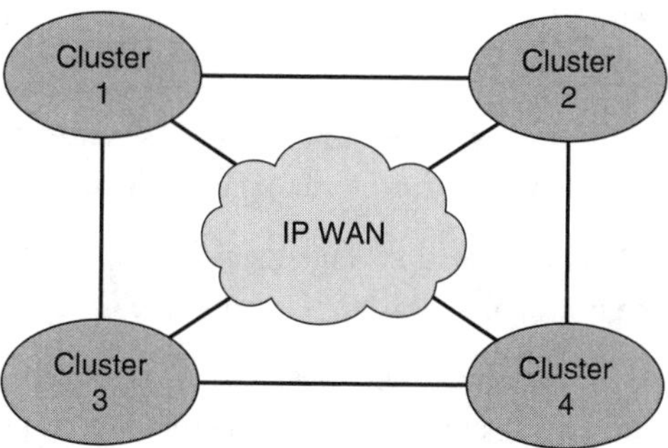

- **Gatekeeper-controlled trunks**—In this case, a single intercluster trunk from each CallManager cluster suffices for communicating with all remote clusters, as shown in Figure 9-5. Similarly, you need only a single H.225 trunk to communicate with multiple H.323 gatekeeper-controlled endpoints. In this configuration, the gatekeeper can dynamically determine the appropriate IP address for the destination of each call to a remote device, and the local Cisco CallManager uses that IP address to complete the call.

Figure 9-5 *Gatekeeper-Controlled Trunk Design*

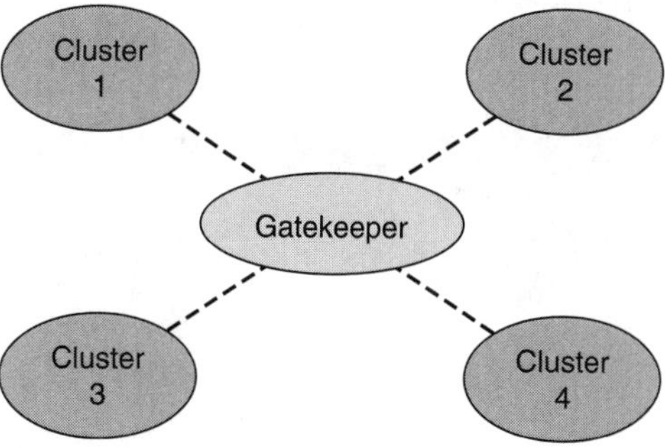

This configuration works well in large and smaller systems. For large systems in which many clusters exist, this configuration helps to avoid the configuration of individual Intercluster Trunks between each cluster. To use this method, choose **Device > Trunk** and choose **Inter-Cluster Trunk (Gatekeeper Controlled)** in Cisco CallManager Administration.

If you configure gatekeeper-controlled trunks, Cisco CallManager automatically creates a virtual trunk device. The IP address of this device changes dynamically to reflect the IP address of the remote device as determined by the gatekeeper.

Complete these steps to configure a nongatekeeper-controlled intercluster trunk:

Step 1 Choose **Trunk** from the Device menu in the Cisco CallManager Administration window.

Step 2 Click the **Add a New Trunk** link and choose **Inter-Cluster Trunk (Non-Gatekeeper Controlled)** from the **Trunk Type** drop-down menu.

Step 3 Cisco CallManager populates the **Device Protocol** field with the appropriate protocol. Click **Next** to continue.

Step 4 The Trunk Configuration window appears, as shown in Figure 9-6. Add the device name. It does not have to be the IP address, but it must be unique throughout the cluster.

Figure 9-6 *CallManager Nongatekeeper-Controlled intercluster trunk Configuration*

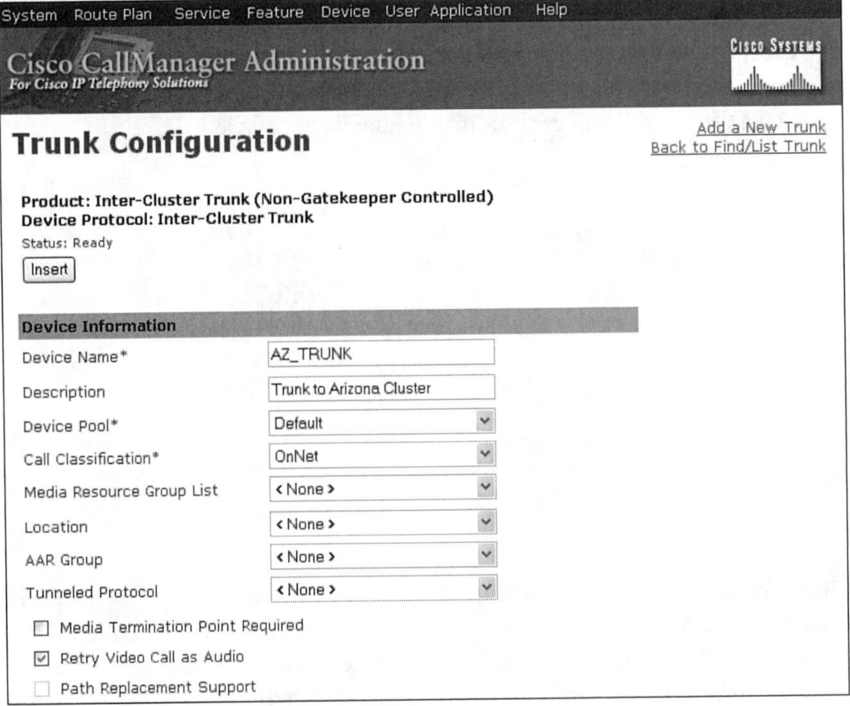

Step 5 At the bottom of the Trunk Configuration window, you can add the IP addresses of up to three Cisco CallManager servers in the remote cluster. You must add the IP address for at least one remote CallManager.

NOTE Configuring gatekeeper-controlled intercluster trunks is covered in Chapter 14, "Implementing Multiple-Site Deployments."

SIP and Cisco CallManager

SIP is specified in Internet Engineering Task Force (IETF) RFC 2543, published in 1999. Since the initial publication, nine *bis* versions (or revisions) have been published, and in 2002, RFC 2543-bis-09 was renumbered to RFC 3261.

SIP is an ASCII-based, application-layer control protocol that can be used to establish, maintain, and terminate multimedia sessions, such as Internet telephony calls between two or more endpoints. SIP works in client/server relationships and in peer-to-peer relationships.

SIP is a VoIP signaling protocol (as are SCCP, MGCP, and H.323) with the following capabilities:

- **Determines the availability of the target endpoint**—If a call cannot be completed because the target endpoint is unavailable, SIP determines whether the called party is connected to a call already or did not answer in the allotted number of rings. SIP then returns a message indicating why the target endpoint was unavailable.
- **Establishes a session between the originating and target endpoints**—If the call can be completed, SIP establishes a session between the endpoints. SIP also supports midcall changes, such as the addition of another endpoint to the conference or the changing of a media characteristic or codec.
- **Handles the transfer**—SIP supports the transfer of calls from one endpoint to another. During a call transfer, SIP establishes a session between the transferee and a new endpoint (specified by the transferring party) and terminates the session between the transferee and the transferring party.
- **Terminates call**—At the end of a call, SIP terminates the sessions among all parties.

SIP Components

A SIP network in a Cisco CallManager environment uses the following components, as shown in Figure 9-7:

- **Cisco SIP proxy server**—The proxy server works as an intermediate device that receives SIP requests from a client and then forwards the requests on behalf of the client. Proxy servers can provide functions such as authentication, authorization, network access control, routing, reliable request retransmission, and security.

- **Redirect server**—The redirect server provides the client with information about the next hop or hops that a message should take, and the client then contacts the next-hop server or user agent server directly.
- **Registrar server**—The registrar server processes requests from user agent clients (UACs) for registration of their current location. Redirect or proxy servers often contain registrar servers.
- **User agent**—A combination of UAC and user agent server (UAS) that initiates and receives calls. A UAC initiates a SIP request. A UAS is a server application that contacts the user when it receives a SIP request. The UAS then returns a response (such as ring, busy, connected, or no answer) on behalf of the user. Cisco CallManager can act as both a server or client (a back-to-back user agent) and can initiate and accept calls simultaneously.

Figure 9-7 *SIP Components*

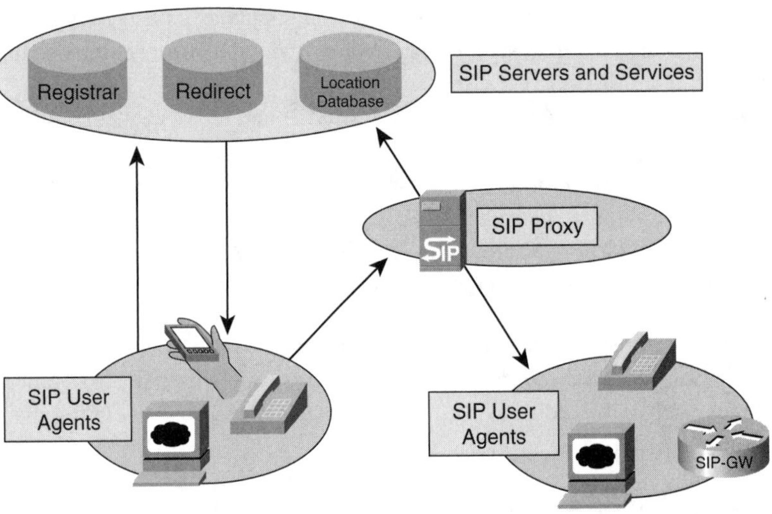

> **NOTE** In the Cisco implementation of the Cisco SIP proxy server, all of the functions of the Redirect and Registrar servers are implemented in a single box. The user agents are shown as any end-user device capable of supporting the SIP protocol.

SIP uses a request-and-response method to establish communications between various components in the network and to ultimately establish a call or session between two or more endpoints. A single session might involve several clients and servers.

Identification of users in a SIP network is by a SIP URL that takes the form sip:*user*@*host*. The *user* part is a username, telephone number, or E.164 address. The *host* part is either a domain name or a numeric network address.

> **TIP** Cisco CallManager 5.X is an appliance-based version of CallManager that implements SIP capabilities to the end-user device using proprietary SIP add-ons to compensate for the current IETF SIP protocol shortcomings.

CallManager SIP Integration and Configuration

Cisco CallManager Release 4.0 introduced a native SIP signaling interface in Cisco CallManager referred to as a SIP trunk. As shown in Figure 9-8, the SIP trunk enables interoperability between Cisco CallManager networks and SIP networks served by a SIP proxy server, and allows any existing devices controlled by Cisco CallManager to communicate with SIP networks. Adding SIP trunks to the CallManager configuration gives CallManager the ability to communicate with voice devices using any of the standards-based VoIP signaling protocols available today.

Figure 9-8 *Cisco CallManager SIP Trunk*

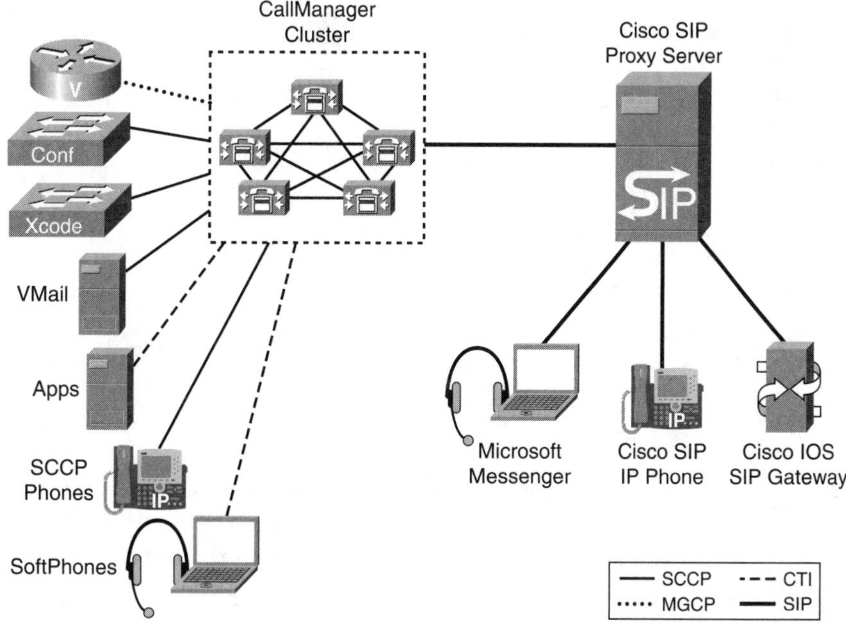

Follow these steps to add a SIP trunk in Cisco CallManager Administration:

Step 1 Choose **Device > Trunk > SIP Trunk** in Cisco CallManager Administration to display the Trunk Configuration window.

Step 2 Click **Add a New Trunk** and choose **SIP Trunk** from the **Trunk Type** drop-down menu. The **Device Protocol** field is automatically filled in.

Step 3 Assign the SIP trunk to the device pools, location, and automated alternate routing (AAR) group as appropriate (example shown in Figure 9-9). The system checks the **Media Termination Point Required** check box by default, and you cannot uncheck it.

Figure 9-9 *Cisco CallManager SIP Trunk Configuration*

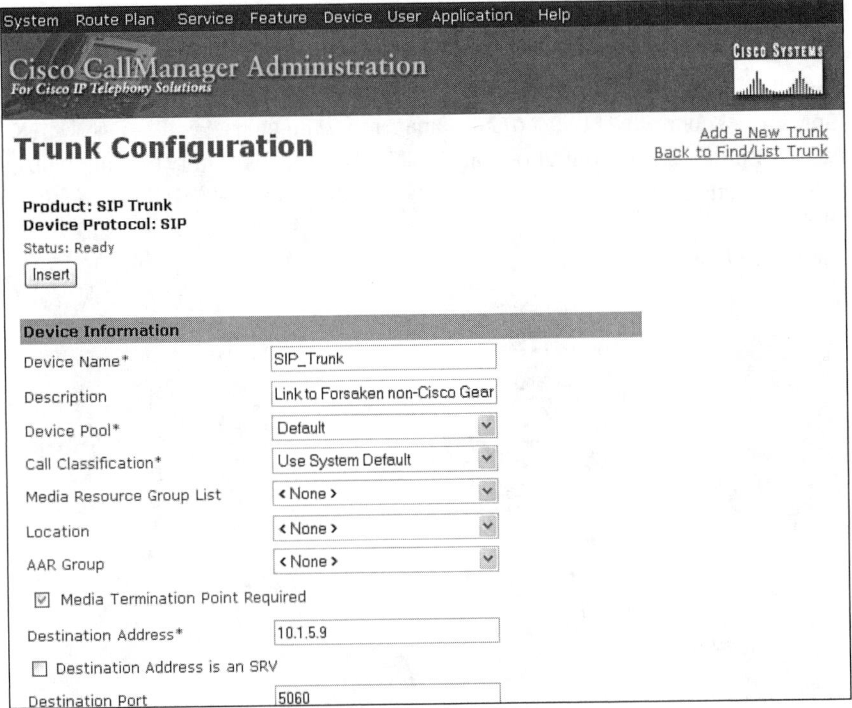

Step 4 The **Destination Address** field indicates the IP address, fully qualified domain name (FQDN), or Domain Name System (DNS) server address of the proxy server. It applies to outgoing calls only; incoming calls do not use the destination address.

Step 5 The **Destination Port** field indicates the port through which to send SIP traffic to the proxy server. The default specifies port 5060, which can be changed to any unique value from 1024 to 65,535.

Step 6 The **Incoming Port** field is the port that Cisco CallManager listens to for incoming SIP traffic. The default specifies port 5060, which can be changed to any unique value from 1024 to 65,535.

> **NOTE** The Destination and Incoming SIP ports act as a positive/negative configuration between the communicating devices. If the destination SIP port is set to 5061, the incoming port on the receiving device must be 5061.

Step 7 Click **Insert** when finished.

Summary

This chapter covered the addition of voice gateways and trunks to the Cisco CallManager configuration. Voice gateways have the ability to connect your Cisco CallManager cluster to networks outside of the local VoIP system. These networks could include the PSTN or other, remote VoIP networks managed by Cisco CallManager or some other third-party vendor.

Cisco CallManager supports direct communication with H.323, MGCP, and SCCP gateways. To support voice networks, gateways should run a software version capable of supporting core voice requirements: DTMF relay, supplementary services, server redundancy, and call survivability. These voice gateways can host analog and digital trunks, allowing them to connect to traditional voice networks. Analog trunks allow a single voice path per port, whereas digital trunks allow a single port to support many voice paths.

In addition to supporting voice gateway configurations, Cisco CallManager also allows you to add trunking mechanisms between voice networks. Trunks perform very similar functions to voice gateways by providing logical paths to other voice networks. However, trunks do not carry voice data (RTP streams). Instead, they provide connection information for devices to contact each other directly, establishing RTP streams without the need for intermediary devices. New to CallManager in versions 4.x is the ability to support SIP trunks, which allows the Cisco CallManager to connect to many third-party voice systems.

Review Questions

You can find the solutions to these questions in Appendix A, "Answers to Review Questions."

1. Which of the following represent an interface you would find on an analog gateway? (Choose two.)
   a. FXS
   b. E&L
   c. T1
   d. FXO
   e. E1

2. Which of the following is *not* a core voice gateway requirement? (Choose two.)
   a. DTMF Relay
   b. inline power support
   c. supplementary service support
   d. SIP trunk support
   e. call survivability
3. Which of the following devices use Skinny signaling? (Choose two.)
   a. Cisco Catalyst 6500 (CatalystOS)
   b. VG224
   c. Cisco IP Phone 7970
   d. Cisco 2801 with a VIC-2FXS interface
4. Which of the following commands could you use to assign all four-digit extensions starting with the number 3 (for example, 3152, 3521, and so on) to a port on an H.323 gateway?
   a. destination-pattern 3
   b. destination-pattern 3 ext 3
   c. destination-pattern 3 ext 4
   d. destination-pattern 3...
   e. destination-pattern 3xxx
5. CallManager 4.1 introduced a new Call Classification feature when configuring gateways. What does this feature accomplish?
   a. It provides advanced logging functions, categorizing the higher importance calls near the top of the log.
   b. It allows or denies calls based on the class of user making the call.
   c. It allows you to restrict conference calls or transfers between local devices and devices off the network.
   d. It allows you to isolate log files for each gateway in the CallManager configuration.
6. You are viewing the configuration of an MGCP router and come across the line **ccm-manager redundant-host 10.1.1.5 10.1.1.6**. What does the IP address 10.1.1.5 represent?
   a. the IP address of the primary Cisco CallManager
   b. the IP address of the secondary Cisco CallManager
   c. the IP address of the tertiary Cisco CallManager
   d. the IP address of the SRST Failover Cisco CallManager

7. What protocol(s) could you use to communicate with a Cisco Catalyst 6500 switch running the NativeIOS image? (Select all that apply.)

   a. MGCP

   b. H.323

   c. Non-IOS MGCP

   d. Skinny

8. What is the difference between configuring a gateway and a trunk in the Cisco CallManager?

   a. Gateways have more security capabilities.

   b. Gateways carry voice traffic; trunks do not.

   c. Trunks allow more flexibility with your connections.

   d. Gateways can only connect to Cisco equipment; trunks can connect to third-party equipment.

9. What is the advantage of using an H.323 gatekeeper in a Cisco IP telephony environment?

   a. Gatekeepers provide more redundancy for your connections.

   b. Gatekeepers ease configuration of Intercluster Trunk connections.

   c. Gatekeepers provide a more centralized security scheme for the voice network.

   d. all of the above

10. What protocol does the H.323 gatekeeper use to provide call admission control?

   a. H.245

   b. H.225

   c. H.225 RAS

   d. SIP

This chapter covers the following topics:

- Identifying the necessary elements for creating external route plans in Cisco CallManager, including gateways and trunks, route groups, route lists, and route patterns
- Explaining how route groups are used to prioritize and group gateways to send external calls out of a preferred path and keep a backup path for redundancy
- Explaining how route lists are used to prioritize route groups that contain different types of gateways that connect to the IP WAN or PSTN
- Explaining how to create route patterns that use wildcards to route calls to gateways or route lists
- Describing how Cisco CallManager analyzes dialed digits to determine where to route calls
- Describing how route groups, route lists, and route patterns are used in a basic route plan to route calls to the IP WAN or PSTN

CHAPTER 10

Cisco Unified CallManager Route Plan Basics

To determine where to route calls, Cisco CallManager requires knowledge of the patterns of digits that users dial to reach a particular telephone number. These patterns include access codes, area codes, and combinations of the digits that are dialed. The route plan is the set of configurable lists that provide Cisco CallManager with the knowledge of where to route calls. Related to call routing is call distribution, which, simply put, is the ability to specify the order and other factors in which Cisco CallManager extends calls to members of a group.

This chapter discusses the basic components of a route plan within Cisco CallManager. Basic components of a route plan include route groups, route lists, and route patterns.

External Call Routing

When you place a call from a Cisco IP Phone, Cisco CallManager analyzes the dialed digits. If the dialed number matches a directory number (DN) that is registered with the Cisco CallManager cluster, Cisco CallManager routes the call to the destination Cisco IP Phone that is associated with the matching DN. This type of call is an internal (or on-cluster) call. Cisco CallManager handles the call internally without the need to route the call to an external PSTN gateway.

IP Phones are not the only devices that can place and receive internal calls; any device that registers a DN with Cisco CallManager can place and receive internal calls. Examples of other devices include the Cisco IP SoftPhone/IP Communicator and analog telephones that are attached to Media Controller Gateway Protocol (MGCP) or Skinny Client Control Protocol (SCCP, or Skinny)–based gateways.

When a Cisco IP Phone dials a number that does not match a registered DN, it assumes that the call is an external (or off-cluster) call. Cisco CallManager then searches its external route table to determine where to route the call. Cisco CallManager uses the concept of route pattern and translation pattern tables to determine where and how to route an external call. The route pattern and translation pattern tables are very similar to the routing table that a Cisco router maintains for routing data.

You can create external route plans based on a three-tiered architecture that allows multiple layers of call routing redundancy as well as digit manipulation. Route patterns match external dial strings, in which a corresponding route list will select available paths for the outbound call based on priority. Cisco refers to these paths as route groups, which are very similar to the trunk group concept in traditional PBX terminology. You can think of a route pattern as a static route with multiple paths that you can prioritize. Figure 10-1 depicts the three-tiered route plan architecture.

Figure 10-1 *Cisco CallManager Route Plan Architecture*

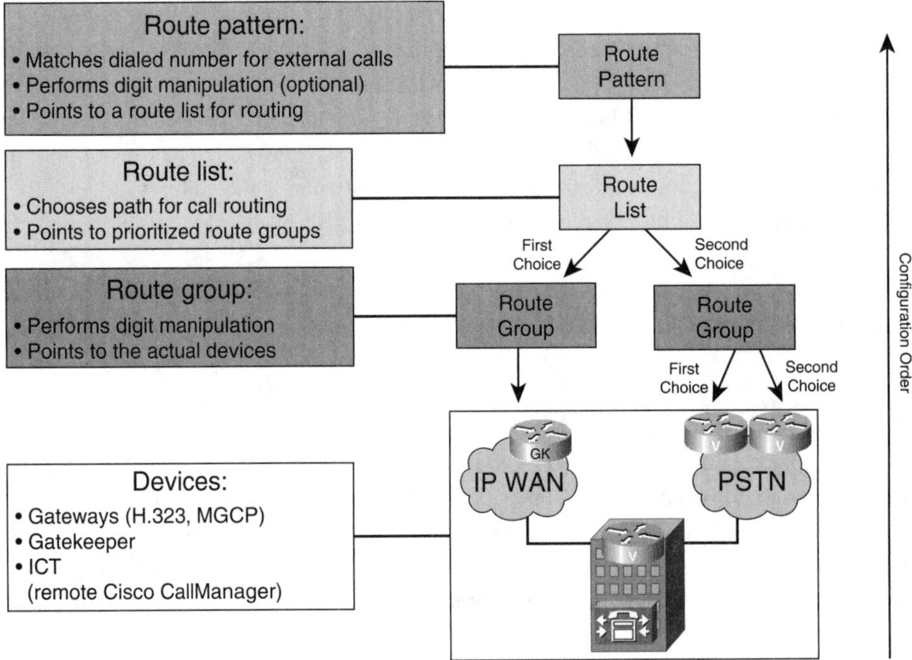

In addition to facilitating multiple prioritized paths for a given dialed number, the route plan can also provide unique digit manipulation for each path, based on the external network requirements. Digit manipulation involves adding or subtracting digits from the original dialed number to accommodate user dial habits and to ensure that the external network or PSTN receives the correct digits to place a call.

Even though the CallManager processes these route plans from the top down (a user dials the route pattern, which directs the call to a route list, then to the preferred route group, and finally to the device), the configuration of the route plan occurs from the bottom up (devices are added, route groups are created from the devices, route lists are created from the route groups, and the pattern points to the list).

Route Plan Configuration Process

The following is the *general* process for route plan configuration. You can construct a route plan using this process:

Step 1 **Add gateway devices**—Create gateway devices using the Device menu.

Step 2 **Build route groups from available devices**—Select and place gateway devices in an ordered list to build a route group.

Step 3 **Build route lists from available route groups**—Select and order route groups into a route list.

Step 4 **Build route pattern**—Build a route pattern and associate it with an available route list or gateway device.

NOTE Chapter 9, "Configuring Cisco Gateways and Trunks," explained the process of adding gateway devices and trunks to the Cisco CallManager configuration. This chapter discusses the route plan configuration process shown in Steps 2 to 4.

The route pattern is the key component in a route plan. The route pattern matches an external dial string and routes the outgoing call to the appropriate gateway. When the dialed digits match a route pattern, Cisco CallManager routes the call to the assigned route list or gateway.

Route Group Overview and Configuration

Route groups and route lists work together to control and enhance external call routing. They also help with implementing cost savings and redundancy, which are among the features of a Cisco IP telephony network.

Route groups are a logical grouping of device gateways, as shown in Figure 10-2. Prioritizing these device gateways allows you to send external calls out of a preferred gateway (possibly across the IP WAN for toll savings) and keep a backup path for external calls (usually the public switched telephone network [PSTN]) if the primary gateway is down or unable to route the call.

Figure 10-2 *Cisco CallManager Route Group Design*

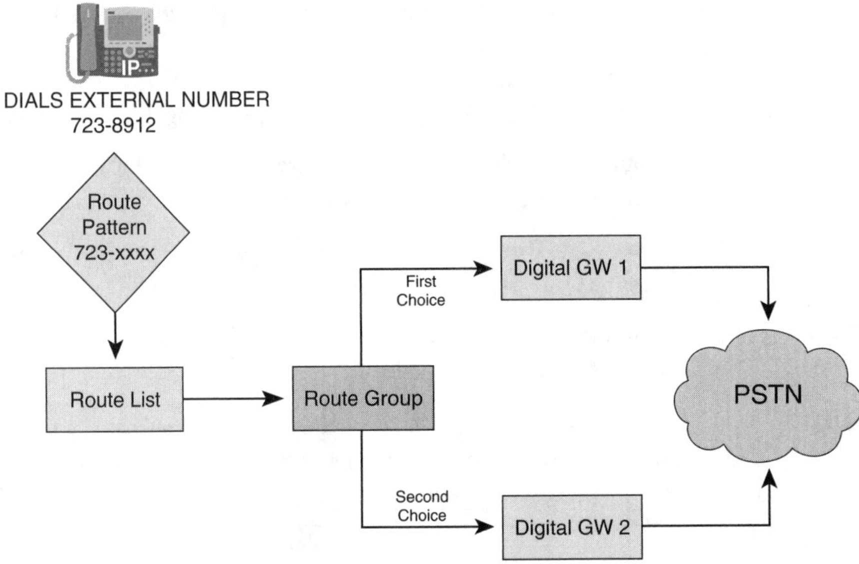

You might encounter a scenario that requires multiple route groups, such as multiple long-distance carriers. Each long-distance carrier offers different rates for long-distance calls on its network. You can use route groups to prioritize the use of the cheaper carrier over the others and retain redundancy if the cheaper carrier cannot route the call for some reason.

Use these steps to configure a route group to the Cisco CallManager configuration:

Step 1 Choose **Route Group** from the **Route Plan > Route/Hunt** menu in the Cisco CallManager Administration window.

Step 2 Click the **Add a New Route Group** link. Give the new route group a name and click **Continue**. It is always best to follow good naming nomenclature (such as PSTN_RG or WAN_RG).

Step 3 Choose a gateway from the **Available Devices** menu to add to the route group. Figure 10-3 demonstrates adding an H.323 PSTN gateway (10.1.5.1) to the PSTN Connection route group for an organization. The route group is a prioritized list of gateways. Place your highest priority gateway at the top of the list using the up and down arrows to the right of the Selected Devices box.

Figure 10-3 *Cisco CallManager Route Group Configuration*

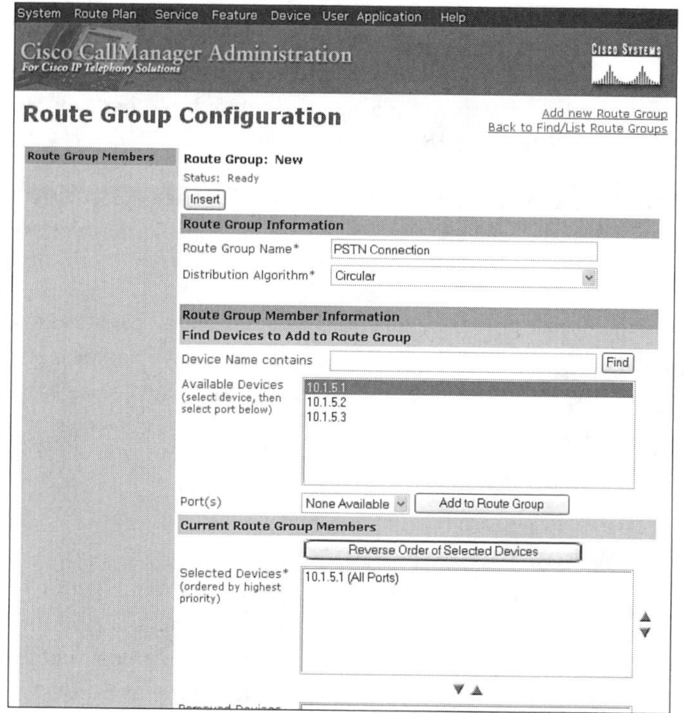

Step 4 Click **Add** or **Update** when finished.

The method that you use to configure route groups depends on the gateway types that you plan to include in the group. Each gateway is an entity; because the CallManager does not know the individual ports on an H.323 gateway, you must add H.323 gateways to a route group as a whole by device. However, because the CallManager knows everything about an MGCP gateway, you can group them by ports, which means that individual ports on MGCP gateways can be entities in a route group.

NOTE The device entities, whether devices in the case of H.323 gateways or ports in the case of MGCP gateways, can be used only once in your route plan configuration. This means that you can only assign them to a single route group. On the other hand, you can assign route groups to multiple route lists. This key fact will play heavily in your route plan design.

In addition, the route group allows you to select the distribution algorithm you want to use. There are two supported distribution algorithms:

- **Circular** (default)—Enables a type of round-robin load balancing for the route group. The first call will go to the first device, the second call to the second, and so on. This is the ideal setting for load distribution across your gateways.
- **Top down**—Uses a strict primary, failover model. The first device listed in the route group is always used unless the gateway is at capacity or unreachable, at which point the second device is used.

You should configure route groups by function. For example, all gateways to the PSTN can belong to one route group, all gateways to long-distance carriers can belong to another (with the cheapest carrier having priority), and all gateways across the IP WAN can belong to another route group. If you want to control routing by gateway instead of by group of gateways or ports, you can set up route groups so that they can contain only one gateway.

Route List Overview and Configuration

Route lists consist of an ordered list of route groups, as shown in Figure 10-4. Route lists expand the route group concept and allow you to prioritize your route groups. Although a gateway or group of ports on a gateway can belong to only a single route group, route groups can belong to any number of route lists. Route groups give you more control over external call routing. In the route plan shown in Figure 10-4, the company has connections to three IntereXchange Carriers (IXCs). They have placed the endpoints into route groups and then prioritized the route groups in a route list to provide least-cost-routing for toll calls.

Figure 10-4 *Cisco CallManager Route List Design*

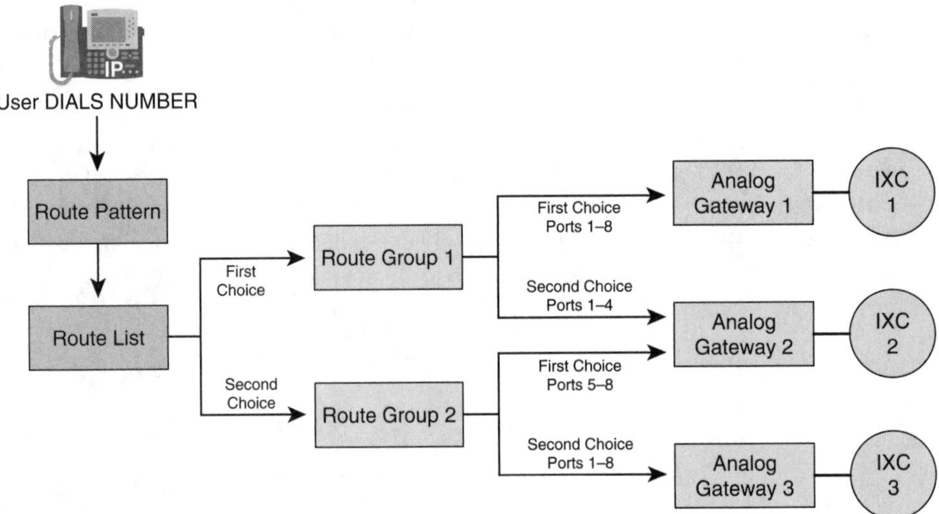

With route lists, you can implement features such as toll bypass and PSTN fallback because within the route list you can prioritize route groups that contain different types of gateways (IP WAN, PSTN, and so on).

Digit manipulation is the key to making toll bypass and PSTN fallback features transparent to your users. Digit manipulation occurs in the form of calling-party and called-party transformations.

Use calling-party transformations to manipulate caller ID information that is presented to the called party. Use called-party transformations to actually manipulate the digits that are dialed. You can apply calling- and called-party transformations at five different levels of the call-routing process: at the originating device, as part of a translation pattern, as part of a route pattern, as part of a route list, or at the terminating device. Calling- and called-party transformations that are set at the route list level override transformations that are set at any other level.

NOTE Calling- and called-party transformations are covered in detail in Chapter 11, "Cisco Unified CallManager Advanced Route Plans."

Complete these steps to configure a route list:

Step 1 From the Route Plan menu in the main Cisco CallManager Administration window, choose **Route/Hunt,** then **Route List**.

Step 2 Click the **Add a New Route List** link. Give the new route list a name and description, and choose the appropriate Cisco CallManager Group. Click **Insert**. It is always best to follow good naming nomenclature (such as PHOENIX_RL or DALLAS_RL).

Step 3 Click the **Add Route Group** button, shown in Figure 10-5, to add the appropriate route groups. This action displays the Route List Detail Configuration window. You can add route groups and set calling- and called-party transformations at this point.

Figure 10-5 *Cisco CallManager Route List Configuration*

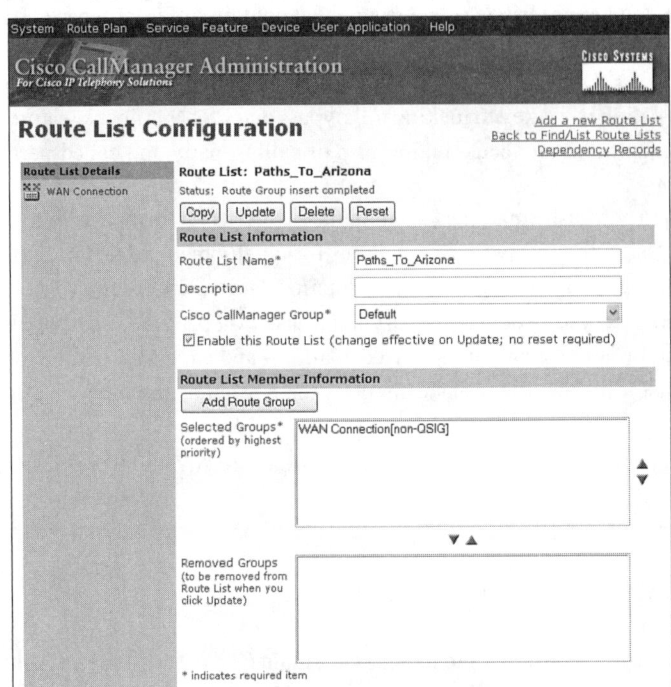

Step 4 Click **Insert** to return to the Route List Configuration window. Click **Add Route Group** again to add additional route groups.

Step 5 Use the up and down arrows to prioritize the route groups.

Route Pattern Concepts and Configuration

In the voice over IP (VoIP) world, route patterns are the equivalent of static routes. The only difference is that route patterns point to E.164 phone numbers (which is the standard defining the international public telecommunication numbering plan used in the PSTN and data networks) instead of IP addresses. External route patterns can point to either an individual gateway or a route list. Here is the call process if the route pattern points to a route list, as shown in Figure 10-6:

1. When a user dials a number, Cisco CallManager analyzes the dialed digits. If the set of digits matches a registered DN, Cisco CallManager routes the call to the internal destination.
2. If the set of digits matches an external route pattern, Cisco CallManager then parses the route list that is associated with that route pattern. The route list contains a prioritized list of route groups, and the route groups contain a prioritized list of voice gateways.

3. If the preferred voice gateway (in the first route group) is unavailable to handle the call, Cisco CallManager passes the call to the next gateway, and so on, until it either finds a gateway to route the call to or exhausts the list of gateways in the route group.

4. If Cisco CallManager exhausts the list of gateways in the route group, it passes the call to the preferred gateway in the next route group in the route list. This process repeats until Cisco CallManager finds a gateway that can handle the call or until it exhausts the list of route groups in the route list. If Cisco CallManager is unable to find a gateway that can take the call, the call fails and the end user receives a fast busy signal.

Figure 10-6 *Cisco CallManager Route Pattern Design*

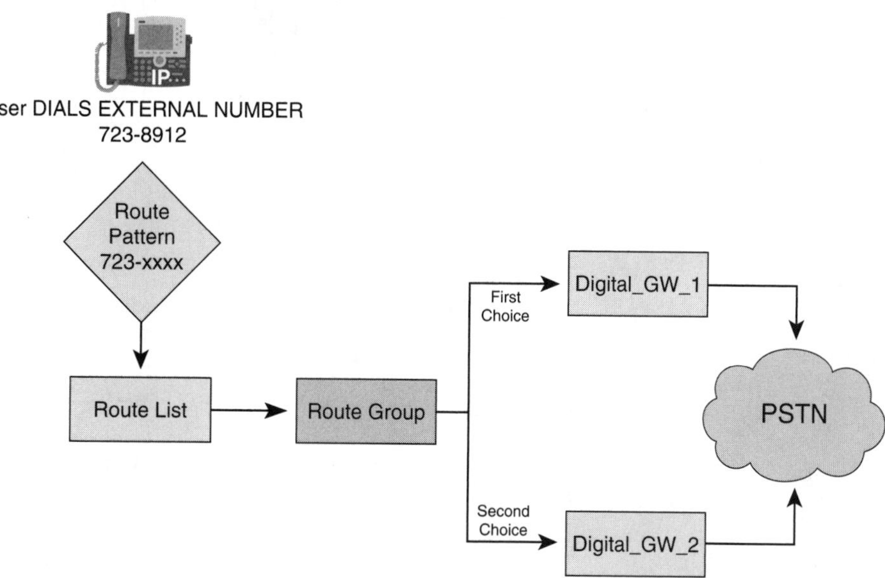

Complete these steps to configure a route pattern in Cisco CallManager:

Step 1 From the Route Plan menu in the Cisco CallManager Administration window, choose **Route/Hunt,** then **Route Pattern**.

Step 2 Click the **Add a New Route Pattern** link.

Step 3 To create a route pattern, enter your route pattern in the **Route Pattern** field, as shown in Figure 10-7, and choose a route list or gateway from the **Gateway or Route List** menu.

> **NOTE** If you point a route pattern directly to a gateway, the gateway is now "used" in the CallManager route plan. Remember, you can only use an endpoint once in the entire route plan. Assigning it to a route pattern keeps it from being assigned to anything else in the route plan. If you have multiple route patterns that used the same gateway, first assign the gateway to a route group. Then, you can create numerous route lists that use the same route group and assign those route lists to the various route patterns.

Figure 10-7 *Cisco CallManager Route Pattern Configuration*

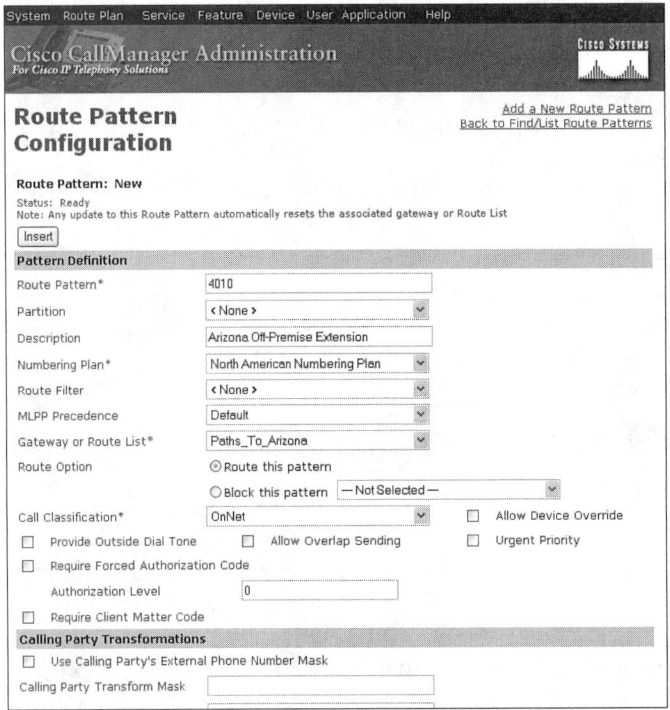

Step 4 If you configure a route pattern to route off-network calls to the PSTN (which most route patterns do), make sure to check the **Provide Outside Dial Tone** check box. This feature plays a second dial tone for users when they dial the outside access code.

TIP When a user dials an outside access code (such as 9) on a legacy PBX, the PBX automatically seizes a trunk connection to the PSTN. The secondary dial tone that the user hears is sent from the PSTN carrier. When a user dials an outside access code in a CallManager environment, the Cisco CallManager generates the secondary dial tone and does not seize a trunk line until the user finishes dialing and CallManager performs digit analysis on the full string.

If Cisco CallManager receives a dial string for which multiple route patterns match, Cisco CallManager must wait for the interdigit timeout (known as the T.302 timer, which is 15 seconds, by default) before applying the longest-match rule and deciding which route pattern to use. You can override the interdigit timeout behavior for a specific route pattern by checking the **Urgent Priority** check box. When a route pattern is marked as urgent, Cisco CallManager immediately routes any outbound calls that match the pattern. This approach avoids the interdigit timeout issue. However, you should use this option very carefully because it can prevent users from reaching certain destinations if it is configured incorrectly. In North America, Urgent Priority is most often used for the 911 and 9911 route patterns.

If your route patterns point to specific gateways and not to route lists, you can set calling-party and called-party transformations at the gateway level. If calling- and called-party transformations are set here and the route pattern points to a route list, Cisco CallManager overrides the gateway-level transformation settings and instead uses the transformation settings that are configured on the route list. Transformation settings are fully discussed in Chapter 11.

Near the bottom of the Route Pattern Configuration window, you will find the ISDN Network Specific Facilities Information Element configuration. This feature allows you to enter the appropriate carrier identification code (up to four digits) to route long-distance calls to specific interexchange carriers on a route pattern-by-route pattern basis.

As of Cisco CallManager Release 4.1, you can classify a route pattern as OnNet or OffNet with an additional option to allow the device associated with the route pattern to override the call classification settings configured in the Route Pattern Configuration window. By checking the **Allow Device Override** check box (shown in Figure 10-7), the gateway or intercluster trunk associated with the route pattern dictates the OnNet/OffNet classification rather than the route pattern.

Route Pattern: Commonly Used Wildcards

A route pattern is a sequence of digits and other alphanumeric characters. If a route pattern contains digits only, it represents a single route pattern match and matches only one destination. By including nonnumeric wildcards in a route pattern, you can allow the route pattern to represent multiple destinations. The purpose of using wildcards is to reduce the number of route patterns that you need to configure. For example, a single route pattern of 1*xxx* would match all dialed numbers from 1000 to 1999. Table 10-1 shows the route pattern wildcards available in Cisco CallManager.

Table 10-1 *Cisco CallManager Route Pattern Wildcards*

Wildcard	Description
X	Matches a single digit. For example, 2xxx matches any number from 2000 to 2999.
@	Matches the entire North American Numbering Plan (NANP). This one wildcard matches all numbers that are valid on the North American PSTN. For example 9@ matches an access code of 9 followed by any number that would be considered valid on the North American PSTN. This is the fastest way to create an external PSTN dial plan. Note that the @ symbol is really a macro representing over 150 individual dial strings. Because of this, using the @ symbol extensively in your route plan can cause significant memory consumption on the Cisco CallManager.
!	Matches one or more digits. Indicates a variable-length dial string that could be any length of digits. The CallManager can only tell if a user is done dialing by waiting for the interdigit timeout (15 seconds by default) or if the user presses the # key on their telephone keypad. This wildcard is typically used to encompass international dialing plans due to their varying lengths.
.	Terminates access code. The "." is not technically a wildcard, but, rather, can separate an access code from a number for easier digit manipulation. For example, the route pattern 9.@ allows an administrator to easily strip the "9" before sending the call to the PSTN.
#	Terminates interdigit timeout. The "#" is also not technically a wildcard, but, rather, a key that a user can use to cause CallManager to skip the typical 15-second interdigit timer and process the call immediately.
[xyz]	Set of matching digits. For example, [458] matches one occurrence of either 4, 5, or 8.
[x-y]	Range of digits. For example, [3-9] matches one occurrence of either 3, 4, 5, 6, 7, 8, or 9. You can use the range notation along with the set notation. For example, [3-69] matches one occurrence of either 3, 4, 5, 6, or 9.
[^x-y]	Exclusion range. If the first character after the open square bracket is a carat, the expression matches one occurrence of any digit (including * and #) except those specified. For example, [^1-8] matches one occurrence of 9, 0, *, or #.
<wildcard>?	A question mark that follows any wildcard or bracket expression matches zero or more occurrences of any digit that matches the previous wildcard. For example, 9[12]? matches the following dial strings: 9, 91, 92, 912, 9122, 92121, and many others. This wildcard is rarely used.
<wildcard>+	A plus sign that follows any wildcard or bracket expression matches one or more occurrences of any digit that matches the previous wildcard. For example, 3[1-4]+ matches 31, 3141, 3333, and many others. This wildcard is rarely used.

TIP The most commonly used wildcards in real-world Cisco CallManager deployments are as follows:

X—Represents a single digit

@—Represents the NANP

!—Represents one or more digits

[x-y]—Number range notation

.—Access code termination

Route Pattern Examples

Table 10-2 illustrates various examples of route pattern wildcard implementations.

Table 10-2 *Route Pattern Examples*

Pattern	Result
1234	Matches 1234
1*1*x*	Matches numbers between 1*10 and 1*19
12*xx*	Matches numbers between 1200 and 1299
13[25-8]6	Matches 1326, 1356, 1366, 1376, 1386
13[^3-9]6	Matches 1306, 1316, 1326
9011!#	Matches any number that begins with 9011, is followed by one or more digits, and ends with #; 901145123# and 90117893271211# are example matches

Although these examples show four-digit extensions, route patterns are more commonly used for external numbers. Route patterns are normally in the form of seven-digit numbers, such as 723-*xxxx*, or longer.

A great example is the 9.@ route pattern. The first digit of the route pattern matches a dialed digit "9," which users commonly use as a code to gain outside access to the PSTN. The second digit "." is used to identify the first digit as an access code and all numbers afterward as the dial string. The third digit "@" is the wildcard that is used to match the North American Numbering Plan. The NANP encompasses a number of dial strings, as presented in Table 10-3.

Table 10-3 *North American Numbering Plan @ Wildcard*

Dial String	Description
Service calls	Service calls are in the form of three- to four-digit numbers that are used to access telephony services such as 911, 411, 611, and so on.
Local calls	Local calls are in the form of a seven-digit number ([2-9]*xx-xxxx*) that is used to dial within your local calling area.
Expanded local calls	Expanded local calls are in the form of a 10-digit number ([2-9]*xx*-[2-9]*xx-xxxx*) that is used to dial expanded-area local calls.
Long-distance calls	Long-distance calls are in the form of a 10-digit number ([2-9]*xx*-[2-9]*xx-xxxx*) that is used to place the calls directly to a long-distance carrier.
Direct-dial long-distance calls	Direct-dial long-distance calls are in the form of an 11-digit number (1-[2-9]*xx*-[2-9]*xx-xxxx*) that is used to place a long-distance call through a local carrier.
International calls	International calls are in the form of 01 1 *xx xxxxxxxxx* where "*xx*" is the country code. The actual length of the dial string depends on which country the user is calling.

Digit Analysis

Call-routing component behavior can be counterintuitive. When a user places a call from a device that is registered with Cisco CallManager, Cisco CallManager must analyze each dialed digit to determine where to route the call. In collecting dialed digits, the call-routing component goes through the following process:

1. Cisco CallManager compares the current sequence of dialed digits against the list of all route patterns and determines which route patterns currently match. Then, Cisco CallManager names the set of route patterns "potentialMatches."
2. If potentialMatches is empty, the user-dialed digit string does not currently correspond with a destination and the calling party will hear a reorder tone.
3. If potentialMatches contains one or more members, the call-routing component determines the closest match. The closest match is the route pattern in potentialMatches that matches the fewest number of route patterns. For example, the dialed digit string 1001 matches both route pattern 1*xxx* and 10*xx*. Although there are 1000 different dialed digit strings that match 1*xxx*, only 100 dialed digit strings match 10*xx*. Therefore, 10*xx* is the closest match.

Digit Collection

Figure 10-8 details a call-routing example in which one route pattern matches the dialed digits exactly. The Cisco CallManager in this example includes the route patterns shown in the figure.

Figure 10-8 *Cisco CallManager Digit Collection*

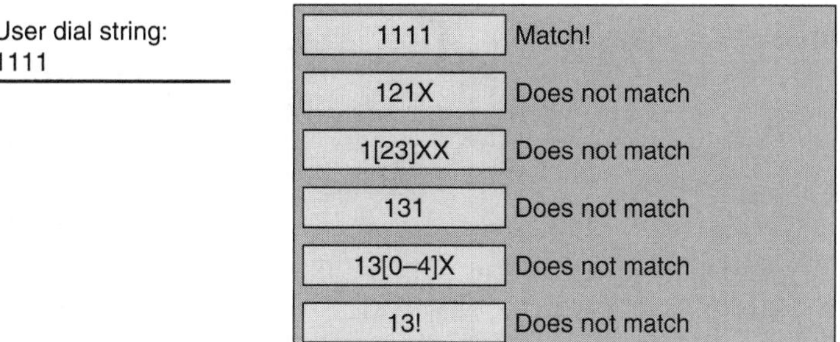

When the user goes off hook, Cisco CallManager begins its routing process. The current set of collected digits is empty. Every route pattern that Cisco CallManager has configured is a potential match at this point. As long as the potentialMatches condition holds true, Cisco CallManager must wait for more digits.

The user now dials a 1. At this time, there are no current matches and every route pattern is still a potential match. The user dials another 1. At this point, Cisco CallManager eliminates route patterns 121*x*, 1[23]*xx*, 131, 13[0-4]*x*, and 13! as potential matches. The only route pattern left is 1111. However, because there are no current matches and the potentialMatches condition is still true, Cisco CallManager must continue to analyze digits. This requirement is in place because the user might continue dialing and dial a string that does not match any entries.

The user dials another 1, which does not change anything. The condition currentMatches is false, and potentialMatches is still true. The user dials 1 again. At this point, the route pattern 1111 is a match, and the currentMatches condition is true. Cisco CallManager removes the route pattern 1111 from the potential matches table. Because there are no more route patterns in the potential matches table, additional dialed digits will not cause Cisco CallManager to match a different route pattern. At this point, Cisco CallManager routes the call to the dialed destination.

Closest Match Routing

Figure 10-9 details a closest-match call-routing example. The Cisco CallManager that is used in this example includes the route patterns shown in the figure.

Figure 10-9 *Cisco CallManager Closest Match Routing*

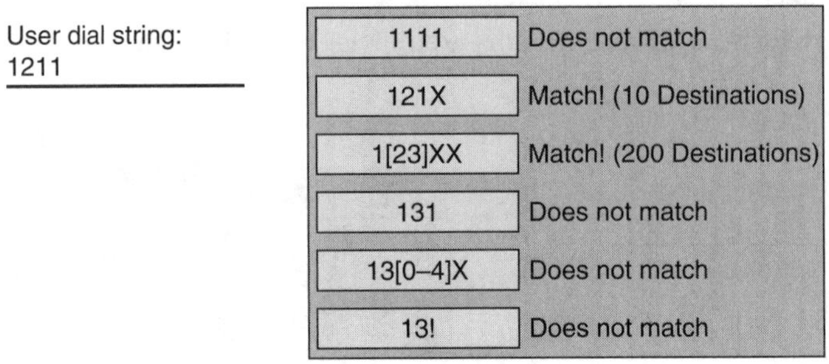

User dial string:
1211

Route Pattern	Result
1111	Does not match
121X	Match! (10 Destinations)
1[23]XX	Match! (200 Destinations)
131	Does not match
13[0–4]X	Does not match
13!	Does not match

The user dials the digits 12. At this point, Cisco CallManager eliminates the route patterns 1111, 131, 13[0-4]*x*, and 13! as potential matches. This leaves route patterns 121*x* and 1[23]*xx* as potential matches. Because there are no current matches and the potentialMatches condition is true, Cisco CallManager continues to analyze digits.

The user dials another 1, which does not change anything. The condition currentMatches is false, and potentialMatches is still true. The user dials 1 again. At this point, the route patterns 121*x* and 1[23]*xx* are current matches, and Cisco CallManager removes them from the potential matches table. Because the potential matches table does not contain additional route patterns, additional dialed digits will not cause Cisco CallManager to match any different route patterns. Now, Cisco CallManager must decide where to route the call based on the route patterns that are available in the current matches table. This is where the closest-match rule is applied. The route pattern 121*x* matches 10 destinations (1210 to 1219). The route pattern 1[23]XX matches 200 destinations (1200 to 1299 and 1300 to 1399). Cisco CallManager then routes the call to the gateway or route list that is associated with the 121*x* route pattern.

Interdigit Timeout

If you configure a Cisco CallManager with route patterns that contain wildcards that match multiple digits, CallManager must often wait for the interdigit timeout to expire before routing the call. The ! wildcard usually represents a variable-length dial string and will never be an exact match for a group of dialed digits. If the user presses # after dialing the last digit, Cisco CallManager does not wait for the interdigit timeout. The Cisco CallManager in this example includes the route patterns shown in Figure 10-10.

Figure 10-10 *Cisco CallManager Interdigit Timeout*

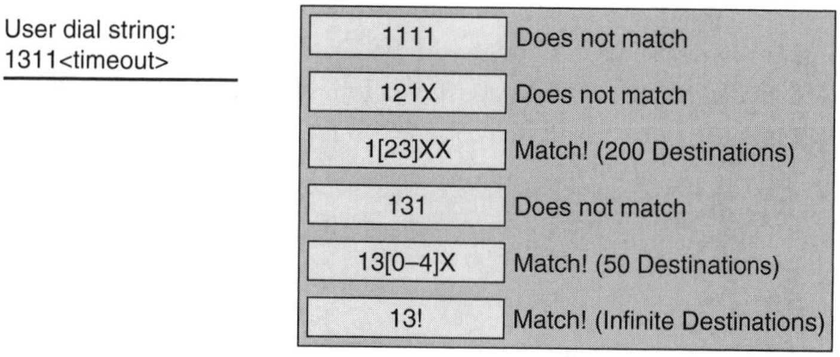

User dial string:
1311<timeout>

1111	Does not match
121X	Does not match
1[23]XX	Match! (200 Destinations)
131	Does not match
13[0–4]X	Match! (50 Destinations)
13!	Match! (Infinite Destinations)

In this example, the user has dialed the string 1311. This action causes Cisco CallManager to eliminate the route patterns 1111, 121*x*, and 131. Cisco CallManager places the route patterns 1[23]*xx*, 13[0-4]*x*, and 13! in the current matches table. The 13! route pattern remains in the potential matches table. The 13! route pattern ensures that the potentialMatches condition is always true because Cisco CallManager has no way of knowing whether the user intends to continue dialing. For example, the user might intend to dial the number 1311555. As long as the potentialMatches condition is true, Cisco CallManager must continue to wait for dialed digits.

In this case, the only event that allows Cisco CallManager to select a destination is an interdigit timeout. When the interdigit timeout timer expires, Cisco CallManager knows that no more digits are forthcoming and can now make a final routing decision. In this example, the user has dialed 1311 and then stopped dialing digits. This action has triggered an interdigit timeout and caused Cisco CallManager to make a final decision based on the following route patterns in the current matches table: 1[23]*xx*, 13[0-4]*x*, and 13!. Because the dial string of 1311 matches multiple route patterns, the closest-match rule is applied.

The route pattern 1[23]*xx* matches 200 destinations (1200 to 1299 and 1300 to 1399). The route pattern 13[0-4]*x* matches 50 destinations (1300 to 1349). The route pattern 13! matches an infinite number of destinations. Cisco CallManager uses this pattern only if it is the only route pattern in the current matches table. The call is routed to the gateway or route list that is associated with the 13[0-4]*x* route pattern.

TIP The system interdigit timeout defaults to 15 seconds. To change it, change the value that is associated with the Cisco CallManager service parameter TimerT302_msec (accessible from **Service > Service Parameters > Cisco CallManager**). This parameter defines the duration of the interdigit timer in milliseconds (ms). The default is 15,000 ms. The lowest configurable value for the T302 timer is 3 seconds (3000 milliseconds). Cisco recommends the value of 5 seconds (5000 milliseconds)for the T302 timer.

Simple Route Plan Example

Figure 10-11 details a simple route plan. In this scenario, the network administrator has configured two gateways for long-distance access to the PSTN (Digital_GW1 and Digital_GW2). Digital_GW1 connects to a carrier that offers a long-distance rate of 7 cents per minute. Digital_GW2 connects to a carrier that offers a long-distance rate of 10 cents per minute.

Figure 10-11 *Simple Route Plan Example*

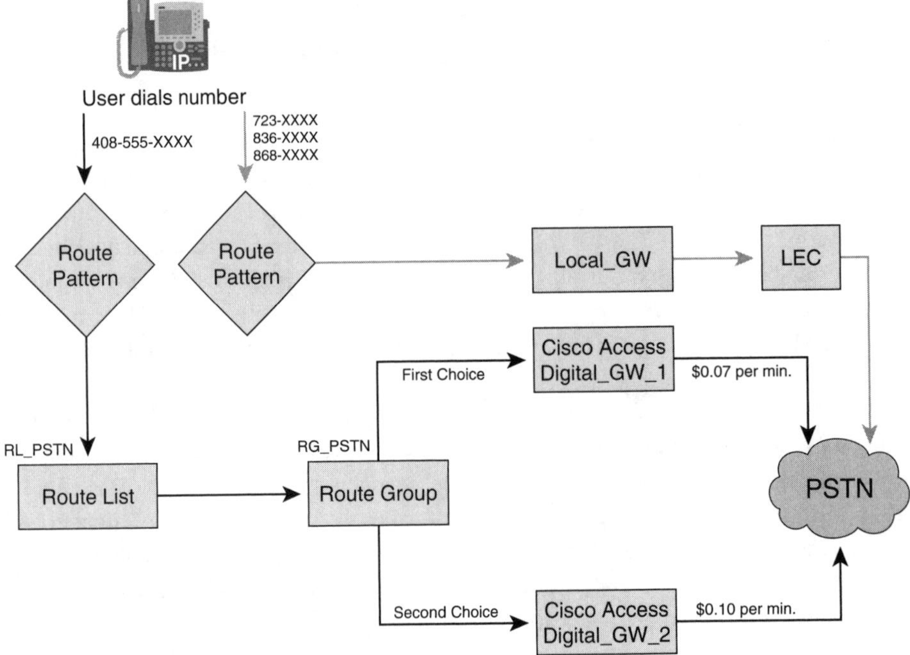

The network administrator has created a route group RG_PSTN to group these gateways and give first priority to Digital_GW1. The route list RL_PSTN uses the route group RG_PSTN. Currently, users need only to call long distance to one destination, which is a remote office in San Jose, California. Therefore, the administrator has created the San Jose route pattern 408-555-XXXX. This route pattern then associates directly with the RL_PSTN route list.

Users also need to dial off-cluster to the PSTN to reach destinations within the local calling area. A separate gateway (Local_GW) connects to the local exchange carrier (LEC) for local PSTN calls. The administrator has defined the route patterns 723-XXXX, 836-XXXX, and 868-XXXX for local calls. These route patterns point directly to the Local_GW gateway for local PSTN access through the LEC.

> **NOTE** You can only use a device in direct Route Patterns or Route Groups in a Cisco CallManager route plan. For example, if you point the route pattern 723-XXXX to a gateway device, you will no longer be able to add that device to a route group. Likewise, if you add a gateway device to a route group, you will no longer be able to point route patterns directly to the gateway device.

Summary

This chapter covered the design and configuration of a basic Cisco CallManager route plan. A route plan is required to route external, or off-cluster, calls in a Cisco IP telephony network. By understanding the call-routing process of Cisco CallManager, you can design your route plan to take advantage of cost considerations and redundancy. A route plan consists of voice gateways and trunks, route groups, route lists, and route patterns.

Route patterns should represent all valid digit streams. Route patterns can be assigned directly to a gateway, or they can be assigned to a route list for more flexibility, such as setting a digital access gateway as the first choice for the least expensive route.

A route list sets the route group usage order. If a route list is used, you must also configure route groups.

A route group sets the access gateway device usage order. This order can be used to select the least expensive route and allows overflow from a busy or failed device to an alternate device.

The route plan configuration order is to add the gateway, add a route group for the gateway, add a route list for the route group, and add route patterns to the route list.

Review Questions

You can find the solutions to these questions in Appendix A, "Answers to Review Questions."

1. When building a Cisco CallManager route plan, which of the following should you configure first?
   a. route pattern
   b. route list
   c. route group
   d. devices/trunks

2. When configuring route groups, you are also given the opportunity to perform digit manipulation using calling- and called-party transformations. (True/False)

3. You are configuring your Cisco CallManager system for an advanced route plan. You access the Device > Gateway menu and verify that you have an H.323 gateway configured at 10.1.1.1 connecting to the PSTN. You then access the Route Pattern Configuration window to add the 9.@ route pattern to the system. When you attempt to associate the H.323 gateway with the route pattern, CallManager does not list the gateway in the drop-down selection box. What is the most likely cause of the problem?

   a. The H.323 gateway must already be used in a route group.

   b. CallManager can only use MGCP gateways to handle PSTN connectivity.

   c. The gateway should have been configured with a public IP address that is valid on the Internet.

   d. There is already a 9.@ route pattern in the CallManager configuration.

   e. You must associate the gateway with a route group because route patterns can only point to route lists.

4. Which interface does a voice gateway provide?

   a. X.25 to SS7

   b. VoIP to H.323

   c. VoIP to PSTN

   d. PSTN to PBX

5. Which of the following contains a list of gateways to use in precedence order?

   a. route group

   b. route list

   c. translation pattern

   d. route pattern

6. Which three of the following are valid wildcards? (Choose three.)

   a. *

   b. !

   c. .

   d. @

7. What can be placed into a route list?

   a. Cisco CallManager servers

   b. route patterns

   c. route groups

   d. devices

8. You are examining a Cisco CallManager route plan and notice the route pattern 34[45]67. Which of the following extensions does this route pattern match?

   a. 344567

   b. 3467

   c. 344

   d. 3467

   e. 34567

9. You have created a route pattern of 4xxx to reach extensions in another CallManager cluster. The calls seem to work fine; however, users complain that they hear a second dial tone after dialing the first digit of the remote extension. What is causing this problem?

   a. The Cisco CallManager assumes all route patterns reach extensions external to the VoIP network (the PSTN) and plays an outside dial-tone automatically.

   b. You need to remove the check from the **Provide Outside Dial-Tone** check box for the route pattern.

   c. You need to check the box for the **Provide Outside Dial-Tone** for the route pattern.

   d. This feature can be disabled through the CallManager Service parameters.

10. You have created the route pattern 7XX!. Which of the following strings match this route pattern? (Select all that apply.)

    a. 7

    b. 71

    c. 712

    d. 7123

This chapter covers the following topics:

- Configuring route filters in Cisco CallManager Administration to reduce the number of route patterns or restrict calling to undesirable locations
- Modifying route patterns to use access codes and discard digit instructions to convert the dialed number to a number that is supported by a national numbering plan
- Configuring transformation masks to manipulate the appearance of the number of the calling party for outgoing calls and to manipulate called numbers for PSTN compatibility
- Configuring translation patterns that manipulate dialed digits before routing a call to enable users to include a uniform dialing plan between offices or to enable hot line functionality
- Describing how to access route plan reports to view a listing of all the Call Park numbers, Call Pickup numbers, conference numbers (such as Meet-Me numbers), route patterns, and translation patterns in the system

CHAPTER 11

Cisco Unified CallManager Advanced Route Plans

Users of any phone system often need to reach a variety of destinations that include calls to extensions located within the same site, to a different site within the same company (sometimes with different dialing plans), and to other companies located within the same country or a different country. Because these calls can take different paths, such as the IP WAN or a preferred public switched telephone network (PSTN) carrier, completing these calls often requires dialing various access codes, numbers of digits, or prefixes. At the same time, it is often prudent to restrict certain destinations for all users, such as 900 numbers.

To require users to understand the specific dialing patterns necessary to reach these various destinations is impractical and inconvenient. Digit manipulation, or the ability of Cisco CallManager to add or subtract digits to comply with a specific internal dial plan or national numbering plan, is the key to providing transparent dialing and creating a unified dialing plan. Implementing route filters in Cisco CallManager Administration blocks access to specified area codes.

This chapter covers route filters, discard digits instructions (DDIs), transformation and translation patterns, and the route plan report to view all route patterns in a Cisco IP telephony clustered solution.

Route Filters

When creating route patterns, you can use the "@" wildcard to represent all the routes defined in the North American Numbering Plan (NANP). Although this is a simple way to provide PSTN access to your internal users, you might be providing far more access than you intend. As shown in Figure 11-1, the NANP includes high-expense patterns such as international dialing access, service numbers (such as 411), and 900 numbers. You can assign route filters to route patterns with the @ route pattern to help reduce the danger that full access to the NANP provides. You can accomplish this reduction by filtering what is included in the @ (or 9.@) route pattern.

Figure 11-1 *@ Route Pattern Without Route Filters*

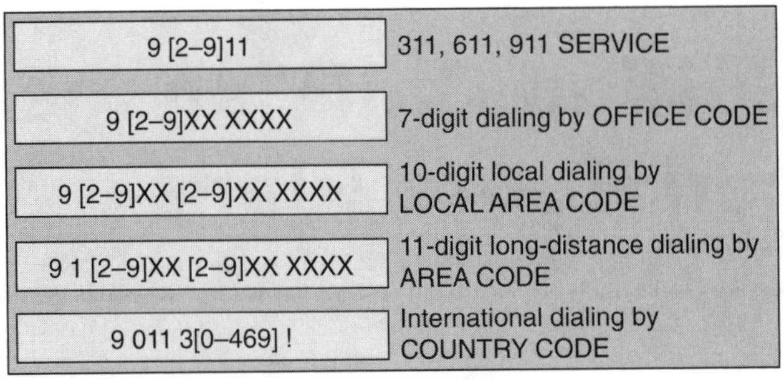

Route Pattern	Description
9 [2–9]11	311, 611, 911 SERVICE
9 [2–9]XX XXXX	7-digit dialing by OFFICE CODE
9 [2–9]XX [2–9]XX XXXX	10-digit local dialing by LOCAL AREA CODE
9 1 [2–9]XX [2–9]XX XXXX	11-digit long-distance dialing by AREA CODE
9 011 3[0–469] !	International dialing by COUNTRY CODE

When using the 9.@ route pattern, Cisco CallManager recognizes that dialing is complete when the user dials 1 + 10 digits (signifying long-distance dialing) or just dials 10 digits (local area codes without the 1). If the number dialed does not begin with a 1, Cisco CallManager considers it a local area code and assumes that dialing is complete after 10 digits.

In an area where seven digits are dialed for local numbers, Cisco CallManager cannot recognize which office exchange codes (NXXs) to use for routing unless you specifically code them as route patterns.

> **NOTE** NXX is the central office (CO) exchange code, which consists of three digits that designate a particular CO or a block of 10,000 subscriber lines. N is any digit between 2 and 9, and X is any digit between 0 and 9.

Generally, telephone company service providers arrange many NXXs in a given area code contiguously where you can use route pattern wildcards to assist in your configuration. Coding these individual route patterns for NXXs can be extremely difficult. You can use a route filter to simplify this procedure.

A route filter called seven-digit dialing is always preconfigured in Cisco CallManager. You should assign this route filter to any 9.@ route pattern in an area that uses seven-digit dialing. This route filter removes all local area codes. If a dialed number does not begin with a 1, then it is a seven-digit number, and Cisco CallManager considers dialing complete after seven digits. This situation requires you to configure local area codes specifically as separate route patterns. Doing so is generally not an issue because the number of area codes in a geographical region is usually small.

> **NOTE** Route filters are only used with the @ route pattern and are not necessary if you have configured a robust dial plan (that does not use the @ route pattern).

Route Filter Tags

You can design and configure route filters using a number of predefined tags in the Cisco CallManager CCMAdmin web utility. Table 11-1 provides a list of tags available to you when implementing route filters.

Table 11-1 *Cisco CallManager Route Filter Tags*

Tag Name	Example Pattern	Description
AREA-CODE	1 214 555 1212	The area code in an 11-digit long-distance call
COUNTRY-CODE	011 33 123456#	The country code in an international call
END-OF-DIALING	011 33 123456#	The #, which terminates interdigit timeout for an international call
INTERNATIONAL-ACCESS	01 1 33 123456#	The initial 01 of an international call
INTERNATIONAL-DIRECT-DIAL	01 1 33 123456#	The digit that denotes the direct-dial component of an international call
INTERNATIONAL OPERATOR	01 0	The digit that denotes the operator component of an international call
LOCAL-AREA-CODE	214 555 1212	The area code in a 10-digit local call
LOCAL-DIRECT-DIAL	1 555 1212	The initial 1 that is required for some 7-digit calls
LOCAL-OPERATOR	0 555 1212	The initial 0 that is required for operator-assisted local calls
LONG-DISTANCE-DIRECT-DIAL	1 214 555 1212	The initial 1 that is required for long-distance direct-dialed calls
LONG-DISTANCE-OPERATOR	0 214 555 1212	The initial 0 that is required for operator-assisted long-distance calls
NATIONAL-NUMBER	011 33 123456#	The national number component of an international call
OFFICE-CODE	1 214 555 1212	The office exchange code of a North American call
SATELLITE-SERVICE	011 88141234#	A specific value that is associated with calls to the satellite country code
SERVICE	1 411	A value that provides access to local telephony provider services

continues

Table 11-1 *Cisco CallManager Route Filter Tags (Continued)*

Tag Name	Example Pattern	Description
SUBSCRIBER	1 214 555 1212	A particular extension that is served by a given exchange
TRANSIT-NETWORK	101 0321 1 214 555 1212	A long-distance carrier code
TRANSIT-NETWORK-ESCAPE	101 0321 1 214 555 1212	The escape sequence that is used for entering a long-distance carrier code

Configuring Route Filters

Route filter configuration occurs in two major steps:

Step 1 Configure route filter with necessary tags and arguments.

Step 2 Apply the route filter to a route pattern or translation pattern.

Just as with access lists on routers, you can create route filters all day and they will never make any difference until you have applied them. Just like an access list, the sole purpose of a route filter is to match criteria; how you apply the route filter determines if the criteria is permitted or denied.

To configure a route filter, use the Cisco CallManager Administration window:

Step 1 Choose the **Route Plan** menu.

Step 2 Choose **Route Filter** from the menu bar.

Step 3 Click the **Add a New Route Filter** hyperlink.

Step 4 Choose **North American Numbering Plan** from the Dial Plan menu.

Step 5 Enter a name in the **Route Filter Name** field. The name can consist of up to 50 alphanumeric characters, and can contain any combination of spaces, periods (.), hyphens (-), and underscore characters (_). Each route filter name must be unique to the route plan.

After you have accomplished these initial steps, the Route Filter Clause Configuration window appears, as shown in Figure 11-2.

Figure 11-2 *Route Filter Clause Configuration Window*

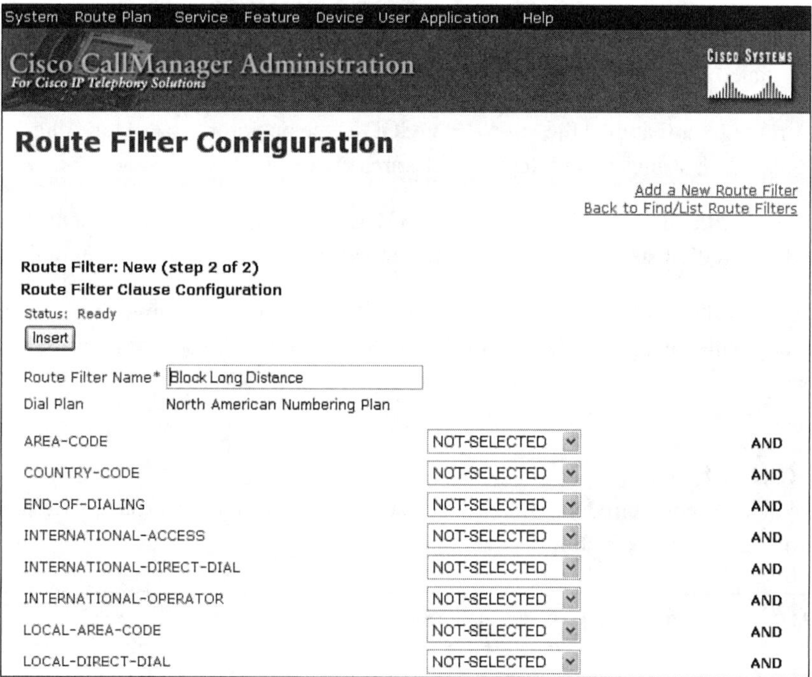

From this point, you can combine your tags with operators to define match conditions. Table 11-2 describes the four operators available when configuring route filters.

Table 11-2 *Cisco CallManager Route Filter Operators*

Operator	Description
NOT-SELECTED	Do not filter calls based on the dialed digit string associated with this tag.
EXISTS	Filter calls when the dialed digit string associated with this tag is found.
DOES-NOT-EXIST	Filter calls when the dialed digit string associated with this tag is not found.
==	Filter calls when the dialed digit string associated with this tag matches the specified value.

The following are examples of match conditions using route filter tags and operators:

- A route filter that uses the tag **AREA-CODE** and the operator **DOES-NOT-EXIST** selects all dialed digit strings that do not include an area code.
- A route filter that uses the tag **AREA-CODE**, the operator = =, and the entry **515** selects all dialed digit strings that include the 515 area code.
- A route filter that uses the tag **AREA-CODE**, the operator = =, and the entry **5[2-9]X** selects all dialed digit strings that include area codes in the range of 520 through 599.
- A route filter that uses the tag **TRANSIT-NETWORK**, the operator ==, and the entry **0288**, along with the tag **TRANSIT-NETWORK-ESCAPE**, the operator ==, and the entry **101**, selects all dialed digit strings with the carrier access code 1010288.

Applying Route Filters

After you have configured the route filter, you must apply them to a route pattern or translation pattern to define the permit or deny action.

> **NOTE** Translation patterns are discussed later in this chapter.

To apply the route filter you have created to a route pattern, perform the following steps:

Step 1 Choose the **Route Plan > Route/Hunt > Route Pattern** menu selection.

Step 2 Choose the **Add a New Route Pattern** hyperlink.

Step 3 Define the route pattern as @ (or 9.@) to represent the NANP.

Step 4 Choose your configured route filter from the **Route Filter** drop-down list, as shown in Figure 11-3.

Figure 11-3 *Applying a Route Filter to a Route Pattern*

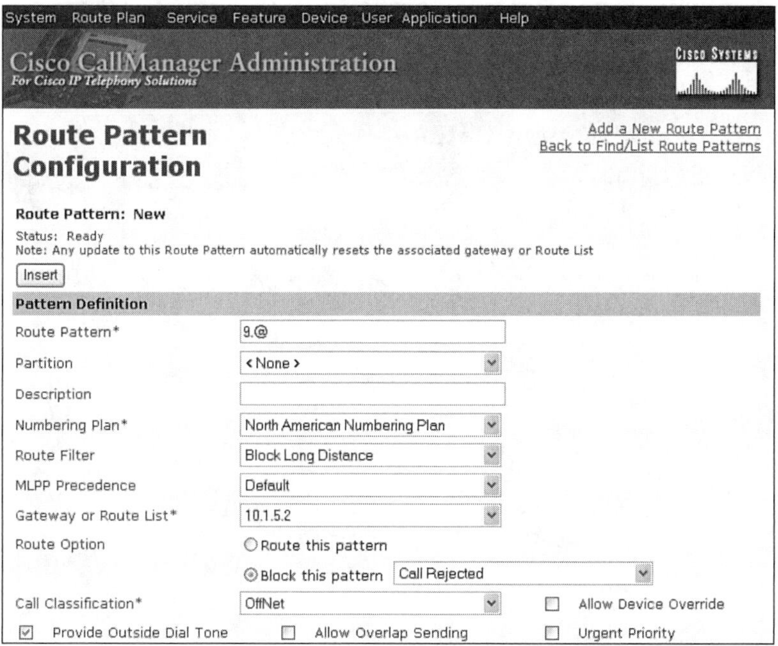

Step 5 Choose a PSTN exit gateway or route list.

Step 6 Select the **Route This Pattern** radio button to allow the numbers matching the filter to route to the PSTN or select the **Block This Pattern** radio button to block the numbers matching the filter from reaching the PSTN.

Practical Route Filter Example

To demonstrate route filter configuration, imagine that a company wanted to create a route filter that kept 1-900 numbers from being made available in the CallManager route plan. The first step would be to create a route filter that matched the area code 900, as shown in Figure 11-4.

Figure 11-4 *Route Filter Matching the 900 Area Code*

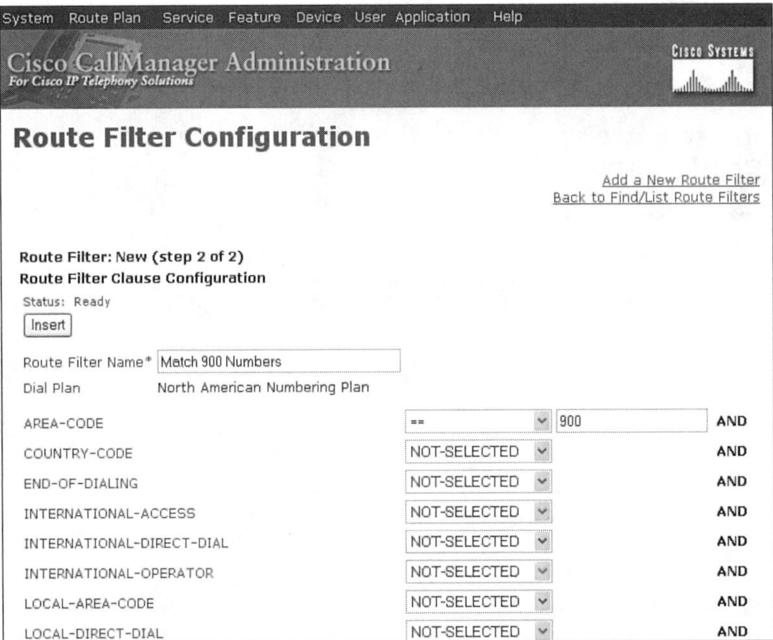

After the route filter has been added to the configuration, you then need to apply it to a route pattern to define the action required. Figure 11-5 illustrates the creation of a 9.@ route pattern (representing the NANP) with the **Match 900 Numbers** route filter applied. The key action rests in the **Route This Pattern** or **Block This Pattern** radio buttons. If you select to **Route This Pattern**, you would add only 900 numbers to the Cisco CallManager route plan. Unless you had a very strange organization, this is not a desired effect. Rather, you would select the **Block This Pattern** radio button to block any numbers containing the 900 area code.

CallManager allows you to configure multiple 9.@ route patterns, provided each has a unique route filter configuration. This provides flexibility when creating your route plan. By combining multiple 9.@ route patterns with unique route filters, you can route (or block) exactly what you want from the CallManager route plan.

> **TIP** You could also accomplish this same objective by creating a route pattern of 1900XXXXXXX and choosing **Block this Pattern** under the route pattern configuration.

Figure 11-5 *Route Pattern Configuration*

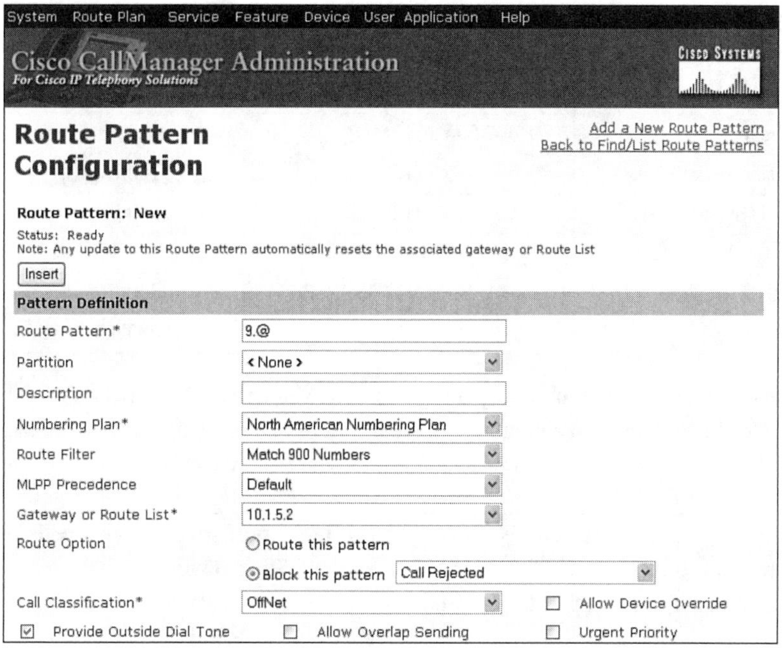

System Route Plan Service Feature Device User Application Help

Cisco CallManager Administration
For Cisco IP Telephony Solutions

Cisco Systems

Route Pattern Configuration

Add a New Route Pattern
Back to Find/List Route Patterns

Route Pattern: New

Status: Ready
Note: Any update to this Route Pattern automatically resets the associated gateway or Route List

Insert

Pattern Definition

Route Pattern*	9.@
Partition	< None >
Description	
Numbering Plan*	North American Numbering Plan
Route Filter	Match 900 Numbers
MLPP Precedence	Default
Gateway or Route List*	10.1.5.2
Route Option	○ Route this pattern
	◉ Block this pattern — Call Rejected
Call Classification*	OffNet — ☐ Allow Device Override

☑ Provide Outside Dial Tone ☐ Allow Overlap Sending ☐ Urgent Priority

Discard Digit Instructions

Discard Digit Instructions (DDIs) allow conversions of a dialed number specific to a national numbering plan. Typically, companies use a route pattern such as 9.@ to access the PSTN. However, only the internal IP telephony network uses the 9 access code to reach the PSTN. If the Cisco CallManager were to keep the access code prefixed to the number to forward to the PSTN, the call would not complete. To avoid this, you can use DDIs to strip extra digits before the call reaches the PSTN.

In general, administrators apply DDIs to route patterns that contain the @ wildcard; however, you can use the DDI PreDot with route patterns that use the "." wildcard even if the route patterns do not contain the @ wildcard. Cisco CallManager applies DDIs to the called-party transformation masks at the route pattern, the route details of a route list, or a translation pattern. DDI identifiers, shown in Figure 11-6, are additive. The DDI **PreDot 10-10-Dialing** combines the effects of each individual identifier. Table 11-3 depicts the most commonly used DDIs in the Cisco CallManager route plan.

Table 11-3 *Cisco CallManager Digit Discard Instructions*

Digit Discard Instructions	If the route pattern is 9.5@... Discarded Digits	Used For
PreDot	95 1 602 555 1212	Access codes
PreAt	95 1 602 555 1212	Access codes
11D/10D@7D	95 1 602 555 1212	Toll bypass
11D@10D	95 1 602 555 1212	Toll bypass
IntlTollBypass	95 011 33 1234 #	Toll bypass
10-10-Dialing	95 1010321 1 602 555 1212	Suppressing carrier selection
Trailing-#	95 1010321 011 33 1234 #	PSTN compatibility

You can configure DDIs at multiple places in the CallManager route plan. One of the more common places is at the route pattern configuration. As shown in Figure 11-6, you can find the DDIs under the Called Party Transformations near the end of the Route Pattern Configuration window.

> **TIP** Digit Discard Instructions applied at the route pattern level are visible to the end user. For example, if the caller dials 914085551212 and the DDI removes the 9, the user will see the number change to 14085551212 on the LCD display of their IP Phone. DDIs applied at the route group level (from within the route list) are not visible to the end user. Applying DDIs at the route group level is covered later in this chapter.

Figure 11-6 *Digit Discard Instructions*

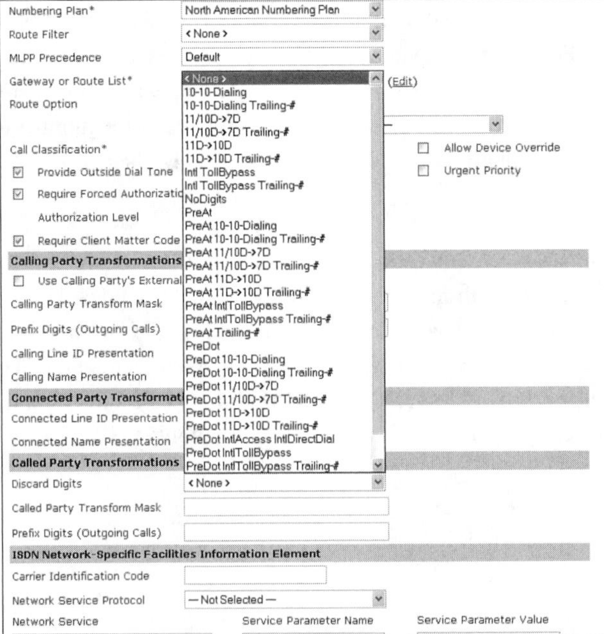

As you can see, CallManager offers a variety of combinations of all the DDIs listed in Table 11-3.

Transformation Masks

Dialing transformations allow the call-routing component to modify either the calling number or the dialed digits of a call. Transformations that modify the calling number are calling-party transformations; transformations that modify the dialed digits are called-party transformations.

Calling-party transformation settings allow you to manipulate the appearance of the calling-party number for outgoing calls. A common application of a calling-party transformation is to use the company external phone number of a calling station in place of the directory number (DN) for outgoing calls. The calling-party number is used for Calling Line Identification (CLID). During an outgoing call, the CLID is passed to each PBX, CO, and interexchange carrier (IXC) as the call progresses. The CLID is also delivered to the calling party when the call is completed.

NOTE Caller ID is also referred to as Automatic Number Identification (ANI) .

Called-party transformation settings allow you to manipulate the dialed digits, or called-party number, for outgoing calls. Examples of manipulating called numbers include appending or removing prefix digits (outgoing calls), appending area codes to calls that are dialed as seven-digit numbers, appending area codes and office codes to interoffice calls that are dialed as four- or five-digit extensions, and suppressing carrier access codes for outgoing calls.

When configuring calling- or called-party transformations, a transformation mask operation allows the suppression of leading digits, the change of some digits while leaving others unmodified, and the insertion of leading digits. A transformation mask requires two pieces of information: the number that you want to mask and the mask itself.

In the transformation mask operation, Cisco CallManager aligns the number with the mask so that the last character of the mask aligns with the last digit of the number. Cisco CallManager uses the corresponding digit of the number wherever the mask contains an X. If the number is longer than the mask, the mask removes the leading digits. Figure 11-7 demonstrates the transformation mask logic.

Figure 11-7 *Transformation Mask Logic*

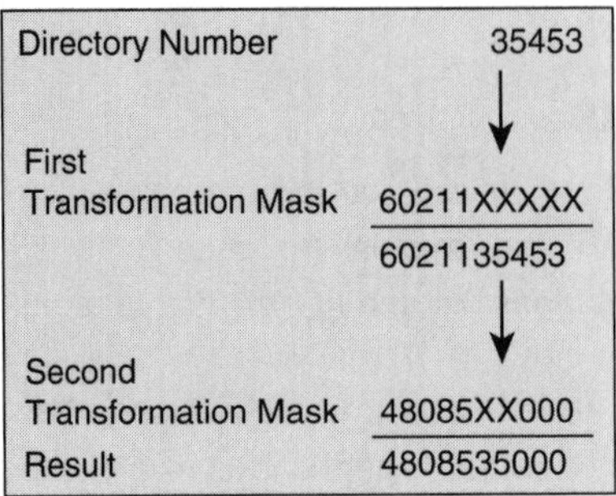

As you can see from Figure 11-7, the initial number (which could be dialed or caller ID information, depending on the type of transformation mask you choose) passes through the first transformation mask. By right-justifying the digits, CallManager passes the number 35453 through the first transformation mask. The digits match to the right-justified X wildcards, causing it to pass through. CallManager prepends the additional digits to the left of the wildcards. As it passes through the second transformation mask, the numbers are again right-justified. This time, only the "35" digits pass through the X wildcards; CallManager replaces the rest of the string with the hard-coded digits to the left and right of the X wildcards.

Calling-Party Transformations

The example in Figure 11-8 shows the applicable settings for calling-party transformations and the order in which Cisco CallManager processes those instructions.

Figure 11-8 *Calling-Party Transformations*

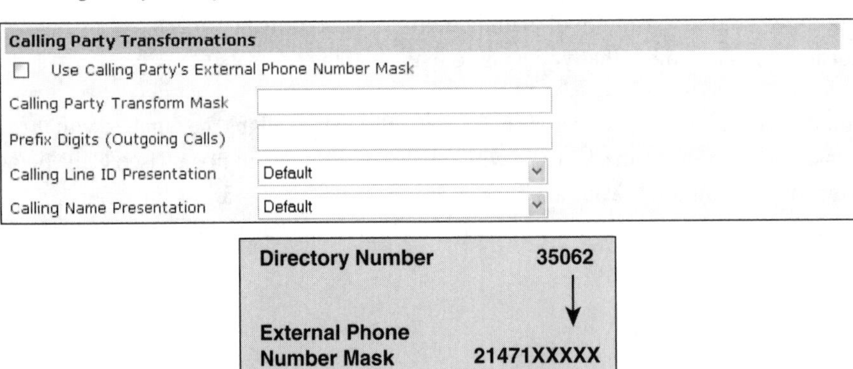

You can configure three types of calling-party transformations in the call-routing component and on route lists:

- Use the external phone number mask, which instructs the call-routing component to use the external phone number of a calling station rather than its DN or the caller ID information. Without the external phone number mask, the calling number might appear as an extension number to the PSTN rather than a fully routable PSTN phone number. You can apply the external phone number mask on a line-by-line basis through the DN configuration screen on the device.
- The calling-party transformation mask allows the suppression of leading digits, leaves other digits unmodified, and inserts leading digits. As shown in Figure 11-8, the post-external phone number mask caller ID information is 2147135062. This passes through the calling-party transformation mask of 40885XX0000, which allows only the numbers "35" to pass through the XX wildcards. The resulting caller ID information is 4088535000.
- Prefix digits allow the prepending of specified digits to the calling number.

Cisco CallManager applies the transformations in the order that is presented in the example.

> **TIP** Remember, the calling-party transformations transform caller ID information (the number of the person who is *calling*).

Called-Party Transformations

The example in Figure 11-9 shows the applicable settings for called-party transformations and the order in which Cisco CallManager processes those instructions.

Figure 11-9 *Called-Party Transformations*

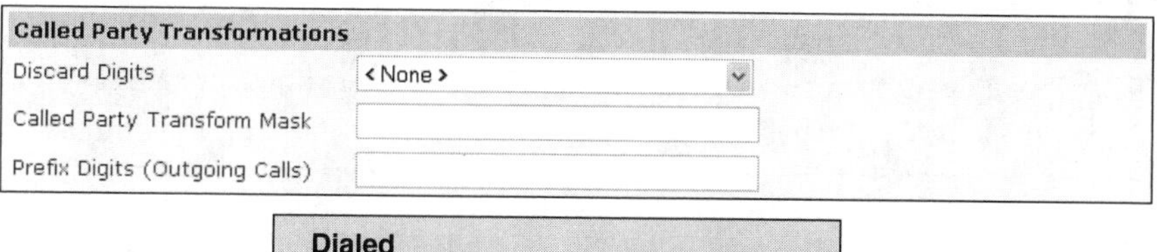

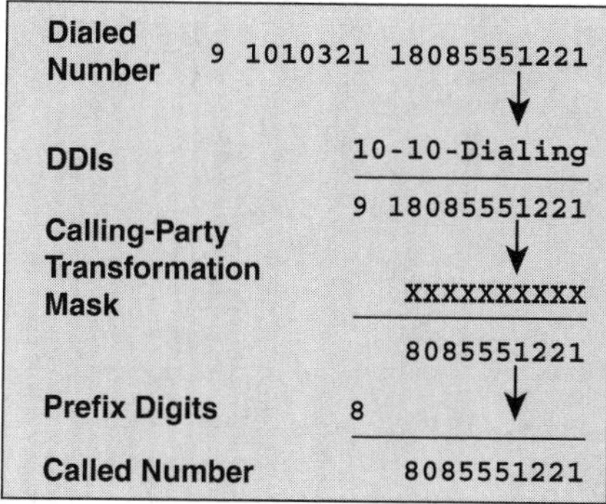

You can configure the following three types of called-party transformations in the call-routing component and on route lists:

- DDIs allow the discarding of digits in the dialed number. Such instructions are critical for implementing toll-bypass solutions. This need arises when Cisco CallManager must convert the long-distance number that the calling party has dialed into a local number. This number allows Cisco CallManager to pass the digits to the PSTN. You can also use DDIs to discard PSTN access codes, such as 9. Figure 11-9 demonstrates the removal of the 10-10-Dialing portions of the call to eliminate other long-distance carriers a user might choose to use.
- The called-party transformation allows the suppression of leading digits, changes the existing digits while leaving others unmodified, and inserts leading digits. Figure 11-9 illustrates the use of a called-party transformation mask consisting of ten "X" wildcards. This has the effect of stripping any preceding digit beyond the ten wildcards (in this case, CallManager strips the 9 and the 1). This might be necessary when configuring toll-bypass on the CallManager. For example, you might have a location that can access the 808 area code without incurring toll charges. You can configure the Cisco CallManager to route the call across the IP WAN then out a LEC.
- Prefix digits allow the prepending of one or more digits to the called number. Figure 11-9 illustrates prefixing an 8 to the front of the original dialed number. This might be required by a PBX at a remote site. For example, the call is transformed using the called-party transformation mask, then prefixed with an 8 and routed across the IP WAN. When the PBX at the remote site received the string, it recognizes the 8 as an outside access code and routes the call to the PSTN LEC.

Cisco CallManager applies the transformation in the order that is presented in the example.

NOTE You could accomplish the same result shown in Figure 11-9 by simply applying a called-party transformation mask of 8XXXXXXXXXX. This is a more efficient method; the called-party transformations shown are used to illustrate the various transformations and the order in which the CallManager applies them.

TIP Remember, the called-party transformations transform dialed-number information (the number that a user *called*).

Configuring Calling- and Called-Party Transformation Masks

You can apply calling- and called-party transformations at the route pattern, route list, or translation pattern configuration windows. The calling-party transformation setting that is used in route lists applies to the individual route groups that make up the list rather than to the entire route list. The calling-party transformation settings that are assigned to the route groups in a route list override any calling-party transformation settings that are assigned to a route pattern that is associated with that route list.

Because you can be more specific, network administrators usually apply transformation masks at the route list level. In this way, you can assign a different transformation mask for each route group in the route list. Transformation masks configured at the route list level have priority over those configured at the route pattern level because they are processed last. If you have configured a transformation at the route pattern level, it becomes more of a "global" translation, that is, as soon as the pattern is matched, the transformation takes effect. As the route pattern sends the call to the route list and the prioritized route group is chosen, the transformations relating to that specific route group apply second, transforming the already transformed number from the route pattern into whatever you have defined.

For example, in the network illustrated in Figure 11-10, a network administrator has two route groups created: the PSTN route group and the IP WAN route group. Both of these route groups contain multiple gateways that connect to their respective networks. When Cisco CallManager forwards a call to a gateway in the PSTN route group, the network administrator applies a mask that transforms the number into an E.164-compliant phone number. However, when Cisco CallManager uses a gateway from the IP WAN route group, Cisco CallManager leaves the number as a four-digit extension.

Figure 11-10 *Transformation Network Design*

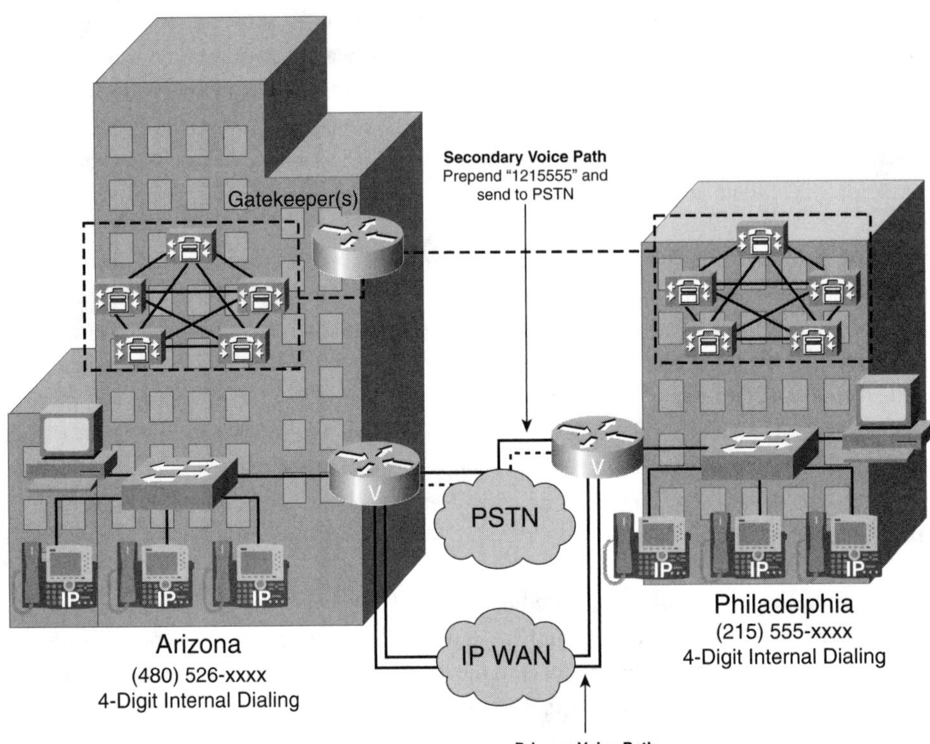

Transformation Example

Figure 11-11 summarizes how transformations to the called-party (dialed digits) and to the calling-party numbers are made within Cisco CallManager. In Figure 11-11, a user dials a number to which Cisco CallManager first applies a calling-party transformation ("calling party" refers to the person who originated the call). This action changes the caller ID number that is displayed on the destination phone. Cisco CallManager then applies a called-party transformation to change the number that is dialed.

Figure 11-11 *Called-Party Transformations*

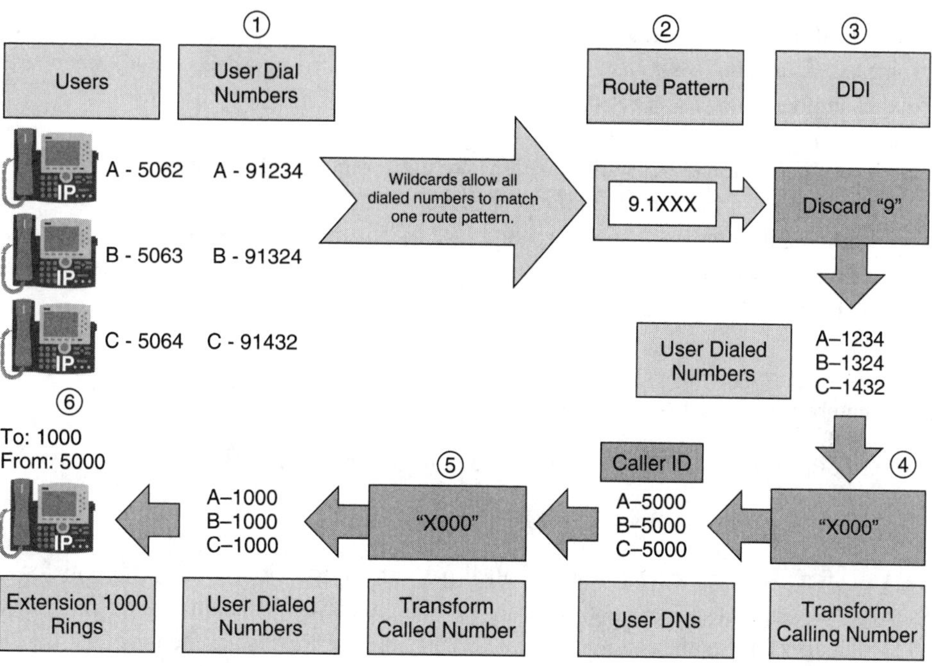

The two transformations are explained in the figure and, for user A specifically, in the following steps:

1. User A has a DN of 5062. This user dials DN 91234.
2. The dialed number matches the route pattern 9.1xxx.
3. The DDIs contain instructions to discard the 9. The dialed number is now 1234.
4. The calling number 5062 now passes through the calling-number transformation mask, which contains instructions to change the last three digits of the calling party number to 000. The new calling number is 5000.
5. Cisco CallManager then passes the called number 1234 through the called-number transformation mask X000, which changes the dialed number to 1000.
6. The result is a calling-party number of 5000 and a called-party number of 1000.

Translation Patterns

Cisco CallManager uses translation patterns to manipulate dialed digits before routing a call. In some cases, the dialed number is not the number that is used by the system. In other cases, the dialed number is not a number that is recognized by the PSTN.

Digit manipulation and translation patterns are used frequently in cross-geographical distributed systems where, for instance, the office codes are not the same at all locations. In these situations, a uniform dialing plan can be created, and translation patterns can be applied to accommodate the unique office codes at each location. The following are additional examples when you can use translation patterns:

- Routing emergency calls to security desks and operator desks (such as sending emergency numbers to a local security office or routing '0' to the local operator extension)
- Hot lines with a need for private line, automatic ringdown (PLAR) functionality
- Extension mapping from the public to a private network

Translation patterns use the results of called-party transformations as a set of digits for a new analysis attempt. The second analysis attempt might match a translation pattern. In this case, Cisco CallManager applies the calling- and called-party transformations of the matching translation pattern and uses the results as the input for another analysis attempt. For example, you have a called-party transformation set up under a route pattern that transforms the dialed number 5555 to 0. You could then have a translation pattern defined to match the dialed number 0 and transform it to an operator extension or hunt group number. To prevent routing loops, Cisco CallManager breaks chains of translation patterns after ten iterations.

Translation Pattern Configuration

Configuration of a translation pattern is similar to configuration of a route pattern. Each pattern has calling- and called-party transformations and wildcard notation. The difference is that when Cisco CallManager applies the translation pattern, it starts the digit-analysis process over and routes the call through a new path if necessary.

To configure a translation pattern, choose the **Route Plan** menu and choose **Translation Pattern**. After you click the **Add a New Translation Pattern** hyperlink, the Translation Pattern Configuration window appears, as shown in Figure 11-12. You can define the route pattern to match (in the Translation Pattern field) and the calling- or called-party transformation settings that you want to apply.

TIP Many new Cisco CallManager administrators get the translation and transformation terms confused. Cisco CallManager allows you to create translation patterns that contain both calling- and called-party transformation masks to modify the caller ID or dialed-number information. Translation patterns are usually used to transform dialed digits, so the called-party transformation masks are more frequently used.

Figure 11-12 *Translation Pattern Configuration Window*

Translation Pattern Configuration

Add a New Translation Pattern
Back to Find/List Translation Patterns

Translation Pattern: New
Status: Ready
Insert

Pattern Definition

Translation Pattern	
Partition	< None >
Description	
Numbering Plan*	North American Numbering Plan
Route Filter	< None >
Calling Search Space	< None >
MLPP Precedence	Default
Route Option	Route this pattern
	Block this pattern — Not Selected —
Provide Outside Dial Tone	Urgent Priority

Calling Party Transformations

Use Calling Party's External Phone Number Mask

Calling Party Transform Mask	
Prefix Digits (Outgoing Calls)	
Calling Line ID Presentation	Default

Practical Use of a Translation Pattern

Figure 11-13 shows an application for translation patterns. When the Direct Inward Dial (DID) range from the CO does not match the internal DN range, you can use a translation pattern to make the connection.

Figure 11-13 *Practical Translation Pattern Example*

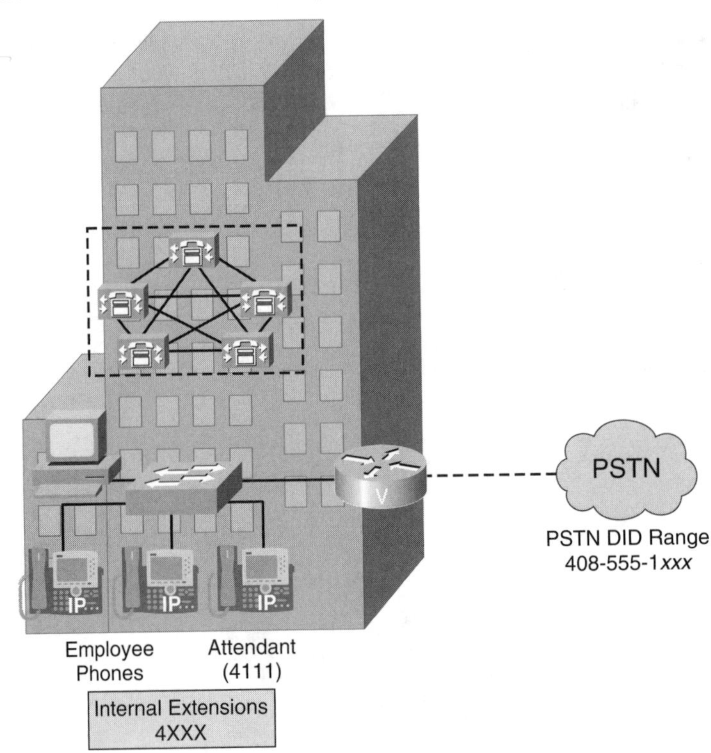

In Figure 11-13, a company has a PSTN DID range of 408-555-1*xxx*. However, all of the internal four-digit extensions begin with 4*xxx*. When the company receives an incoming call, the company could use DDIs to remove the 555 from the beginning of the number. However, the 1*xxx* extension still remains. Instead, the translation pattern could apply a 4XXX called-party transformation mask. This mask would convert the 1*xxx* external DID range to a 4*xxx* internal range. After Cisco CallManager applies the transformation mask, it reanalyzes the dialed number and directs it to the correct internal extension. So, to summarize (and simplify), the following configuration would be created:

Translation Pattern: 40855551XXX
Called-Party Transformation Mask: 4XXX
Resulting Phone Number: 4XXX

If a call came into the DID 4085551111, CallManager would convert the dialed digits to 4111.

Route Plan Report

The route plan report is a listing of all the Call Park numbers, Call Pickup numbers, conference numbers (such as Meet-Me numbers), route patterns, and translation patterns in the system. The route plan report allows you to view either a partial or full list and go directly to the associated configuration windows. You can accomplish this by selecting a route pattern, partition, route group, route list, Call Park number, Call Pickup number, conference number, or gateway.

The route plan report allows you to save report data into a comma-separated values (CSV) file that you can import into other applications (such as Microsoft Excel). The CSV file contains more detailed information than the web pages, including DNs for phones, route patterns, and translation patterns.

To generate a route plan report, use the **Route Plan > Route Plan Report** selection. The Route Plan Report window shown in Figure 11-14 appears. From here, you can either generate a route plan report to view in the web interface or click the **View in File** hyperlink to download the route plan as a CSV file.

Figure 11-14 *Generating a Route Plan Report*

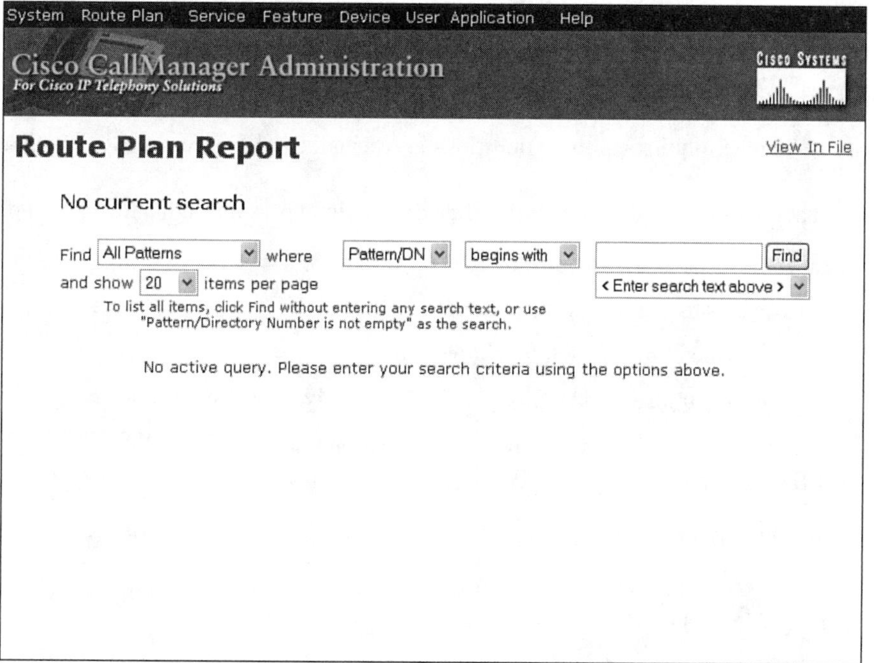

Summary

This chapter covered the design and configuration of an advanced Cisco CallManager route plan. The concepts started by using the route filter configurations to screen the 9.@ NANP route pattern. By default, the @ wildcard includes numbers that might be undesirable for a corporate entity. By using route filters, you can limit the number of patterns that are added when creating a PSTN dial-plan using the @ wildcard.

You can also use discard digit instructions (DDIs) to manipulate the digits sent to a destination, especially the PSTN. Most corporations have a number that is dialed (such as 9) to indicate an outside PSTN call. You can use DDIs to strip this access code before the call leaves to the PSTN. You can use DDIs in a number of circumstances to properly transform incoming or outgoing calls, many of which are seen in Chapters 12-14.

You can use calling- and called-party transformations to change caller ID information (calling) or dialed digits (called). These masks give you complete flexibility to transform this information however you see fit. Because you can apply them at nearly every level of the CallManager route plan, you can make differing modifications to dialed-number information depending on the gateway the CallManager decides to use to route the call. Translation patterns can also be added to the route plan for last resort modifications using calling- or called-party transformations.

Review Questions

You can find the solutions to these questions in Appendix A, "Answers to Review Questions."

1. What does Cisco CallManager do when dialed digits pass through a translation pattern?
   a. extends the call to the destination
   b. forwards the call to a route pattern
   c. selects the closest match to that pattern
   d. sends the transformed digits through digit analysis one more time
2. When DN 1111 calls and a calling transformation mask of 972555XXXX is applied, which CLID is sent?
   a. 1111
   b. 5551111
   c. 9725551111
   d. 19725551111

3. What are the final digits that Cisco CallManager sends when the discard digits instruction PreDot is applied to the 9808.5550150 pattern?

   a. 98085550150

   b. 5550150

   c. 95550150

   d. 8085550150

4. You have created a route filter called "Match 900 numbers" where you have defined a condition, "AREA-CODE == 900". What must you do to put this route filter into effect?

   a. You need to apply the route filter to a route pattern and select the allow or deny action.

   b. You need to apply the route filter to a route list and select the allow or deny action.

   c. You need to create a transformation pattern.

   d. Nothing needs to be done; the route filter takes effect as soon as it is inserted into the configuration.

5. You apply the DDI 11D@10D to the route pattern 16025551212. What digit(s) are discarded?

   a. 1

   b. 1602

   c. 1602555

   d. 555

6. You are editing the properties for the 9.@ route pattern. You apply a calling-party transformation mask of 8. What does this accomplish?

   a. The dialed digits are prefixed with an 8.

   b. The caller ID information is prefixed with an 8.

   c. The dialed digits are transformed into an 8.

   d. The caller ID information is transformed into an 8.

7. What information does a called-party transformation mask modify?

   a. the long-distance code information

   b. the dialed-digit information

   c. the caller ID information

   d. It depends where the mask is applied.

8. You apply a prefix digit of 99 and a calling-party transformation mask of 555XXXX under a PSTN route pattern. A user at extension 5123 dials a PSTN number; what information is displayed for the caller ID information on the external phone?

a. 555

b. 99555

c. 5555123

d. 995555123

e. 5559912

9. You have created a route pattern of 4xxx to reach extensions in another CallManager cluster. To properly forward the number, you have added a prefix-digit transformation of 8. In addition, you created a translation pattern of 8.xxxx that applies a PreDot DDI. What dialed-number information does the Cisco CallManager forward?

a. The dialed digits will forward to the other side as 4xxx.

b. The dialed digits will forward to the other side as 84xxx.

c. The dialed digits will forward to the other side as xxx.

d. The CallManager will play a fast busy signal.

10. Which transformation changes caller ID information?

a. translation patterns

b. calling-party transformations

c. called-party transformations

d. route patterns

This chapter covers the following topics:

- Defining call-distribution components and algorithms
- Describing how hunting differs from forwarding and how the Call Coverage feature extends hunting to allow final forwarding if hunting exhausts
- Configuring line groups, hunt lists, and hunt pilots to create a hunt group
- Configuring hunting with internal and external forwarding support specifications for busy, no answer, and no call coverage
- Given usage scenarios, determining the hunting and forwarding behavior that results

CHAPTER 12

Configuring Hunt Groups and Call Coverage

Many businesses have sales or service support departments that service inbound calls from customers. These businesses typically need several phone lines and a method to make the lines work together. If one representative is busy or not available, calls will be routed to other members of the group until it is answered or forwarded to an auto-attendant or voice mail. Hunt groups are the mechanisms that help these businesses manage inbound calls. A hunt group is a group of telephone lines that are associated with a common number. When a call comes in to the number associated with the hunt group, the call cycles through the group of lines until an available line is found. This process is known as hunting.

This chapter discusses how to configure hunt groups and enable the Call Coverage feature to ensure that the calling party will receive final forwarding treatment if hunting fails (that is, when no hunt party answers, either because the hunt has exhausted the list of hunt numbers or because it has timed out).

Call Distribution Components

Line groups, hunt lists, and hunt pilots work together to provide call-distribution capabilities in Cisco CallManager Administration. Call distribution is the ability of a caller to dial a number and have the call extended in an ordered manner to members of a group. An example of this functionality is a company 800 number to reach a company technical support department.

A line group contains directory numbers (DNs) and designates the order in which DNs are chosen.

A hunt list contains one or more prioritized line groups.

A hunt pilot is a number that is associated with a hunt list. The hunt pilot can be called directly (for example, to a technical support hotline for a company), or can be reached through forwarding (for example, a caller places a direct call to a technical support group member, and if that member is not available, the call is forwarded to the hunt pilot number). Figure 12-1 demonstrates the proper design of the Cisco CallManager call distribution components.

Figure 12-1 *Cisco CallManager Call Distribution Components*

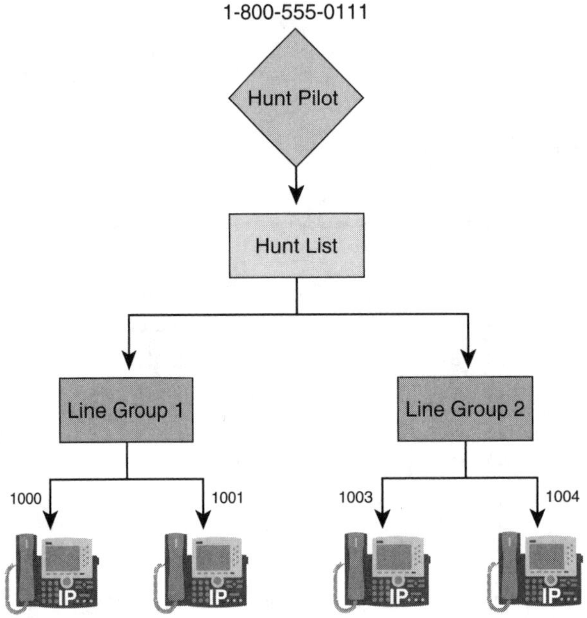

Line Groups

A line group allows you to designate the distribution mechanism where DNs are chosen.

Line groups contain the following components, shown in Figure 12-2:

- **Members**—Directory numbers that are in one of these states:
  - — **Idle**—Not serving any call
  - — **Available**—Serving an active call but able to accept new calls
  - — **Busy**—Unable to accept any calls
- **Distribution Algorithm**—A method for distributing calls to members.
- **Ring No Answer Reversion (RNAR) timeout value**—A mechanism for determining how to handle calls that go unanswered. The RNAR is a value, in seconds, after which Cisco CallManager will distribute a call to the next available or idle member of this line group or to the next line group if the call is not answered and if the first hunt option, **Try Next Member; Then, Try Next Group in Hunt List**, is chosen. The RNAR timeout applies at the line-group level to all members.

- **Hunt options**—The ability to roll past members who are busy, not available, or do not answer, continuing until the call is answered or options are exhausted.

Figure 12-2 *Line Group Components*

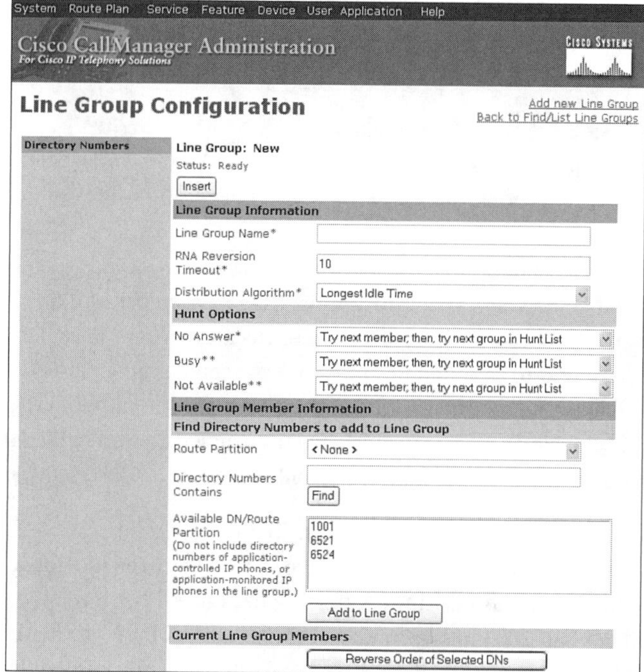

Cisco CallManager distributes a call to idle or available members of a line group based on the call-distribution algorithm and on the RNAR setting.

Call-Distribution Algorithms

Line groups contain an algorithm that controls how calls that come in on the hunt pilot are distributed to members, as follows:

- **Top down**—If you choose this distribution algorithm, Cisco CallManager distributes a call to idle or available members starting from the first idle or available member of a line group to the last idle or available member. Referring to Figure 12-3, a top-down distribution algorithm would extend the next call to 1000, then to 1001 (if 1000 was unavailable), then to 1002 (if 1001 was unavailable), then to 1003 (if 1002 was unavailable). The next incoming call would then be sent back to 1000 to start the process over again.

Figure 12-3 *Call-Distribution Algorithms*

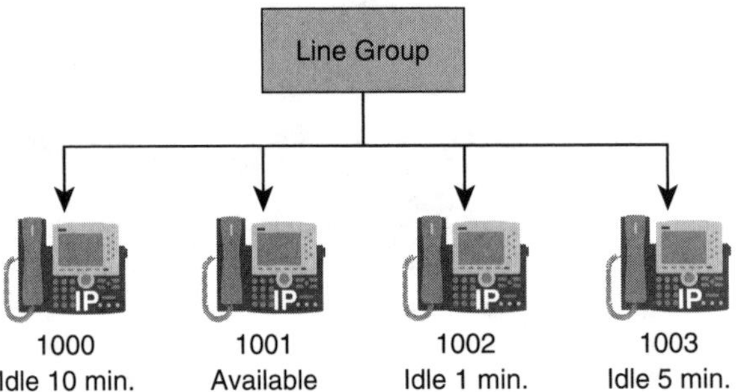

- **Circular**—If you choose this distribution algorithm, Cisco CallManager distributes a call to idle or available members starting from the (*n*+1)th member of a line group, where the *n*th member is the last member to receive a call. Because of this, Circular distribution is commonly referred to as round robin. If the *n*th member is the last member of a line group, Cisco CallManager distributes a call starting from the top of the line group. Referring to Figure 12-3, assume that Cisco CallManager extended the last call to 1002 (*n*). The next call that comes in on the hunt pilot number would go to 1003 (*n* + 1).
- **Longest idle time**—If you choose this distribution algorithm, Cisco CallManager distributes a call starting from the member of a line group who has been idle longest to the member who has been idle for the shortest time. Referring to Figure 12-3, assume that 1000 has been idle for 10 minutes and 1003 has been idle for 5 minutes. A longest idle time distribution mechanism would extend the call to 1000, and the next incoming call would go to 1003.
- **Broadcast**—If you choose this distribution algorithm, Cisco CallManager distributes a call to all idle or available members of a line group simultaneously.

Hunt Options

Hunt options configured in the line group apply to members in one of the three states: no answer, busy, or not available. Not available is a state triggered by the Do Not Disturb (DND) line state, covered later in the chapter. For a given distribution algorithm, the hunt option specifies where CallManager should distribute a call next if a member of a line group is busy, does not answer, or is not available. The Line Group Configuration window provides the following options for each of the three hunt options:

- **Try Next Member, Then, Try Next Group in Hunt List** (Default)—Distributes a call to idle or available members. If all lines respond with no answer (or busy or not available), try the next line group in a hunt list.

- **Try Next Member, But Do Not Go to Next Group**—Distributes a call to idle or available members. Stops hunting upon reaching the last member of the current line group.
- **Skip Remaining Members, and Go Directly to Next Group**—Skips the remaining members of current line group when the RNAR timeout value elapses for the first member (or first member is busy or not available). Hunting proceeds to the next line group in a hunt list.
- **Stop Hunting**—Stops hunting after trying to distribute a call to the first member of current line group if the member does not answer (or first busy member or first unavailable member).

TIP Distributing the call to other line groups can be useful in an environment where you have Tier 1 and Tier 2 tech support. If all the lines in Tier 1 are busy, the call can spill over to the Tier 2 group. In addition, the Tier 2 employees will see the call redirect information so they can answer the call appropriately.

Call Distribution Scenarios: Top-Down Example

Figure 12-4 shows an example of a line group (Line Group 1) with the following setup information:

- **Line Group 1**—Contains DNs 1000, 1001, and 1002
- **Distribution algorithm**—Top down
- **RNAR timeout**—10 seconds. After 10 seconds, Cisco CallManager will distribute a call to the next available or idle member of this line group or to the next line group if the call is not answered and if the first hunt option, Try Next Member; Then, Try Next Group in Hunt List, is chosen.
- **Hunt Options**—
  - **RNA**—Try Next Member; Then, Try Next Group in Hunt List
  - **Busy**—Try Next Member; Then, Try Next Group in Hunt List
  - **Not available**—Try Next Member; Then, Try Next Group in Hunt List

Figure 12-4 *Call Distribution Example*

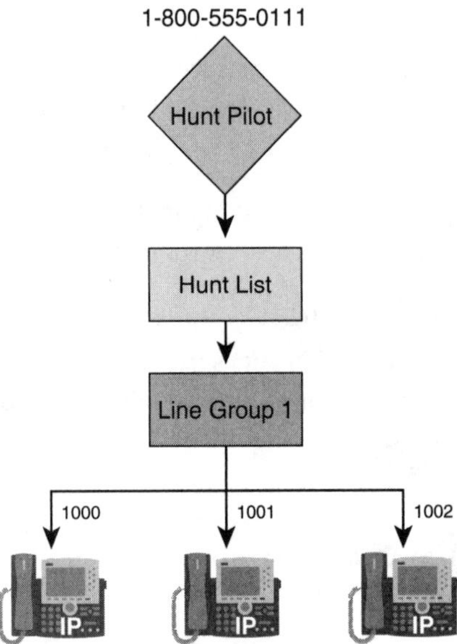

The call flow is as follows:

1. Caller calls hunt pilot 1-800-555-0155.
2. 1000 rings and is not answered for 10 seconds (RNAR timeout).
3. The call extends next to 1001, following the top-down algorithm and RNAR setting.
4. 1001 rings for 3 seconds.
5. 1001 is answered.

Hunting and Forwarding

Hunting differs from call forwarding, although both allow calls to be redirected. Hunting allows Cisco CallManager to extend a call to one or more lists of numbers, where each such list can specify a hunting order that is chosen from a configurable set of algorithms. When a call extends to a hunt party from these lists and the party fails to answer or is busy, hunting resumes with the next hunt party. (The next hunt party varies depending on the current hunt algorithm.) Hunting thus ignores the Call Forward No Answer (CFNA) or Call Forward Busy (CFB) settings for the attempted party.

Call forwarding allows detailed control as to how to extend (*divert* and *redirect* are equivalent terms for *extend*) a call when a called party fails to answer or is busy and hunting is not taking place. For example, if the CFNA setting for a line is set to a hunt pilot number, an unanswered call to that line diverts to the hunt pilot number and thus begins a hunt.

Starting with Cisco CallManager Release 4.1, Cisco CallManager offers the ability to redirect a call when hunting fails (that is, when hunting terminates without any hunt party answering, either because the list of hunt numbers exhausts or because the hunt process times out). If used, this final redirection constitutes a Call Forwarding action. Therefore, the Hunt Pilot Configuration window in Cisco CallManager Administration (choose **Route Plan > Route/Hunt > Hunt Pilot**) includes call forwarding configuration concepts that are similar to those found in the Directory Number Configuration window (Forward No Answer/Forward Busy).

In Cisco CallManager Release 4.0, hunting stops either when one of the hunt parties answers the call or when the hunt list is exhausted. When hunting stops due to exhaustion, the caller receives a reorder tone (or an equivalent announcement).

Configuring Line Groups, Hunt Lists, and Hunt Pilots

To access the line group, hunt list, and hunt pilot configuration windows in Cisco CallManager Administration Release 4.1, choose **Route Plan > Route/Hunt**, as shown in Figure 12-5.

Figure 12-5 *Hunt Configuration Menu*

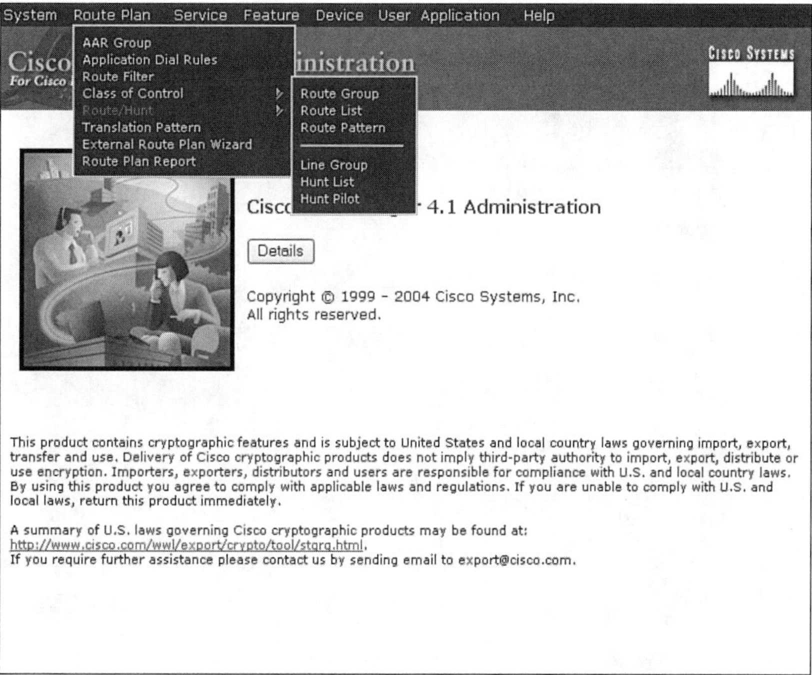
System Route Plan Service Feature Device User Application Help
AAR Group
Application Dial Rules
Route Filter
Class of Control
Route/Hunt
Translation Pattern
External Route Plan Wizard
Route Plan Report
Route Group
Route List
Route Pattern
Line Group
Hunt List
Hunt Pilot
Cisco Systems
4.1 Administration
Details
Copyright © 1999 - 2004 Cisco Systems, Inc.
All rights reserved.
This product contains cryptographic features and is subject to United States and local country laws governing import, export, transfer and use. Delivery of Cisco cryptographic products does not imply third-party authority to import, export, distribute or use encryption. Importers, exporters, distributors and users are responsible for compliance with U.S. and local country laws. By using this product you agree to comply with applicable laws and regulations. If you are unable to comply with U.S. and local laws, return this product immediately.
A summary of U.S. laws governing Cisco cryptographic products may be found at:
http://www.cisco.com/wwl/export/crypto/tool/stqrg.html.
If you require further assistance please contact us by sending email to export@cisco.com.

When configuring hunting, follow this general process:

Step 1 Create the line groups, add members, and configure the distribution algorithm and hunt options.

Step 2 Create the hunt list and add the line groups.

Step 3 Create the hunt pilot, associate the hunt list with the hunt pilot, and configure hunt forward settings.

These steps are covered in more detail in the following topics.

Configuring Line Groups

The general process for configuring a line group follows. The DNs that will become the members of the line group must already exist in the database before you can complete this procedure.

Step 1 Choose **Route Plan > Route/Hunt > Line Group**.

Step 2 Click **Add a New Line Group**. The Line Group Configuration window shown in Figure 12-6 appears.

Figure 12-6 *Line Group Configuration Window*

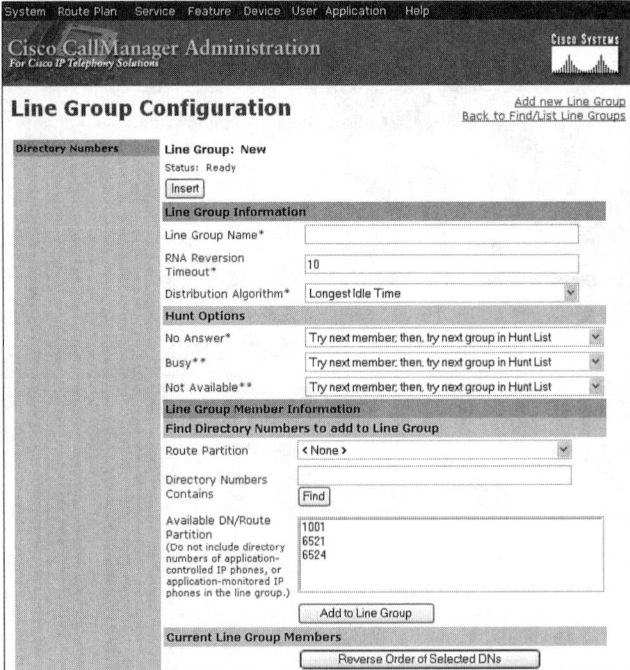

Step 3 Enter a name in the **Line Group Name** field. The name can contain up to 50 alphanumeric characters and can contain any combination of spaces, periods (.), hyphens (-), and underscore characters (_). Ensure that each line group name is unique to the route plan.

Step 4 Configure the distribution algorithm, hunt options, and RNAR timeout as desired, or leave them at their default values.

Step 5 Click **Insert**.

To add members to the line group, follow this procedure:

Step 1 If you need to locate a DN, choose a route partition from the **Route Partition** drop-down list, enter a search string in the **Directory Number Contains** field, and click **Find**. To find all DNs that belong to a partition, leave the **Directory Number Contains** field blank and click **Find**.

Step 2 A list of matching DNs is displayed in the **Available DN/Route Partition** pane.

Step 3 In **the Available DN/Route Partition** pane, select a DN to add and click **Add to Line Group** to move it to the **Selected DN/Route Partition** pane. Repeat this step for each member that you want to add to this line group.

Step 4 In the **Selected DN/Route Partition** pane, choose the order in which the new DNs will be accessed in this line group. To change the order, click a DN and use the up and down arrows to the right of the pane.

Step 5 Click **Update** to add the new DNs and to update the DN order for this line group.

TIP A single DN can be a member of multiple Line Groups

Notice the RNA Reversion Timeout (RNAR), which defaults to 10 seconds. This is the time, in seconds, after which Cisco CallManager will distribute a call to the next available or idle member of a line group or to the next line group if the call is not answered and if the first hunt option, **Try Next Member; Then, Try Next Group in Hunt List**, is chosen.

Configuring Hunt Lists

To add a hunt list in Cisco CallManager Administration 4.1, follow these steps:

Step 1 Choose **Route Plan > Route/Hunt > Hunt List**.

Step 2 Click **Add a New Hunt List**.

Step 3 In the **Hunt List Name** field, enter a name. The name can comprise up to 50 alphanumeric characters and can contain any combination of spaces, periods (.), hyphens (-), and underscore characters (_). Ensure that each hunt list name is unique to the route plan.

Step 4 Choose a Cisco CallManager group from the drop-down list. The group must already exist in the database; you cannot create a new group from this window.

Step 5 To add this hunt list, click **Insert**. The Hunt List Configuration window shown in Figure 12-7 appears.

Figure 12-7 *Hunt List Configuration Window*

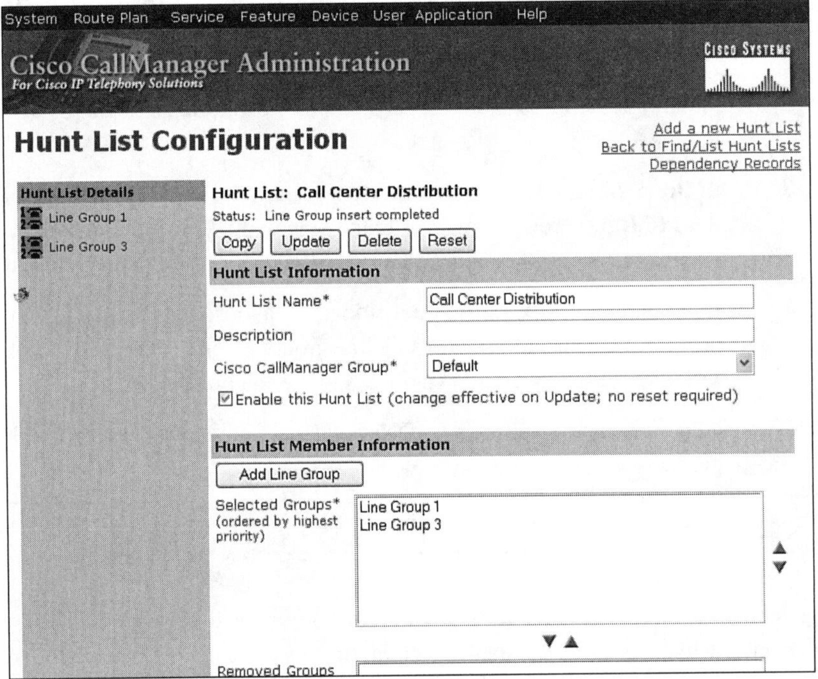

NOTE After clicking the **Insert** button, a popup message reminds you that you must add at least one line group to this hunt list for it to accept calls.

Step 6 The Hunt List Configuration window displays the newly added hunt list.

Step 7 Add at least one line group to the new hunt list. To add a line group, click **Add Line Group**. The Hunt List Detail Configuration window is displayed.

Step 8 From the **Line Group** drop-down list, choose a line group to add to the hunt list.

Step 9 To add the line group, click **Insert**. The line group name is displayed in the Hunt List Details list on the left side of the window.

Step 10 To add more line groups to this list, click **Add Line Group** and repeat Step 6 and Step 7.

Step 11 When you are finished adding line groups to the hunt list, click **Update**.

Step 12 Click **Reset** to reset the hunt list. When the popup windows are displayed, click **OK**.

Cisco CallManager accesses line groups in the order in which they are shown in the hunt list. You change the access order of line groups by selecting a line group from the **Selected Groups** pane and clicking the up or down arrow on the right side of the pane to move the line group up or down in the list.

Configuring Hunt Pilots

Before you create a hunt pilot, ensure that the following items are configured in Cisco CallManager:

- Hunt list
- Partition (unless you are using None)
- Route filter (unless you are using None)

You can then perform the following steps to configure a hunt pilot:

Step 1 Choose **Route Plan > Route/Hunt > Hunt Pilot**.

Step 2 Click **Add a New Hunt Pilot**. The Hunt Pilot Configuration window shown in Figure 12-8 appears.

Figure 12-8 *Hunt Pilot Configuration Window*

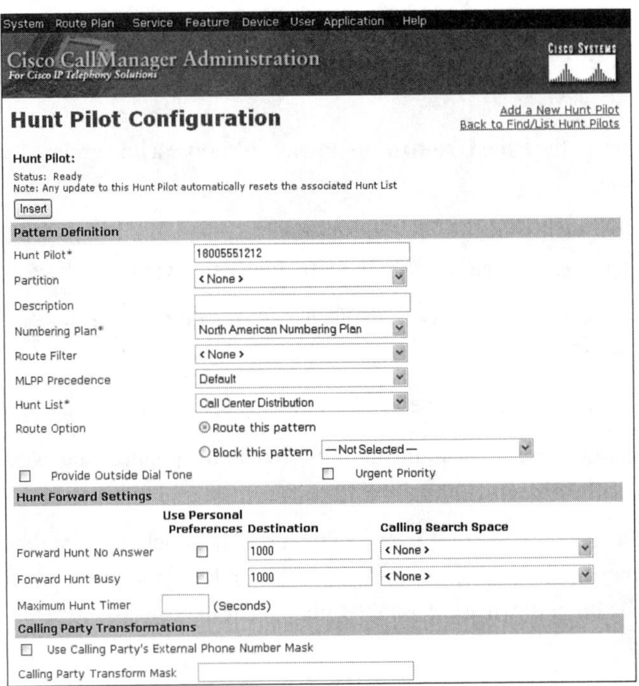

Step 3 Enter the hunt pilot number in the **Hunt Pilot** number field.

Step 4 Assign the hunt pilot to a hunt list using the **Hunt List** drop-down menu.

Step 5 (Optional) Assign the hunt pilot to a partition and configure other settings, such as hunt forward, as desired.

> **NOTE** If you do not configure Hunt Forward Settings for Forward Hunt No Answer and Forward Hunt Busy, CallManager returns a reorder tone if all members assigned to the hunt pilot are unavailable.

> **TIP** The **Use Personal Preferences** check box under the Hunt Forward Settings enables the Call Forward No Coverage settings in the Directory Number Configuration page for the original called number that forwarded the call to this hunt pilot. If checked, CallManager ignores the Destination and Calling Search Space settings configured under the hunt pilot.

The Hunt Pilot Configuration window also allows you to define a Maximum Hunt Timer (in seconds), which dictates the length of time a call to the hunt pilot number will search through members. This setting overrides the Ring No Answer Reversion (RNAR) setting configured under the line group. For example, if you have three members of a line group configured for a RNAR setting of 10 seconds per member, the call hunts for a maximum of 30 seconds before returning a status of No Answer from the line group. However, if you have defined a Maximum Hunt Timer of 25 seconds on the Hunt Pilot Configuration window (shown in Figure 12-8), the call would stop hunting through the line group after moving through the first two members (10 seconds each) and ringing for 5 seconds on the third member.

Summary

This chapter covered the design and configuration of a Cisco CallManager hunt group. You can use hunt groups to define a group of DNs to search through for an incoming call. This is useful in an extraordinarily large number of environments, from receptionist pools for incoming calls to technical support help desk representatives.

Configuring hunt groups is very similar to configuring the CallManager route plan. The configuration is performed from the bottom up, first starting by adding member DNs to a line group and choosing the distribution algorithm. You can then group one or more line groups into a hunt list, which is nothing more than an ordered list of line groups to which CallManager should distribute calls. You will finally create the hunt pilot, which defines a trigger DN and points to the hunt list that should receive the incoming calls.

Review Questions

You can find the solutions to these questions in Appendix A, "Answers to Review Questions."

1. In addition to checking the **Use Personal Preferences** check box in the Hunt Forward Settings section of the Hunt Pilot Configuration window, what else must be configured to enable final forwarding for a call that is forwarded to the hunt pilot?

   a. maximum hunt timer and RNAR timers in the Line Group Configuration window

   b. the Call Forward No Coverage settings for the original called number that forwarded the call to the hunt pilot

   c. the **Destination and Calling Search Space** fields in the Hunt Forward Settings section of the Hunt Pilot Configuration window

   d. the Forward Busy and Forward No Answer settings for the original called number that forwarded the call to the hunt pilot

2. Assume a line group with five members: party 1 (DN 5001), party 2 (DN 5002), party 3 (DN 5003), party 4 (DN 5004), and party 5 (DN 5005). The top-down distribution algorithm is applied to the line group. Party 3 answered the last call that came in on the hunt pilot. To which party will Cisco CallManager extend the next call that comes into the hunt pilot?

   a. 1

   b. 2

   c. 3

   d. 4

   e. 5

3. A hunt group has been configured with a maximum hunt timer of 15 seconds on the Hunt Pilot Configuration window. However, the line group with five members has been configured with a RNA reversion timeout value of 5 seconds. When an incoming call comes in for the hunt group, how long will the hunting process occur before the call is forwarded?

   a. 5 seconds

   b. 15 seconds

   c. 25 seconds

   d. 40 seconds

4. Which of these components are absolutely required to configure a hunt group? (Select all that apply.)

   a. hunt pilot

   b. hunt list

   c. line group

   d. route list

   e. gateway

   f. route pattern

5. If a line group member DN is marked as an available line, what state is it in?

   a. It is not serving a call at this time.

   b. It is serving a call but can accept a new call.

   c. It is serving a call but cannot accept a new call.

   d. It cannot accept any calls.

6. Which of the following call distribution algorithms rings all members of the line group at the same time?

   a. multicast

   b. broadcast

   c. group

   d. circular

7. You are looking through a hunt group configuration in Cisco CallManager. Under the line group configuration window, you notice that the **No Answer** hunt option is configured with the **Stop Hunting** selection. What does this cause?

   a. The CallManager will hunt to the first member in the line group and stop if the member is unavailable.

   b. The CallManager will hunt through the current line group and stop if the members are unavailable.

   c. The CallManager will hunt through all the line groups and stop if the members are unavailable.

   d. The CallManager will not hunt through the line group, but will divert the call to the call forward settings.

8. A hunt pilot receives a call and passes it down to the hunt list, which distributes the call to three members of a line group. The call returns from the line group with a busy status. Under the call forwarding section of the hunt pilot, the **Use Personal Preferences** check box is checked for both the **No Answer** and **Busy** fields. How does the CallManager handle the call?

   a. The call is forwarded to the destination defined under the Forward Hunt Busy section of the hunt pilot.

   b. The call is forwarded to the destination defined under the Call Forward Busy section of the calling party.

   c. The call is forwarded to the destination defined under the Call Forward Busy section of the original called party.

   d. The call is forwarded to the destination defined under the Call Forward No Coverage section of the calling party.

   e. The call is forwarded to the destination defined under the Call Forward No Coverage section of the original called party.

9. When configuring a CallManager hunt group, which option should you configure first?
   a. member DNs
   b. line group
   c. hunt list
   d. hunt pilot
10. By default, how are calls routed through a hunt group?
   a. Calls match the hunt pilot DN and hunt through the members listed in the first line group defined in the hunt list.
   b. Calls match the hunt pilot DN and hunt through the members listed in all line groups defined in the hunt list.
   c. Calls match the hunt pilot DN and hunt to the first member listed in the first line group defined in the hunt list.
   d. Calls match the hunt pilot DN and forward to the defined number in the call coverage area.

This chapter covers the following topics:

- Defining Class of Service as it relates to users of a phone system
- Defining partitions and calling search spaces and identifying the components of each
- Configuring partitions and calling search spaces in Cisco CallManager to assign calling privileges to users and devices
- Defining time-of-day routing and identifying its uses and components
- Configuring time-of-day routing to control call routing based on the time of day, day of week, and day of year when the call was made

CHAPTER 13

Implementing Telephony Call Restrictions and Control

An important dial plan consideration is the assignment and enforcement of calling privileges. You might want company executives to have different calling privileges than receptionists, or employee phones to have different calling privileges than lobby phones. You might also want to place further restrictions on the times that these privileges are available, for example, by allowing international calls to be placed only during business hours to prevent unauthorized use after hours. Partitions, calling search spaces, and time-of-day routing are the primary class of control components that enable you to assign and enforce calling privileges.

This chapter discusses how to deploy calling restrictions and control by using Cisco CallManager partitions, calling search spaces, and time-of-day routing.

Class of Service Overview

Class of Service (CoS) is a collection of calling permissions and restrictions that you assign to individual users or groups of users. (The terms *calling permissions* and *calling restrictions* are used interchangeably in this chapter.)

> **NOTE** CoS as it applies to telephony networks holds a completely different meaning than its application in quality of service (QoS). CoS in telephony means the implementation of calling restrictions, whereas CoS in data networking means the application of a data link layer marking in a data frame.

Examples of class-of-service permissions are as follows:

- One class of users can place toll calls during normal business hours, but not at other times.
- Lobby phone users can dial the local emergency numbers and campus extensions, but cannot dial local, long-distance, or international numbers.
- Receptionists can dial anywhere within the company and all local area codes, but cannot dial long-distance or international numbers.
- Executives can call anywhere except 900 area codes.

Cisco CallManager uses partitions, calling search spaces, and time-of-day routing to implement class-of-service restrictions.

Partitions and Calling Search Spaces Overview

A partition is a group of directory numbers (DNs) with similar accessibility. A calling search space defines which partitions are accessible to a particular device. A device can call only the DNs located in the partitions that are part of its calling search space.

A partition comprises a logical grouping of directory numbers (DNs) and route patterns with similar reachability characteristics. Items that are placed in partitions include DNs and route patterns (or anything else that has a directory number). For simplicity, partition names usually reflect their characteristics, such as "NYLongDistancePT," "NY911PT," and so on.

A calling search space is an ordered list of partitions that Cisco CallManager digit analysis looks at before a telephone call is placed. Calling search spaces then determine the partitions that calling devices, such as Cisco IP Phones, Cisco IP SoftPhones, and gateways, can reach when attempting to complete a call. If a device attempts to reach a route pattern or DN that is not contained in one of the partitions in its calling search space, it receives a fast busy signal (or a prerecorded message played by the annunciator service).

Items that can be placed in partitions all have a dialable pattern, which includes phone lines, route patterns, translation patterns, computer telephony integration (CTI) route group lines, CTI port lines, voice-mail ports, and Meet-Me conference numbers. In short, you can place absolutely *anything* that has a directory number into a partition. To do this, you group common numbers together. For example, you could create an internal number partition (perhaps named INTERNAL_PT) that contains all numbers internal to the organization, an emergency partition (named EMERGENCY_PT) that contains route patterns representing emergency numbers such as 911, and a local PSTN partition (named LOCAL_PT) that contains route patterns representing local PSTN numbers. By doing this, you have grouped the numbers to assign the calling restrictions. By default, everything belongs to the <NONE> partition (or no partition assignment), which is why there are no calling restrictions.

Conversely, you can assign a calling search space to all devices capable of dialing a call, such as telephones, telephone lines, gateways, and applications (via their CTI route groups or voice-mail ports). The calling search space contains nothing more than an ordered list of partitions. When you assign a calling search space to a device, that device can reach whatever is in the partitions listed in the calling search space. For example, you could create a calling search space named INT_EMG_CSS that contains just the internal and emergency partitions (INTERNAL_PT and

EMERGENCY_PT mentioned in the previous paragraph). By assigning this to an IP Phone, you will have restricted it to only dialing internal extensions and emergency numbers.

NOTE Regardless of the calling search space assigned, all devices are able to reach any number assigned to the <NONE> partition. Because of this, Cisco recommends that you should never leave numbers assigned to the <NONE> partition.

As shown in Figure 13-1, the DNs of lobby phones and break room phones are placed into partition A. Partitions B, C, D, E, and F contain the route patterns to reach local numbers, long-distance numbers, international numbers, and company extensions.

Figure 13-1 *Partition and Calling Search Space Example*

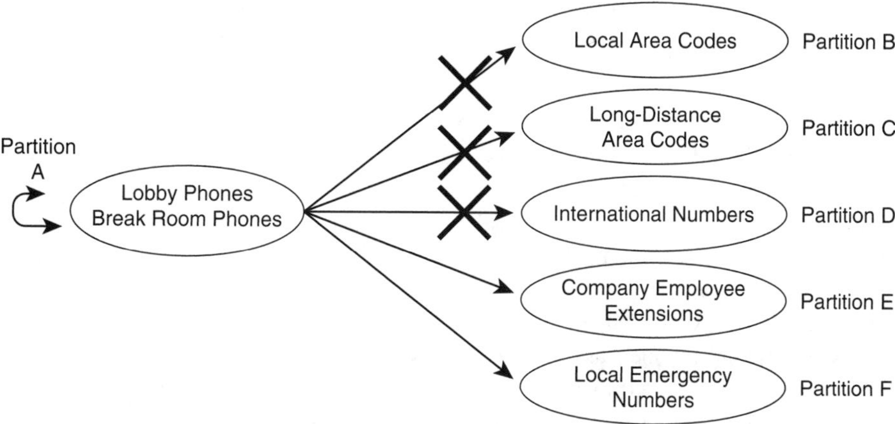

The calling search space for the lobby phones includes only the partitions containing the company extensions and the local emergency numbers. Therefore, a lobby phone located in partition A has a calling search space containing partition A, E, and F and can dial only company destinations, including the break room (in other words, devices belonging to the same partition) and local emergency numbers (for example, 911 in the United States).

NOTE In addition to assigning calling search spaces to the phone or directory number, you can assign calling search spaces to the call forwarding fields of an IP Phone (call forward busy, call forward no answer, and so on). This allows you to place different calling restrictions beyond normal calling when a user forwards their phone.

Calling Search Spaces Applied to Gateways and Intercluster Trunks

In addition to applying calling search spaces to the IP Phones in the network, you must also apply them to the gateways and intercluster trunks. By default, the gateways and intercluster trunks of the network are assigned a calling search space of <NONE>. This calling search space can only access the directory numbers and route patterns assigned to the <NONE> partition.

> **TIP** The default state of ALL devices in the CallManager cluster is the following:
>
> Partition: <NONE>
>
> Calling Search Space: <NONE>
>
> Even though it might appear as though these mean "no assignment," there is an unconfigurable partition and calling search space called <NONE>. The <NONE> calling search space only has access to the devices in the <NONE> partition. As you begin to assign directory numbers and route patterns to partitions other than <NONE>, any devices with the <NONE> calling search space (default) will lose access to the reassigned numbers.

The previously mentioned tip warrants special consideration when dealing with gateways and intercluster trunks. Because these devices are assigned the default calling search space of <NONE>, they will begin to lose access to the cluster directory numbers as you assign them to other partitions. The directory numbers that the gateways and intercluster trunks have access to affect inbound calls to the cluster.

For example, you could create a calling search space named INT_LOC_CSS that only allowed access to directory numbers assigned to the Internal (INTERNAL_PT) and Local PSTN (LOCAL_PT) partitions. If this INT_LOCAL_CSS calling search space were applied to an Intercluster Trunk to a remote CallManager cluster, any calls coming *inbound* from the remote cluster would only be able to reach the internal and local PSTN extensions. This feature is useful when you do not have administrative control of the remote cluster but have the need to configure call restrictions into your cluster from the remote devices.

> **NOTE** This feature works identically for gateway devices configured in the CallManager cluster. The calling search space applied to gateway devices affect calls coming *inbound* (into the cluster) from the gateway. It does not affect calls outbound to the gateway from the devices in the cluster.

Partition Configuration

To configure partitions, choose **Route Plan** > **Class of Control** > **Partition**. When the Find and List Partition window appears, click the **Add a New Partition** link. The Partition Configuration window that is shown in Figure 13-2 appears. From here, you can add a maximum of 75 partitions at a time using the following syntax:

<partitionName>**,** <description>

Figure 13-2 *Partition Configuration Window*

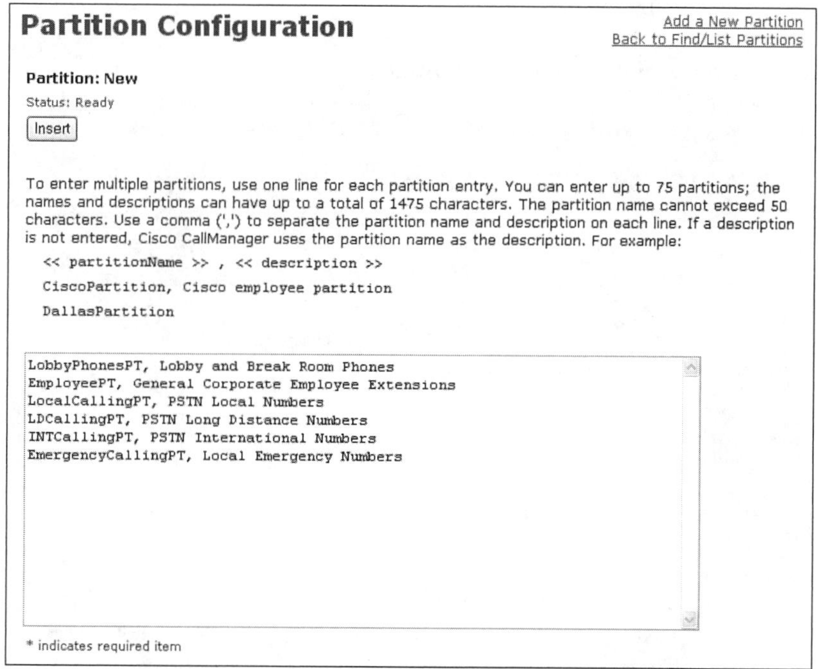

Partition Configuration
Add a New Partition
Back to Find/List Partitions
Partition: New
Status: Ready
Insert
To enter multiple partitions, use one line for each partition entry. You can enter up to 75 partitions; the names and descriptions can have up to a total of 1475 characters. The partition name cannot exceed 50 characters. Use a comma (',') to separate the partition name and description on each line. If a description is not entered, Cisco CallManager uses the partition name as the description. For example:
<< partitionName >> , << description >>
CiscoPartition, Cisco employee partition
DallasPartition
LobbyPhonesPT, Lobby and Break Room Phones
EmployeePT, General Corporate Employee Extensions
LocalCallingPT, PSTN Local Numbers
LDCallingPT, PSTN Long Distance Numbers
INTCallingPT, PSTN International Numbers
EmergencyCallingPT, Local Emergency Numbers
* indicates required item

> **NOTE** **Class of Control** is a new submenu item under the **Route Plan** menu in Release 4.1 of Cisco CallManager. The **Class of Control** submenu includes partitions, calling search spaces, and time-of-day routing items.

Cisco CallManager Administration requires that you enter the partition name. However, adding a description for the partition can be useful for documentation purposes.

Using partitions allows you to group DNs with similar characteristics together. For example, the network administrator at ABC Company must allow certain individuals to call the DNs in the 1*xxx* and 2*xxx* ranges. Before assigning the DNs to a partition, the administrator must first configure the partitions using the Partition Configuration window in Cisco CallManager Administration. The administrator could add the necessary partitions using the following format:

- DN_1XXX, Directory Numbers 1000-1999
- DN_2XXX, Directory Numbers 2000-2999

After the administrator adds the partitions, DNs must be assigned. To do this, the administrator must enter the configuration mode of the telephones or route patterns that have the DNs, proceed to the Directory Number Configuration window, and choose the newly created partition from the menu, as shown in Figure 13-3.

Figure 13-3 *Assigning a Directory Number to a Partition*

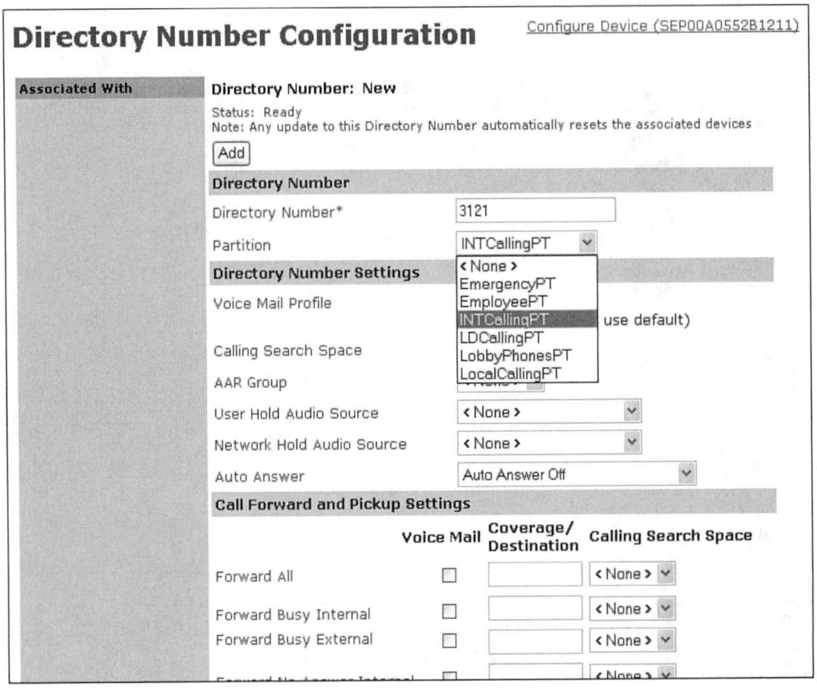

Calling Search Space Configuration

After configuring the partitions, you can configure the calling search spaces that contain a prioritized list of the available partitions. Figure 13-4 shows the Calling Search Space Configuration window in Cisco CallManager Administration (choose **Route Plan > Class of Control > Calling Search Space**).

You can use the arrows between the **Available Partitions** and **Selected Partitions** panes to choose the partitions that you want to add to the calling search space. You can reorder partitions by using the arrows to the right of the **Selected Partitions** panes. To reduce call-processing time, place the partitions with the most frequently used numbers at the top of the Selected Partitions list with the exception of critical partitions. Emergency number partitions or partitions containing blocked numbers are usually placed near the top of the list.

Figure 13-4 *Calling Search Space Configuration Window*

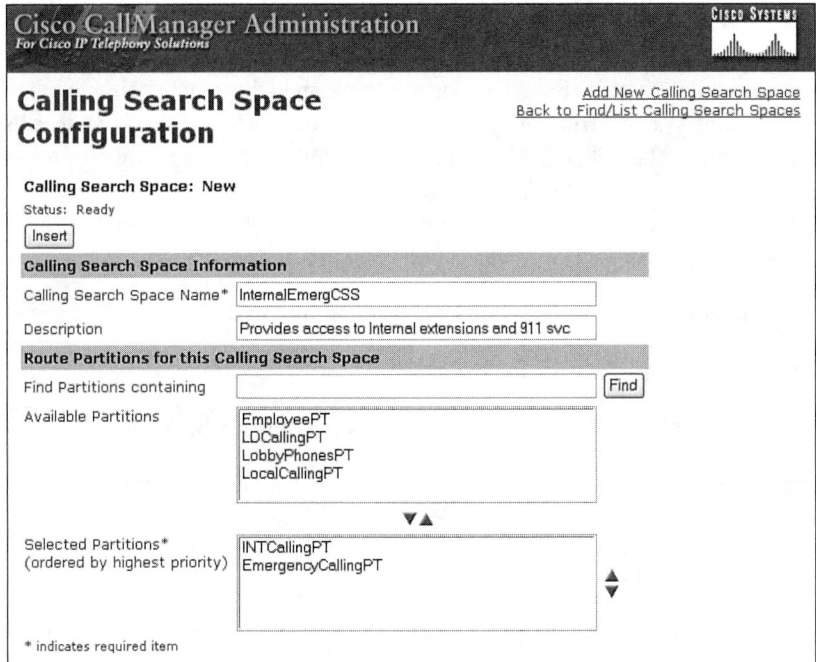

The calling search space gives you the ability to place any number of calling restrictions on the IP telephony network. For example, to restrict access to the 1XXX and 2XXX partitions, the network administrator from the ABC Company must create a calling search space that is named "1XXX_Only_CSS" and add the DN_1XXX partition to this calling search space. The administrator then creates another calling search space named "2XXX_Only_CSS" and adds the DN_2XXX partition to this calling search space. Finally, the administrator creates a calling search space named "All_DNs_CSS" and adds both the DN_1XXX and DN_2XXX partitions to this calling search space.

After configuring the calling search spaces, the administrator assigns them to the various network devices. For example, telephone A is assigned the 1XXX_Only_CSS calling search space, which means that telephone A can call only the DNs that are assigned to the partition DN_1XXX. By assigning telephone B to the 2XXX_Only_CSS calling search space, the administrator restricts telephone B from calling any numbers outside of the DN_2XXX partition. If the administrator assigns telephone C to the All_DNs_CSS calling search space, telephone C can call the DNs that are assigned to both partitions DN_1XXX and DN_2XXX.

Time-of-Day Routing Overview

Time-of-day routing, introduced in Release 4.1 of Cisco CallManager, routes calls to different locations based on the time of day when a call is made. For example, during business hours, calls can route to a pilot number (linked to a hunt group), and after hours, calls can go directly to a voice-messaging system. Time-of-day routing also provides the ability to route calls based on the time-of-day or based on a specific day, such as December 25. The following are practical applications of how you could use time-of-day calling restrictions:

- Allow international calls only during office hours.
- Block international calls based on local caller's time zone.
- Block international calls on holidays.
- Allow international calls only during office hours of the caller's time zone.
- Implement a least-cost routing system by choosing the cheapest provider for a specific time of day.
- Route calls after hours to a home number or voice mail.
- Any application where you want to control the calling search space based on the time of the day.

Time-of-day settings are assigned to partitions. After the administrator has configured the time-of-day settings and assigned them to partitions, the time-of-day feature filters the calling search space through time-of-day settings that are defined for each partition in the calling search space.

The time-of-day feature is applied when a called number is validated. Cisco CallManager filters the partitions contained in the calling search space of the originating device, and the called number is validated against this filtered calling search space. Keep in mind that you can assign a calling search space to a voice gateway. This could, as an example, allow you to reroute all incoming calls from the PSTN to the IP telephony network based on time-of-day restrictions.

To implement time-of-day routing in Cisco CallManager, you must understand the concept of time periods and time schedules.

Time Periods

A time period comprises a start time and end time. The available start times and end times are 15-minute intervals on a 24-hour clock, from 00:00 to 24:00. In addition, a time period requires definition of a repetition interval. Repetition intervals are the days of the week (for example, Monday through Friday) or a day of the calendar year (for example, June 9).

The following are examples of four time periods:

- Time period *weekdayhrs_TP* as 08:00 to 17:00 from Monday to Friday.
- Time period *weekendhrs_TP* as 08:00 to 17:00 on Saturday and Sunday.
- Time period *newyears_TP* as 00:00 to 24:00 on January 1.
- Time period *noofficehours_TP* as no hours on Saturday and Sunday. For this time period, the associated partition is not active on Saturday and Sunday.

Time Schedule

A time schedule consists of a group of defined time periods that the administrator associates with a partition.

After the administrator selects a time period for association with a time schedule, the time period remains available for association with other time schedules.

Figure 13-5 shows an example of a time period *RegEmployees_TS* with time periods *weekdayhrs_TP*, *newyears_TP* and *noofficehours_TP* associated with it.

Figure 13-5 *Time Schedule Example*

Time Periods	Start–End	Repetition
weekdayhrs_TP	08:00–17:00	M–F
weekendhrs_TP	08:00–17:00	Sat–Sun
newyears_TP	00:00–24:00	January 1
noofficehours_TP		Sat–Sun

Time Schedule	Time Periods
RegEmployees_TS	*weekdayhrs_TP* *newyears_TP* *noofficehours_TP*

Partition	Time Schedule
CiscoAustin_PT	*RegEmployees_TP*

The administrator associates time schedules with a partition. Partitions contained within the calling search space are available based on time-of-day settings. Cisco CallManager filters the calling search space through the time-of-day settings defined for each of the partitions in the calling search space.

Time-of-Day Routing Effect on Users

If time-of-day routing is enforced, users cannot set certain Call Forward All (CFA) numbers at certain times. For example, the user A calling search space for forwarding includes a time-of-day-configured partition that allows international calls from 8:00 to 17:00 (5:00 p.m.). User A wants to configure his CFA number to an international number. User A can set this number only during the 8:00 to 17:00 time period because, outside these hours, the system does not find the international number in the partition that is used to validate the CFA number.

If the user sets the CFA during office hours when it is allowed, and the user receives a call outside office hours, the caller hears a fast busy signal.

In addition, users cannot reach DNs in some partitions that are configured for time-of-day routing and that are not active during the time of the call, depending upon the configuration of partitions. Users will not be able to reach the route or translation patterns in partitions configured with time-of-day routing that are not active at the time of the call.

Configuring Time-of-Day Routing

To access the time-of-day routing configuration components, choose **Route Plan > Class of Control > Time Period** or **Route Plan > Class of Control > Time Schedule**. Figure 13-6 illustrates these options.

Figure 13-6 *Time-of-Day Routing Configuration*

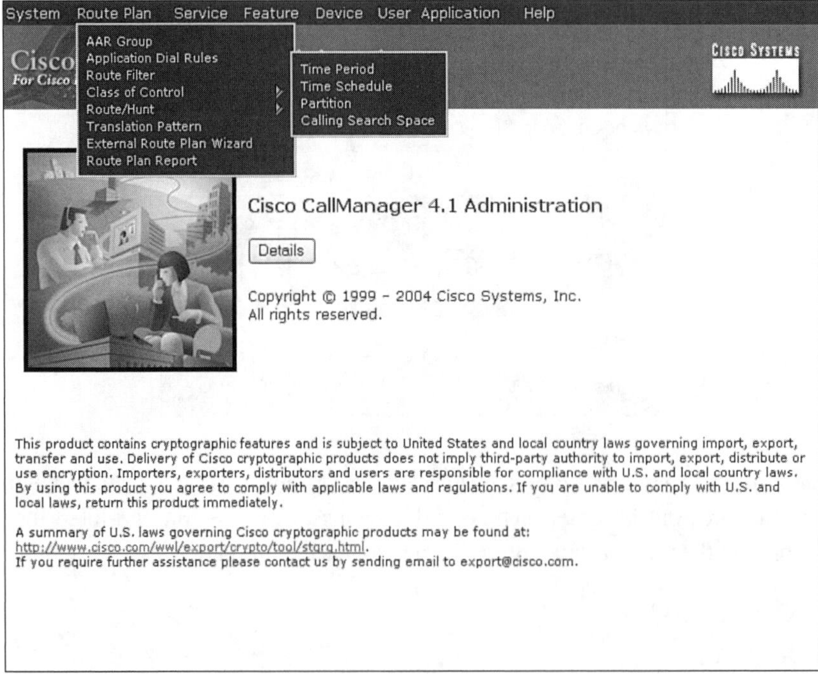
System Route Plan Service Feature Device User Application Help
AAR Group
Application Dial Rules
Route Filter
Class of Control
Route/Hunt
Translation Pattern
External Route Plan Wizard
Route Plan Report
Time Period
Time Schedule
Partition
Calling Search Space
Cisco Systems
Cisco CallManager 4.1 Administration
Details
Copyright © 1999 - 2004 Cisco Systems, Inc.
All rights reserved.
This product contains cryptographic features and is subject to United States and local country laws governing import, export, transfer and use. Delivery of Cisco cryptographic products does not imply third-party authority to import, export, distribute or use encryption. Importers, exporters, distributors and users are responsible for compliance with U.S. and local country laws. By using this product you agree to comply with applicable laws and regulations. If you are unable to comply with U.S. and local laws, return this product immediately.
A summary of U.S. laws governing Cisco cryptographic products may be found at:
http://www.cisco.com/wwl/export/crypto/tool/stqrg.html.
If you require further assistance please contact us by sending email to export@cisco.com.

To configure time-of-day routing, follow these steps:

Step 1 Create the individual time periods.

Step 2 Create the time schedule and assign the time periods to it.

Step 3 Assign the time schedule to a partition.

Configuring Time Periods

To add and configure a time period, follow this procedure:

Step 1 In the menu bar, choose **Route Plan > Class of Control > Time Period**.

Step 2 Click **Add a New Time Period**.

Step 3 Enter the time period name, start time, end time, and repetition interval.

Step 4 To add the new time period, click **Insert**.

The message "Status: Insert completed" appears.

Step 5 To add more time periods, click **Add a New Time Period** and repeat this procedure.

Figure 13-7 shows an example of a time period named OfficeHoursTP, a start time of 08:00, an end time of 17:00, and a weekly repetition interval of every Monday through Friday.

Figure 13-7 *Time Period Configuration Window*

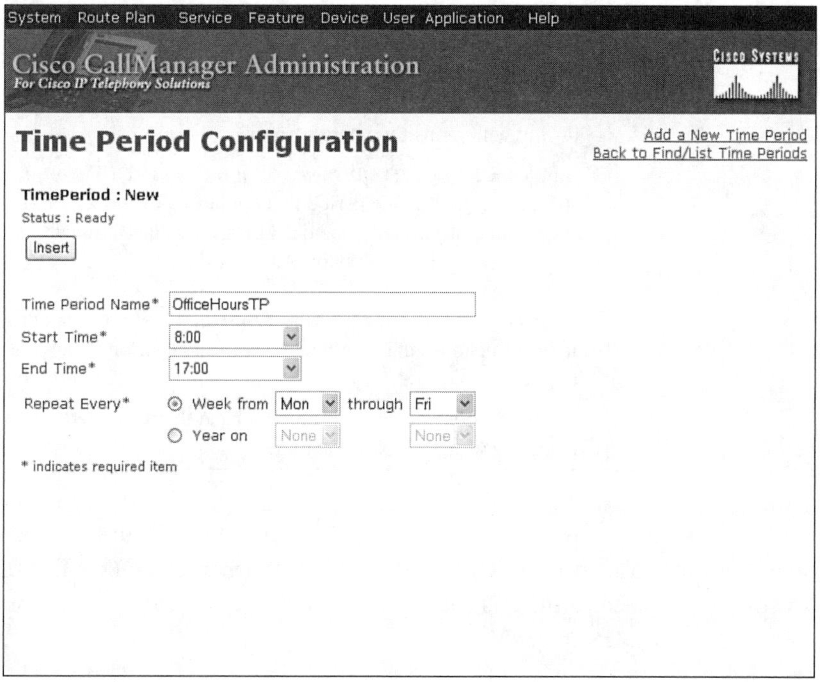

Table 13-1 provides a list of options available to you when implementing time periods.

Table 13-1 *Time Period Options*

Parameter	Description
Time Period Name	Enter a name in the **Time Period Name** field. The name can include up to 50 alphanumeric characters and can contain any combination of spaces, periods (.), hyphens (-), and underscore characters (_). Ensure that each time period name is unique to the plan. Use concise and descriptive names for your time periods. The hours_or_days format usually provides a sufficient level of detail and is short enough to enable you to quickly and easily identify a time period. For example, office_M_to_F identifies a time period for the business hours of an office from Monday to Friday.
Start Time	Time when this time period starts. The available start times are 15-minute intervals throughout a 24-hour day. The default value is No Office Hours. No Office Hours means that the selected partition will not be active for the defined day of year or days of week. To start a time period at midnight, choose the **0:00** value.
End Time	Time when this time period ends. The available end times are 15-minute intervals throughout a 24-hour day. The default value is No Office Hours. To end a time period at midnight, choose the **24:00** value.
Repeat Every	Click one of the radio buttons to set a schedule: • **Week From**—If you click the **Week From** radio button, use the drop-down menus next to **From** and **Through** to choose the days of the week during which this time period applies. Examples: Choose a **From** value of **Mon**(day) and a **Through** value of **Fri**(day) to define a time period that applies from Monday to Friday. Choose a **From** value of **Sat**(urday) and a **Through** value of **Sat**(urday) to define a time period that applies only on Saturdays. • **Year On**—If you click the **Year On** radio button, use the drop-down menus to choose the month and day of the year on which this time period applies. Example: Choose the month **Jan**(uary) and the day **1** to define a time period that applies yearly on New Year's Day.

Figure 13-8 shows how to create a time period using the **No Office Hours** time interval and a repetition interval with a specific day of the year defined. When the **No Office Hours** time interval is selected, the associated partition is not active for the defined days of the week or day of the year—in this example, December 25.

Figure 13-8 *Creating a Christmas Time Period*

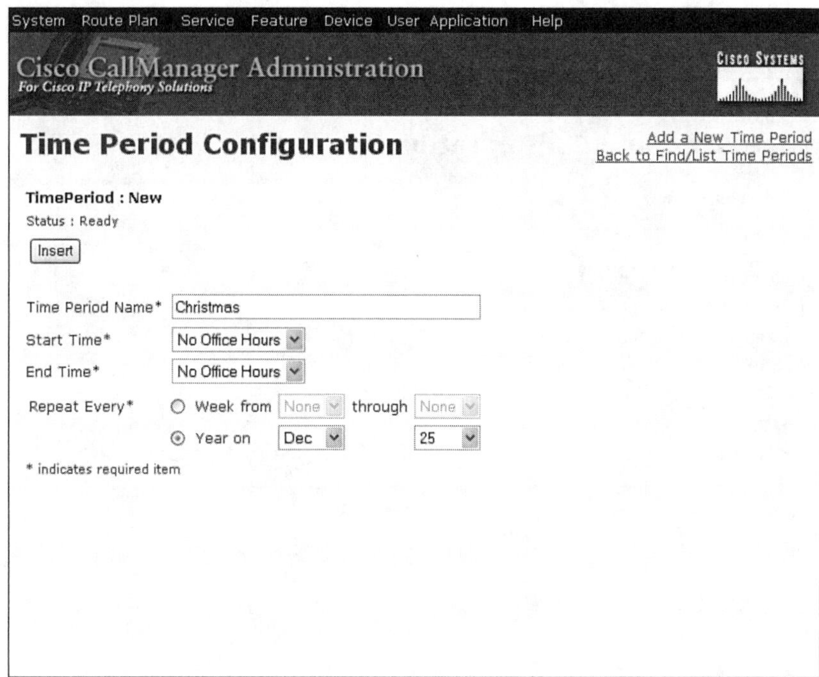

Use the **No Office Hours** time interval and the **Year On** repetition interval for days, such as Christmas, New Year's Day, and national holidays, when for example, the company is closed, certain departments are closed, or certain employees are on holiday.

Configuring Time Schedules

After the time periods are created, you can create the time schedule:

Step 1 In the menu bar, choose **Route Plan > Class of Control > Time Schedule**.

Step 2 Click **Add a New Time Schedule**.

Step 3 Name the time schedule in the **Time Schedule Name** field.

Step 4 Choose the desired time periods from the **Available Time Periods** pane, shown in Figure 13-9, and use the down arrow to move them to the **Selected Time Periods** pane. Move any time periods you do not want in the **Selected Time Periods** pane to the **Available Time Periods** pane.

Figure 13-9 *Creating a Time Schedule*

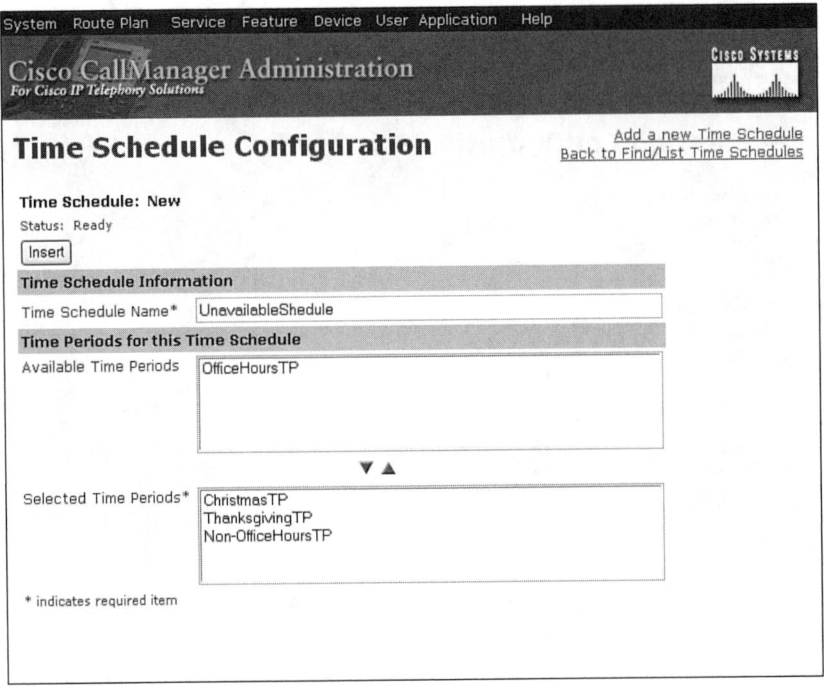

Step 5 To add the new time schedule, click **Insert** (or **Update** if the time schedule already exists and you are changing it).

The message "Status: Insert completed" appears.

Step 6 To add more time schedules, click **Add a New Time Schedule** and repeat this procedure.

Applying Time Schedules

Associating the time schedule (collection of time periods) to a partition is the final step in configuring time-of-day routing. A time schedule is not activated until it is assigned to a partition. In Cisco IOS software, this process is similar to creating an access control list (ACL) that does not become activated until it is assigned to an interface.

TIP Cisco CallManager allows you to create duplicate route patterns as long as they are assigned to different partitions. This grants the flexibility to create a route pattern and assign it to a partition for which you have assigned specific time-of-day restrictions for some users. You can then create an identical route pattern and assign it to a partition without time-of-day calling restrictions for other users. You can control user access privileges through the partition you assign to their calling search space.

You can create a new partition from the Partition Configuration window and assign the time schedule to it or assign the time schedule to an existing partition, as shown in Figure 13-10. The process is the same:

Step 1 From the **Time Schedule** drop-down menu, choose a time schedule to associate with this partition.

Step 2 Choose either the time zone of the originating device or any specific time zone for a time schedule. The system checks the chosen time zone against the time schedule when the call is placed to directory numbers in this partition.

Figure 13-10 *Assigning a Time Schedule to a Partition*

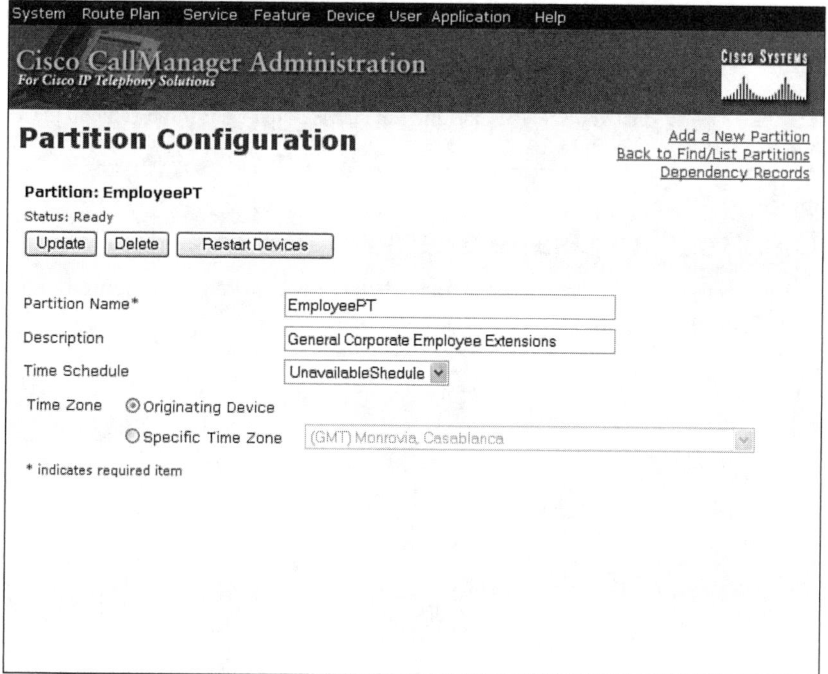

Table 13-2 provides a list of available options when applying a time schedule to a partition.

Table 13-2 *Time Schedule Application Options*

Parameter	Description
Time Schedule	From the drop-down menu, choose a time schedule to associate with this partition. The associated time schedule specifies when the partition is available to receive incoming calls. The default value specifies **None**, which means that time-of-day routing is not in effect and the partition remains active at all times. In combination with the time zone value in the following field, associating a partition with a time schedule configures the partition for time-of-day routing. The system checks incoming calls to this partition against the specified time schedule.
Time Zone	Choose one of the following options to associate a partition with a time zone: • **Originating Device**—If you choose this option, the system checks the partition against the associated time schedule with the time zone of the calling device. • **Specific Time Zone**—If you choose this option, choose a time zone from the drop-down menu. The system checks the partition against the associated time schedule at the time that is specified in this time zone. These options all specify the time zone. When there is an incoming call, the current time on the Cisco CallManager is converted into the specific time zone that you set. This specific time is validated against the value in the **Time Schedule** field.

Time-of-Day Routing Usage Scenario

Figure 13-11 shows an example of how time-of-day routing can be configured to route calls after office hours to a home number.

Figure 13-11 *Time-of-Day Routing Usage Scenario*

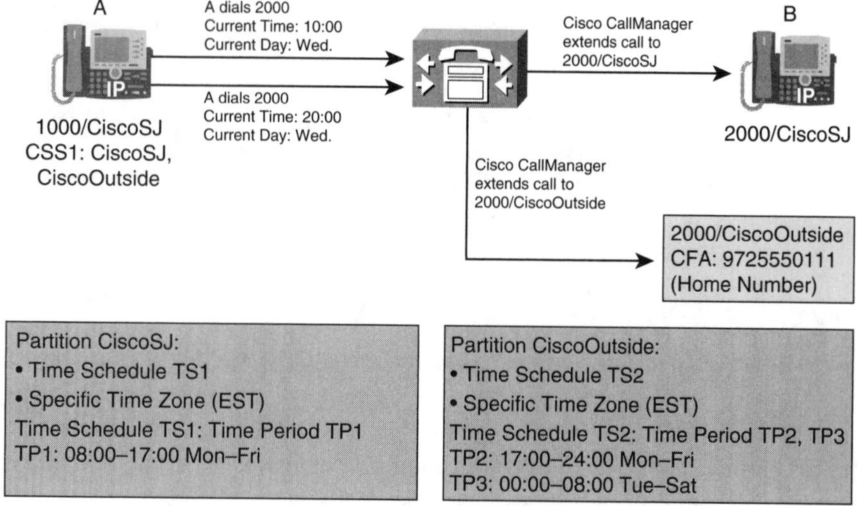

The setup is as follows:

- Partition CiscoSJ is configured with the time schedule TS1 and the specific time zone Eastern Standard Time (EST).
  - — Time period TP1 is associated with time schedule TS1.
  - — The TP1 start time is 08:00, the end time is 17:00, and the repetition interval is Monday through Friday.
- Partition CiscoOutside is configured to use time schedule TS2 and the specific time zone EST.
  - — Time periods TP2 and TP3 are associated with time schedule TS2.
  - — The TP2 start time is 17:00, the end time is 24:00, and the repetition interval is Monday through Friday.
  - — The TP3 start time is 10:00, the end time is 08:00, and the repetition interval is Tuesday through Saturday.
- The user A calling search space is CSS1. CSS1 contains the CiscoSJ and CiscoOutside partitions.

Call flow is as follows:

- User A at extension 1000 calls 2000 at 10:00 a.m. Wednesday. The partition CiscoSJ is active at that time (TP1), so the call is forwarded to 2000.
- User A at extension 1000 calls 2000 at 20:00 (8:00 p.m.) Wednesday. The partition CiscoSJ is not active at that time. However, the partition CiscoOutside is active then (TP2), and the calling search space CSS1 contains a pattern to reach the user B home phone number 9725550111, which enables user B to set CFA to forward incoming calls to a home number.

Summary

This chapter covered the concepts and configuration of Cisco CallManager calling restrictions. Class of Service (CoS) is necessary in nearly every corporate environment to implement telephony policies for end users. Cisco CallManager implements CoS through partitions and calling search spaces. A partition is a group of DNs with similar accessibility characteristics, whereas a calling search space defines which partitions are accessible to a particular device (such as an IP Phone or gateway).

To configure partitions and calling search spaces, create the partition and assign the appropriate DNs to the partition. You must then create a calling search space containing the partitions you want to be reachable and apply the calling search space to the affected IP Phones or gateway devices.

Time-of-day routing routes calls to different locations based on the time of day or day of the year when a call is made. To configure time-of-day routing, create the necessary time periods, create a time schedule containing similar time periods, and assign the time schedule and time zone to a partition.

Review Questions

You can find the solutions to these questions in Appendix A, "Answers to Review Questions."

1. The Partition Configuration window in Cisco CallManager Administration contains which two parameters associated with time-of-day routing? (Choose two.)
   a. start and end times
   b. repetition interval
   c. time zone
   d. time period
   e. time schedule

2. Which time period would be configured to allow access to user A during user A's weekday office hours (assuming user A works from 8:00 a.m. to 5:00 p.m.)?

   a. 08:00 to 17:00 Monday to Friday and the time zone of the originating device

   b. 08:00 to 17:00 Monday to Friday and the time zone of user A

   c. no office hours Saturday and Sunday and the time zone of the originating device

   d. no office hours Saturday and Sunday and the time zone of user A

3. Which of the following items can be assigned to a partition? (Choose three.)

   a. phones

   b. directory numbers

   c. gateways

   d. route patterns

   e. translation patterns

4. Describe the order of Class of Service configuration.

   a. DNs are placed in partitions, partitions are placed in calling search spaces, and calling search spaces are assigned to the calling device.

   b. DNs are placed in calling search spaces, calling search spaces are placed in partitions, and partitions are assigned to the calling device.

   c. DNs are placed in calling search spaces, calling search spaces are placed in partitions, and calling search spaces are assigned to the calling device.

   d. IP Phones and gateways are placed in partitions, partitions are placed in calling search spaces, and both the partition and calling search spaces are assigned to the calling device.

5. To which of the following devices can you assign a calling search space? (Choose three.)

   a. gateways

   b. IP Phones

   c. directory numbers (phone lines)

   d. route patterns

6. How does CallManager process a call from a device configured with a calling search space?

   a. It processes the call by looking through the partitions in the calling search space from the bottom of the list to the top.

   b. It processes the call by looking through the partitions in the calling search space from the top of the list to the bottom.

   c. It processes the call by first looking through the partitions in the calling search space of the called device followed by the partitions in the calling search space of the calling device.

   d. It processes the call by first looking through the partitions in the calling search space of the calling device followed by the partitions in the calling search space of the called device.

7. When configuring time-of-day routing, which of the following should be created first?

   a. time schedules

   b. time agendas

   c. time routes

   d. time periods

8. You want to implement time-of-day routing restrictions. One group of users should only be able to call PSTN numbers from 8:00 a.m. to 5:00 p.m. Another group of users should be able to call the PSTN anytime. How could this be configured?

   a. You must create two sets of PSTN route patterns. One set should be added to the partition restricted by the 8:00 a.m. to 5:00 p.m. time schedule. The other set should be added to a partition not restricted by a time schedule. A calling search space containing the restricted partition is then assigned to the users limited to 8:00 a.m. to 5:00 p.m. PSTN calling and a calling search space containing the unrestricted partition is assigned to the users able to reach the PSTN anytime.

   b. You must create one set of PSTN route patterns. This set is added to a partition restricted by the 8:00 a.m. to 5:00 p.m. time schedule and a partition not restricted by a time schedule. A calling search space containing the restricted partition is then assigned to the users limited to 8:00 a.m. to 5:00 p.m. PSTN calling and a calling search space containing the unrestricted partition is assigned to the users able to reach the PSTN anytime.

   c. You must create one set of PSTN route patterns. This set is added to a partition restricted by the 8:00 a.m. to 5:00 p.m. time schedule. A calling search space containing the restricted partition is then assigned to the users limited to 8:00 a.m. to 5:00 p.m. PSTN calling and a calling search space that does not contain the restricted PSTN partition is assigned to the users able to reach the PSTN anytime.

   d. This functionality is not currently supported in Cisco CallManager 4.x versions.

9. How is time-of-day routing applied to an end user?
   a. Restrictions are applied to the user's partition.
   b. Restrictions are applied directly to the user's DN.
   c. Restrictions are applied to a partition contained in a user's calling search space.
   d. Restrictions are applied to a user's calling search space.
10. You want to create a time period that matches the Christmas holiday every year. What time period selection criteria would you use to accomplish this?
    a. Repeat Every Day On...
    b. Repeat Every Week From...
    c. Repeat Every Year From...
    d. Repeat Every Year On...

This chapter covers the following topics:

- Describing why call admission control is important to maintain voice QoS across an IP WAN
- Describing how the locations feature in Cisco CallManager provides call admission control for centralized call-processing environments
- Configuring locations-based call admission control in a centralized call-processing deployment to limit the number of active calls and prevent oversubscribing the bandwidth on the IP WAN links
- Explaining what AAR is, how it works, and the requirements for configuring Cisco CallManager for AAR
- Describing how a gatekeeper can reduce the number of intercluster trunks that are required in a distributed call-processing environment
- Identifying the communication procedures between an H.323 gatekeeper and H.323 endpoint, including discovery, registration, admission, and bandwidth requests
- Configuring gatekeeper-based call admission control in a distributed call-processing deployment to limit the number of active calls and prevent oversubscribing the bandwidth on the IP WAN links
- Describing how SRST provides Cisco CallManager failover capabilities
- Configuring SRST on a supported gateway and in Cisco CallManager so that the SRST router assumes call-processing duties should the WAN link fail

CHAPTER 14

Implementing Multiple-Site Deployments

Implementing multiple-site IP telephony deployments over an IP WAN requires additional planning to ensure the quality and availability of voice calls. When an IP WAN connects IP telephony clusters, a mechanism must exist to control the audio quality and video quality of calls over the IP WAN link by limiting the number of calls that are allowed on that link at the same time. Call admission control is the mechanism that ensures that voice calls do not oversubscribe the IP WAN bandwidth and affect voice quality.

When the priority queue of IP WAN bandwidth is consumed, a mechanism must exist to automatically reroute calls over the public switched telephone network (PSTN) without requiring the caller to hang up and redial the called party. Automated Alternate Routing (AAR) is a Cisco CallManager feature that automatically reroutes calls through the PSTN or other networks when priority bandwidth is insufficient in a centralized call-processing deployment.

NOTE Referring to the priority queue of IP WAN bandwidth does not necessarily encompass the entire amount of WAN bandwidth available. Rather, it encompasses the amount of bandwidth you have set aside for high-priority traffic (including voice).

If connectivity with Cisco CallManager is lost, Cisco IP Phones become unusable for the duration of the failure. Cisco Survivable Remote Site Telephony (SRST) overcomes this problem and ensures that the Cisco IP Phones offer continuous service by providing call handling support for Cisco IP Phones directly from the Cisco SRST router.

This chapter describes the operation and configuration of call admission control, AAR, and SRST.

Call Admission Control

Call admission control (CAC) provides you with mechanisms to control the volume of calls between two endpoints. Controlling the number of calls, or the amount of bandwidth that is required between two endpoints, is key to maintaining quality of service (QoS) for all existing and new calls. As shown in Figure 14-1, a WAN might only have enough bandwidth provisioned to support two calls. If the CallManager were to send a third call over the IP WAN, all calls experience poor quality.

Figure 14-1 *Call Admission Control Example*

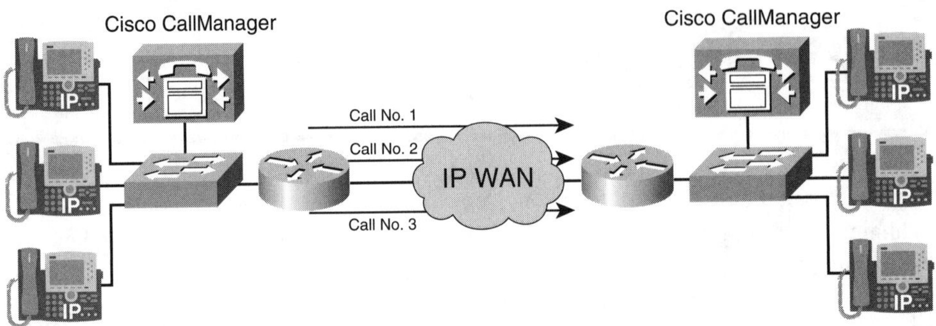

You can provision the network to carry a specific amount of real-time traffic. Any traffic that exceeds the provisioned bandwidth will subject all real-time traffic to delay, jitter, and possibly packet loss. The coder-decoder (codec) used for the call determines the bandwidth calculations used with call admission control.

Using Cisco CallManager, the following two types of call admission are possible:

- **Locations-based call admission control**—The locations feature of Cisco CallManager provides a simplified call admission control scheme for centralized call-processing systems. A centralized system uses a single Cisco CallManager cluster to control all of the locations.
- **Gatekeeper-based call admission control**—A gatekeeper device provides call admission control for distributed call-processing systems. In a distributed system, each site contains its own call-processing capability.

Locations-Based Call Admission Control

Cisco CallManager provides a simple locations-based call admission control mechanism for hub-and-spoke topologies, used primarily for centralized call processing.

The locations feature in Cisco CallManager lets you specify the maximum amount of audio bandwidth (for audio calls) and video bandwidth (for video calls) that is available for calls to and from each location. This specification limits the number of active calls and limits oversubscription of the priority bandwidth on the IP WAN links.

NOTE Video calls are discussed in further detail in Chapter 28, "Introducing IP Video Telephony."

For the purpose of calculating bandwidth for call admission control, Cisco CallManager assumes that each call stream consumes the following amount of bandwidth:

- A G.711 call uses 80 kbps.
- A G.722 call uses 80 kbps.
- A G.723 call uses 24 kbps.
- A G.728 call uses 16 kbps.
- A G.729 call uses 24 kbps.
- A Global System for Mobile Communication (GSM) call uses 29 kbps.
- A wideband call uses 272 kbps.

Locations work in conjunction with regions to define the characteristics of a network link. Locations define the amount of available bandwidth for the link, and regions define the type of compression (G.711, G.723, or G.729) that is used on the link.

For example, in Figure 14-2, three locations are specified: San Jose (unlimited bandwidth), New York (256 kbps), and Dallas (64 kbps). Cisco CallManager continues to admit new calls to a link as long as sufficient bandwidth is still available. Thus, if the link to the New York location in this example has 256 kbps of available bandwidth, that link can support three G.711 calls at 80 kbps each and ten G.723 or G.729 calls at 24 kbps each. If any additional calls are received that would exceed the bandwidth limit, the system rejects them, the calling party receives a reorder tone, and a text message is displayed on the phone.

Figure 14-2 *Location-Based Call Admission Control Example*

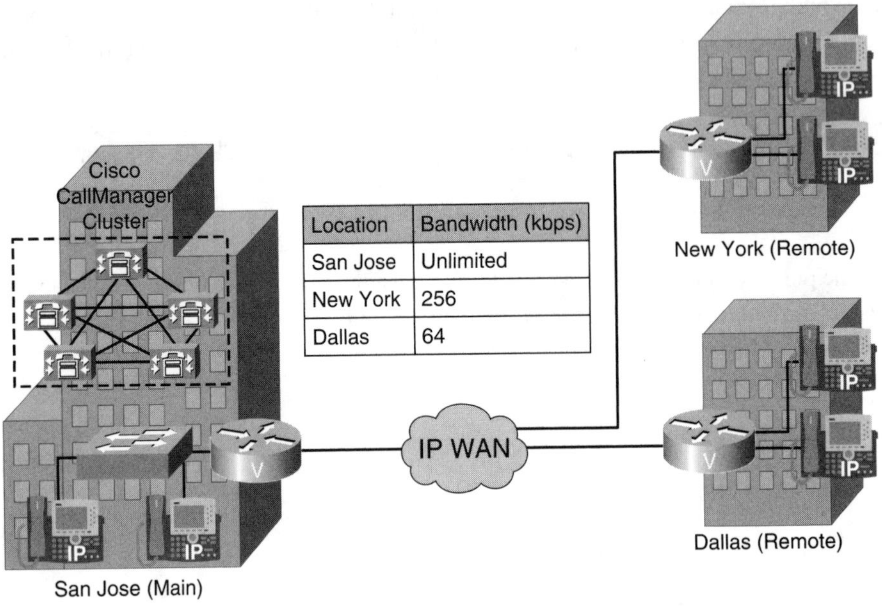

Cisco CallManager Cluster

Location	Bandwidth (kbps)
San Jose	Unlimited
New York	256
Dallas	64

New York (Remote)

IP WAN

Dallas (Remote)

San Jose (Main)

Configuring Location-Based Call Admission Control

Configuring location-based call admission control in Cisco CallManager is a relatively simple process. Before you can accurately configure locations, you must ensure you have configured all the devices at remote locations to use a common codec when calling across the WAN. You can accomplish this through the region configuration assigned to the device pool of the remote phones. After you have accurately assigned the codec, follow these steps to configure locations in Cisco CallManager:

Step 1 Choose **System > Location** to configure a separate location for each IP WAN link to which you want to apply call admission control. As shown in Figure 14-3, allocate the maximum available bandwidth for calls across the link to that location.

Step 2 In the individual device configuration windows, configure the telephones and other devices and assign each of them to the appropriate device pool and location, as shown in Figure 14-4.

Figure 14-3 *Configuring Locations*

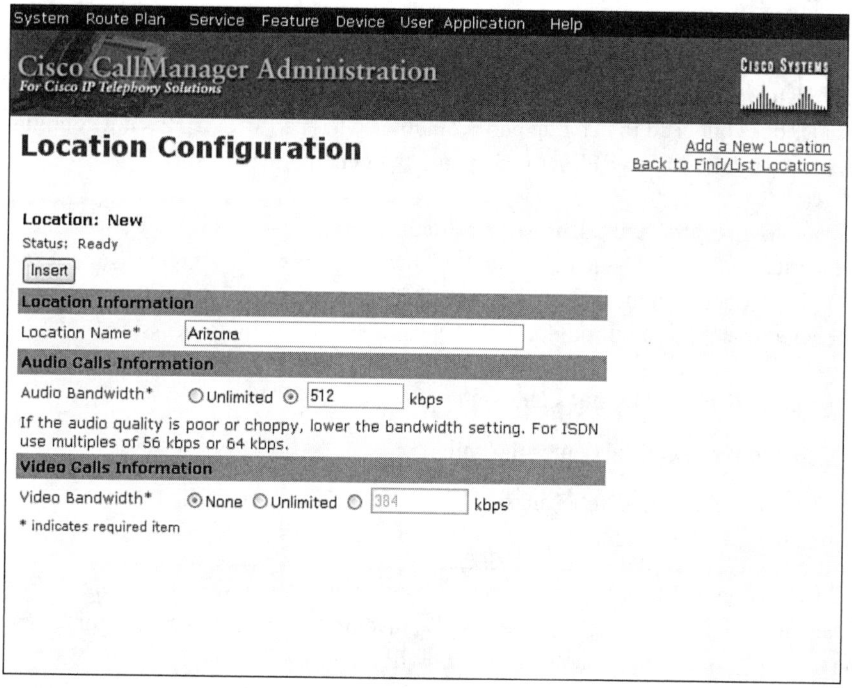

System Route Plan Service Feature Device User Application Help

Cisco CallManager Administration
For Cisco IP Telephony Solutions

Cisco Systems

Location Configuration

Add a New Location
Back to Find/List Locations

Location: New
Status: Ready
Insert

Location Information
Location Name* Arizona

Audio Calls Information
Audio Bandwidth* Unlimited 512 kbps
If the audio quality is poor or choppy, lower the bandwidth setting. For ISDN use multiples of 56 kbps or 64 kbps.

Video Calls Information
Video Bandwidth* None Unlimited 384 kbps
* indicates required item

Figure 14-4 *Assigning Devices to a Location*

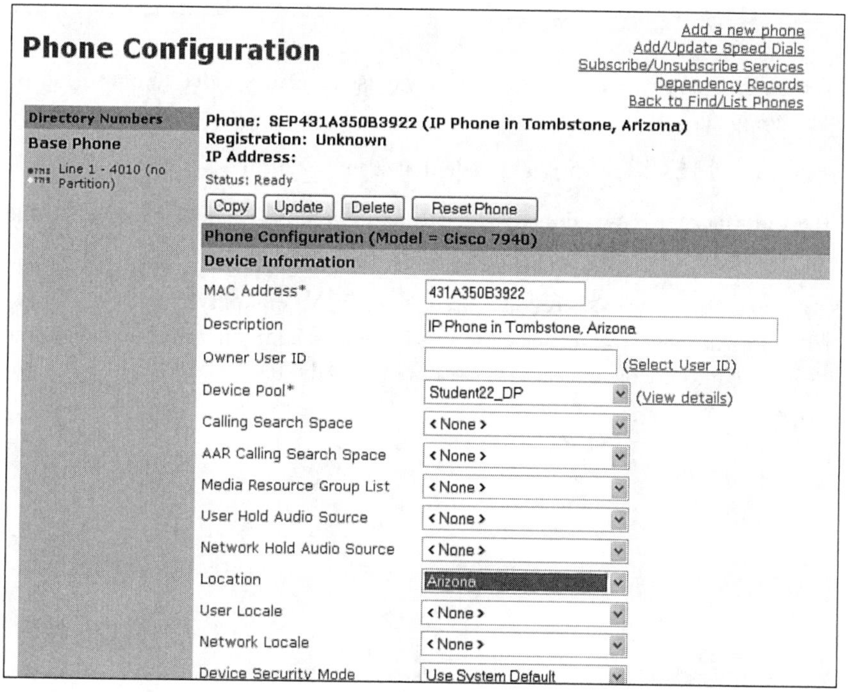

Phone Configuration

Add a new phone
Add/Update Speed Dials
Subscribe/Unsubscribe Services
Dependency Records
Back to Find/List Phones

Directory Numbers
Base Phone
Line 1 - 4010 (no Partition)

Phone: SEP431A350B3922 (IP Phone in Tombstone, Arizona)
Registration: Unknown
IP Address:
Status: Ready
Copy Update Delete Reset Phone

Phone Configuration (Model = Cisco 7940)
Device Information

MAC Address*	431A350B3922
Description	IP Phone in Tombstone, Arizona
Owner User ID	(Select User ID)
Device Pool*	Student22_DP (View details)
Calling Search Space	< None >
AAR Calling Search Space	< None >
Media Resource Group List	< None >
User Hold Audio Source	< None >
Network Hold Audio Source	< None >
Location	Arizona
User Locale	< None >
Network Locale	< None >
Device Security Mode	Use System Default

AAR Overview

Automated Alternate Routing (AAR) is a mechanism used in conjunction with location-based call admission control. AAR allows calls to be rerouted through the PSTN by using an alternate number when Cisco CallManager blocks a call due to insufficient location bandwidth. With AAR, the caller does not need to hang up and redial the called party. If AAR is not configured, the user gets a reorder tone and the IP Phone displays "Not enough bandwidth."

AAR applies to centralized call-processing deployments. For instance, if a telephone in a company headquarters calls a telephone in branch B (shown in Figure 14-5) and the available bandwidth for the WAN link between the branches is insufficient (as computed by the locations mechanism), AAR can reroute the call through the PSTN using the following process:

1. Phone A (DN = 2345) dials On-Net to phone B (DN = 1234).
2. Call admission control denies the call.
3. The external phone number mask 215-555-XXXX is added. The result is a fully qualified number, 215-555-1234.

> **NOTE** When working with the external phone number mask, it is important to keep straight which mask the CallManager will use when invoking AAR. When AAR redirects a call across the PSTN, it will always use the *destination* IP Phone's external phone number mask to transform the called number. The *source* IP Phone's external phone number mask will be used to transform the caller ID information.

4. The prefix used to access the PSTN gateway is 9, and 1 is added to the string for numbering plan compatibility. These values are configured in the AAR group.
5. 9-1-215-555-1234 is the new alternate dial string.
6. The CallManager passes the new dial string through the route plan and sends the call across the PSTN.

AAR is transparent to users. It is configured so that users dial only the on-net (for example, four-digit) directory number (DN) of the called phone and no additional user input is required to reach the destination through the alternate network (such as the PSTN).

Figure 14-5 *AAR Scenario*

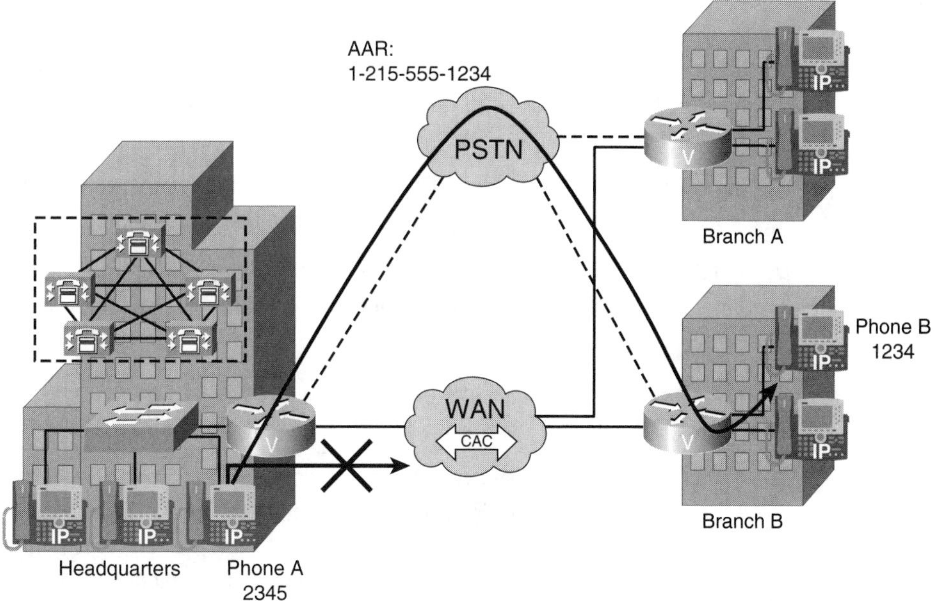

Keep the following requirements and caveats in mind when applying AAR:

- AAR requires call admission control based on locations and regions; AAR will function only if the WAN bandwidth is consumed.
- The IP Phone that originates a call should be in the same location as the gateway that routes the call to the PSTN.
- The called IP Phone and the gateway that terminates the call from the PSTN should be in the same location.
- If a call originates from a device in one location and terminates to a non-IP Phone in another location, AAR will not function. A voice-mail port on another vendor device also does not use AAR.
- If a call originates from a Cisco computer telephony integration (CTI) route point, AAR will not function.
- AAR does not work with SRST, which means that AAR will not function in the case of a WAN failure.

Configuring AAR

Configuring Cisco CallManager for AAR requires the following steps:

Step 1 Configure the locations. Use locations to implement call admission control in a centralized call-processing system. Cisco CallManager requires that the locations be arranged in a hub-and-spoke topology.

Step 2 Configure the regions. Use regions to specify the type of compression and the amount of bandwidth used within a region and between regions.

Step 3 Assign devices to a region and location. Use device pools to define sets of common characteristics—in this case, the region setting—for devices in a specific location.

Step 4 Enable AAR clusterwide. Ensure that the Automated Alternate Routing Enable service parameter is set to True.

Step 5 Configure AAR groups. For each AAR group, enter the prefix digits that are used for AAR within the AAR group, in addition to the prefix digits used for AAR between a given AAR group and other AAR groups. Devices such as gateways, telephones (by means of DNs), and trunks associate with AAR groups.

Step 6 Configure the calling search space for AAR. Cisco CallManager uses the AAR calling search space to reroute calls when there is no available bandwidth on the WAN.

Step 7 Configure the endpoints as follows:

- Assign devices to the AAR group.
- Assign the external line mask to the DN.
- Assign devices to the AAR calling search space.

Steps 1 through 3 involve the location configuration, which was discussed earlier in this chapter. The AAR configuration steps starting with Step 4 are covered in detail in the following subtopics.

Enabling AAR in the CallManager Cluster

To access the settings for AAR throughout the cluster, open the **Service > Service Parameters** window for the Cisco CallManager service. You can use the Microsoft Internet Explorer Find feature to quickly locate the Automated Alternate Routing Enable service parameter, shown in Figure 14-6. Ensure this value is set to True. The default value for this service parameter is False.

Figure 14-6 *Automated Alternate Routing Service Parameters*

Clusterwide Parameters (System - CCM Automated Alternate Routing)		
Parameter Name	**Parameter Value**	**Suggested Value**
Automated Alternate Routing Enable*	True	False
AAR Groups Initialization Timer (sec)*	90	90

In addition, you can access the **Service Parameters > CallManager > Clusterwide Parameters (Device–Phone)** window (shown in Figure 14-7) to modify the two fields used to configure the messages that appear on the end user's IP Phone if there is no WAN bandwidth available or if AAR reroutes the call over the WAN.

Figure 14-7 *Automated Alternate Routing End-User Notification Messages*

AAR Group Configuration

If a user dials an internal number that goes to another location and the WAN is busy, the call should be rerouted over the PSTN. To place a call over the PSTN, Cisco CallManager needs the fully qualified number, not the internal DN, to reroute the call.

The destination number might require a prefix for an Off-Net access code (for example, 9) to be routed properly by the dial plan of the origination branch. Furthermore, if the point of origin is located in a different Numbering Plan Area (NPA, or area code), the network might require a prefix of 1 as part of the dialed string. Cisco CallManager uses the internal DN, the external phone number mask of the called DN, and the prefix to determine the alternate number for routing the call over the PSTN.

When configuring AAR, place the DNs in AAR groups. As shown in Figure 14-8, for each pair of AAR groups, you can configure prefix digits to add to the DNs for calls between the two groups, including prefix digits for calls originating and terminating within the same AAR group. For example, if a user in the California_AAR group dials a user in the Arizona_AAR group (shown in Figure 14-8) and the IP WAN connection bandwidth was oversubscribed, the CallManager would redirect the call over the PSTN connection, prefixing the digits "91" to the DN (which is also combined with the external phone number mask, discussed in the upcoming section).

Figure 14-8 *Automated Alternate Routing Group Configuration Window*

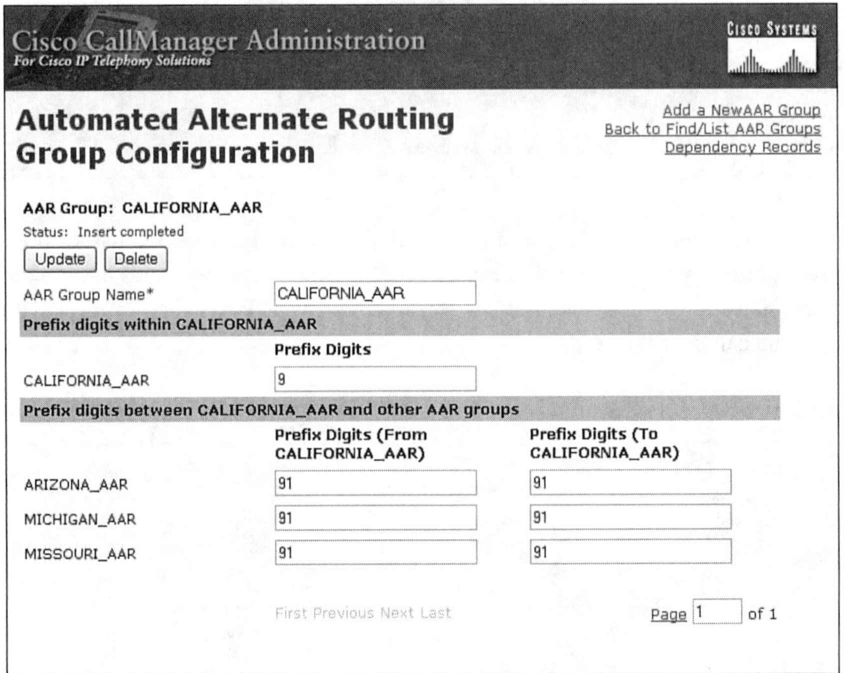

As a general rule, place DNs in the same AAR group if they share all of the following characteristics:

- A common off-net access code (for example, 9)
- A common PSTN dialing structure for interarea calls (for example, 1-NPA-N*xx*-*xxxx* in North America)
- A common external phone number mask format

For example, assume that both the San Francisco and New York sites share all of the preceding characteristics. The DNs for San Francisco and New York can be placed into a single AAR group, and the group can be configured such that AAR calls placed within this AAR group are prefixed with 91. For phone A in San Francisco to reach phone B in New York (at 212-555-1212), the AAR group configuration prefixes 91 to the dialed string, yielding a completed string of 91-212-555-1212.

Complete these steps to add an AAR group:

Step 1 From the menu bar, choose **Route Plan > AAR Group**.

Step 2 Click **Add a New AAR Group**.

Step 3 Enter a name in the **AAR Group Name** field.

Step 4 Click **Continue**.

Step 5 In the **Prefix Digits Within** field for the group being added, enter the prefix digits to use for AAR within this AAR group.

Step 6 In the Prefix Digits Between the group being added and Other AAR Groups area, complete the following fields:

- **Prefix Digits (From)**—Enter the prefix digits to use for AAR when routing a call from this group to a device that belongs to another AAR group.

> **NOTE** Prefix digits that are entered in this field for the originating AAR group are also added in the **Prefix Digits (To)** field of the AAR destination group.

- **Prefix Digits (To)**—Enter the prefix digits to use for AAR when you are routing a call to this group from a device that belongs to another AAR group.

> **NOTE** Prefix digits entered in this field for the destination AAR group are also added in the **Prefix Digits (From)** field of the AAR originating group.

Step 7 Click **Insert** to add this AAR group.

Configuring Endpoints for AAR

Most of the setup process for AAR occurs when configuring the endpoints and gateways for AAR. This process can be completed in three steps:

Step 1 Configure the DN to use the AAR group, as shown in Figure 14-9. An AAR group setting of **None** specifies that no rerouting of blocked calls will be attempted.

Figure 14-9 *Configuring DNs for AAR Groups*

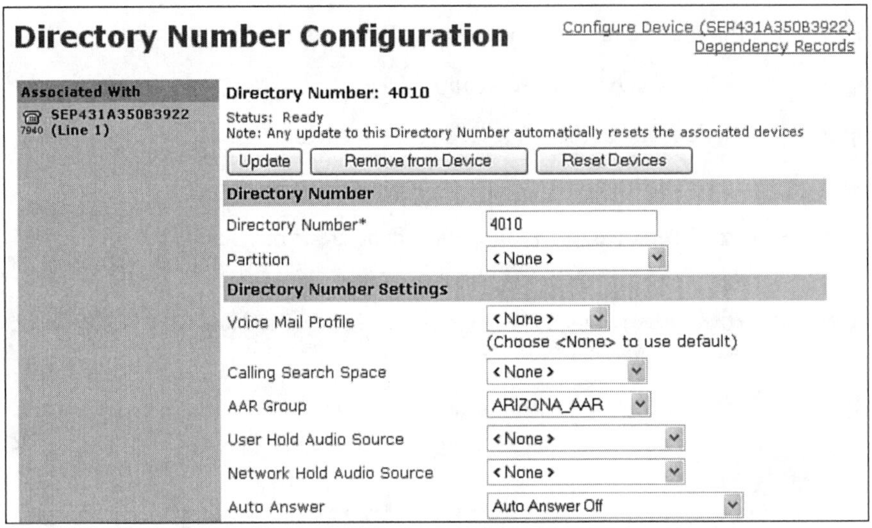

Directory Number Configuration
Configure Device (SEP431A350B3922)
Dependency Records
Associated With
SEP431A350B3922
7940 (Line 1)
Directory Number: 4010
Status: Ready
Note: Any update to this Directory Number automatically resets the associated devices
Update | Remove from Device | Reset Devices
Directory Number
Directory Number* 4010
Partition < None >
Directory Number Settings
Voice Mail Profile < None >
(Choose <None> to use default)
Calling Search Space < None >
AAR Group ARIZONA_AAR
User Hold Audio Source < None >
Network Hold Audio Source < None >
Auto Answer Auto Answer Off

Step 2 Assign the external phone number mask to the DN.

The rerouting of calls requires using a destination DN that is routable through the alternate network (for example, the PSTN). AAR uses the dialed digits to establish the on-cluster destination of the call and then combines them with the external phone number mask of the called party. The combination of these two elements must yield a fully qualified number that is routable by the alternate network.

The destination number might require a prefix for an off-net access code (for example, 9) to be routed properly by the origination branch dial plan. Furthermore, if the point of origin is located in a different NPA, a prefix of 1 might be required as part of the dialed string. You should add these prefix digits in the AAR Group Configuration window rather than the external phone number mask.

For example, assume that phone A in San Francisco (DN = 2345) dials an on-net DN (1234) configured on phone B in New York. If locations-based call admission control denies the call, AAR retrieves the external phone number mask of the New York phone (212-555-XXXX) and uses it to derive the fully qualified number (212-555-1234) that is routable on the PSTN.

The PSTN routing of a call from San Francisco to New York requires a 1 as a prefix to the phone number. It is recommended that this prefix not be included as part of the external phone number mask because it would be displayed as part of the calling line Identification (CLID, or caller ID) for any calls made by the phones to an off-net destination. Instead, it is recommended that the 1 be added as part of the AAR group configuration.

Configure the external phone number mask on the IP Phone DN by choosing **Device > Phone**, and then selecting the phone and the line you want to configure. Figure 14-10 illustrates this configuration.

Figure 14-10 *Configuring DNs for AAR Groups*

Line Settings for this Device	
Display (Internal Caller ID)	
Line Text Label	
External Phone Number Mask	480555XXXX
Message Waiting Lamp Policy	Use System Policy
Ring Setting (Phone Idle)	Use System Default
Ring Setting (Phone Active)**	Use System Default

Indicate the phone number (or mask) that is used to send caller ID information when a call is placed from this line. A maximum of 30 numeric and X characters can be added. The Xs represent the DN and must appear at the end of the pattern. For example, if you specify a mask of 972813XXXX, an external call from extension 1234 displays a caller ID number of 9728131234.

TIP Remember, the external phone number mask should always be the number the DN you are configuring through the PSTN. If your organization does not use Direct Inward Dial (DID) ranges, you should configure the external phone number mask as the location's general number, allowing a receptionist to redirect the call to the internal extension.

Step 3 Configure the phone (or gateway) to use the AAR calling search space.

With AAR, the AAR calling search space was introduced. With this special parameter, the caller rights can be adjusted for this special event when AAR is used. Cisco CallManager looks at the AAR calling search space to determine whether the device has the right to call over the PSTN. For example, if the originating calling device can reach only internal phones with the configured calling search space, then it is possible with the AAR calling search space to allow calls from that device to be rerouted using the PSTN. In this case, the AAR calling search space grants additional permissions to route the call when the IP WAN is down.

The AAR calling search space specifies the collection of route partitions that are searched to determine how to route a collected (originating) number that is blocked because of insufficient bandwidth. You can assign the AAR calling search space to the phone from the Phone Configuration window, as shown in Figure 14-11.

Figure 14-11 *Configuring AAR Calling Search Space*

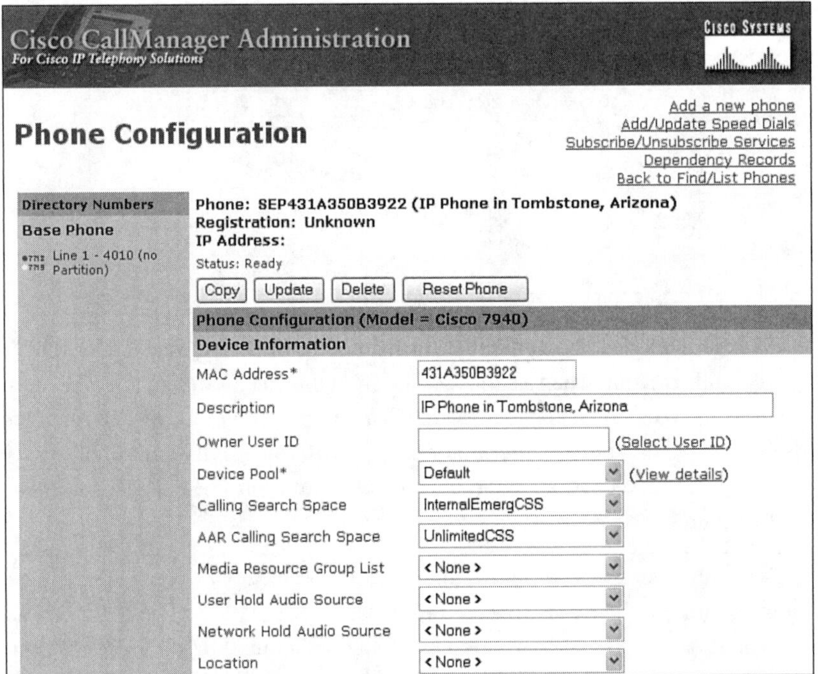

Gatekeeper-Based Call Admission Control

Gatekeeper call admission control reduces configuration overhead by eliminating the need to configure separate individual intercluster trunks between clusters. A gatekeeper can determine the IP addresses of devices that are registered with it, or you can enter the IP addresses explicitly. It uses these IP addresses to refer calls between endpoints (an endpoint could be an entire Cisco CallManager cluster). For example, a call could originate from one CallManager cluster where the route plan indicates to forward the call to the gatekeeper. The gatekeeper responds with the real IP address of the CallManager in another cluster that manages the extension the call is attempting to reach.

If you choose the gatekeeper method of call admission control, you will need to set up an Intercluster Trunk (gatekeeper-controlled) or H.225 trunk (gatekeeper-controlled). These trunks are configured to point to the gatekeeper device and are included in the dial plan for your network.

When you configure gatekeeper-controlled trunks, Cisco CallManager automatically creates a virtual trunk device. The IP address of this device changes dynamically to reflect the IP address of the remote device as determined by the gatekeeper. For example, if the gatekeeper forwards the call to another CallManager cluster, the endpoint IP address for the virtual trunk device points to the CallManager server in the remote cluster.

> **NOTE** Much of the H.323 gatekeeper configuration is covered in *Cisco Voice Gateways and Gatekeepers* (ISBN: 1-58705-258-x) from Cisco Press. The gatekeeper configuration discussed in this book is directly related to the Cisco CallManager integration.

Gatekeeper Communication

For a Cisco CallManager to use an H.323 gatekeeper, a new communication exchange occurs between the gatekeeper and the Cisco CallManager. The first process that an endpoint must go through is gatekeeper discovery. An endpoint achieves gatekeeper discovery either manually or through autodiscovery.

Autodiscovery uses multicast to discover the gatekeeper. A gatekeeper request (GRQ) is multicast, and any gatekeeper that can accept a registration returns a gatekeeper confirmation (GCF). If a gatekeeper cannot accept a registration, it returns a gatekeeper reject (GRJ). This exchange is illustrated in Figure 14-12.

Figure 14-12 *Gatekeeper Discovery*

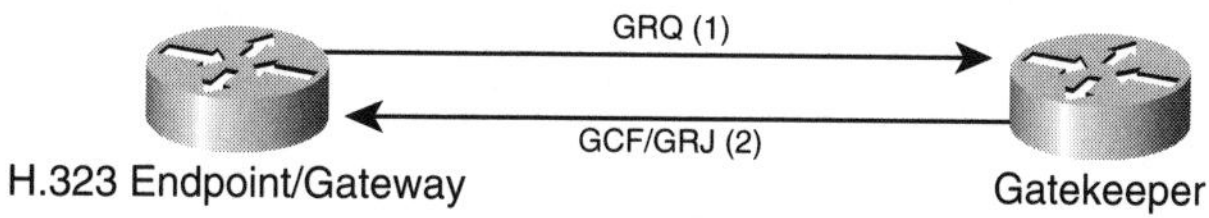

> **NOTE** Although the exchange shown in Figure 14-12 is supported on most H.323 endpoints and gateways (as it is defined in the H.323 standard), Cisco CallManager does not support gatekeeper discovery messages. Because the gatekeeper can play such an integral role in the CallManager route plan, H.323 gatekeepers must be manually configured rather than dynamically discovered.

After the discovery process has completed, the Cisco CallManager must register with the gatekeeper. A Cisco IOS gatekeeper supports two types of registration:

- Full registration
- Lightweight registration

An endpoint must always use a full registration during the initial registration process. An endpoint can use lightweight registration to maintain registration. Should an endpoint become unregistered with the gatekeeper, a full registration is required.

Full registration requires the endpoint to register any E.164 address, H.323 identifier, device type, and other possible parameters each time that it registers. This procedure involves additional processing load on a gatekeeper every time an endpoint registers or renews its registration. The registration request (RRQ) includes the time between renewal of registrations or Time to Live (TTL), and the gatekeeper can replace this value or return this value unchanged.

NOTE You can make the returned TTL value configurable with Cisco IOS Software Release 12.1.5T and later.

The lower the TTL value, the higher the load on the gatekeeper processing the registration. The impact of a higher value is that it takes longer for the gatekeeper to become aware that an endpoint has lost connectivity. Use 30 to 300 seconds, depending on design requirements.

When the endpoint sends a full RRQ to the gatekeeper, the gatekeeper responds with a registration confirmation (RCF) to accept or a registration rejection (RRJ) to refuse, as illustrated in Figure 14-13. The gatekeeper can refuse the registration for many reasons, such as duplicate E.164 or H323 identifiers or ambiguous information.

Figure 14-13 *Gatekeeper Registration and Unregistration*

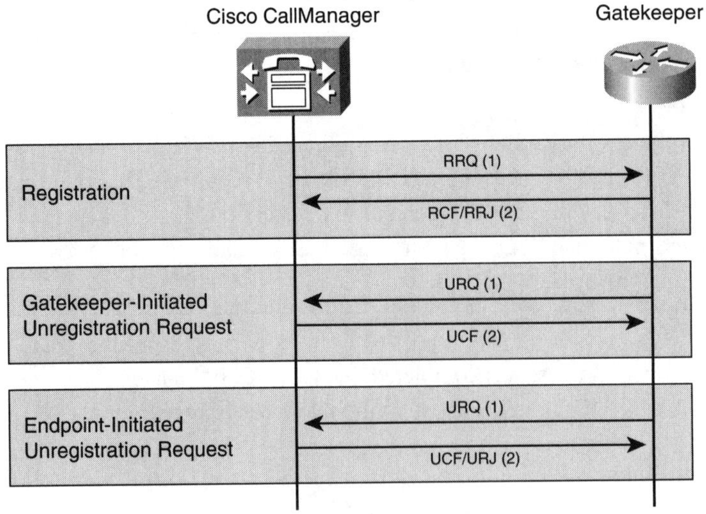

An endpoint registration has a finite life. Before the TTL expires, the endpoint is required to renew its registration by sending an RRQ. If the TTL expires and the gatekeeper has not received an RRQ from the endpoint, the endpoint becomes unregistered.

Lightweight registration reduces the processing load on the gatekeeper during registration renewal. The gatekeeper receives an RRQ with the keepalive bit set and the minimum required information from the endpoint. If the gatekeeper accepts the renewal, the gatekeeper returns an RCF to the endpoint and resets the TTL timer. If the gatekeeper rejects the renewal with an RRJ, the endpoint becomes unregistered.

If the endpoint is unregistered, the endpoint must start the gatekeeper discovery and registration process again.

At any time, an endpoint or a gatekeeper can cancel a registration with an unregister request (URQ), normally used during configuration changes.

An endpoint or gatekeeper sends an unregister confirmation (UCF) in response to a URQ. If an unregistered endpoint sends a URQ to a gatekeeper, the gatekeeper responds with an unregister reject (URJ) to indicate the error. Cisco IOS gatekeepers, Cisco IOS gateways, and Cisco CallManager support lightweight registration.

After the Cisco CallManagers from multiple clusters register with the gatekeeper, the gatekeeper device can perform admission and bandwidth control between the clusters. Telephony endpoints (Cisco IP Phones or Cisco IP SoftPhones) send an admission request (ARQ) to the gatekeeper to initiate a call, as shown in Figure 14-14. The ARQ contains an H.323 identifier or the E.164 address of a destination or called party that it wants to reach. Also contained within the ARQ message are the call bandwidth (not including the header overhead), the source E.164 address, and the H.323 identifier of the calling party.

The gatekeeper will respond to the ARQ with either an admission confirmation (ACF) or an admission reject (ARJ). The gatekeeper sends the ACF if the requested bandwidth is available and the called endpoint is found. The ACF contains the IP address of the endpoint. On receipt of an ACF from the gatekeeper, the endpoint sends a setup message directly to the other endpoint, using the IP address returned in the ACF. If bandwidth is unavailable or if the called endpoint is not registered, the gatekeeper sends an ARJ.

When an endpoint terminates a call, the endpoint is required to indicate the termination to the gatekeeper and return the used bandwidth. The endpoint sends a disengage request (DRQ) to the gatekeeper to indicate that the call is complete. The gatekeeper responds with a disengage confirmation (DCF) and returns the previously used bandwidth to the pool.

Figure 14-14 *Gatekeeper Admission Control*

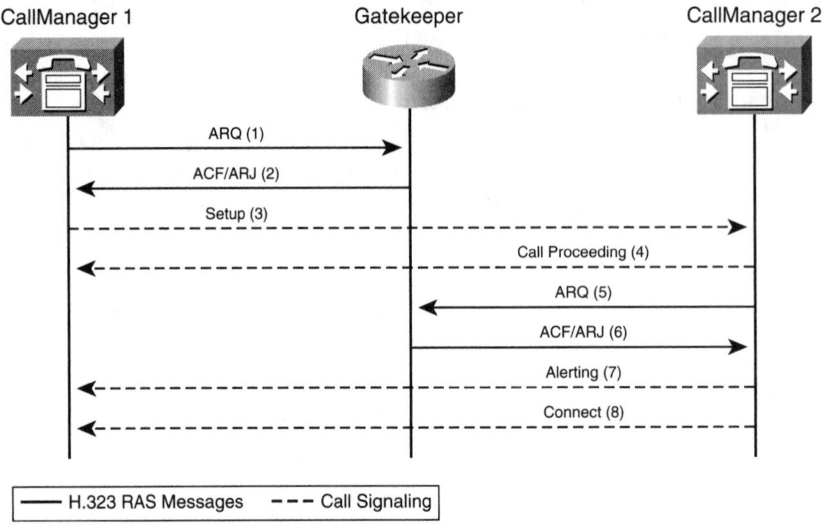

The gatekeeper can also clear the call by sending a DRQ to the endpoint, forcing the endpoint to clear the call with the other endpoint and return a DCF.

If during the duration of the call the bandwidth requirement changes, because of a changing codec or additional media channels opening or closing, the endpoint can request or release the bandwidth by sending a bandwidth request (BRQ). The gatekeeper responds with a bandwidth confirmation (BCF) if the bandwidth is available or with a bandwidth reject (BRJ) if the bandwidth is not available, as shown in Figure 14-15.

Figure 14-15 *Gatekeeper Disengage Bandwidth Control*

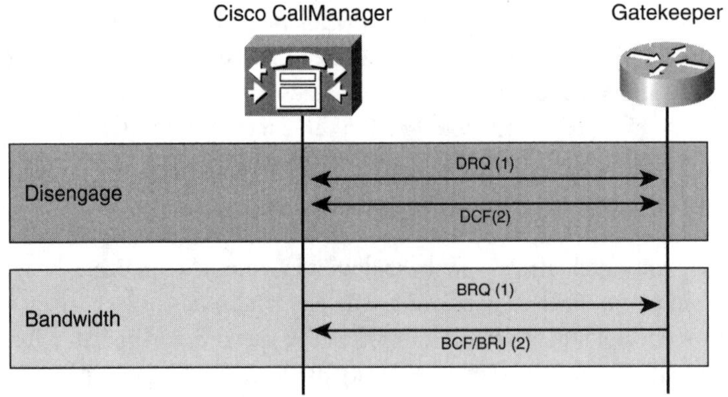

Gatekeeper-Based Call Admission Control Configuration

The general recommendation is to use separate Cisco routers as dedicated gatekeepers in your network in a number appropriate for your topology. Cisco also supports clustering the gatekeeper routers using H.323 clustering with the Gatekeeper Update Protocol (GUP). You can configure a gatekeeper with the appropriate Cisco IOS feature set, such as the Enterprise Plus/H323 MCM feature set.

> **TIP** Other feature sets of the IOS have begun adding gatekeeper support. The best way to find out what feature set you should download is to use the Cisco feature navigator utility available at http://www.cisco.com/go/fn.

The following are the four general steps for configuring call admission control using gatekeepers and trunks:

Step 1 On the gatekeeper device, configure the appropriate zones and bandwidth allocations for the various Cisco CallManager nodes that will route calls to it.

Example 14-1 shows a sample Cisco IOS gatekeeper simple configuration.

Example 14-1 *Sample H.323 Gatekeeper Basic Configuration*

```
Router(config)# gatekeeper
Router(config-gk)# zone local SJGK1 cisco.com
Router(config-gk)# zone prefix SJGK1 408*
Router(config-gk)# gw-type-prefix 1#* default-technology
Router(config-gk)# bandwidth total zone SJGK1 512
Router(config-gk)# bandwidth session zone SJGK1 256
```

Table 14-1 describes these commands.

Table 14-1 *Cisco IOS Gatekeeper Commands*

Command	Description
`Gatekeeper`	Enters gatekeeper configuration mode.
`zone local SJGK1 cisco.com`	Specifies the zone name controlled by the gatekeeper. In this case, cisco.com is the zone controlled by gatekeeper SJGK1.
`zone prefix SJGK1 408*`	Associates the digits 408 with the local zone SJGK1.
`gw-type-prefix 1#* default-technology`	Configures a technology prefix in the gatekeeper. Cisco gatekeepers use technology prefixes to route calls when there are no E.164 addresses registered (by a gateway) that match the called number. With the default technology prefix option, the Cisco gatekeeper assigns a default gateway or gateways for routing unresolved call addresses. This assignment is based on the registered technology prefix of the gateways.

continues

Table 14-1 *Cisco IOS Gatekeeper Commands (Continued)*

Command	Description
`bandwidth total zone SJGK1 512`	Specifies the maximum bandwidth available in zone SJGK1 as 512 kbps.
`bandwidth session zone SJGK1 256`	Specifies the maximum bandwidth allowed for a session in zone SJGK1 as 256 kbps.

Step 2 Configure gatekeeper settings in Cisco CallManager Administration. Make sure that the hostname or IP address is set the same way on each Cisco CallManager. You can register multiple gatekeepers per Cisco CallManager cluster.

You can add gatekeepers to the CallManager configuration by accessing the **Device > Gatekeeper Configuration** window. When you click on **Add a New Gatekeeper**, the configuration window shown in Figure 14-16 appears. Table 14-2 describes the configuration options.

Figure 14-16 *Configuring a Gatekeeper Reference in Cisco CallManager*

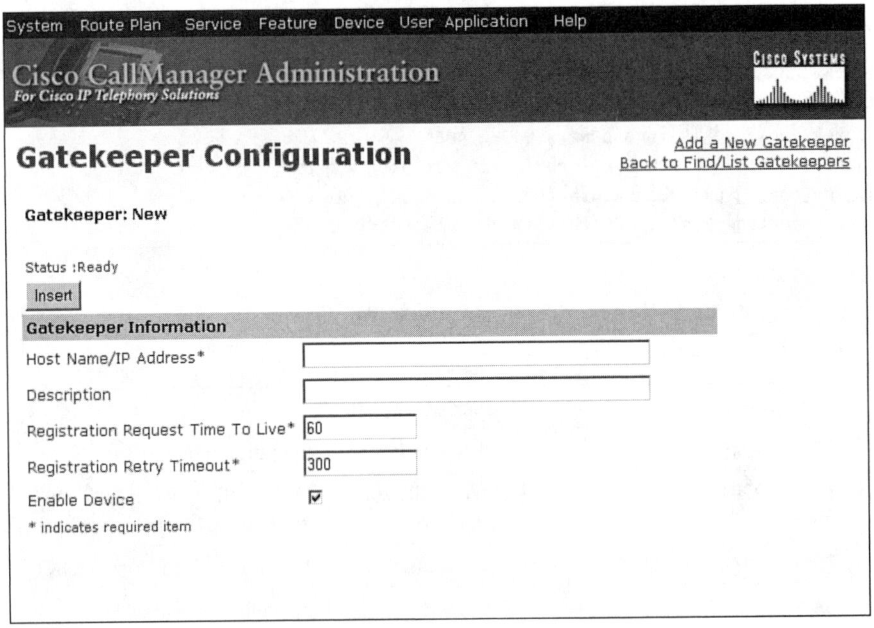

Table 14-2 *Cisco CallManager Gatekeeper Configuration Options*

Field	Description
Host Name/IP Address*	Enter the IP address or hostname of the gatekeeper in this required field (IP address preferred).
Registration Request Time to Live	Do not change this value unless a Cisco Technical Assistance Center (TAC) engineer instructs you to do so. The default value specifies 60 seconds. The **Registration Request Time to Live** field indicates the time that the gatekeeper considers a registration request (RRQ) valid. The system must send a keepalive RRQ to the gatekeeper before the RRQ TTL expires. Cisco CallManager sends an RRQ to the gatekeeper to register and subsequently to maintain a connection with the gatekeeper. The gatekeeper may confirm (RCF) or deny (RRJ) the request.
Registration Retry Timeout*	Do not change this value unless a Cisco TAC engineer instructs you to do so. Enter the time in seconds. The default value specifies 300 seconds. The **Registration Retry Timeout** field indicates the time that Cisco CallManager waits before retrying gatekeeper registration after a failed registration attempt.

* Indicates required item

Step 3 Configure the appropriate intercluster trunks or H.225 trunks to specify gatekeeper information. The H.225 trunk allows connectivity to H.323 Cisco IOS gateways. The intercluster trunk provides specific Cisco functionality for calls between Cisco CallManager clusters.

After you have added the necessary gatekeeper(s) to the CallManager configuration, you can add trunks connecting to the gatekeeper device. Cisco CallManager supports two types of gatekeeper-controlled trunks:

- **H.225 trunk (Gatekeeper Controlled)**—In an H.323 network that uses gatekeepers, use an H.225 trunk with gatekeeper control to configure a connection to a gatekeeper for access to other Cisco CallManager clusters and to H.323 devices (which could connect to third-party networks). An H.225 trunk can communicate with any H.323 gatekeeper-controlled endpoint. When you configure an H.323 gateway with gatekeeper control in Cisco CallManager Administration, use an H.225 trunk. To use this method, choose **Device** > **Trunk** and then choose **H.225 Trunk (Gatekeeper Controlled)**.
- **Inter-Cluster Trunk (Gatekeeper Controlled)**—In a distributed call-processing network with gatekeepers, use an Intercluster Trunk with gatekeeper control to configure connections between clusters of Cisco

CallManager systems. Gatekeepers provide call admission control and address resolution for intercluster calls. A single Intercluster Trunk can communicate with all remote clusters. To use this method, choose **Device > Trunk** and then choose **Inter-Cluster Trunk (Gatekeeper Controlled)** in Cisco CallManager Administration.

You can add gatekeeper-controlled H.225 and intercluster trunks to the Cisco CallManager configuration using the same process as adding non-gatekeeper controlled trunks, which was discussed in Chapter 10, "Cisco Unified CallManager Route Plan Basics." The trunk should point to the gatekeeper device rather than the remote cluster and be configured for the appropriate default technology prefix and local zone name that you have configured on the gatekeeper device, as shown in Figure 14-17.

Figure 14-17 *Configuring a Gatekeeper-Controlled Trunk*

Gatekeeper Information	
Gatekeeper Name*	10.5.1.9
Terminal Type*	Gateway
Technology Prefix	1#
Zone	PHOENIX

NOTE The two different types of gatekeeper-controlled trunks have caused much confusion with CallManager administrators. The Intercluster Trunk is a Cisco proprietary trunking method that allowed communication between Cisco CallManager clusters. This type of trunk is only necessary when communicating with clusters running Cisco CallManager 3.2 or earlier. The H.225 trunk is an industry standard trunking method used to communicate with any type of H.323-compliant device, including CallManager clusters since version 3.3 and Cisco CallManager Express platforms.

Step 4 Configure a route pattern to route calls to each gatekeeper-controlled trunk.

After you have added the gatekeeper-controlled trunks to the configuration, you can include them in the Cisco CallManager route plan just like any other device.

Survivable Remote Site Telephony

In a centralized deployment model, if a WAN connection fails, remote IP Phones cannot make calls. This weakness can be a serious problem when it comes to emergency calls.

A simple way of solving this problem is to provide limited call-processing capabilities in the remote office router. Cisco IP Phone enhancements grant the ability to rehome to the call-processing functions in the local router upon WAN failure detection. This solution is Cisco Survivable Remote Site Telephony (SRST).

The Cisco SRST feature provides call-handling support on the gateway router for attached Cisco IP Phones when a Cisco CallManager or WAN link fails. On restoration of the Cisco CallManager or WAN link, the Cisco CallManager resumes the call-handling capabilities for the IP Phones. The implementation of this feature is transparent to the end user, with the exception of the notification that a user receives on the IP Phones that it is in fallback mode.

The SRST-enabled router supports the following:

- IP Phone-to-IP Phone calls (at the local site)
- IP Phone-to-PSTN calls
- Direct Inward Dialing (DID)
- Multiple lines per IP Phone
- Multiple line appearance across IP Phones
- Call hold and pickup on a shared line
- Transfer of local calls
- Caller ID information
- Speed dialing
- Last-number redial
- Call transfer without consultation (local to router only)
- Call hold and resume
- Multiple extensions (up to six extensions per IP Phone on Cisco 7960 IP Phones)
- Multiple line appearances, with up to 24 appearances per system
- Distinctive ringing
- Extension class of service (CoS)
- Full interworking with Cisco gatekeeper functionality
- Voice-mail support (only to local answering machine)

- Billing support using call detail records (CDRs)
- Dual-line mode
- Music on Hold

SRST goes into effect when Cisco IP Phones detect that they are no longer receiving responses to their keepalive packets from the Cisco CallManager, as shown in Figure 14-18. The Cisco IP Phones can be configured to register with the router as a backup call-processing source. The SRST software in the router automatically activates and builds a local database of all Cisco IP Phones attached to it, up to the stated maximum. The SRST router now performs all local call setup and processing, call maintenance, and call termination.

Figure 14-18 *SRST Failover Process*

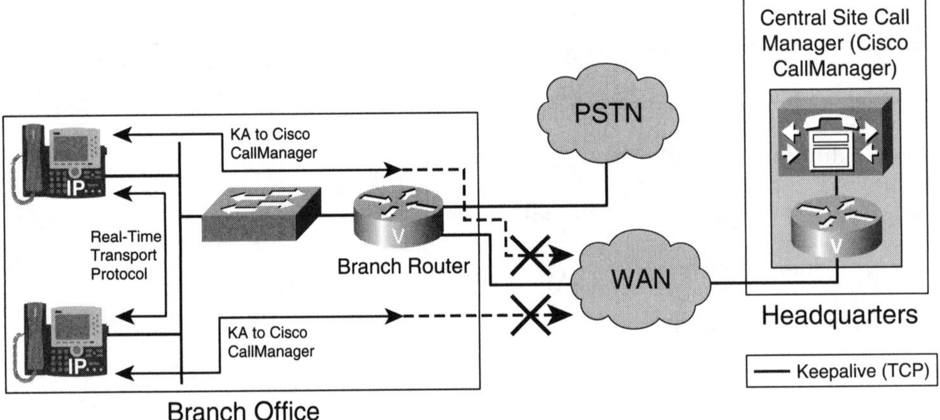

When the WAN link resumes, the IP Phones detect keepalive responses from the central Cisco CallManager and revert to the central Cisco CallManager for primary call setup and processing. As IP Phones rehome to the Cisco CallManager, the SRST router purges its call-processing database and reverts to standby mode. Calls in progress continue without interruption. IP Phones in use during WAN link recovery rehome to the Cisco CallManager after the calls terminate.

SRST Router Configuration

The most common application of SRST is to maintain basic IP telephony functionality for the IP Phones at remote branch offices when the WAN link fails or the Cisco CallManager at headquarters is no longer available. The remote branch router activates SRST functions and takes over communication with the IP Phones. IP Phones are able to call each other and make off-net calls to the PSTN. In addition, the most basic telephone functions, such as hold and transfer, are still available.

There is one global command (with a series of subcommands) to configure for SRST, the **call-manager-fallback** command. Example 14-2 shows a sample SRST configuration.

Example 14-2 *SRST Sample Configuration*

```
Router(config)#call-manager-fallback
Router(config-cm-fallback)#access-code fxo 9
Router(config-cm-fallback)#default-destination 4312
Router(config-cm-fallback)#dialplan-pattern 1 345555….
Router(config-cm-fallback)#ip source-address 10.1.1.2 port 2000
Router(config-cm-fallback)#keepalive 30
Router(config-cm-fallback)#max-ephones 24
Router(config-cm-fallback)#max-dn 48
Router(config-cm-fallback)#transfer-pattern 525...
Router(config-cm-fallback)#voicemail 4001
```

Table 14-3 describes the function of these commands.

Table 14-3 *Cisco SRST Command Descriptions*

Command	Description
access-code	Defines access codes for outgoing calls.
default-destination	Defines or disables the default destination DN for ringing on unknown called number (typically used for incoming PSTN calls).
dialplan-pattern	Defines an E.164 telephone number prefix. This command defines the number of digits sent from the provider for incoming calls and dictates how many digits should be forwarded to the phones. In the sample syntax, the provider is sending ten-digit DID numbers and the internal office is using four-digit extensions.
ip source-address	Defines an IP address and port for the SRST router. This command dictates which internal IP address should expect to receive Skinny messages when the CallManager connection is lost.
keepalive	Defines the keepalive timeout period to unregister IP Phones.
max-dn	Specifies the maximum DNs supported on the IP Keyswitch.
max-ephones	Specifies the maximum number of IP Phones.
transfer-pattern	Defines valid call transfer destinations off the VoIP network. By default, SRST allows transfers only between devices registered to the same SRST router.
voicemail	Sets the voice-mail access number called when the Messages button is pressed.

SRST Reference Configuration

After you input the necessary Cisco IOS SRST gateway configuration, you must then configure the Cisco CallManager to recognize the gateway as an SRST reference. The CallManager will then deliver the SRST reference to the IP Phone through the configuration file on the TFTP server.

> **NOTE** If the IP Phones at a remote location use their default gateway as the SRST router, it is not necessary to configure SRST references. In the IP Phone's device pool configuration, you can select the **Use Default Gateway** option to point the IP Phones to the correct SRST device.

To configure SRST references, choose the **System** menu in the Cisco CallManager Administration utility and then choose **SRST**. When the Find and List SRST References window appears, click the **Add a New SRST Reference** link in the upper-right area of the window. A window similar to the one shown in Figure 14-19 should appear. To create a valid SRST reference, you must enter values in the following fields you input:

- **SRST Reference Name**—This value is a logical name that you can use when referencing the SRST gateway. It does not need to match the name assigned to the gateway.
- **IP Address**—This value is the IP address that the Cisco IP Phone should use when contacting the SRST gateway. The IP Phone itself must be able to reach this IP address.
- **Port**—This value is the port number that the IP Phone should use when contacting the SRST reference. By default, this uses TCP port you input 2000.

Figure 14-19 *SRST Reference you input Configuration Window*

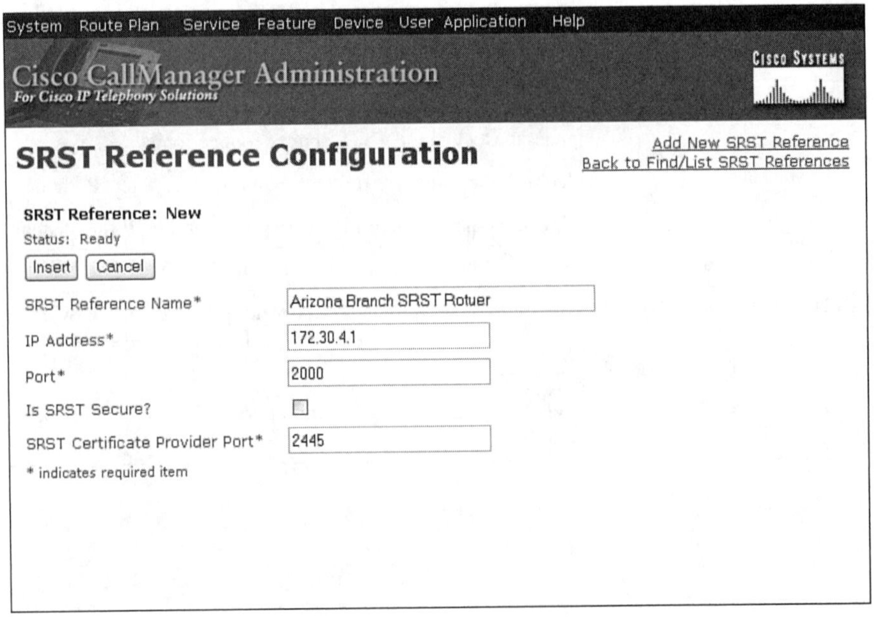

The **Is SRST Secure?** check box and the **SRST Certificate Provider Port** field are used for configuring the Cisco CallManager portion of a secure SRST-enabled gateway connection. Secure SRST allows Cisco CallManager to authenticate with a secure SRST-enabled gateway and add the SRST-enabled gateway certificate to the Cisco CallManager database. The TFTP server adds the SRST certificate to the phone cnf.xml file and sends the file to the phone. A secure phone then uses a secure connection to interact with the SRST-enabled gateway. Phone security is discussed in Chapters 26, "IPT Authentication and Encryption Fundamentals" and 27, "Configuring IPT Authentication and Encryption."

After you create the input SRST reference in Cisco CallManager, you must assign the SRST reference to the Cisco IP Phone. Cisco CallManager creates this assignment through the device pool. In the Device Pool Configuration window, click the **SRST Reference** drop-down arrow to choose the SRST reference that the IP Phone should use. If you want the Cisco IP Phone to use its default gateway as the SRST reference, you can choose the **Use Default Gateway** option from the menu. Using this option can simplify your SRST configuration.

NOTE Each router platform supports a different maximum number of IP Phones. Up-to-date information on these numbers can be gathered from the SRST administration guide available on the Cisco website you input.

Summary

This chapter covered the concepts and configuration of Cisco CallManager in a multiple-site deployment. Call admission control (CAC) mechanisms are necessary in this type of deployment to control the volume of calls between two endpoints, which is key to maintaining QoS of all calls.

Cisco CallManager supports two models of CAC: location-based CAC for centralized call-processing environments and gatekeeper-based CAC for distributed call-processing environments. Locations-based CAC is configured on the Cisco CallManager and allocates a specific audio and video bandwidth amount to each location. IP Phones are then assigned to their respective locations on a per-device basis.

Automated Alternate Routing (AAR) is a mechanism used with location-based CAC to automatically reroute calls to the PSTN (or other network) when there is insufficient bandwidth on the primary voice path. Configuring AAR entails configuring AAR groups and assigning the external phone number mask to the DN assigned to each AAR-capable device.

In a distributed call-control environment, multiple Cisco CallManager clusters can exist. This design requires an independent authority that can control the WAN bandwidth and call routing between clusters. The H.323 gatekeeper is used to satisfy this requirement. Gatekeepers are configured in the IOS software and added to the Cisco CallManager configuration to support gatekeeper-controlled trunks. These trunks are then included in the Cisco CallManager route plan to route outside of the cluster.

The final topic discussed in this chapter addresses the failover capabilities of remote sites in a centralized CallManager environment. Survivable Remote Site Telephony (SRST) provides call-handling support for IP Phones when the Cisco CallManager or WAN link fails. SRST is configured on an IOS-based router and added to the Cisco CallManager configuration as an SRST reference. The SRST reference is assigned to end devices through their device pool.

Review Questions

You can find the solutions to these questions in Appendix A, "Answers to Review Questions."

1. Which is a benefit associated with gatekeeper call admission control?
   a. no requirement to configure Cisco IOS commands on the gatekeeper
   b. no requirement to configure an Intercluster Trunk between clusters
   c. provides emergency call-handling capability if the WAN link fails
   d. provides call admission control over the intranet in addition to the WAN
2. Without call admission control, what happens to existing calls when the next call oversubscribes the WAN?
   a. All calls are dropped.
   b. Voice quality on all calls degrades.
   c. Voice quality on the last call degrades.
   d. Nothing happens if the router is configured for QoS.
3. Which two characteristics are associated with the distributed call-control environment? (Choose two.)
   a. Intercluster Trunk to each Cisco CallManager cluster
   b. gatekeeper-controlled trunks
   c. maximum bandwidth determined on the Cisco CallManager
   d. zones and bandwidth allocation configured on the gatekeeper
4. How do the Cisco IP Phones in a branch site know how to register to a gateway running SRST?
   a. The IP Phones stop receiving keepalive packets from the SRST gateway.
   b. The IP address is configured on the gateway and passed to the IP Phone.
   c. The gateway IP address is specified in the SRST Reference Configuration window and assigned to a device pool.
   d. The device pool contains the IP address reference to the SRST gateway.

5. Using the Cisco CallManager locations feature, how many simultaneous audio calls can be placed over a given WAN link with 128 kbps of available bandwidth using a G.729 codec?

   a. two

   b. three

   c. four

   d. five

6. AAR derives the alternate dial string used to route the call over the PSTN from which three of the following? (Choose three.)

   a. DN

   b. external phone number mask

   c. AAR calling search space

   d. MAC address

   e. PSTN prefix

   f. AAR group

7. Which command is used to initiate SRST capabilities on an IOS-based router?

   a. telephony-service

   b. call-fallback

   c. call-manager-fallback

   d. ccm-communication

8. You are working in a location-based CallManager deployment. Phone A (DN=3423) dials on-net to Phone B (DN=3420). The location-based CAC denies the call and AAR initiates. Which external phone number mask will be used by AAR to complete the call?

   a. Phone A

   b. Phone B

   c. the gateway at the calling site

   d. the gateway at the called site

9. What is the default state of AAR in a CallManager cluster?

   a. AAR is enabled, but must be configured by an administrator.

   b. AAR is enabled and preconfigured, provided the administrator has entered the correct external phone number masks under the applicable DNs.

   c. AAR is disabled until a feature license is applied.

   d. AAR is disabled.

10. You have AAR configured in a cluster to divert calls to the PSTN should the IP WAN become unusable. To test the configuration, you disconnect the WAN and place a call to an alternate site. The CallManager returns a reorder tone. You are sure the digit transformation settings are configured correctly; what is the most likely cause of this problem?

a. AAR does not function in a distributed call-control environment.

b. The AAR calling search space does not provide the necessary privileges to complete the call.

c. The standard calling search space does not provide the necessary privileges to complete the call.

d. AAR does not function during a WAN failure.

Part IV: VoIP Features

This chapter covers the following topics:

- Activating all necessary Cisco CallManager services that are used in media resources
- Configuring conference bridge resources to enable ad hoc and Meet-Me conferencing between IP Phones
- Describing the services that MTP resources provide
- Identifying the Cisco CallManager resources that are required for the annunciator feature
- Configuring transcoder resources in Cisco CallManager and on a Cisco access gateway to provide codec conversion
- Configuring audio sources for MoH and assigning user and network MoH to IP Phones
- Allocating media resources to devices using MRGs and MRGLs

CHAPTER 15

Media Resources

Conferencing, music on hold (MoH), and informational tones and spoken word progress tones are important business phone services. Media resources provide these and other services in a Cisco CallManager IP telephony deployment. This chapter describes how to configure and allocate media resources to include conferencing, Media Termination Points (MTPs), the annunciator, transcoders, and MoH within a Cisco CallManager solution.

Introduction to Media Resources

A media resource is a software-based or hardware-based entity that performs media processing functions on the voice streams to which it is connected. Media-processing functions include mixing multiple streams to create mixed, unicast output streams (conferencing), passing the stream from one connection to another (Media Termination Point), converting the data stream from one compression type to another (transcoding), streaming voice progress tones (annunciation), and music on hold.

Every Cisco CallManager contains a software component called a Media Resource Manager (MRM) that communicates with MRMs on other Cisco CallManager servers. The MRM locates a media resource to connect the media streams and to complete the feature. The MRM manages the following media resource types:

- Conference bridge
- MTP
- Annunciator
- Transcoder
- MoH server

NOTE To act as a Media Resource Manager, you must activate the Voice Media Streaming Application service on the Cisco CallManager server. This service is discussed in detail later in this chapter.

Your Cisco CallManager servers can also participate in the media-processing functions in the cluster. After Cisco CallManager is installed, you must activate these two Cisco CallManager services:

- **Cisco IP Voice Media Streaming Application**—The Cisco IP Voice Media Streaming Application provides voice media streaming functionality for Cisco CallManager for use with MTP, the annunciator, conferencing, and MoH. The Cisco IP Voice Media Streaming Application relays messages from Cisco CallManager to the IP voice media streaming driver. The driver handles the Real-Time Transport Protocol (RTP) streaming.
- **Cisco MoH Audio Translator**—The Cisco MoH Audio Translator service converts audio source files, which can be in .WAV or .MP3 format, into the appropriate MoH source file for various coder-decoders (codecs) so that the MoH feature can use them.

To activate the required services in Cisco CallManager, access the administration web page and choose **Application > Cisco CallManager Serviceability**. In the Serviceability window, choose **Tools > Service Activation**. You can activate the services on any server that you choose.

Conference Bridge Resources

A conference bridge is a resource that joins multiple participants into a single call. Depending on the conference bridge you are using, each conference call is limited to a certain number of participants and specific codecs. There is a one-to-one correspondence between media streams that are connected to a conference and participants who are connected. The conference bridge mixes the streams together and creates a unique output stream for each connected party. The output stream for a given party is the composite of the streams from all connected parties minus its own input stream.

Cisco CallManager supports both hardware and software conference bridges. Hardware and software conference bridges can be active at the same time.

Hardware-enabled conferencing provides the ability to support voice conferences using hardware resources. Digital signal processors (DSPs) convert multiple voice over IP (VoIP) packets into streams that are mixed into a single conference call stream. The DSPs support both Meet-Me and ad hoc conferences. Hardware conference devices can provide a mixing of multiple codecs on the same conference call for G.711, G.729, G.723, Global System for Mobile Communication (GSM) Full Rate (FR), and GSM Enhanced Full Rate (EFR). Not all hardware resources support all of these codecs, but they all support at least G.711 and G.729, which are the two codecs supported by all modern Cisco IP Phones.

Software conferences use the resources of Cisco CallManager. A software conference bridge is capable of mixing G.711 audio streams and Cisco Wideband audio streams. Any combination of Wideband or G.711 a-law and mu-law streams can be connected to the same conference.

Conference bridges enable both ad hoc and Meet-Me voice conferencing:

- **Ad hoc conference**—A user, known as the conference controller, adds participants to a conference by calling the new participant and pressing the **Confrn** softkey. Alternatively, the conference controller can press the **Select** softkey and then press the **Join** softkey to make it an ad hoc conference. Up to 15 established calls can be added to the ad hoc conference (16 total). Only the conference controller can add participants to an ad hoc conference. An ad hoc conference can continue if the conference controller hangs up, but new participants cannot be added. When only two participants remain in conference, the conference terminates and the two remaining participants are reconnected directly as a point-to-point call. This action saves conference resources.
- **Meet-Me conference**—A user, known as the conference controller, presses the **MeetMe** button or softkey and establishes the conference. The administrator must configure a directory number (DN) or range of DNs in Cisco CallManager Administration. The conference controller provides the DN to the participants, and at the appointed time, participants dial the DN to join the conference. Participants can leave the conference by hanging up. If the conference controller hangs up, the conference continues if there are least two participants on the bridge.

NOTE The Meet-Me conference functionality included with Cisco CallManager is very basic and does not provide scheduling and/or security capabilities. The Cisco Meeting Place or Meeting Place Express software can be used for this functionality.

Conference Bridge Hardware

Table 15-1 identifies the conference bridge types that exist in Cisco CallManager 4.1 Administration. For each conference bridge type, the table lists the supported product or application, the supported codecs, and the maximum number of participants.

Table 15-1 *Conference Bridge Hardware*

Cisco CallManager Resource Type	Conferences Resource	Codecs	Max. Participants per Conference
Cisco Conference Bridge	WS-SVC-CMM	G.711 mu-law, G.711 a-law, G.729 annex A and annex B, and G.723.1	8 per conference, 64 conferences per port adapter

continues

Table 15-1 *Conference Bridge Hardware (Continued)*

Cisco CallManager Resource Type	Conferences Resource	Codecs	Max. Participants per Conference
Cisco Conference Bridge Hardware	WS-X6608-T1 WS-X6608-E1	G.711, G.723, G.729, GSM FR, GSM EFR	1 CFB–32 users to 10 CFB–3 users For G.711 or G.729a: 256 streams total per module, 32 streams maximum per port
Cisco Conference Bridge Software	Cisco IP Voice Media Streaming App.	G.711, Cisco Wideband	64–Ad Hoc 128–Meet-Me
Cisco IOS Conference Bridge	NM-HDV	G.711, G.729	6
Cisco IOS Enhanced Conference Bridge	NM-HD NM-HDV2 WS-SVC-CMM-ACT	G.711, G.729, GSM FR, GSM EFR G.711, G.729, or G723	8
Cisco Video Conference Bridge (IP/VC-35xx)	IP/VC-35xx	Numerous audio and video coding schemes	Varies by platform

Brief descriptions of the conference resources follow:

- **WS-SVC-CMM**—This conference bridge type, when configured with the ACT port adapter, supports the Cisco Catalyst 6500 Series and Cisco 7600 Series Communication Media Module (CMM). This conference bridge type supports up to eight parties per conference and up to 64 conferences per port adapter. This conference bridge type supports the following codecs: G.711 mu-law, G.711 a-law, G.729 annex A and annex B, and G.723.1. This conference bridge type supports ad hoc conferencing.

- **WS-X6608-T1 and WS-X6608-E1**—The WS-X6608-T1 and WS-X6608-E1 provide eight digital T1 or E1 interfaces for public switched telephone network (PSTN) and PBX gateway access, transcoding, and conference bridging. Each one of these eight T1/E1 ports can be used for either WAN/PSTN connectivity or to provision the DSP resources for media resource support, but not both at the same time.

- **Cisco IP Voice Media Streaming Application**—The Cisco IP Voice Media Streaming Application provides voice media streaming functionality for the Cisco CallManager for use with MTP, conferencing, and MoH. The Cisco IP Voice Media Streaming Application relays messages from the Cisco CallManager to the IP voice media streaming driver. Supporting services using the Cisco CallManager are limited to G.711 only (with the exception of streaming MoH) because the CallManager is not capable of performing transcoding functions.

- **NM-HDV**—The NM-HDV network modules (NMs) provide conferencing, transcoding, voice termination, and a voice WAN interface card (VWIC) slot, and include the NM-HDV-2E1-60, NM-HDV-2T1-48, NM-HDV-FARM-C36, NM-HDV-FARM-C54, and NM-HDV-FARM-C90. The NM-HDV modules are first generation DSP farms. Much of this functionality has been merged into the NM-HD and NM-HDV2 modules.
- **NM-HD**—The NM-HD modules include the NM-HD-1V, NM-HD-2V, and NM-HD-2VE. The NM-HD-1V has one video interface card (VIC) slot and supports one analog or BRI VIC. The NM-HD-2V has two VIC slots and supports two analog or BRI VICs (or any combination). The NM-HD-2VE has two VIC slots and supports two analog or BRI VICs or two digital VWICs (or any combination).
- **NM-HDV2**—The NM-HDV2 supports up to eight voice channels of analog or BRI voice. The NM-HDV2 supports a VIC/VWIC slot that can be fitted with either digital or analog or BRI voice/WAN interface cards, and supports up to 60 channels of digital voice or four channels of analog voice. The NM-HDV2-1T1/E1 adds support for one built-in T1 or E1 port and supports up to 90 channels of digital voice or 30 channels of digital voice and four channels of analog voice. The NM-HDV2-2T1/E1 adds support for two built-in T1 or E1 ports and supports a maximum of 120 channels of digital voice or 60 channels of digital voice and four channels of analog voice.
- **NM-HD-2VE**—The NM-HD-2VE supports analog, BRI, T1, E1, voice, and data WANs and up to 48 channels (G.711 codec).
- **IP/VC-3500 Series**—The Cisco IP/VC 3500 Series Video Multipoint Conference Unit is a dual multimedia bridge that provides videoconferencing. The videoconference bridge provides audio and videoconferencing functions for video Cisco IP Phones, H.323 endpoints, and audio-only Cisco IP Phones with the VT Advantage package. The Cisco IP/VC 3500 Series includes the Cisco IP/VC 3511, the Cisco IP/VC 3521 BRI Videoconferencing Gateway, and the IP/VC 3526 PRI Videoconferencing Gateway. For large or centralized videoconferencing deployments, the scalable, multifunctional IP/VC 3540 Series Videoconferencing System offers the combination of MCUs, a videoconferencing gateway, a rate matching module, and a data collaboration server. Each product in the series supports a number of audio and video codecs (H.261, H.263, H.263++, and H.264); these vary by platform.

Table 15-2 provides additional detail about audio conference bridges.

Table 15-2 *Conference Bridge Hardware*

<table>
<tr><th>Conference Type in Cisco CallManager</th><th>Number of Participants and Bridges</th><th>Resource</th></tr>
<tr><td>Hardware</td><td>For G.711 or G.729a:
• 256 streams total per module and 32 streams maximum per port.
• Bridges can range from 10 bridges with 3 participants to 1 bridge with 32 participants.
For all GSM:
• 192 streams per module and 24 streams per port</td><td>WS-X6608-T1
WS-X6608-E1</td></tr>
<tr><td>CallManager Software (Cisco IP Voice Media Streaming Application)</td><td>IP Voice Media Streaming Application on a standalone server:
• 128 streams.
• Ad hoc conference bridges can range from 42 bridges with 3 participants to 2 bridges with 64 participants.
• A Meet-Me conference is 1 bridge with up to 128 participants.
IP Voice Media Streaming Application coresident with Cisco CallManager:
• 48 streams.
• Bridges can range from 16 bridges with 3 participants to 1 bridge with 48 participants.</td><td>Software</td></tr>
<tr><td>Cisco IOS software</td><td>• 3 bridges per PVDM-12
• 3, 6, 9, or 15 bridges per NM
• Maximum of 6 participants per bridge
For information on the PVDM2-8, PVDM2-16, PVDM2-32, PVDM2-48, and PVDM2-64, refer to the "Hardware Resources for MTP, Conferencing, and Transcoding" section of the Cisco IP Telephony Solution Reference Network Design (SRND) for Release 4.1 at: http://www.cisco.com/go/srnd</td><td>NM-HDV</td></tr>
<tr><td>Enhanced Cisco IOS software</td><td>The total number of conference sessions is limited by the capacity of the entire system, the Cisco CallManager, and the codec. Further details can be found in the "Cisco Enhanced Conferencing and Transcoding for Voice Gateway Routers" data sheet at: http://www.cisco.com/en/US/products/ps5855/products_data_sheet0900aecd801b97a6.html</td><td>NM-HD
NM-HDV2</td></tr>
</table>

> **NOTE** The hardware and capacities described in Table 15-2 are accurate at the time of this writing; however, Cisco is continually adding new hardware and making improvements on existing hardware. To ensure accuracy when provisioning your network, refer to the latest CallManager SRND documentation available at http://www.cisco.com/go/srnd.

Conference Bridge Hardware CallManager Configuration

You must add hardware-based conference bridges to the Cisco CallManager configuration for the cluster to utilize them. The process of adding conference bridge resources differs, based on the type of conference resources you are adding. As an example, the following steps demonstrate the addition of a WS-X6608 as a DSP farm resource to the Cisco CallManager configuration:

Step 1 Choose **Service > Media Resource > Conference Bridge** and then choose **Add a New Conference Bridge**.

Step 2 Choose **Cisco Conference Bridge Hardware** in the **Conference Bridge Type** field. The Conference Bridge Configuration window shown in Figure 15-1 appears.

Figure 15-1 *Cisco Conference Bridge Hardware Configuration*

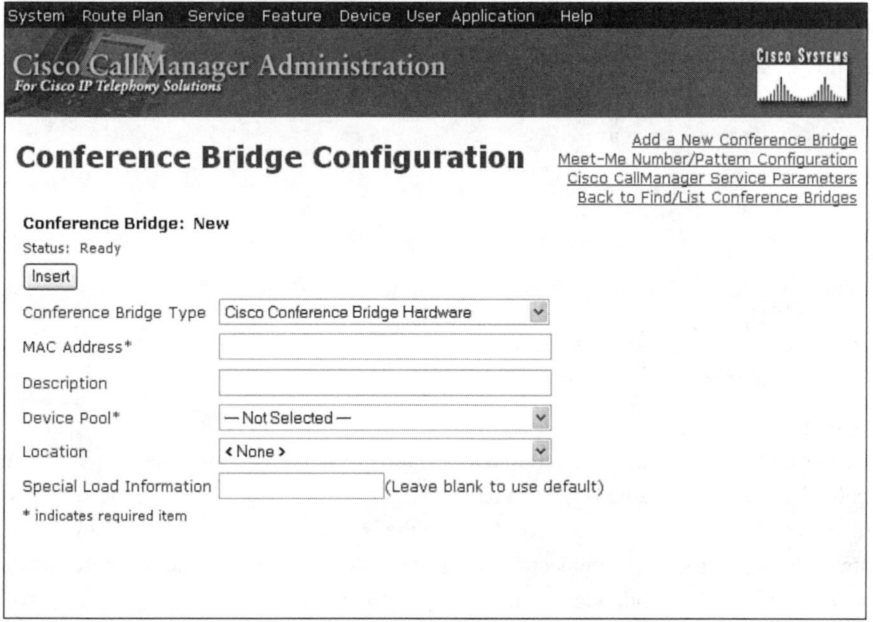

Step 3 Add the MAC address of the WS-X6608 port that will be used for conferencing.

On the WS-X6608, the port must be pointed toward the Cisco TFTP server to obtain the configuration file and a list of the Cisco CallManager servers within the Cisco IP telephony network to use for registration. Use the **set port voice interface** command on Cisco Catalyst switches running the Catalyst operating system to point the port toward the Cisco TFTP server (usually the publisher server).

The following example disables Dynamic Host Configuration Protocol (DHCP) on port 3/1 of a 6608 port, assigns an IP address, subnet mask, VLAN number, and default gateway, and points the port to the Cisco TFTP server (in bold):

```
set port voice interface 3/1 dhcp disable 172.16.10.201 255.255.255.0 vlan 15 tftp
172.16.10.5 gateway 172.16.10.1
```

NOTE Any Cisco CallManager servers in the cluster that have the Voice Media Streaming Application service activated will automatically be listed and used as a software-based conference resource. If you do not want a CallManager server to participate in conference bridge processing (to save resources), you can remove it as a conference bridge server by deleting the CallManager server in the Conference Bridge Configuration window.

Media Termination Point Resources

Media Termination Points (MTPs) are used to extend supplementary services to H.323 endpoints that do not support the H.323 Version 2 (H.323v2) OpenLogicalChannel and CloseLogicalChannel request features with the EmptyCapabilitiesSet feature. Supplementary services are features such as:

- Call Hold
- Call Transfer
- Call Park
- Conferencing

An MTP is an entity that accepts two full-duplex G.711 streams. It bridges the media streams together and allows them to be set up and torn down independently. Simply put, the MTP allows a call to be held (maintained) when a user places it on hold due to one of the services mentioned previously. The streaming data received from the input stream on one connection is passed to the output stream on the other connection, and vice versa. In addition, the MTP transcodes G.711 a-law to G.711 mu-law, and vice versa, and adjusts packet sizes as required by the two connections.

When needed, an MTP is allocated and connected into a call on behalf of an H.323 endpoint. After being inserted, the media streams are connected between the MTP and the H.323 device, and these connections are present for the duration of the call. The media streams connected to the other side of the MTP can be connected and disconnected as needed to implement features such as hold, transfer, and so forth.

Cisco CallManager requires an RFC 2833 dual-tone multifrequency (DTMF)-compliant MTP device to make Session Initiation Protocol (SIP) calls. The current standard for SIP uses in-band payload types to indicate DTMF tones. Cisco components such as Skinny-based IP Phones support only out-of-band payload types. Thus, an RFC 2833-compliant MTP device monitors for payload type and acts as a translator between in-band and out-of-band payload types. With the MTP device, any service that requires a media change (such as call hold) happens transparently.

Table 15-3 provides additional detail about MTP resources.

Table 15-3 *Media Termination Point Resources*

MTP Type	Limitations
Cisco IOS Software Enhanced Media Termination Point	This type supports Cisco 2600XM, 2691, 2811, 2821, 2851, 3660, 3725, 3745, 3825, and 3845 access routers and the following MTP cases: For a software-only implementation that does not use DSP but has the same packetization time for devices that support G.711-to-G.711 or G.729-to-G.729 codecs, this implementation can support up to 500 sessions per gateway. For a hardware-only implementation with DSP for devices that use G.711 codec only, 200 sessions can occur per NM-HDV2 and 48 sessions can occur per NM-HD. Cisco IOS Software Enhanced Media Termination Point does not support RFC 2833 (DTMF relay). This type can support Network Address Translation (NAT) in a service provider environment to hide the private address. In Cisco CallManager Administration, ensure that you enter the same MTP name that exists in the gateway command-line interface (CLI).
Cisco CallManager Media Termination Point Software (Voice Media Streaming Application)	A single MTP provides a default of 48 MTP (user-configurable) resources, depending on the speed of the network and the network interface card (NIC). For example, a 100-Mbps network card/NIC can support 48 MTP resources. For a 10-Mbps network card/NIC, approximately 24 MTP resources can be provided; however, the exact number of MTP resources that are available depends on the resources that are being consumed by other applications on that server, the speed of the processor, network loading, and various other factors. The Cisco IP Voice Media Streaming Application supports RFC 2833.

MTP Configuration

By default, any Cisco CallManager software-based MTP resources are automatically added to the cluster when you have activated the Voice Media Streaming Application on a server. If you do not want a CallManager server to participate in MTP processing (which saves resources), delete the server from under the MTP Configuration window. Hardware-based MTP resources (known as Cisco IOS Enhanced Software Media Termination Points) must manually be added to the cluster.

To configure or add an MTP, choose **Service > Media Resource > Media Termination Point** from the Cisco CallManager Administration console and click **Add a New Media Termination Point**. The Media Termination Point Configuration window shown in Figure 15-2 appears.

Figure 15-2 *Media Termination Point Configuration Window*

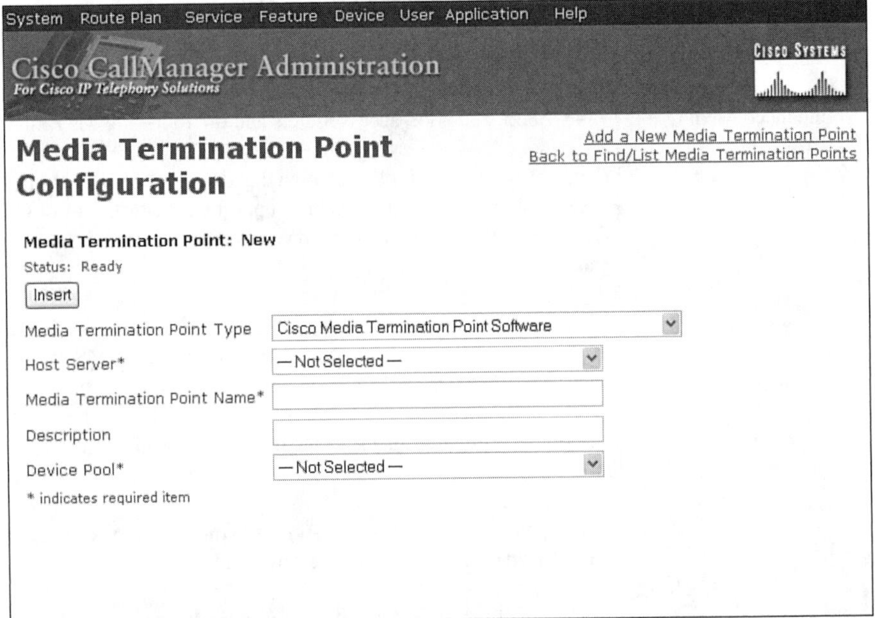

From here, you can choose to add a software- or hardware-based conference bridge to the CallManager cluster configuration. Table 15-4 describes the configuration options available from this window.

Table 15-4 *Media Termination Point Configuration Options*

Field	Description
Media Termination Point Type	Choose the MTP type, either Cisco IOS Enhanced Software Media Termination or Cisco Media Termination Point Software.
Host Server	Choose the server to run MTP (for software-based MTPs only).

Table 15-4 *Media Termination Point Configuration Options (Continued)*

Field	Description
Media Termination Point Name	Enter an MTP name, up to 15 alphanumeric characters.
Description	Enter a description for MTP.
Device Pool	Choose your preferred device pool or choose **Default**.

Annunciator Resources

An annunciator uses the Cisco IP Voice Media Streaming Application service and enables Cisco CallManager to play prerecorded announcements (.wav files) and tones to Cisco IP Phones, gateways, and other configurable devices. The annunciator enables Cisco CallManager to alert callers as to why a call has failed. The annunciator can also play tones for some transferred calls and some conferences.

In conjunction with Cisco CallManager, the annunciator device provides multiple one-way, RTP stream connections to devices such as Cisco IP Phones and gateways. For example, a user at extension 1001 dials extension 2503, an invalid number. The system cannot complete the call. The annunciator device plays a one-way RTP stream to extension 1001: "Your call cannot be completed as dialed. Please consult your directory and call again or ask your operator for assistance. This is a recording."

The annunciator plays the announcement or tone to support the following conditions:

- **Announcement**—For devices that are configured for Cisco CallManager Multilevel Precedence Preemption (MLPP).
- **Barge tone**—Before a participant joins an ad hoc conference.
- **Ringback tone**—When you transfer a call over the PSTN through a Cisco IOS gateway, over an H.323 Intercluster Trunk, or to the SIP client from an SCCP phone, the annunciator plays the tone because the gateway cannot play the tone when the call is active.

To add an annunciator to the Cisco CallManager, you must activate the Cisco IP Voice Media Streaming Application service on the server where you want the annunciator to exist in the cluster.

Table 15-5 shows sample annunciator announcements.

Table 15-5 *Sample Annunciator Announcements*

Condition	Announcement
An equal- or higher-precedence call is in progress.	"Equal- or higher-precedence calls have prevented the completion of your call. Please hang up and try again. This is a recording."
A precedence access limitation exists.	"Precedence access limitation has prevented the completion of your call. Please hang up and try again. This is a recording."
A service interruption occurred.	"A service disruption has prevented the completion of your call. In case of emergency, call your operator. This is a recording."

For a single annunciator, Cisco CallManager sets the default maximum to 48 simultaneous streams, as indicated in the annunciator service parameters (accessed under the service parameters for the Voice Media Streaming Application). It is recommended that you not exceed 48 annunciator streams on a coresident server where the Cisco CallManager and Cisco IP Voice Media Streaming Application services run. If the server has only 10-Mbps connectivity, lower the setting to 24 simultaneous streams.

If the annunciator runs on a standalone server where the Cisco CallManager service does not run, the annunciator can support up to 255 simultaneous announcement streams. If the standalone server has dual CPUs and a high-performance disk system (as in the case of the 7845 MCS server), the annunciator can support up to 400 simultaneous announcement streams. You can add multiple standalone servers to support the required number of streams.

Each annunciator can support G.711 a-law, G.711 mu-law, wideband, and G.729 codec formats. A separate .wav file exists for each codec that is supported.

Annunciator Configuration

Because the annunciator service requires access to a large amount of audio files, only the Cisco CallManager can act as an annunciator in the cluster. There are no hardware-based resources that exist. When you activate the Cisco IP Voice Media Streaming Application service in Cisco CallManager Serviceability, Cisco CallManager automatically adds the annunciator device to the server configuration.

The annunciator configuration is almost identical to the MTP configuration. Minimally, you must select a host server, enter the annunciator name, and assign the annunciator to a device pool, as shown in Figure 15-3.

Figure 15-3 *Annunciator Configuration Window*

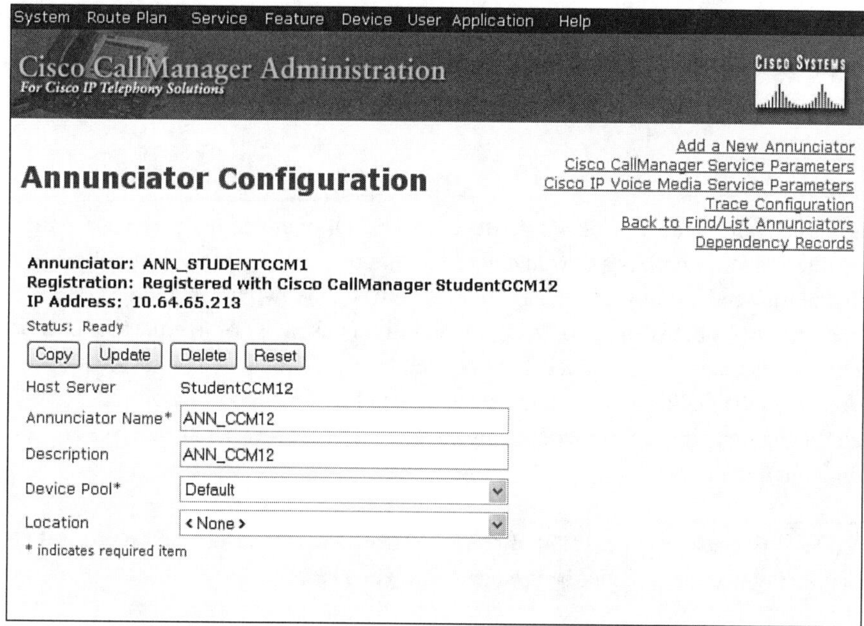

Each annunciator registers with only one Cisco CallManager at a time. The system might have multiple annunciators, depending on your configuration, each of which can register with different Cisco CallManager servers, depending on the device pool to which you have assigned the annunciator service. Each annunciator belongs to a device pool. The device pool associates the secondary (backup) Cisco CallManager and the region settings.

When you update or configure the annunciator service parameters, the changes automatically occur when the annunciator becomes idle, when no active announcements are played.

Transcoder Resources

A transcoder device takes the output stream of one codec and converts the voice streams to another compression type. For example, a transcoder can take an output stream from a G.711 codec and convert it to a G.729 stream. Depending on the hardware resources you are using, transcoders for Cisco CallManager convert between G.711, G.723, G.729, and GSM codecs. A transcoder device provides additional capabilities and can be used to enable supplementary services for H.323 endpoints.

Figure 15-4 shows a transcoder device (XCODE) enabling communication between two different codecs and providing MTP services for H.323 endpoints.

Figure 15-4 *Transcoder Operation*

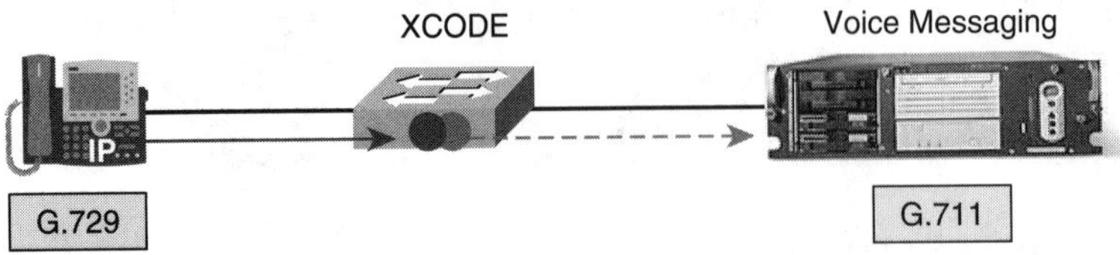

The Cisco CallManager invokes a transcoder on behalf of endpoint devices when the two devices use different voice codecs and would normally not be able to communicate. When inserted into a call, the transcoder converts the data streams between the two incompatible codecs to enable communications between them. The transcoder remains invisible to either the user or the endpoints that are involved in a call. For example, a user could be communicating across the IP WAN using the G.729 codec to a legacy voice-mail server supporting only G.711. Cisco CallManager can invoke transcoding resources to convert between the codecs and allow communication to occur.

NOTE Because of the amount of resources necessary to perform transcoding, Cisco CallManager servers cannot be used as transcoding resources.

Table 15-6 shows the currently available transcoding resources and the resource capabilities of each.

Table 15-6 *Transcoder Resource Capabilities*

<table>
<tr><th>Resource</th><th>From Codec</th><th>To Codec</th></tr>
<tr><td rowspan="2">WS-X6608-T1,
WS-X6608-E1</td><td>G.723. G.729a, GSM FR, GSM EFR</td><td>G.711 a-law or mu-law</td></tr>
<tr><td>G.711 a-law or mu-law</td><td>G.723. G.729a, GSM FR, GSM EFR</td></tr>
<tr><td rowspan="2">NM-HDV and
NM-HDV-
FARM</td><td>G.729, G.729a, G.729b, G.729ab</td><td>G.711 a-law or mu-law</td></tr>
<tr><td>G.711 mu-law</td><td>G.729, G.729a, G.729b, G.729ab</td></tr>
<tr><td rowspan="2">NM-HD and
NM-HDV2</td><td>G.729, G.729a, G.729b, G.729ab,
GSM FR, GSM EFR</td><td>G.711 a-law or mu-law</td></tr>
<tr><td>G.711 a-law or mu-law</td><td>G.729, G.729a, G.729b, G.729ab,
GSM FR, GSM EFR</td></tr>
<tr><td>WS-SVC-CMM</td><td colspan="2">This type provides transcoding between any combination of the following codecs:
• G.711 a-law and G.711 mu-law
• G.729 annex A and annex B
• G.723.1
• GSM (FR)</td></tr>
</table>

NOTE Cisco is continually adding transcoding-capable devices to their product line. For the latest information on transcoding resources, check the Cisco website.

Transcoder Configuration

To configure or add a new transcoder, choose **Service > Media Resource > Transcoder**, click **Add a New Transcoder** (shown in Figure 15-5), and then follow this general procedure:

Step 1 Choose the appropriate transcoder type: Cisco Media Termination Point Hardware, Cisco IOS Media Termination Point, Cisco IOS Enhanced Media Termination Point, or Cisco Media Termination Point (WS-SVC-CMM).

Step 2 For Cisco Media Termination Point Hardware or Cisco Media Termination Point (WS-SVC-CMM), enter a MAC address, which must be 12 characters.

Step 3 For Cisco Media Termination Point (WS-SVC-CMM) transcoders, choose a subunit from the drop-down list (not shown in the figure).

Step 4 Choose a device pool. For more detailed information on the chosen device pool, click **View Details**.

Step 5 Enter any special load information into the **Special Load Information** field or leave it blank to use the default. Valid characters include letters, numbers, dashes, dots (periods), and underscores.

Step 6 For Cisco Media Termination Point (WS-SVC-CMM) transcoders, choose a maximum capacity from the drop-down list (not shown in the figure).

Figure 15-5 *Transcoder Configuration Window*

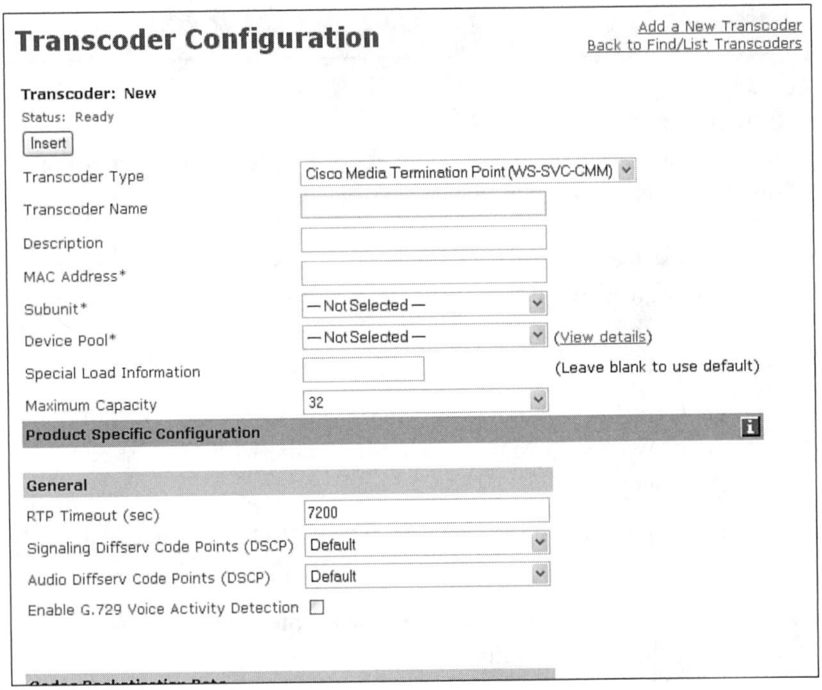

Transcoder Configuration

Add a New Transcoder
Back to Find/List Transcoders

Transcoder: New
Status: Ready
Insert

Transcoder Type: Cisco Media Termination Point (WS-SVC-CMM)
Transcoder Name
Description
MAC Address*
Subunit*: — Not Selected —
Device Pool*: — Not Selected — (View details)
Special Load Information (Leave blank to use default)
Maximum Capacity: 32

Product Specific Configuration

General
RTP Timeout (sec): 7200
Signaling Diffserv Code Points (DSCP): Default
Audio Diffserv Code Points (DSCP): Default
Enable G.729 Voice Activity Detection

> **NOTE** The preceding procedure shows the CallManager transcoder configuration for the WS-SVC-CMM module. The configuration fields for each type of transcoding resource are unique.

Music on Hold Resources

The integrated Music on Hold (MoH) feature provides On-Net and Off-Net users with on hold music from a streaming source. The MoH feature has two hold types:

- **User hold**—A user presses the **Hold** button or **Hold** softkey.
- **Network hold**—A user activates the transfer, conference, or Call Park feature, which automatically activates the hold feature before performing the operation.

MoH is customizable so that it plays specific recordings, based on the DN that is used to place the caller on hold or the line number that the caller has dialed. Recorded audio or a live audio stream can be configured as audio sources.

The MoH feature requires the use of a server that is part of a Cisco CallManager cluster. You can configure the MoH server in either of the following ways:

- **Coresident deployment**—In a coresident deployment, the MoH feature runs on any server (either publisher or subscriber) in the cluster that is also running the Cisco CallManager software. Because MoH shares server resources with Cisco CallManager in a coresident configuration, this type of configuration drastically reduces the number of simultaneous streams that an MoH server can send.
- **Standalone deployment**—A standalone deployment places the MoH feature on a dedicated server within the Cisco CallManager cluster. The sole function of this dedicated server is to send MoH streams to devices within the network. A standalone deployment allows for the maximum number of streams from a single MoH server.

Table 15-7 provides details on the number of MoH sessions and codecs that are supported for each server platform.

Table 15-7 *Transcoder Resource Capabilities*

Server Platform	Codecs Supported	MoH Sessions Supported
Cisco MCS 7815 Cisco MCS 782*x* (all models) Cisco MCS 7830 (all models) Cisco SPE-310 Hewlett-Packard DL320 IBM xSeries 33x (all models)	G.711 (a-law and mu-law) G.729a Wideband audio	Coresident server: 20 MoH sessions Standalone MoH server: 50 MoH sessions
Cisco MCS 7835 (all models) Cisco MCS 7845 (all models) Hewlett-Packard DL380 IBM xSeries 34x (all models)	G.711 (a-law and mu-law) G.729a Wideband audio	Coresident server: 20 MoH sessions Standalone MoH server: 250 MoH sessions

The maximum session limits apply to unicast, multicast, or simultaneous unicast and multicast sessions. The limits represent the recommended maximum sessions that a platform can support.

Creating Audio Source Files

Figure 15-6 shows the interactions among the audio translator, default MoH TFTP server, and MoH server. The large boxes in the figure represent cluster components that might reside on a single server or on three separate servers. This figure also shows how the MoH server processes the added audio source file.

Figure 15-6 *Creating Audio Source Files*

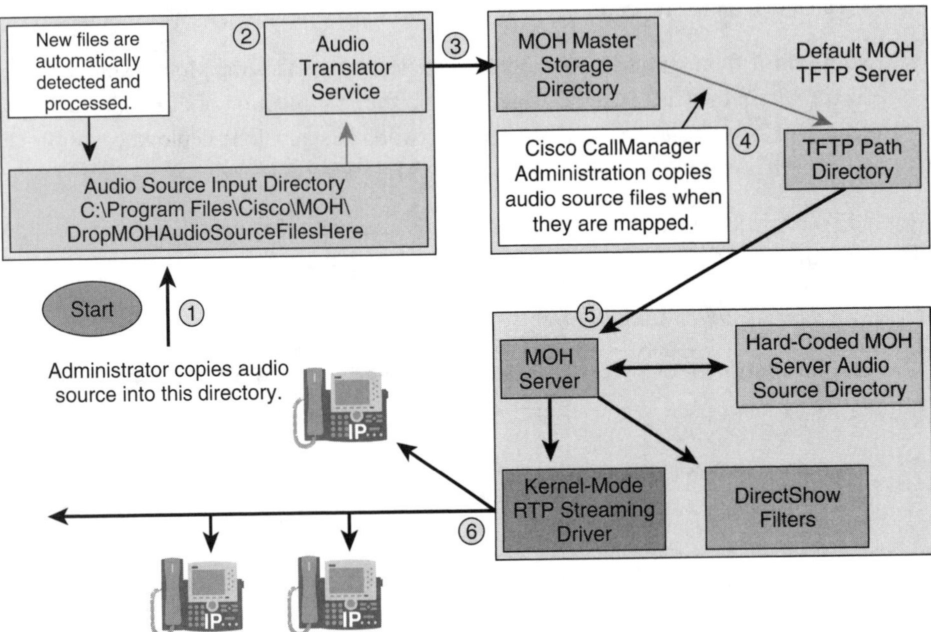

In creating an audio source, the following sequence takes place, as shown in the figure:

Step 1 The network administrator drops the audio files into the C:\Program Files\Cisco\MoH\DropMoHAudioSourceFilesHere directory path. Standard .wav and MP3 files are valid input.

NOTE It takes approximately 30 seconds to convert a 3-MB MP3 file.

Step 2 Cisco CallManager automatically detects and translates the files.

Step 3 The output and source files are moved into the default MoH TFTP server holding directory. This holding directory is the same as the default TFTPMoHFilePath with \MoH appended.

NOTE It is not recommended that the audio translator service be used during production hours because the service will consume 100 percent of the CPU.

Step 4 The network administrator assigns an audio source number to the audio source file. The corresponding audio source files are then copied to a directory that is one level higher in the directory structure (which is the default TFTP path) to make them available to the MoH servers.

Step 5 The MoH servers download the needed audio source files and store them in the hard-coded directory C:\Program Files\Cisco\MoH.

Step 6 The MoH server then streams the files using DirectShow and the kernel-mode RTP driver as needed or requested by Cisco CallManager.

Configuring MoH

The Cisco CallManager MoH Configuration is a six-step process:

Step 1 Configure the audio translator.

Step 2 Configure the MoH server.

Step 3 Add and configure audio source files.

Step 4 Set MoH servicewide settings.

Step 5 Find and configure the fixed audio source.

Step 6 Assign audio source IDs.

Step 1: Configure the Audio Translator

An MoH audio translator service converts administrator-supplied audio sources to the proper format for the MoH server to use. The audio translator uses two parameters, an input directory and an output directory. You can configure the input directory, which defaults to:

C:\Program Files\Cisco\MoH\DropMoHAudioSourceFilesHere, on a per-service basis.

The output directory, a clusterwide parameter, contains a Universal Naming Convention (UNC) name to a shared directory on the default MoH TFTP directory. For whichever directory is specified, append \MoH.

To display the Service Parameters Configuration window, choose **Service > Service Parameters** in Cisco CallManager Administration, choose the server that will provide MoH (typically, the publisher if not a standalone server), and choose Cisco MoH Audio Translator for the service. Figure 15-7 illustrates this configuration.

Figure 15-7 *Cisco MoH Audio Translator Service Configuration*

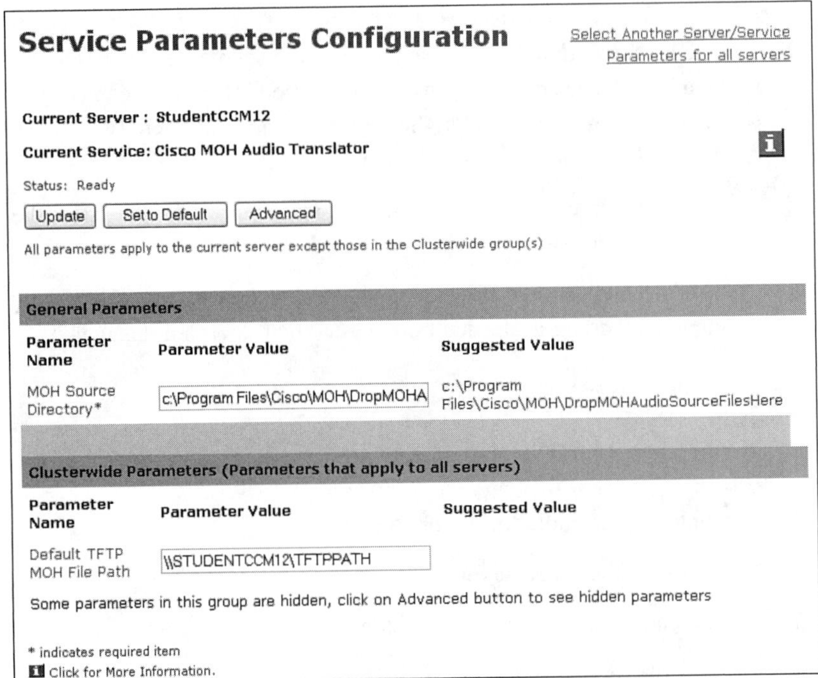

After you configure the audio translator service, you can drop your MoH audio source files (in .wav or .mp3 format) into the drop directory you specify. As soon as you copy the files into the directory, the CallManager's audio translator service immediately goes to work converting the files into the various audio codecs compatible with the VoIP network.

CAUTION Converting the audio source files into audio codec format can cause massive processor utilization on the CallManager server, potentially keeping it at 100 percent utilization for a short time (depending on the size and number of audio source files you copy). Cisco highly recommends doing this conversion during network off-hours.

TIP Be sure to copy the MoH audio source files into the drop directory. If you move the files (by dragging and dropping them from a source on the same hard disk partition, such as the desktop), the files retain their original permissions rather than inheriting the permissions of the parent directory. If the permissions are not set correctly, the CallManager will not be able to convert the audio files.

Step 2: Configure the MoH Server

Figure 15-8 shows the MoH Server Configuration window. The MoH server can be configured for unicast or multicast. Multicast MoH conserves system resources. Multicast allows multiple users to use the same audio source stream to provide MoH. Multicast audio sources associate with an IP address. To use multicast audio for MoH, your network must be configured to support multicast traffic. In addition, the audio source is always playing. Users placed on hold will typically join the audio source midstream; if you have announcements that play at the beginning of the audio stream, they might be missed.

Figure 15-8 *Cisco MoH Server Configuration*

Music On Hold (MOH) Server Configuration

Add a New Music On Hold Server
Configure Audio Sources
Trace Configuration
Back to Find/List Music On Hold Servers
Dependency Records

Music On Hold Server: MOH_STUDENTCCM1
Registration: Registered with Cisco CallManager StudentCCM12
IP Address: 10.64.65.213
Status: Ready

Copy Update Delete Reset

Device Information

Host Server	StudentCCM12
Music On Hold Server Name*	MOH_STUDENTCCM1
Description	
Device Pool*	Default
Location	< None >
Maximum Half Duplex Streams*	250
Maximum Multicast Connections*	30
Fixed Audio Source Device	
Run Flag*	Yes

Multicast Audio Source Information

☐ Enable Multicast Audio Sources on this MOH Server

Base Multicast IP Address	0.0.0.0
Base Multicast Port Number	0 (Even numbers only)
Increment Multicast on	⦿ Port Number ○ IP Address

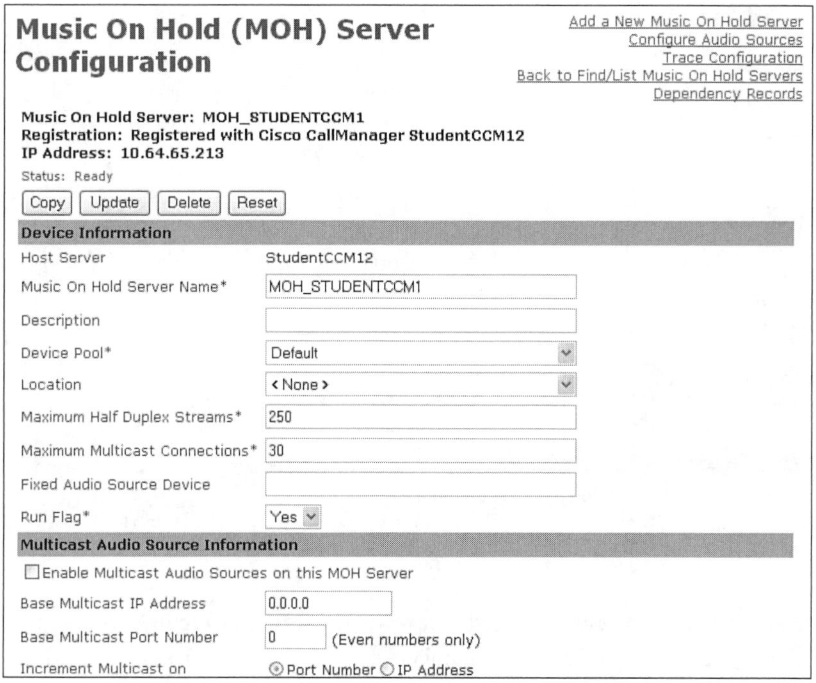

Unicast MoH, the system default, uses a separate source stream for each user or connection. Users connect to a specific device or stream. If your network supports multicast traffic, you can deploy

MoH services much more efficiently. Cisco recommends using a locally scoped multicast address (239.x.x.x) to ensure MoH multicast traffic does not stream over the IP WAN unnecessarily.

Choose **Service > Media Resource > Music On Hold Server** to display the Music On Hold (MoH) Server Configuration window.

Step 3: Add and Configure Audio Source Files

The next step in configuring MoH is to add and configure the audio source files that the CallManager has converted (by adding .wav or .mp3 files to the directory shown in Step 1) to audio source IDs. Choose **Service > Media Resource > Music On Hold Audio Source** to display the Music On Hold (MoH) Audio Source Configuration window, shown in Figure 15-9.

Figure 15-9 *Configuring Audio Source Files*

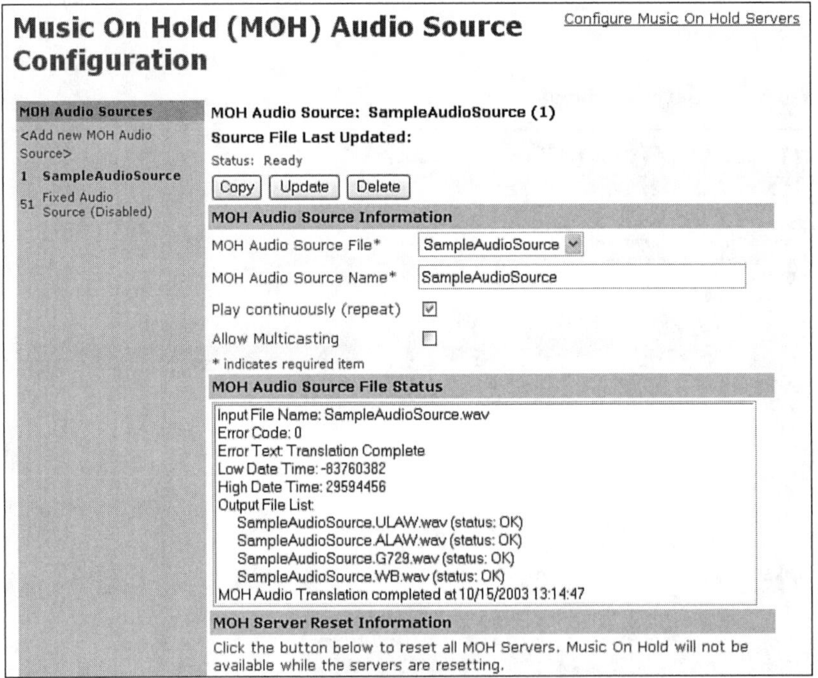

To add audio source files, click the **Add New MoH Audio Source** link, choose an MoH Audio Stream Number unique in the cluster (numbers range from 1 to 50), assign the MoH Audio Source File to the number, and click **Insert**. The **Play Continuously (Repeat)** check box should always be checked to ensure music loops when the end of the file is reached. If multicast capabilities are necessary, you must check the **Allow Multicasting** check box. If the **Play Continuously (Repeat)** and **Allow Multicasting** check boxes are both unchecked, the audio file stops playing when it reaches the end and the network administrator must stop and start the server to reset the MoH server.

The MoH Audio Source File Status window shows the conversion status and indicates whether the audio file translated correctly or had errors.

Step 4: Set MoH Servicewide Settings

To set the MoH servicewide settings, open the **Service Parameters Configuration** window, choose an MoH server, and choose the **Cisco IP Voice Media Streaming App** option. The Service Parameters Configuration window for MoH appears, as shown in Figure 15-10.

Figure 15-10 *Voice Media Streaming Application Service Parameters*

Conference Bridge (CFB) Parameters

Parameter Name	Parameter Value	Suggested Value
Call Count*	48	48
Run Flag*	True	True

Media Termination Point (MTP) Parameters

Parameter Name	Parameter Value	Suggested Value
Call Count*	48	48
Run Flag*	True	True

Clusterwide Parameters (Parameters that apply to all servers)

Parameter Name	Parameter Value	Suggested Value
Supported MOH Codecs*	711 mulaw 711 alaw 729 Annex A	711 mulaw
Default TFTP MOH IP Address*	STUDENTCCM12	
IP Type of Service to Cisco CallManager*	0x68	0x68

* indicates required item

Click for More Information.

The **Supported MoH Codecs** field is set to the codecs that are supported by the MoH servers in the cluster. This field defaults to G.711 mu-law during the installation. You can enable multiple codecs by pressing the **Ctrl** key while selecting the codecs.

The **Default TFTPMOH IP Address** field is set to the IP address or computer name of the default MoH TFTP server.

> **NOTE** Compressed codecs (such as G.729) are designed to handle Latin-based speech patterns. Music on hold audio does not translate well through codecs of this nature and the degradation in music quality is very perceptible.

Step 5: Find and Configure the Fixed Audio Source

One of your options for MoH is a fixed music source (attached via a sound card). This could be an external CD player, jukebox, iPod, or any device that can connect through the Line In or Microphone port of your sound card. You will need the exact name (case sensitive) of the fixed audio source device to complete the fixed audio source configuration in Cisco CallManager.

> **NOTE** CallManager MCS servers do not ship with sound cards. A list of supported sound cards can be found in the CallManager SRND available at http://www.cisco.com/go/srnd.

To find the name of the fixed audio source, open Control Panel and choose **Sounds and Multimedia**. Choose the **Audio** tab. You can use any sound-recording device name that appears in the Preferred Device menu, shown in Figure 15-11. In addition, be sure to open the Recording Control window, and click the **Volume** button in the Sound Recoding area. Verify that the **Line In, Microphone, or CD Audio** check box is checked and the volume has been adjusted to an appropriate level (this might require some testing in your IPT environment).

Figure 15-11 *Fixed Audio Source Windows Sound Properties*

To allow Cisco CallManager to use the fixed audio source, you must link the CallManager configuration with the Windows sound device. After you have located the sound-recording device name that appears in the Windows Control Panel, you must open the Audio Source File Configuration window (by choosing **Service > Media Resource > Music On Hold Audio Source**) and select the Fixed Audio Source (this will always be audio source ID 51). The window shown in Figure 15-12 appears.

Figure 15-12 *Fixed Audio Source CallManager Configuration*

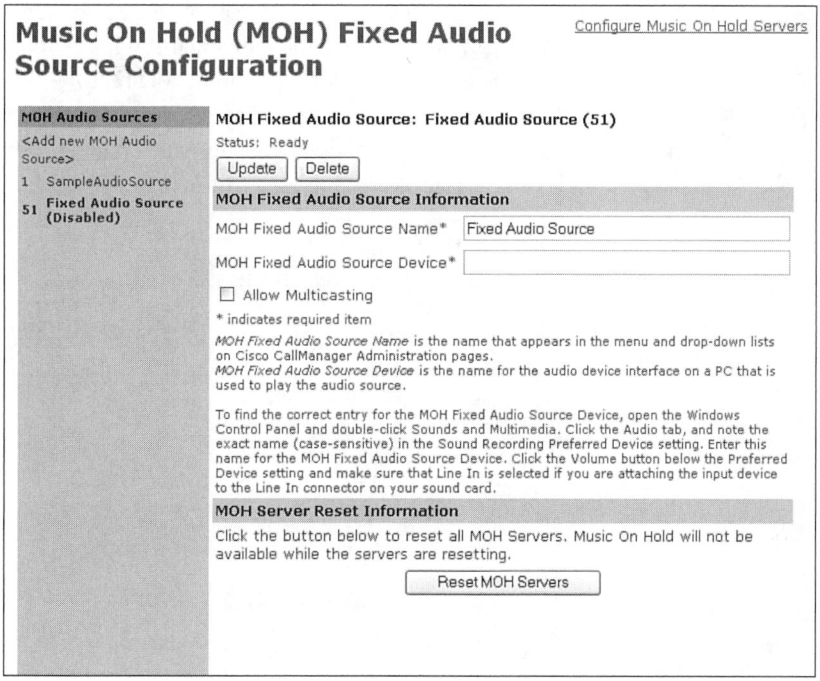

The MoH Fixed Audio Source Device name is case sensitive and must be entered exactly as it appears in the Sounds and Multimedia Properties window, including any spaces or symbols that appear in the name. If the **Allow Multicasting** check box is checked, and the G.729 codec is enabled, 5 to 7 percent of the CPU resources will be consumed. This setting is global for all MoH servers. If the fixed audio source does not exist on a server, it cannot be used.

The Fixed Audio Source option affects all of the MoH servers that have an MoH fixed audio source device by the selected name.

NOTE The FCC considers music on hold a type of broadcasting. Copyrighted music must be licensed for prerecorded and live audio sources. Failure to comply with this law can result in significant fines.

Step 6: Assigning Audio Source IDs

For your users to use the MoH sources you have configured, you must assign the audio source IDs to the IPT devices. An audio source ID represents an audio source on the MoH server. The audio source can be either a file on a disk or a fixed device from which a source stream obtains the streaming data. Each audio source (represented by an audio source ID) can stream in unicast and multicast mode.

The device that activates the hold will determine which audio source ID the caller will listen to. You can assign the MoH audio source IDs to a group of devices by assigning them through the device pool (choose **System > Device Pool**), through the individual IP Phones (choose **Device > Phone**), or for specific directory numbers (choose **Device > Phone > Directory Number**). If you assign the audio sources at both the device pool and IP Phone levels, the IP Phone settings override the device pool. Likewise, the directory number assignments overrule both the IP Phone and device pool settings. Figure 15-13 illustrates assigning the audio source IDs at the IP Phone level.

Figure 15-13 *Assigning Audio Source IDs to an IP Phone*

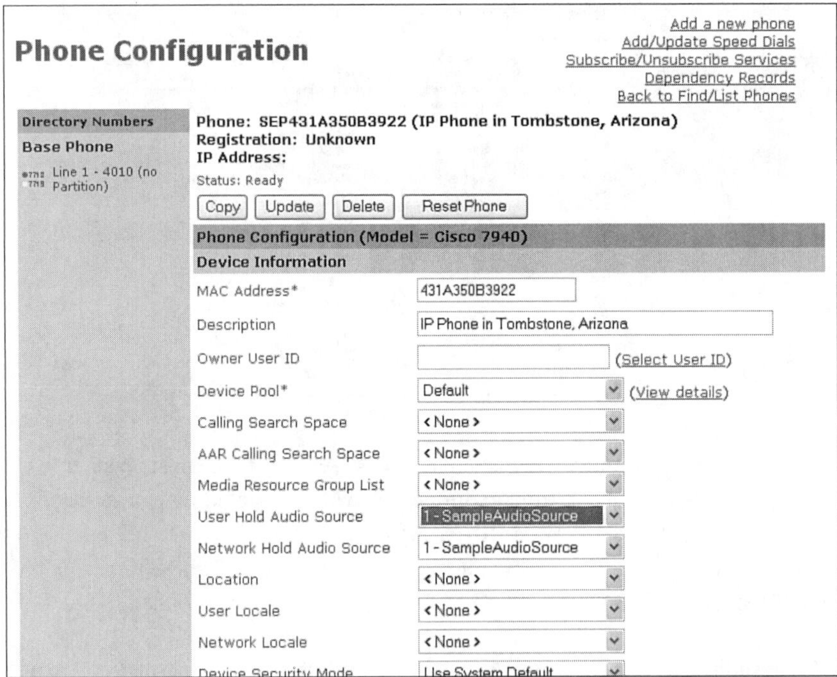

Media Resource Management

Media Resource Management (MGM) is an integral component of Cisco CallManager. The MRM system controls and manages the media resources within a cluster, allowing all Cisco CallManager servers within the cluster to share media resources.

The MRM enhances Cisco CallManager features by making it easier for Cisco CallManager to deploy transcoder, annunciator, conferencing, MTP, and MoH resources. MRM distribution throughout the Cisco CallManager cluster uses these resources to their full potential, which makes the Cisco CallManager cluster more efficient and more economical.

The reasons that resources are shared include the following:

- To enable hardware and software devices to coexist within a Cisco CallManager
- To enable Cisco CallManager to share and access the resources that are available in the cluster
- To enable Cisco CallManager to perform load distribution within a group of similar resources
- To enable Cisco CallManager to allocate resources based on administrative preference

Media Resource Design

Cisco CallManager Media Resource Groups (MRGs) and Media Resource Group Lists (MRGLs) provide a way to manage resources within a cluster.

Figure 15-14 shows the hierarchical ordering of media resources and how MRGs and MRGLs are similar to route groups and route lists. When a device needs a media resource, it searches its own MRGL first. If a media resource is not available, the device searches the default list, which includes all of the media resources that have not been assigned to an MRG. After a resource is assigned to an MRG, it is removed from the default list.

Figure 15-14 *Media Resource Design*

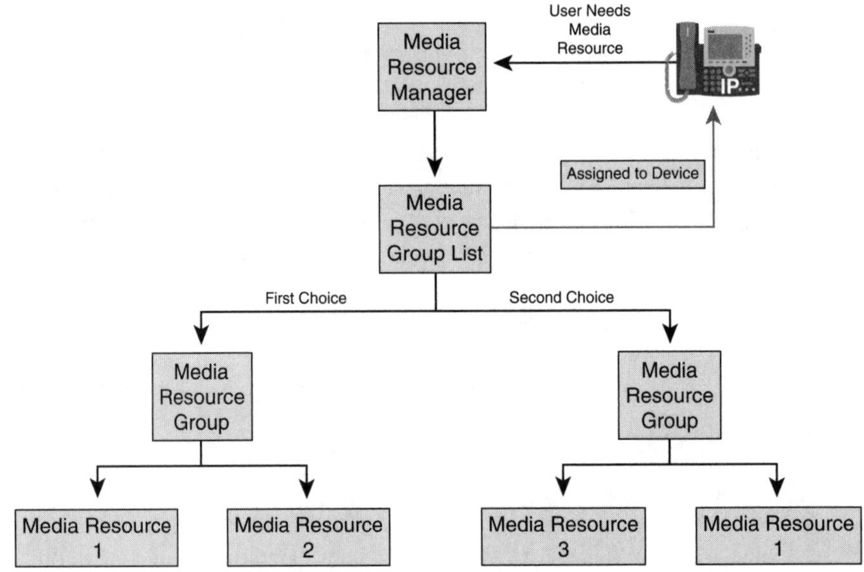

> **NOTE** By default, CallManager assigns all media resources in the cluster to the default media resource group. If you decide to keep this default, you will have no control over what media resources are used in your IPT environment.

Media Resource Groups

MRGs define logical groupings of media resources. Cisco CallManager provides a default list of media resources. The default list of media resources includes all of the media resources that have not been assigned to an MRG. If media resources have been configured but no MRGs have been defined, all media resources are on the default list, and all media resources are available to all Cisco CallManager servers within a given cluster.

Figure 15-15 shows how media resources are allocated to devices when they are listed in an MRG. The default media resources shown for a Cisco CallManager include MOH1, MTP1, XCODE1, XCODE2, and XCODE3. The MRM distributes the load evenly among the transcoder resources in its default MRG for calls that require a transcoder resource.

Figure 15-15 *Default Media Resource Group Behavior*

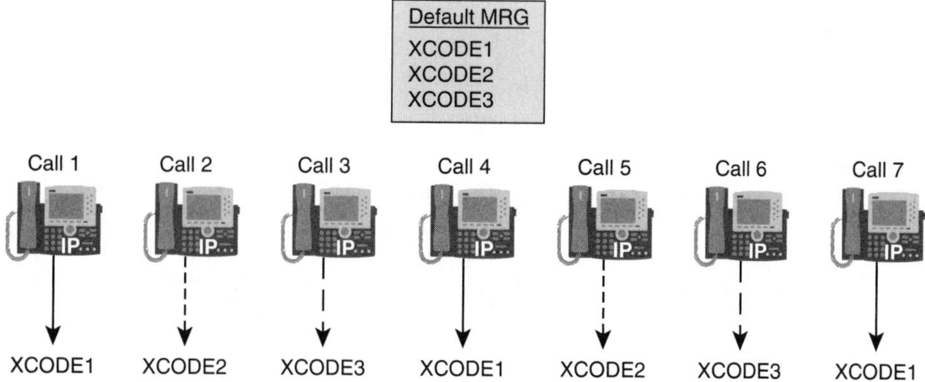

This is the allocation order for incoming calls that require a transcoder resource:

- Call 1 uses XCODE1.
- Call 2 uses XCODE2.
- Call 3 uses XCODE3.
- Call 4 uses XCODE1.
- Call 5 uses XCODE2.
- Call 6 uses XCODE3.
- Call 7 uses XCODE1.

Media Resource Group Configuration

Configuring an MRG is similar to configuring a route group. Choose **Service > Media Resource > Media Resource Group** to display a Media Resource Group Configuration window, like that shown in Figure 15-16. Enter a name and description for the MRG and then add the media resources by moving them from the Available Media Resource section to the Selected Media Resource section. To allow for a more flexible configuration, Cisco CallManager will allow you to assign media resources to multiple MRGs.

Figure 15-16 *Media Resource Group Configuration Window*

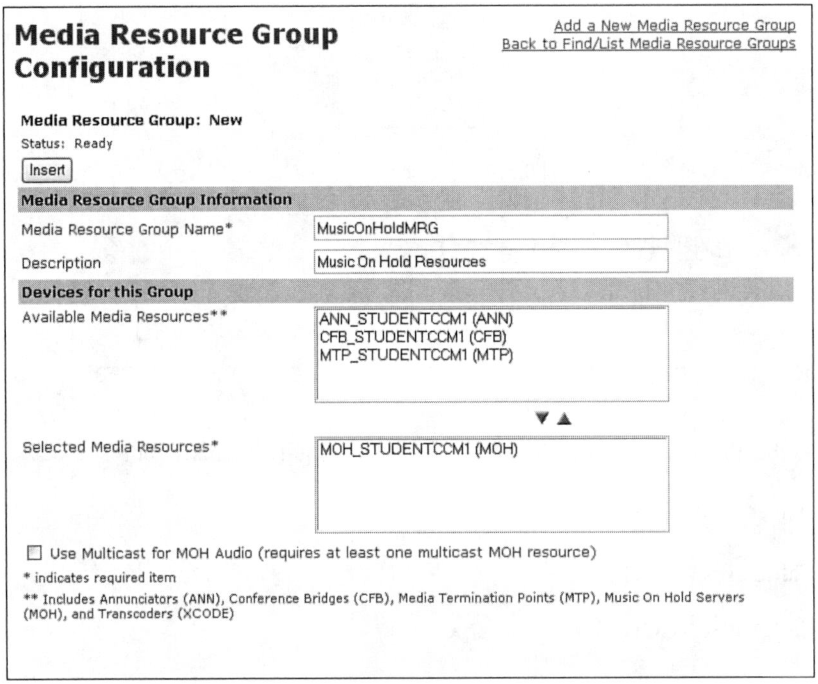

Media Resource Group Configuration

Add a New Media Resource Group
Back to Find/List Media Resource Groups

Media Resource Group: New
Status: Ready
Insert

Media Resource Group Information

Media Resource Group Name* MusicOnHoldMRG
Description Music On Hold Resources

Devices for this Group

Available Media Resources** ANN_STUDENTCCM1 (ANN) CFB_STUDENTCCM1 (CFB) MTP_STUDENTCCM1 (MTP)

Selected Media Resources* MOH_STUDENTCCM1 (MOH)

Use Multicast for MOH Audio (requires at least one multicast MOH resource)

* indicates required item

** Includes Annunciators (ANN), Conference Bridges (CFB), Media Termination Points (MTP), Music On Hold Servers (MOH), and Transcoders (XCODE)

Media Resource Group List Configuration

After you have added MRGs to the CallManager configuration, they can be grouped together and assigned to the IP Phones through MRGLs. Configuring an MRGL is similar to configuring a route list. Choose **Service > Media Resource > Media Resource Group List** to display the Media Resource Group List Configuration window, shown in Figure 15-17. Enter a name for the MRGL and choose the MRGs you want to add to the MRGL. Keep in mind that this is an ordered list. The resources in the MRGs at the top of the list have the most priority.

Figure 15-17 *Media Resource Group List Configuration Window*

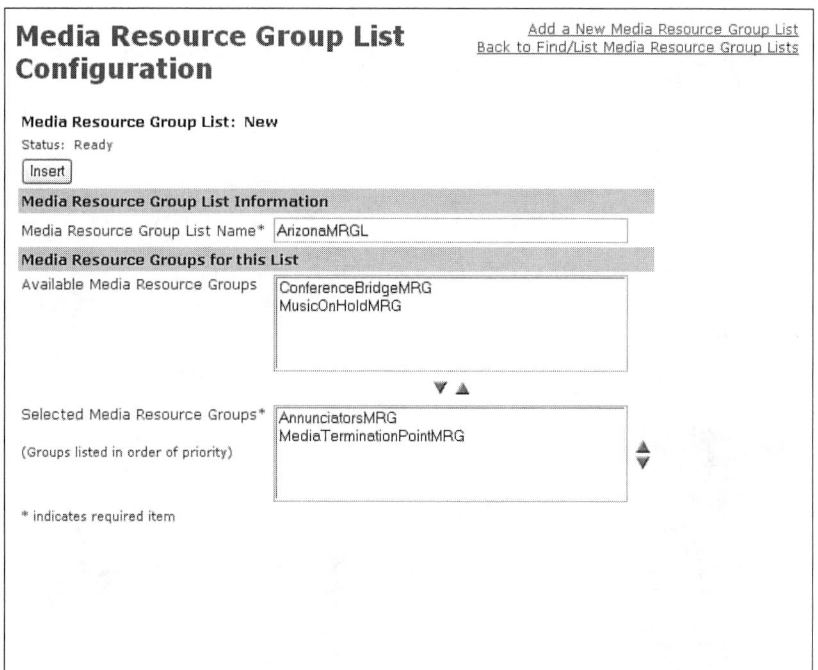

Assigning Media Resource Group Lists

There are two levels at which MRGLs can be assigned to devices. The higher-priority MRGL level is configured at the device. For example, a Cisco IP Phone is configured in the Phone Configuration window in Cisco CallManager Administration. The lower-priority level is an optional parameter of the device pool. If an MRGL is not configured at the device level, it uses the MRGL that is configured at the device pool level first, and then, if there are no resources available, it tries to use resources in the default list. If a device does have an MRGL that is configured at the device level, that MRGL is used first.

The last MRGL is the default MRGL. A media resource that is not assigned to an MRG is automatically assigned to the default MRGL. The default MRGL is always searched and it is the last resort if no resources are available in the device-based MRGL and the device pool MRGL or if no MRGLs are configured at any level.

NOTE If all media resources have been placed in MRGs, there will be no resources remaining in the default MRG pool. If a device does not have a particular resource made available in its MRGL, access to that resource is restricted. Whatever services the missing resource(s) support will be unavailable on the device.

MRGL Design Strategy: Grouping Resources by Type

Figure 15-18 shows how conference resources are allocated when resources are grouped by type and the software conference resource group is listed *after* the hardware conference resource group in the MRGL.

The media resources are assigned to three MRGs:

- **Hardware MRG**—XCODE1, XCODE2, HW-CONF1, and HW-CONF2
- **Software MRG**—MTP1, MTP2, SW-CONF1, and SW-CONF2
- **MOH MRG**—MOH1 and MOH2

Figure 15-18 *Grouping Resources by Type*

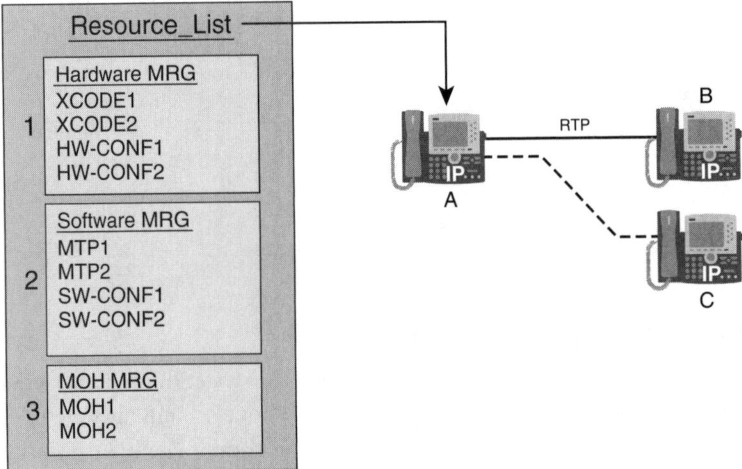

An MRGL called Resource_List was created and the MRGs assigned to it in this order: Hardware MRG, Software MRG, and MoH MRG.

In this arrangement, when a conference is needed, Cisco CallManager allocates the hardware conference resources first. The software conference resources are not used until all of the hardware conference resources have been exhausted.

MRGL Design Strategy: Grouping Resources by Location

Figure 15-19 shows media resources that are grouped by location. Devices use the media resources in their location before using the media resources at the central site (hub).

Figure 15-19 *Grouping Resources by Location*

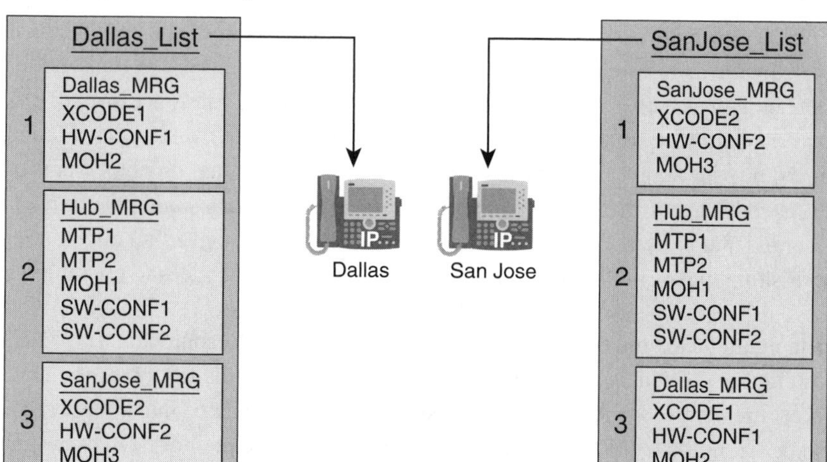

This example is for multiple-site WAN deployments that use centralized call processing. All Cisco CallManager and software resources are located at the central site. For devices at the Dallas and San Jose locations, it is more efficient to use media resources that reside physically at the location than to use a resource across the WAN.

Media resources are assigned to these three MRGs:

- **Hub_MRG**—MTP1, MTP2, MOH1, SW-CONF1, and SW-CONF2
- **Dallas_MRG**—XCODE1, HW-CONF1, and MOH2
- **SanJose_MRG**—XCODE2, HW-CONF2, and MOH3

In this example, the network administrator has created a Dallas_List MRGL and assigned the MRGs so that the resources are available in this order: local hardware resources first (Dallas_MRG), software resources second (Hub_MRG), and distant hardware resources third (SanJose_MRG).

The network administrator has also created a SanJose_List MRGL and assigned the MRGs so that the resources are available in this order: local hardware resources first (SanJose_MRG), software resources second (Hub_MRG), and distant hardware resources third (Dallas_MRG).

Lastly, the administrator has assigned an IP Phone in Dallas to use the Dallas_List MRGL and an IP Phone in San Jose to use the SanJose_List MRGL. With this arrangement, the IP Phone in Dallas will use the Dallas_List resources before using the central site or the SanJose_List resources.

Summary

This chapter covered the concepts and configuration of Cisco CallManager media resources and media resource management. Media resources provide services such as transcoding, conferencing, music on hold (MoH), and media termination. Conference bridges resources can be software or hardware solutions that allow ad hoc and Meet-Me conferences. Media termination resources provide supplementary services to H.323 endpoints that do not support the H.323v2 OpenLogicalChannel and CloseLogicalChannel request features. Annunciator resources play prerecorded announcements and tones. Transcoder resources convert an output stream from one compression type to another, allowing devices using different codecs to communicate.

By default, all media resources are added to a default Media Resource Group (MRG) that cannot be modified or deleted. As you create new MRGs and add media resources to them, those media resources are removed from the default MRG. MRGs are organized into an ordered list in a Media Resource Group List (MRGL), which is assigned to a device pool or devices to grant access to a specific set of media resources in the cluster.

Review Questions

You can find the solutions to these questions in Appendix A, "Answers to Review Questions."

1. Which of these descriptions best describes MRGLs?
   a. an ordered list of media resources
   b. an ordered list of media gateways
   c. an ordered list of Media Resource Groups
   d. an ordered list of media servers
2. The Media Resource Manager manages which two resource types? (Choose two.)
   a. call dispatcher service
   b. Voice Media Streaming Application
   c. transcoder
   d. multiplexer

3. Which of the following is needed to add a 6608 hardware conference bridge into a Cisco CallManager?

   a. MAC address
   b. IP address
   c. port address
   d. Meet-Me number
   e. directory number

4. Annunciator resources require that which service be activated?

   a. Cisco MoH Audio Translator
   b. Cisco IP Voice Media Streaming Application
   c. Cisco Messaging Interface
   d. Cisco CDR Insert
   e. Cisco TFTP

5. A user is having a conversation with her friend. A manager walks by and the user quickly presses the conference button to make it look as if she were initiating a business-related conference call. What music is the user's friend hearing while the conference call is being initiated?

   a. whatever music is defined for the user hold option on the user's device pool or IP Phone
   b. whatever music is defined for the network hold option on the user's device pool or IP Phone
   c. The user hears no music because conference calls do not have MoH features.
   d. It depends on the route plan.

6. What is the default MoH streaming setting on a Cisco CallManager server?

   a. unicast
   b. multicast
   c. broadcast
   d. None, the MoH server must be configured before MoH functionality exists.

7. A user has an MRGL assigned at both the device pool and IP Phone level. When the user presses the transfer button on their phone, the MGM searches for a resource based on which criteria?

   a. the MTP resource listed first in the first MRG of the device pool MRGL

   b. the MTP resource listed first in the first MRG of the IP Phone MRGL

   c. the MTP resource listed first in the last MRG of the device pool MRGL

   d. the MTP resource listed first in the last MRG of the IP Phone MRGL

8. You have not created any MRGs or MRGLs in your Cisco CallManager cluster configuration. How does the MGM manage the media resources that are available?

   a. The media resources are unavailable to users until they have been assigned to an MRG.

   b. The media resources are assigned to the default MRG, which cannot be modified or deleted. The MRM will use a round-robin load-balancing system for these resources.

   c. The media resources are assigned to the default MRG, which cannot be modified or deleted. The MRM will use hardware-based resources first and software-based resources second.

   d. The media resources are assigned to the default MRG. The default MRG must then be added to an MRGL, which is assigned to the end devices.

9. Which of the following media resource functions can the Cisco CallManager server NOT perform?

   a. annunciator

   b. conference bridge

   c. Media Termination Point

   d. Music on Hold

   e. transcoding

10. Which audio source ID is always reserved for the fixed audio source in the Cisco CallManager cluster?

    a. 1

    b. 21

    c. 51

    d. 99

This chapter covers the following topics:

- Describing core Cisco IP Phone features of Cisco CallManager, including hold, redial, transfer, speed dialing and abbreviated dialing, and Auto Answer
- Describing enhanced IP phone features of Cisco CallManager, such as multiple calls per line appearance, Direct Transfer, Call Join, and Immediate Divert
- Defining standard and nonstandard softkey templates and creating nonstandard softkey templates and assigning them to Cisco IP Phones
- Configuring Cisco CallManager to enable Call Park, Call Pickup, and Cisco Call Back
- Configuring Cisco CallManager to enable Barge and Privacy on a shared line
- Configuring Cisco CallManager to enable users to subscribe to IP phone Services from their Cisco IP Phones

CHAPTER 16

Configuring User Features, Part 1

Administrators need to have a working knowledge of the various options that are available for Cisco IP Phones to ensure that all of the desired features and functions are available to users and that they are properly configured. This chapter, the first of two on features, discusses many of the Cisco IP Phone features that are available to users in a Cisco IP telephony solution. The chapter includes a discussion of core and enhanced IP phone features: Call Park, Call Pickup, Cisco Call Back, Barge, Privacy, and Cisco IP Phone Services. The chapter explains the purpose of each feature and describes how to configure and use the feature.

Basic IP Phone Features

Cisco CallManager software extends enterprise telephony features and capabilities to packet telephony network devices, such as Cisco IP Phones, media-processing devices, voice over IP (VoIP) gateways, and multimedia applications. Four basic IP phone features do not require configuration in Cisco CallManager and are activated when the user presses a softkey on the IP phone:

- **Hold**—Places an active call on hold. Hold requires no configuration, unless you want to use music on hold (MoH). When you put a call on hold, the call remains active even though you and the other party cannot hear one another. You can answer other calls while a call is on hold. Engaging the hold feature generates music or a beeping tone (called "tone on hold").

- **Redial**—Redials the last number dialed. To redial the most recently dialed number, press the **Redial** softkey. Doing so without lifting the handset activates the speakerphone or headset. To redial a number from a line other than your primary line, select the desired line button and then press **Redial**.

- **Transfer**—Transfers an active call to another directory number (DN) through use of the **Transf** softkey. This can be a blind transfer, where the call is cut over directly to another extension, or a consultative transfer, where a temporary ad hoc conference call is created to allow all parties to speak before a transfer occurs.

- **Call Waiting**—Lets users receive a second incoming call on the same line without disconnecting the first call. When the second call arrives, the user receives a brief call waiting indicator tone.

Speed Dial and Abbreviated Dial Configuration

Speed dialing provides quick access to frequently dialed numbers. Abbreviated dialing, introduced in Cisco CallManager Release 4.0, extends speed dial functionality by enabling a user to configure up to 99 speed dial entries on a telephone. When a user lifts the handset, the **AbbrDial** softkey appears. The user can access any speed dial entry by entering the appropriate index, either one or two digits, followed by pressing the **AbbrDial** softkey.

You can configure speed dials or abbreviated dials in Cisco CallManager Administration. You can access this configuration by clicking **Device > Phone**, selecting the phone you want to configure, and clicking the **Add/Update Speed Dials** link in the upper-right corner. A window similar to that shown in Figure 16-1 opens. Configure abbreviated dials just as you would configure speed dials. Users (or administrators) can configure speed dials from the User Options web page (https://<server IP address>/ccmuser).

Figure 16-1 *Configuring IP Phone Speed Dials*

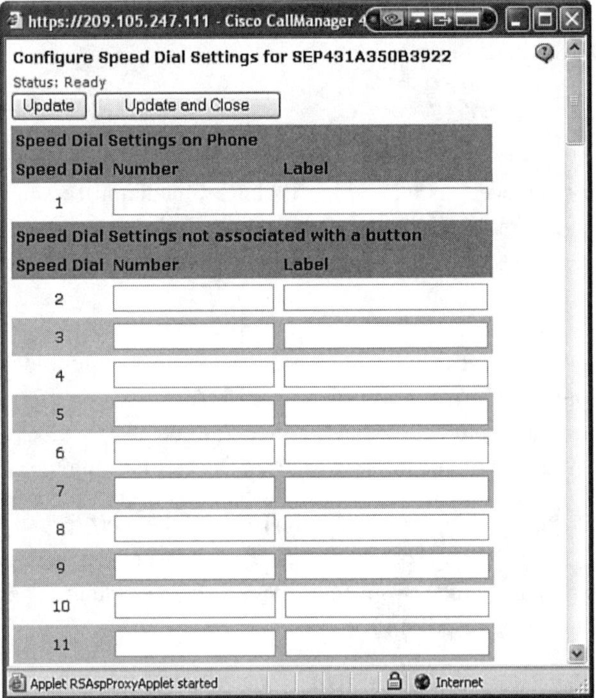

Auto Answer Configuration

Auto Answer is a feature that causes the speakerphone or headset to go off hook automatically when an incoming call is received. You can program this feature on a telephone-by-telephone basis. To configure Auto Answer, choose the device that you want to enable, and then choose **Auto Answer** under the Directory Number Settings. A window appears similar to that shown in Figure 16-2. You can choose Auto Answer Off, Auto Answer with Headset, or Auto Answer with Speakerphone. Using the Auto Answer with Headset feature works well for support desks because it delays the call by one second and plays a tone in the ear of the user with the headset to notify them of an incoming call.

Figure 16-2 *Configuring Auto Answer*

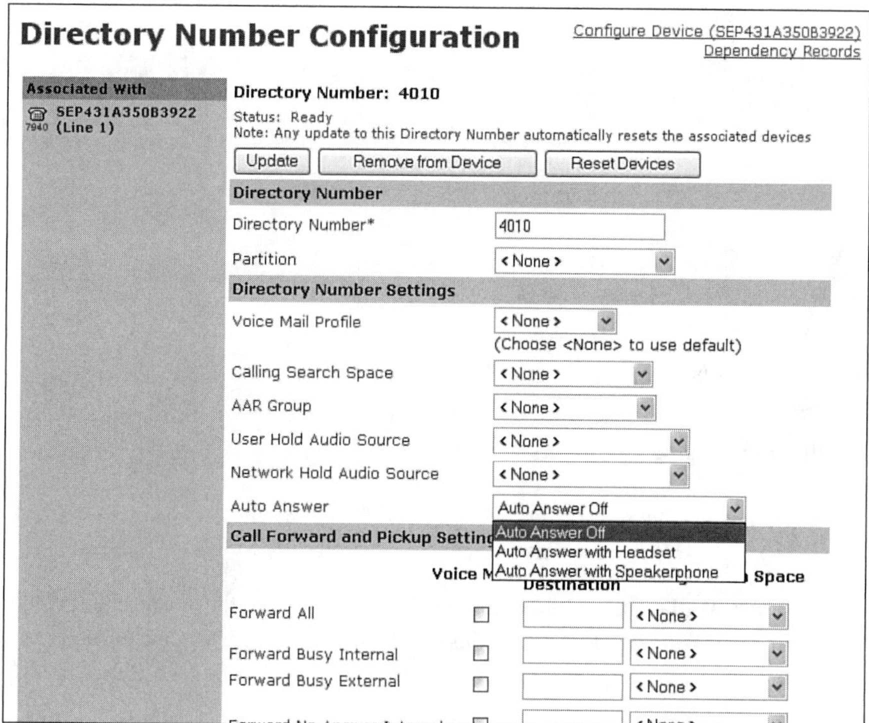

Call Forward and Configurable Call Forward Display Configuration

Call forwarding allows an administrator or user to configure a Cisco IP Phone so that all calls that are destined for that IP phone ring at another telephone or go directly to voice mail. To access the call forwarding options, choose **Device > Phone**, then select a phone and select a line to display the call forwarding parameters shown in Figure 16-3.

Figure 16-3 *Configuring Call Forwarding*

Call Forward and Pickup Settings

	Voice Mail	Coverage/ Destination	Calling Search Space
Forward All	☐		< None >
Forward Busy Internal	☐		< None >
Forward Busy External	☐		< None >
Forward No Answer Internal	☐		< None >
Forward No Answer External	☐		< None >
Forward No Coverage Internal	☐		< None >
Forward No Coverage External	☐		< None >

No Answer Ring Duration (seconds)

Call Pickup Group < None >

MLPP Alternate Party Settings

Target (Destination)

Calling Search Space < None >

No Answer Ring Duration (seconds)

Line Settings for all Devices

Alerting Name

Line Settings for this Device

Display (Internal Caller ID)

Line Text Label

External Phone Number Mask

The call forwarding options are as follows:

- **Forward All**—The settings in this row of fields specify the forwarding treatment for calls to this DN if the DN is set to forward all calls. Specify the following values:
  - **Voice Mail**—Check this check box to use settings in the Voice Mail Profile Configuration window. When this check box is checked, Cisco CallManager ignores the settings in the **Coverage/Destination** and **Calling Search Space** fields.
  - **Coverage/Destination**—This setting indicates the DN to which all calls are forwarded. Use any dialable phone number, including an outside destination.
  - **Calling Search Space**—This setting allows you to specify different calling restrictions for call forwarding. Otherwise, the same calling restrictions applied in the IP phone calling search space also apply to call forwarding.
- **Other call forwarding settings**—Starting with Cisco CallManager Release 4.1, the administrator can specify different call forwarding treatment based on whether the caller is external or internal for no answer, busy, and no coverage conditions.

> **NOTE** Call Forward Busy, Call Forward No Answer, and Call Forward No Coverage for external and internal calls and the interaction of the No Coverage option is covered in detail in Chapter 12, "Configuring Hunt Groups and Call Coverage."

- **Configurable call forwarding display**—Starting with Cisco CallManager Release 4.0, the administrator can configure call forwarding information display options to the original dialed number, to the redirected dialed number, or to both (these settings are not shown in Figure 16-3). You can enable or disable the caller name or caller number and present this information to the display of the forwarded party. The display option is configured for each line appearance.

Softkey Templates

Softkeys extend the functions of nearly all Cisco IP Phones (with the exception of the 7902). As shown in Figure 16-4, softkeys are buttons along the side and bottom of the IP phone liquid crystal display (LCD) that point to functions and feature options on the LCD screen. Softkeys change depending on the status of the phone.

Figure 16-4 *Softkeys Available on 7940, 7960, and 7970 Cisco IP Phones*

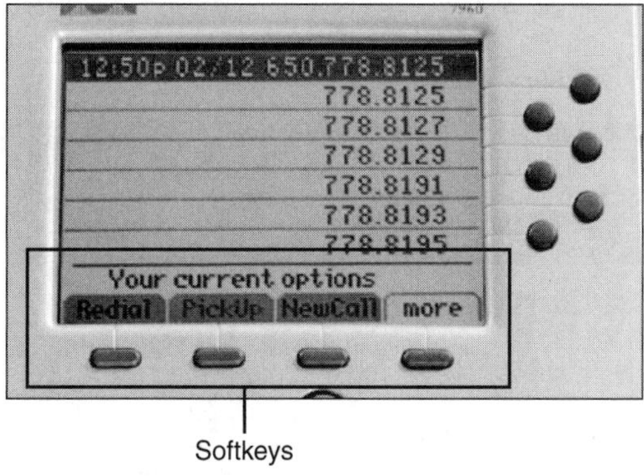

Cisco CallManager provides softkey templates for administrator convenience. Softkey templates group softkeys that are used for common call-processing functions and applications. You can use these default softkey templates to provide standard softkey definitions for devices, or you can create custom templates.

Cisco CallManager, starting with Release 4.0, includes these five standard softkey templates:

- Standard IPMA Assistant
- Standard User

- Standard Feature
- Standard IPMA Manager
- Standard IPMA Shared Mode Manager

You cannot delete or modify these standard templates. However, you can create custom (nonstandard) templates to meet the needs of your organization.

Adding Softkey Templates

To create a nonstandard softkey template, you must first copy a standard template and make the modifications desired to this copy. Choose **Device > Device Settings > Softkey Templates** to access softkey templates. The Find and List Softkey Templates window shown in Figure 16-5 appears. Choose the standard template and click the **Copy** button. The Softkey Template Configuration window then displays the softkey template name, description, and applications that are associated with the template. You must rename the template with a new descriptive name. After you have entered a unique name, click the **Insert** button. The standard template is copied, and when you choose **Back to Find/List Softkey Templates**, the new softkey template is displayed. After the nonstandard template is made, application softkeys can be added or removed from the template.

Figure 16-5 *Standard Softkey Template Listing*

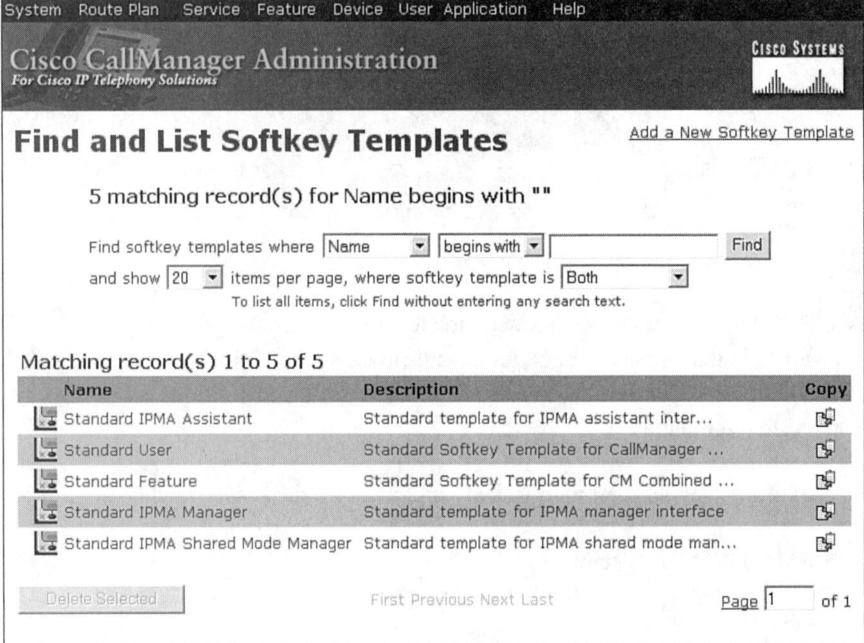

Modifying Softkey Availability and Positioning

You can add or delete softkeys or modify softkey positions in a nonstandard softkey template to customize the appearance of the softkeys on Cisco IP Phones. In the **Softkey Templates** field, choose the template in which you want to add or delete softkeys or modify the softkey positions. In the upper-right corner of the window, click the **Configure Softkey Layout** link. As shown in Figure 16-6, the Softkey Layout Configuration window is displayed with call states on the left and the Selected Softkeys pane on the right. You can select the softkeys that you want displayed for each call state.

Figure 16-6 *Modifying Softkey Availability and Positioning*

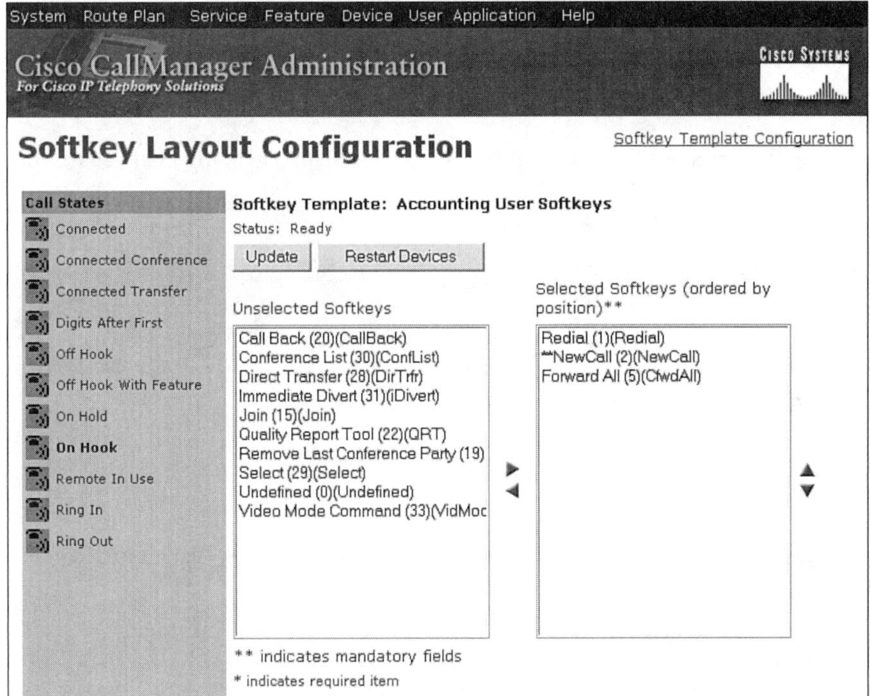

To add softkeys, select a softkey from the Unselected Softkeys pane and click the right arrow to move it to the Selected Softkeys pane. If the number of softkeys exceeds 16, an error message is displayed that states that you must remove some of the softkeys before continuing. To delete softkeys, select a softkey from the Selected Softkeys pane and click the left arrow to move it to the Unselected Softkeys pane. Click **Update** after completing either procedure.

To modify softkey positions, use the up and down arrows to rearrange the positions of the selected softkeys (the top position corresponds to the leftmost softkey on the IP phone). To save the modifications that you have made to the template, click **Update**.

After making modifications to softkey templates, you must restart the devices that are using the template.

Assigning Softkey Templates to Devices

You can assign softkey templates to devices in several ways. The template can be assigned in the Device Pool Configuration window (**System** > **Device Pool**), through a user device profile (**Device** > **Device Settings** > **Device Profile**), or on the device itself (**Device** > **Phone**).

For example, you might have a (standard or nonstandard) softkey template that you assign to a device pool to configure the majority of phones in your cluster, a different softkey template that you use for a feature that requires a device profile (for example, Extension Mobility), and a different softkey template that includes the Barge, Privacy, and Immediate Divert softkeys that you assign to a device belonging to a manager.

Figure 16-7 illustrates the Accounting User Softkeys template being assigned to a device pool.

Figure 16-7 *Assigning Softkey Templates to Devices*

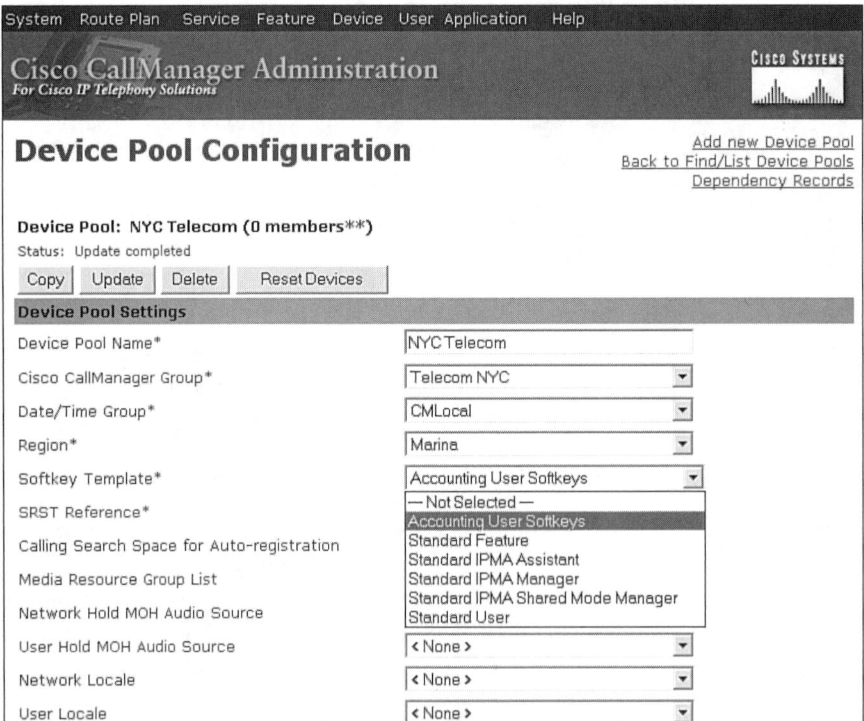

Deleting Softkey Templates

Standard templates cannot be deleted. Only nonstandard templates can be deleted. If you want to delete a nonstandard softkey template, the template cannot be in use by any device in the Cisco CallManager system. If the softkey template is assigned to a device pool, user profile, or Cisco IP Phone, you will receive an error message stating that the template is in use when you attempt to delete it. You must remove the template from all devices before the template can be deleted.

To determine whether a softkey template is in use, click the **Dependency Records** link, located in the upper-right corner of the Softkey Template Configuration window. By default, CallManager disables the dependency records function because of its high CPU consumption on CallManager servers.

> **NOTE** Dependency records functionality causes high CPU usage when it is used. After it has been enabled, this task executes at below-normal priority and might take time to complete because of the dial plan size and complexity, CPU speed, and CPU requirements of other applications.

To enable dependency records, follow these steps:

Step 1 Choose **System > Enterprise Parameters**.

Step 2 Scroll to the CCMAdmin Parameters area of the window.

Step 3 From the **Enable Dependency Records** drop-down menu, choose **True**.

A message box displays a message about the consequences of enabling the dependency records. Read the information carefully before clicking OK.

Step 4 Click **OK**. The field displays **True**.

Step 5 Click **Update**.

Step 6 Close the browser that you are using; then, reopen the browser. This action makes the parameter take effect for the entire system.

Enhanced IP Phone Features

The following features are considered fairly new features to the IP Telephony environment. They are supported in the CallManager 4.x versions and later.

Multiple Calls per Line Appearance

Cisco CallManager Release 4.0 and later enable multiple calls to exist on the same line. This feature eliminates the need to create multiple instances of the same directory number in different partitions to allow users to share a line and still be able to receive and place multiple calls out of the same line. Cisco CallManager will now support up to 200 active calls on a single line and one connected call per telephone at any time.

Two configuration settings enable multiple line appearances and are configured from the Directory Number Configuration window, as shown in Figure 16-8:

- **Maximum Number of Calls**—This setting configures the maximum number of calls inbound or outbound per line appearance. You can configure up to a potential of 200 calls for a line on a device, with the limiting factor being the total number of calls that are configured on the device. As you configure the number of calls for one line, the number of calls that are available for another line decrease. The default specifies 4.
- **Busy Trigger**—This setting, which works in conjunction with Maximum Number of Calls and Call Forward Busy (CFB), determines the maximum number of calls to be presented at the line. If the maximum number of calls is set to 50 and the busy trigger is set to 40, then incoming call 41 is rejected with a busy cause code (and will be forwarded if CFB is set). If this line is shared, all the lines must be busy before incoming calls will be rejected.

Figure 16-8 *Multiple Line Appearance Configuration*

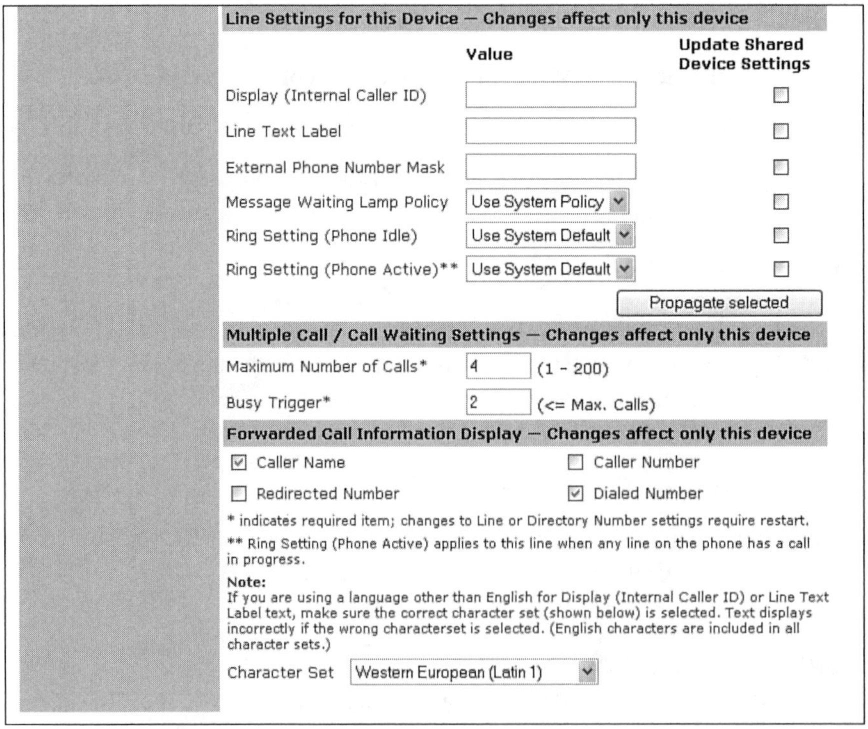

In Figure 16-8, the maximum number of calls is set to 4 and the busy trigger is set to 2. With this configuration, four calls can be active at a given time. If two calls are active, and a third call comes in, it is forwarded to the Call Forward Busy destination. The users, however, can place up to two more outbound calls before the line is at capacity. Keep in mind that multiple lines are needed to use various other features such as call transfer and conference.

Direct Transfer

Direct Transfer, which was introduced in Cisco CallManager 4.0, joins two established calls (defined as a call in the hold or connected state) into one call and drops the feature initiator from the call. Direct Transfer does not initiate a consultation call and does not put the active call on hold.

To implement Direct Transfer, the Direct Transfer initiator selects two calls at the Cisco IP Phone and presses the **DirTrfr** softkey, shown in Figure 16-9. The two calls are joined immediately and directly, and no conference resources are inserted. The initiating user is not included in the call after the transaction is complete, and the call is released from the IP phone of the initiator.

Figure 16-9 *Direct Transfer*

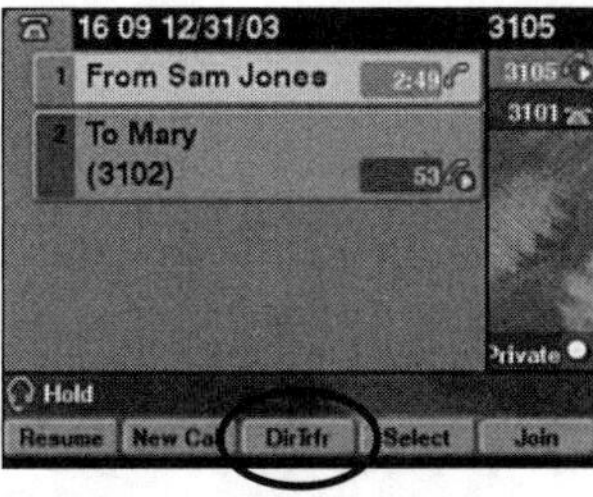

The following steps illustrate the user sequence of events in a typical Direct Transfer call:

Step 1 Sam and Kim are participating in an active call.

Step 2 Sam asks Kim to transfer him to Mary.

Step 3 Kim puts Sam on hold.

Step 4 Kim calls Mary.

Step 5 Kim touches the line that Sam is using (Cisco IP Phone 7970 only) or uses the **Select** softkey to select that line.

Step 6 Kim presses the **DirTrfr** key, and Sam and Mary are immediately connected.

Call Join

Introduced in Cisco CallManager Release 4.0, the Call Join feature enables a user to link up to 15 established calls (for a total of 16) in a conference. Call Join does not create a consultation call (does not put the active call on hold).

To implement Call Join, the user chooses an active or held call and, using either the rocker key (Cisco IP Phones 7960 and 7940) and the **Select** softkey or the touch screen (Cisco IP Phone 7970), selects the appropriate line and then presses the **Call Join** softkey so that the selected calls and the join initiator are joined in an ad hoc conference. Figure 16-10 illustrates this process. The initiator can leave the Call Join session at any time, and the conference stays active. Only the initiator of the Call Join session can add participants to the conference or drop them from it.

Figure 16-10 *Call Join*

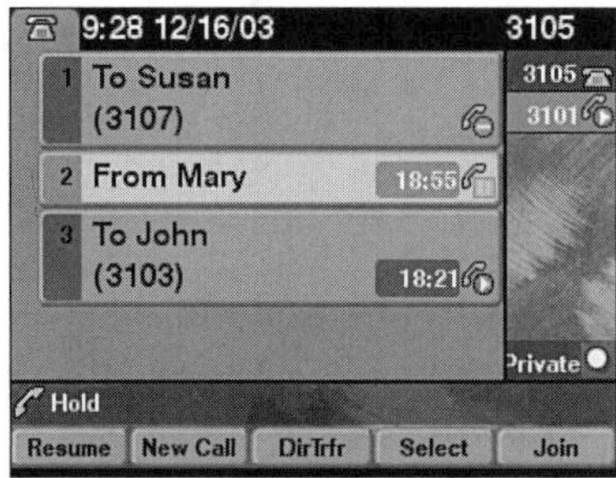

Immediate Divert to Voice Mail

The Immediate Divert feature is a feature that was introduced in Cisco CallManager Release 4.0. This feature allows you to immediately divert a call to a voice-messaging system. When the call is diverted, the line becomes available to make or receive new calls.

Immediate Divert supports an incoming call in the call-offering (ring in), call-on-hold, or call-active state. Immediate Divert supports an outgoing call in the call-on-hold or call-active state.

You can access the Immediate Divert feature by using the **iDivert** softkey, shown in Figure 16-11. This softkey can be applied to any Cisco IP Phone that can accept softkeys. Configure this softkey by using the Softkey Template Configuration window (discussed in the following section) of Cisco CallManager Administration.

Figure 16-11 *Immediate Divert to Voice Mail*

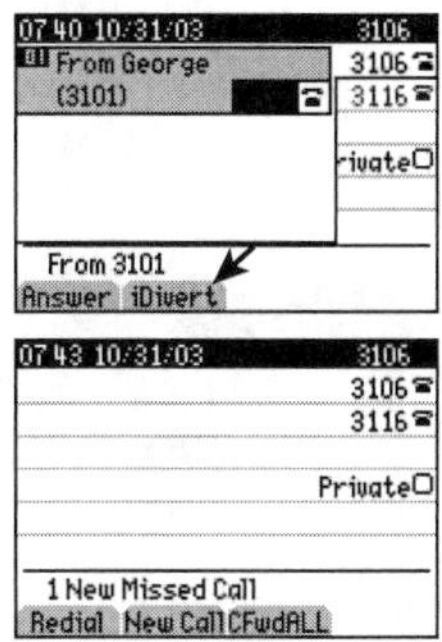

Immediate Divert requires the following components:

- Cisco CallManager Release 4.0 or later
- Cisco IP Phones (models 7905, 7912, 7920, 7940, 7960, or 7970)

Call Park

The Call Park feature allows you to put a call on hold so that it can be retrieved from another telephone in the Cisco CallManager cluster.

For example, the ABC Department Store, which has an overhead paging system, is using the Call Park feature. A call for an employee on the floor comes in to a cashier desk. The cashier can park the call and announce the Call Park code on the overhead paging system, and the employee on the floor can pick up the call by using the Call Park code on a nearby telephone.

If you are on an active call on your telephone, you can park the call to a Call Park extension by pressing the **Park** softkey. The Cisco IP Phone will display the Call Park number that it assigned to your active call on the IP phone (the number will display on screen for 10 seconds, by default). Someone (or you) on another phone in your system can then dial the Call Park extension to retrieve the call.

Before the Call Park feature functions in your IPT network, a Call Park number or range must be configured for the cluster. When you invoke the Call Park feature, it is assigned a Call Park code. A user uses this code to pick up the call from another Cisco IP Phone on the same Cisco CallManager to which the original IP Phone is registered. When you assign the Call Park number or range to a partition, you can limit access to the Call Park feature based on the device calling search space. You should ensure that the Call Park number or range is unique throughout the Cisco CallManager cluster.

You can configure the Call Park feature by choosing **Feature > Call Park**. Select the **Add a New Call Park Number** hyperlink in the upper-right corner of the screen. The Call Park Configuration window shown in Figure 16-12 appears. Configure the Call Park number or range (CallManager accepts the same wildcards as you can use in a route pattern) and choose **Insert**.

Figure 16-12 *Configuring Call Park*

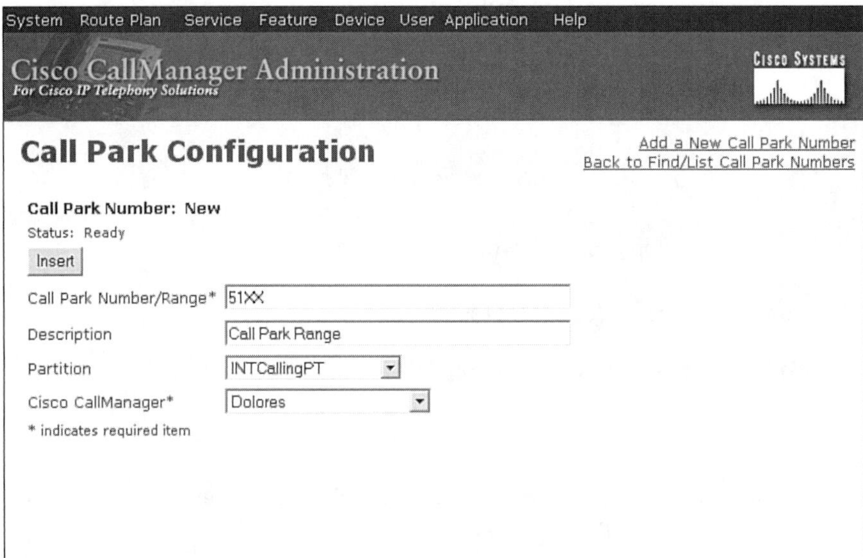

Call Pickup and Group Call Pickup

The purpose of Call Pickup is to enable a group of users who are seated near each other to cover incoming calls as a group. When a member of the group receives a call and is not available to answer it, any other member of the group can pick up the call from their own phone.

Three types of Call Pickup exist:

- **Call Pickup**—Enables users to pick up incoming calls on any telephone within their own group. When the users press the **Call Pickup** button or **PickUp** softkey, Cisco CallManager automatically dials the appropriate Call Pickup number.

- **Group Call Pickup**—Enables users to pick up incoming calls on any telephone within their own group or in another group. Users press the **Group Call Pickup** button or **GpickUp** softkey and dial the appropriate group number for Call Pickup. (The reason that users manually enter a number with Group Call Pickup but not with Call Pickup is because more than one group can exist and Cisco CallManager needs to know which one to dial. With Call Pickup, in effect, there is only one number corresponding to one group.)
- **Other Group Call Pickup**—Allows users to pick up incoming calls in a group that is associated with their own group. This type of Call Pickup is covered in the next subtopic.

Other Group Call Pickup

Cisco CallManager Release 4.1(3) added support for Other Group Call Pickup. Other Group Call Pickup allows users to pick up incoming calls in a group that is associated with their own group. Cisco CallManager automatically searches for the incoming call in the associated groups to make the call connection when the user activates this feature from a Cisco IP Phone. Use the softkey **OPickup** for this type of Call Pickup.

When more than one associated group exists, the priority of answering calls for the associated group goes from the first associated group to the last associated group. For example, groups A, B, and C associate with group X, and the priority of answering calls goes to group A, then B, and then C.

Usually, within the same group, the longest alerting call (longest ringing time) is picked up first if multiple incoming calls occur in that group. For Other Group Call Pickup, priority takes precedence over the ringing time if multiple associated pickup groups are configured.

Both the idle and off-hook call states make the three softkeys **Pickup**, **GPickup**, and **OPickup** available.

Call Pickup Configuration

To configure Call Pickup, you must first add and configure the Call Pickup number and then assign the Call Pickup number to the desired DNs. Follow this procedure to add a Call Pickup number and group in Cisco CallManager Administration:

Step 1 Choose **Feature > Call Pickup**.

Step 2 In the upper-right corner of the window, click the **Add a New Call Pickup Number** link.

Step 3 The Pickup Group Configuration window opens, as shown in Figure 16-13.

Figure 16-13 *Configuring Call Pickup*

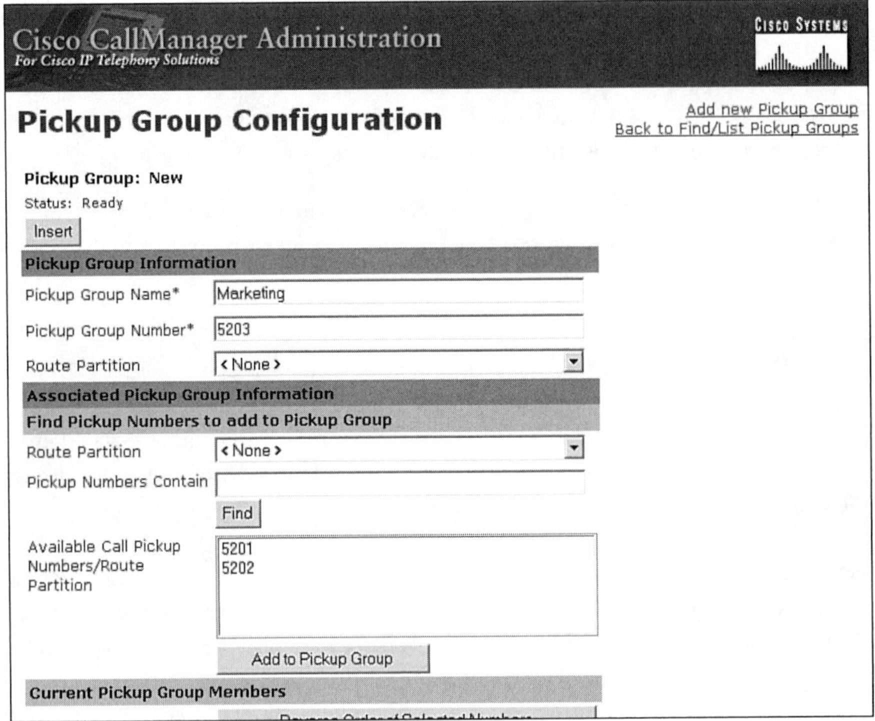

Step 4 Enter a unique pickup group name and unique pickup group number.

Step 5 Assign the pickup group to a route partition as desired.

Step 6 Click **Insert** to save the new Call Pickup Group number in the database.

Step 7 Access the directory number you want to assign to the Call Pickup Group (**Device > Phone > Select DN**) and assign the Call Pickup Group, as shown in Figure 16-14.

AutoCall Pickup

You can automate Call Pickup, Group Call Pickup, and Other Group Call Pickup by setting the service parameter Auto Call Pickup Enabled to True (available in CallManager 4.1(3)). (Choose **Service** > **Service Parameters**, and choose the publisher server and Cisco CallManager for the service.)

When this parameter is enabled, Cisco CallManager automatically connects users to the incoming call in their own pickup group, in another pickup group, or in a pickup group that is associated with their own group after users press the appropriate softkey on the phone. This action reduces keystrokes.

Figure 16-14 *Assigning DNs to a Call Pickup Group*

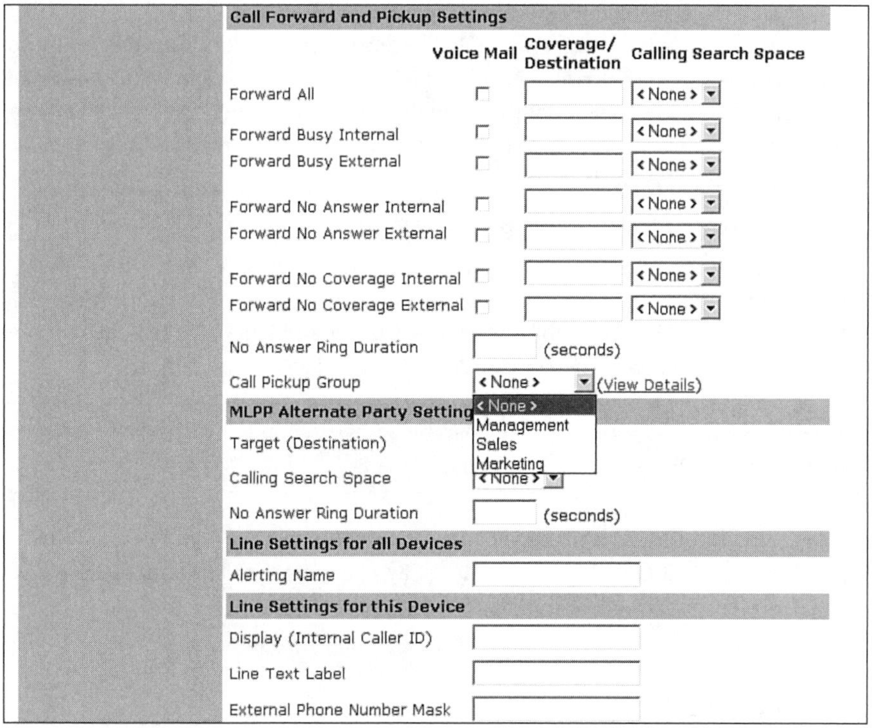

Automated Call Pickup connects the user to an incoming call in the user's own group. When the user presses the **Pickup** softkey on the phone, Cisco CallManager locates the incoming call in the group and completes the call connection. If automation is not enabled, the user must press the softkeys **Pickup** and **Answer** to make the call connection. You can also use this feature to connect the user to an incoming call in another pickup group. The user presses the **GPickup** softkey on the phone, and then dials the DN of the other pickup group. Upon receiving the DN, Cisco CallManager completes the call connection. If automation is not enabled, the user must press the softkeys **GPickup** and **Answer** and dial the DN of the other pickup group to make the call connection.

Automated Other Group Call Pickup connects the user to an incoming call in a group that is associated with the user's own group. The user presses the **OPickup** softkey on the phone. The Cisco CallManager automatically searches for the incoming call in the associated groups in the sequence that the administrator entered in the Pickup Group Configuration window and completes the call connection after the call is found. If automation is not enabled, the user must press the softkeys **OPickup** and **Answer** to make the call connection.

Cisco Call Back

The Cisco Call Back feature allows you to receive call-back notification on your Cisco IP Phone when a called-party line becomes available. To receive call-back notification, a user presses the **CallBack** softkey upon receiving a busy or ringback tone. You can activate call-back notification on a line on a Cisco IP Phone within the same Cisco CallManager cluster as your telephone. You cannot activate call-back notification if the called party has forwarded all calls to another extension (Call Forward All [CFA] feature).

For example, IP phone user A calls IP phone user B in the same cluster. If IP phone B is busy or there is no answer, IP phone user A activates the Cisco Call Back feature through the **CallBack** softkey. When IP phone B becomes available, IP Phone A receives an audible alert and visual notification that the DN is available. Cisco CallManager remembers the dialed number, so IP phone user A can then press the **Dial** softkey to reach IP phone user B.

> **NOTE** The Cisco Call Back feature requires Cisco CallManager Release 3.3 or later and a Cisco IP Phone that supports softkeys.

To configure Cisco Call Back, create a new softkey template (or modify one of your existing templates). Next, configure the softkey layout by choosing the **On Hook** call state and the **CallBack** option, as shown in Figure 16-15. Then, choose **Ring Out**, include the CallBack option by making sure that it is at the top of the list, and click **Update**.

Figure 16-15 *Configuring Call Back*

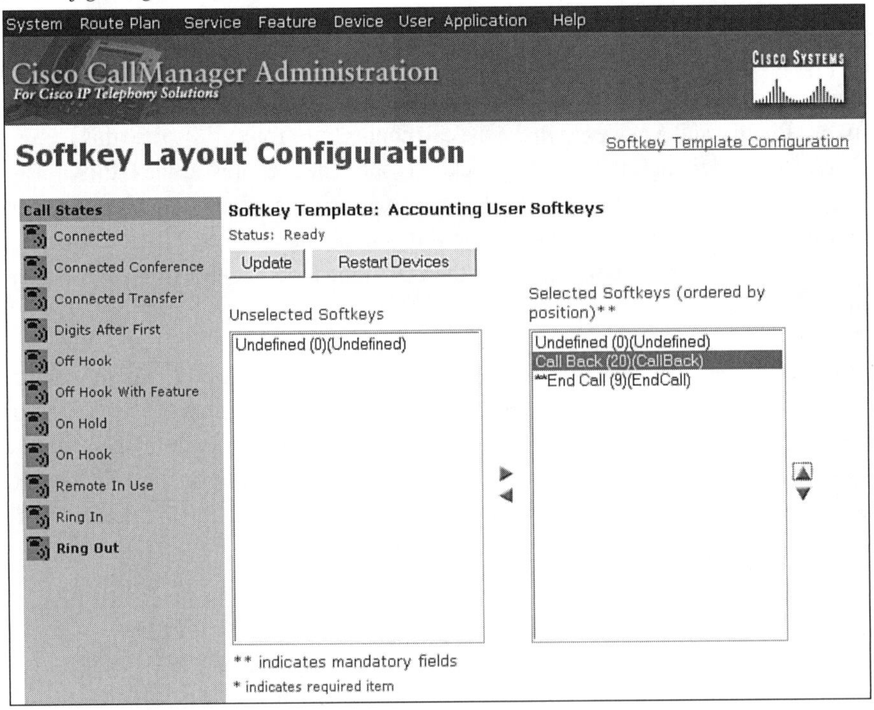

Barge and Privacy

Using the Barge feature, users can add themselves to an existing call on a shared line. Two types of Barge are available in Cisco CallManager Release 4.0:

- **Barge using built-in conference; Barge softkey**—Barge uses the built-in conference capability of the target IP phone. Barge also uses the Standard User or Standard Feature softkey template (both contain the **Barge** softkey). When a Barge is being set up, no media interruption occurs and the only display change to the original call is a spinning circle that is displayed at the right side of the prompt status message window at the target device.
- **Barge using shared conference; cBarge softkey**—Conference Barge (cBarge) uses a shared conference bridge. No standard softkey template includes the **cBarge** softkey. To allow users to access the **cBarge** softkey, the administrator must add it to a nonstandard softkey template and then assign the softkey template to a device.

When you press the **cBarge** softkey, a Barge call is set up by means of the shared conference bridge, if it is available. The original call is split and then joined at the conference bridge, which causes a brief media interruption. The call information for all parties changes to Barge. The barged call becomes a conference call with the Barge target device as the conference controller. The conference controller can add more parties to the conference or can drop any party. When only two parties are left in the conference, they experience a brief interruption and then are reconnected as a point-to-point call, which releases the shared conference resources.

When the initiator uses Barge to join the call, it becomes a three-way call. If the initiator hangs up, the original call remains active. If the target hangs up, the caller who used Barge and the other party connect in a point-to-point call. If the other party hangs up, the original call and the barged call are released.

The Privacy feature was introduced in Cisco CallManager Release 4.0. With Privacy, administrators can enable or disable the ability of users with telephones that share the same line (DN) to view call status and to barge the call. Administrators enable or disable Privacy for each telephone.

The Barge and Privacy features have some restrictions, including the following:

- Built-in Barge supports a three-way Barge maximum, G.711 voice, and the Cisco IP Phone 7940, 7960, and 7970 models.
- Barge and Privacy require Cisco CallManager Release 4.0.

Barge requires a shared line appearance. Cisco CallManager considers a DN on more than one device in the same partition to be a shared line appearance. One example of a shared line appearance is when a DN appears on line 1 of a manager telephone and also on line 2 of an assistant telephone. Another example of a shared line is a single incoming 800 number that is set up to appear as line 2 on every help desk telephone in an office.

These guidelines are helpful when using shared line appearances with Cisco CallManager:

- You can create a shared line appearance by assigning the same DN and partition to different lines on different devices.
- If other devices share a line, the words "Shared Line" are displayed in red next to the DN in the Directory Number Configuration window in Cisco CallManager Administration.
- If you change the calling search space, call waiting, or call forward and pickup settings on any device that uses the shared line, the changes are applied to all of the devices that use that shared line.
- To stop sharing a line appearance on a device, you can change the DN or partition number for the line and update the device. (Deletion removes the DN on the current device only. The deletion does not affect the other devices.)
- Do not use shared line appearances on any Cisco IP Phone that will be used with the Attendant Console.
- Do not use shared line appearances on any Cisco IP Phone 7960 that requires the Auto Answer capability.

Configuring Barge

To configure Barge with a built-in conference bridge, follow these steps:

Step 1 Assign the Standard User or Standard Feature softkey template (both contain the **Barge** softkey) to each device that accesses Barge by using the built-in conference bridge.

Step 2 To enable Barge clusterwide for all users, choose **Service > Service Parameters** for the Cisco CallManager service and set the Built-In Bridge Enable clusterwide service parameter to **On**. Alternatively, configure Barge for each telephone by setting the **Built-In Bridge** field in the Phone Configuration window on the device itself.

Step 3 Set the Party Entrance Tone to **True** if you desire tones when a Barge occurs.

> **NOTE** To configure Barge using a shared conference resource (rather than the built-in IP phone conference resources), just add the Conference Barge (**cBarge**) softkey to the Remote In Use call state of the device's softkey template.

Configuring Privacy

Recall that when Privacy is enabled, users on a shared line can enable or disable the ability of other users on the shared line to view call status and to barge the call.

To configure Privacy, follow these steps:

Step 1 Set the optional Privacy Setting clusterwide service parameter for Cisco CallManager to **True**.

NOTE Do not set this parameter if only a few users need access to Privacy (see Step 3).

Step 2 For each phone button template for which you want to enable Privacy, add Privacy to one of the feature buttons, as shown in Figure 16-16.

Figure 16-16 *Call Privacy Phone Button Template Configuration*

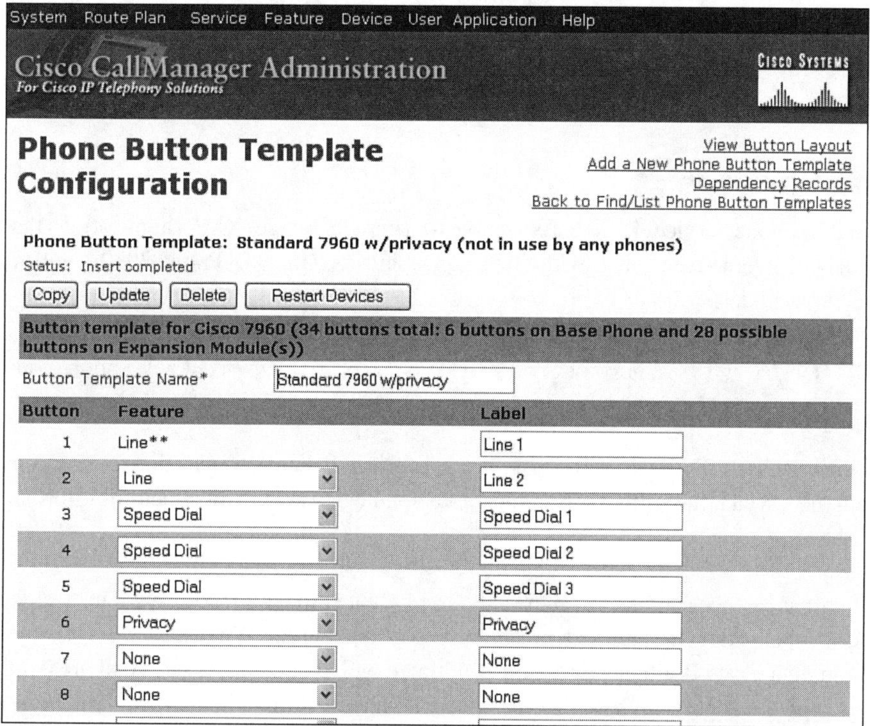

Step 3 For each telephone user who wants to enable Privacy, choose **On** in the **Privacy** drop-down menu in the Phone Configuration window. If you have configured Privacy clusterwide, you can leave the Privacy setting at Default or set it to Off to selectively disable privacy.

Step 4 For each telephone user who wants to enable Privacy, choose the phone button template that contains the Privacy feature button that you created in Step 2.

Figure 16-17 shows the phone display when the Privacy feature is assigned to a feature button. When Privacy is enabled, the **Privacy** button changes display—a black circle appears inside the **Privacy** field. Now, when the other user on the shared line goes off hook on the shared line, the **Barge** softkey does not appear.

Figure 16-17 *Call Privacy Phone Display*

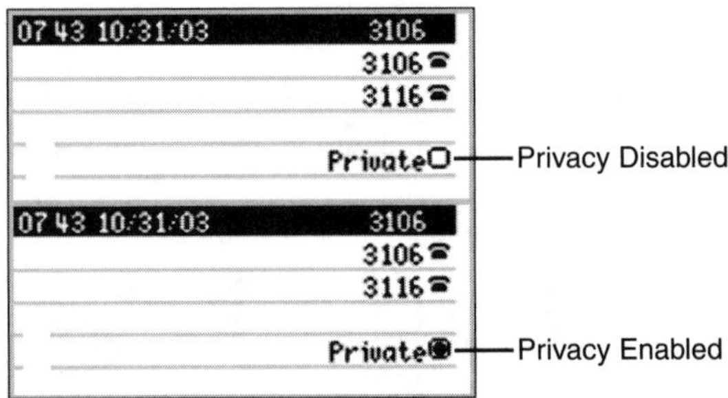

IP Phone Services

Cisco IP Phone Services include Extensible Markup Language (XML) applications that enable the display of interactive content with text and graphics on Cisco IP Phone 7970, 7960, 7940, 7912, and 7905 models.

NOTE Cisco IP Phones 7912 and 7905 support only text-based XML applications.

Using the Cisco IP Phone, you can deploy customized client services that users can interact with from the keypad, the softkeys, or a rocker key and can use to display helpful information on the IP phone.

A user can access a service from the supported phone model in two ways. The user can press the button labeled **Services** to use a preconfigured phone button. When a user presses the **Services** button on a Cisco IP Phone, a session is initiated and a menu of services that are configured for the telephone appears. When the user selects a service from the listing, the telephone display is updated.

In addition to adding a service so that it is available to users on their telephones, you can assign the service to a phone button that is configured as a service URL button. This option gives the user one-button access to the service without using the **Services** button on the IP phone. With Cisco CallManager Release 4.0 or later, you can use any line or speed dial button for one-touch access to selected XML services such as MyFastDials or to access critical XML applications such as those that check inventory levels.

The following list provides examples of services that can be supplied to Cisco IP Phones:

- Conference room scheduler
- E-mail and voice-mail messages list
- Daily and weekly schedule and appointments
- Personal Address Book entries
- Weather reports
- Company news
- Flight status

You can create customized Cisco IP Phone applications for your site by using the Cisco IP Phone Services Software Development Kit (Cisco XML SDK).

Configuring IP Phone Services

You can add services to Cisco CallManager by using the Cisco IP Phone Services Configuration window. After services are configured in Cisco CallManager Administration, users or administrators can subscribe to these services for the devices to which they have access.

To add an IP phone Service, complete the following steps:

Step 1 Choose **Feature** > **Cisco IP Phone Services**.

Step 2 In the upper-right corner of the window, click the **Add a New IP Phone Service** link. The Cisco IP Phone Services Configuration window is displayed, as shown in Figure 16-18.

Figure 16-18 *Cisco IP Phone Services Configuration Window*

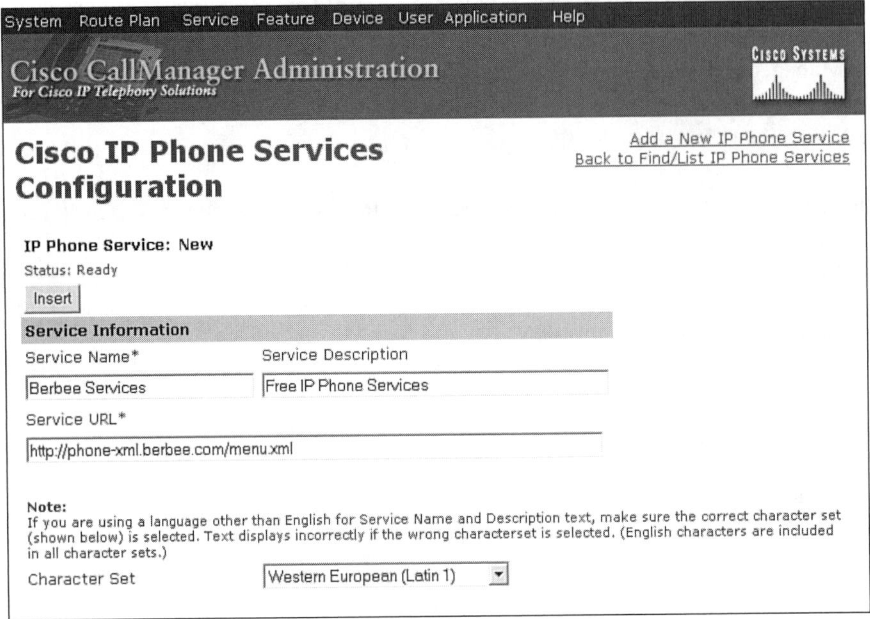

Step 3 Enter the appropriate settings. This list describes the information that must be configured for each service:

- **Service Name**—Enter the name of the service as it will be displayed on the menu of available services in the Cisco IP Phone User Options application. Enter up to 32 characters for the service name.
- **Service Description (optional)**—Enter a description of the content that the service provides to help users decide whether they want to subscribe to the service. (This parameter is not shown in the figure because the service has already been added.)
- **Service URL**—Enter the URL of the server where the Cisco IP Phone Services application is located. Make sure that this server remains independent of the servers in your Cisco CallManager cluster. Do not specify a Cisco CallManager server or any server that is associated with Cisco CallManager (such as a TFTP server or directory database publisher server).
- **Character Set**—If you are using a language other than English for the service name or description, choose the character set for that language.

Step 4 To add the service, click **Insert**.

TIP You can use the service URL shown in Figure 16-18 to obtain free XML services, including stock quotes, weather reports, and news from Berbee, a Cisco partner.

To add the service URL button to an IP phone, follow these steps after you add the service to Cisco CallManager:

Step 1 Customize a phone button template by configuring a Service URL button, as shown in Figure 16-19.

Figure 16-19 *IP Phone Service Line Button Configuration*

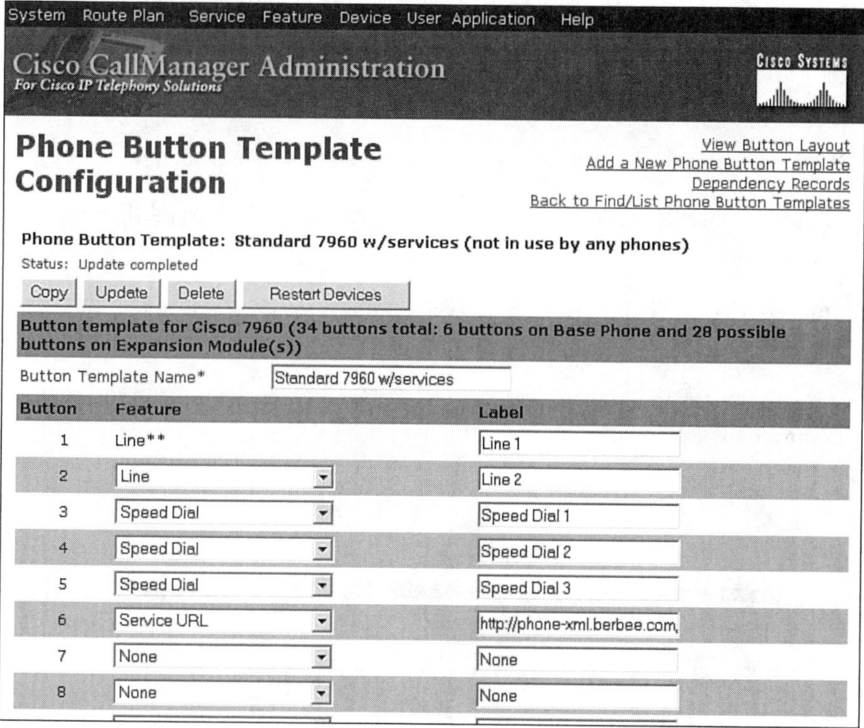

Step 2 Add the customized phone button template to the telephone.

Step 3 Choose **Device > Phone**.

Step 4 To locate a specific telephone, enter the search criteria and click **Find**.

Step 5 Choose the telephone to which you want to add a service URL button.

Step 6 On the upper-right side of the window, click the **Add/Update Service URL Buttons** link.

Step 7 From the **Service** drop-down menu, choose the service that you want to add to the telephone.

Step 8 To add the service to the telephone button, click **Update**, or click **Update and Close** to add the service to the phone button and return to the Phone Configuration window.

Services Phone Display Examples

The Cisco IP Phones have extensive XML display capabilities (especially the 7970 and 7971 models). Here is a list of typical Cisco IP Phone Services displays, as demonstrated in Figure 16-20:

- **Menu**—The menu enables the user to scroll through a list of menu items and make choices.
- **Text**—The text from a web page can be delivered for the user to view.
- **Input**—Input enables the user to enter information using the keypad. The 7970 and 7971 also support touch screen input.
- **Image**—Cisco IP Phone Services can deliver images in black and white and in shades of gray. Color images are available over Cisco IP Phones with a color display.
- **Directory**—Cisco IP Phone Services can deliver a corporate directory to enable users to conveniently locate and dial other employees.
- **Graphical**—Cisco IP Phone Services can display graphics as well as text.

Figure 16-20 *IP Phone Service Display Examples*

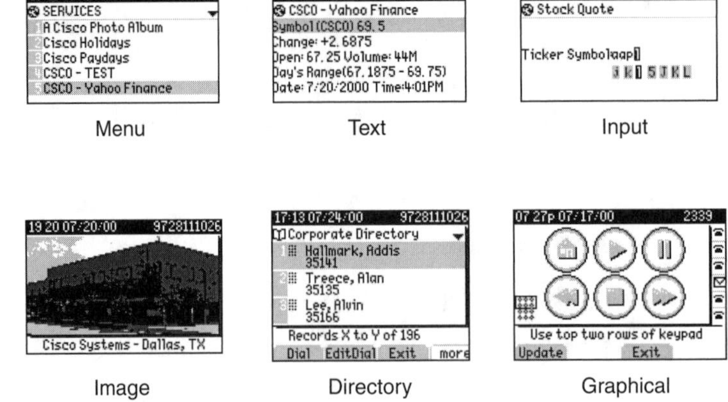

Summary

This chapter covered the concepts and configuration of Cisco CallManager end-user features. The Cisco CallManager core features include hold, redial, and transfer. By default, these features are available on any Cisco IP Phone. In addition, you can configure additional features to be made available through an IP phone's softkey template. The softkey templates choose the availability and order of the feature buttons on an end-user IP phone.

In addition to supporting core features, the Cisco CallManager supports enhanced features, including Call Join, multiple calls per line appearance, and Immediate Divert. Call Park enables a call to be picked up on a different phone than the one it came in on, whereas Call Pickup enables users to cover incoming calls as a group. Configuring Cisco Call Back allows a user to receive call-back notification when a called-party line becomes available. Barge adds a user to a call that is already in progress, whereas Privacy disables the Barge capability.

Finally, Cisco IP Phone Services enable the display of interactive content with text and graphics on XML-capable Cisco IP Phones.

Review Questions

You can find the solutions to these questions in Appendix A, "Answers to Review Questions."

1. What are two requirements for users to be able to view weather reports, airline arrival and departure times, stock quotes, or other Cisco IP Phone Services that the system administrator has made available to them?

   a. Subscribe to the service in the User Options pages.

   b. Enable CTI Application Use.

   c. Go to http://<server_name>/Services.asp.

   d. Press the **Services** button on the Cisco IP Phone.

2. Which three of these areas can you use to assign a softkey template to a device?

   a. Location

   b. Device defaults

   c. Device pools

   d. User profile

   e. Region

   f. Device

3. Which phone feature requires no administrator configuration?

   a. Call Park
   b. Transfer
   c. Barge
   d. Privacy

4. For which softkey is the initiating user NOT included in the call after the transaction is completed?

   a. DirTrfr
   b. Barge
   c. cBarge
   d. Join

5. Barge requires which of the following?

   a. Privacy
   b. Shared line appearance
   c. Attendant Console
   d. Standard User softkey template
   e. Cisco IP Phone 7960

6. Which of the following features allow a user to answer a ringing phone automatically through their speakerphone?

   a. Call Pickup
   b. Group Call Pickup
   c. Other Call Pickup
   d. Auto Answer

7. You have configured the shared extension 1005 to support 30 maximum calls, and to initiate a busy trigger when the calls have reached 15. Michael is using the shared DN 1005 and picks up the extension to make an outgoing call. The current number of individuals using the line is 15. What does Michael hear?

   a. A fast-busy signal
   b. An automated message
   c. A dial tone
   d. A single beep, followed by silence

8. You would like to provide Call Back capabilities to everyone in your organization. All IP phones are configured to use the Standard User softkey template. What would be the easiest way to provide Call Back capabilities to the users?

   a. Add the **Call Back** softkey to the Ring Out and On Hook call states of the standard user template.

   b. Create a new softkey template, add the **Call Back** softkey to the Ring Out and On Hook call states, and assign the softkey template to all users in your organization.

   c. Configure the Call Back XML service and allow users to subscribe from the CCMUser web pages.

   d. Assign the users to the Standard IPMA Manager softkey template.

9. Which of the following accurately describes the Group Call Pickup feature?

   a. Group Call Pickup allows users to pick up a ringing phone located within their Call Pickup Group.

   b. Group Call Pickup allows users to pick up a ringing phone located within their own Call Pickup Group or another Call Pickup Group.

   c. Group Call Pickup allows users to pick up a ringing phone in their pickup group or another pickup group without dialing a group number.

   d. Group Call Pickup allows users to pick up a call on hold by dialing the appropriate extension.

10. A user notices that their shared line appearance is currently in use. Out of curiosity, the user presses a softkey. Immediately, the user is in a conference call with the parties currently using the shared line appearance. Which softkey did the user press?

    a. Barge

    b. Privacy

    c. cBarge

    d. iBarge

This chapter covers the following topics:

- Configuring Cisco CallManager Extension Mobility to enable users to log in to any Cisco IP Phone and obtain their default device profiles
- Configuring FAC and CMC to manage call access and accounting
- Configuring Call Display Restrictions to selectively allow or restrict the display of calling- or connected-line information
- Configuring MCID to report a call of a malicious nature
- Describing the purpose of MLPP

CHAPTER 17

Configuring User Features, Part 2

Administrators need to have a working knowledge of the various options that are available for Cisco IP Phones to ensure that all of the desired features and functions are available to users and that they are properly configured. This lesson, the second of two parts on features, discusses many Cisco IP Phone features that are available to users in a Cisco IP telephony solution. The chapter includes a discussion of Cisco CallManager Extension Mobility, Call Display Restrictions, Forced Authorization Codes (FAC), Client Matter Codes (CMC), Malicious Call Identification (MCID), and Multilevel Precedence and Preemption (MLPP) features.

Cisco CallManager Extension Mobility

Cisco CallManager Extension Mobility is an approach to organizing work environments so that workspaces—including offices, cubicles, and desks—are not permanently assigned to individuals. Instead, employees "check into" an office space by performing a login process at the Cisco IP Phone where they want to receive their calls. Following the login, the IP Phone is assigned the appropriate direct telephone number with all of its characteristics (ring type, speed dialing, and so on). Environments where employees do not routinely conduct business in the same office space every day, such as sales offices, commonly use Cisco CallManager Extension Mobility. It is often referred to as "hoteling."

Cisco CallManager provides a standard login service. The login service can be expanded by using a set of Extensible Markup Language (XML) requests over HTTP. Third parties (including customers and integrators) can replace the login user interface with one of their own design. For example, capabilities can be added to the standard login service such as authenticating via smart card readers or automating the login process according to a "desk sharing" web application.

Because Cisco CallManager Extension Mobility is enabled by XML-based services, it is available only on Cisco IP Phones.

Extension Mobility Example

Figure 17-1 illustrates an example of Extension Mobility.

Figure 17-1 *Extension Mobility in Action*

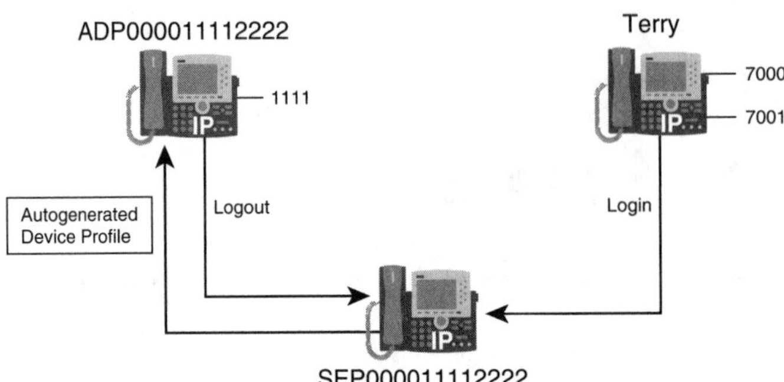

Terry has configured a user device profile called Terry. This profile has a line appearance with a directory number (DN) of 7000 and another with a DN of 7001. Terry is logging in to device SEP000011112222, which has an autogenerated device profile, ADP000011112222, as its default device profile. The default device profile is configured with a single-line appearance with the DN of 1111.

When Terry logs in, the device restarts and displays lines 7000 and 7001. It no longer has line 1111 assigned to it. All of the speed dials and services configured for Terry replace those that are normally on SEP000011112222.

When Terry logs out, the device restarts and loads the autogenerated device profile.

Configuring Extension Mobility

Configuring Extension Mobility is no small chore. In earlier versions of Cisco CallManager, Extension Mobility was only available by purchasing separate server software. In CallManager 4.x versions, Cisco has integrated these server functions into a CallManager service managed by the Tomcat Web Application Manager. Your first step in configuring Extension Mobility is to use the Cisco CallManager Serviceability tool Service Activation to activate the Cisco CallManager Extension Mobility service, as shown in Figure 17-2.

Figure 17-2 *Extension Mobility Service Activation*

Service Activation

Control Center

Servers	Server: MICHIGAN_PUB
MICHIGAN_PUB	Status: Ready
Michigan_Sub	Update · Set Default

Service Name	Activation Status
NT Service	
☑ Cisco CallManager	Activated
☑ Cisco Tftp	Activated
☑ Cisco Messaging Interface	Activated
☑ Cisco IP Voice Media Streaming App	Activated
☑ Cisco CTIManager	Activated
☑ Cisco Telephony Call Dispatcher	Activated
☑ Cisco MOH Audio Translator	Activated
☑ Cisco RIS Data Collector	Activated
☑ Cisco Database Layer Monitor	Activated
☑ Cisco CDR Insert	Activated
☑ Cisco Extended Functions	Activated
☑ Cisco Serviceability Reporter	Activated
☑ Cisco CTL Provider	Activated
☐ Cisco Certificate Authority Proxy Function	Deactivated
Tomcat Web Service	
☑ Cisco Extension Mobility	Activated
☑ Cisco IP Manager Assistant	Activated
☑ Cisco WebDialer	Activated

TIP The Tomcat Web Application Manager is an open-source application manager originally designed for the Apache web server. It allows you to start and stop applications (or Java servlets) without starting and stopping the entire web server. It can be accessed at http://<CCM_Server_IP>/manager/list.

Using the Tomcat Manager window, stop and start the Cisco CallManager Extension Mobility service at http://<Cisco Extension Mobility server>/manager/list, where *Cisco Extension Mobility server* specifies the IP address of the server that has the Cisco CallManager Extension Mobility service running on it. Figure 17-3 illustrates the Tomcat Web Application Manager.

Figure 17-3 *Tomcat Web Application Manager*

Tomcat Web Application Manager

Message: OK - Started application at context path /emservice

Applications

Path	Display Name	Running	Sessions	
/art		true	0	Start Stop Reload Remove
/emapp		true	0	Start Stop Reload Remove
/emservice	Cisco Extension Mobility Service	true	0	Start Stop Reload Remove
/ma	Cisco IP Manager Assistant	true	0	Start Stop Reload Remove
/manager	Tomcat Manager Application	true	0	Start Stop Reload Remove
/wdsoap	Apache-SOAP	true	0	Start Stop Reload Remove
/webdialer		true	0	Start Stop Reload Remove

Install

Path: Config URL: WAR URL: Install

Server

Server Version	JVM Version	JVM Vendor	OS Name	OS Version	OS Arch
Apache Tomcat/4.1.12	1.4.2_05-b04	Sun Microsystems Inc.	Windows 2000	5.0	x86

When the service is activated, configure the following elements to enable Cisco CallManager Extension Mobility:

- Cisco CallManager Extension Mobility service parameters
- A device profile for a Cisco IP Phone model
- A device profile for a Cisco IP Phone user
- A new user
- Add the Extension Mobility service
- Update Cisco IP Phones to support Extension Mobility

To avoid problems with deploying Cisco CallManager Extension Mobility, be sure to follow these configuration guidelines:

- Configure a device profile default for each Cisco IP Phone model in a cluster that you want to support Cisco CallManager Extension Mobility.
- If you want to enable all IP Phones within a Cisco CallManager cluster with Cisco CallManager Extension Mobility, do not allow the users to control these telephones.

— When users go to their Cisco CallManager User Options web page to change their services, they must choose Device Profiles from the **Select a Device to Configure** drop-down list. They cannot control an individual IP Phone or modify the settings for an individual IP Phone.

— As administrator, you can change the services for an IP Phone by using Cisco CallManager Administration. After making the changes, if you update the configuration using the main menu (not the popup menu), you must reset the IP Phone for the changes to take effect. This action ensures that the new snapshot is stored as the logout profile.

- If a particular user controls a device, for example, the user's office telephone, do not allow anyone else to log in to that device.

Cisco CallManager Extension Mobility Service Parameters

Figure 17-4 shows the service parameters for the Cisco CallManager Extension Mobility service.

Figure 17-4 *Extension Mobility Service Parameters*

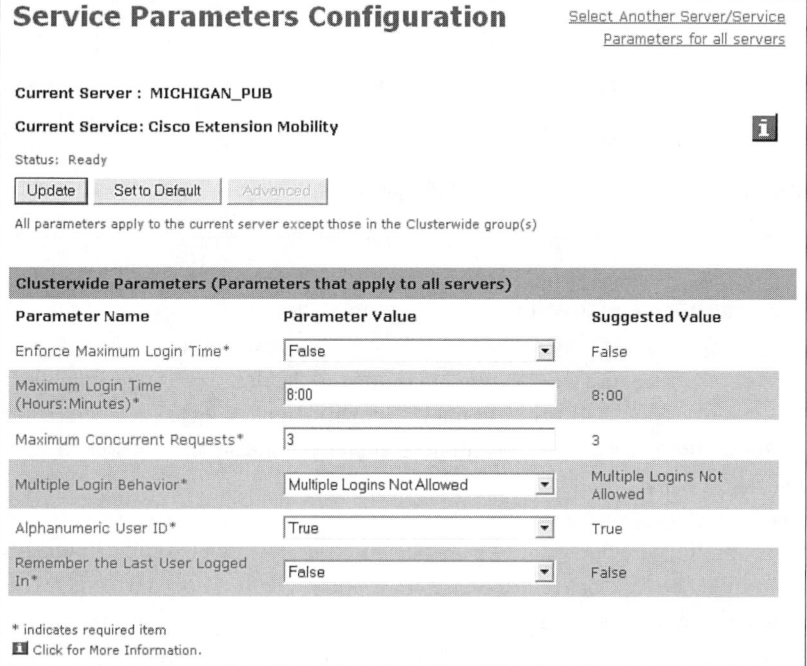

To access this window, choose **Service > Service Parameters** and from the **Service** drop-down menu, choose **Cisco Extension Mobility**. Table 17-1 defines the settings in the Service Parameters Configuration window.

Table 17-1 *Cisco Extension Mobility Service Parameters*

Parameter	Description
Enforce Maximum Login Time	When set to True, this parameter enforces a maximum login time. If set to False, no time limit is set on logins.
Maximum Login Time (Hours:Minutes)	This parameter is the maximum amount of time a user is allowed to remain logged in to a device. The maximum allowable value is 168:00, entered as HHH:MM. Note that :MM is also an acceptable format for durations under 1 hour. This parameter is ignored if the Maximum Login Time parameter is set to False.
Maximum Concurrent Request	This parameter specifies the maximum number of login or logout operations that can occur simultaneously. This maximum prevents the Cisco CallManager Extension Mobility service from consuming excessive system resources.
Multiple Login Behavior	This parameter specifies the behavior for multiple attempted logins by the same user on different devices. The choices are to allow, not to allow, and to cause a previous login to automatically log out.
Alphanumeric User ID	Choose True to allow Cisco CallManager to accept alphanumeric Cisco CallManager Extension Mobility logins or False to force numeric logins only.
Remember the Last User Logged In	When set to True, this parameter remembers the last user to log in.

Configuring a Default Device Profile

Device profiles are very similar to user profiles in Microsoft administration. A user profile consisted of a user's entire workstation environment: the desktop background, the screen saver, the files on the desktop, and so on. In the IPT environment, a device profile defines the common settings for an IP Phone: the phone button template, the music on hold source, the softkey template, and so on.

The device profile default is a clusterwide default used for each Cisco IP Phone that will be supported by Cisco CallManager Extension Mobility. The IP Phone takes on the device profile default whenever a user logs in to an IP Phone model for which the user has no device profile. To access this window, from the Cisco CallManager Administration, choose **Device > Device Settings > Device Profile Default**. From the left column, click the device profile, or if adding a new profile, click **Add a New Device Profile Default**, and the Device Profile Default Configuration window shown in Figure 17-5 appears.

Figure 17-5 *Extension Mobility Default Device Profile*

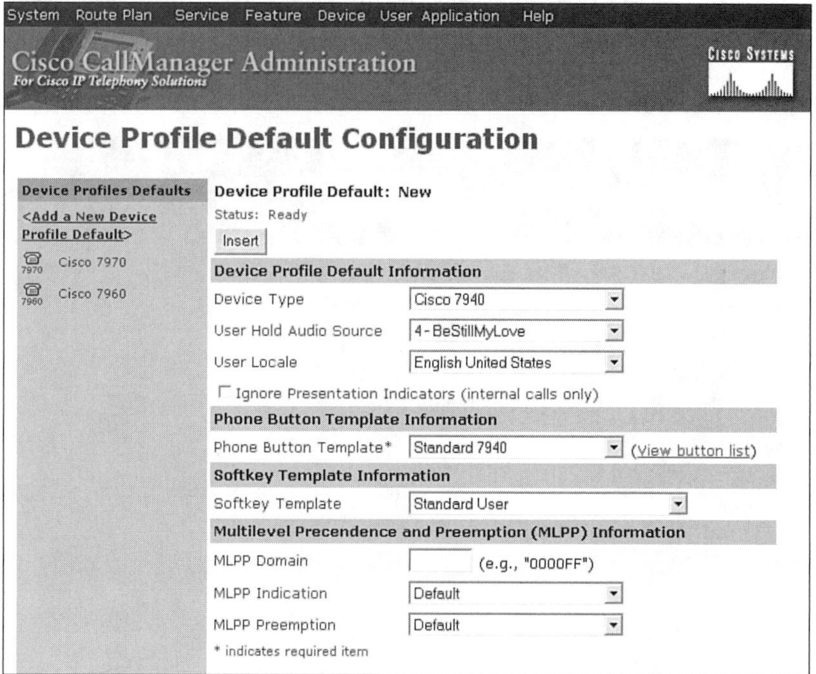

If you do not choose an audio source in the **User Hold Audio Source** field, Cisco CallManager uses the audio source that is defined in the device pool. If the device pool does not specify an audio source ID, the system default is used.

The **User Locale** field identifies a set of detailed information to support users, including language and font. Cisco CallManager makes this field available only for IP Phone models that support localization.

Configuring User Device Profiles

After you have created the default device profile(s) for the IP Phones, you must now create your user profiles. These profiles will be capable of moving between Cisco IP Phones as the user logs in and out of various devices. These profiles correspond on a 1:1 basis with Extension Mobility users in your network. The user device profile contains attributes such as name, description, phone button template, expansion modules, directory number, subscribed services, and speed dial information.

To access this window from Cisco CallManager Administration, choose **Device > Device Settings > Device Profile**. To add a new user device profile, choose **Add a New User Device Profile**. The User Device Profile Configuration window shown in Figure 17-6 appears.

Figure 17-6 *Creating User Device Profiles*

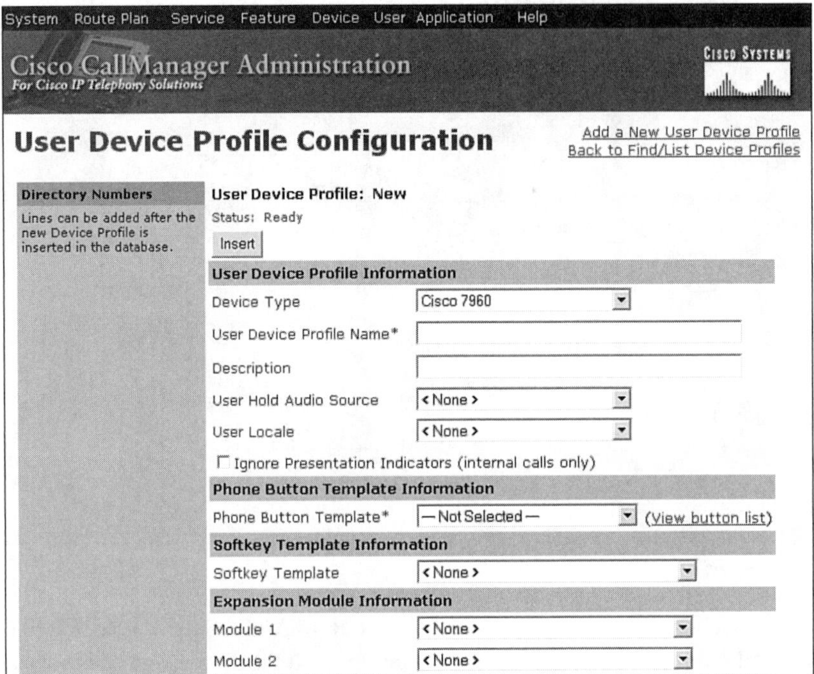

From here, you can select the user device type and add DNs to the profile, just like you were configuring a user IP Phone.

> **NOTE** Device profiles are created for specific devices and only work on specific devices. For example, a device profile created for a 7960 IP Phone will not be able to log in to a 7940 or 7970 IP Phone.

Associating Users with Device Profiles

New users must be configured before they can use Cisco CallManager Extension Mobility. To add a new user for Cisco CallManager Extension Mobility, follow these steps:

Step 1 In Cisco CallManager Administration, choose **User > Add a New User**.
The new user creation window appears, as shown in Figure 17-7.

Figure 17-7 *Adding a New User*

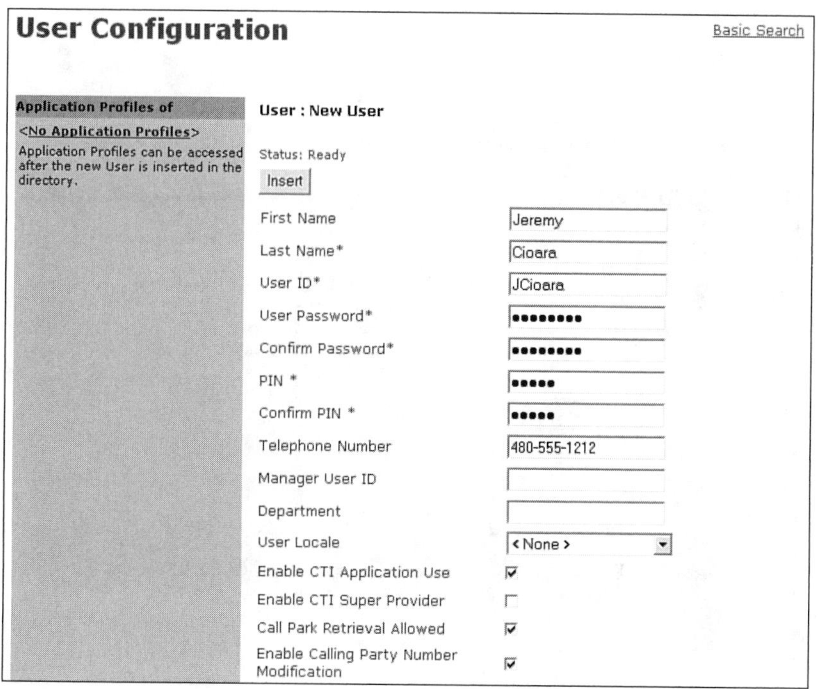

Step 2 In the Add a New User window, enter the first name, last name, and username.

Step 3 In the **User Password** and **Confirm Password** fields, enter a password.

Step 4 In the **PIN** field, enter a numeric personal identification number (PIN). Confirm the PIN.

Step 5 Enter the user telephone number.

Step 6 Click **Insert,** and the window refreshes. From the left pane, choose **Cisco Extension Mobility**.

Step 7 Associate the user device profile with the user account, as shown in Figure 17-8, and then click the **Update Selected** button.

Figure 17-8 *Associating Device Profiles with User Accounts*

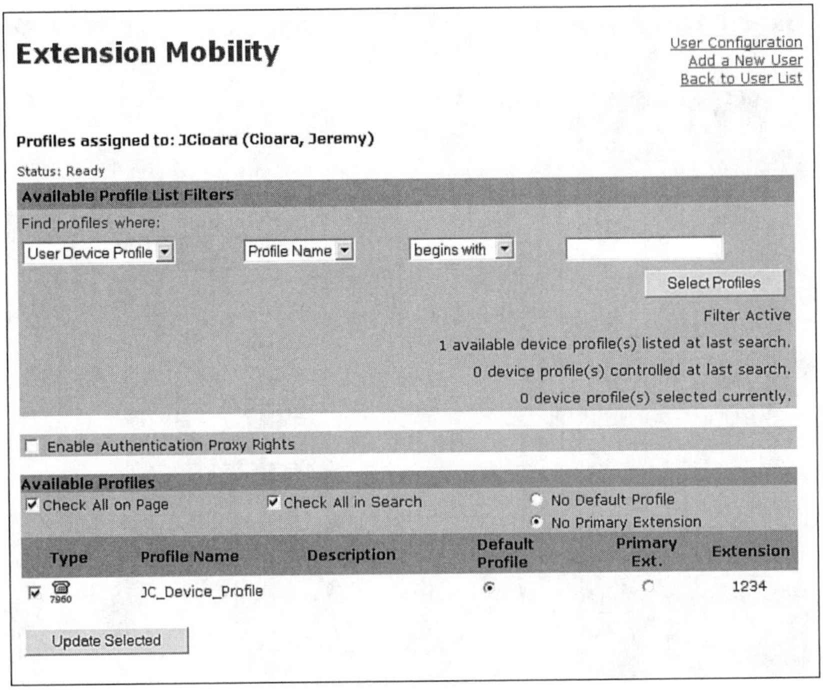

Creating the Extension Mobility Service

Cisco implemented the Extension Mobility feature as an additional service in Cisco CallManager. Because of this, for the IP Phones to support Extension Mobility, you must make it available as a service in the Cisco CallManager and add the new service as an IP Phones subscription. To accomplish this, perform the following steps:

Step 1 In Cisco CallManager Administration, choose **Feature > Cisco IP Phone Services**.

Step 2 Click **Add a New IP Phone Service** in the upper-right corner of the window.

Step 3 Choose a logical name such as "Extension Mobility" for the service name.

Step 4 As shown in Figure 17-9, in the Service URL, enter the following string: **http://<CCM_IP>/emapp/EMAppServlet?device=#DEVICENAME#**

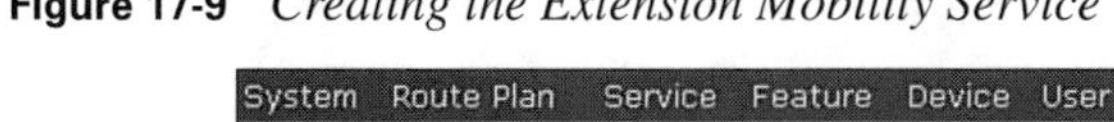

Figure 17-9 *Creating the Extension Mobility Service*

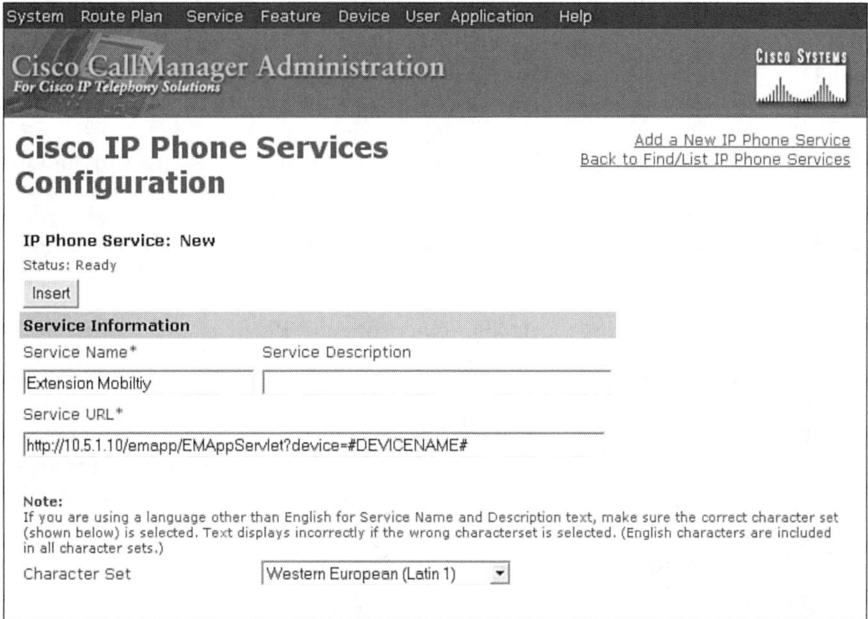

> **CAUTION** The Extension Mobility service URL must be entered *exactly* as shown, substituting the IP address of the CallManager running the Extension Mobility service for CCM_IP. This URL is case sensitive.

> **TIP** To provide redundancy for a Cisco IP Phone service, use a CallManager hostname rather than an IP address. If that CallManager fails, the services will automatically failover to a secondary Cisco CallManager. Be sure you have configured the IP Phone for DNS support if you choose to do this.

Step 5 Click the **Insert** button. The Extension Mobility service is now saved.

Updating Cisco IP Phones to Add Extension Mobility Support

The final step in configuring Extension Mobility is to configure the Cisco IP Phones with the correct service and profile information. If you do not subscribe the phones to the Extension Mobility service, they will be stuck on the default profile without users having the ability to log in with their custom profiles. To subscribe an IP Phone to the Extension Mobility service, perform the following steps:

Step 1 Enter the device configuration mode for the Cisco IP Phone you want to configure for Extension Mobility support.

Step 2 Click the **Subscribe/Unsubscribe Services** link in the upper-right of the screen.

Step 3 Using the drop-down menu, select the Extension Mobility service you created and click **Continue**.

Step 4 Click **Subscribe** to add the service to the IP Phone configuration.

Step 5 On the phone configuration window, scroll to the bottom and click the **Enable Extension Mobility Feature** check box.

Step 6 At the **Log Out Profile** field, select **Use Current Device Settings** to use the default profile you configured, as shown in Figure 17-10.

Figure 17-10 *Configuring the IP Phone for Extension Mobility*

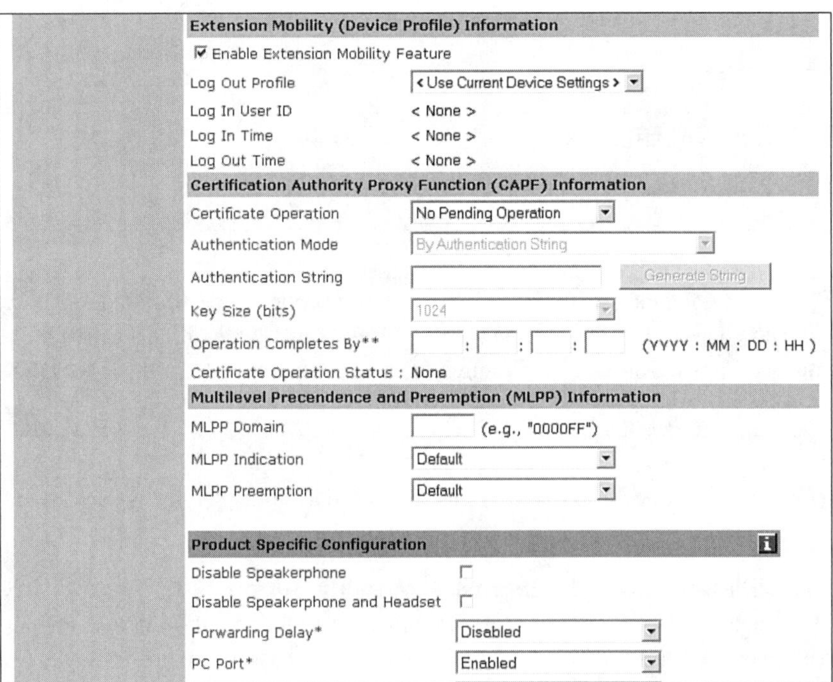

NOTE Cisco CallManager gives you two options for the **Log Out Profile** field: **Use Current Device Settings**, which uses the default device profile you configured for the IP Phone, or **Select a User Device Profile**, which allows you to configure a unique user profile for the IP Phone. Cisco strongly advises against using a user profile for this purpose.

Step 7 Click **Update** to save the changes.

NOTE You should also modify the Extension Mobility parameters on the default device profile for the service subscription to be available at all times.

Client Matter Codes and Forced Authentication Codes

Forced Authentication Codes (FACs) and Client Matter Codes (CMCs) allow you to manage call access and accounting. CMCs are often referred to as account codes and assist with call accounting and billing for billable clients. FACs regulates the types of calls that certain users can place.

The CMC feature benefits law offices, accounting firms, consulting firms, and other businesses or organizations that need to track the length of the call for each client. To use the CMC feature, users must enter a client matter code to reach certain dialed numbers.

You can use FAC for colleges, universities, or any business or organization when limiting access to specific classes of calls proves beneficial. Likewise, when you assign unique authorization codes, you can determine which users placed calls.

FAC Concepts

For each user, you specify an authorization code, and then you enable FAC for relevant route patterns by checking the appropriate check box and specifying the minimum authorization level for calls through that route pattern.

When you enable FAC through route patterns in Cisco CallManager Administration, users must enter an authorization code to reach the intended recipient of the call. When a user dials a number that is routed through a FAC-enabled route pattern, the system plays a tone that prompts for the authorization code. Figure 17-11 illustrates the FAC process, which follows these steps:

Step 1 A user dials a number that goes to a FAC-enabled route pattern.

Step 2 Cisco CallManager tells the phone to play the tone.

Step 3 The user enters the authorization code, followed by the # key.

> **NOTE** The pound sign (#) at the end of the client matter code cancels the interdigit timeout. If users do not append the # to the authorization code or client matter code, the system waits for the T302 timer to extend the call (**System > Service Parameters** for the Cisco CallManager service). The default for the T302 timer is 15 seconds.

Step 4 The call is extended to the exiting gateway.

Step 5 CallManager generates a Call Detail Record (CDR) flagged with the FAC number.

Figure 17-11 *FAC Process*

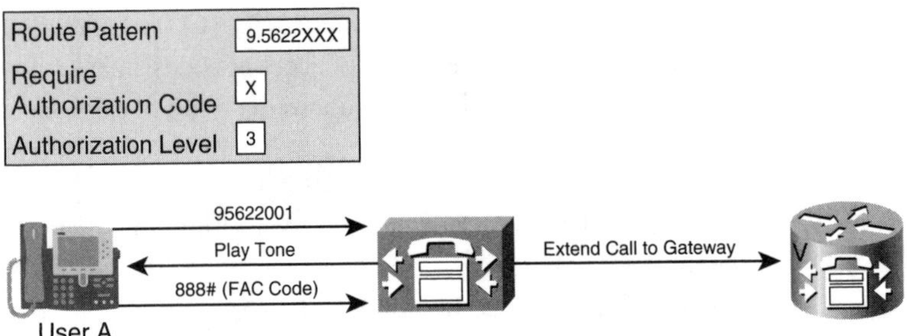

In Cisco CallManager Administration, you can configure various levels of authorization. Users are given codes that assign them a certain authorization level. Route patterns are then assigned authorization levels. If the user authorization code does not meet the level of authorization that is specified to route the dialed number, the user receives a reorder tone. If the authorization is accepted, the call is placed. The name of the authorization writes to Call Detail Records (CDRs), so that you can organize the information by using CDR Analysis and Reporting (CAR), which generates reports for accounting and billing.

To implement FAC, you must devise a list of authorization levels and corresponding descriptions to define the levels. You must specify authorization levels in the range from 0 to 255. Cisco allows authorization levels to be arbitrary, so that you define what the numbers mean for your organization. For example, you could configure authorization levels as follows:

- Configure an authorization level of 10 for interstate long-distance calls in North America.
- Because intrastate calls often cost more than interstate calls, configure an authorization level of 20 for intrastate long-distance calls in North America.
- Configure an authorization level of 30 for international calls.

CMC Concepts

You apply CMC through route patterns, and you can configure multiple client matter codes. When a user dials a number that is routed through a CMC-enabled route pattern, a tone prompts the user for the client matter code. When the user enters a valid code, the call is placed; if the user enters an invalid code, a reorder tone is played. CMC is written to the CDR, so you can collect the information by using CAR, which generates reports for client accounting and billing.

> **TIP** The FAC and CMC features are very similar and often confused. Cisco created the FAC primarily to prevent toll fraud and to limit and track the users able to make calls by authorization levels. CMC is a nearly identical feature allowing organizations to track calls based on the CMC code dialed rather than authorization level.

Figure 17-12 shows a basic CMC call where the route pattern 8.@ is configured to require the user to enter a client matter code:

Step 1 When the user dials 8-214-555-0134, the dialed string matches the 8.@ route pattern.

Step 2 Cisco CallManager plays a "zip-zip" tone to prompt the user to enter the client matter code associated with the dialed string, in this example, 1234.

Step 3 If the user enters 1234 followed by the # key, the call is immediately extended to the voice gateway. If the user does not enter a code or enters the wrong code, the user hears a reorder tone, and the call is not extended.

Step 4 Because the user entered a valid code, Cisco CallManager extends the call to the voice gateway for call completion.

Step 5 Cisco CallManager generates a CDR with the associated client matter code for client-tracking and reporting purposes.

Figure 17-12 *CMC Process*

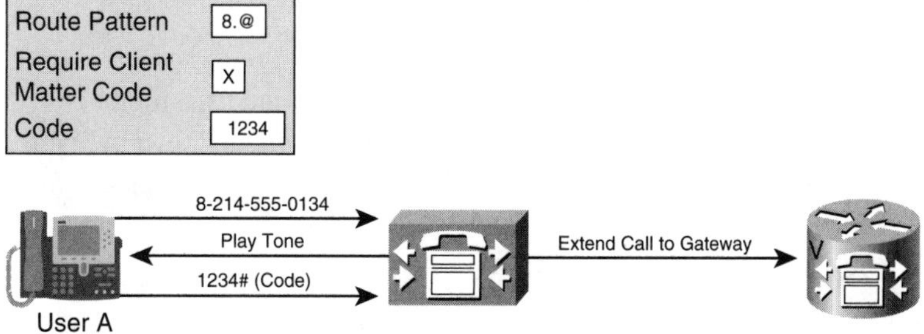

CMC and FAC can be implemented together for a given route pattern. For example, you can allow only certain users to have authorization to place certain long-distance calls, and then require the user to enter a CMC for that call. The tones for CMC and FAC sound the same to the user, so the feature tells the user to enter the authorization code after the first tone and enter the account code after the second tone.

FAC and CMC Configuration

To implement CMC or FAC, you can perform the following steps:

Step 1 If using CMCs, create a document with a list of CMCs and associated client names that you want to track. If using FACs, create a document listing the authorization levels you want to create and the authorization levels required for restricted route patterns.

Step 2 Insert the CMC or FAC codes by using Cisco CallManager Administration (choose **Feature > Client Matter Code** or **Feature > Forced Authorization Code**).

Step 3 To enable FAC or CMC, update route patterns by selecting **Require Client Matter Code** or **Require Forced Authorization Code** and entering the level of FAC required.

Step 4 Update dial plan documents as necessary.

Step 5 Provide information to users and explain how the feature works.

Creating CMC Codes

Complete the following steps to add CMCs in Cisco CallManager Administration:

Step 1 In Cisco CallManager Administration, choose **Feature > Client Matter Code**.

Step 2 In the upper-right corner of the window, click the **Add a New Client Matter Code** link.

Step 3 In the **Client Matter Code** field, enter a unique code of no more than 16 digits that users will enter when placing a call, as shown in Figure 17-13. The client matter code displays in the CDRs for calls that use this code.

Figure 17-13 *CMC Configuration*

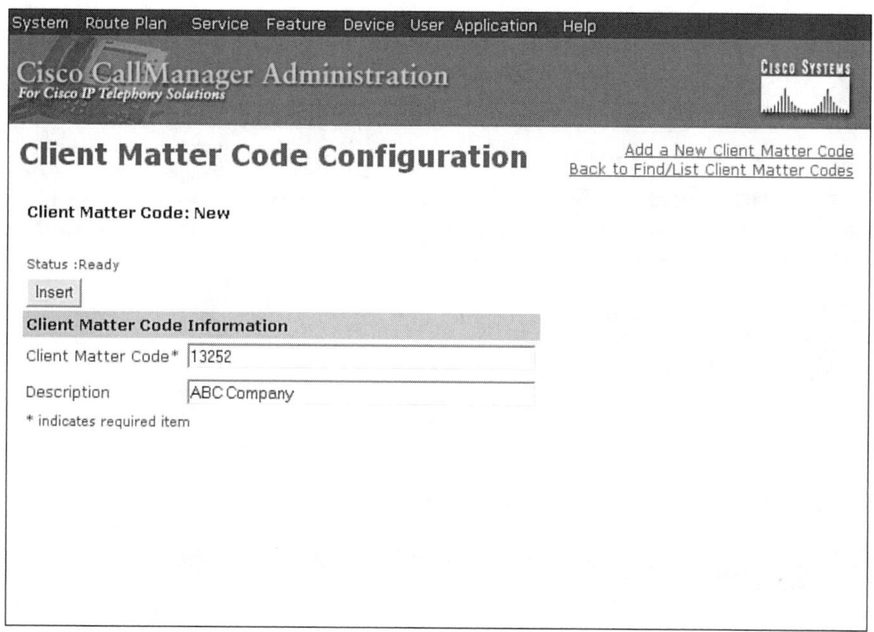

Step 4 In the **Description** field, enter a name of no more than 50 characters. This optional field associates a client code with a client.

Step 5 Click **Insert**.

Creating FAC Codes

Complete the following steps to add FACs in Cisco CallManager Administration:

Step 1 In Cisco CallManager Administration, choose **Feature > Forced Authorization Code**.

Step 2 In the upper-right corner of the window, click the **Add a New Forced Authorization Code** link.

Step 3 In the **Authorization Code Name** field, enter a logical name representing the authorization, as shown in Figure 17-14.

Figure 17-14 *FAC Configuration*

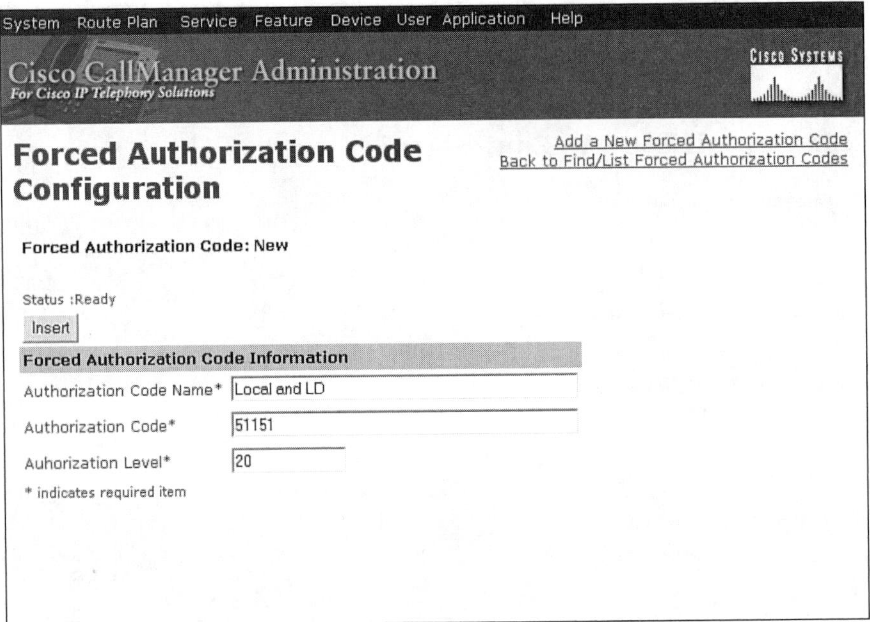

Step 4 In the **Authorization Code** field, enter the code users will dial to obtain this level of authorization.

Step 5 In the **Authorization Level** field, enter the level of authorization the user obtains if they enter the authorization code.

Step 6 Click **Insert**.

Enabling Route Patterns for FAC and CMC

Complete the following steps to enable route patterns for FAC and CMC:

Step 1 In Cisco CallManager Administration, choose **Route Plan > Route/Hunt > Route Pattern**.

Step 2 Open the properties window for the route pattern you want to modify.

Step 3 If you are configuring the route pattern for CMC, check the **Require Client Matter Code** check box, as shown in Figure 17-15.

Step 4 If you are configuring the route pattern for FAC, check the **Require Forced Authorization Code** check box and enter the level of authorization required to access this route pattern.

Step 5 Click **Update**.

Figure 17-15 *Route Pattern Configuration*

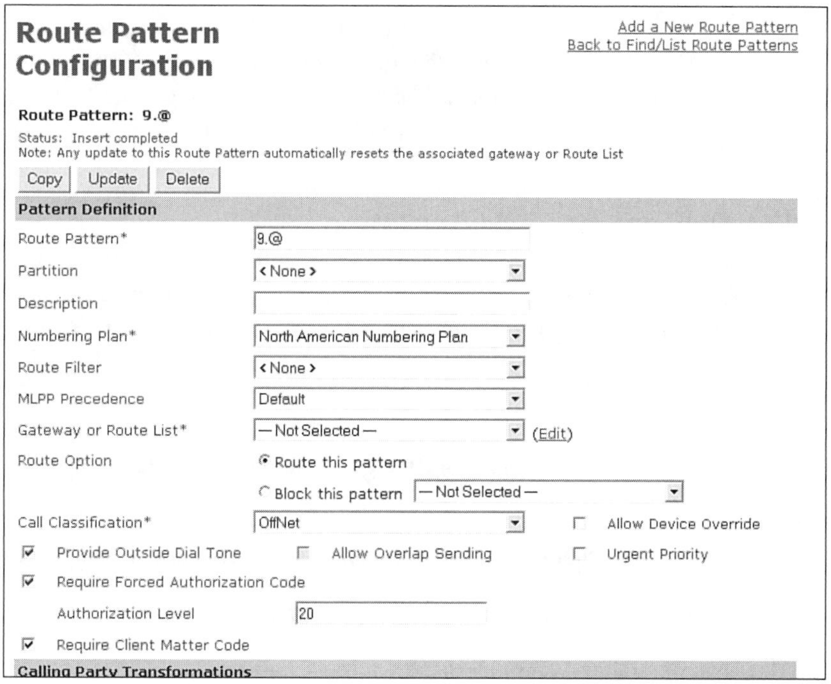

Route Pattern Configuration

Add a New Route Pattern
Back to Find/List Route Patterns

Route Pattern: 9.@

Status: Insert completed
Note: Any update to this Route Pattern automatically resets the associated gateway or Route List

Copy | Update | Delete

Pattern Definition

Route Pattern*	9.@
Partition	< None >
Description	
Numbering Plan*	North American Numbering Plan
Route Filter	< None >
MLPP Precedence	Default
Gateway or Route List*	— Not Selected — (Edit)
Route Option	Route this pattern
	Block this pattern — Not Selected —
Call Classification*	OffNet ☐ Allow Device Override

☑ Provide Outside Dial Tone ☐ Allow Overlap Sending ☐ Urgent Priority

☑ Require Forced Authorization Code

Authorization Level 20

☑ Require Client Matter Code

Calling Party Transformations

Call Display Restrictions

The Call Display Restrictions feature allows you to selectively display or restrict the calling and connected (called party) line information. A hotel environment frequently requires this functionality and might have the following needs:

- For calls between a guest room and the front desk, both the room and the front desk should see both the calling-party information and the called-party information.
- For calls between guest rooms, the rooms should not see the call information of other rooms displayed.
- For calls between guest rooms and other hotel extensions (such as a clubhouse), only the rooms should see the call information displayed.
- For external calls from the public switched telephone network (PSTN) to the front desk or guest rooms, the call information of the caller should not be displayed if the display settings are restricted.

- For all calls to the front desk, the call information of internal calls should be displayed.

In Cisco CallManager Release 4.0 and later, the calling-party and connected-party presentation can be controlled by the configuration at the translation pattern level. Starting with Cisco CallManager Release 4.1, this functionality was extended by adding a new setting at the device level that enables the device to ignore the caller ID restrictions of the other party for internal calls.

Understanding Calling Line ID Presentation

Cisco CallManager uses the **Calling Line ID Presentation** field information as a supplementary service to allow or restrict display of the telephone number of the originating caller on a call-by-call basis. Choose one of the following options to allow or restrict the display of the telephone number of the calling party on the IP Phone display of the called party for this translation pattern, shown in Figure 17-16:

- **Default**—This option does not change the presentation of the calling-party identification information.
- **Allowed**—Cisco CallManager allows the display of the calling-party name or number.
- **Restricted**—Cisco CallManager blocks the display of the calling-party name or number.

Figure 17-16 *Calling Line ID Presentation Restrictions in Translation Patterns*

Numbering Plan*	North American Numbering Plan
Route Filter	< None >
Calling Search Space	< None >
MLPP Precedence	Default
Route Option	Route this pattern
	Block this pattern —Not Selected—
Provide Outside Dial Tone	Urgent Priority
Calling Party Transformations	
Use Calling Party's External Phone Number Mask	
Calling Party Transform Mask	
Prefix Digits (Outgoing Calls)	
Calling Line ID Presentation	Restricted
Calling Name Presentation	Restricted
Connected Party Transformations	
Connected Line ID Presentation	Allowed
Connected Name Presentation	Allowed
Called Party Transformations	
Discard Digits	< None >
Called Party Transform Mask	
Prefix Digits (Outgoing Calls)	

* indicates required item.

If the incoming call goes through a translation pattern or route pattern and the Calling Line ID Presentation setting is allowed or restricted, the system modifies the calling-line presentation with the translation or route pattern setting.

Understanding Connected Line ID Presentation

Cisco CallManager uses the **Connected Line ID Presentation** field information as a supplementary service to allow or restrict the display of the telephone number of the called party on a per-call basis. Choose one of the following options to allow or restrict the display of the telephone number of the connected party on the telephone of the calling party for this translation pattern, as shown in Figure 17-16:

- **Default**—This option does not change the presentation of the connected-line identification information.
- **Allowed**—Cisco CallManager allows the display of the connected-party name or number.
- **Restricted**—Cisco CallManager blocks the display of the connected-party name or number.

If the incoming call goes through a translation or route pattern and the **Connected Line ID Presentation** field is set to **Allowed** or **Restricted**, the system modifies the connected-line presentation indicator with the translation or route pattern setting.

Understanding Ignore Presentation Indicators

The **Ignore Presentation Indicators** check box, introduced in CallManager 4.1, gives you the flexibility to overrule internal caller ID restrictions on a device-by-device basis. To activate this check box, access the IP Phone where you want to remove caller ID restrictions and place a check in the **Ignore Presentation Indicators (Internal Calls Only)** check box, shown in Figure 17-17. When this feature is active, the following caller ID modifications take place:

- Cisco CallManager always displays the call information of the remote party if the other party is internal, regardless of the other calling- and called-party presentation settings.
- Cisco CallManager does not display the call information of the remote party if the other party is external and the display presentation is restricted.

Figure 17-17 *Setting Ignore Presentation Indicators Option for Select Devices*

Phone Configuration (Model = Cisco 7940)	
Device Information	
MAC Address*	431A350B3922
Description	IP Phone in Tombstone, Arizona
Owner User ID	(Select User ID)
Device Pool*	Student22_DP (View details)
Calling Search Space	< None >
AAR Calling Search Space	< None >
Media Resource Group List	< None >
User Hold Audio Source	< None >
Network Hold Audio Source	< None >
Location	< None >
User Locale	< None >
Network Locale	< None >
Device Security Mode	Use System Default
Signal Packet Capture Mode	None
Packet Capture Duration	60
Built In Bridge	Default
Privacy	Default
☑ Retry Video Call as Audio	
☑ Ignore Presentation Indicators (internal calls only)	
Phone Button Template Information	

Ignore Presentation Indicators Option

Configuring Caller ID Restrictions

Because each IPT environment can be so different, it is impossible to create exact caller ID restriction steps that apply to all organizations. Instead, complete the following general steps if you want to use Call Display Restrictions:

Step 1 Configure partitions and calling search spaces before you add a translation pattern.

Step 2 Configure translation patterns with different levels of display restrictions.

Step 3 Check the **Ignore Presentation Restriction (Internal Calls Only)** check box for IP Phones such as lobby phones when you want to ensure that the call information display for internal calls is always visible.

Step 4 Configure individual, associated translation patterns for each individual Call Park directory number to work with the Call Park feature.

Malicious Call Identification

Malicious Call Identification (MCID), available starting with Cisco CallManager Release 4.0, is an internetwork service that allows users to initiate a sequence of events when they receive calls with a malicious intent from another network (typically, the PSTN). The user who receives a disturbing call can invoke the MCID feature by using a softkey or feature code while connected to the call. The MCID service immediately flags the call as a malicious call with an alarm notification to the Cisco CallManager administrator. The MCID service flags the CDR with the MCID notice and sends a notification to the off-net PSTN that a malicious call is in progress.

The MCID service is an ISDN PRI service, when using PRI connections to the PSTN. The MCID service includes two components:

- **MCID-O**—An originating component that invokes the feature at the request of the user (victim) and that sends the invocation request to the connected network
- **MCID-T**—A terminating component that receives the invocation request from the connected network and responds with a success or failure message that indicates whether the service can be performed

Typically, each function runs in separate network entities, and the two service components communicate with each other to allow two networks to identify a call as malicious.

Cisco CallManager supports only the originating component at this time.

> **TIP** MCID is a PRI-based service. If your organization does not use PRI PSTN connections, MCID can still flag calls with malicious intent in the CallManager CDRs.

Configuring MCID

MCID, which is a system feature, comes standard with Cisco CallManager software. MCID does not require special installation or activation.

To configure MCID, follow these general procedures:

Step 1 Ensure that the CDR flag is set to True.

Step 2 Configure the alarm.

Step 3 Configure a softkey template with the **Malicious Call Trace** softkey.

Step 4 Assign the MCID softkey template to an IP Phone.

Step 5 Notify users that the MCID feature is available.

Configuring CallManager to Support CDRs

To enable Cisco CallManager to flag a CDR with the MCID indicator, you must enable the CDR flag. Use the following procedure in Cisco CallManager Administration to enable the CDR flag:

Step 1 From the drop-down list, choose **Service > Service Parameters**.

Step 2 Choose the Cisco CallManager server name.

Step 3 In the **Service** field, choose **Cisco CallManager**. The Service Parameters Configuration window appears.

Step 4 In the System area, set the **CDR Flag Enabled** field to **True** if it is not already enabled, as shown in Figure 17-18.

Figure 17-18 *Configuring CallManager Service Parameters to Support CDRs*

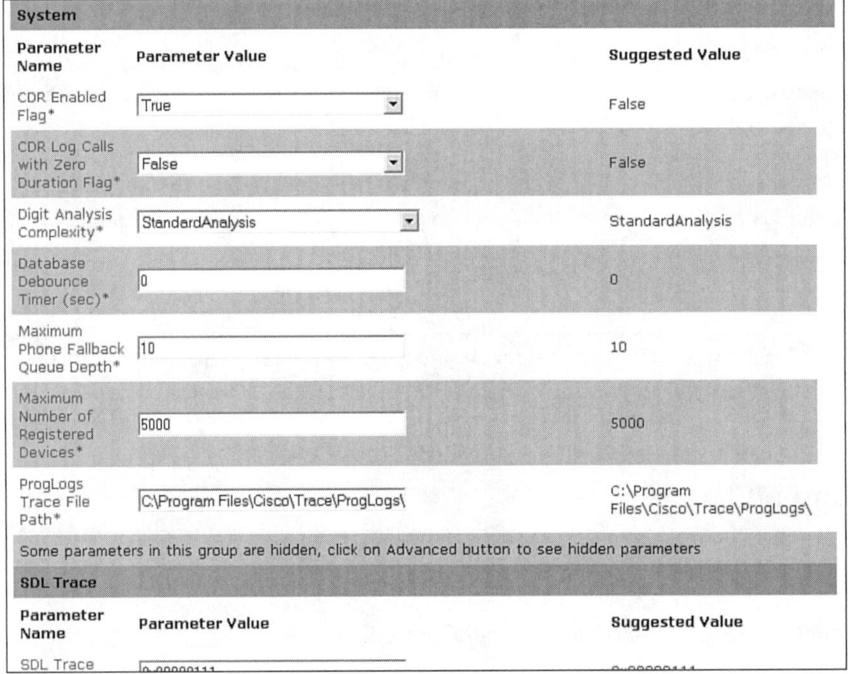

System

Parameter Name	Parameter Value	Suggested Value
CDR Enabled Flag*	True	False
CDR Log Calls with Zero Duration Flag*	False	False
Digit Analysis Complexity*	StandardAnalysis	StandardAnalysis
Database Debounce Timer (sec)*	0	0
Maximum Phone Fallback Queue Depth*	10	10
Maximum Number of Registered Devices*	5000	5000
ProgLogs Trace File Path*	C:\Program Files\Cisco\Trace\ProgLogs\	C:\Program Files\Cisco\Trace\ProgLogs\

Some parameters in this group are hidden, click on Advanced button to see hidden parameters

SDL Trace

Parameter Name	Parameter Value	Suggested Value
SDL Trace		

Step 5 If you have made a change, click **Update**.

Configuring MCID Alarms

To provide for the MCID alarm information to appear in the Event Viewer, you need to enable the alarm event level. Use Cisco CallManager Serviceability and the following procedure to activate alarms for MCID:

Step 1 Choose **Application > Serviceability**. The Cisco CallManager Serviceability application opens.

Step 2 Choose **Alarm > Configuration**. The Alarm Configuration window is displayed.

Step 3 From the list, choose the Cisco CallManager server.

Step 4 In the **Configured Services** drop-down list, choose **Cisco CallManager**. The Alarm Configuration window updates with configuration fields.

Step 5 Under Event Viewer, in the **Alarm Event Level** drop-down list, choose **Informational**, as shown in Figure 17-19.

Figure 17-19 *Configuring MCID Alarms in Windows 2000 Event Viewer*

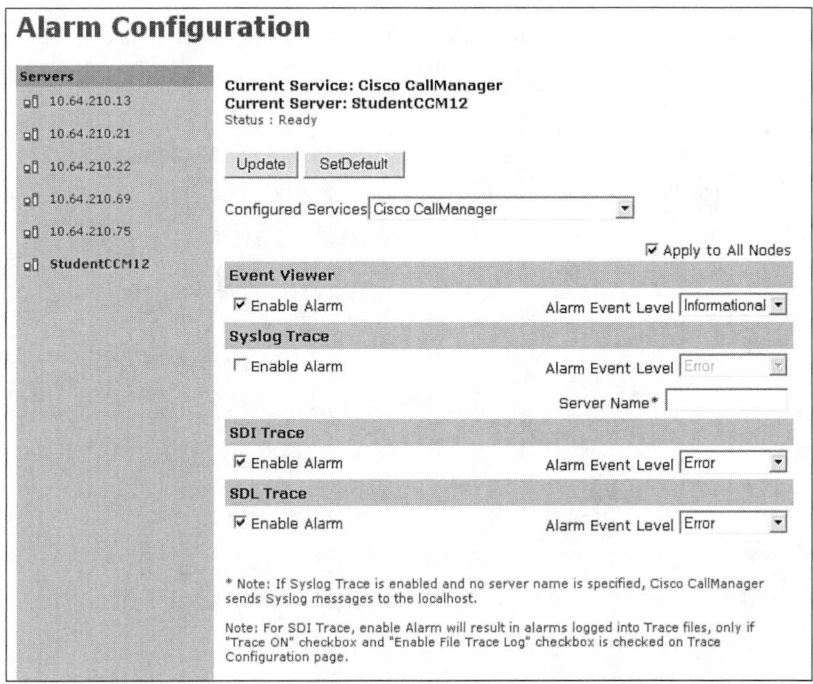

Step 6 Under Event Viewer, check the **Enable Alarm** check box.

Step 7 If you want to enable the alarm for all nodes in the cluster, check the **Apply to All Nodes** check box.

Step 8 Click **Update** to turn on the informational alarm.

Adding the MCID Softkey

For users to trigger MCID alerts, you must add the appropriate softkey to the softkey template configured for their IP Phones. Use this procedure in Cisco CallManager Administration to add the **Malicious Call** softkey to a template:

Step 1 Choose **Device** > **Device Settings** > **Softkey Template**. The Find and List Softkey Templates window appears.

Step 2 Select the Softkey Template assigned to your users. If your users are using one of the built-in softkey templates, you will need to create a new softkey template, as described in Chapter 16, "Configuring User Features, Part 1."

Step 3 In the upper-right corner of the window, click the **Configure Softkey Layout** link. The Softkey Layout Configuration window appears.

Step 4 In the Call States area on the left, choose **Connected**. The list in the Unselected Softkeys pane changes to display the available softkeys for this call state.

Step 5 In the Unselected Softkeys pane, choose **Toggle Malicious Call Trace**, as shown in Figure 17-20.

Step 6 To move the softkey to the Selected keys pane, click the right arrow.

Step 7 Click **Update** to ensure that the softkey template is configured.

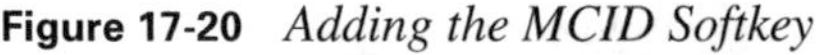

Figure 17-20 *Adding the MCID Softkey*

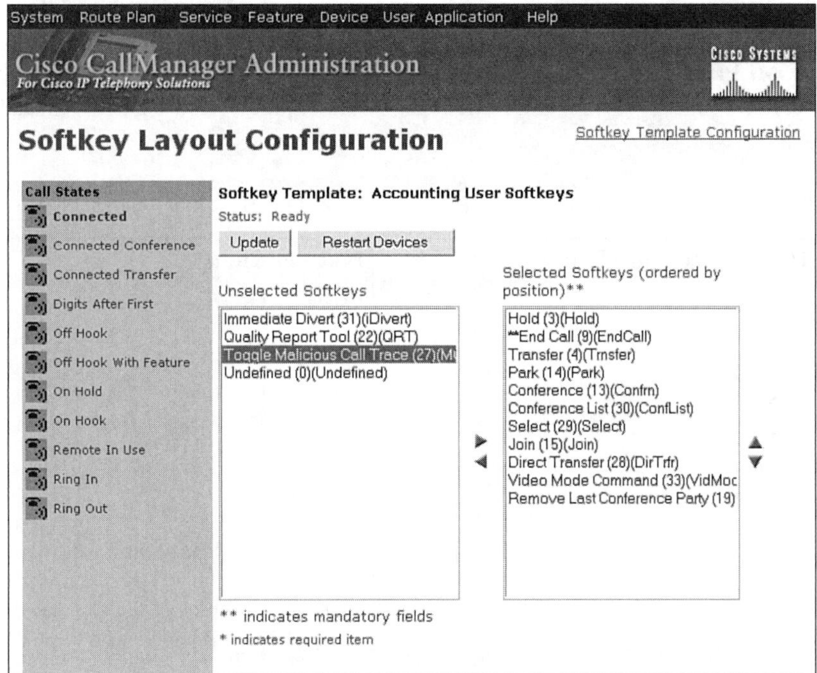

Multilevel Precedence and Preemption

Most telephone systems are designed to accommodate busy-hour traffic. However, should an emergency occur, chances are that everyone would attempt to make a telephone call at the same time, and this behavior could overwhelm the system. In a national emergency or when network performance has degraded, an organization might want to give certain individuals calling precedence over others to implement emergency plans.

The MLPP feature, introduced in Cisco CallManager Release 4.0, allows placement of priority calls. *Precedence* is the priority level that is associated with a call. *Preemption* is the process that terminates existing calls of lower precedence and extends a call of higher precedence to or through (in the case of a gateway) the target device.

Cisco CallManager provides indication signals (tones and displays) to MLPP-enabled devices to ensure that the calling and called parties are aware of an MLPP call. MLPP-indication-enabled devices can play preemption tones and receive MLPP preemption announcements that the announcement server (annunciator) generates when there is a high-precedence call. The precedence ringback and ringer have a different cadence than the regular ringback and ringer.

MLPP indication settings are configured in the device windows in Cisco CallManager Administration.

The six MLPP precedence levels presented in Table 17-2 are available in the Translation Pattern Configuration window of Cisco CallManager Administration (**Route Plan > Translation Pattern**).

MLPP Precedence Levels

MLPP Precedence Setting	Precedence
Highest	Executive Override Starting in Cisco CallManager Release 4.1, Executive Override is the highest precedence level and has a precedence setting of 0. Six precedence levels are available, 0 through 5.
Second highest	Flash Override (In Cisco CallManager Release 4.0, Flash Override is the highest precedence level and has a precedence setting of 0. Five precedence levels are available in Release 4.0, 0 through 4.)
Third highest	Flash
Fourth highest	Immediate
Fifth highest	Priority
Sixth highest	Routine
Does not override the incoming precedence level but rather lets it pass unchanged	Default

Calls with a precedence level higher than Routine are considered precedence calls.

As an MLPP example, Phone B (extension 3116) is on a call with no precedence. Phone A (extension 3101) attempts to place a call to Phone B. Because Phone B is on a call, the call is forwarded to voice mail. Phone A hangs up and dials a Flash Override code of 555+3116. This action causes a preemption annunciator message to play on Phone B. Phone B hangs up and hears the precedence ring. Phone B picks up the call from Phone A, and a precedence call is established.

Summary

This chapter covered the concepts and configuration of Cisco CallManager enhanced end-user features. A highly desired feature supported in Cisco CallManager is Extension Mobility. This feature enables users to temporarily access their Cisco IP Phone configuration from other Cisco IP Phones. This allows you to assign users roaming phone profiles and keep them from being tied to a physical location.

Client Matter Codes (CMC) and Forced Authorization Codes (FAC) allow you to manage call access and accounting. CMC codes are generally used to track calls on a per-client or per-department basis, whereas FAC authorization levels are used to prevent toll fraud from internal users.

Malicious Call Identification (MCID) allows users to invoke a softkey to initiate a series of events when they receive a threatening call. This even can range from flagging a CDR record in the CallManager database to notifying an emergency response group on the PSTN.

Call Display Restrictions give you the ability to control the caller ID information passed between devices on the IPT network. Finally, Multilevel Precedence and Preemption (MLPP) give you the ability to allow placement of higher-priority calls over lower-priority calls.

Review Questions

You can find the solutions to these questions in Appendix A, "Answers to Review Questions."

1. When a user logs in to a Cisco IP Phone using the Cisco CallManager Extension Mobility feature, what is pushed to the IP Phone?
   a. the device profile associated with the physical port
   b. an automatically generated device setting
   c. a temporary default phone button template
   d. the device profile associated with the user
2. Which two of the following are requirements to implement the MCID feature in a Cisco CallManager deployment? (Choose two.)
   a. PRI service
   b. critical alarm level
   c. MCID-T
   d. Cisco Emergency Responder Service
   e. Defense Switched Network

3. What should you instruct users to do if they receive a fast-busy tone after accidentally entering an invalid client matter code?

   a. wait for the prompt and rekey the correct code

   b. call technical support

   c. enter the correct code within 3 seconds

   d. enter the authorization code first

   e. press the **Speed Dial** button

   f. hang up and try the call again

4. Which four configuration items would enable a user (User A) in a hotel guest room to view the name and number of a caller and prevent the caller from viewing the user A caller ID information? (Choose four.)

   a. Connected Line ID Presentation Restricted

   b. Connected Line ID Presentation Allowed

   c. Connected Name Presentation Restricted

   d. Connected Name Presentation Allowed

   e. Calling Line ID Presentation Restricted

   f. Calling Line ID Presentation Allowed

   g. Calling Name Presentation Restricted

   h. Calling Name Presentation Allowed

5. A user logs in to a phone using the CallManager Extension Mobility functionality. They later move to a different location and attempt to log in to another Cisco IP Phone while remaining logged in to the original phone. What behavior occurs if the CallManager Extension Mobility service parameters are left in the default configuration

   a. The user will not be able to log in to the second phone.

   b. The user will be able to log in to the second phone and remain logged in to the first IP Phone.

   c. The user will be able to log in to the second phone and be automatically logged out of the first IP Phone.

   d. The user will have to wait 8 hours for the first phone to log out before they are able to automatically log in at the second.

6. You are configuring a CallManager-based IPT network for a customer. They want to require users to dial traceable PIN numbers assigned to differing authorization levels to reach PSTN numbers causing toll charges. What Cisco CallManager feature will accomplish this?

   a. CMC

   b. CAC

   c. FAQ

   d. FAC

7. How is a user able to trigger MCID functions on any given call?

   a. by dialing the MCID sequence configured in CallManager

   b. by signaling using a hook-flash sequence on the phone

   c. by pressing the **MCID** softkey

   d. any of the above

8. What is the highest MLPP level you can assign in CallManager 4.1?

   a. Priority

   b. Immediate

   c. Flash

   d. Executive Override

   e. Flash Override

9. You want to allow a Cisco IP Phone to override the call display restrictions configured inside your agency. What configuration setting will allow this?

   a. the Calling Line ID Presentation configuration from the translation pattern configuration

   b. the Calling Line ID Presentation configuration from the device configuration

   c. the Ignore Presentation Indicators configuration from the translation pattern configuration

   d. the Ignore Presentation Indicators configuration from the device configuration

10. You have created a default device profile for a Cisco IP Phone 7960. How do you assign this default device profile to your devices to enable Extension Mobility support?

   a. Do nothing, the default device profile is automatically assigned.

   b. You need to select the devices CallManager should apply the device profile to using the device profile Find/List Phones dialog box.

   c. You must select the Use Current Device Settings for the Logged Out profile of the device.

   d. You must create a specific user profile and assign it to the phone as the default.

This chapter covers the following topics:

- Explaining the features and functions of the Cisco CallManager Attendant Console
- Defining the key Cisco CallManager Attendant Console components and explaining their operation
- Explaining the basic operation of call routing and call queuing as it relates to Cisco CallManager Attendant Console
- Describing the Cisco CallManager Attendant Console redundancy process
- Configuring the server portion of Cisco CallManager Attendant Console
- Installing and configuring the client portion of Cisco CallManager Attendant Console
- Using the user and administrative features of Cisco CallManager Attendant Console

CHAPTER 18

Configuring Cisco Unified CallManager Attendant Console

Enterprises today can choose to route inbound telephone calls through numerous methods. These methods are either completely automated, manually directed, or some hybrid of automated and manual operation. An automated operation uses an application that can accept inbound calls, query the caller for destination information, and rapidly dispatch the call without operator intervention. A manual operation handles each inbound caller through a specially trained and equipped operator who assesses the purpose of the call and intended destination and uses tools to dispatch the call.

There are benefits associated with each method. Handling each inbound caller through an operator can lead to a heightened sense of customer satisfaction and, in many cases, a more reliably dispatched call. Automation of inbound call dispatch is efficient and affordable.

An operator or receptionist can use the Cisco CallManager Attendant Console to accept inbound calls, query the caller for destination information, and rapidly dispatch the call without operator intervention. For businesses that desire operator intervention, Cisco CallManager Attendant Console is designed to more efficiently automate both the user operations and the administrative operations of a manual attendant function. Cisco CallManager Attendant Console has an additional benefit over traditional consoles and line extenders because each user line is monitored, as opposed to monitoring only a select few in a time-division multiplexing (TDM)–based system.

This chapter covers the features, operation, installation, and configuration of Cisco CallManager Attendant Console on both Cisco CallManager and on the Attendant Console station.

Introduction to Cisco CallManager Attendant Console

Cisco CallManager Attendant Console, a client/server application installed on a PC, allows you to set up an Attendant Console to use with Cisco IP Phones. Employing a graphical user interface, the Attendant Console uses speed dial buttons and quick directory access to look up telephone numbers, monitor line status, and direct calls. A receptionist or administrative assistant can use the Attendant Console to handle calls for a department or company, or other employees can use it to manage their own telephone calls.

The Attendant Console installs on a PC with IP connectivity to the Cisco CallManager system. The Attendant Console works with a Cisco IP Phone that is registered to a Cisco CallManager system. Multiple Attendant Consoles can connect to a single Cisco CallManager system. When a server fails, the Attendant Console automatically fails over to another specified server in the cluster.

The Cisco CallManager Attendant Console client application is shown in Figure 18-1. The client is downloadable from the Cisco CallManager plug-in web page. (Choose **Applications > Install Plugins**, and click **Cisco CallManager Attendant Console.**) The client installs on end-user systems running Microsoft Windows 98, Me, 2000, and XP. The installation program places a Cisco CallManager Attendant Console icon on the attendant desktop and can also be accessed using **Start** > **Programs**.

Figure 18-1 *Cisco CallManager Attendant Console*

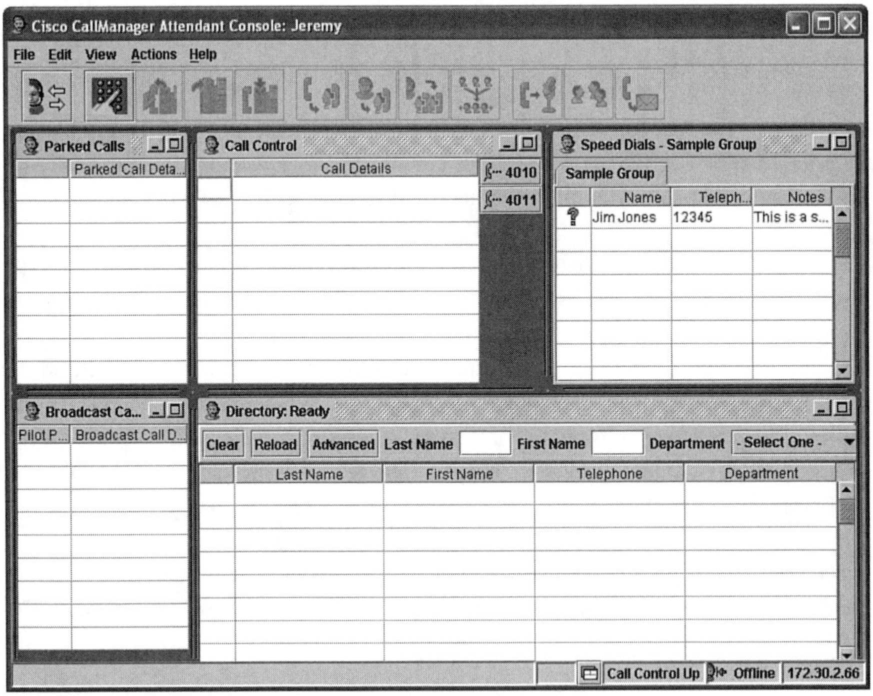

Terms and Definitions

Table 18-1 defines the terminology used for the Cisco CallManager Attendant Console application.

Table 18-1 *Cisco Attendant Console Terminology*

Term	Definition
Cisco CallManager Attendant Console client	Client application; web browser user interface; maximum of 96 clients per Cisco CallManager cluster
Cisco CallManager Attendant Console user	Cisco CallManager database entry; represents the Cisco CallManager Attendant Console client; one per client
Cisco Telephony Call Dispatcher	Server application; distributes calls, monitors line state, and performs call control; one per Cisco CallManager
Hunt group	Ordered list of directory numbers (DNs) to which Cisco TCD distributes calls; maximum of 32 per Cisco CallManager cluster
Pilot number or pilot point	DN that points to a hunt group; one per hunt group
Hunt group member	Either a DN (extension) or user-line pair; maximum of 16 per hunt group

The Telephony Call Dispatcher and Attendant Console Directory

The following sections provide additional detail about the Cisco Telephony Call Dispatcher (TCD) and the Cisco CallManager Attendant Console Directory.

Cisco Telephony Call Dispatcher

As shown in Figure 18-2, the Attendant Console application registers with and receives call-dispatching services from Cisco TCD. Cisco TCD, a Cisco CallManager service, provides communication among Cisco CallManager servers, Attendant Consoles, and the Cisco IP Phones that are used with the Attendant Consoles.

Cisco TCD handles Attendant Console requests for the following items:

- Call dispatching from pilot point to the appropriate hunt group destination
- Line status (unknown, available, on hook, or off hook)
- User directory information (Cisco TCD stores and periodically updates directory information for fast lookup by the Attendant Console.)

Cisco TCD monitors the status of internal devices and telephones only. An Attendant Console user cannot see the line state for a telephone that is connected to a gateway.

Figure 18-2 *Telephony Call Dispatcher Service*

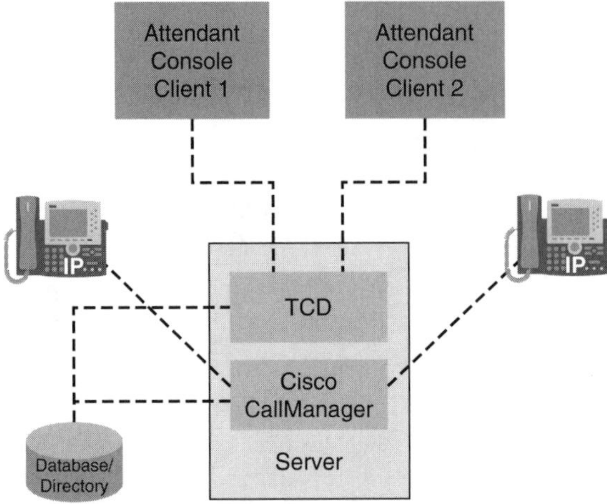

Cisco CallManager Attendant Console Directory

The CallManager Attendant Console directory is used to allow the Attendant Console application to maintain an active list of the corporate directory of users. Using this list, a receptionist can verify the state of any IP phone in the corporation and transfer calls simply by dragging and dropping the active call to the applicable user in the directory.

The Attendant Console server reads and caches the user directory entries at startup. After an initial handshake determines whether the directory entries have changed since the previous login, the Attendant Console downloads the user list. The Attendant Console also downloads the user list when the interval in the **Directory Reload Interval** field in the Attendant Settings dialog box expires or when the user clicks the **Reload** button in the Directory window.

The Attendant Console searches the following files (in order) for the user list:

- The user list file that is specified in the **Path Name of Local Directory File** field in the Attendant Settings dialog box on the attendant PC.
- The CorporateDirectory.txt file in the user list directory on the Cisco CallManager Attendant Console server. You can create the CorporateDirectory.txt file if your user list is located on a directory server that is separate from the Cisco CallManager server.
- The AutoGenerated.txt file that is generated by the Cisco TCD service and stored in the user list directory on the Cisco CallManager Attendant Console server. If the Directory Sync Period service parameter does not equal zero, Cisco TCD generates the AutoGenerated.txt file when the Cisco TCD service starts and when the directory synchronization period expires.

To modify the Directory Sync Period service parameter, choose **Service > Service Parameters**. Choose the appropriate server from the Server drop-down list and choose the Cisco Telephony Call Dispatcher Service from the Service drop-down list.

The user list file is in Comma-Separated Values (CSV) format and contains the following information:

- Last name
- First name
- Telephone number
- Department

Pilot Points and Hunt Groups

A pilot point, a virtual DN that is never busy, alerts Cisco TCD to receive and direct calls to hunt group members. A hunt group consists of a list of destinations that determine the call redirection order.

For Cisco TCD to function properly, make sure that the pilot point number is unique throughout the system (it cannot be a shared line appearance and will probably be the corporate primary DID number). When configuring the pilot point, you must choose one of the following routing options:

- **First Available Hunt Group Member**—Cisco TCD goes through the members in the hunt group in order until it finds the first available destination for routing the call. (You can choose this routing option from the Pilot Point Configuration window in Cisco CallManager Administration.)
- **Longest Idle Hunt Group Member**—This feature arranges the members of a hunt group in order from longest to shortest idle time. Cisco TCD finds the member with the longest idle time and, if available, routes the call. If not, Cisco TCD continues to search through the group. This feature evenly distributes the incoming call load among the members of the hunt group. (You can choose this routing option from the Pilot Point Configuration window in Cisco CallManager Administration.)
- **Circular Hunting**—Cisco TCD maintains a record of the last hunt group member to receive a call. When a new call arrives, Cisco TCD routes the call to the next member in the hunt group. Most people know this as round-robin hunting. (You can choose this option from the Attendant Console Configuration Tool.)

- **Broadcast Hunting**—When a call arrives at the pilot point, Cisco TCD answers the call, places the call on hold, adds the call to the queue, and displays the call in the Broadcast Calls pane on ALL Attendant Console applications. While on hold, the caller receives music on hold (MoH), if it is configured. Any attendant can answer the call from the Broadcast Calls pane. (You can choose this option from the Attendant Console Configuration Tool.)

Call Routing and Call Queuing

The following sections discuss the basic operation of call routing and call queuing as they relate to Cisco CallManager Attendant Console.

Call Routing

Figure 18-3 shows the interaction of the Cisco CallManager Attendant Console components in a basic call-routing example when a call is made to a number that is configured as a pilot point and associated with a hunt group. In this example, 4000 is a support number associated with a support hotline.

Figure 18-3 *Attendant Console Call Routing Example*

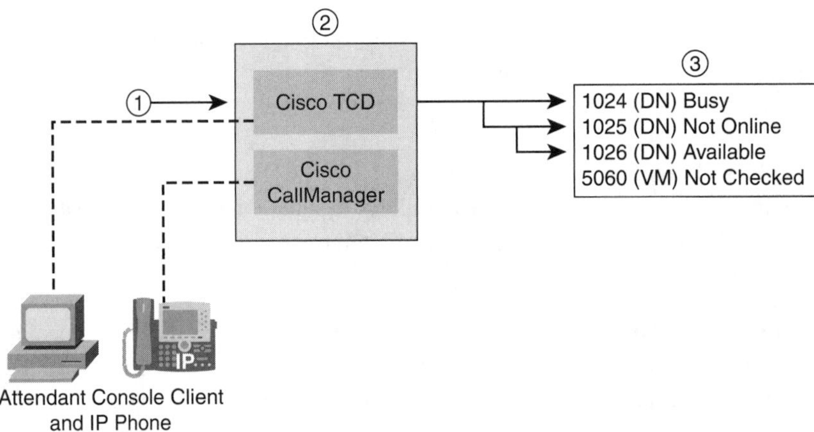

The process numbered in Figure 18-3 is as follows:

1. Cisco TCD receives a call and directs it to the pilot point, DN 4000.
2. Because 4000 is a pilot point and First Available Hunt Group Member is specified as the call-routing option, the Cisco TCD that is associated with the pilot point checks the members of the hunt group in order, beginning with the first member, to determine where to route the call. DN 1024 is busy, DN 1025 is busy, and DN 1026 is available.

3. Cisco TCD routes the call to the first available DN, which is 1026. Because 1026 is available, Cisco TCD never checks the 5060 voice-mail pilot point number. If all numbers would have been busy, the call would forward to the voice-mail extension.

Call Queuing

You can configure a pilot point to support call queuing so that when a call comes to a pilot point and all hunt groups members are busy, Cisco CallManager Attendant Console sends calls to a queue. While in the queue, callers hear MoH if you have chosen an audio source from the Network Hold Audio Source and the User Hold MoH Audio Source drop-down lists in the Device Pool window. The attendants cannot view the queued calls, with the exception of Broadcast groups (covered in the "Attendant Console GUI: Broadcast Calls" section later in this chapter). When a hunt group member becomes available, Cisco TCD redirects the call to that hunt group member. This sequence of events is reflected in Figure 18-4.

Figure 18-4 *Attendant Console Call Queuing Example*

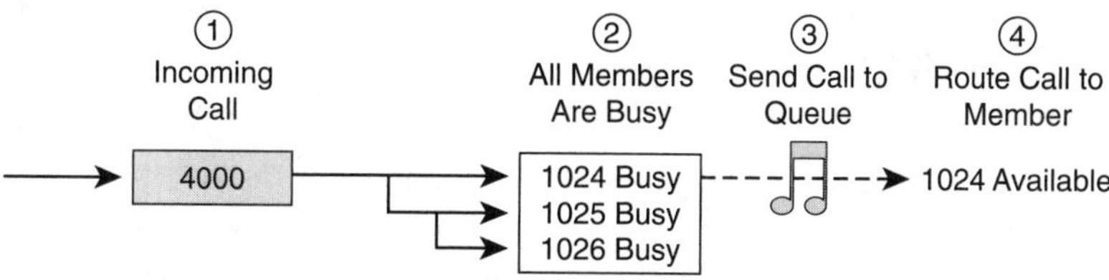

You enable queuing for a pilot point using the Cisco CallManager Attendant Console Configuration Tool. You also use the tool to configure the queue size, which is the number of calls that are allowed in the queue, and the hold time, which is the maximum time (in seconds) that Cisco TCD keeps a call in the queue. Configuring the Cisco CallManager Attendant Console Configuration Tool is covered in the "Using the Attendant Console Configuration Tool" section later in this chapter.

If the queue is full, Cisco TCD routes calls to the "always-route" hunt group member that is specified in the Hunt Group Configuration window. If you do not specify an always-route member, Cisco TCD drops the call when the queue size limit is reached. If the call is in the queue for longer than the hold time, the call is redirected to the always-route member. If an always-route member is not configured, no action occurs. Configuring the Always Route option in the Hunt Group Configuration window is covered in the "Hunt Group Configuration" section later in the chapter.

Server and Administration Configuration

Follow this general procedure to configure the Cisco CallManager server to support the Cisco CallManager Attendant Console:

Step 1 **Add Cisco CallManager Attendant Console users.** These individual users will use the Cisco CallManager Attendant Console application. They are not the same as directory users that you configure in the User area of the Cisco CallManager Administration window.

Step 2 **Create the ac user and associate all pilot point devices with the user.** You must configure one user named "ac" and associate the attendant IP Phones and the pilot points with the user. If you do not configure this user, the Attendant Console cannot interact with Cisco CTIManager, and the attendant cannot receive calls.

Step 3 **Configure the pilot point for the Cisco CallManager Attendant Console.** The pilot point is a DN that provides access to Cisco CallManager Attendant Console users indirectly through hunt groups. The pilot point usually maps to the general company number (switchboard number), but it can use a DN outside of the Direct Inward Dial (DID) range.

Step 4 **Configure hunt groups.** Hunt groups consist of Cisco CallManager Attendant Console users or DNs. When adding a Cisco CallManager Attendant Console user with multiple line numbers to the hunt group, you must specify which line to use.

Step 5 **Activate Cisco TCD and CTIManager services.** Verify that the Cisco TCD service activates and runs on all servers that are running the Cisco CallManager service. Verify that the Cisco CTIManager service activates and runs on at least one server in the cluster.

Step 6 **Access the Attendant Console Configuration Tool.** At a minimum, change the default username and password of the ac user and, optionally, configure queuing and assess other hunting options not available directly from the Pilot Point Configuration window in Cisco CallManager Administration.

Adding Attendant Console Users

You must add users through the Cisco CallManager Attendant Console User Configuration window and assign them a password *before* they can log in to a Cisco CallManager Attendant Console client. Complete the following procedure to add a user:

Step 1 Open the Cisco CallManager Attendant Console User Configuration window and choose **Service > Cisco CM Attendant Console > Cisco CM Attendant Console User**.

Step 2 In the upper-right corner of the window, click the **Add a New Attendant Console User** link. The Attendant Console User Configuration window shown in Figure 18-5 appears.

Figure 18-5 *Adding an Attendant Console User*

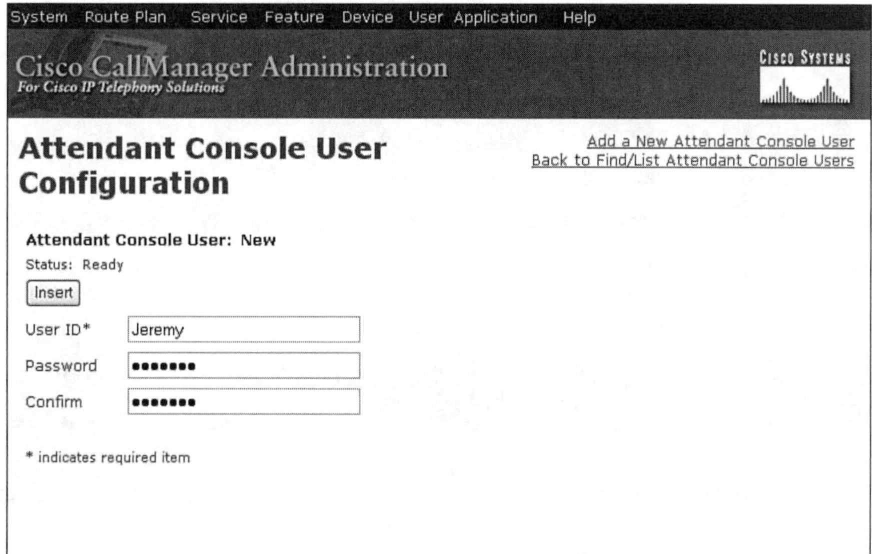

Step 3 Create user accounts for each Cisco CallManager Attendant Console user by entering the appropriate user ID (username) and password for each account.

Step 4 Click **Insert** when you are finished.

Adding the "ac" User

You must create one generic user, the ac user, and associate the attendant Cisco IP Phones and the pilot points with the ac user. This user is designed to give the Attendant Console and related Cisco IP Phones CTI permissions with the CallManager cluster. When you configure the ac user, the Cisco CallManager Attendant Console can then interact with the Cisco CTIManager service on the Cisco CallManager server. Perform the following procedure to configure the ac user:

Step 1 Choose **User > Add a New User** in the Cisco CallManager Administration window.

Step 2 Enter **ac** in the **First Name** and **Last Name** fields.

Step 3 Enter **ac** in the **User ID** field.

Step 4 Enter **12345** in the **User Password** field.

Step 5 Enter **12345** in the **Confirm Password** field.

Step 6 "ac" and "12345" are mandatory default settings when first configuring the Attendant Console user.

Step 7 Enter a personal identification number (PIN) and telephone number.

Step 8 Check the **Enable CTI Application Use** check box. You must check this box for the Cisco CallManager Attendant Console to interact with Cisco CTIManager.

Step 9 Check the **Call Park Retrieval Allowed** check box. The user configuration should now resemble the settings shown in Figure 18-6.

Figure 18-6 *Adding the Attendant Console "ac" User*

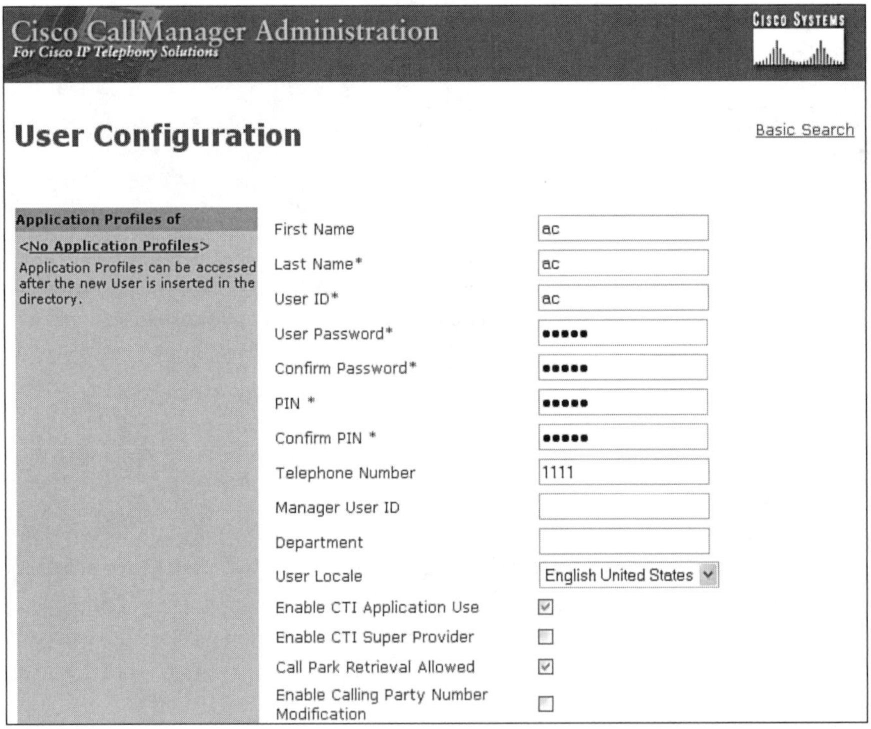

Step 10 Click **Insert**.

Step 11 Associate all attendant Cisco IP Phones and pilot points with the ac user.

> **TIP** To enhance the security of your deployment, you should change the username and password of the "ac" user to something beyond the default. To make this change, run the **acconfig.bat** file located in the C:\Program Files\Cisco\CallManagerAttendant\bin directory on the CallManager server. Specific instructions for accomplishing this are in the "Using the Attendant Console Configuration Tool" section later in this chapter.

Pilot Point Configuration

You must configure pilot points and hunt groups through the Cisco CallManager Administration window before Cisco TCD can route calls. In Cisco CallManager Administration, choose **Service > Cisco CM Attendant Console > Pilot Point** and in the upper-right corner, click the **Add a New Pilot Point** link to open the Pilot Point Configuration window.

Table 18-2 defines the settings in the Pilot Point Configuration window shown in Figure 18-7.

Figure 18-7 *Pilot Point Configuration*

System Route Plan Service Feature Device User Application Help
Cisco CallManager Administration
For Cisco IP Telephony Solutions
Cisco Systems
Pilot Point Configuration
Add a New Pilot Point
Back to Find/List Pilot Points
Pilot Point: New
Pilot Number: Not Assigned
Status: Ready
Insert
Pilot Name* Reception_PLT
Device Pool* Default
Partition < None >
Calling Search Space < None >
Pilot Number * 5100
Route Calls to First Available Hunt Group Member
Location < None >
* indicates required item

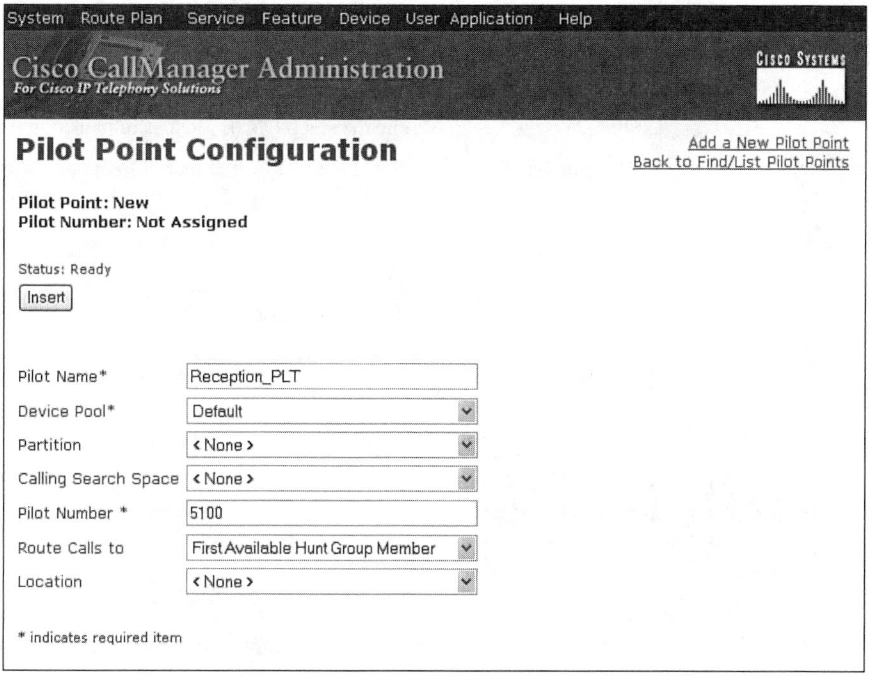

Table 18-2 *Pilot Point Configuration Fields*

Field	Description
Pilot Name	Enter up to 50 alphanumeric characters, including spaces, to specify a descriptive name for the pilot point.
Device Pool	Assign the pilot point to a device pool. The device pool has the Cisco CallManager whose Cisco TCD service will service this pilot point.
Partition	Choose the partition to which the pilot point belongs. Make sure that the pilot point that you enter in the **Pilot Number** field is unique within the partition that you choose. If you do not want to restrict access to the pilot number, choose None for the partition.
Calling Search Space	To designate the partitions that the pilot point searches when it attempts to route a call, choose a calling search space from the drop-down list.
Pilot Number	Enter a DN into this field to designate a DN for this pilot point. Verify that this number is unique throughout the system; it cannot be a shared line appearance.
Route Calls To	Choose the mechanism to distribute calls to hunt group members: • Choose the **First Available Hunt Group Member** option to route incoming calls to the first available member of a hunt group. This is the default setting. • Choose the **Longest Idle Hunt Group Member** option to order members based on the length of time that each DN or line has remained idle. If the voice-mail number is the longest-idle member of the group, Cisco TCD will route the call to voice mail without first checking the other members of the group. If you want to use the Circular Hunting or Broadcast Hunting routing options, use the Attendant Console Configuration Tool.
Location	Designates a Call Admission Control (CAC) location for the pilot point to be used with bandwidth control.

TIP If the pilot point is not the main or general telephone number, the main number can go to a translation pattern, allowing CallManager to transform the call to the attendant pilot number.

Hunt Group Configuration

After you configure the pilot point, you must configure the hunt group. A hunt group consists of a list of destinations (either DNs, or Cisco CallManager Attendant Console user or line numbers) that determine the call-redirection order.

In Cisco CallManager Administration, choose **Service > Cisco CM Attendant Console > Hunt Group**. The Hunt Group Configuration window appears. In the shaded column on the left, click the pilot point for which you want to add hunt group members. You can then add member directory numbers by clicking the **Add Member** button, entering the directory number you want to add, and selecting **Update**. You can also add the Attendant Console users to the hunt group. Adding by user has the added benefit of allowing whatever phone is associated with the Attendant Console user to be included in the hunt group rather than just the specific extension. Figure 18-8 shows an example of this configuration.

Figure 18-8 *Hunt Group Configuration*

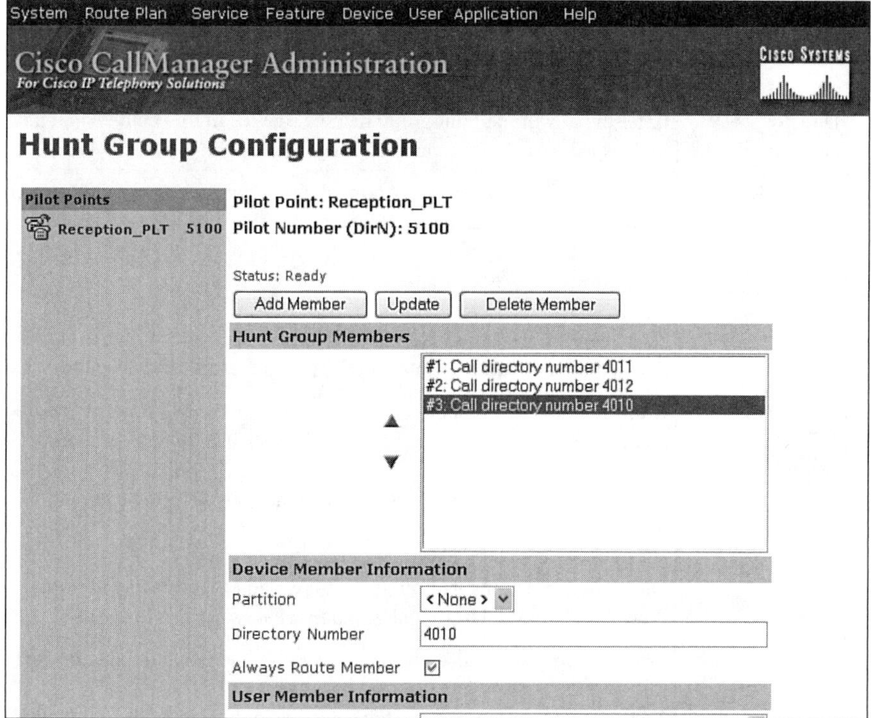

Table 18-3 defines the settings in the Hunt Group Configuration window.

Table 18-3 *Hunt Group Configuration Fields*

Field	Description
Partition	If a hunt group member is a DN, you can click the drop-down arrow to view the values for the **Partition** field and then choose the appropriate option. Enter the DN in the **Directory Number** field in the Device Member Information section. The partition designates the route partition to which the DN belongs. If the DN for this hunt group member is in a partition, you must choose a partition. If the DN is not in a partition, choose **None**.
Directory Number	Enter the DN of the hunt group member device in this field. When the DN is not in the specified partition, an error message appears.
Always Route Member	Always Route Member is an optional check box that applies to DNs only. If this check box is checked, Cisco TCD always routes the call to this hunt group member, regardless of whether it is busy. Cisco TCD does not check whether the line is available before routing the call. To manage overflow conditions, check this check box for voice-messaging or Auto Attendant numbers that handle multiple simultaneous calls.
User Name	If the hunt group member is a user and line number, fill in only the **User Name** and **Line Number** fields in the User Member Information section. From the drop-down list, choose Attendant Console users who will serve as hunt group members. Only Attendant Console users who are added in the Cisco CallManager Attendant Console User Configuration window appear in this list.
Line Number	From the drop-down list, choose the appropriate line numbers for the hunt group. You can add the same user to the same line only once within a single hunt group. For example, you cannot add Mary Brown, Line 1, more than once in the hunt group.

If you have configured queuing, and the queue is full, Cisco TCD routes calls to the always-route hunt group member that is specified in the Hunt Group Configuration window. If you do not specify an always-route member, Cisco TCD drops the call when the queue size limit is reached. If the call is in the queue for longer than the hold time, the call is redirected to the always-route member.

Activating Cisco TCD and CTIManager Services

Before the Cisco CallManager is able to support the Attendant Console clients, you must activate the Cisco Telephony Call Dispatcher and CTIManager services. To activate these services, follow this procedure:

Step 1 In the Cisco CallManager Administration window, choose **Application > Cisco CallManager Serviceability**. The Cisco CallManager Serviceability window appears.

Step 2 Choose **Tools > Service Activation**. The Service Activation window displays the list of servers.

Step 3 From the Servers list, choose the server where Cisco CallManager is running. The Service Activation window shown in Figure 18-9 appears.

The window displays the service names for the server that you chose and the activation status of the services. Verify the active status of the Cisco Telephony Call Dispatcher and CTIManager services, or follow the remaining steps to activate them.

Figure 18-9 *TCD and CTIManager Service Activation*

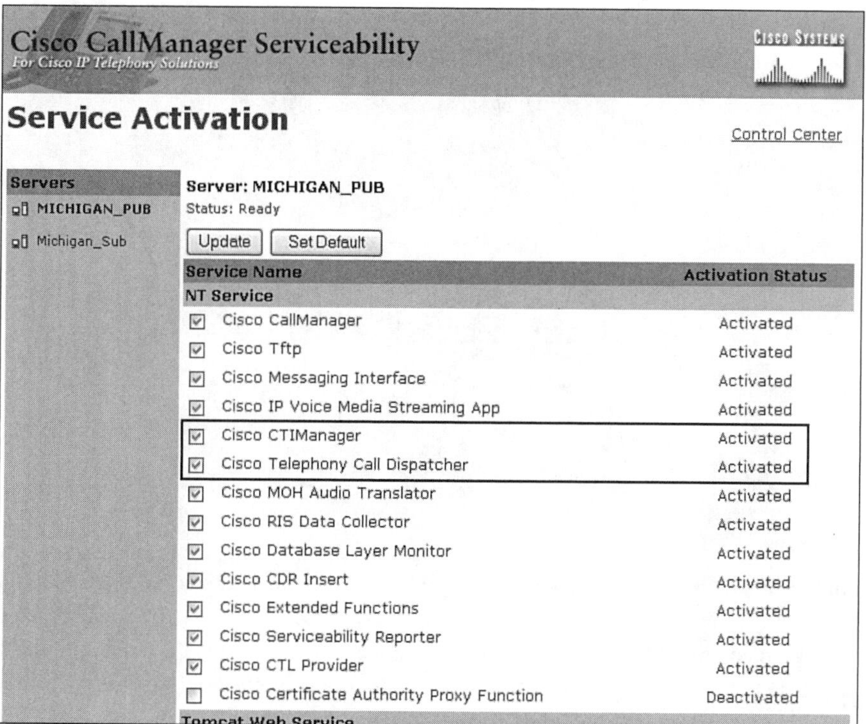

Step 4 Check the check boxes next to the Cisco Telephony Call Dispatcher and CTIManager services.

Step 5 Click **Update**.

Using the Attendant Console Configuration Tool

The Attendant Console Configuration Tool is a simple utility found on the Cisco CallManager server that you can use to perform these tasks:

- Set the JTAPI username and password beyond the default values of ac and 12345.
- Set directory values.
- Enable call queuing for a pilot point and set the maximum hold time.
- Configure circular hunt groups and broadcast hunt groups.

The Attendant Console Configuration Tool is somewhat hidden on the Cisco CallManager hard drive. To access the tool, open the **acconfig.bat** file, which is located in the C:\Program Files\Cisco\CallManagerAttendant\bin directory on the Cisco CallManager Attendant Console server. The Edit Server Properties dialog box shown in Figure 18-10 opens.

Figure 18-10 *Attendant Console Configuration Tool - Basic Tab*

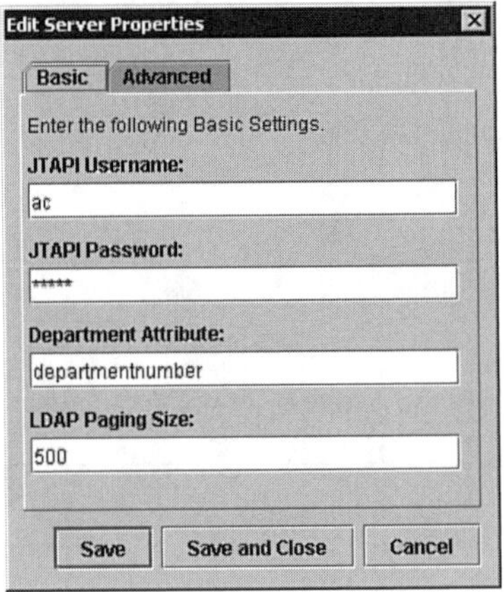

From the **Basic** tab, you can change the default ac username and password to something else.

The **Advanced** tab (shown in Figure 18-11) enables you to access additional hunting options not available in the CallManager Administration Hunt Group Configuration window: enable queuing, change the queue size (the default is 32 calls), and change the hold time (the default is 0, which keeps calls in the queue until an attendant becomes available).

Figure 18-11 *Attendant Console Configuration Tool - Advanced Tab*

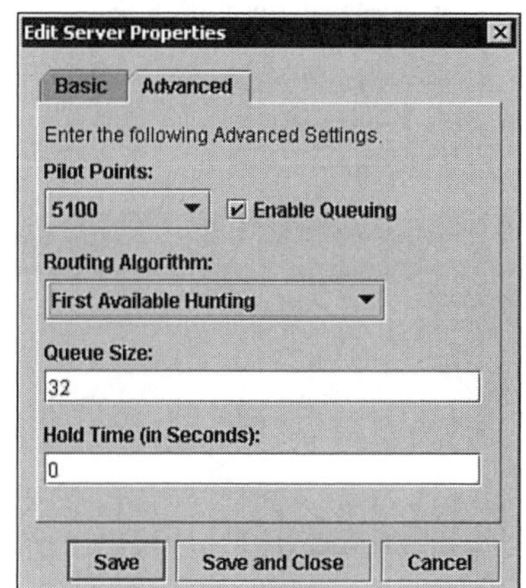

TIP Making changes in the Attendant Console Configuration Tool might require a restart of the CTIManager and Cisco TCD services for the changes to take effect. On rare occasions, a complete restart of the CallManager server might be required.

Installing and Configuring the Attendant Console Client

After you activate Cisco TCD and CTIManager services and configure the Cisco CallManager Attendant Console in Cisco CallManager Administration, you are ready to install and configure the Cisco CallManager Attendant Console plug-in on each attendant PC.

The following steps provide the PC requirements for the Attendant Console:

Step 1 Verify that the PC is running Microsoft Windows 2000 or Windows XP and has network connectivity to the Cisco CallManager.

Step 2 Install the Cisco CallManager Attendant Console plug-in on each attendant PC.

- Download the Cisco CallManager Attendant Console plug-in by choosing **Application > Install Plugins** in the Cisco CallManager Administration window.
- Save the CiscoAttendantConsoleClient.exe file to the local machine.
- Launch the CiscoAttendantConsoleClient.exe file.

Step 3 As soon as the Attendant Console application launches, the settings window appears. Configure the Cisco CallManager Attendant Console settings on the attendant PC, as shown in Figure 18-12.

- Specify the IP address of the Cisco CallManager TCD server and the DN of the associated IP phone, and click **Save**.
- Provide the username and password.

Figure 18-12 *Configuring the Attendant Console Client*

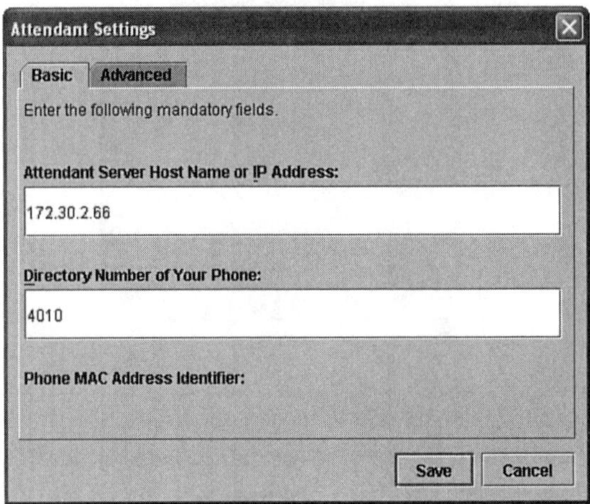

After you install the Cisco CallManager Attendant Console, the user is ready to start the application. After opening the Cisco CallManager Attendant Console application, the user will have to log in and then go online. The user is then ready to answer calls.

To launch the application on the PC where the Attendant Console is installed, choose **Start > Programs > Cisco CallManager > Cisco CallManager Attendant Console** or click the **Cisco CallManager Attendant Console** icon on the desktop.

TIP Receiving the message "Initialization of Call Control Failed. Retrying…" upon opening the Attendant Console indicates a problem with the ac user account.

Cisco Attendant Console Features

As shown in Figure 18-13, the features of the Cisco CallManager Attendant Console are menu-driven. You can use the associated shortcut keys to access all of the menu functions.

Figure 18-13 *Attendant Console Client User Interface*

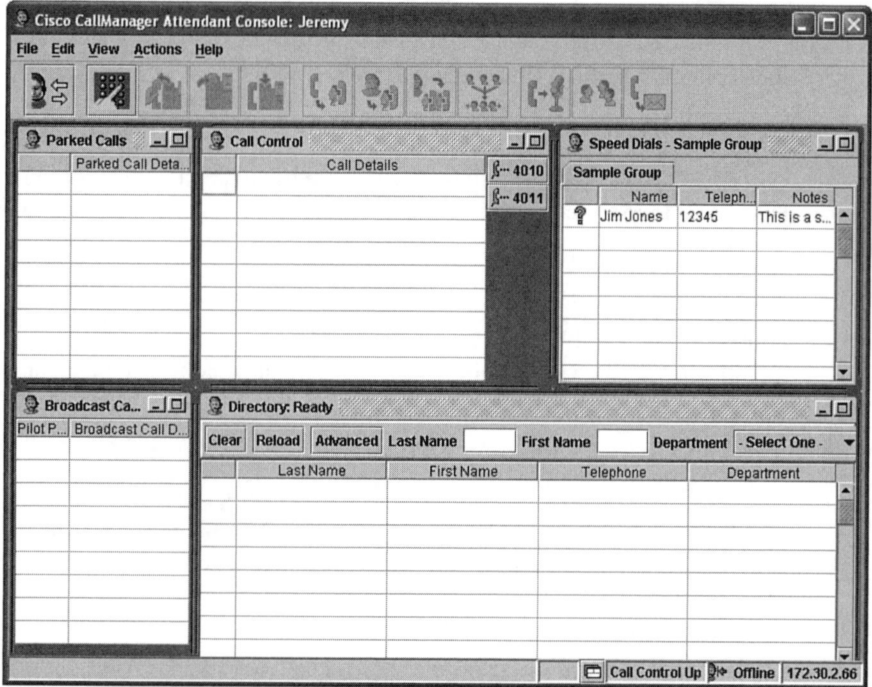

The following is a description of the menus:

- **File menu**—From the File menu, you can go online or offline, log out, and exit the program.
- **Edit menu**—From the Edit menu, you can create your own keyboard shortcuts. You can also add, modify, and delete speed dial entries or groups and view or revise settings, which is an optional task.
- **View menu**—From the View menu, you can change the size of the text in the windows or the color on the console.
- **Actions menu**—You perform call-control tasks through the Actions menu or the Action Key shortcuts shown in Figure 18-13. This menu includes many feature options, such as answering calls, transferring calls, parking calls, and enabling other features on the system.
- **Help menu**—Cisco CallManager Attendant Console provides online help and easy access to the latest Cisco CallManager Attendant Console plug-in for an upgrade.

The Cisco CallManager Attendant Console efficiently automates the user and the administrative operations of a manual attendant function. It has an intuitive and configurable GUI to handle calls and monitor line state.

In a system with hundreds or thousands of users, a Cisco CallManager Attendant Console operator can accept calls and perform a directory lookup by selecting the field title in the Directory section and typing in the first few characters of the last name, first name, or department of the user. A directory search returns information that matches the query.

An operator can view the status of a user line (busy, idle, or ringing) and advise the caller of the line state. The operator can then transfer the call to the user by either initiating a traditional transfer sequence through the Transfer icon or dragging and dropping the call from the selected loop to the desired user record.

Attendant Console GUI: Call Control

The Call Control window, shown in Figure 18-14, has the following two components:

- **Call Details pane**—This component includes the line status, the DN of the incoming call, the name of the person (if available), the operator DN, and the elapsed time display.
- **Operator Line buttons**—This component includes the line status and the DN of the attendant Cisco IP Phone, displayed in the upper-right corner of the window.

Figure 18-14 *Attendant Console GUI: Call Control Window*

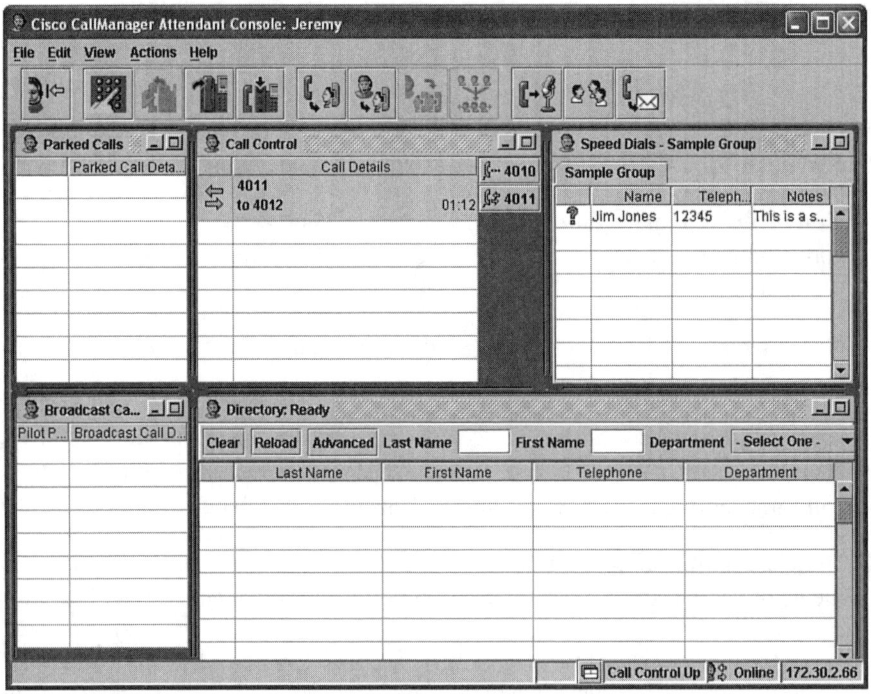

The Call Details pane displays the lines on the Cisco IP Phone that the Cisco CallManager Attendant Console controls. The number of lines configured depends on the type of configuration. For example, if you have a Cisco IP Phone 7960 with two attachments of the Cisco IP Phone 7914 Expansion Module, and you associate a DN with each line, then a total of 34 lines can be displayed. Each of the lines will show a line status symbol describing the current state of the line. The various line statuses are described in Figure 18-15.

Figure 18-15 *Attendant Console GUI: Line Status Symbol*

Line Status	
Line Status	Corresponding Icon
A call is ringing on the line.	
The line is active.	
The line is held.	
The line is idle.	
The status of the line is unknown.	

Attendant Console GUI: Custom Speed Dials

The Speed Dials pane (shown in Figure 18-16) is located in the upper-right corner of the screen and contains DNs and labels customized by the user of the Attendant Console. By clicking a speed dial button, you place a call from the currently selected attendant line to the associated DN. Speed dials can be added or deleted quickly by dragging and dropping users from the corporate directory.

Figure 18-16 *Attendant Console GUI: Speed Dials*

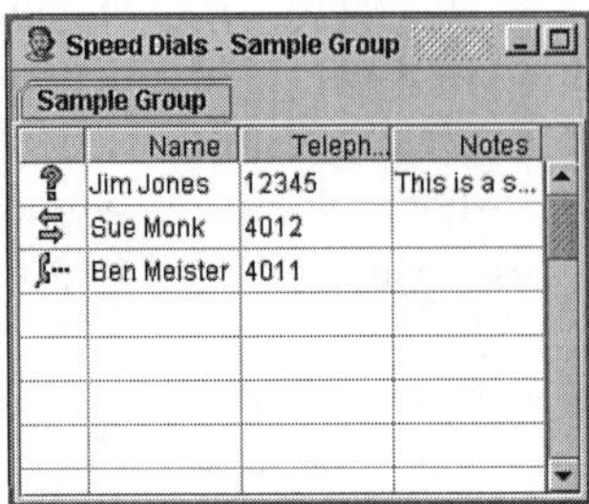

Attendant Console GUI: Directory Lookup

The Directory pane (shown in Figure 18-17) is located in the lower-right corner of the screen. By clicking a displayed directory entry, you place a call from the currently selected attendant line to the associated DN.

Figure 18-17 *Attendant Console GUI: Directory Lookup*

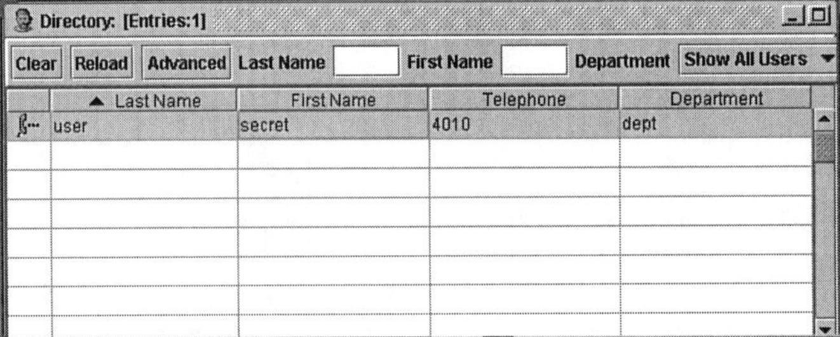

Attendant Console GUI: Parked Calls

From the Parked Calls pane (shown in Figure 18-18), you can view and pick up all calls that have been parked by all attendants that are connected to the attendant server. If the call is not answered, you can revert the parked calls in these ways:

- Right-click the call that you want to park, and then click **Revert Park** from the context-sensitive menu.
- Click the call that you want to park, and then click the **Revert Park** button on the Call Control toolbar.
- Click the call that you want to park, and then choose **Revert Park** from the Actions menu.
- On the PC keyboard, press **Ctrl-P.**

Figure 18-18 *Attendant Console GUI: Parked Calls*

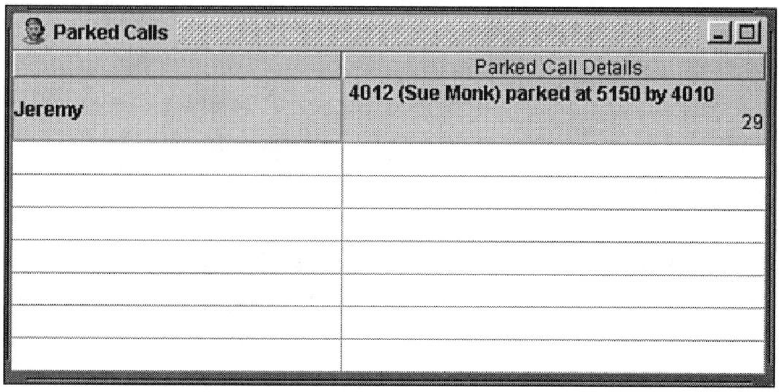

Attendant Console GUI: Broadcast Calls

Broadcast hunting enables Cisco CallManager Attendant Console to answer calls and place them in a queue. The Attendant Console displays the queued calls to all available attendants after inserting the calls into the Broadcast Calls pane (shown in Figure 18-19).

Figure 18-19 *Attendant Console GUI: Broadcast Calls*

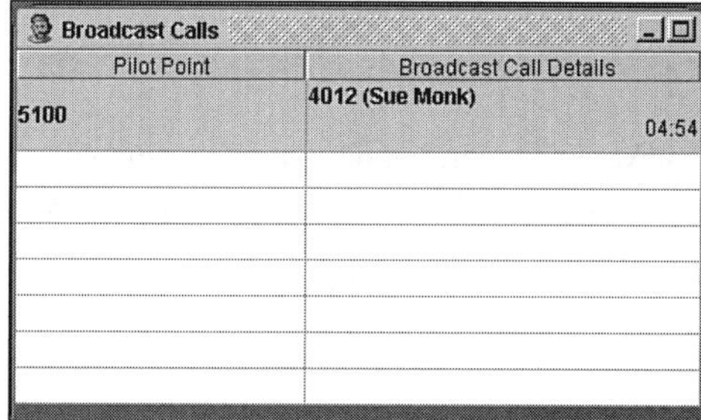

Any attendant in the hunt group that is online can answer the queued calls. Cisco TCD does not automatically send the calls to an attendant. When an attendant answers a call, Cisco TCD removes the call from the Broadcast Calls pane and displays it in the Call Control pane of the attendant who answered the call.

> **NOTE** For Broadcast Calls to appear in the Attendant Console window, the attendants *must* be added to the Broadcast Queue hunt group using the attendant's username and line number rather than direct phone extension.

Summary

This chapter covered the concepts and configuration of Cisco CallManager Attendant Console. The Attendant Console is a client/server application that allows you to manage a high volume of calls through a GUI installed on a client PC. The key Attendant Console components include the Cisco TCD and CTIManager, Attendant Console client software, Attendant Console user, pilot points, and hunt groups.

The Cisco TCD provides call routing for incoming calls to the pilot point. You can configure the pilot point for standard call routing or for queuing. If configured for standard call routing, the pilot point receives the incoming call and works through the hunt group ordered list until it finds a free call attendant. If configured for queuing, the TCD holds incoming calls, allowing the attendants to answer the calls as they become available.

You can install the Attendant Console client by accessing the Cisco CallManager Administration plug-in window. Configuring the client requires simply specifying the CallManager server IP address and the attendant DN. The Attendant Console uses a GUI, which is fairly simple to use and includes a vast number of features.

Review Questions

You can find the solutions to these questions in Appendix A, "Answers to Review Questions."

1. Match the Cisco CallManager Attendant Console terms with the answer choice that is most closely associated with the term.

Term	Answer
1. Pilot point	
2. Hunt group	
3. Queue	
4. Distribution algorithm	
5. Cisco TCD	

a. First available hunt group member

b. Dispatches calls

c. List of ordered destinations

d. Virtual number

e. Holding place

2. When you configure Cisco CallManager Attendant Console server in Cisco CallManager Administration, what should you do to prevent calls from being dropped when the queue is full?

   a. Configure the queue size limit to 1024.

   b. Configure an always-route member.

   c. Configure a hold time.

   d. Configure a pilot point.

3. Which two services must be activated for Cisco CallManager Attendant Console to function properly?

   a. Cisco IP Voice Media Streaming Application

   b. Cisco CTL Provider

   c. Cisco TCD

   d. Cisco MOH Audio Translator

   e. Cisco CTIManager

4. Which item can be configured from the Pilot Point Configuration window in Cisco CallManager Administration?

   a. Queue size

   b. Hold time

   c. Longest-idle distribution algorithm

   d. Circular distribution algorithm

5. How many hunt groups can you have in a Cisco CallManager cluster?

   a. 10

   b. 16

   c. 32

   d. 48

6. Which of the following hunting types allow the Attendant Console clients to receive a list of currently queued calls and accept them as they become available?

   a. Circular Hunting

   b. Broadcast Hunting

   c. First Available Hunting

   d. Longest Idle Hunting

7. To allow the Attendant Console client to function in the cluster, you must create a user with the username ________ and the password _________.

   a. global, cisco
   b. ac, 12345
   c. ac, cisco
   d. global, 12345

8. How do you access the Attendant Console Configuration Tool?

   a. By using the **Service > Cisco CM Attendant Console** menu in the CallManager Administration window
   b. Through the Cisco CallManager Serviceability utility
   c. By accessing the Properties window of the Attendant Console client application
   d. By executing the acconfig.bat file on the CallManager server hard drive

9. A corporate operator has parked a call at extension 5529. After a few minutes, the operator notices that the call has not been answered. How can the operator revert the Call Park process?

   a. Right-click on the parked call in the Attendant Console software and choose **Revert Park**.
   b. Dial the parked number from the handset and answer the call to retrieve it.
   c. Call the CallManager administrator to revert a parked call.
   d. CallManager 4.x does not offer this capability.

10. You are adding an Attendant Console user to the CallManager configuration. You click **User > Add a New User** and fill out the user information. What additional option should you select for this user?

   a. Enable CTI Application Use
   b. Enable CTI Super User
   c. Call Park Allowed
   d. You should not be adding an Attendant Console User this way.

This chapter covers the following topics:

- Describing the features of Cisco IPMA and its two modes
- Explaining the function of the components that make up the Cisco IPMA architecture
- Configuring Cisco IPMA for shared-line mode
- Configuring the manager divert target for call forwarding
- Using the Assistant Console interface to place and receive calls

CHAPTER 19

Configuring Cisco IP Manager Assistant

Senior managers frequently employ assistants who have as one of their duties the management of telephone activities for the manager or for a group of managers. The assistant normally sets up conferences for the manager and also places, answers, and transfers calls. This assistant (and to some extent, the managers) need a different set of features than other users. In addition to the ability to handle the call activities of the manager, the assistant needs to be able to monitor that call activity when the manager is on a call, in a meeting, or does not want to be disturbed; to communicate with the manager using an intercom; and to change features and settings for the manager.

Cisco IP Manager Assistant (IPMA) is an application that provides these capabilities to managers and assistants. This chapter discusses the features and functions of Cisco IPMA, how to configure the feature, and the end-user applications that constitute the application-manager configuration and Assistant Console.

Cisco IP Manager Assistant Overview

Cisco IPMA enables managers and their assistants to work together more effectively. When configuring Cisco IPMA, you can configure Cisco CallManager users as managers or assistants. An assistant user handles calls on behalf of a manager or group of managers.

Cisco IPMA provides specific features for both managers and assistants. The features consist of enhancements to IP phone capabilities for the manager and desktop interfaces that are primarily used by the assistant. These enhancements give the assistant a type of "joint control" over the manager's lines in a similar style as shared-line extensions.

Cisco IPMA supports two modes of operation: proxy-line support (Cisco CallManager Release 3.3 or later) and shared-line support (Cisco CallManager Release 4.0 or later). The Cisco IPMA service supports both proxy-line and shared-line support in a given cluster. The difference between these operation types is covered in the following sections.

CallManager supports Cisco IPMA on Cisco IP Phone 7970, 7960, and 7940 models.

Cisco IPMA with Proxy-Line Support

Cisco IPMA with proxy-line support intercepts calls that are made to managers and routes them to the assistant or to preconfigured targets that are based on preconfigured call filters. Because the Cisco IPMA service intercepts calls that are made to managers who are using proxy-line mode, it requires configuration of partitions, calling search spaces, route points, and translation patterns.

The Cisco IPMA Configuration Wizard enables you to automatically create the partitions, calling search spaces, route points, and translation patterns that are required for proxy-line mode. The wizard also creates Bulk Administration Tool (BAT) templates for the Cisco IPMA manager telephone, the Cisco IPMA assistant telephone, and all other user telephones. The Cisco IPMA Configuration Wizard can be run only one time; however, you can make corrections and additions manually in Cisco CallManager Administration.

Cisco CallManager Release 4.x supports the existing proxy-line configuration in earlier versions of Cisco CallManager, but Release 4.x features such as Barge, Privacy, Call Join, Direct Transfer, and multiple calls per line require the shared-line mode.

In the proxy-line mode, a manager can be assisted by only one assistant at a time. The proxy-line IPMA configuration is now considered a "legacy" IPMA support method.

Cisco IPMA with Shared-Line Support

Cisco IPMA with shared-line support enables the assistant to share the primary line of the manager (the assistant and the manager have the same DN configured on one line). In this support mode, there is no call routing; calls for the manager ring on both the manager line and the assistant line.

The Cisco IPMA Configuration Wizard is not used in Cisco IPMA with shared-line mode because there is no need to configure route points, partitions, calling search spaces, or translation patterns. The Cisco IPMA in shared-line mode also supports Cisco CallManager features such as multiple calls per line, Call Join, Direct Transfer, Privacy, and Barge.

The manager telephone uses the softkey template called Standard IPMA Shared Mode Manager. This template has the following softkeys:

- **DND**—Do not disturb; turns the ringer off. The manager telephone and the assistant's IPMA console display the DND state.
- **ImmDiv**—Immediate Divert; diverts the selected call to a preconfigured target (typically the assistant).
- **TransferToVM**—Transfer to voice mail; redirects the selected call to the voice mail of the manager.

One manager can be configured to have up to ten assistants. The manager IP phone will have speed dials for all the configured assistants, allowing the manager to reach the assistants quickly. Optionally, you can configure a dedicated incoming intercom line on the manager telephone to the assistant(s). Cisco IP Phone Services are not supported in shared-line mode for managers.

Table 19-1 summarizes the key differences between the Cisco IPMA shared-line and proxy-line modes.

Table 19-1 *Shared-Line and Proxy-Line Modes Compared*

Feature	Shared	Proxy
Number of Managers per Assistant	Up to 33	Up to 33
Number of Assistants per Manager	Up to 10	One at a time
IP Phone Services Support on Manager Phone	No	Yes
Barge, Privacy, Join, Direct Transfer, and Multiple Calls Per Line	Yes	No
Configuration	Simple	Complex

Cisco IP Manager Assistant Architecture

The Cisco IPMA feature architecture includes the Cisco IPMA service, the desktop interfaces, and the Cisco IP Phone interfaces, as shown in Figure 19-1.

Figure 19-1 *Cisco CallManager IPMA Architecture*

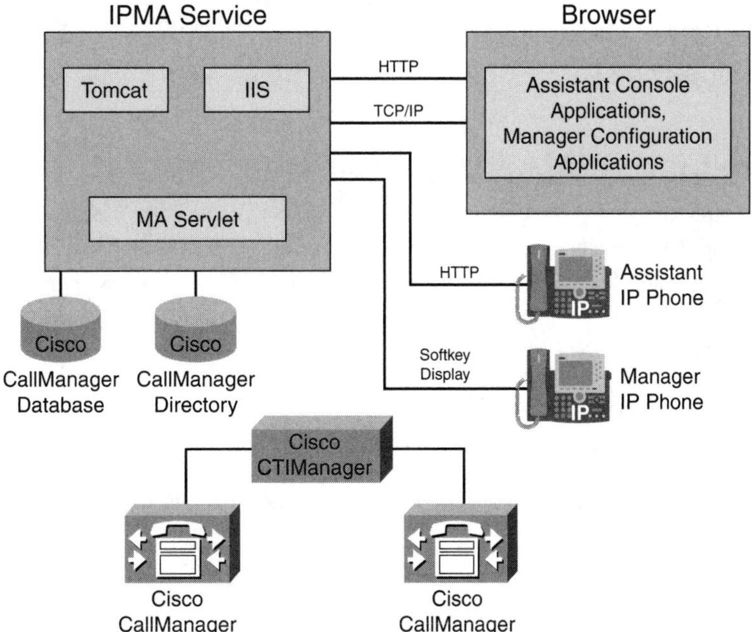

The following is a brief definition for each of the IPMA services:

- **Cisco IPMA service**—The Cisco Tomcat web server loads the Cisco IPMA service, a servlet. Cisco Tomcat, a Microsoft Windows NT service, is installed as part of the Cisco CallManager installation. The Cisco IPMA service performs the following tasks:
  - Hosts the web pages that the manager uses for configuration
  - Communicates to a Cisco CallManager cluster through Cisco CTIManager for third-party call control; Cisco IPMA requires only one computer telephony integration (CTI) connection for all users in a cluster
  - Accesses data from the database and directory
  - Supports the Assistant Console application
- **Desktop interface**—Cisco IPMA supports the following desktop interfaces for managers and assistants (accessed from the PC):
  - **Assistant Console**—Used for call control, login, assistant preferences, monitoring the call activity of managers, and keyboard shortcuts
  - **Manager Configuration**—Used for configuring the Immediate Divert target and to configure the Send All Calls target and filters (proxy-line mode only)
- **Cisco IP Phone interface**—Assistants and managers use softkeys to access Cisco IPMA features.

> **NOTE** A Cisco IP Phone 7960 or 7970 that is running Cisco IPMA can be equipped with a Cisco IP Phone 7914 Expansion Module.

Configuring Cisco IPMA for Shared-Line Support

In Cisco CallManager 4.x versions, proxy-line support is still available; however, it is considered a legacy configuration method due to its complexity and lack of feature support. Newer IPMA deployments use the shared-line support configuration. Follow these six steps to configure Cisco IPMA:

Step 1 Activate the Cisco IPMA service.

Step 2 Configure the appropriate service parameters.

Step 3 Restart the Cisco IPMA service from the Tomcat web page.

Step 4 Configure a Cisco IPMA manager and assign an assistant.

Step 5 Access Manager Configuration to set a divert target for calls.

Step 6 Install the IPMA Assistant Console on the IPMA Assistant's PC.

IPMA Step 1: Activating the Cisco IPMA Service

The CallManager installation process installs the Cisco IPMA service on all Cisco CallManager systems; however, you will still need to activate the service on the servers where you want to use IPMA. Cisco supports one active and one backup IPMA server in a cluster.

To activate the Cisco IPMA service, follow these steps:

Step 1 In the Cisco CallManager Administration window, choose **Application > Cisco CallManager Serviceability**. The Cisco CallManager Serviceability window opens.

Step 2 Choose **Tools > Service Activation**. The Service Activation window displays the list of servers.

Step 3 From the Servers pane, choose the server on which you want to activate Cisco IPMA.

Step 4 Check the **Cisco IP Manager Assistant** check box, shown in Figure 19-2, and click **Update**.

Figure 19-2 *Activating the Cisco IPMA Service*

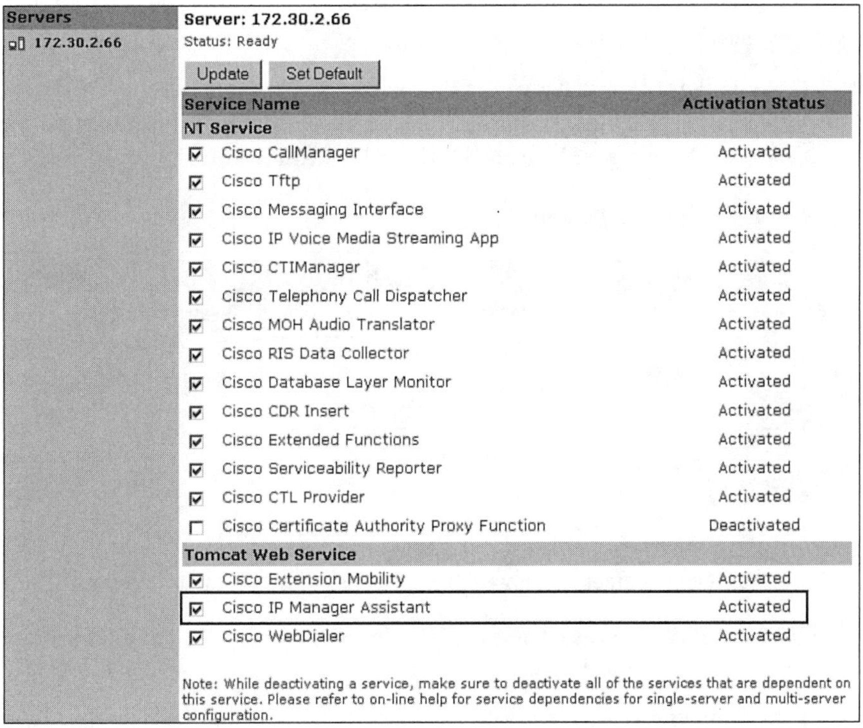

IPMA Step 2: Configuring Service Parameters

Configuring the Cisco IPMA-related service parameters enables automatic configuration of some IP phone features for the manager's and assistant's telephones. These features are the softkey template and Auto Answer with speakerphone for the intercom line.

Service parameters for the Cisco IPMA service consist of two categories: general and clusterwide. Specify clusterwide parameters once for all Cisco IPMA services. Specify general parameters for each Cisco IPMA service that is installed.

Set the Cisco IPMA service parameters by first using Cisco CallManager Administration to access them at **Service > Service Parameters**. Next, choose the server where the Cisco IPMA application resides, and then choose the Cisco IPMA service.

Cisco IPMA includes the following service parameters that must be configured:

- The general parameters, shown in Figure 19-3, include the following:
  - — **Cisco CTIManager (Primary) IP Address**—No default. Enter the IP address of the primary Cisco CTIManager that will be used for call control.
  - — **Cisco CTIManager (Backup) IP Address**—No default. The administrator must manually enter this IP address.
  - — **Route Point Device Name for Proxy Mode**—No default, necessary only if configuring proxy-mode sharing. Choose the Cisco IPMA route point device name (which you configure by using **Device > CTI Route Point**).

Figure 19-3 *IPMA General Service Parameters*

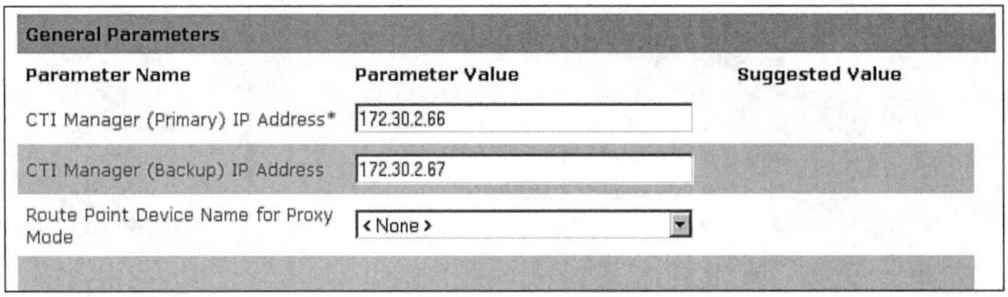

General Parameters

Parameter Name	Parameter Value	Suggested Value
CTI Manager (Primary) IP Address*	172.30.2.66	
CTI Manager (Backup) IP Address	172.30.2.67	
Route Point Device Name for Proxy Mode	< None >	

- The clusterwide parameters, shown in Figure 19-4, include the following:
  - — **Cisco IPMA Server (Primary) IP Address**—No default. The administrator must manually enter this IP address.
  - — **Cisco IPMA Server (Backup) IP Address**—No default. The administrator must manually enter this IP address.

— **Cisco IPMA RNA (Ring No Answer) Forwarding Flag**—The default specifies False. If the parameter is set to True, an assistant telephone that is not answered forwards to another assistant telephone.

— **Cisco IPMA RNA Timeout**—The default specifies 10 seconds. RNA timeout determines how long an assistant telephone can go unanswered before the call is forwarded to another assistant telephone. If Call Forward No Answer (CFNA) and RNA timeout are both configured, the first timeout to occur takes precedence.

— **Desktop Heartbeat Interval**—The default specifies 30 seconds. This interval timer specifies how long it takes for failover to occur on the assistant desktop.

Figure 19-4 *IPMA Clusterwide Service Parameters*

Clusterwide Parameters (Parameters that apply to all servers)

Parameter Name	Parameter Value	Suggested Value
Cisco IPMA Server (Primary) IP Address*		
Cisco IPMA Server (Backup) IP Address		
Cisco IPMA Server Port*	2912	2912
Desktop Heartbeat Interval (sec)*	30	30
Desktop Request Timeout (sec)*	30	30
Cisco IPMA RNA Forwarding Flag*	False	False
Cisco IPMA RNA Timeout (sec)*	10	10

Clusterwide Parameters (Softkey Templates)

Parameter Name	Parameter Value	Suggested Value
Assistant Softkey Template	Standard IPMA Assistant	Standard IPMA Assistant
Manager Softkey Template for Proxy Mode	Standard IPMA Manager	Standard IPMA Manager
Manager Softkey Template for Shared Mode	Standard IPMA Shared Mode Manager	Standard IPMA Shared Mode Manager

Cisco IPMA includes the following softkey template parameters that must be configured as clusterwide parameters if you want to use Cisco IPMA automatic configuration for managers and assistants:

- **Assistant Softkey Template**—The default specifies the Standard IPMA Assistant softkey template. This parameter specifies the softkey template that is assigned to the assistant device during Cisco IPMA assistant automatic configuration.

- **Manager Softkey Template for Shared Mode**—The default specifies the Standard IPMA Shared Mode Manager softkey template.

IPMA Step 3: Restarting the Cisco IPMA Service

After you have made changes to the IPMA service parameters, you must restart the Cisco IPMA service. The Cisco IPMA service runs as an application on Cisco Tomcat. To start or stop the Cisco IPMA service, log in to the Tomcat Web Application Manager window by using administrator privileges. The URL of the Tomcat Web Application Manager web page is http://<IPMA server>/manager/list, where <IPMA server> specifies the IP address of the server that has the IPMA service running on it. After you access this URL, the web page shown in Figure 19-5 appears. To restart the service, just click the **Stop** link followed by the **Start** link (or just click the **Reload** link) for the Cisco IP Manager Assistant service.

Figure 19-5 *Restarting the Cisco IPMA Service*

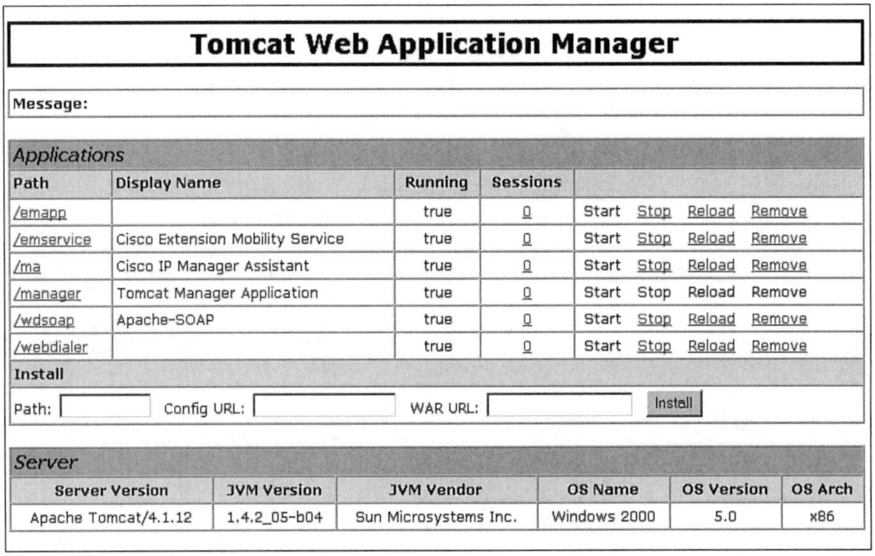

Tomcat Web Application Manager

Message:

Applications

Path	Display Name	Running	Sessions	
/emapp		true	0	Start Stop Reload Remove
/emservice	Cisco Extension Mobility Service	true	0	Start Stop Reload Remove
/ma	Cisco IP Manager Assistant	true	0	Start Stop Reload Remove
/manager	Tomcat Manager Application	true	0	Start Stop Reload Remove
/wdsoap	Apache-SOAP	true	0	Start Stop Reload Remove
/webdialer		true	0	Start Stop Reload Remove

Install

Path: Config URL: WAR URL: Install

Server

Server Version	JVM Version	JVM Vendor	OS Name	OS Version	OS Arch
Apache Tomcat/4.1.12	1.4.2_05-b04	Sun Microsystems Inc.	Windows 2000	5.0	x86

The Tomcat Web Application Manager requires Cisco CallManager Release 4.0 or later. It enables you to start or stop an existing application without having to shut down and restart Tomcat, which restarts all applications that rely on Tomcat. If you have earlier versions of Cisco CallManager, you will need to stop and then start Tomcat by choosing **Start > Programs > Administrative Tools > Services > Cisco Tomcat**. Right-click on **Cisco Tomcat** and choose **Restart**.

IPMA Step 4: Configuring Managers and Assistants

Now that you have configured the IPMA services in Cisco CallManager, you can begin creating the managers and their assistants. You should first configure Cisco IPMA manager information before configuring Cisco IPMA information for an assistant.

Perform the following procedure to configure a Cisco IPMA manager and assign an assistant to the manager. Before performing these steps, the managers and assistants must already exist in the Cisco CallManager directory, be associated with their respective devices, and have a shared line appearance.

Step 1 Choose **User** > **Global Directory**.

Step 2 To find the user who will be the Cisco IPMA manager, click the **Search** button or enter the username in the field and click the **Search** button.

Step 3 To display user information for the chosen manager, click the username. The User Configuration window opens.

Step 4 To configure Cisco IPMA information for the manager, click **Cisco IPMA** from the Application Profiles menu.

If this is the first time that this user is being configured for Cisco IPMA, the User Configuration window displays a message to continue configuration for a manager or to cancel if the user being configured is not a manager (shown in Figure 19-6). Click the **Continue** button.

Figure 19-6 *Configuring IPMA Manager*

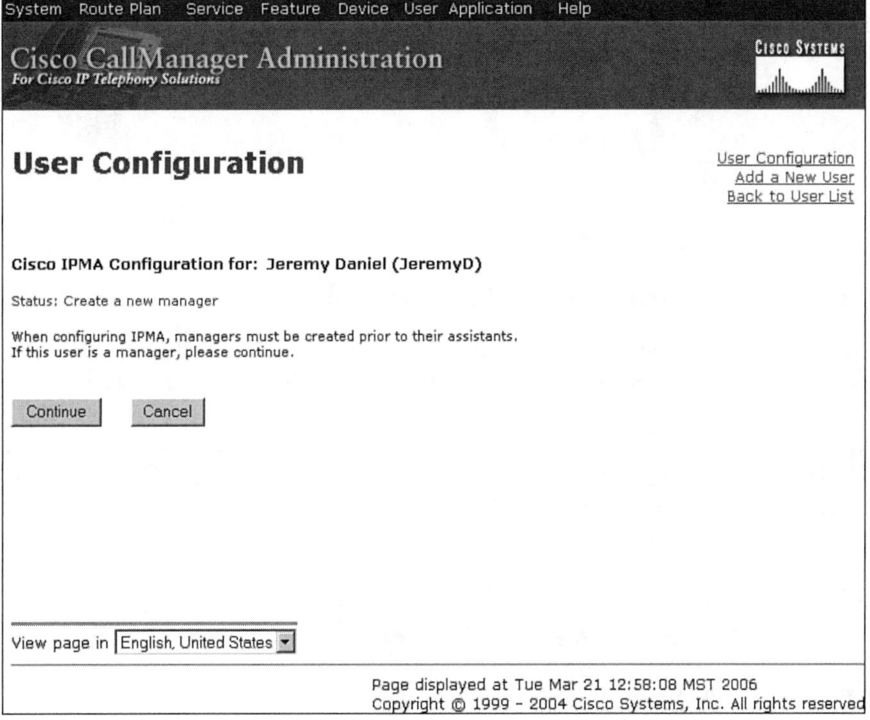

Step 5 The User Configuration window is displayed again and this time contains manager configuration information, such as device name and profile, Cisco IPMA-controlled lines, and intercom line (shown in Figure 19-7).

Figure 19-7 *Configuring IPMA Manager*

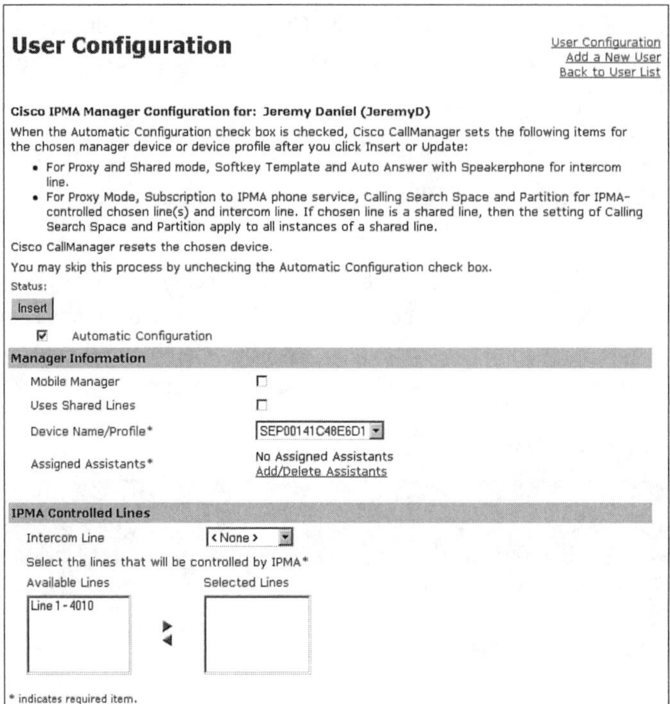

Step 6 Check the **Uses Shared Lines** check box.

Step 7 To associate a device name or device profile with a manager, choose the device name or device profile from the **Device Name/Profile** drop-down list.

NOTE If the manager telecommutes, check the **Mobile Manager** check box and optionally choose **Device Profile** to support Extension Mobility functions.

Step 8 From the **Intercom Line** drop-down list, choose the intercom line appearance for the manager, if applicable.

Step 9 From the Available Lines pane, select a line that you want to be controlled by Cisco IPMA and click the right arrow. The line appears in the Selected Lines pane. Configure up to five Cisco IPMA-controlled lines.

NOTE The Cisco IPMA-controlled lines (selected) must always be the shared-line DN.

Step 10 To automatically configure the softkey template and Auto Answer with Speakerphone for the intercom line of the manager telephone, check the **Automatic Configuration** check box. Automatic configuration configures the softkey template and intercom line on the manager telephone or device profile.

Step 11 In the User Configuration window, click the **Add/Delete Assistants** link. The Assign Assistants window opens.

Step 12 To find an assistant, click the **Search** button or enter the specific name (either the full name or partial string) or user ID of the assistant in the search field.

A list of available assistants is displayed in the window, as shown in Figure 19-8.

Figure 19-8 *Assigning IPMA Assistants*

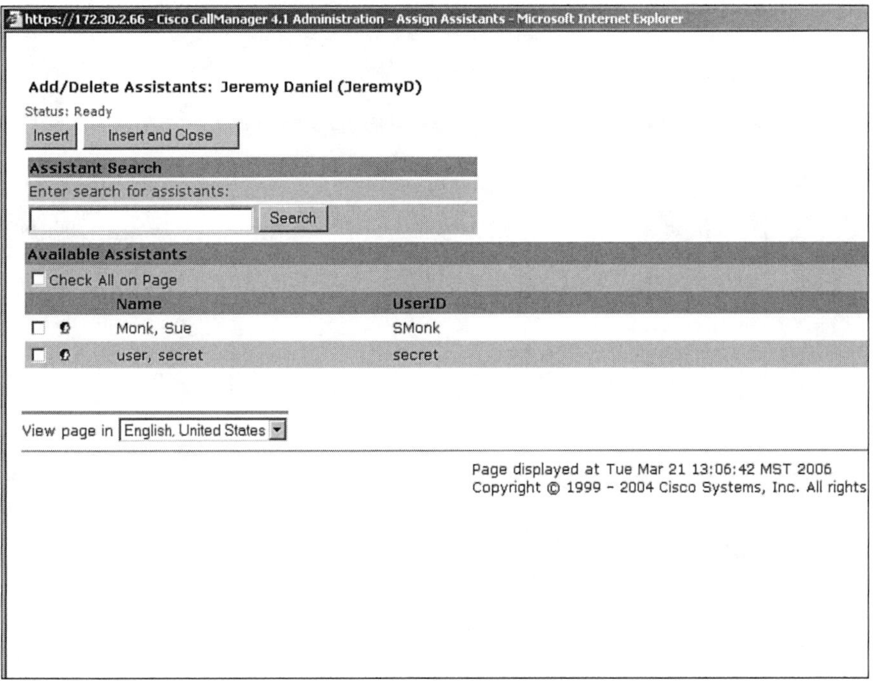

Step 13 Check the check box next to the name of the assistant(s) that you want to assign to the manager. A manager can have a maximum of ten assigned assistants.

Step 14 To save and continue, click the **Insert** button; otherwise, to return to the Cisco IPMA Manager Configuration window, click the **Insert and Close** button.

The User Configuration window displays the manager configuration, and the assistant that you configured is displayed in the Assigned Assistants list, as shown in Figure 19-9.

Figure 19-9 *Completed IPMA Manager Window*

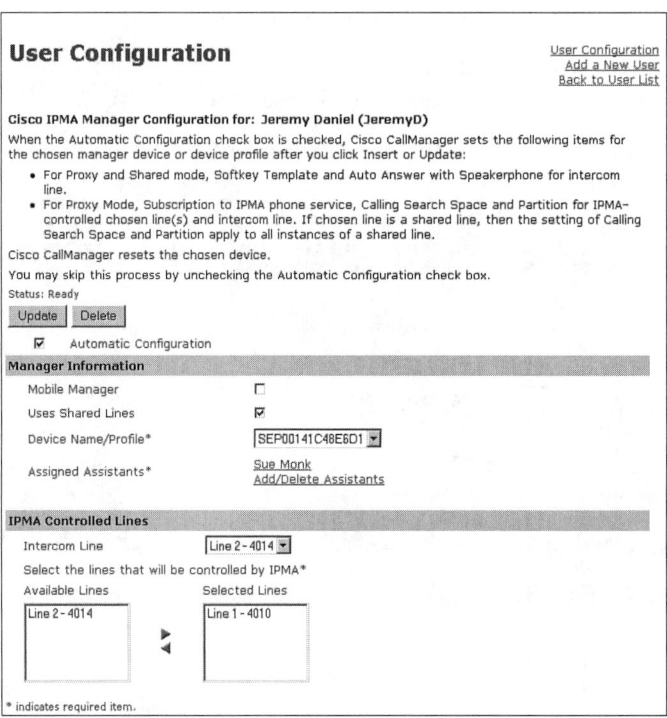

IPMA Step 5: Configuring Call Divert Target

Managers can modify manager preferences from the Manager Configuration window at **https://<ipma-server-address>/ma/desktop/maLogin.jsp** (shown in Figure 19-10). Managers can access this window from a website; assistants can access it from the Assistant Console (**Manager > Configuration**).

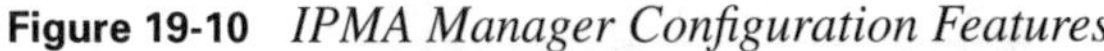

Figure 19-10 *IPMA Manager Configuration Features*

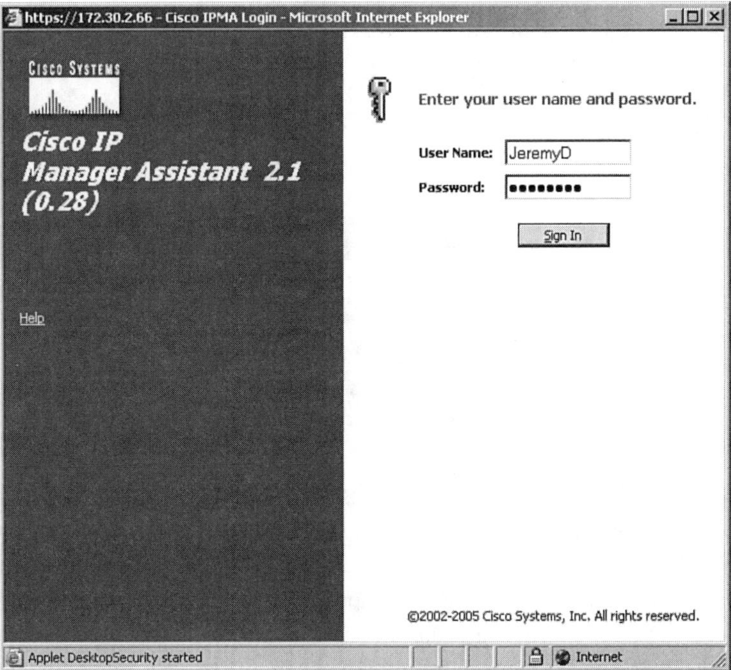

Managers using Cisco IPMA in shared-line mode can set up a divert target and forward calls as they come in by using the **ImmDiv** softkey. The divert screen is automatically displayed when you access the Manager Configuration URL. By default, the divert target is the active assistant for the manager. Managers and assistants can change this target by entering a valid telephone number in the **Directory Number** field. Enter the number exactly as you would dial it from the manager's office telephone, as shown in Figure 19-11.

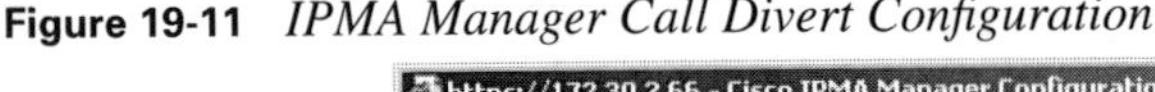

Figure 19-11 *IPMA Manager Call Divert Configuration*

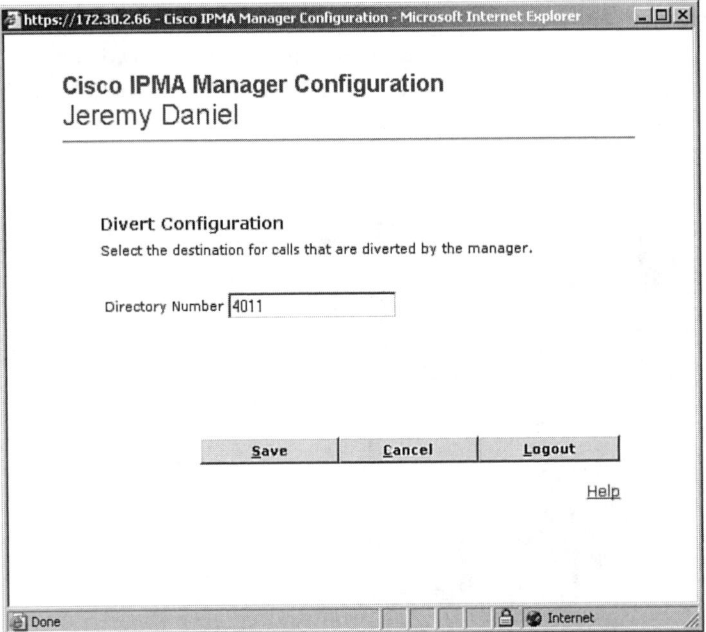

IPMA Step 6: Installing the IPMA Assistant Console

The IPMA Assistant Console uses a very similar look and feel to the Attendant Console application discussed in Chapter 18, "Configuring Cisco Unified CallManager Attendant Console." However, these applications are not the same and must be installed from different locations. To install the IPMA Assistant Console, access the following URL: **http://<IPMA server>/ma/Install/IPMAConsoleInstall.jsp**, where <IPMA Server> is the CallManager server running the IPMA service. An automated Java installation script runs and installs the IPMA Assistant Console. By default, this script places shortcuts to the application in the Windows Start menu and on the desktop.

When running the Assistant Console, the assistant logs in using standard user credentials, and a window similar to that shown in Figure 19-12 opens. From here, the assistant can view and control all manager lines for which you have given the assistant authority.

Figure 19-12 *IPMA Assistant Console*

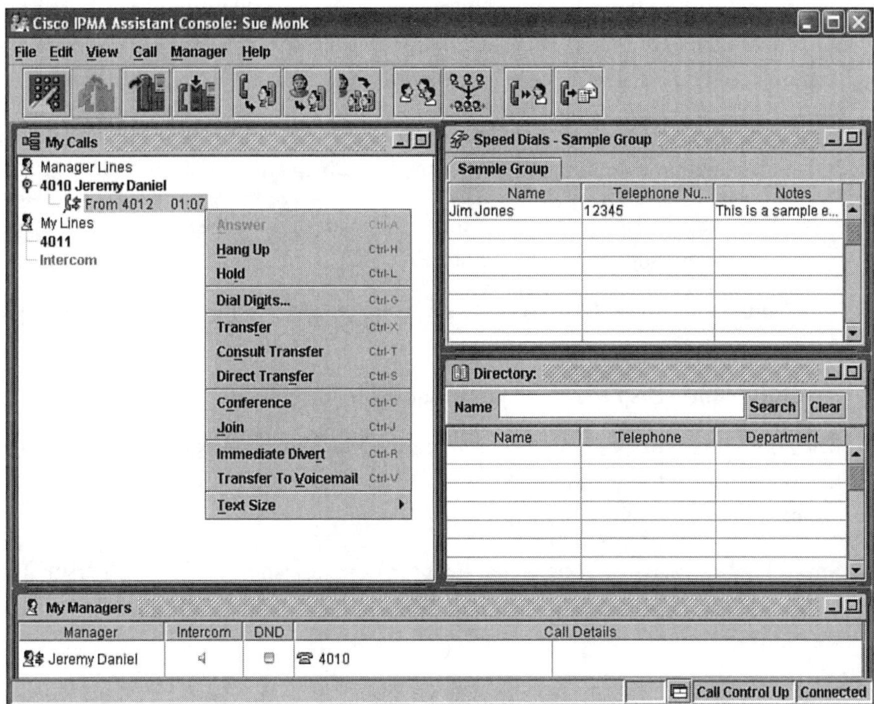

The Assistant Console application includes the following features:

- **Menu bar**—The menu bar is located along the top of the Assistant Console. You can use the menu bar as follows:
  - — **File**—Go online or offline, log in or log out, and exit the console.
  - — **Edit**—Create and edit speed dials, personalize keyboard shortcuts, change the Immediate Divert target, set preferences, and access administrator settings.
  - — **View**—Specify text size and color schemes and refresh the default layout.
  - — **Call**—Dial, answer, hang up, place on hold, transfer, divert, or add conference participants to a call.
  - — **Manager**—Place an intercom call to a manager, access the Manager Configuration window, and enable or disable features for a manager.
  - — **Help**—Access online help.

- **Call control buttons**—Call control buttons are the row of icons that are located along the top or side of the console. Roll your mouse over a call control button to see a description of its function. You can use the call control buttons to perform numerous tasks, such as hold, resume, transfer, join a call, hold a conference, Immediate Divert, and so on.
- **My Calls panel**—The Assistant Console displays calls for the assistant and managers in the My Calls panel. Each telephone line is displayed beneath one of the following headings:
  - **My Lines**—Displays any currently active call that the assistant placed or received using the assistant's own telephone line
  - **Manager Lines**—Displays active calls that the assistant is handling or can handle on behalf of the manager
  - **Intercom**—Displays the status of intercom lines, if applicable
- **My Managers panel**—Assistants can use the My Managers panel in the Assistant Console to monitor call activity and feature status for each manager. Assistants can also enable and disable manager features from this panel.
- **Speed Dials panel**—The speed dial feature allows assistants to set up a personal phone book on the Assistant Console and to place calls and perform other call-handling tasks using speed dial numbers.
- **Directory panel**—Use the directory to search for a coworker, and then use the search results to place and handle calls.
- **Status bar**—The status bar is located along the bottom of the Assistant Console screen and displays the following system information:
  - **Connected or Not Connected**—Indicates the status of the assistant's connection to the Cisco IPMA server
  - **Online or Offline**—Indicates the availability of the assistant to managers
  - **Call Control Up or Call Control Down**—Indicates the availability of call-handling features
  - **Filtering Down**—Indicates the availability of call-filtering features (proxy mode)

Summary

This chapter covered the concepts and configuration of Cisco CallManager IP Manager Assistant (IPMA) features. The IPMA supports proxy-line (legacy) and shared-line configurations. Because of the complexity of configuring proxy-line environments, CallManager 4.x administrators typically use shared-line configurations. Configuring the Cisco IPMA consists of configuring service parameters, configuring a Cisco IPMA manager, and assigning the assistant. After you have configured the base settings, you can then allow managers to access the IPMA Manager Configuration window to choose the assistant who should receive their diverted calls. The attendants can also install the IPMA Assistant Console on their PC to manage multiple manager extensions using an Assistant Console–style graphic interface.

Review Questions

You can find the solutions to these questions in Appendix A, "Answers to Review Questions."

1. Managers can do which of the following when they access Cisco IPMA Manager Configuration in shared-line mode?
   a. Configure speed dials.
   b. Change the divert target.
   c. Assign an assistant.
   d. Subscribe to services.
2. When you configure Cisco IPMA in shared-line mode, the Cisco IPMA-controlled line must always be which line?
   a. Intercom
   b. Assistant's primary
   c. Shared DN
   d. Proxy
   e. Speed dial
3. Which statement is most closely associated with Cisco IPMA shared-line mode?
   a. Supports newer features such as Call Join, Privacy, and Direct Transfer
   b. Uses call filters and partitions to route calls to the assistant
   c. Uses the Standard IPMA Manager softkey template
   d. Uses Cisco Tomcat to load the Cisco IPMA service

4. Which of the following Cisco IP Phones can you use with a Cisco IPMA Configuration? (Choose two.)

   a. Cisco 7912

   b. Cisco 7970

   c. Cisco 7940

   d. Cisco 7900

5. What is the maximum number of assistants per manager if you are using shared-line IPMA mode?

   a. 1

   b. 10

   c. 16

   d. 32

   e. 48

6. The IPMA Service is run as a servlet in what parent web server software?

   a. Microsoft IIS

   b. Apache Tomcat

   c. Netscape Webservices

   d. IBM Websphere

7. After modifying the IPMA service parameters, what must you do to ensure IPMA operates properly?

   a. Add managers and assistants through the IPMA wizard.

   b. Create partitions.

   c. Restart the MA Servlet through the Tomcat web server.

   d. Restart the IPMA service through the Serviceability control center.

8. When configuring IPMA, which of the following must you do first?

   a. Add IPMA assistants.

   b. Add IPMA managers.

   c. Install the IPMA Assistant Console.

   d. Access the IPMA Manager Configuration web pages.

9. How is the IPMA Assistant Console installed?

   a. The Assistant Console is downloaded from the CallManager Plug-Ins window and customized for the assistant.

   b. It can be downloaded from the Cisco website using a valid CCO account.

   c. It is installed automatically when the assistant logs in to their IP phone.

   d. It is installed from a custom IPMA page managed by the Tomcat web server.

10. How does the IPMA service communicate to all servers in a CallManager cluster?

   a. Using SQL replication

   b. Through the CTIManager

   c. By using Skinny Messages

   d. Through the TSP interface

Part V: IPT Security

This chapter covers the following topics:

- Identifying security threats to the Windows operating system
- Explaining the Cisco security and hot fix policy for keeping the operating system up to date
- Explaining how the optional operating system security script and manual security settings provide more stringent security controls to the hardened Windows operating system
- Identifying the antivirus protection software that is approved for use on a Cisco CallManager server
- Explaining the features and functions of Cisco Security Agent as they relate to securing Cisco CallManager
- Defining and administering a password policy for the administrator password
- Explaining how to protect Windows against the most common exploits
- Explaining common security practices and settings that are not recommended on Cisco CallManager

CHAPTER 20

Securing the Windows Operating System

The telephony system is a business-critical, system, 24 hours a day, seven days a week, to all companies. Such critical environments must be as secure as possible to avoid breakdowns related to failures in the system or attacks involving the network. The Microsoft Windows 2000 Server Operating System is the base of Cisco CallManager 3.X and 4.X versions. This chapter discusses options for hardening and securing the Cisco CallManager operating system and gives students an overview of possible vulnerabilities and of practices for tightening security in the Cisco IP Telephony Operating System.

NOTE Cisco Unified CallManager 5.X versions use Red Hat Linux as a base operating system. This operating system is inaccessible as the 5.X versions of CallManager run as an appliance.

Threats Targeting the Operating System

When you are securing an operating system, several threats should be considered. Bugs in the operating system, as well as in the services and applications that come with the operating system, can pose severe security threats. Because applications are installed on top of the operating system, even well-written and secure applications can be affected by vulnerabilities in the underlying operating system. Built-in networking services and applications are especially sensitive because they are exposed to remote attacks. That vulnerability also applies to the IP stack in the Windows operating system. The IP stack has a strategic importance and, unfortunately, also a long tradition of more and less severe security issues. These issues result not only from the particular implementation of the IP protocol, but also from the lack of security mechanisms in the protocol itself. As shown in Figure 20-1, password and account policies as well as insecure Windows configuration settings pose security concerns in the foundation Cisco CallManager operating system.

Figure 20-1 *Threats Targeting the Windows Operating System*

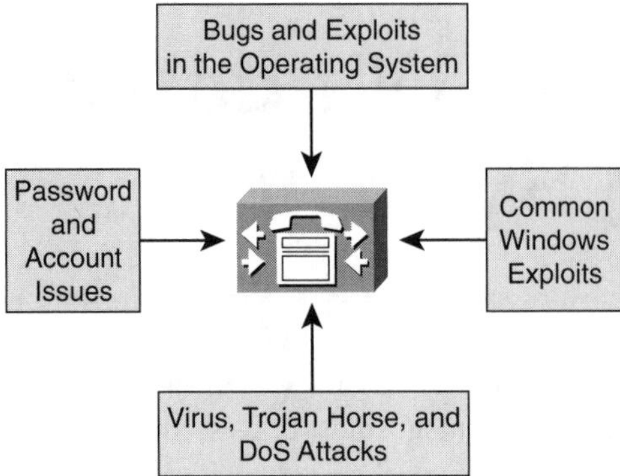

Microsoft Windows, as the most popular operating system, is well-known to the public. As a result, many known issues are related to its password policies as well as vulnerabilities in the operating system default settings. An attacker might try to log in to the operating system using the Administrator account with commonly used passwords. In Microsoft networking, File and Print Sharing services can be used (and might have been turned on by default in some versions of Windows) to allow access to file shares without any security checking.

Another threat to the system is malicious code execution by viruses, worms, or Trojan horses. Protection against these threats consists of blocking the threats from the system and detecting and eliminating attacks that were not blocked.

Finally and extremely important is the fact that server-operating systems are vulnerable to denial of service (DoS) attacks. If the server operating system cannot resist DoS attacks, an attacker can tear down the whole IP telephony infrastructure with a single, focused attack against Cisco CallManager nodes. Besides other methods (separating the server network from other parts of the network and establishing access control), the server itself should be hardened to resist at least simple and common DoS attacks.

Lowering the Threats in Windows Operating System

You can divide the possible countermeasures against attacks to the operating system itself into measures that eliminate vulnerabilities to certain threats and methods to protect the system against attacks exploiting the remaining vulnerabilities.

The following are practices to reduce possible vulnerabilities:

- Harden the Windows operating system with Cisco operating system upgrades.
- Deploy the Cisco security and hot fix policy.

- Implement a secure Windows password policy.
- Protect against common exploits involving Windows.
- Protect against attacks from the network by using the following:
  — Antivirus software
  — Cisco Security Agent

To protect against bugs and exploits involving Microsoft Windows, Cisco provides an already hardened version of the Windows operating system called Cisco IP Telephony Operating System. You must keep the Windows 2000 Server up to date to secure the operating system against new security holes. For that reason, Cisco provides operating system upgrades and hot fixes. Cisco CallManager and other Cisco IP telephony applications require these upgrades to function properly.

Cisco uses the Cisco IP Telephony Operating System in several Cisco IP Telephony Application Server components, such as Cisco CallManager, Cisco Emergency Responder (ER), Cisco IP Contact Center (IPCC), and Cisco Interactive Voice Response (IVR). Cisco builds the IP Telephony Operating System upgrades on top of each other and they are incrementally more secure. The upgrades provide changes to, for example, the IP stack, file system, Registry, access control lists (ACLs), and dynamic link library (DLL) engines.

NOTE Before you run an operating system upgrade provided by Cisco, read the release notes for that upgrade carefully. The operating system upgrade might not apply to your installation and could harm the running applications. Before upgrading, verify that you are using the proper operating system upgrade for your Cisco CallManager version. It is also a good practice to consider making a backup before upgrading the Cisco IP Telephony Operating System.

Cisco IP Telephony Operating System upgrades can be downloaded from Cisco.com at http://www.cisco.com/cgi-bin/tablebuild.pl/cmva-3des (requires CCO account).

Security and Hot Fix Policy

Cisco closely monitors security bulletins from Microsoft and evaluates them based on the impact to Cisco CallManager and other IP telephony applications.

When Microsoft posts a security patch, Cisco determines whether the patch affects applications and operating system components in Cisco CallManager and applications that share the same operating system installation process. Cisco then tests the relevant patches to verify correct operation with Cisco applications. This is a list of applications and operating system components that might be affected by a patch:

- Microsoft Windows 2000 Server (including any Windows component or subcomponent installed by Cisco)
- Microsoft Internet Information Server (IIS)
- Microsoft Internet Explorer
- Microsoft Structured Query Language (SQL) Server 2000

CAUTION The operating system upgrades provided by Cisco are not the same as upgrades provided by Microsoft. The operating system upgrades and patches provided by Cisco are tailored for IP telephony applications. If a Microsoft service pack (SP) or hot fix is installed for the Cisco IP Telephony Operating System, the applications running on the Cisco IP Telephony Operating System might be adversely affected.

The security patch and hot fix policy for Cisco CallManager specifies that any applicable patch deemed Severity 1 or Critical must be tested and posted to Cisco.com within 24 hours as a hot fix. All other applicable patches are consolidated and posted once a month as incremental service releases. Notification tools (e-mail service) for providing automatic notification of new fixes, operating system updates, and patches for Cisco CallManager and associated products are also available:

- **Cisco CallManager Notification Tool**—This e-mail service provides automatic notification of new fixes, operating system updates, and service releases that are available for Cisco CallManager and related products, including Cisco CallManager Attendant Console, Cisco IP Manager Assistant (IPMA), and Bulk Administration Tool (BAT). To subscribe, go to http://www.cisco.com/cgi-bin/Software/Newsbuilder/Builder/VOICE.cgi and follow the instructions on the web page.
- **Cisco Product Security Incident Response Team (PSIRT) Advisory Notification Tool**—This e-mail service provides automatic notification of all Cisco security advisories released by Cisco PSIRT. Advisories that describe security issues that directly impact Cisco products provide a set of actions required to repair these products. To subscribe, go to http://www.cisco.com/en/US/products/products_security_vulnerability_policy.html and follow the instructions on the web page.

NOTE The Cisco IP Telephony Operating System configuration and patch process does not currently allow an automated patch-management process.

Operating System Hardening

One of the most important steps in securing an IP telephony server is installing all the applicable product or component security updates and then making sure that they are kept up to date. Cisco provides three types of updates for the Cisco IP Telephony Operating System:

- **Operating system upgrade**—Comprehensive upgrade to all components of the operating system that is released two to three times a year, including Microsoft Windows 2000 SPs, Internet Explorer SPs, BIOS, firmware, drivers, Microsoft hot fixes, security configuration changes, third-party software that is installed in the base operating system, and configuration changes to match the currently shipping operating system version.
- **Operating system service releases**—Primarily a comprehensive roll-up of security hot fixes that are released the third Tuesday of each month when needed to deliver new security hot fixes. The operating system service release occasionally contains nonsecurity hot fixes or configuration changes needed to resolve a defect in the operating system.
- **Critical hot fixes**—When Microsoft releases a hot fix that is critical for Cisco IP telephony products, Cisco tests the hot fix and posts it to Cisco.com within one business day of the release by Microsoft.

An IP telephony server must be used for IP telephony purposes only. The server should not be used as a common file server that stores user data or has user applications, such as Microsoft Office products, installed on it. File-share access has to be limited to the absolute minimum needed (for instance, to access log files and generate reports). Strict file access control has to be deployed, and auditing of network file access should be enabled. This practice also eliminates the need to add user accounts to the server; only administrator and auditor accounts should exist. If network file access is not needed at all, it should be disabled to enhance the security of the server.

The more services that are running on a server, the more likely it is that vulnerabilities can be exploited by an attacker. To minimize this risk, only the services that are needed should be activated. Many services that are not needed have already been disabled in the Cisco hardened version of the Microsoft Windows 2000 Server operating system.

To make Cisco CallManager even more secure, Cisco provides additional security scripts and information on how to protect the Cisco IP Telephony Operating System against common threats.

Do not install any other application on the servers unless it is approved software, such as Cisco Security Agent or antivirus products. A hardened IP telephony server has to be stripped down to run only the services and applications that are needed for its operation.

IP Telephony Operating System Security Scripts

Cisco IP Telephony Operating System 2.6 and later includes scripts and information guides on additional security settings. These security guides and scripts provide additional security settings beyond those that are installed by default in the Cisco IP Telephony Operating System. The settings in the optional security script have not been included by default and are not intended for all customers to use. When planning to use the optional security script, consider these points:

- The optional security script settings are supported only for Windows 2000 servers that are running Cisco CallManager Release 3.3(2) and later.
- The optional security script settings might have an adverse impact on some of the other Cisco IP telephony applications that use this operating system, on the interaction between Cisco CallManager servers and some other Cisco IP telephony applications, and on some supported third-party software.
- Because these settings are not installed by default, they receive only a limited amount of testing.
- Only experienced Windows administrators should apply the optional security script or manual settings.

> **CAUTION** Applying the optional security script can destroy collocated applications, such as Cisco IPCC Express, Cisco IP IVR, and Cisco IP Queue Manager (IP QM)!

As shown in Figure 20-2, the optional security script and some additional information are available in the C:\utils\SecurityTemplates folder.

The script file is a batch job that can be started by clicking the CCM-OS-OptionalSecurity.cmd file. Before doing so, read the CCM-OS-OptionalSecurity-Readme.htm file to identify possible issues with applications running on the operating system:

- The CCM-OS-OptionalSecurity-Readme.htm file contains information on what the CCM-OS-OptionalSecurity script is changing in the operating system and provides additional security settings that can be configured manually.
- Some of the optional security settings cause upgrades to fail. Therefore, if the Cisco IP Telephony Operating System optional security settings have been installed on the server and you want to upgrade the server, read the "Before CallManager Upgrade" guide. It includes a checklist of all settings to which you must revert for the upgrade to work.

Figure 20-2 *CallManager Security Script Templates*

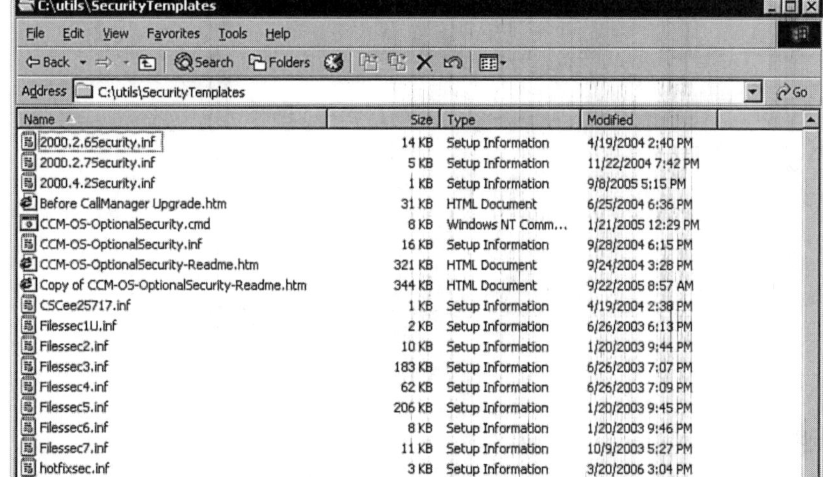

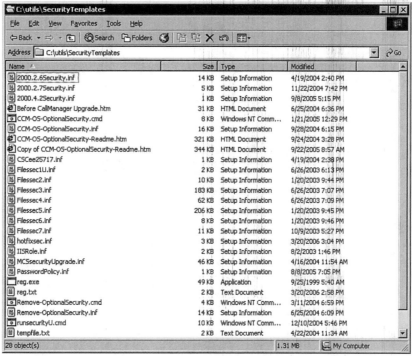

In addition, Cisco has provided an additional security script in the C:\utils directory, shown in Figure 20-3. This script is called the IP security filter and will block the fixed Windows 2000 and SQL ports. Read the IPSec-W2KSQL-Readme.htm file for instructions on how to use the IP security filter.

Figure 20-3 *CallManager SQL Security Script Template*

C:\utils

File Edit View Favorites Tools Help

Address C:\utils

Name	Size	Type	Modified
FormatTracePart.exe	292 KB	Application	12/30/2004 2:04 PM
getmac.exe	11 KB	Application	12/2/1999 3:53 PM
instsrv.exe	62 KB	Application	12/2/1999 1:53 PM
ipsecpol.exe	54 KB	Application	11/4/1999 9:47 AM
ipsecutil.dll	25 KB	Application Extension	11/17/1999 12:56 PM
ipsec-W2KSQL.cmd	9 KB	Windows NT Comm...	4/12/2004 7:20 PM
IPSec-W2KSQL-Readme.htm	55 KB	HTML Document	4/12/2004 7:21 PM
J2RE1.4.2_04.exe	13,368 KB	Application	4/30/2004 7:40 PM
kill.exe	10 KB	Application	11/30/1999 10:40 PM
LastLogin.cmd	2 KB	Windows NT Comm...	2/5/2004 11:15 AM
LastLogin	1 KB	Shortcut	12/28/2004 1:48 PM
MCSVer.exe	56 KB	Application	2/27/2004 12:19 PM
MSCOMCT2.OCX	633 KB	ActiveX Control	5/22/2000 12:00 AM
mscomctl.ocx	1,042 KB	ActiveX Control	5/22/2000 12:00 AM
msvcp60.dll	393 KB	Application Extension	8/6/2000 12:04 PM
MSVCP60D.DLL	505 KB	Application Extension	8/28/2000 11:00 PM
MSVCRTD.DLL	425 KB	Application Extension	7/14/2000 11:00 PM
netset.exe	85 KB	Application	12/2/1999 1:53 PM
now.exe	61 KB	Application	12/2/1999 1:53 PM
PASSEXP.CMD	1 KB	Windows NT Comm...	3/31/2004 5:49 PM
PASSEXP2.VBS	1 KB	VBScript Script File	3/31/2005 5:30 PM
ptree.msi	444 KB	Windows Installer P...	11/4/1999 11:38 AM
pulist.exe	54 KB	Application	12/2/1999 3:54 PM
report.vbs	1 KB	VBScript Script File	1/17/2004 6:31 PM
scanreg.exe	60 KB	Application	12/2/1999 3:54 PM
sclist.exe	6 KB	Application	11/12/1999 1:48 AM

56 object(s) 18.9 MB My Computer

The security script provides the following benefits:

- Blocking the fixed Windows 2000 and SQL ports adds an extra layer of protection from viruses, worms, and hackers. A provided script eases the creation of the IP security filter. You must customize the script with the IP addresses that the organization wants to allow through the filter. For example, the Cisco CallManager uses SQL ports allowing every IP address to connect to these port numbers. The IPSec-W2KSQL script would allow SQL connections only from the IP addresses defined in the script. These consist mostly of the other Cisco CallManager servers in the cluster and applications that need direct access to the database, for example, to the call detail record (CDR) tables.
- Using this IP security filter increases the management overhead of the servers. If the IP infrastructure changes or additional servers are added to the Cisco IP telephony solution, the permit lists on all the servers will need to be updated.

NOTE The name of the IPSec-W2kSQL file has nothing to do with the IPsec virtual private network (VPN) umbrella standard.

File-Sharing Considerations

To secure the access to file shares, limit access to the absolute minimum number of users who need it, as shown in Figure 20-4. Check the share permissions on all shared folders, for example, the CDR and TFTPPath folders. Avoid assigning share permissions for the Everyone group. You can find detailed information on how to secure file shares in the CCM-OS-OptionalSecurity-Readme guide, located in the folder C:\Utils\SecurityTemplates.

Figure 20-4 *Managing CallManager Share Permissions*

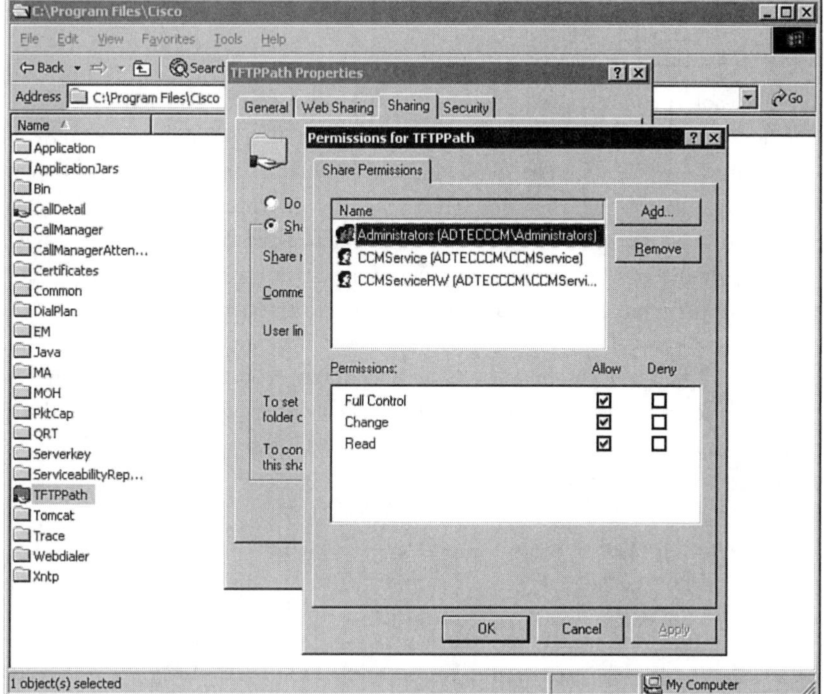

Antivirus Protection

In addition to hardening the Cisco IP Telephony Operating System by using built-in tools, you should protect the system by using antivirus software. This practice will defend against attacks by viruses, Trojan horses, and worms. Make sure that the software itself and the virus definition files are kept up to date so that the newest viruses can be detected. Disable heuristic scanning in any antivirus software because it can block Cisco CallManager web pages from operating. Cisco currently supports these antivirus products on the Cisco IP Telephony Operating System:

- McAfee VirusScan Enterprise 4.5, 7.0, and 7.1
- Symantec AntiVirus Corporate Edition 7.61, 8.0, and 8.1

- Trend Micro ServerProtect v5

The list of the latest supported antivirus software is available at http://www.cisco.com/en/US/products/sw/voicesw/ps556/prod_bulletin0900aecd800f8572.html.

> **NOTE** Heuristic scanning refers to the ability of the software to flag suspicious files or attachments because they resemble known viruses. Heuristic scanning uses behavior-based rules to identify and block new viruses without requiring you to first download a patch.

Cisco Security Agent

In addition to antivirus protection, you must protect the operating system against other threats from the network, such as DoS attacks. For these issues, Cisco provides Cisco Security Agent software to install on every Cisco CallManager system. The Cisco Security Agent implements the host-based intrusion prevention system (HIPS), which provides an additional layer of protection against known and unknown attacks. At the same time, CSA provides security services not offered by the host operating system. Examples of these services are personal firewall protection, software keylogger detection, and abnormal application behavior protection.

Cisco Security Agent is designed to protect the endpoint from network-borne attacks, and it enforces its protection rules on several levels. One of them is the protection of the underlying operating system from potentially hostile applications. Cisco Security Agent provides three basic areas of operating system protection:

- **Protection of operating system integrity**—Cisco Security Agent policy rules always prohibit access to sensitive system files and Registry settings. For example, no application can change files in the Windows system folder.
- **Prevention or restriction of application misbehavior resulting from injection of hostile code or other network attacks**—Several policy rules are dynamic and allow or disallow local resource access based on the behavior of the application and, hence, its potential "hostility." For example, if a client application accesses the network, it is automatically considered less trusted and its access to local resources is further restricted.
- **Endpoint, or "personal" firewalls**—Cisco Security Agent can allow or deny network access to any local application, and, hence, minimize access to and from the system, enforcing the least-privilege rule.

Cisco Security Agent (CSA) operates independently of native operating system functions, providing an independent layer of protection that prevents attacks even when the native operating system access control methods are breached. You should never deploy the CSA in place of strong host security, but as an additional protective layer to provide protection methods not available in the host operating system.

The rationale behind the behavioral approach is that although the number of methods and exploits to attack a system is extremely large, the number of possible consequences of these attacks is relatively small. For example, a web server can be persuaded by the attacker to execute a local file or an executable attachment in an e-mail attempting to access the Windows Registry. CSA can recognize application behavior leading to or following an attack and prevent the malicious actions. This ability is also why CSA does not require constant updates; its policies need to be updated only if a completely different class of attacks is created, which is relatively rare.

CSA for IP telephony servers is available in two versions:

- **Headless agent**—This version comes with a set of rules for a specific server platform, such as Cisco CallManager; no further configuration is necessary.
- **Managed agent**—This version has to be configured with rules for the appropriate IP telephony servers. Predefined rules can be downloaded from Cisco.com.

CAUTION Do not use the headless agent when running Cisco CallManager with collocated applications, such as Cisco IPCC Express, Cisco IP IVR, or Cisco IP QM, because the fixed policy of the headless agent will not support these applications (and as a consequence they will not work properly).

Cisco Security Headless Agent

The free headless agent has a fixed security policy and no centralized reporting capabilities. For each type of IP telephony server, a different (predefined) agent kit is available for the headless agent. The headless agent is configured with appropriate policies and exceptions for a typical supported configuration of that server. The headless agent should be used in environments where centralized reporting is not required or practical and the IP telephony servers are aligned with Cisco specifications for installed software and system and application configuration and where they feature no add-ons that might conflict with the security rules of the headless agent.

NOTE The headless agent is also commonly referred to as the standalone CSA agent on the Cisco website.

Cisco Security Managed Agent

The managed version of CSA uses CiscoWorks VPN/Security Management Solution (VMS) and CSA Management Center (MC) for centralized policy distribution and allows event correlation and reporting. As with the headless agent, which comes in different configurations for different types of IP telephony servers, CSA MC also allows the administrator to load predefined, application-specific policies for each IP telephony server type.

NOTE Cisco offers a free, predefined policy for the CSA Managed Agent that deploys the same CallManager security standards as the standalone CSA.

The managed agent should be used in environments where centralized reporting is required, where servers do not use a typical configuration (for example, with nondefault TCP or UDP ports) or have special application requirements (for example, custom systems management software), or where the default policies need to be augmented with site-specific protection requirements.

Deployment of the managed agent also allows the use of CSA Profiler, an expert add-on tool that can, to a large extent, automate generation of custom application policies. This add-on would allow an expert CSA administrator to further enhance the built-in policies and confine every IP telephony application to a sandbox, similar to the functions that the built-in Restrictive MS IIS Module and Restrictive MS SQL Server Module provide for those two applications.

The CSA Profiler must be purchased separately, but it does not require any other software to be installed on the profiled servers.

CSA Supported Applications

CSA is available for Cisco CallManager Release 3.2(3), 3.3, and later. To use CSA for another Cisco IP telephony application, check the CSA administration manual to determine whether Cisco supports CSA for that particular application.

This is a list of software add-ons that are supported with CSA on the same server:

- BMC PATROL
- Concord eHealth Monitor
- Diskeeper Server Standard Edition 8.0.478.0
- HP OpenView Operations Agent 7.1
- HP OpenView Performance Manager 3.3
- Integrated Research PROGNOSIS
- McAfee VirusScan 7.0
- Micromuse Netcool

- NAI ePolicy Agent
- NetIQ Vivinet Manager
- RealVNC VNC
- Symantec AntiVirus Corporate Edition 8.0
- Trend Micro AntiVirus
- Windows Terminal Services

NOTE The Cisco Security Agent headless agent and the Cisco Security Agent policies for the Cisco Security Agent MC are both available at http://www.cisco.com/cgi-bin/tablebuild.pl/cmva-3des (Cisco CCO account required).

CSA Protection

The CSA default operating system protection rules for IP telephony servers provide basic operating system hardening and integrity protection and contain rule exceptions for supported add-on applications. In regard to local resource access control, these policies can be summarized as follows:

- Allow specific actions required by basic operating system processes
- Protect the integrity of the system binaries and other sensitive files from local applications
- Protect the integrity of the system Registry from local applications
- Allow all other actions (including network access and access to local files as dictated by the native security of the local host, for example, file ACLs in Windows)

In addition to these basic rules, many other rule modules constitute the total CSA protection policy of a system.

CSA Guidelines

At the minimum, for each server, deploy the headless CSA, as shown in Figure 20-5. The built-in operating system protection policies are sound and generally do not require tuning for enhanced protection, except where dictated by the site policy.

Figure 20-5 *Headless (or Standalone) CSA Interface*

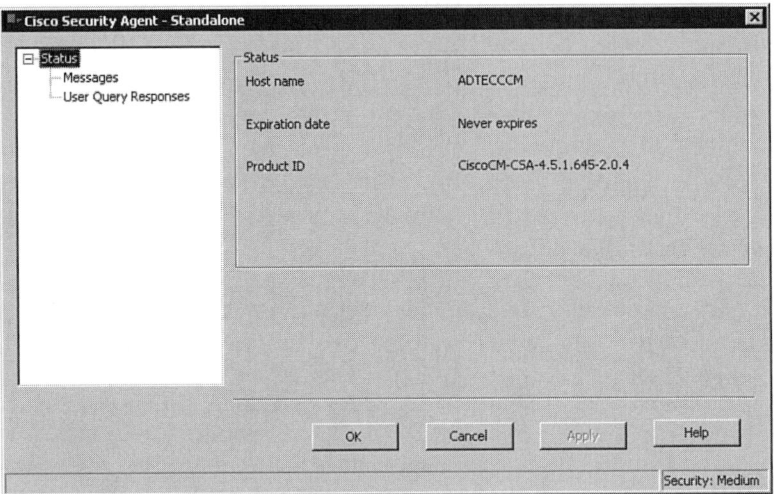

So-called "false positives," events that are erroneously classified as attacks, are very likely when using unsupported server add-ons, such as system management and unsupported antivirus software. To eliminate this erroneous behavior, deploy the managed agent and add the requested permissions for these applications so that CSA will not consider them to be malicious.

CSA also provides personal firewall functions by restricting network connections to the server. The headless agent has a fixed policy that allows all inbound connections to the server, and this cannot be changed. If you want to use CSA to control network connectivity to the server, you have to use the managed agent. Alternatively, you could use native Windows IP security filtering or rely solely on packet filtering by network devices, such as routers or firewalls.

CSA by default allows the agent service to be stopped by the local administrator (using the **net stop csagent** command). When using the managed version of CSA, you can apply an agent policy that blocks the local administrator from stopping the agent.

> **TIP** The CSA should be installed on the Cisco CallManager server after you have applied the security template. Otherwise, the CSA will think many security template modifications are attacks on the CallManager server.

Administrator Password Policy

One of the easiest and most frequently used attacks against Microsoft operating systems is to try to log in to the Administrator account, using various well-known passwords. To block that security hole, consider using strong password policies, renaming the Administrator account, and other mechanisms to protect the Administrator account.

The Windows operating system gives administrators the ability to assign restrictions to password and account policies, as shown in Figure 20-6.

Figure 20-6 *Implementing Password Restrictions in Windows 2000*

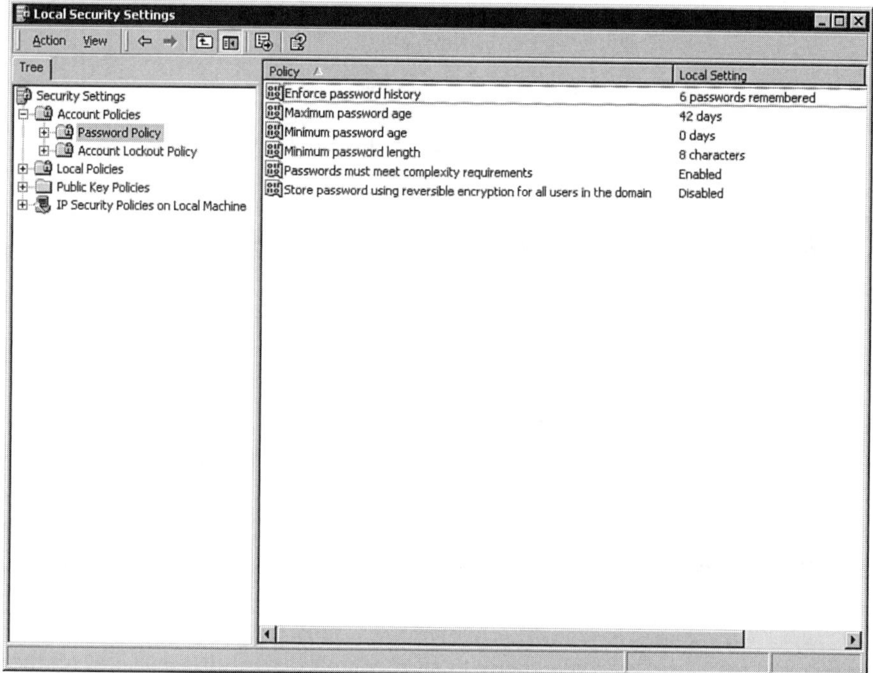

A general rule is not to create any user accounts on an IP telephony server. Only administrators and operators should have access to the server. Make sure that these accounts have complex passwords. If a password is too simple, not kept secret, or not changed for a long period, it can be discovered and misused by unauthorized people. The account policy settings should not be modified, because setting the lockout policies can adversely affect the system during the next upgrade (requiring a new installation from scratch). Consider these issues:

- Setting the account policy is more important for servers with user accounts because otherwise the administrator has no control over the frequency of password changes by the users.
- The Minimum Password Length parameter determines how short passwords can be. If it is set to zero, blank passwords are allowed. It is recommended that you set this value to at least eight characters.

- The Passwords Must Meet Complexity Requirements parameter determines whether password complexity is enforced. If this setting is enabled, passwords must meet these requirements:
  - — The password is at least six characters long.
  - — The password contains characters from at least three of these categories:
  - — English uppercase characters (A through Z)
  - — English lowercase characters (a through z)
  - — Base-10 digits (0 through 9)
  - — Nonalphanumeric characters (For example: $, !, %, #, &)
  - — The password does not contain three or more characters from the username.

To configure the password policy for an account, complete these steps:

Step 1 From the Cisco CallManager server, click **Start**.

Step 2 Choose **Settings**.

Step 3 From the Settings menu, choose **Control Panel**.

Step 4 When the Control Panel window opens, click **Administrative Tools**.

Step 5 In the Administrative Tools window, click **Local Security Policy**.

Step 6 When the Local Security Settings window opens, click **Account Policy**.

Step 7 Click **Password Policy**.

You can configure the password policies to meet complexity requirements and set the minimum length of the password.

> **TIP** You should apply the password complexity settings before you install the Cisco CallManager application. If the passwords applied in the installation process do not fit the complexity requirements, the Cisco CallManager services will no longer be able to start.

Account and Password Considerations

When giving individual users the ability to log in to the Cisco IP Telephony Operating System as administrators, you should create a separate account for each user and put each into the Administrators group. Doing so enables tracking of changes made to the Cisco IP Telephony Operating System. In addition, you could change the default administrator account to a decoy

Administrator account that has no rights but is strictly monitored (by enabling auditing of login attempts or usage of that account).

NOTE Cisco CallManager installations and upgrades currently require the Administrator account to be used. Before installing or upgrading Cisco CallManager, rename the decoy Administrator account and change the name of the real Administrator account back to "Administrator" on all Cisco CallManager servers in the cluster.

Some corporate security policies require separating the system auditors from the system administrators. To enable more accurate auditing information regarding the identity of an administrator, it is a good practice to create individual accounts for each administrator and make them members of the Administrator group. In addition, separate administration from auditing by creating separate auditor accounts. Auditor accounts should have full rights to logs but should not have any other administrative permission, whereas administrator accounts should have only read access to log files.

Follow general security guidelines for accounts and passwords, such as removing unnecessary accounts and requiring complex passwords, but also harden the server by applying password protection to complementary metal oxide semiconductor (CMOS) access, screen savers, and Hewlett-Packard Integrated Lights-Out (iLO) access (used for out-of-band server management).

NOTE More information on iLO can be found at http://h71028.www7.hp.com/enterprise/cache/98327-0-0-225-121.aspx.

Common Windows Exploits

A hardened Cisco IP Telephony Operating System can successfully defend against many common Windows exploits. Some active services cannot be disabled because Cisco CallManager uses them. To secure these areas, you must design the IP telephony-ready network properly and choose the proper roles for the Cisco CallManager nodes in the cluster. You need to protect Windows against some of the most common exploits.

One common exploit involves Extensible Markup Language (XML) applications running on HTTP (TCP port 80). Most XML applications go to the Internet to get their data. Because of this, Cisco recommends that you off-load XML services to a dedicated server that is isolated (as much as possible) from the rest of the network.

The most important task for Microsoft IIS issues is to turn off IIS on all subscribers. IIS is the parent process for HTTP, Simple Mail Transfer Protocol (SMTP), and FTP. Eighty percent of the attacks against Windows are against the IIS parent process. Turn off IIS on the subscribers, where all of the active call processing is taking place, and run it only on the publisher for administration purposes. This practice will minimize the threats against Windows by 80 percent and actually bring it closer to parity with what is considered to be the normal security settings of UNIX or Linux operating systems.

In a Cisco CallManager cluster, different servers can have different roles and, hence, do not need the same active services. One server could act as a pure management server by providing access only to Cisco CallManager Administration web pages, while other servers are providing call-routing functions and others are being used for applications such as phone services. Because IIS is a common target, run it only where needed: at the Cisco CallManager Publisher. During upgrades, IIS will also be needed on subscribers but will automatically be started when needed as long as the service is set to manual rather than disabled. Therefore, set IIS to manual on all subscribers and keep the setting automatic only at the publisher.

CAUTION IIS needs to be available during upgrades. If you have set the IIS Startup Type option to Disabled, the upgrade will fail.

Table 20-1 shows what will happen during a Cisco CallManager upgrade when the IIS service is set to different options.

Table 20-1 *Behavior of Cisco CallManager During an Upgrade*

IIS Service Parameter	Resulting Upgrade Behavior
Enabled	The upgrade will work with no interference.
Disabled	The upgrade will fail; no message is displayed.
Manual and Stopped	The upgrade will stop, a message that the IIS is not running will pop up, the IIS service will start, and the upgrade will continue. On the next reboot, the IIS service will be in the Manual and Stopped state again.
Manual and Running	The upgrade will work with no interference.

Finally, to avoid attacks against the Dynamic Host Configuration Protocol (DHCP) server, which, in most installations, is used to provide IP settings, push DHCP services as close to the endpoints as possible. This might include using an intelligent Cisco switch or router for DHCP services.

Security Taboos

After you have protected Cisco CallManager against common Windows exploits such as attacks on IIS, there are additional security settings that, from the point of view of a Windows administrator, are nice to have but that are not recommended in a Cisco CallManager environment. Some of the settings that a Windows administrator would normally implement on the servers could cause the Cisco CallManager installation to fail, increase the system downtime of the Cisco CallManager server, and delay troubleshooting efforts.

Table 20-2 describes common Windows security settings never to be done in any circumstance on a Cisco CallManager server.

Table 20-2 *Windows Security Settings Not to Be Done in Any Circumstance*

Security Setting	Reason It Is Not Allowed
Do not delete, disable, or rename any service accounts.	Services like Cisco CallManager or SQL might not function.
Do not change "password never expires" on service accounts created by Cisco.	Services might not start.
Do not change any file, folder, or Registry key permissions unless documented.	A high probability exists that Cisco CallManager will not function.
Do not set the CMOS power-on password.	The server will not boot after power failure until the password is entered.
Do not delete, disable, or rename the IUSR_Guest or IWAM_Guest accounts.	Some IIS virtual directories require them.
Do not disable parent paths in IIS.	Some Cisco CallManager web pages will no longer work.
Do not remove the IIS application mappings for .asp, .cer, .cdx, and .asa.	Some Cisco CallManager web pages will no longer work.
Do not install unapproved third-party software, utilities, or agents.	Issues with Cisco support arise.

In addition to the security settings never to be implemented, Cisco also lists a few security settings that are not recommended. Table 20-3 describes these settings.

Table 20-3 *Not Recommended Windows Security Settings*

Security Setting	Reason It Is Not Recommended
Join an Active Directory domain	Role-based administrator not supported Complexity of Active Directory group policies (too many possible permutations)
Shutdown if Unable to Write Security Log	Not ideal for a strategic application

continues

Table 20-3 *Not Recommended Windows Security Settings (Continued)*

Security Setting	Reason It Is Not Recommended
Disable crash control	Disabling Dr. Watson crash dumps adds complexity to forensic troubleshooting
Convert disk D from FAT to NTFS	Same server recovery will not work
Clear page file at reboot	Reboots can take 30 minutes or longer
Account lockout after N failed login attempts	Disables low-level service accounts

NOTE Cisco CallManager Release 4.x uses the following service accounts: CCMCDR, CCMService, CCMServiceRW, CCMUser, and SQLSvc.

CAUTION If the Cisco CallManager is integrated into the Microsoft Active Directory, the installation will lose its Cisco TAC support.

Summary

This chapter covered the security concepts and protection of the foundation Cisco CallManager operating system. There are many security threats targeting Microsoft Windows operating systems. Because of this, Cisco has modified the default Windows 2000 security settings and released their own Cisco IP Telephony Operating System, prehardened against many common attacks and intrusions. To enhance this security, you should consider using the optional security scripts located on the CallManager hard drive. Adding approved antivirus protection software can prevent intrusion by viruses, worms, and Trojan horses.

Cisco also provides a free, standalone version of their Cisco Security Agent, preconfigured for a CallManager installation. Installing this can protect the server from network intrusions, software modifications, and DoS attacks.

In addition to all these security supplicants, you should also consider using complex passwords and account policies for all administrative and auditing accounts. However, you should not rename accounts or modify passwords of services related to the Cisco CallManager. Cisco also has a list of security taboos that should be avoided on the Cisco CallManager to ensure you do not invalidate your TAC support contracts.

Review Questions

You can find the solutions to these questions in Appendix A, "Answers to Review Questions."

1. When are critical hot fixes and patches to the Cisco IP Telephony Operating System posted on Cisco.com for download?
   a. 24 hours after the announcement from Microsoft
   b. Monthly in a consolidated security release
   c. With the next operating system upgrade
   d. These should be downloaded from Microsoft as soon as they appear.
2. Which feature should not be enabled when using antivirus protection software?
   a. Full-scan
   b. Heuristic scan
   c. E-mail scan
   d. Pagefile scan
3. Which Cisco-provided software tool protects Cisco CallManager against malicious applications?
   a. CDR
   b. CER
   c. CSA
   d. CRM
4. Which parameter has to be set on all service accounts?
   a. Complex password requirement
   b. Minimum password length of six characters
   c. Password never expires
   d. Enforce password history
5. What Microsoft service is most commonly attacked?
   a. DNS service
   b. DHCP service
   c. IIS service
   d. Active Directory service

6. Which setting on the Cisco IP Telephony Operating System is supported on the CallManager platform but not recommended by Cisco?
   a. Delete the IUSER_Guest account
   b. Delete SQL service accounts
   c. Install third-party utilities
   d. Disable Dr. Watson
7. What automated method does Cisco support for security updates and hot fixes to the CallManager server?
   a. Receiving e-mail updates from the Cisco CallManager Notification Tool
   b. Downloading updates directly from Microsoft using the Windows Update Services
   c. Using the CSA standalone automatic update feature
   d. Downloading updates directly from Cisco using the automated Cisco Update Services
8. Which of the following files represent an automated security script that will add additional Cisco approved security to the CallManager server? (Choose two.)
   a. CCM-OS-OptionalSecurity.cmd
   b. CSA_SecurityScript.cmd
   c. IPSec-W2KSQL.cmd
   d. SecurityTemplace_CCM4xx.cmd
9. Which of the following antivirus platforms is NOT supported by Cisco for installation on a Cisco CallManager platform?
   a. McAfee VirusScan Enterprise
   b. Symantec AntiVirus Corporate Edition
   c. Trend Micro ServerProtect
   d. WebX SecureServer
10. Which of the following does the headless CSA protect against? (Choose two.)
    a. Operating system file integrity
    b. Restriction of network-aware, locally installed applications to local resources
    c. Protection against virus infection
    d. Protects against preconfigured inbound network connections to the CallManager server

This chapter covers the following topics:

- Explaining the threats targeting remote Cisco CallManager Administration and other applications
- Explaining how HTTPS provides secure remote communication and logins to Cisco CallManager Administration
- Describing HTTPS certificate details, using Microsoft IIS to save a certificate to a trusted folder, and copying the certificate to a file
- Describing how MLA provides multiple levels of security to Cisco CallManager Administration
- Enabling MLA and assigning a password to the superuser
- Defining a functional group and identifying the two types of functional groups
- Defining a user group and identifying how its privileges are mapped to functional groups
- Creating a new functional group and a new user group and assigning an access privilege level to the members of the user group

CHAPTER 21

Securing Cisco Unified CallManager Administration

By securing communication with the Cisco CallManager using Secure HTTP (HTTPS), a hacker cannot listen to the data stream during HTTP sessions. In addition, in large voice environments, it is important to distribute the various administration tasks. Cisco CallManager Multilevel Administration Access allows you to assign different authorization levels to administrators. This chapter discusses both the concepts and configuration of HTTPS and MLA on your Cisco CallManager servers.

Threats Targeting Remote Administration

In releases earlier than Cisco CallManager Release 4.1, HTTP is the standard protocol for accessing the Cisco CallManager Administration web pages. If an attacker intercepts the connection and looks for the username and password of the administrator, the attacker can find the relevant information easily because CallManager does not encrypt the connection. Beginning with Cisco CallManager Release 4.1, HTTPS (RFC 2818) is the standard protocol for accessing the Cisco CallManager Administration pages, without installing or configuring any additional security parameters.

To add to the security woes, the default Cisco CallManager Administrator account is the same as the Microsoft Windows Administrator account. If a hacker learned this login information, the hacker could not only access the Cisco CallManager Administration pages, but could also log in to the operating system of the Cisco CallManager server with full access to all information. To address this issue, Cisco has added Multilevel Administration Access (MLA), giving CallManager an alternate user database to manage administrative privileges.

Securing CallManager Communications Using HTTPS

HTTPS secures communication between the browser on the client PC and a web server. It allows authentication of the web server (to ensure the client is not accessing an impersonating website) and protects communication between the client and the web server. All packets are signed to provide integrity, so that the receiver has a guarantee that the packets are authentic and have not been modified during transit. In addition, all packets are encrypted to provide privacy, so that sensitive information can be sent over untrusted networks. These Cisco CallManager applications support HTTPS:

- Cisco CallManager Administration
- Cisco CallManager Serviceability
- Cisco IP Phone User Options web pages
- Bulk Administration Tool (BAT)
- Tool for Auto-Registered Phones Support (TAPS)
- Cisco Call Detail Record (CDR) Analysis and Reporting (CAR)
- Trace Collection Tool
- Real-Time Monitoring Tool (RTMT)

When you are using HTTPS for browsing to Cisco CallManager Administration and user options web pages, communication is secure. A hacker who sniffs the communication will find it very difficult to re-create any information from the sniffed packets.

HTTPS secures not only the username and passwords in the communication, but also configuration changes in Cisco CallManager Administration and other applications, such as Cisco CallManager Serviceability. If a user configures parameters such as call forwarding or speed dials on the user options web pages, the client and IIS communicate in a secure way.

HTTPS Certificates

HTTPS uses certificates for web server authentication. Certificates provide information about a device and are signed by an issuer, the Certificate Authority (CA). By default, Cisco CallManager uses a self-signed certificate, but it also allows you to use a certificate issued by a company CA or even an external CA such as VeriSign. The file where the Cisco CallManager HTTPS certificate is stored is C:\Program Files\Cisco\Certificates\httpscert.cer.

> **TIP** A self-signed certificate provides the same functions as a certificate issued by a recognized CA. The only problem that occurs with a self-signed certificate is that client web browsers issue warning or caution messages the first time they access the secured website. For internal and intranet server use, this should not cause any major problems.

The certificate will be used on the IIS default website that hosts the Cisco CallManager virtual directories, which include the following:

- CCMAdmin and CCMUser
- CCMService
- Administration Serviceability Tool (AST)
- BAT and TAPS
- RTMTReports
- CCMTraceAnalysis
- PktCap
- Administrator Reporting Tool (ART)
- CCMServiceTraceCollectionTool

To use a certificate issued by a CA after a Cisco CallManager installation or upgrade, delete the self-signed certificate and install the CA signed certificate instead.

NOTE For more information on how to obtain a certificate from an external CA, contact a vendor of Internet certificates such as VeriSign or consult with the administrator of your company CA (if using your own CA).

Accessing CallManager When Using Self-Signed Certificates

The first time that a user accesses Cisco CallManager Administration or other Cisco CallManager applications after the Cisco CallManager Release 4.1 installation or upgrade from a browser client, a Security Alert dialog box (shown in Figure 21-1) asks whether the user trusts the server. When the dialog box appears, clicking the buttons results in these actions:

- **Yes**—Trust the certificate for the current web session only. The Security Alert dialog box will display each time you access the application.
- **No**—Cancel the action. No authentication occurs, and the user cannot access the Cisco CallManager Administration pages.
- **View Certificate**—Start certificate installation tasks, so that the certificate is always trusted. After you install the certificate, the Security Alert dialog box no longer appears when you access the Cisco CallManager Administration pages.

Figure 21-1 *Self-Signed Certificate Security Alert*

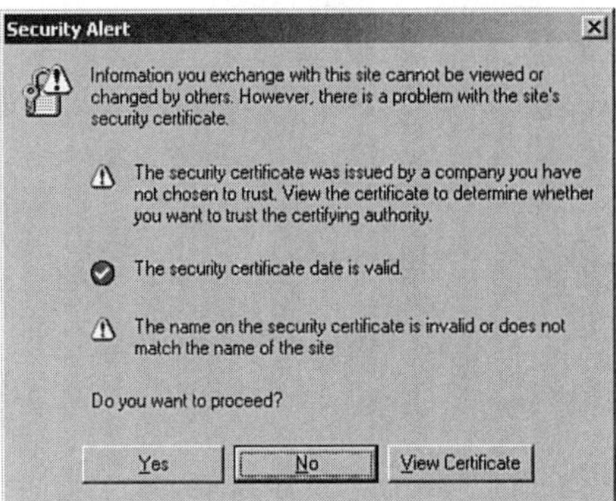

Click the **View Certificate** button. The Security Alert dialog box appears and the Certificate window opens, shown in Figure 21-2. The **General** tab shows brief information about the certificate, such as the issuer and the validation. For more detailed information, click the **Details** tab. Another way to get information about the certificate is to check the certificate directly on the Cisco CallManager. On the Cisco CallManager publisher, right-click the certificate name in C:\Program Files\Cisco\Certificates\httpscert.cer and choose **Open**. It is not possible to change any data in the certificate.

Figure 21-2 *Viewing the SSL Certificate*

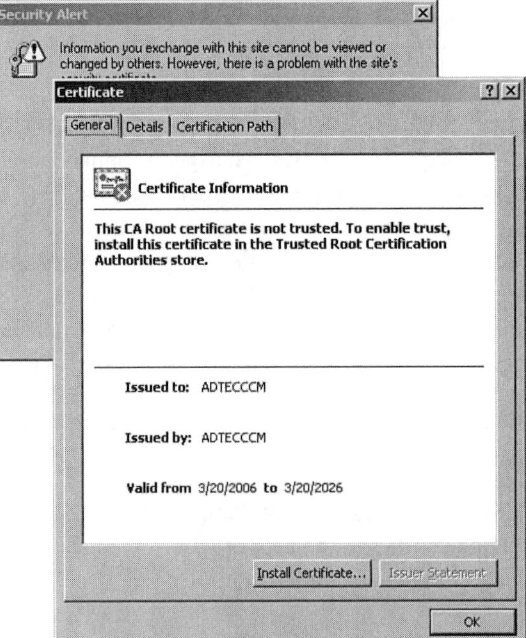

To keep from seeing the security warning each time you navigate to the Cisco CallManager server, click the **Install Certificate** button. By walking through the Microsoft Windows Certificate Import Wizard, you will import the CallManager self-signed certificate into your local certificate store. This keeps Microsoft Internet Explorer from prompting you with a security warning each time you access the CallManager Administration interface.

Multilevel Administration

Prior to the availability of MLA, there was only one administrator login. Administrators had full read and write access to Cisco CallManager configuration. An administrator could change any parameter in the database or directory that is accessible through the Cisco CallManager Administration and Cisco CallManager Serviceability pages. The entire system could be disabled with a few mouse clicks that accidentally modified data to which the user did not need access.

MLA provides multiple levels of security to Cisco CallManager Administration. Cisco CallManager menus are grouped in functional groups. Users are grouped in user groups. MLA permits you to grant only the privileges required to a selected group of users and to limit access to the configuration menu for a particular user group.

Different access levels can be assigned to each functional group, such as no access, read-only access, and full access. The access rights can be set for every configured user group. MLA also provides audit logs of user logins and access to and modifications to Cisco CallManager configuration data.

Before installing MLA, Cisco CallManager administrators logged in using a local Windows 2000 Administrator account. After you have enabled MLA, usernames and passwords are stored in a Lightweight Directory Access Protocol (LDAP) directory and provide the basis for login authentication.

During enabling, MLA creates a predefined user called CCMAdministrator. The Windows Registry stores the user ID and the encrypted password of the CCMAdministrator user. Thus, even when the LDAP directory is unavailable, the CCMAdministrator user can log in to Cisco CallManager Administration. Only the CCMAdministrator ID and password are stored in the Windows Registry.

MLA was introduced with the Cisco CallManager Release 3.2(2c) and had to be separately installed. With Cisco CallManager Release 4.0 and later, MLA is integrated in Cisco CallManager but disabled by default.

> **NOTE** If you are upgrading from an earlier version of Cisco CallManager to Cisco CallManager release 4.0 or later and already have MLA installed and enabled, CallManager migrates your existing MLA configuration to the new MLA version and keeps it enabled. However, the upgrade process resets the existing CCMAdministrator password to a random password (displayed at the end of the upgrade).

Enabling MLA

The Enable MultiLevelAdmin enterprise parameter designates whether MLA is enabled. This enterprise parameter can be found in the Cisco CallManager menu **User > Access Rights > Configure MLA Parameters**, shown in Figure 21-3. You can set the Enable MultiLevelAdmin parameter to True (enabled) or False (disabled); False is the default value.

Figure 21-3 *Enabling MLA*

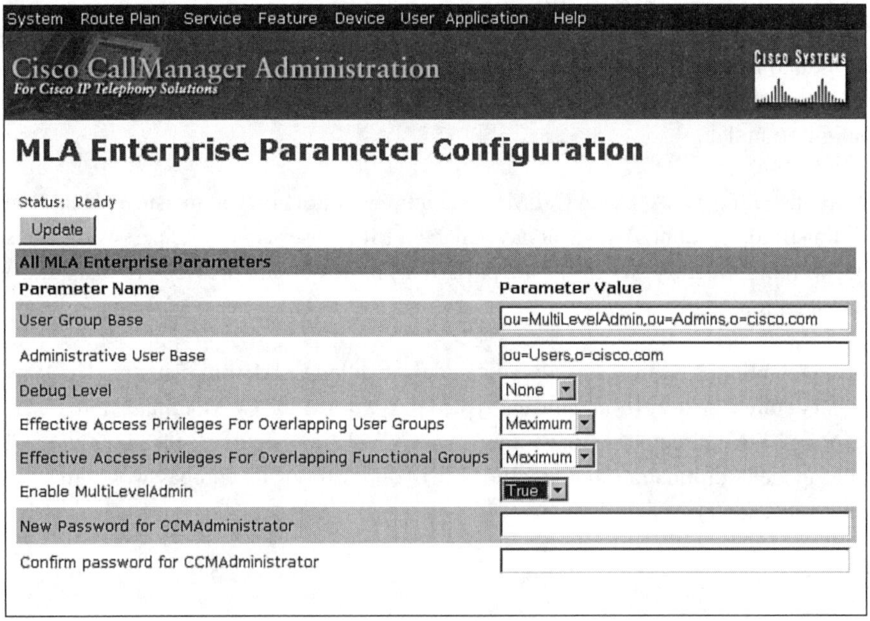

When you choose True, enter a new password at the New Password for CCMAdministrator prompt and reenter the password at the Confirm Password for CCMAdministrator prompt. Only the CCMAdministrator user can now log in to Cisco CallManager; the Windows NT Administrator account no longer has access rights to Cisco CallManager Administration.

When the Enable MultiLevelAdmin enterprise parameter value is modified, the World Wide Web Publishing Service has to be restarted. Then, reopen the browser and reauthenticate with Cisco CallManager by using the new CCMAdministrator account.

MLA Functional Groups

Cisco MLA uses two group management functions: user groups and functional groups. A user group simply contains user accounts. A functional group consists of a collection of Cisco CallManager system administration submenus. All the web pages that compose each functional group belong to a common administrative menu. Two types of functional groups exist:

- Standard functional groups, which are the default functional groups
- Custom-based functional groups

Standard functional groups are created as a part of MLA during Cisco CallManager installation and cannot be modified or deleted. They contain typical permissions assigned to sublevel Cisco CallManager administrators. You can define your own custom-based functional groups to allow a group of administrators access to specific Cisco CallManager Administration menus.

When you enable Cisco CallManager MLA, a complete set of standard functional groups becomes available (shown in Figure 21-4):

- Standard Plugin
- Standard User Privilege Management
- Standard User Management
- Standard Feature
- Standard System
- Standard Service Management
- Standard Service
- Standard Serviceability
- Standard Gateway
- Standard RoutePlan
- Standard Phone

Figure 21-4 *Built-In MLA Functional Groups*

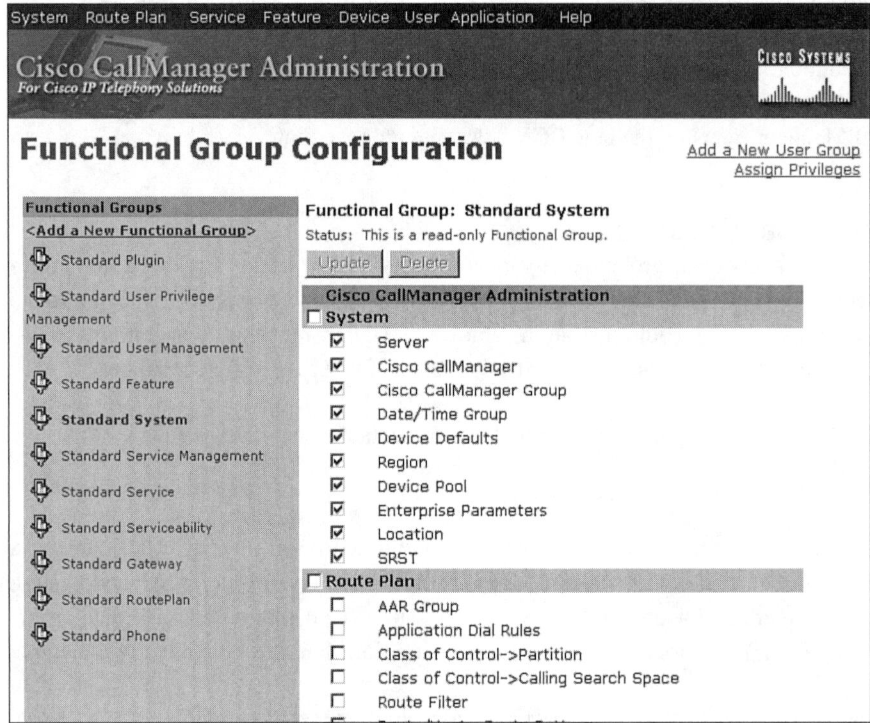

> **CAUTION** In the Standard System functional group, all submenus of the Cisco CallManager System menu, such as Server, Cisco CallManager, Cisco CallManager Group, and so on, are enabled. A user with full access rights in the Standard System functional group could, for example, change the IP address of the server. Be careful when you assign access rights to the fundamental Cisco CallManager menus.

MLA User Groups

Various user groups are predefined and have no members assigned when you enable MLA. The CCMAdministrator user can add users to these groups, set the access rights for the user groups, and configure additional named user groups as needed. To add users, select the relevant user group and click the **Add a User to Group** hyperlink in the upper-right corner of the administration window.

These user groups are created at the time of installation (shown in Figure 21-5):

- PhoneAdministration
- ReadOnly
- ServerMonitoring
- SuperUserGroup
- ServerMaintenance
- GatewayAdministration

Figure 21-5 *Built-In MLA User Groups*

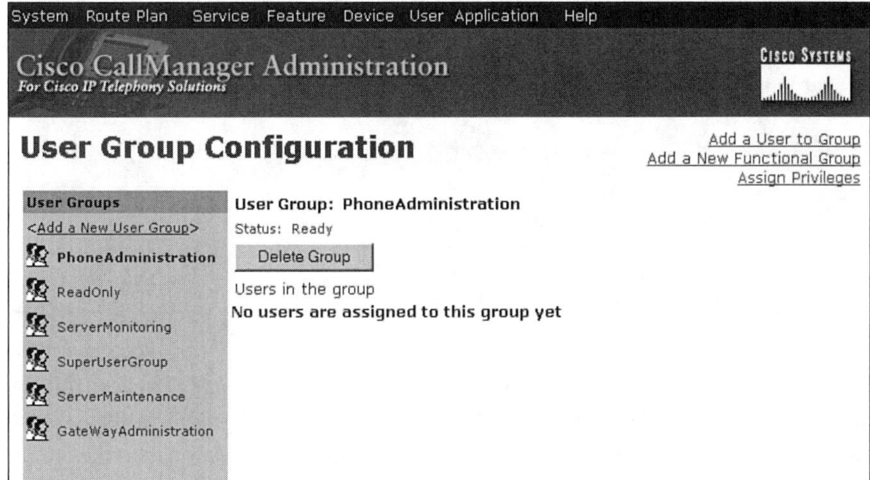

Assigning MLA Access Privileges

After users are added to a user group, access privileges are then set for each functional group. The functional group defines the Cisco CallManager menus that can be used by the relevant user group.

Figure 21-6 shows the items in the CallManager Administration Device menu that are enabled for the Standard Phone functional group.

Figure 21-6 *Device Menu Access for the Standard Phone Functional Group*

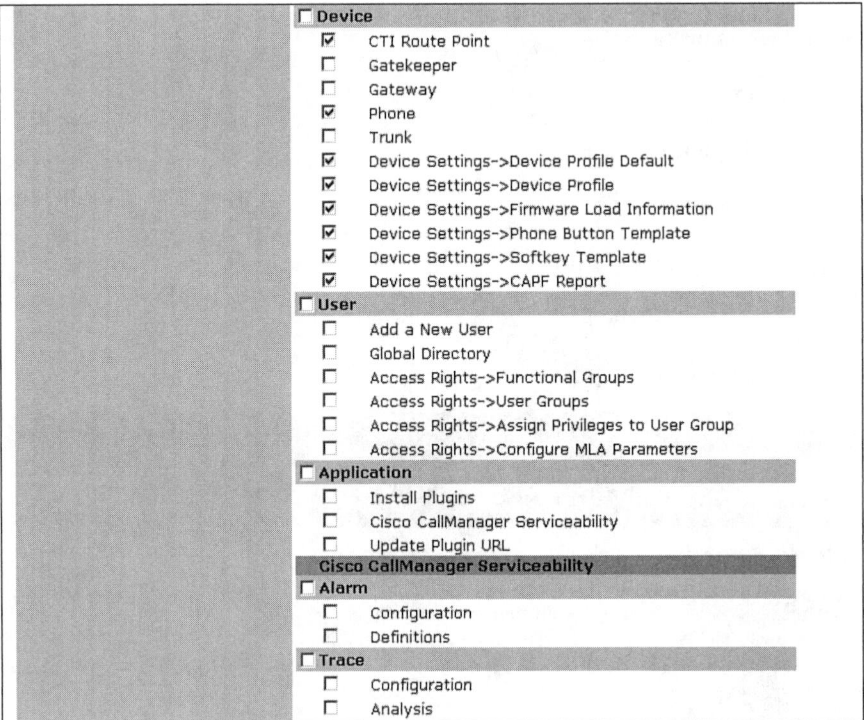

As shown in Figure 21-7, the PhoneAdministration user group has full access rights to the Standard Phone and the Standard User Management functional groups. This means that a user assigned to the PhoneAdministration user group can add, change, or delete the configuration of the computer telephony integration (CTI) points and phones. A user in the PhoneAdministration user group can also access all Device Settings submenus.

Creating New MLA Functional and User Groups

Cisco CallManager allows you to configure MLA groups outside the built-in defaults to provide custom administration functions for your organization. For example, imagine you had a sublevel administrator who should only have rights to change the music on hold preferences for your users. To configure a custom administrative level for this administrator, you could follow these general steps:

Step 1 Create a new functional group and assign privileges.

Step 2 Create a new user group and assign privileges.

Step 3 Verify proper operation.

Figure 21-7 *Assigning Rights to User Groups*

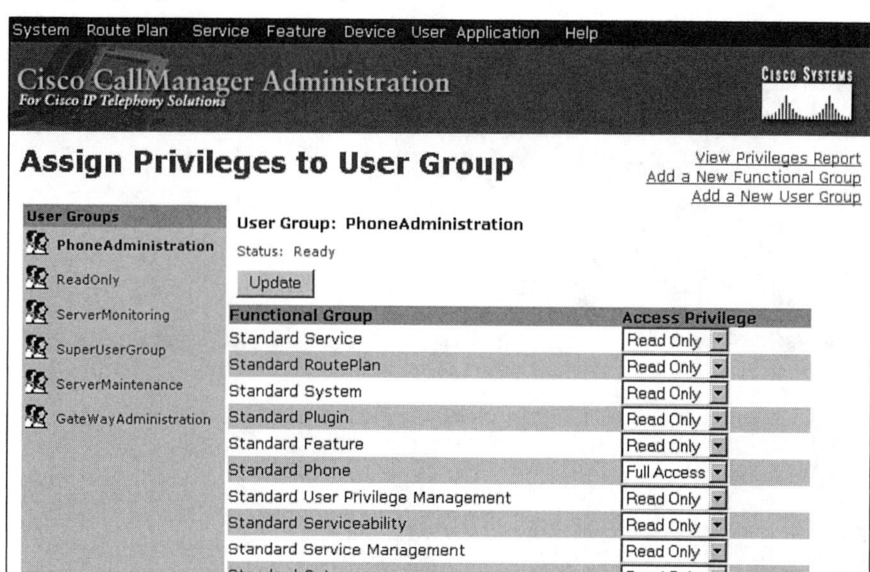

Initially, you would need to create a new functional group for the subadministrator defining the areas of the CallManager Administration to which they have access. You could follow this procedure to add a new functional group:

Step 1 Choose **User > Access Rights > Functional Group**, and click **Add a New Functional Group**.

Step 2 In the **Functional Group Name** field, enter the name of a new functional group (in this example, Music Only, shown in Figure 21-8).

Figure 21-8 *Adding a New Functional Group*

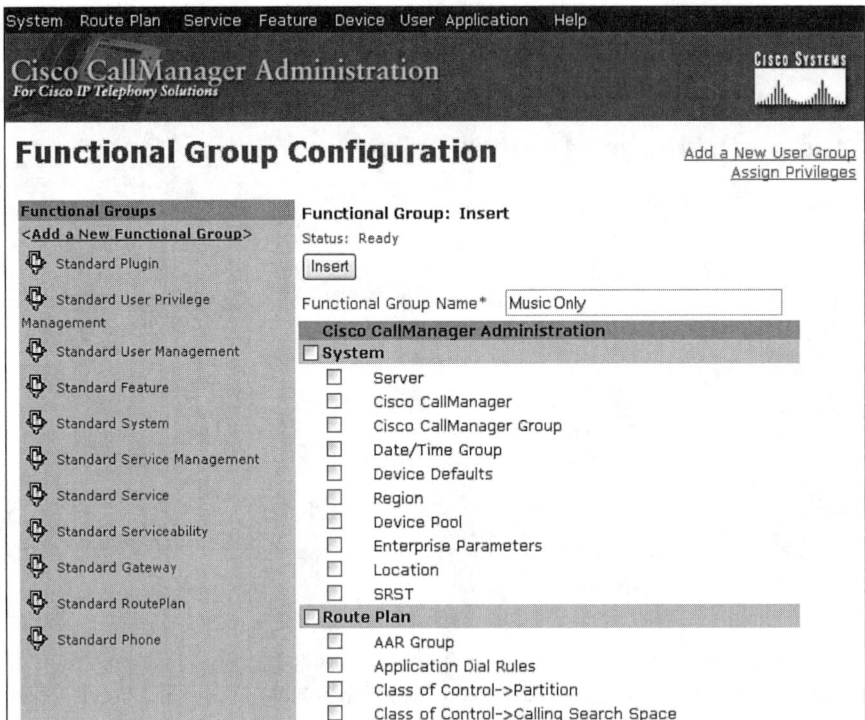

Step 3 Check the check box next to the menu that you want to include in the new functional group. In this example, check only the **Media Resource->Music on Hold Audio Source** check box under Service, as shown in Figure 21-9, and click **Insert**. Figure 21-9 results from scrolling down near the bottom of the screen shown in Figure 21-8.

Figure 21-9 *Assigning Functional Group Menus*

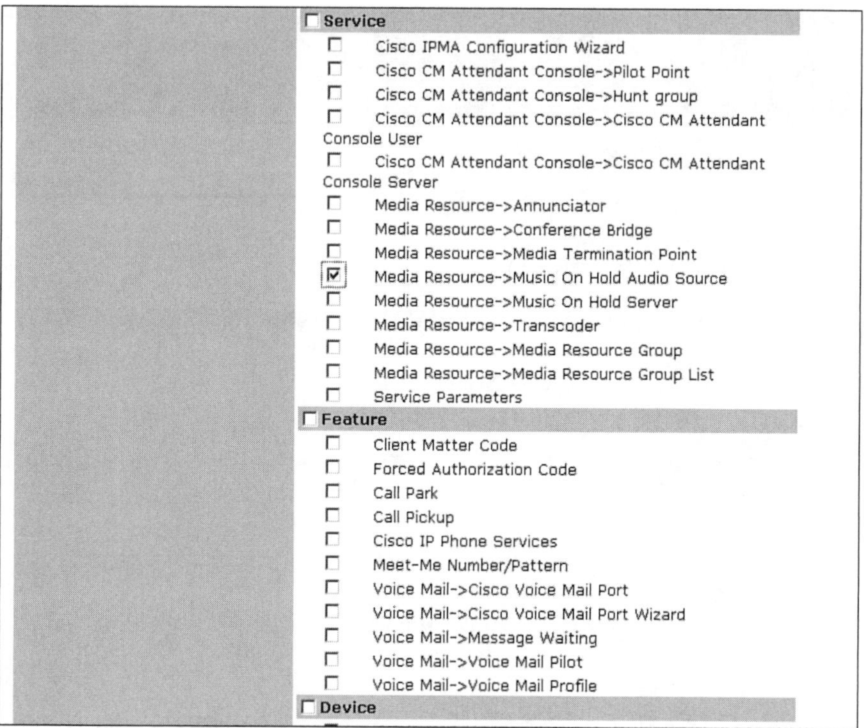

After you have added the functional group to the configuration, you can create a user group for the administrator and assign the necessary functional group privileges. To create the user group, complete the following steps:

Step 1 Choose **User > Access Rights > User Group**, and click **Add a New User Group**.

Step 2 In the **User Group Name** field, enter the name of the new user group (in this example, MusicDJ), and click **Insert**.

Step 3 Click **Add a User to Group,** and enter the username (which must already have been configured in Cisco CallManager Administration). In this example, the user JeremyD was chosen from the directory, shown in Figure 21-10.

Figure 21-10 *Adding a New User Group*

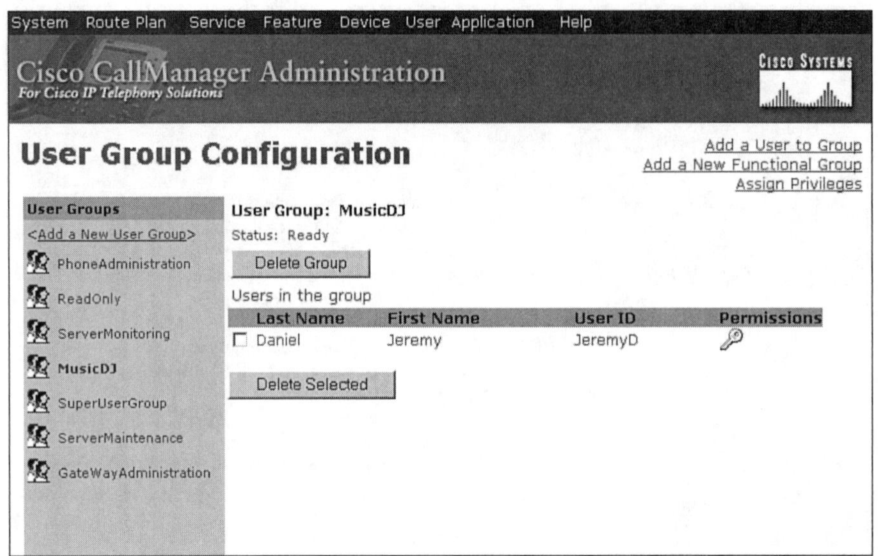

Now that you have created the user group, you can assign the necessary privileges to the music administrator:

Step 1 Choose **User > Access Rights > Assigning Privileges to User Group.**

Step 2 Click the name of the user group to which you want to assign privileges. In this case, the MusicDJ user group is chosen.

Step 3 Choose the privilege level for each functional group within the user group. Three privilege levels are available from the drop-down list: **No Access**, **Read Only**, and **Full Access**. In this case, the MusicDJ user group is assigned **Full Access** for the functional group Music Only (shown in Figure 21-11). After you have selected the necessary permissions for the functional groups, click **Update**.

Figure 21-11 *Assigning User Group Permissions*

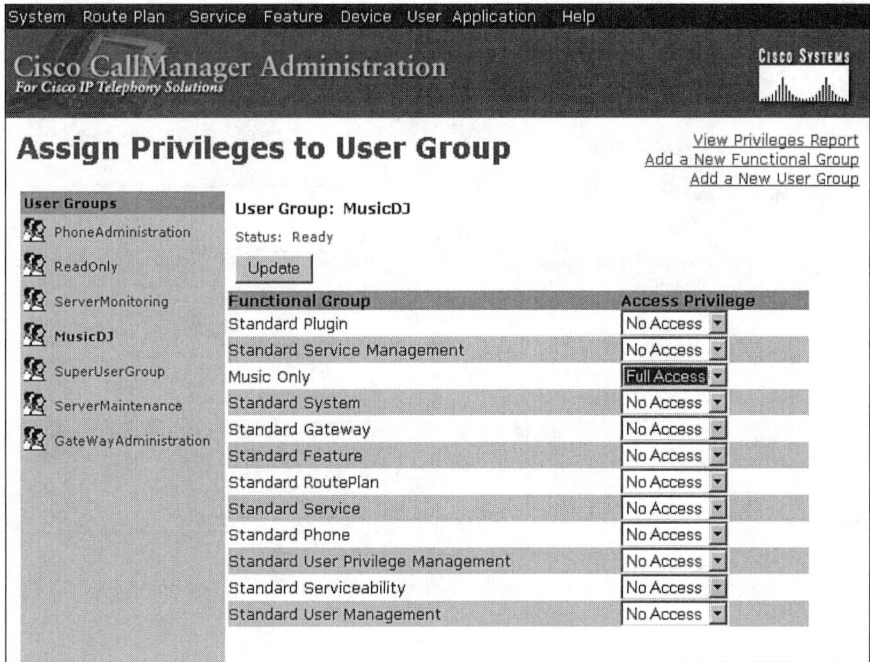

Finally, the last step in this configuration is to verify and test the privileges. To verify whether a specific user has the correct access rights, click the **Key** symbol in the Permission column in the User Group Configuration window. In Figure 21-12, the user JeremyD was chosen, and, therefore, the MusicDJ user group is displayed with the configured access rights. The privileges report shows that JeremyD has no access to any functional group except the Music Only group, to which he has full access.

Figure 21-12 *Verifying User Permissions*

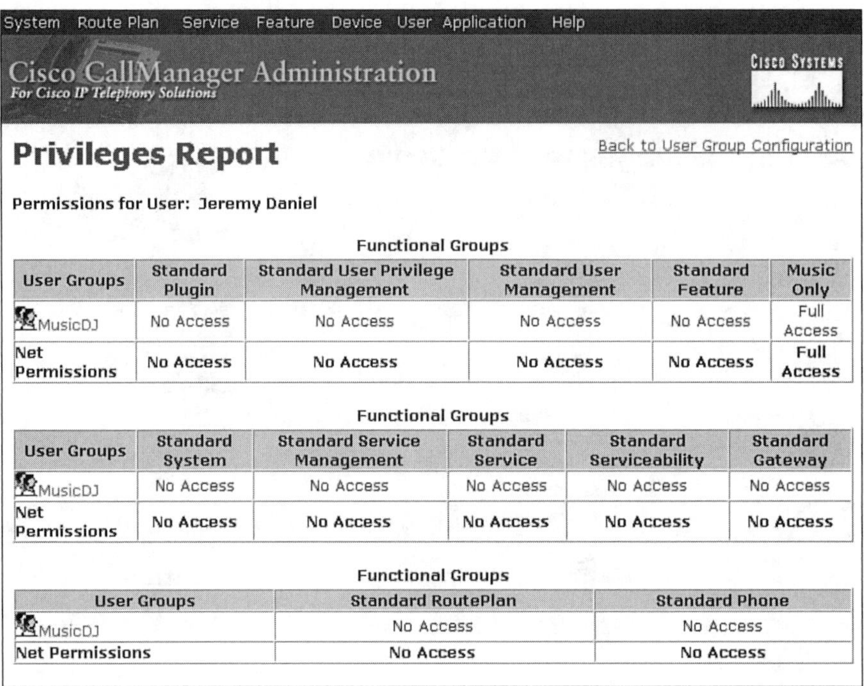

To test the privileges, you can log in using a user account assigned to the specific user group you want to test. After logging in, attempt to access allowed and disallowed areas of the CallManager Administration. Disallowed pages will appear as shown in Figure 21-13. Allowed pages will function normally, unless you have assigned them Read-Only access.

Figure 21-13 *Testing User Permissions*

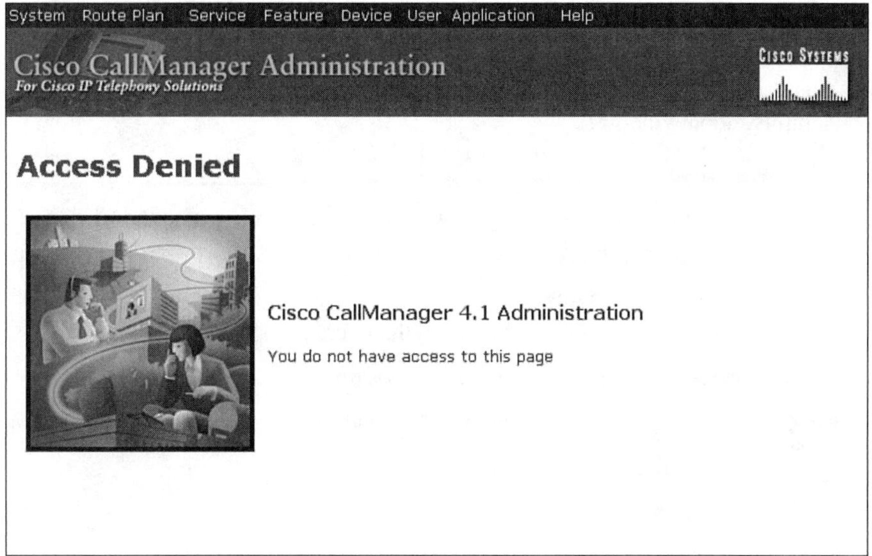

Summary

This chapter covered the security concepts and protection of the Cisco CallManager Administration web pages. In CallManager versions earlier than 4.1, HTTP was the rule for administration access. This could open the CallManager servers to packet sniffing attacks. HTTPS secures the connection between the browser and IIS. With CallManager releases 4.1 and later, the server uses a self-signed certificate, which protects communication, but can cause warning messages in client web browsers.

To increase the administrative security of the system, Cisco has released the Multilevel Administration Access (MLA) utility for Cisco CallManager 3.2 and later. MLA allows you to give users different access rights for Cisco CallManager Administration. Upon enabling MLA, the old Windows 2000 Administrator account will be disabled from CallManager access. Standard MLA functional groups are created with the MLA installation and can be supplemented by custom functional groups. User groups unite access privileges to functional groups.

Review Questions

You can find the solutions to these questions in Appendix A, "Answers to Review Questions."

1. What is the danger when browsing unsecured and without MLA to the Cisco CallManager Administration window?
   a. There is no risk.
   b. With a sniffed username and password, a hacker can log in to the Cisco CallManager Administration window only.
   c. With a sniffed username and password, a hacker can log in to the Cisco CallManager Administration window as well as to the operating system.
   d. The hacker can only listen to the conversation.
2. How do you browse securely to the CallManager Administration window?
   a. http://CM-IP/SecureCCMAdmin
   b. https://CM-IP/CCMAdmin
   c. https://CM-IP/TTL/CCMAdmin
   d. https://CM-IP/SSL/CCMAdmin
3. Which of the following is not a valid access level in MLA?
   a. No access
   b. Read-only
   c. Read-write
   d. Full access
4. After you enable MLA, what is the new administrator account?
   a. MLAAdministrator
   b. Administrator
   c. Windows NT Administrator account
   d. CCMAdministrator
5. Which functional group is not a default group?
   a. Standard Device
   b. Standard Service
   c. Standard Gateway
   d. Standard Plugin
   e. Standard RoutePlan

6. Which user group is not a default group?

   a. PhoneAdministration

   b. FullAccess

   c. SuperUserGroup

   d. GatewayAdministration

   e. ServerMaintenance

7. By default, client web browsers using HTTPS-secured administration will receive warning messages. Why do these warning messages exist?

   a. Because the Cisco CallManager uses 40-bit encryption

   b. Because the Cisco CallManager uses a self-signed certificate

   c. Because the Cisco CallManager uses weak encryption

   d. Because there is a name conflict on the certificate

8. Where are the normal user accounts for MLA stored?

   a. LDAP Directory

   b. A local file

   c. CallManager Administration

   d. The Windows Registry

9. Where is the CCMAdministrator user account for MLA stored?

   a. LDAP Directory

   b. A local file

   c. CallManager Administration

   d. The Windows Registry

10. What is the default state of Cisco MLA? (Choose two.)

    a. Disabled for a clean CallManager install

    b. Enabled for a clean CallManager install

    c. Enabled if upgrading from a previous MLA version that was enabled

    d. Disabled if upgrading from a previous MLA version that was enabled

This chapter covers the following topics:

- Explaining how legitimate devices can be exploited for fraudulent use of the IP PBX system to make toll calls
- Using partitions and calling search spaces, restricting call forwarding based on user classes, and restricting voice-mail transfers to internal destinations
- Explaining the usage of blocking commonly exploited area codes
- Configuring Cisco CallManager to route calls to different locations based on the time of day when a call is made
- Designing and implementing FAC to require user authorization for different classes of calls
- Providing external call transfer blocking by setting service parameters and configuring gateways, trunks, and route patterns as OffNet devices
- Configuring Cisco CallManager Administration to drop a conference call when the conference creator leaves the call or when the last OnNet party leaves

CHAPTER 22

Preventing Toll Fraud

Business consumers have more control over their telecommunications services than ever before. New technologies provide more information and more flexibility in how businesses use their telecommunications services. Unfortunately, the shift in control has made businesses and telephone companies more susceptible to toll fraud and led to an increase in fraud. This chapter discusses ways to prevent toll fraud in a company.

Toll Fraud Exploits

A company telephony system can be subject to toll fraud by company employees or by external people who try to find vulnerabilities in the system. The first group, employees, simply ignores policies, hoping that their activities will not be detected because it is difficult to differentiate between business calls and private calls based on the dialed number. The other group of people, the external callers, is more technically oriented. They try to find vulnerabilities in network devices, including IP telephony systems. Sometimes, they do not even specifically look for voice systems; they just exploit whatever system over which they can get control.

The main difference between these two groups is the way in which you can mitigate the "attack." In the case of external attackers, the key is to prevent unauthorized access to the system and its devices. For authorized users of the system, the administrator has to very carefully limit the technical abilities and features of the system without compromising the flexibility and efficiency of its users.

There are also some features in a telephony system that can be misused. These include call forward and call transfer settings and voice-mail transfer options. If the features that are commonly used for toll fraud are well protected, users might try to exploit the system using other features. As an example, if a user is not allowed to transfer an external call to another external destination, the user could try to set up a conference call for these two parties and then leave the conference.

Usually, an administrator has to accept the fact that toll fraud cannot be eliminated completely. The only way to achieve complete elimination would be to block all external calls and disable all features that would allow employees to place calls outside the company. This technique might be feasible for single-function telephones, such as public telephones located in a lobby, but is not desirable for telephones used by standard employees. Therefore, only those calls that can be clearly identified as nonbusiness calls will be blocked. However, in many cases, you cannot judge in advance whether the call being placed is business-related or private.

Figure 22-1 shows different types of toll fraud.

Figure 22-1 *Forms of Toll Fraud*

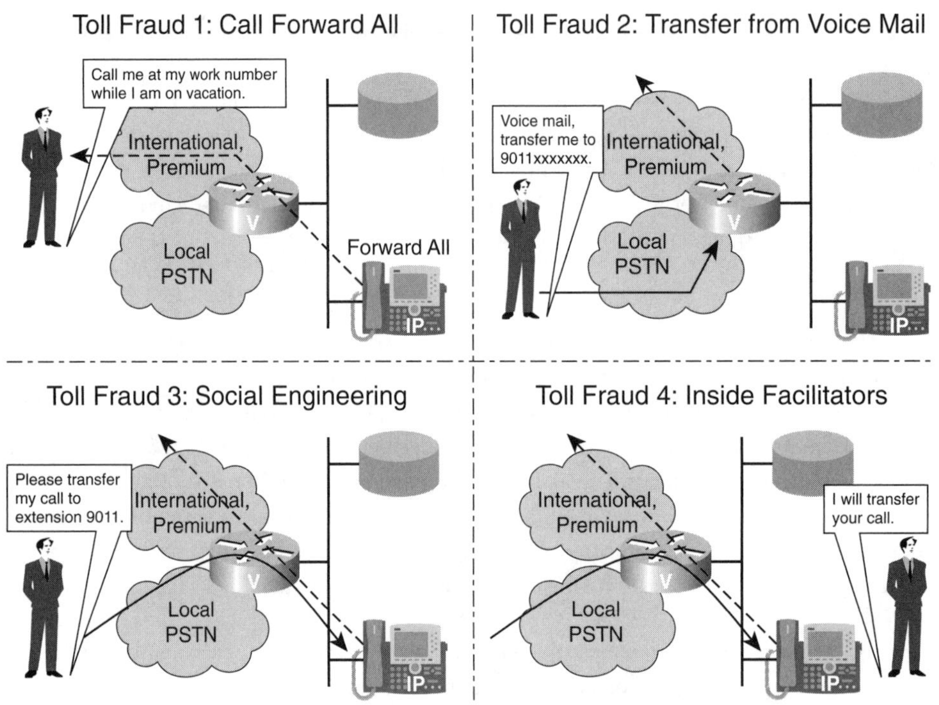

The following list explains these types of toll fraud:

- **Call Forward All (CFA)**—The first example describes a scenario in which an employee forwards the office number to, for example, an international or mobile number. This employee then tells friends to call the office number. The call is forwarded to the number that the employee specified, making the company pay the costs of the calls.

- **Transfer from voice mail**—The second toll fraud example shows an attacker making an external call to the voice-mail system, which forwards the call to an international premium destination. The attacker is billed only for a local call, whereas the company, from which the call is forwarded, pays for the international call.
- **Social engineering**—The third example shows a scenario in which an attacker calls from outside the company and uses social engineering tricks (for instance, pretending to be an employee working from home) to be transferred to an external number, such as 9011. The 011 prefix (plus 9 being the typical number dialed in corporations for outside dial tone) is used in the United States to place international calls. This attacker is also charged only for a local call, whereas the company again pays for the connection to an international telephone number.
- **Inside facilitators**—The fourth example is very similar to the third one. But in this case, an employee inside the company transfers the external call to another external number. In this case, the toll fraud has an internal source.

Preventing Call Forward and Voice-Mail Toll Fraud Using Calling Search Spaces

Call Forward All (CFA) is a feature in Cisco CallManager that allows an internal number (for example, an employee office number) to be forwarded to an external number (for example, an international number, mobile number, or premium number). For example, an employee can call the office number, which is then forwarded to the number specified in the forwarding field. This number can be an international or premium number. The user can configure the setting using the web interface, so the forwarding configuration can be set up and removed very easily from home or elsewhere. CFA exploits can be avoided by applying a calling search space to the CFA feature. As shown in Figure 22-2, the administrator has applied a calling search space named IntLocCSS (which allows only internal and local PSTN calls) to the CFA field.

Figure 22-2 *Restricting Call Forward All*

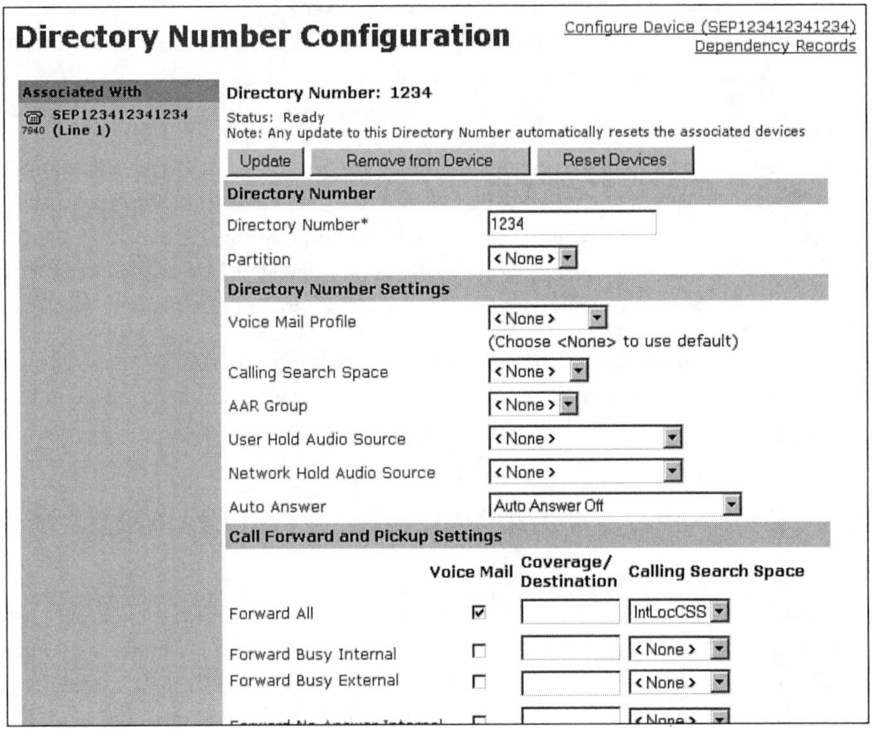

Directory Number Configuration

Configure Device (SEP123412341234)
Dependency Records

Associated With
SEP123412341234
7940 (Line 1)

Directory Number: 1234
Status: Ready
Note: Any update to this Directory Number automatically resets the associated devices

Update | Remove from Device | Reset Devices

Directory Number

Directory Number* 1234
Partition < None >

Directory Number Settings

Voice Mail Profile < None > (Choose <None> to use default)
Calling Search Space < None >
AAR Group < None >
User Hold Audio Source < None >
Network Hold Audio Source < None >
Auto Answer Auto Answer Off

Call Forward and Pickup Settings

	Voice Mail	Coverage/ Destination	Calling Search Space
Forward All	☑		IntLocCSS
Forward Busy Internal	☐		< None >
Forward Busy External	☐		< None >

> **NOTE** The only call forwarding ability available to the user (from either the CCMUser pages or the IP phone) is Call Forward All. By applying the calling search space to only this field, you have effectively restricted user forwarding.

Voice-mail systems, which can transfer a call to an extension, can be misused in a similar way if they are configured to allow transfer of calls when the called party is not available. If such transfers are not limited, a caller could connect to the voice-mail system by a local call and then transfer to the public telephony network (for example, a long-distance number). Voice-mail forwarding exploits can be avoided by applying a calling search space to the voice-mail port in the Cisco CallManager configuration. As shown in Figure 22-3, the administrator has applied the same IntLocCSS calling search space to the voice-mail port.

Figure 22-3 *Restricting Voice-Mail Forwarding*

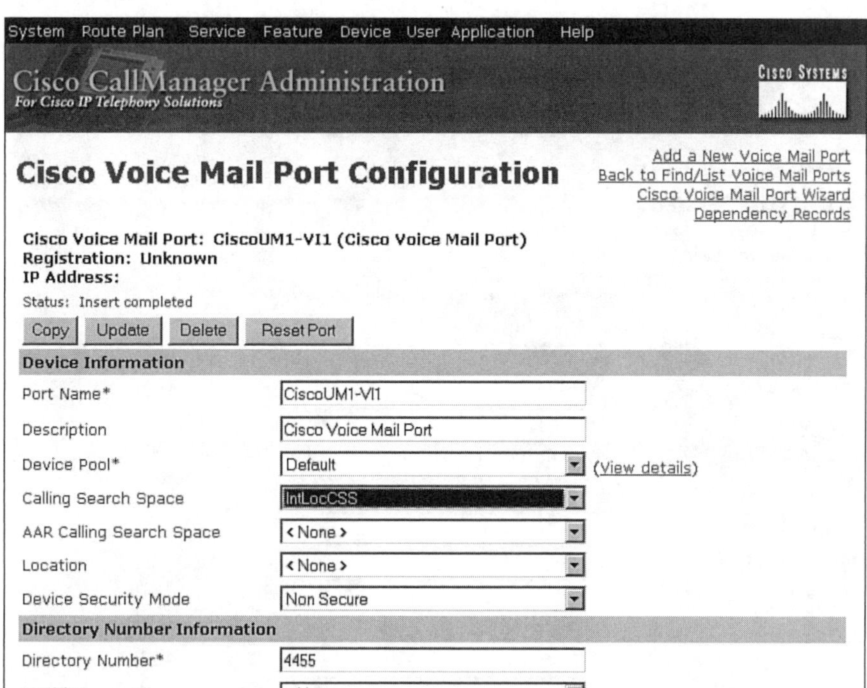

Blocking Commonly Exploited Area Codes

When blocking commonly exploited area codes, create a unique route pattern for each area code that you want to block. You can create different restriction levels; for example, general employees are not allowed to call these numbers, but executives and managers are allowed to. Use different route filters, partitions, and calling search spaces to generate restriction levels. As a general recommendation to prevent toll fraud, you should block as many numbers as possible. For the example shown in Figure 22-4, all calls to the Bahamas are blocked. For each number that you want to block, create a route pattern that explicitly blocks the number. Often, the decision as to whether a number should be blocked or allowed depends on company policies or simply on whether it is necessary to call the number.

Figure 22-4 *Restricting Specific Area Codes*

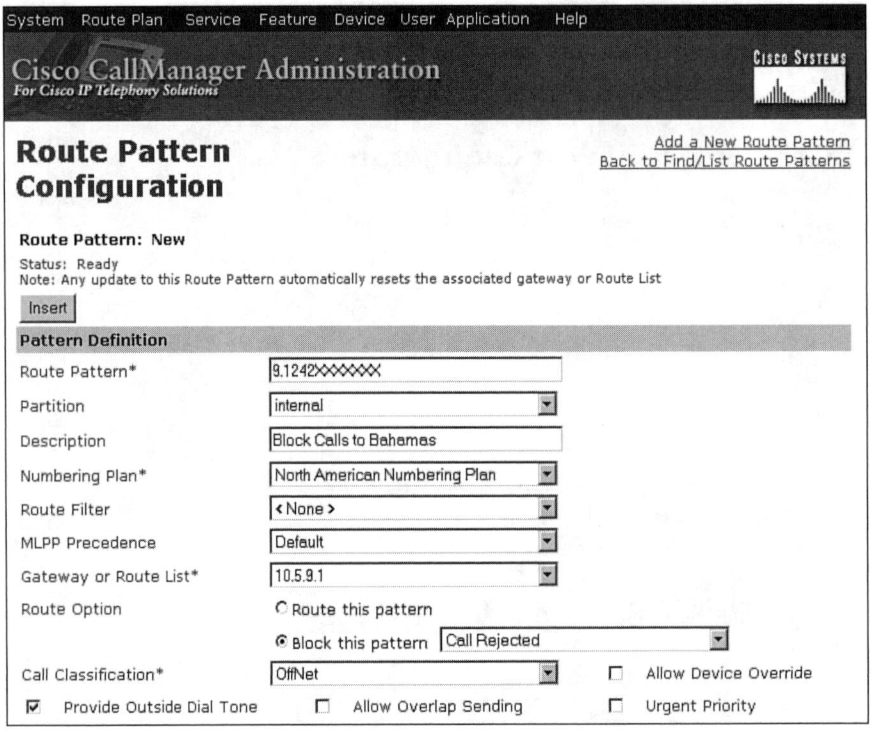

Table 22-1 shows some of the most commonly exploited area codes that you might want to block. It is not an exhaustive list, and some of these area codes might not apply to your organization.

Table 22-1 *Commonly Exploited North American Area Codes*

Country	Area Code	Blocked Cisco CallManager Pattern
Anguilla	264	9.1264xxxxxxx
Antigua/ Barbuda	268	9.1268xxxxxxx
Bahamas	242	9.1242xxxxxxx
Barbados	246	9.1246xxxxxxx
Bermuda	441	9.1441xxxxxxx
British Virgin Islands	284	9.1284xxxxxxx
Cayman Islands	345	9.1345xxxxxxx
Dominica	767	9.1767xxxxxxx
Dominican Republic	809	9.1809xxxxxxx

Table 22-1 *Commonly Exploited North American Area Codes (Continued)*

Country	Area Code	Blocked Cisco CallManager Pattern
Grenada	473	9.1473xxxxxxx
Jamaica	876	9.1876xxxxxxx
Montserrat	664	9.1664xxxxxxx
Puerto Rico	787	9.1787xxxxxxx
St. Kitts & Nevis	869	9.1869xxxxxxx
St. Lucia	758	9.1758xxxxxxx
St. Vincent & the Grenadines	784	9.1784xxxxxxx
Toll Charge	900 976	9.1900xxxxxxx 9.1976xxxxxxx
Trinidad & Tobago	868	9.1868xxxxxxx
Turks & Caicos Islands	649	9.1649xxxxxxx
U.S. Virgin Islands	340	9.1242xxxxxxx

In the worldwide country code numbering scheme, several countries do not use their own country codes.

These numbers have the same format as the NANP—[access code] [area code] [number] (for example, 9.142*xxxxxxx*)—but a call to one of these destinations results in an international toll charge.

Administrators should make sure that all of the devices in the IP telephony network can reach only the destinations that they should be able to reach. For example, a lobby phone should not be able to call international numbers. In situations in which individuals in your organization have legitimate business in one of these countries, the recommendation is to explicitly configure route patterns that will match those businesses, while still blocking the area code as a whole.

Using Time-of-Day Routing

With the 4.1 release of Cisco CallManager, time-of-day routing routes calls to different locations based on the time of day when a call is made. For example, User A wants to configure the CFA number to an international number. User A can set this number only during the 8:00 a.m.-to-5:00 p.m. time period because outside these hours the system does not find the international number in the partition that is used to validate the CFA number.

Time-of-day routing can be used for other purposes as well. With time-of-day routing, a least-cost routing system can be designed to choose the cheapest provider for a specific time of day. For example, assume that there are two telephony providers, ABC and XYZ. Between 8 a.m. and 1 p.m., provider ABC is the cheaper provider, so Cisco CallManager routes calls over this provider during that period. After 1 p.m., provider XYZ becomes the cheaper provider, so the Cisco CallManager uses this provider then.

NOTE A complete description of time-of-day routing and its configuration can be found in Chapter 13, "Implementing Telephony Call Restrictions and Control."

Using FAC and CMC

Forced Authorization Codes (FAC) became available in Cisco CallManager Release 3.3(4). It is not included in Cisco CallManager Release 4.0 but has been included since Cisco CallManager Release 4.1. In Cisco CallManager Administration, various levels of authorization can be configured. With FAC, sensitive destinations can be "secured" by requiring use of authorization codes for such destinations. When a call is routed through a FAC-enabled route pattern, Cisco CallManager plays a tone and requests an authorization code. If the authorization code entered by the user does not meet or exceed the level of authorization that is specified to route the dialed number, the user receives a reorder tone. If the authorization is accepted, the call is routed. The authorization is logged to call detail records (CDRs) so that the information can be used by the CDR Analysis and Reporting (CAR) tool to generate reports for accounting and billing.

FAC is useful for colleges and universities or any business or organization for which limiting access to specific classes of calls proves beneficial. An additional benefit is that when you assign unique authorization codes, the users who can place calls can be determined. For example, for each user, a unique authorization code can be specified.

Enable FAC for relevant route patterns by checking the appropriate check box and specifying the minimum authorization level for calls through that route pattern. After updating the route patterns in Cisco CallManager Administration, the dial plan documents have to be updated to define the FAC-enabled route patterns and configured authorization level.

To implement FAC, devise a list of authorization levels and corresponding descriptions to define the levels. Authorization levels must be specified in the range of 0 to 255. Cisco allows authorization levels to be arbitrary, so define what the numbers mean for your organization. Before defining the levels, review the following examples of levels that can be configured for a system:

- Configure an authorization level of 10 for intrastate long-distance calls in North America.
- Because interstate calls often cost more than intrastate calls, configure an authorization level of 20 for interstate long-distance calls in North America.

- Configure an authorization level of 30 for international calls.

TIP Incrementing authorization levels by 10 establishes a structure that provides scalability when more authorization codes need to be added. The range for authorization codes is from 0 to 255.

Client Matter Codes (CMC) can also be used by companies to keep track of private calls placed by their employees. For example, a company could allow employees to place private calls using the company telephony infrastructure but require the employee to pay the cost. External route patterns (for example, those for long-distance and international calls and those for the 900 area code) can be configured to request a Client Matter Code to be entered and, therefore, to be logged accordingly.

This feature does not prevent users from making private calls using business telephones, but it allows a company to have a policy that does not deny private calls in general but requests that users identify them as such and pay for them. In both situations (denying private calls in general or permitting them if properly flagged), additional tools (logging, reporting) are needed to detect improper usage.

When CMC is configured, users hear a tone prompting them to enter any valid Client Matter Code. The CDR will include the code that is entered for later processing.

CMC was first available in Cisco CallManager Release 3.3(4). It is not included in Cisco CallManager Release 4.0 but has been included since Cisco CallManager Release 4.1.

NOTE A complete description of Forced Authorization Codes (FAC) and Client Matter Codes (CMC) and their configuration can be found in Chapter 17, "Configuring User Features, Part 2."

Restricting External Transfers

Call transfer is typically a feature that employees use to transfer *from* internal DNs *to* internal DNs. When calls are transferred to an external destination, very often the reason is that the caller whose call is transferred does not have permission to dial that external destination. The operator or an employee, for instance, could be asked to transfer a call of a colleague who is home on vacation to an international destination. Or an employee who is not allowed to call international numbers could ask a colleague who is allowed to call international numbers to transfer the call to that international number. An employee could also save money by having family members call the employee in the office when they need to place costly calls. All that the employee has to do is to transfer the call for them. To eliminate the cost of their call to the office of the employee, the employee could even hang up and call them back before transferring the call.

You can configure Cisco CallManager to block external-to-external call transfers. This configuration involves setting a simple service parameter and configuring gateways, trunks, and route patterns as OffNet (external) devices. After you have configured this, external-to-external call transfers will not be allowed. This feature provides an OnNet or OffNet alerting tone to the terminating end of the call (determined by the configuration of the device as either OnNet or OffNet). For incoming calls, trunks or gateways determine OffNet versus OnNet classification. For outgoing calls, the route pattern determines OffNet versus OnNet status.

NOTE The external call transfer restriction requires the Cisco CallManager Release 4.1 or later software component.

Defining OnNet and OffNet

Cisco CallManager classifies internal and external calls as OnNet and OffNet. A call coming from an external PSTN is classified as an OffNet call. A call that is placed internally (from one telephone to another, or between two Cisco CallManager clusters, where the call is routed over the WAN) is classified as an OnNet call, as illustrated in Figure 22-5. When you are using Automated Alternate Routing (AAR) in OnNet or OffNet implementations, it is important to know from where the call is coming. With AAR, the source can be either the WAN connection or the PSTN connection. This can cause restrictions when a call is rerouted. For example, if a user attempts to call across the IP WAN and AAR reroutes the call through the PSTN, the called party will not be able to transfer the call to another external phone number due to the Block OffNet to OffNet Transfers service parameter.

Figure 22-5 *OnNet Versus OffNet Calls*

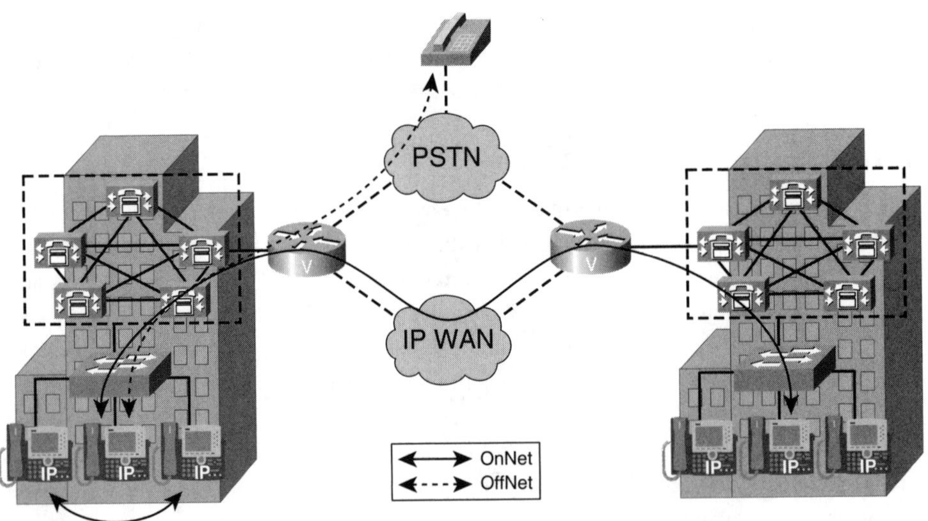

You can configure gateways and trunks as OnNet (internal) or OffNet (external) by using gateway configuration, using trunk configuration, or setting a clusterwide service parameter to classify devices automatically. When the feature is used in conjunction with the clusterwide service parameter **Block OffNet to OffNet Transfer**, the configuration determines whether calls can transfer over a gateway or trunk.

These devices can be configured as OnNet and OffNet to Cisco CallManager, as shown in Figure 22-6:

- H.323 gateway
- Media Gateway Control Protocol (MGCP) Foreign Exchange Office (FXO) trunk
- MGCP T1/E1 trunk
- Intercluster trunk
- Session Initiation Protocol (SIP) trunk

Figure 22-6 *Configuring a Gateway as OnNet or OffNet*

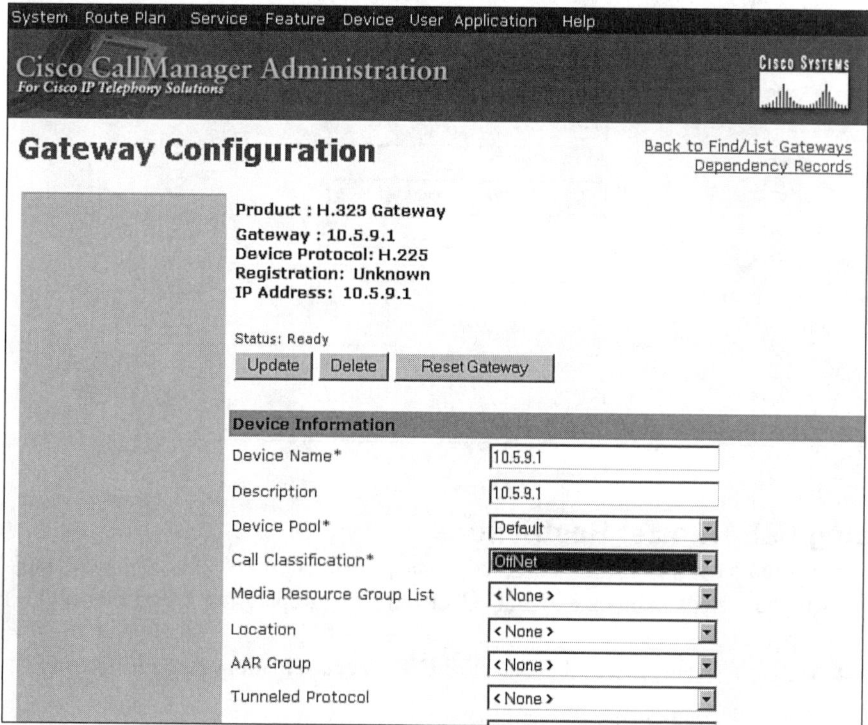

By default, all gateways use OffNet classification.

To classify an outgoing call as OnNet or OffNet, you can set the **Call Classification** field in the Route Pattern Configuration window to **OnNet** or **OffNet**, as shown in Figure 22-7. You can override the route pattern setting and use the trunk or gateway setting by checking the **Allow Device Override** check box in the Route Pattern Configuration window. All route patterns default to **OffNet** if the **Provide Outside Dial Tone** check box is checked. If the check box is unchecked, the route pattern defaults to **OnNet**.

Figure 22-7 *Configuring a Route Pattern as OnNet or OffNet*

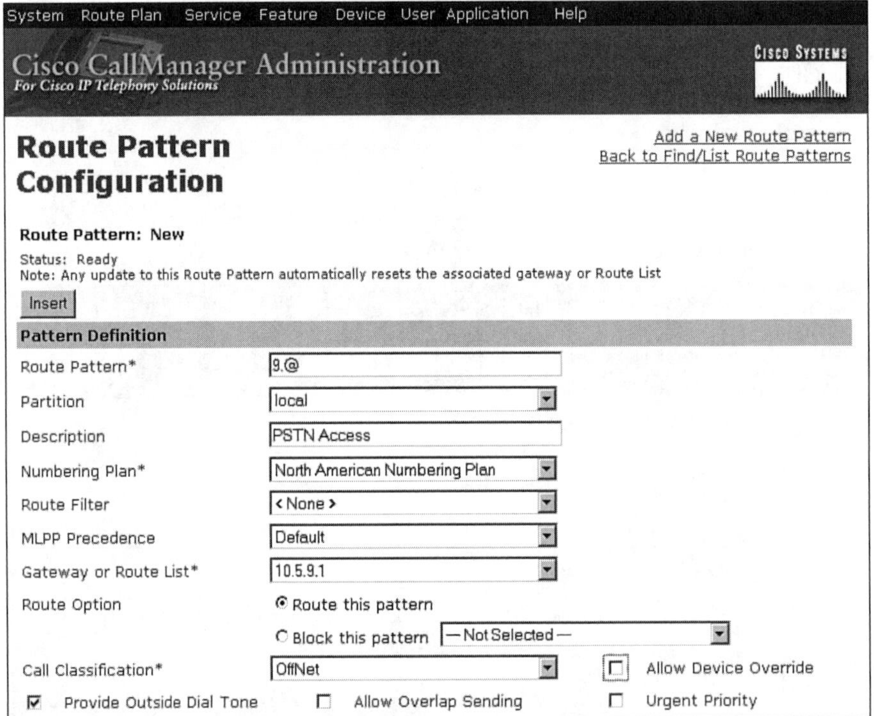

Configuring Call Transfer Restrictions

Now that you have seen the method used to categorize gateways and route patterns, you can complete these steps to block external calls from being transferred to external devices:

Step 1 You can specify the OnNet or OffNet classification on the following:

- Route patterns
- Intercluster trunks
- Gateways

Step 2 For incoming calls, configure individual gateways or trunks as **OffNet**.

Step 3 For outgoing calls, configure the route pattern **Call Classification** field as **OffNet**. Note that you can choose the **Allow Device Override** check box under the route pattern to allow the associated gateway to dictate whether the outgoing call is OnNet or OffNet.

Step 4 Set the **Block OffNet to OffNet Transfer** clusterwide CallManager service parameter shown in Figure 22-8 to **True**.

Figure 22-8 *Setting the Block OffNet to OffNet Service Parameter*

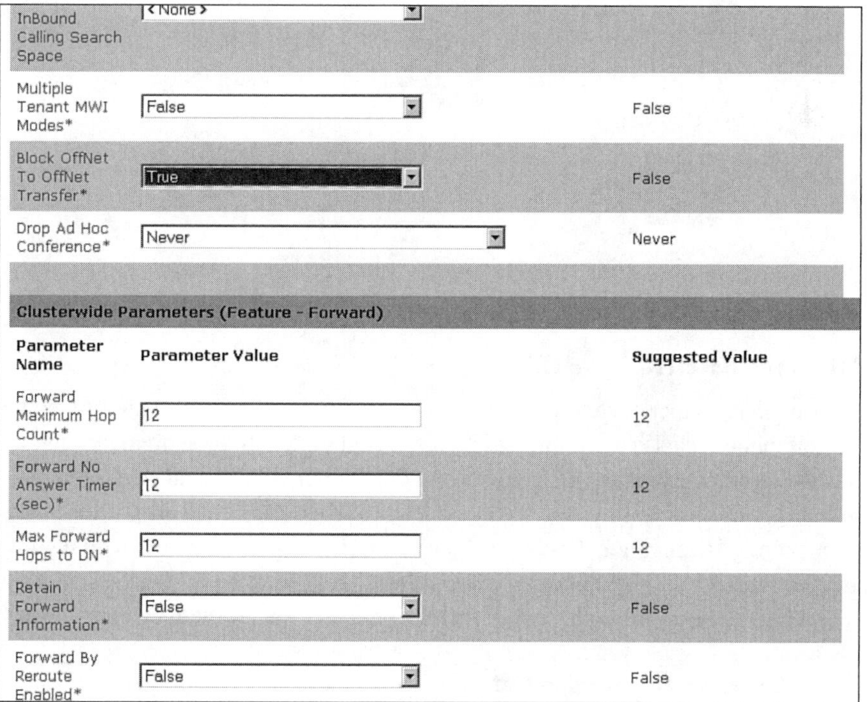

Call Transfer Restriction Example

In the Cisco CallManager configuration shown in Figure 22-9, the route pattern that is used to reach the external destinations is classified as an OffNet pattern. The gateway is also classified as OffNet. The service parameter **Block OffNet to OffNet Transfer** in the Cisco CallManager service parameters is set to **True**. Thus, the attempt by party A to call party B and transfer the call to party C will not work because OffNet-to-OffNet call transfers are restricted.

Figure 22-9 *Blocking OffNet-to-OffNet Calls*

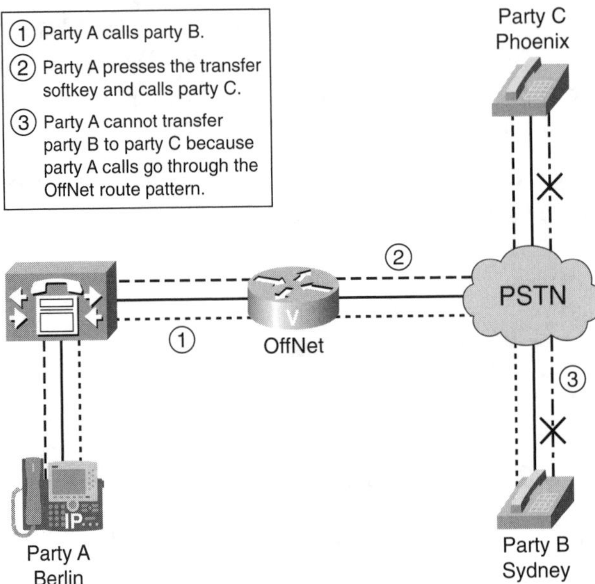

Dropping Conference Calls

As seen earlier, another method that a user can use for toll fraud is the ad hoc conferencing feature of their IP phone. This is accomplished by dialing multiple OffNet individuals into a conference call and then exiting from the call, leaving the OffNet individuals connected. Beginning in Cisco CallManager Release 3.3(4), you can configure the conference call to drop when its creator leaves the conference. Beginning in Cisco CallManager Release 4.1, you can also configure the value **When No OnNet Parties Remain in the Conference**. Determine the OnNet status for each party by checking the device or route pattern that the party is using, as with call transfer restrictions.

IP phones are always classified as OnNet devices. Gateways, trunks, and route patterns can be classified either as OnNet or as OffNet.

Valid values for the **Drop Ad Hoc Conference** CallManager service parameter, shown in Figure 22-10, are as follows:

- **Never**—The conference call stays active even when the conference creator hangs up. This behavior retains the original behavior of the conference feature. This is the default value.
- **When Conference Creator Drops Out**—When the conference creator hangs up, the conference call is dropped. When the conference creator transfers, redirects, or parks the call and the retrieving party hangs up, the conference is also dropped.

- **When No OnNet Parties Remain in the Conference**—When the last OnNet party in the conference hangs up, the conference is dropped.

Figure 22-10 *Configuring Drop Ad Hoc Conference Service Parameter*

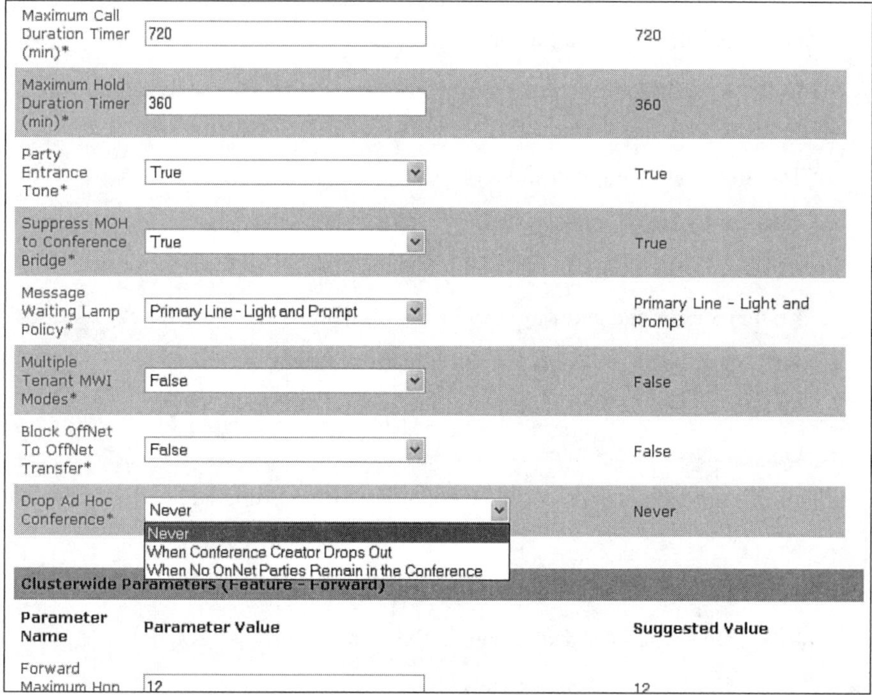

Summary

This chapter discussed combating voice network toll fraud using the Cisco CallManager. Sources of toll fraud can be external or internal. The attacks typically focus on using the call forwarding and conference features to avoid toll charges. You can stop call forwarding fraud through partitions and calling search spaces. An additional method you can integrate to restrict call transfers is the built-in CallManager ability to restrict OffNet-to-OffNet transfers.

You should also block commonly exploited area codes using route patterns. In addition, you can use FAC and CMC to restrict or track the users making toll calls. Time-of-day routing is used to change user permissions to place calls at certain hours or days. Finally, you can configure CallManager to drop ad hoc conferences when no OnNet parties remain on the call or when the conference creator drops out.

Review Questions

You can find the solutions to these questions in Appendix A, "Answers to Review Questions."

1. Which two of the following are typical sources of toll fraud?
   a. Voice mail-to-voice mail transfer
   b. Call Forward All
   c. Transfer from voice mail
   d. Transfer to an internal destination
   e. Transfer to a conference system
2. When you are restricting external call transfers, which statement is correct?
   a. Route patterns and gateways can be classified as OnNet or OffNet.
   b. Calls must be classified to use call transfer restrictions.
   c. Only restricted OnNet-to-OffNet transfers and OffNet-to-OffNet transfers can be used.
   d. Only OnNet devices must be classified.
3. Which two service parameters can be configured when using ad hoc conference restrictions?
   a. Never
   b. When First OnNet Party Leaves the Conference
   c. When No OffNet Parties Remain in the Conference
   d. When Conference Creator Drops Out
4. What is the default value for the Drop Ad Hoc Conference service parameter?
   a. Never
   b. Drop Ad Hoc Conference When Creator Leaves
   c. When No OnNet Parties Remain in the Conference
   d. When No OffNet Parties Remain in the Conference
5. What is the purpose of FACs?
   a. Time-based call routing
   b. Restricting call routing to destinations based on the time of day
   c. Restricting call routing to destinations based on user codes
   d. Restricting call routing to destinations based on OnNet or OffNet classification

6. Why is it important to block commonly exploited area codes when you want to restrict international calls?

   a. Commonly exploited countries have special premium numbers as country codes.

   b. Commonly exploited countries have special country codes that look like area codes of the United States.

   c. Countries such as the Bahamas can be reached either over the country code or over an area code.

   d. When these numbers are not blocked, they are treated like normal local telephone calls.

7. What automated method does Cisco support for security updates and hot fixes to the CallManager server?

   a. Receiving e-mail updates from the Cisco CallManager Notification Tool

   b. Downloading updates directly from Microsoft using the Windows Update Services

   c. Using the CSA standalone automatic update feature

   d. Downloading updates directly from Cisco using the automated Cisco Update Services

8. Which of the following describes the configuration of time-of-day routing?

   a. Create a time period, and then assign the time period to the calling search space.

   b. Create time periods, add the time periods to a time schedule, assign the time schedule to a partition, and assign the partition to a calling search space.

   c. Create time schedules, add the time schedules to a time period, create partitions, assign the partitions to a calling search space, and then assign the time period to the calling search space.

   d. Create a time period, add the time period to a time schedule, create partitions, assign the partitions to a calling search space, and then assign the time schedule to the calling search space.

9. Which of the following requires a code to be dialed, which is typically tracked to a specific department or user, before making outgoing calls? (*Hint:* This code can be used to make all outgoing calls.)

   a. CBC

   b. FAQ

   c. FAC

   d. CMC

10. Which of the following devices can be classified as OnNet or OffNet? (Choose three.)

   a. Route pattern
   b. Route group
   c. Route list
   d. Trunks
   e. Gateways
   f. IP phones

This chapter covers the following topics:

- Identifying potential threats against IP phones and the attack tool or method
- Explaining how signed firmware images prevent rogue or incorrect images from being placed on the IP phone
- Configuring parameters in the Phone Configuration window of Cisco CallManager Administration to harden the IP phone
- Explaining how disabling the PC port, the **Settings** button, and web access help secure the IP phone
- Explaining how, by ignoring gratuitous ARP, the IP phone can help prevent a man-in-the-middle attack
- Explaining how blocking the PC from accessing the voice VLAN through the IP phone prevents eavesdropping on the voice conversation
- Explaining how authentication and encryption on Cisco CallManager and the IP phones prevent identity theft of the phone or Cisco CallManager server, data tampering, and call-signaling and media-stream tampering

CHAPTER 23

Hardening the IP Phone

The IP phone is a target for attacks just like all other components of the network. Very often endpoints, such as IP phones, are not protected; only servers and network infrastructure devices are hardened. This is not a good practice because IP phones have default settings that make them vulnerable to certain attacks. However, several options are available to harden IP phones and, thus, protect them against various attack and infiltration methods. This chapter discusses these methods.

Threats Targeting Endpoints

As shown in Figure 23-1, there are many attack paths against an IP phone, including a connection through the network or through the integrated switch port to which a PC is attached. Corrupt images and altered configuration files can sabotage the IP telephony environment. Further attacks can be started from an infiltrated IP phone that is generally trusted and has access to the network. The physical access to the IP phone can be misused for violations of the IP phone integrity and the privacy of the user. Information can be gathered by browsing to the IP phone as well. In addition, IP phone conversations are vulnerable to various attacks when the network has been infiltrated, so the privacy of calls must be protected.

Figure 23-1 *Attacks Against IP Phone Endpoints*

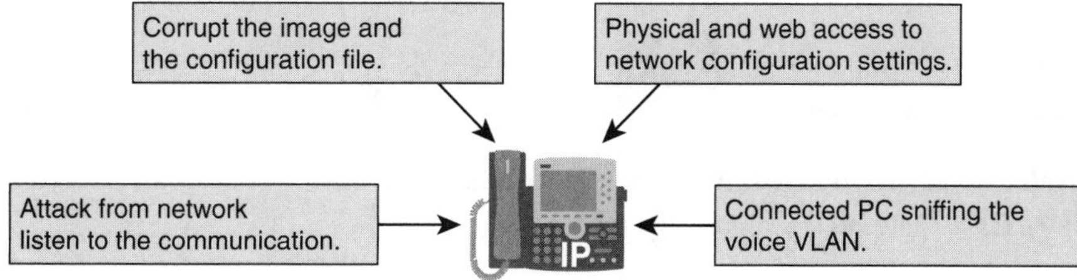

Endpoints are a common target of attacks because they are usually less protected than strategic devices, such as servers or network infrastructure devices. If an attacker gets control of an endpoint, such as an IP phone, the attacker could use that device as a jumping-off point for further attacks. Because the endpoints are trusted devices and have certain permissions in the network, an attacker can use them to target devices that they would not be able to reach directly. To get control of an IP phone, an attacker could try to modify the image and configuration file (for example, by spoofing the TFTP server or by replacing the file on the TFTP server itself or while in transit).

Another major threat is eavesdropping on conversations. If an attacker has physical access to the IP phone, the attacker can "tap the wire," either by connecting between the IP phone and the switch or by connecting to the PC port of the IP phone. If the attacker does not have physical access to the IP phone or its network connection, the attacker could launch a man-in-the-middle attack from any network between two communicating endpoints. In a man-in-the-middle attack, the attacker pretends to be a neighboring system (such as the default gateway when the communication is between two IP networks or a peer on the same IP network) and, hence, receives all packets. A common type of man-in-the-middle attack is to use gratuitous Address Resolution Protocol (ARP) for redirection of packets at the MAC address layer.

A lot about the IP phone and the telephony infrastructure can be learned just by looking into the network settings or browsing to the built-in HTTP server of the IP phone. This information contains Dynamic Host Configuration Protocol (DHCP), Domain Name System (DNS), default router, TFTP, and Cisco CallManager addresses. With this information, a hacker can direct an attack at the TFTP or Cisco CallManager server, because Windows hosts are generally more vulnerable than network components.

Overall, attacks on the endpoints can be broken down into four major categories:

- Eavesdropping on VoIP conversations
- Modifying the IP phone image
- Attacking system and CallManager services
- Hacking network devices and services

The simplest way to eavesdrop on the conversations of a user is to tap the wire between the IP phone and the PC attached to it. A variety of tools exist to accomplish this feat:

- **Ettercap**—A suite for man-in-the-middle attacks that allows sniffing and on-the-fly manipulation of data
- **Voice Over Misconfigured Internet Telephones (VOMIT)**—A tool that can create .wav files from captured G.711 conversations
- **Ethereal**—A sniffer and network protocol analyzer that allows both capturing conversations and converting them to playable files

An attacker could also try to get control of an IP phone by modifying the IP phone image or configuration file. This attack is carried out either at the TFTP server by manipulating the files themselves or by replacing the content while it is in transit. For the first method, the attacker needs access to the directory of the TFTP server; for the second, the attacker has to launch a successful man-in-the-middle attack.

The hacker might want to direct the attack at the most critical telephony components: the servers. An easy way to gather information about the IP addresses of critical components (such as the Cisco CallManager addresses, default gateway address, TFTP server address, DNS server address, and voice VLAN ID) is to retrieve them from the IP phone. This retrieval can be done locally at an IP phone by using the **Settings** button or by connecting to the IP address of the IP phone with a web browser. From the retrieved information, the hacker can build a topology map, associate it with services, and use the topology map to attack relevant devices.

If the attacker manages to get access to network devices, such as routers and switches, the attacker could redirect traffic to any destination using various kinds of tunnels. These include Generic Route Encapsulation (GRE), IPsec, Layer 2 Protocol Tunneling (L2TP), or Switched Port Analyzer (SPAN).

Blocking Endpoint Attacks

Cisco IP Phones are network devices that receive an IP address assignment. This allows them to communicate on the network, but also opens them to attack from network intruders. The following sections discuss mitigation techniques you can employ to protect the IP phone devices.

Stopping Rogue Images from Entering IP Phones

Cisco IP Phone image authentication was introduced with Cisco CallManager Release 3.3(3). In this and later releases, phone images are signed by Cisco manufacturing. Such a signature proves the authenticity of the origin, and the Cisco IP Phone will not accept images that are not published by Cisco manufacturing. The image also contains information about the IP phone model, so an IP phone will not accept an image for a different model. Since the introduction of image authentication, the current image verifies the signature of a new image. Only if the new image is properly signed by Cisco manufacturing is the new image accepted.

Cisco IP Phone configuration file authentication was introduced with Cisco CallManager Release 4.0 for Cisco IP Phone 7940, 7960, and 7970 models. The configuration files are signed by Cisco CallManager. The phone now verifies the signature and accepts the new configuration file only if it is properly signed by Cisco CallManager. Cisco IP Phone configuration file authentication requires additional configuration and hardware (Universal Serial Bus [USB] security tokens) and is not on by default.

IP phones will reject images with invalid signatures. They verify that the signature really validates the corresponding file whether it was obtained from an attacker or from the legitimate TFTP server. Since the introduction of this feature, the actual (current) image used in the phone includes the code to accept new images only if they have a valid signature. The actual image also includes the public key that is needed to verify the signature of new images. This way, only images that have been signed with the correct private key (owned by Cisco engineering) can be loaded. This also means that after you load the first image that features signature verification, you cannot load an older image that does not include a valid signature. This limitation guarantees that no image that has been tampered with can be loaded to your phone.

With image signature information about the IP phone model having been added to the image as well, the IP phone can verify that the image that is loaded is not for a different phone model. Before the introduction of this feature, a phone became inoperable if an image for another model was loaded, whereas today, such a wrong image is simply not accepted.

Disabling Phone Settings in Cisco CallManager Administration

The product-specific configuration parameters of Cisco IP Phones are set by default to achieve the greatest functionality but are considered insecure. To secure Cisco IP Phones, these settings can be modified:

- **Disable Speakerphone** and **Disable Speakerphone and Headset**—Disable these features to prevent eavesdropping on conversations in the office.
- **PC Port**—Disable the PC port to prevent a PC from connecting to the network via the IP phone switch.
- **Settings Access**—Disable or restrict access to the IP phone settings to avoid the risk that details about the network infrastructure could be exposed.
- **Gratuitous ARP**—Disable this feature to prevent gratuitous ARP-based man-in-the-middle attacks.
- **PC Voice VLAN Access**—Disable this feature to stop the IP phone from forwarding voice VLAN traffic to the PC.
- **Web Access**—Disable access to the IP phone from a web browser to avoid the risk that details about the network infrastructure could be exposed.

Disabling PC Port and Settings Access

The PC port is typically disabled in special areas such as a lobby or areas where no additional PC access is allowed. It is not a common setting, though, because it entails a major functionality constraint. Disabling the settings access prevents users from gathering information about, for example, DHCP server, TFTP server, default router, and Cisco CallManager IP addresses. Cisco CallManager Release 4.1 and later releases offer the Restricted option for settings access. With restricted access, the user can modify the contrast and ringer settings but cannot see any other information.

You can access both of these settings through the IP Phone Configuration window in Cisco CallManager Administration, as shown in Figure 23-2.

Figure 23-2 *Modifying IP Phone Security Settings*

Operation Completes By**	[ ] : [ ] : [ ] : [ ] (YYYY : MM : DD : HH)
Certificate Operation Status : None	
Multilevel Precendence and Preemption (MLPP) Information	
MLPP Domain	[ ] (e.g., "0000FF")
MLPP Indication	Default
MLPP Preemption	Default
Product Specific Configuration	
Disable Speakerphone	☐
Disable Speakerphone and Headset	☐
Forwarding Delay*	Disabled
PC Port*	Enabled
Settings Access*	Enabled
Gratuitous ARP*	Enabled
PC Voice VLAN Access*	Enabled
Video Capabilities*	Disabled
Auto Line Select*	Disabled
Web Access*	Enabled

* indicates a required item.
** Indicates time on Publisher.

Back to top of page
Back to Find/List Phones

Disabling IP Phone Web Access

You can use a web browser to connect to the HTTP server of the IP phone by simply browsing to the IP address of the phone, as shown in Figure 23-3. The HTTP server displays similar information that can be viewed directly on the IP phone using the **Settings** button, enhanced by some additional statistics. A hacker can use the intelligence gained by discovering the network configuration to direct attacks at the most critical telephony components, such as Cisco CallManager and the TFTP server. Therefore, from a security perspective, it is recommended that you disable web access to the phone. When web access is disabled, the IP phone will not accept incoming web connections and, hence, does not provide access to sensitive information.

> **NOTE** Disabling web access at the IP phone stops Extensible Markup Language (XML) push applications from working. If you want to use XML push applications on some IP phones (for instance, for an emergency notification application), you cannot disable web access to the IP phone.

Figure 23-3 *Cisco IP Phone Built-in Web Server*

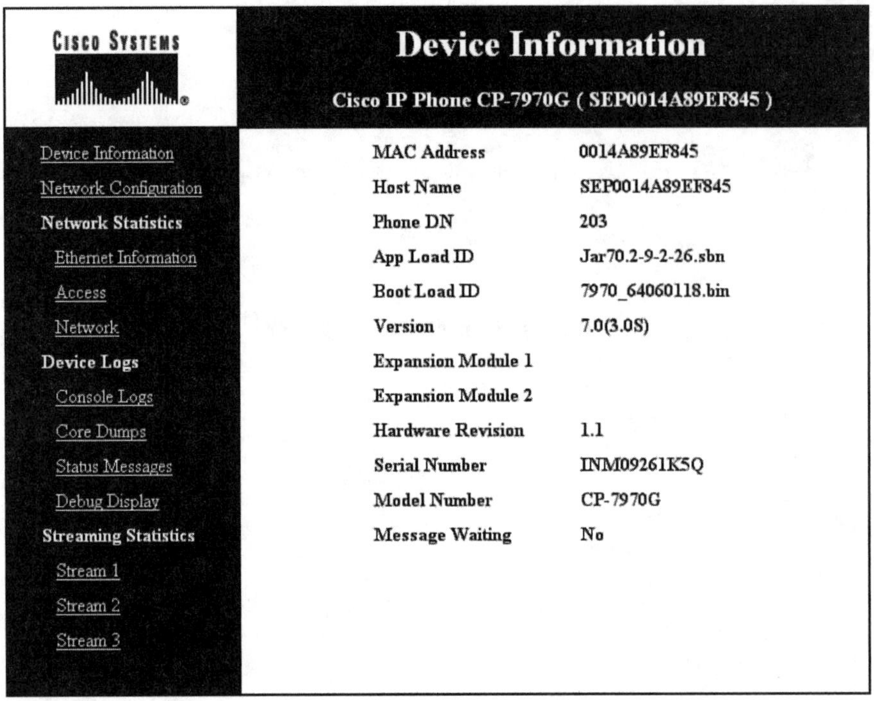

CISCO SYSTEMS

Device Information

Cisco IP Phone CP-7970G (SEP0014A89EF845)

Device Information
Network Configuration
Network Statistics
Ethernet Information
Access
Network
Device Logs
Console Logs
Core Dumps
Status Messages
Debug Display
Streaming Statistics
Stream 1
Stream 2
Stream 3

MAC Address	0014A89EF845
Host Name	SEP0014A89EF845
Phone DN	203
App Load ID	Jar70.2-9-2-26.sbn
Boot Load ID	7970_64060118.bin
Version	7.0(3.0S)
Expansion Module 1	
Expansion Module 2	
Hardware Revision	1.1
Serial Number	INM09261K5Q
Model Number	CP-7970G
Message Waiting	No

Ignoring Gratuitous ARP

Usually, ARP operates in a request-and-response fashion. When a station needs to know the MAC address of a given IP address, it sends an ARP request. The device with the corresponding IP address replies and, thus, provides its MAC address. All receiving devices update their ARP cache by adding the IP and MAC address pair. Gratuitous ARP packets are packets that announce the MAC address of the sender even though this information has not been requested. This technique allows receiving devices to update their ARP caches with the information. Usually, such gratuitous ARP messages are sent after the MAC address of a device has changed to avoid packets being sent to the old MAC address until the related entry has timed out in the ARP caches of the other devices. Gratuitous ARP, however, can also be used by an attacker to redirect packets in a man-in-the-middle attack.

Figure 23-4 illustrates a gratuitous ARP attack against an IP phone. By default, Cisco IP Phones accept gratuitous ARP messages and update their ARP cache whenever they receive a gratuitous ARP packet.

Figure 23-4 *Manipulating Gratuitous ARP to Accomplish a Man-in-the-Middle Attack*

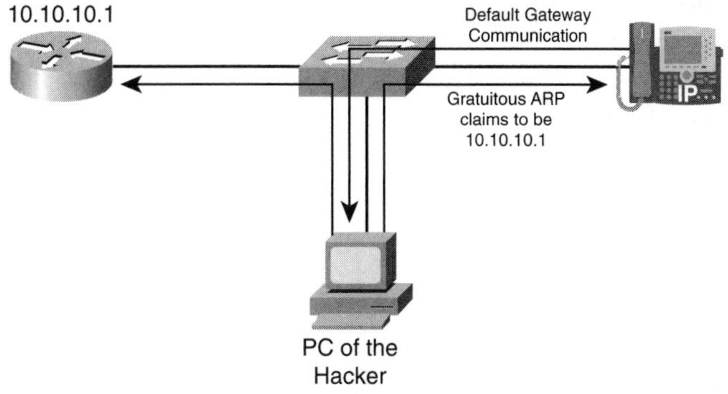

The attacker located in the VLAN of the IP phone repeatedly sends out gratuitous ARP packets announcing its MAC address to be the MAC address of the default gateway of the IP phone. The IP phone accepts the information, updates its ARP cache, and forwards all packets meant for the default gateway to the attacker. With tools such as Ettercap, the hacker can copy or modify the information and then relay it to the real default gateway. The user does not notice that someone is listening to the data stream as long as the hacker does not significantly increase the delay and does not drop packets.

In this example, only traffic from the IP phone toward the default gateway is sent to the attacker, but if the attacker also impersonates the IP phone toward the router, the attacker could control bidirectional traffic. In this case, the router would also have to listen to gratuitous ARP packets.

NOTE There are several methods to prevent gratuitous ARP attacks in the network. You can disable it on end devices or you can use features such as Dynamic ARP Inspection (DAI) and IP Source Guard on Catalyst switches. You can find more information about DAI and IP Source Guard in your Cisco IOS or Cisco Catalyst operating system switch configuration guide.

To prevent gratuitous ARP-based attacks against an IP phone, the gratuitous ARP feature of the IP phone should be disabled. This setting is found at the bottom of the IP Phone Configuration window, as shown in Figure 23-2.

Disabling Voice VLAN Access

By default, an IP phone sends all traffic that it receives from the switch out its PC port. This enables the PC to see not only the traffic of the native VLAN, the data VLAN, but also to see the traffic of the voice VLAN. When the PC receives voice VLAN traffic, the traffic can be captured and, hence, the conversation can be sniffed.

Further, the PC can also send packets to the voice VLAN if they are tagged accordingly. This breaks the separation of voice VLANs and data VLANs, because the PC that is supposed to have access to the data VLAN only is now able to send packets to the voice VLAN, bypassing all access-control rules (access control lists [ACLs] in routers or firewalls) that might be enforced between the two VLANs.

Usually, the PC does not need access to the voice VLAN, and, therefore, you should block PC access to the voice VLAN.

NOTE Some applications, such as call recording or supervisory monitoring in call centers, require access to the voice VLAN. In such situations, you should not disable the PC Voice VLAN Access setting.

To block the PC from accessing the voice VLAN, set the PC Voice VLAN Access configuration parameter shown in Figure 23-2 to Disabled. When a phone is configured this way, it will not forward voice VLAN-tagged traffic to the PC when it receives such frames from the switch. In addition, the phone will not forward voice VLAN-tagged traffic to the switch if it receives such frames from the PC. Although this setting is recommended from a security perspective, it makes troubleshooting more difficult because you cannot analyze voice VLAN traffic from a PC connected to the PC port of the IP phone. Whenever you need to capture voice VLAN traffic to analyze network problems, you will have to sniff the traffic on the network devices. On Cisco Catalyst switches, you can configure SPAN ports to duplicate traffic from certain ports or VLANs to another port where you attach the PC that is running your protocol analyzer. Remote SPAN (RSPAN) even allows you to send the selected traffic to another switch for remote analysis.

NOTE Cisco 7912 IP Phones do not currently support disabling PC voice VLAN access.

Enabling IP Phone Encryption and Authentication

Cisco CallManager Release 4.0 introduced certificate-based authentication and encryption of signaling and media. Skinny Call Control Protocol (SCCP), used between the IP phone and Cisco CallManager for call signaling, can be secured by Transport Layer Security (TLS), formerly known as Secure Sockets Layer (SSL). This protects the signaling channels from most types of attacks. The media stream between two IP phones is protected with Secure Real-Time Transfer Protocol (SRTP), which encrypts and authenticates the voice data. A hacker cannot modify the packets and is not able to listen to the audio stream because it is now encrypted.

NOTE Because of its complexity, IP phone encryption and authentication is discussed fully in Chapters 24 through 27.

Summary

This chapter discussed the potential threats against Cisco IP Phones and the attack tools or methods a hacker can use. Hackers typically begin with the weakest points in the network, such as Cisco IP Phones. To combat this, the IP phones can validate images and configuration updates using signature security. Cisco administrators can disable access to the **Settings** button and built-in web server to prevent hackers from viewing key network information. In addition, disabling gratuitous ARP prevents man-in-the-middle attacks.

Finally, it is a good practice to disable the PC port of an IP phone if no PC is attached to it, and generally block access to the voice VLAN to avoid unauthorized network access.

Review Questions

You can find the solutions to these questions in Appendix A, "Answers to Review Questions."

1. What could be of interest to a hacker planning to attack an IP phone?
   a. The attacker can learn about the IP telephony environment.
   b. The attacker can start attacks from the IP phone.
   c. With a modified image and configuration file, the attacker can bring down the Cisco CallManager.
   d. The attacker can sabotage a special user.
2. Which IP phone does not support configuration file authentication?
   a. Cisco IP Phone 7920
   b. Cisco IP Phone 7940
   c. Cisco IP Phone 7960
   d. Cisco IP Phone 7970
3. In which window are IP phone security settings configured?
   a. Directory Number Configuration
   b. Phone Configuration
   c. Phone Security Configuration
   d. Product Specific Configuration
4. How do you browse to the built-in web server of an IP phone?
   a. http://IP-Phone's-IP-address
   b. https://IP-Phone's-IP-address
   c. https://IP-Phone's-IP-address/CCMAdmin
   d. https://IP-Phone's-IP-address/Admin

5. Which statement is not true about gratuitous ARP attacks?
   a. Gratuitous ARP is a man-in-the-middle attack.
   b. Gratuitous ARP attackers usually operate from the Internet.
   c. Gratuitous ARP is normally used for HSRP.
   d. Ettercap is a tool used for gratuitous ARP attacks.
6. Which of the following statements about authentication and encryption is not true?
   a. It was introduced with Cisco CallManager Release 4.0.
   b. Media streams use SRTP.
   c. Signaling uses Secure SCCP.
   d. TLS was formerly known as SSL.
7. Which of the following network information cannot be found out from a Cisco IP Phone?
   a. DHCP server address
   b. DNS server address
   c. TFTP server address
   d. Intranet server address
   e. Cisco CallManager address
8. You want to prevent users from accessing the PC port of a 7912 IP Phone. What option is available to you?
   a. Use the Cisco CallManager Phone Configuration window to disable the PC port.
   b. Use the CallManager service parameters to disable all PC ports.
   c. Use the Bulk Administration Tool to disable the PC port for all 7912 IP Phones.
   d. Fill the PC port of the phone with glue.
9. Which of the following was the predecessor of Transport Layer Security?
   a. IPsec
   b. SSL
   c. DES
   d. AES

10. What must you do to implement signed firmware validation on the Cisco IP Phones?

a. Nothing; the feature is already enabled since CCM 3.3(3).

b. Change the signed firmware setting from the Phone Configuration window.

c. Change the signed firmware setting from the CallManager service parameters.

d. Change the signed firmware setting from the IP phone itself.

This chapter covers the following topics:

- Defining cryptography and explaining the four cryptographic services: confidentiality, integrity, authentication, and nonrepudiation
- Explaining the basic operation and uses of symmetric encryption algorithms and identifying the common algorithms in use today
- Explaining the basic operation and uses of asymmetric encryption algorithms and identifying the common algorithms in use today
- Explaining how hash functions provide data integrity and listing common hash functions in use today
- Defining digital signatures and explaining how they provide identity and integrity

CHAPTER 24

Understanding Cryptographic Fundamentals

Configuring Cisco CallManager for security is relatively straightforward; however, the underlying security services, algorithms, and operations are often not well-known to the Cisco CallManager administrators who must secure the Cisco CallManager installation. This chapter provides information about cryptographic fundamentals. It helps you understand the elements that are the basis of cryptography in the data world.

What Is Cryptography?

Cryptography is the science of transforming readable messages into an unintelligible form and the later reversal of that process. The application is to send the transformed, unreadable message over an untrusted channel. In the data world, this untrusted channel very often is a public network, such as the Internet.

Cryptography provides four services:

- **Data authenticity**—This service should guarantee that the message comes from the source that it claims to come from. When an application such as e-mail or protocols such as IP do not have any built-in mechanisms that prevent spoofing of the source, cryptographic methods can be used for proof of sources.

- **Data confidentiality**—This service provides privacy by ensuring that messages can be read only by the receiver.

- **Data integrity**—This service ensures that the messages are not altered in transit. With data integrity, the receiver can verify that the received message is identical to the sent message and that no manipulation was done.

- **Data nonrepudiation**—This service allows the sender of a message to be uniquely identified. With nonrepudiation services in place, a sender cannot deny having been the source of that message.

All these services are based on encryption and authentication methods. However, for different applications, different kinds of encryption and authentication techniques are used. Figure 24-1 illustrates examples of the four services.

Figure 24-1 *Services of Cryptography*

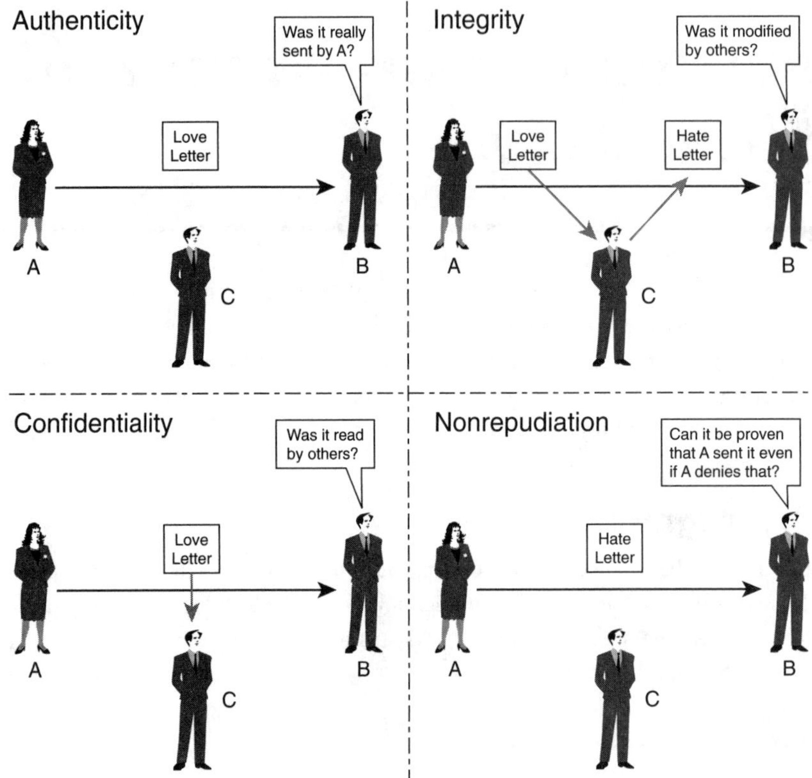

These scenarios are possible:

- **Authenticity**—If B receives a love letter that says it is coming from A, how can B be sure that it was really sent by A and not someone else? Without any reliable service that ensures authenticity of the source, user B will never know.
- **Confidentiality**—On the other hand, if there are means of guaranteeing the authenticity of the source, B might be afraid that somebody else read the love letter while it was in transit, resulting in a loss of privacy. This problem could be solved by a service providing confidentiality.
- **Integrity**—If B were to receive a hate letter, formed in a way that it proved the authenticity of the source, how can B know that the content has not been modified in transit? A service that ensures integrity of the message is needed to eliminate this kind of threat.
- **Nonrepudiation**—However, if B receives a hate letter from A that seems to be authentic, can B prove to others that it must have been sent by A? A nonrepudiation service is needed in this case.

It might appear that the authenticity service and the nonrepudiation service are fulfilling the same function. Although both address the question of the proven identity of the sender, there is a small difference in the two, which is sometimes quite important: When the receiver needs to be sure about the authenticity of the source, the method and the means that are used to achieve the proof of authenticity can be available to both the sender and the receiver. Because the receiver knows that he or she was not the source, it does not matter that the sender and receiver both know how to treat a message to provide authenticity of the source.

If, however, the receiver has to prove the source of the sender to others, it is not acceptable that the receiver know how the sender treated this message to prove authenticity because the receiver could then have pretended to be the sender.

An example for authenticity versus nonrepudiation is data exchange between two computers of the same company versus data exchange between a customer and a web shop. When the two computers do not have to prove to others which of them sent a message, but just need to make sure that whatever was received by one was sent by the other, the two computers can *share* the same way of transforming their messages. This practice is not acceptable in business applications such as a web shop. If the web shop knows how a customer transforms messages to prove authenticity of the source, the web shop could easily fake "authentic" orders. Therefore, in such a scenario, the sender must be the only party having the knowledge how to transform messages. Then, the web shop can prove to others that the order must have been sent by the customer. The customer could not argue that the order was faked by the web shop when the web shop does not know how to transform the messages from the customer to make them authentic.

Authentication and Encryption

Authentication functions are used to provide authenticity, integrity, and nonrepudiation. To achieve this, the sender adds (appends) verification data to the actual data. The authenticated data can be information about the sender (such as its identity) or the information that should be passed from the sender to the receiver itself. The receiver checks the verification data added by the sender and, if successful, can confirm authenticity.

There are various ways to create the verification data, the most common being Hash-based Message Authentication Code (HMAC) or digital signatures.

Confidentiality functions are provided by encryption. More precisely, the transformation of cleartext to ciphertext is called encryption, whereas the transformation of the ciphertext back to the original cleartext is called decryption.

Encryption utilizes an encryption algorithm and keys. If the key that is used to encrypt the data and the key that is used to decrypt the data is the same, the encryption algorithm is considered symmetric (with symmetric keys). If the encryption and decryption keys are different, the encryption algorithm is asymmetric (with asymmetric keys).

Although the encryption algorithms are usually well-known, the keys that are used for the encryption have to be secret. Symmetric keys have to be known by both endpoints that want to use a symmetric encryption algorithm for their data exchange. With asymmetric encryption, the sender needs to know only the encryption key, whereas the receiver needs to know only the decryption key.

Desirable features of an encryption algorithm are as follows:

- **Resistance to cryptographic attacks**—The algorithm itself must be trusted by the cryptographic community and there must be no shortcut to decipher data other than knowing or guessing the decryption key.
- **Variable key lengths and scalability**—The longer the encryption key, the longer it will take attackers to break it if they try all the possible keys (for example, a 16-bit key = 2^{16} = 65,536 possible keys, whereas a 56-bit key = 2^{56} = 71,892,000,000,000,000 possible keys). Scalability provides flexible key length, and the strength or speed of encryption can be selected as needed.
- **Avalanche effect**—When only a small part of the plaintext message is changed (a few bits), and that small change causes its ciphertext to change completely, the algorithm has an avalanche effect. The avalanche effect is a desired feature because it allows very similar messages to be sent over an untrusted medium, with their encrypted (ciphertext) messages being completely different.

Symmetric Encryption

Symmetric encryption has two main characteristics: It is very fast (compared to asymmetric encryption) and uses the same key for encryption and decryption, as shown in Figure 24-2. As a consequence, the *same* key has to be known by the sender and the receiver. To ensure confidentiality, nobody else is allowed to know the key. Such keys are also called *shared secrets*.

Figure 24-2 *Symmetric (Shared Secret) Encryption*

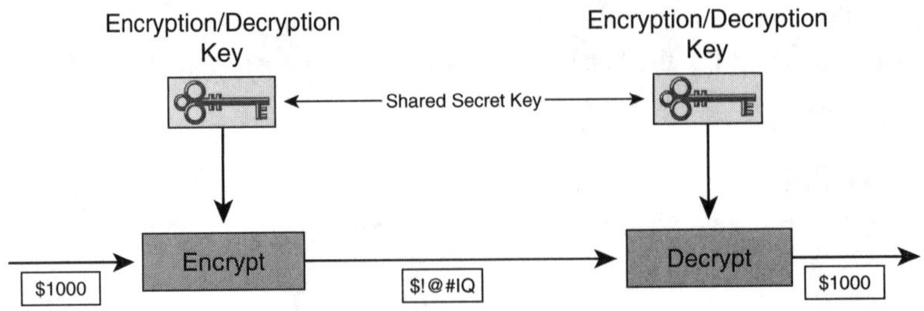

Symmetric encryption has been used for decades, and several algorithms are commonly used. Among the best-known and most widely trusted symmetric encryption algorithms are Triple Data Encryption Standard (3DES), Advanced Encryption Standard (AES), International Data Encryption Algorithm (IDEA), the RC series (RC2, RC4, RC5, RC6), Software Encryption Algorithm (SEAL), and Blowfish. They are all based on the same concept: They have two types of input (the cleartext and the key) and produce unreadable output (the ciphertext). For decryption, the ciphertext and the key are the input data and the original cleartext is the output.

Symmetric algorithms are usually very simple in their structure, therefore quite fast, and as a consequence, they are often used for wire-speed real-time encryption in data networks. They are, in their essence, based on simple mathematical operations and can be easily hardware-accelerated using specialized encryption application-specific integrated circuits (ASICs). Typical applications are e-mail, IPsec, Secure Real-Time Transfer Protocol (SRTP), or Secure HTTP (HTTPS).

Keys should be changed frequently because they could be discovered otherwise, and loss of privacy would be the consequence. The "safe" lifetime of keys depends on the algorithm, the volume of data for which they are used, the key length, and the time period for which the keys are used. The key length is usually 128 to 256 bits. Because of the limited lifetime (usually hours to days) and the fact that each pair of devices should use a different key, key management is rather difficult.

Symmetric Encryption Example: AES

For a number of years, the industry recognized that Data Encryption Standard (DES) would eventually reach the end of its useful life. In 1997, the AES initiative was announced, and the public was invited to propose encryption schemes, one of which could be chosen as the encryption standard to replace DES.

On October 2, 2000, the U.S. National Institute of Standards and Technology (NIST) announced the selection of the Rijndael cipher as the AES algorithm. The Rijndael cipher, developed by Joan Daemen and Vincent Rijmen, has a variable block length and key length. The algorithm currently specifies how to use keys with lengths of 128, 192, or 256 bits to encrypt blocks with lengths of 128, 192, or 256 bits (all nine combinations of key length and block length are possible). Both block length and key length can be extended very easily to multiples of 32 bits, allowing the algorithm to scale with security requirements of the future. The U.S. Department of Commerce approved the adoption of AES as an official U.S. government standard, effective May 26, 2002.

AES was chosen to replace DES and 3DES because they are either too weak (DES, in terms of key length) or too slow (3DES) to run on modern, efficient hardware. AES is, therefore, more efficient on the same hardware (much faster, usually by a factor of around five compared to 3DES), and is more suitable for high-throughput, low-latency environments, especially if pure software encryption is used. However, AES is a relatively young algorithm, and, as the golden rule of cryptography states, a more mature algorithm is always more trusted. 3DES is, therefore, a more conservative and more trusted choice in terms of strength, because it has been analyzed for around 30 years. AES has also been thoroughly analyzed during the selection process, and is considered mature enough for most applications.

AES is the algorithm for encrypting both IP phone-to-Cisco CallManager communication (signaling with Transport Layer Security [TLS] protection) and phone-to-phone and phone-to-gateway (media with SRTP protection) channels in Cisco IP telephony.

Asymmetric Encryption

Asymmetric algorithms (also sometimes called public-key algorithms) are designed in such a way that the key used for encryption is different from the key used for decryption, as shown in Figure 24-3. The decryption key cannot (at least in any reasonable amount of time) be calculated from the encryption key and vice versa.

Figure 24-3 *Asymmetric (Public Key) Encryption*

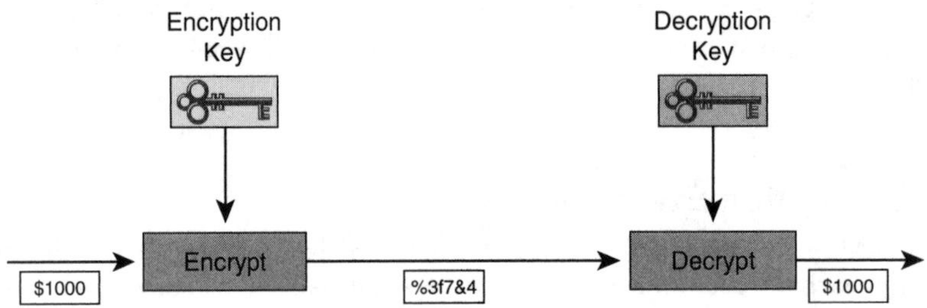

The main feature of asymmetric encryption algorithms is that the encryption key (often called the *public key*) does not have to be secret; it can be published freely and anyone can use this key to encrypt data. The corresponding decryption key (often called the *private key*) is known only to a single entity that can decrypt data encrypted with the encryption key. Therefore, when you need to send an encrypted message to someone else, you first obtain the public (encryption) key of the other person and transform the message with it. Only the recipient knows the private (decryption) key and can, therefore, decrypt the message.

Asymmetric algorithms are relatively slow (up to 1000 times slower than symmetric algorithms). Their design is based on computational problems, such as factoring extremely large numbers or computing discrete logarithms of extremely large numbers.

The best-known asymmetric cryptographic algorithms are the Rivest, Shamir, and Adleman (RSA); ElGamal; and elliptic curve algorithms. RSA is recommended because it is widely trusted for its resistance against attacks and well-known internals. Because of their lack of speed, asymmetric encryption algorithms are usually used to protect small quantities of data (such as digital signatures or key exchange). Key exchange allows you to use the slower, more secure asymmetric algorithm to protect the exchange of a faster symmetric key algorithm over a public network, such as the Internet.

Key management tends to be simpler compared to symmetric (secret key) algorithms. As stated earlier, with asymmetric encryption, each device has a pair of keys (public and private). The public key of each device has to be publicly available (known by all other devices) to allow a full mesh of encrypted communication, whereas with symmetric encryption different symmetric keys have to be safely distributed for each combination of two peers. Asymmetric keys are usually used for a longer time (months to years).

Symmetric Encryption Example: RSA

Ronald L. Rivest, Adi Shamir, and Leonard M Adleman invented the RSA algorithm in 1977. It was a patented public-key algorithm, and its patent expired in September 2000, putting the algorithm in the public domain. Of all the public-key algorithms proposed over the years, RSA is still the most strongly preferred.

RSA has withstood years of extensive cryptoanalysis, and although analysis has neither proven nor disproven the security of the RSA algorithm, it does suggest a justifiable confidence. The security of RSA is based on the difficulty of factoring very large numbers, that is, breaking them into multiplicative factors. If an easy method of factoring these large numbers were discovered, the effectiveness of RSA would be destroyed (and, as a side effect, mathematics might take a huge leap). RSA keys are usually 1024 to 2048 bits long.

RSA, like all asymmetric encryption algorithms, can be used in two different ways:

- **Confidentiality**—The sender encrypts the data with the public key of the receiver. This guarantees that only the receiver can decrypt the data.
- **Authenticity of digital signatures**—The sender uses its private key to sign (encrypt) the data. Such a signature can be verified by everybody because only the public key is needed to verify (decrypt) the signature.

RSA is used for device authentication (IP phone to Cisco CallManager and vice versa) in Cisco IP telephony.

Hash Functions

Hash functions are used for several cryptographic applications. They can be used for secure password verification or storage and are also a base component for data authentication.

Hashing is a one-way function of input data, which produces fixed-length output data, the digest. The digest uniquely identifies the input data and is cryptographically very strong, that is, it is impossible to recover input data from its digest, and if the input data changes just a little, the digest (fingerprint) changes substantially (avalanche effect). Therefore, high-volume data can be identified by its (shorter) digest. For this reason, the digest is called a fingerprint of the data. Given only a digest, it is not computationally feasible to regenerate the data that was used to compute the digest.

Figure 24-4 illustrates how hashing is performed. Data of arbitrary length is input to the hash function, and the result of the hash function is the fixed-length hash (digest, fingerprint). Hashing is similar to the calculation of cyclic redundancy check (CRC) checksums, except that it is much stronger from a cryptographic point of view. With CRC, given a CRC value, it is easy to generate data with the same CRC. However, with hash functions, this is not computationally feasible for an attacker.

Figure 24-4 *Hashing Process*

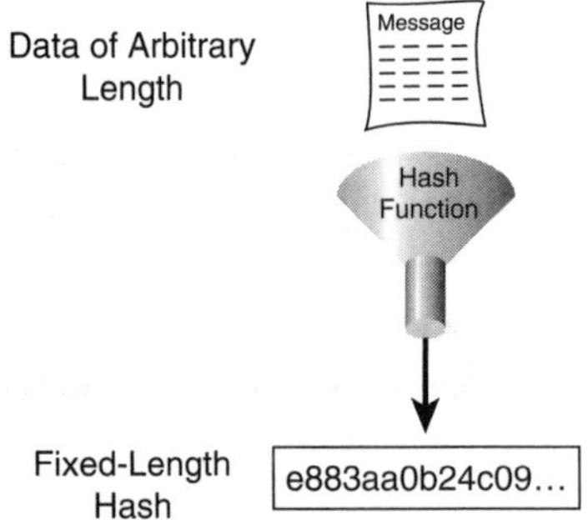

The two best-known hashing functions are these:

- Message Digest 5 (MD5), with 128-bit digests
- Secure Hash Algorithm 1 (SHA-1), with 160-bit digests

There is considerable evidence that MD5 might not be as strong as originally envisioned and that collisions (different inputs resulting in the same fingerprint) are more likely to occur than designed for. Therefore, MD5 should be avoided as an algorithm of choice and SHA-1 should be used instead.

NIST developed SHA, the algorithm specified in the Secure Hash Standard. SHA-1 is a revision to SHA that was published in 1994; the revision corrected an unpublished flaw in SHA. Its design is very similar to the MD4 family of hash functions developed by Rivest. The algorithm takes a message of no less than 264 bits in length and produces a 160-bit message digest. The algorithm is slightly slower than MD5, but the larger message digest makes it more secure against brute-force collision and inversion attacks.

Figure 24-5 illustrates hashing in action. The sender wants to ensure that the message will not be altered on its way to the receiver. The sender uses the message as the input to a hashing algorithm and computes its fixed-length digest or fingerprint. This fingerprint is then attached to the message (the message and the hash are cleartext) and sent to the receiver. The receiver removes the fingerprint from the message and uses the message as input to the same hashing algorithm. If the hash computed by the receiver is equal to the one attached to the message, the message has not been altered during transit.

Figure 24-5 *Hashing Example*

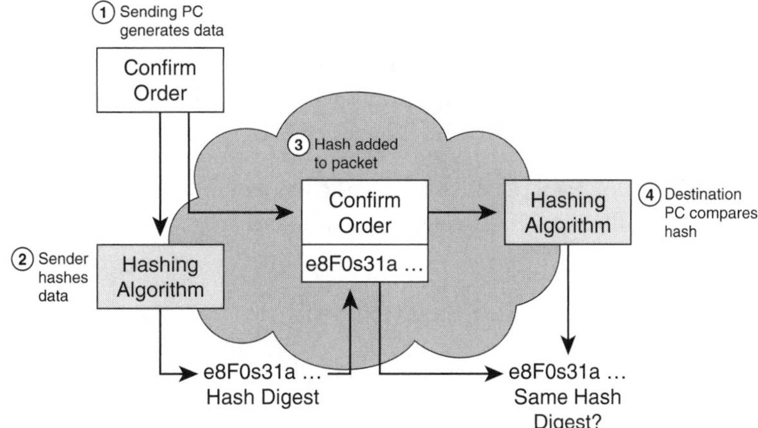

Be aware that there is no security added to the message in this example. When the message traverses the network, a potential attacker could intercept the message, change it, recalculate the hash, and append the newly recalculated fingerprint to the message (a man-in-the-middle interception attack). Hashing only prevents the message from being changed accidentally (that is, by a communication error). There is nothing unique to the sender in the hashing procedure; therefore, anyone can compute a hash for any data, as long as they know the correct hash algorithm.

Thus, hash functions are helpful to ensure that data was not changed accidentally but cannot ensure that data was not deliberately changed. For the latter, you need to employ hash functions in the context of Hash-based Message Authentication Code (HMAC). They will extend hashes by adding a secure component.

HMAC uses existing hash functions, but with the significant difference of adding an additional secret key as the input to the hash function when calculating the digest (fingerprint). Only the sender and the receiver share the secret key, and the output of the hash function now depends on the input data and the secret key. Therefore, only parties who have access to that secret key can compute or verify the digest of an HMAC function. This defeats man-in-the-middle attacks and also provides authentication of data origin. If only two parties share a secret HMAC key and use HMAC functions for authentication, the receiver of a properly constructed HMAC digest with a message can be sure that the other party was the originator of the message because that other party is the only other entity possessing the secret key. However, because both parties know the key, HMAC does not provide nonrepudiation. For the latter, every entity would need its own secret key instead of having a secret key shared between two parties.

HMAC functions are generally fast and are often applied in these situations:

- To provide a fast proof of message authenticity and integrity among parties sharing the secret key, such as with IPsec packets or routing protocol authentication
- To generate one-time (and one-way) responses to challenges in authentication protocols (such as PPP Challenge Handshake Authentication Protocol [CHAP], Microsoft NT Domain, and Extensible Authentication Protocol-MD5 [EAP-MD5])
- To provide proof of integrity of bulk data, such as with file-integrity checkers (for example, Tripwire), or with document signing (digitally signed contracts, Public Key Infrastructure [PKI] certificates)

Some well-known HMAC functions are as follows:

- Keyed MD5, based on the MD5 hashing algorithm, which should be avoided
- Keyed SHA-1, based on the SHA-1 hashing algorithm, which is recommended

Cisco IP telephony uses SHA-1 HMAC for protecting signaling traffic and media exchange.

Digital Signatures

Digital signatures are verification data appended to the data that is to be signed. They provide three basic security services in secure communications:

- **Authenticity of digitally signed data**—Authentication of source, proving that a certain party has signed the data in question.
- **Integrity of digitally signed data**—Guarantee that the data has not changed since being signed by the signer.
- **Nonrepudiation of the transaction**—The recipient can take the data to a third party, which will accept the digital signature as a proof that this data exchange really did take place. The signing party cannot repudiate (that is, deny) that it has signed the data.

Digital signatures are usually based on asymmetric encryption algorithms to generate and verify digital signatures. Compared to using asymmetric encryption for confidentiality, the usage of the keys is reversed when creating digital signatures: The private key is used to create the signature, and the public key is used to verify the signature.

Because digital signatures are based on asymmetric (slow) algorithms, they are not used today to provide real-time authenticity and integrity guarantees to network traffic. In network protocols, they are usually used as a proof of endpoint (client, server, and phone) identity when two entities initially connect (for example, an IP phone authenticating to Cisco CallManager, or a Cisco VPN Client authenticating to a Cisco VPN Concentrator). For real-time protection of authenticity and integrity, which do not require nonrepudiation (for example, signaling messages between IP phones and a Cisco CallManager, or IPsec packet protection), HMAC methods are used instead.

Digital Signatures and RSA

Digital signatures require a key pair for each device that wants to create signatures. One key is used to create signatures and the other is used to verify signatures. RSA can be used for that purpose. The usage of the RSA keys for digital signatures is opposite to their usage for encryption:

- **Digital signatures**—The signer uses its private key to sign (encrypt) data. The signature is checked by a recipient who is using the public key of the signer to verify (decrypt) the signature.
- **Encryption**—The sender encrypts the data with the public key of the receiver. This guarantees that only the receiver can decrypt the data because the encrypted data can only be decrypted by the holder of the private key.

RSA is extremely slow and not designed for real-time encryption of a large volume of data. Therefore, when it is used to create signatures, the data that is to be signed is first hashed, and only the hash digest is signed by RSA (encrypted with the public key). This practice significantly improves performance because RSA transforms only the fingerprint of the data (not all of the data). The signature and verification process, illustrated in Figure 24-6, is as follows:

Step 1 The signer makes a hash (fingerprint) of the document, which uniquely identifies the document and all its contents.

> **NOTE** A hash of the data is created for two reasons: First, RSA is extremely slow, and it is more efficient to sign only the (shorter) fingerprint than to sign the whole of the data. Next, if the transferred information should be out-of-band verified, it is simpler to compare the shorter fingerprint than to compare all the transferred information.

Step 2 The signer encrypts the hash only with its private key.

Step 3 The encrypted hash (the signature) is appended to the document.

Step 4 The verifier obtains the public key of the signer.

Step 5 The verifier decrypts the signature with the public key of the signer. This process unveils the assumed hash value of the signer.

Step 6 The verifier makes a hash of the received document (without its signature) and compares this hash to the decrypted signature hash. If the hashes match, the document is authentic (that is, it has been signed by the assumed signer) and has not been changed since the signer signed it.

Figure 24-6 *RSA Signature Process*

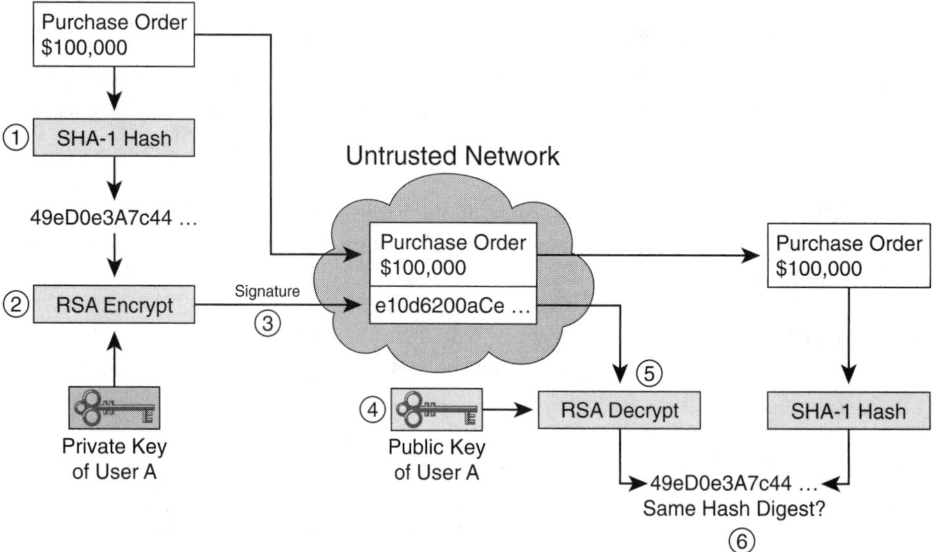

Summary

This chapter discussed the concepts behind cryptography. Cryptography is the science of transforming cleartext into ciphertext and transforming the ciphertext back into cleartext. Symmetric encryption is one of the fastest encryption methods because it uses the same key for both encryption and decryption. With symmetric encryption, a different key is needed for each pair of devices. Asymmetric encryption uses a different key for encryption and decryption. When using asymmetric encryption, each device needs a pair of keys: one public and one private.

Hashes are one-way functions that can be used to authenticate data by adding a secret value to the data being sent. Digital signatures sign data by using the private, asymmetric encryption, key to encrypt fingerprints (hashes) of the data.

Review Questions

You can find the solutions to these questions in Appendix A, "Answers to Review Questions."

1. Which two of the following are not cryptographic services?
   a. Authenticity
   b. Confidentiality
   c. Integrity
   d. Nonrepudiation
   e. Resistance against DoS
   f. Defense in depth
2. Which two statements about symmetric encryption are true?
   a. Symmetric encryption is a good choice for real-time encryption of bulk data.
   b. Symmetric encryption is commonly used to sign asymmetric keys.
   c. Symmetric encryption uses asymmetric keys.
   d. RSA is an example of a symmetric encryption algorithm.
   e. ASE is an example of a symmetric encryption algorithm.
   f. With symmetric encryption, the encryption key equals the decryption key.
3. Which two statements about asymmetric encryption are true?
   a. Asymmetric encryption is considerably faster than symmetric encryption.
   b. Asymmetric encryption keys should have about half the lifetime of symmetric encryption keys.
   c. With asymmetric encryption, the private key can only encrypt data, whereas the public key can only decrypt data.
   d. With asymmetric encryption, either of the two keys can be used for encryption and the opposite key can be used for decryption.
   e. NSA is an example of an asymmetric encryption algorithm.
   f. Asymmetric encryption is often used to create signatures.

4. Which two statements about hash functions are true?
   a. A hash digest can never be reverted to the hashed data.
   b. It is computationally difficult to revert a hash digest to the hashed data.
   c. Data can be encrypted if hashed with a secret key.
   d. Data can be signed by appending a hash of the data.
   e. AES can use SHA-1 for data encryption.
   f. AES can use MD5 for hashing data.
5. Which of the following statements does not apply to digital signatures?
   a. Digital signatures provide data authenticity.
   b. Digital signatures provide data integrity.
   c. Digital signatures provide nonrepudiation.
   d. Digital signatures do not provide data confidentiality.
   e. Digital signatures are based on asymmetric cryptographic algorithms.
   f. Digital signatures are created by hashing the result of an asymmetric encryption.
6. Which of the following represent a more reliable hashing algorithm?
   a. DES
   b. 3DES
   c. AES
   d. SHA-1
   e. RSA
   f. MD5
7. You are looking for a method that can prove to others that a certain source sent some data. What cryptography method accomplishes this?
   a. Nonrepudiation
   b. Authentication
   c. Confidentiality
   d. Integrity
   e. Encryption

8. Which of the following is not a symmetric encryption algorithm?

   a. AES
   b. RSA
   c. DES
   d. Blowfish

9. When using asymmetric encryption, which key is transmitted from the sending to the receiving host?

   a. Public key
   b. Private key
   c. Shared secret key
   d. No keys are transmitted

10. When using asymmetric encryption, the public key is a reverse encryption algorithm of the private key. What is to keep a host from capturing the public key and generating the opposite algorithm to find the private key?

    a. The public key is never communicated to another host.
    b. The public key is first encrypted with a shared secret key.
    c. Asymmetric keys are always paired with symmetric keys to ensure the algorithm cannot be broken.
    d. It is feasibly impossible to find the opposite formula with just the public key.

This chapter covers the following topics:

- Describing the problem of secure, scalable distribution of public keys and presenting PKI as a solution
- Explaining the concept of a trusted introducer
- Explaining certificates, CAs, certification paths, certificate trust, and revocation lists
- Explaining the certificate enrollment procedure
- Explaining PKI certificate revocation
- Explaining the use of PKI in existing applications

CHAPTER 25

Understanding the Public Key Infrastructure

Cisco CallManager Release 4.0 and later supports many security features that are based on a Public Key Infrastructure (PKI) solution. In earlier releases, Cisco CallManager did not use PKI-like features, and many Cisco CallManager administrators are not familiar with PKI. This chapter discusses the concept of a PKI, its components, and its applications.

The Need for a PKI

Scalable and secure key exchange is the main issue when deploying cryptography. Depending on the cryptographic algorithm that is used, there are different needs. In symmetric encryption, the keys should be changed frequently. They are shared between two peers. But how can you exchange these keys safely between the peers? Symmetric keys should be known only by the two peers using them, and, therefore, *confidentiality* must be ensured for the key exchange.

In asymmetric encryption, the public key of a device has to be known by all other devices (made public). But how can you distribute the public keys safely to your devices? You have to ensure that the public keys that are exchanged over the network are authentic, and hence *authenticity* must be ensured for that key exchange.

Key Exchange in Symmetric Cryptography

When exchanging keys in symmetric cryptography, you have two possible options: You can use out-of-band manual key exchange or you can use in-band automated key exchange.

Manual key exchange is the simplest method of exchanging secret keying material. However, it does not scale and often relies on the human operator to perform the procedure securely. Every peer with which the entity wants to exchange encrypted traffic must go through a one-time manual key exchange. After the keys are generated, the two parties exchange the keys manually, through a secure channel (for example, by telephone or in person). This process should include an out-of-band method of authentication to ensure that the keys were exchanged unaltered with the correct party. This concept is often applied when using authenticated routing protocol updates, where the symmetric key that is used for the authentication has to be entered on all participating routers. If multiple router administrators are involved, they can exchange the symmetric key in person or use some other protected channel (such as encrypted e-mail and Secure Shell [SSH Protocol]).

Most key exchanges are automated and do not require any human intervention. A couple of good methods for automatic key exchange are heavily used in modern cryptosystems. One of them is the Diffie-Hellman algorithm, which allows two peers to compute the same value (key) without exchanging all information that is needed for that computation. Another method is to send the actual symmetric keys but encrypt them using an asymmetric encryption algorithm first. In Cisco IP telephony, asymmetric encryption algorithms are used to exchange symmetric keys securely.

Key Exchange Protected by Asymmetric Encryption

When using asymmetric encryption to secure the automated exchange of symmetric keys, the keys are encrypted with the public key of the receiver and then sent over the untrusted network. Only the receiver can decrypt the message (the keys) because only the receiver knows the corresponding private key. This solution relies on the knowledge of public keys of all possible peers at all the participating devices.

In the example shown in Figure 25-1, user A wants to use symmetric encryption with user B.

Figure 25-1 *Using Asymmetric Cryptography to Securely Exchange Symmetric Keys*

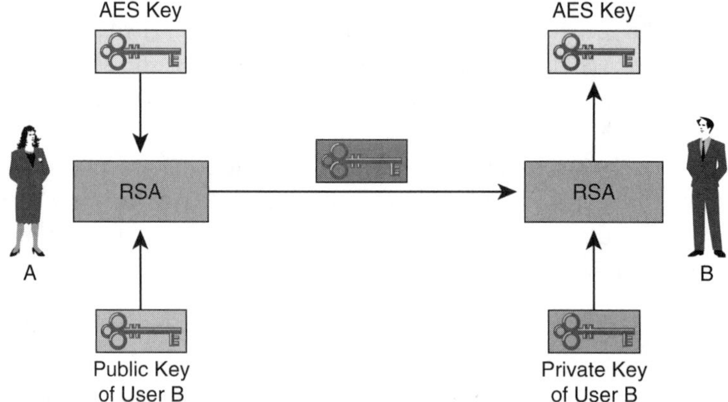

For secure key exchange, asymmetric encryption will be used in this way:

Step 1 User A generates the symmetric key.

Step 2 User A encrypts the symmetric key with the public RSA key of user B and sends the encrypted key over the untrusted network to user B.

Step 3 User B decrypts the key using his private RSA key.

Step 4 Now both of them know the symmetric key and can start using it for encrypting their communication channel.

As mentioned previously, this solution assumes that user A knows the public key of user B.

The Pitfall of Asymmetric Key Exchange

Asymmetric algorithms offer the advantage of one of the keys being public, which simplifies key exchange and distribution. The pitfall of this approach is not obvious at first glance. Obtaining the public key from another person can be very tricky. Although it is true that public keys are public information and can be published in a well-known directory, an extremely important issue remains: When you receive a public key from someone, how do you really know it belongs to that person?

When a public key is requested or is sent over an untrusted network, an attacker could intercept that key and substitute another public key for it. This man-in-the-middle attack would cause the message sender to encrypt all messages with the public key of the attacker. A mechanism is, therefore, needed that allows verification of the relationship between a name of an entity and its public key. The PKI is the solution to this problem and allows such systems to scale, although, on a smaller scale, alternative, manual solutions can be devised.

PKI as a Trusted Third-Party Protocol

PKI does not eliminate the need for authenticity when exchanging public keys in an asymmetric encryption environment, but PKI solves the scalability issues associated with that process. It uses the concept of a single, trusted introducer. Instead of securely exchanging all public keys among all devices, only the public key of the trusted introducer has to be securely distributed to all devices, as shown in Figure 25-2. This is usually done by downloading the public key and then verifying it out of band. The trusted introducer performs the role of authentication for the devices: If the devices are authenticated by the trusted introducer, they are considered authenticated to each other. If they are not authenticated by the trusted introducer, they are not authenticated to each other. Essentially, the devices have an explicit (configured) trust to believe anything the trusted introducer tells them.

Figure 25-2 *Using the Public Key of the Trusted Introducer*

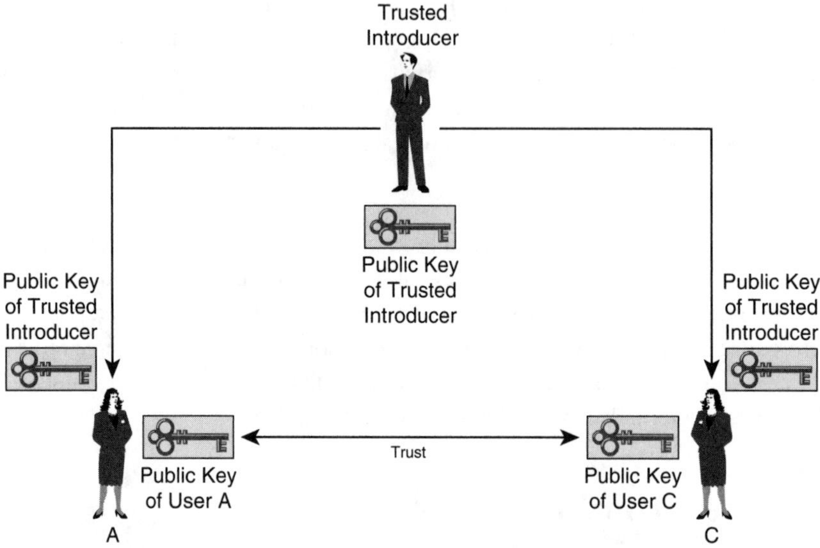

When all devices know the authentic key of the introducer, the introducer can guarantee the authenticity of the public keys of all devices by using a certificate for each device in the topology. The certificate includes information about the identity of a device and its public key. The (publicly trusted) introducer then signs the certificates of the individual devices, and the devices can directly distribute their public keys by sending their certificates. A device receiving such a certificate can verify it by checking the signature of the issuer (the introducer).

Every user in the system trusts information provided by the introducer. In practice, this is accomplished by digital signatures. Anything that the introducer signs is considered to be trusted. To verify the signatures of the trusted introducer, each user of this system must first obtain the public key of the trusted introducer. To become a part of the trust system, all end users enroll with the introducer; that is, they submit their identity and their public key to the introducer, as shown in Figure 25-3.

Figure 25-3 *Exchanging Public Keys*

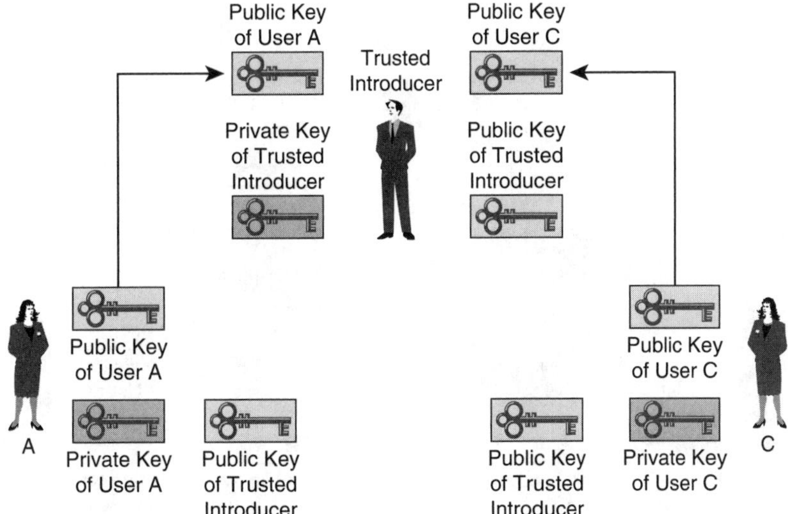

The trusted introducer then verifies the identity and public key of each enrolling user and, if they are correct, the trusted introducer digitally signs the submitted public key with the private key of the introducer. The result is a kind of "document" (certificate) for each user that includes the identity (name) of the user and the public key of the user. The trusted introducer provides each user with a signed document, containing the name and public key of the user, bound together by the signature of the trusted introducer. As shown in Figure 25-4, each user now possesses a public and private key pair, the public key of the trusted introducer, and a document with the identity and public key of the user. This document is signed by the trusted introducer.

Figure 25-4 *Generation of a PKI Certificate*

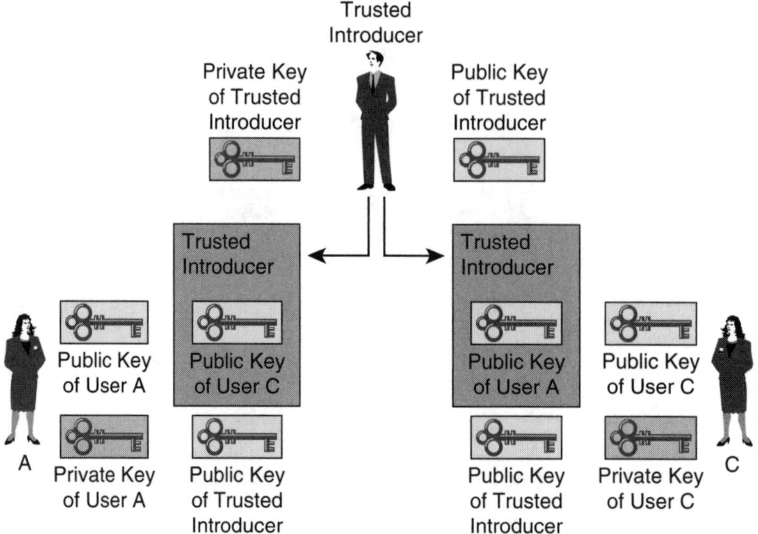

Because all users now have their own documents containing the correct name and public key, signed by the trusted introducer, and the public key of the trusted introducer, they can verify all data signed by the trusted introducer. The entities can now (independently of the trusted introducer) establish point-to-point trusted relationships by exchanging information about themselves in the form of that document.

In practice, this means that at this stage the end users can mutually exchange signed public keys over an insecure medium and use the digital signature of the trusted introducer as the protection mechanism for the exchange. Again, the signature of the trusted introducer is trusted because it can be verified (the entities have the public key of the trusted introducer), and the trusted introducer and its operations are considered to be secure.

PKI Entities

A PKI is the service framework needed to support large-scale public key–based technologies. The PKI is a set of all the technical, organizational, and legal components needed to establish a system that enables large-scale use of public key cryptography to provide authenticity, confidentiality, integrity, and nonrepudiation services.

Two very important terms need to be defined when talking about a PKI:

- A *Certificate Authority* (CA) is the trusted third party (trusted introducer) that signs the public keys of all end entities (PKI users).

- A *certificate* is a document that, in essence, binds the name of the entity and its public key that has been signed by the CA, so that every other entity will be able to trust it.

> **NOTE** Certificates are not secret information and do not need to be encrypted in any way. The idea is not to hide anything but to ensure the authenticity and integrity of the information contained in the certificate.

Another term that is often used with a PKI is *certificate revocation list* (CRL). The CRL is a list of certificates that should not be trusted anymore. Examples of when a certificate is added to the CRL ("revoked") include exposure or loss of the private key. A PKI user who receives a certificate should verify the CRL to ensure that the received certificate is not on the list of revoked certificates.

Many vendors offer CA servers as a managed service or as an end-user product:

- Microsoft Windows 2000/2003 Certificate Services (http://www.microsoft.com) is a Windows Server add-on that allows an organization to set up its own CA server.
- VeriSign (http://www.verisign.com) offers outsourced PKI services.
- Entrust Technologies (http://www.entrust.com) offers both PKI products and outsourcing services.
- The CA Proxy Function (CAPF) in Cisco CallManager can act as a standalone CA.

X.509v3 Certificates

X.509 is the ubiquitous and well-known standard that defines basic PKI data formats, such as certificate and CRL format, to enable basic interoperability. This format is already extensively used in the infrastructure of the Internet. X.509 is used for these applications:

- With secure web servers for website authentication in the Secure Sockets Layer (SSL) protocol
- With web browsers for services that implement client certificates in the SSL protocol
- With user mail agents that support mail protection using the Secure/Multipurpose Internet Mail Extensions (S/MIME) protocol
- In IPsec virtual private networks (VPNs) where certificates can be used as a public key distribution mechanism for Internet Key Exchange (IKE) Rivest, Shamir, and Adleman (RSA)–based authentication

Figure 25-5 shows an example certificate format, following X.509 Version 3 (X.509v3). The most important pieces of information contained in the certificate are these:

- Subject X.500 Name (Name of the holder)
- Subject Public Key Information (Public key)
- CA Signature

Other fields include these:

- Certificate serial number
- Validity period of the certificate
- Signature Algorithms

Figure 25-5 *Sample X.509 Certificate Format*

Certificate Format Version	Version 3
Certificate Serial Number	12457801
Signature Algorithm Identifier for CA	RSA with SHA-1
Issuer X.500 Name	C=US O=Cisco CN=CA
Validity Period	Start=04/01/04 Expire=04/01/09
Subject X.500 Name	C=US O=Cisco CN=CCMCluster001
Subject Public Key Information	756ECE0C9ADC7140...
Extension(s) (v3)	
CA Signature	2C086C7FE0B6E90DA396AB...

Self-Signed Certificates

In a PKI system, all public keys are distributed in a form of a certificate, including the certificate of the trusted introducer, the CA. The obvious question is: Who signs the certificate of the CA, if it is itself the signer of all other certificates? In reality, the CA also issues a certificate to itself, just to have a consistent format for distributing its public key. This process is how the end entities obtain the public key of the CA—by obtaining its self-signed certificate. The signature of a self-signed certificate of the CA cannot be verified using the standard method (verification by using the public key of the signer) because that public key should actually be protected by the signature. Therefore, other methods (such as manual verification) are needed to ensure the authenticity of a CA certificate.

Sometimes end entities also sign their own certificates. This happens if that particular end entity is not a part of a PKI but uses a PKI-enabled application. For example, a web server could generate a private and public RSA key and sign its public key with its private key to create a self-signed certificate. This certificate could then be used in Secure HTTP (HTTPS), where the web server would present a self-signed certificate to the connecting web browser. However, how does the web browser verify the presented certificate, if it was not issued (signed) by a known CA for which the web browser has a locally available certificate? This web server certificate, therefore, cannot be accepted automatically, but needs to be verified using some other method (such as the manual, out-of-band verification that is also used in pre-PKI protocols).

- Organizations will typically use self-signed certificates internally to save on the continual cost of obtaining certificates from a publicly known Certificate Authority (CA). This causes web browser clients to initially display warning messages when connecting to a server using a self-signed certificate.

PKI Enrollment

PKI enrollment is the process of adding a PKI user (such as a person, a device, or an application) to the PKI. The enrollment is done in the following way:

Step 1 An enrolling user obtains the CA certificate (self-signed) in which the public key of the CA is embedded. This public key will be used to verify the digital signature on certificates of the other entities.

Step 2 The enrolling user sends its identity information and public key to the CA.

Step 3 The CA verifies (authenticates) the user, signs the submitted information, and returns the signed data in the form of a certificate.

Step 4 The user verifies the returned certificate using the public key of the CA from the previously obtained CA certificate.

The enrollment procedure is the initial step of establishing trust between a user and the CA. If the process is executed over an untrusted network, it would be vulnerable to man-in-the-middle attacks. Therefore, it has to be secured in such cases.

Man-in-the-Middle PKI Enrollment Attack

Without any additional protection for the enrollment process, a man-in-the-middle attack can be used to spoof identities. The attacker could replace the submitted public key of the user with the public key of the attacker, causing the CA to possibly issue a certificate to the attacker instead of to the legitimate user. The attacker could replace the real CA certificate with the false CA certificate of the attacker when the end user requests the certificate of the CA. The end user would then trust the CA of the attacker instead of the real CA.

> **NOTE** The attacker would replace only the public key of the user, not the identity (name) of the user. When the CA issues the certificate, the attacker can pretend to be the user by presenting the certificate with the name of the user but the public key of the attacker.

Secure PKI Enrollment

To mitigate the risk of interception and key substitution during enrollment, the enrollment procedure needs to incorporate two out-of-band authentication procedures:

- Verification by the enrolling PKI user that the correct CA certificate has been received
- Verification by the CA that it has received the correct enrollment information from the enrolling PKI user

This can be done by out-of-band exchange of fingerprints of the messages (certificates). If the out-of-band received fingerprint matches the fingerprint of the received message, the message is authentic. However, if the enrollment is completed over a secure network, where interception is not possible, those security procedures might be relaxed or omitted completely.

To verify that the correct CA certificate has been received, a local hash (fingerprint) of the received information is calculated, as shown in Figure 25-6. This fingerprint is compared to the true CA certificate fingerprint, obtained over the telephone or another secure channel. If they match, the true CA certificate has been received.

When the user submits identity and public key information, a local hash (fingerprint) of the submitted information is calculated again. The CA also performs a hashing procedure of the received information. The CA then compares its hash of the received information to the hash of the user of the submitted information over the telephone or any other secure channel. If the two hashes match, the CA has received an unmodified enrollment request.

Figure 25-6 *Manually Securing PKI Enrollment*

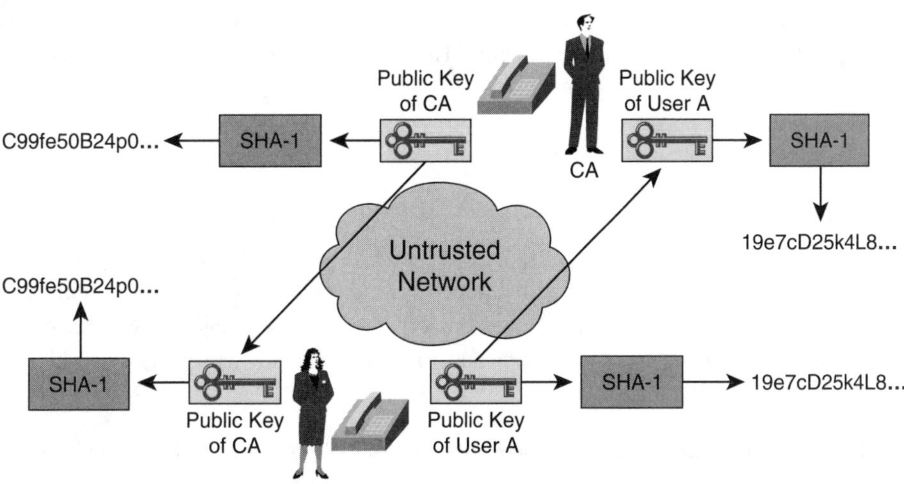

PKI Revocation and Key Storage

A certificate and the public key included in the certificate and its associated private key have a lifetime. When a certificate is issued, the CA sets the lifetime of the certificate. The lifetime of certificates is usually relatively long (months to years). But how do you handle a situation in which a key becomes compromised before its expiration? This would happen if, for instance, an intruder steals a server's private key. In such a case, all other entities have to know not to trust that private key (and its corresponding public key).

The most common reasons why a certificate should not be trusted anymore include the following:

- Private key compromise
- Contract termination for that PKI user
- Loss of private keys (for instance, because of device replacement)

A PKI can offer such a solution by revoking a certificate. Certificate revocation is the announcement that a private key is not trustworthy anymore. You can revoke a certificate using different methods.

PKI Revocation Methods

Keys that are not trusted anymore could be manually revoked by deleting the certificates and the corresponding keys on all affected systems. This process does not scale, so a form of automatic revocation is needed.

Automatic revocation can be achieved by different methods:

- **Certificate revocation lists (CRLs)**—These lists contain all certificates that are no longer valid. The CRL is signed by the CA and has a lifetime. It is stored in a Lightweight Directory Access Protocol (LDAP)-accessible directory or on a web server and made publicly available. It is the duty of the end user to download a fresh CRL after the lifetime of the current CRL has expired. Whenever an end user wants to use a certificate, it should be checked against the downloaded CRL.
- **Online Certificate Status Protocol (OCSP)**—OCSP is a protocol designed for real-time verification of certificates against a database of revoked certificates. Upon receipt of a certificate of another user, the end user or device queries the OCSP server in real time to verify whether the received certificate has been revoked. OCSP is newer and not yet widely used in network infrastructures.

The main advantage of OCSP over CRLs is that it ensures up-to-date information because of the real-time verification of the certificate. CRLs might contain stale information because they are issued periodically, usually every couple of hours. If a key is compromised, a window of vulnerability exists until the end user downloads a new CRL listing the certificate of the compromised system. To at least limit this window of vulnerability, the CRL lifetime is used.

Key Storage

Secret (for symmetric algorithms) and private (for asymmetric algorithms) keys must be stored securely because forgery and loss of privacy could result if their secrecy is compromised. The measures taken to protect a secret or private key must be at least equal to the required security of the messages encrypted with that key. Ideally, keys are never stored in cleartext form or in user-accessible storage.

Keys, especially long-term keys (such as RSA), should be protected especially well. They are very often stored on nonvolatile storage media:

- **Hard drives**—For example, storing private RSA keys on a PC
- **Flash memory**—Sometimes, in the form of a Personal Computer Memory Card International Association (PCMCIA) card
- **Read-only memory (ROM)**—For example, encryption keys that are hard-coded in hardware

Ideally, RSA keys are stored on Smart Cards or tokens where all key-related operations are done so that the key itself does not even have to leave that device.

Smart Cards and Smart Tokens

A Smart Card or smart token is essentially a small computer, capable of performing basic cryptographic operations and containing the protected secret keys within its internal memory. The host computer, to which the Smart Card reader is attached, simply passes challenges to the card, which, for example, computes an authentication response. This technique ensures that the private key never leaves the card and provides one of the strongest key-protection methods available today.

Any PKI-based application that uses certificates to distribute public keys can store the relevant private key on a Smart Card instead of in some less well-protected memory (such as the hard disk of the end user). The application software then off-loads all public key operations to the Smart Card.

In Cisco IP telephony, the private RSA key used to sign the Certificate Trust List (CTL) is stored on a smart token and never leaves it. The smart token is a small computer that can sign data fed to it over the Universal Serial Bus (USB) interface.

> **NOTE** More information on Smart Card and smart token technology can be found at http://www.opencard.org, http://www.chipcard.ibm.com, and http://www.gemplus.com.

PKI Example

Among the first applications of a PKI were web browsers and web servers using SSL. With these applications, the web server authenticates to the browser using a PKI system. HTTPS is widely used on the Internet today and whenever secure web communication is needed (for example, online banking and e-commerce).

Transport Layer Security (TLS) is the successor of SSL and is application-independent, hence not limited to HTTP traffic. TLS is very similar to SSL and also uses a PKI system to provide secure communication.

S/MIME, used for secure messaging, is another example of an application that relies on a PKI.

PKI and SSL/TLS

If a web server runs sensitive applications, SSL or TLS is used to secure the communication channel between the client and the server. A company that needs to run a secure web server (a server supporting authenticated and encrypted HTTP sessions) first generates a public and private key on the web server. The public key is then sent to one of the Internet CAs, which, after verifying the identity of the submitter, issues a certificate to the server by signing the public key of the web server with the private key of the CA.

Internet CAs are mainly run by either specialized private companies (such as VeriSign), telecommunications companies, or governments. The certificates of those CAs are embedded at installation into client operating systems (such as Microsoft Windows) or inside browsers (such as Mozilla). The collection of embedded CA certificates serves as the trust anchor for the user. The user can then verify the validity of signatures of any other certificate signed using the public keys contained in those CA certificates.

Web Server Certificate Exchange

Figure 25-7 shows part of the list of the CA certificates embedded in the web browser. To see the CA certificates installed in your computer, open Microsoft Internet Explorer, choose **Tools > Internet Options,** choose the **Content** tab, click **Publishers,** and choose the **Trusted Root Certification Authorities** tab.

Figure 25-7 *Default Trusted Root Certificate Authorities in Windows XP*

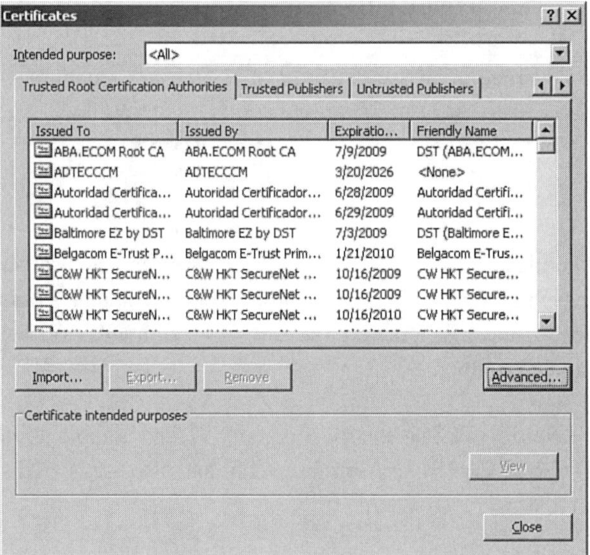

When a browser contacts a secure web server using HTTPS, the first step of the protocol is to authenticate the web server—to verify that the browser indeed has connected to the correct web server, as desired by the user. Figure 25-8 depicts an example in which a user connects to https://www.amazon.com.

Figure 25-8 *Web Server Certificate Verification*

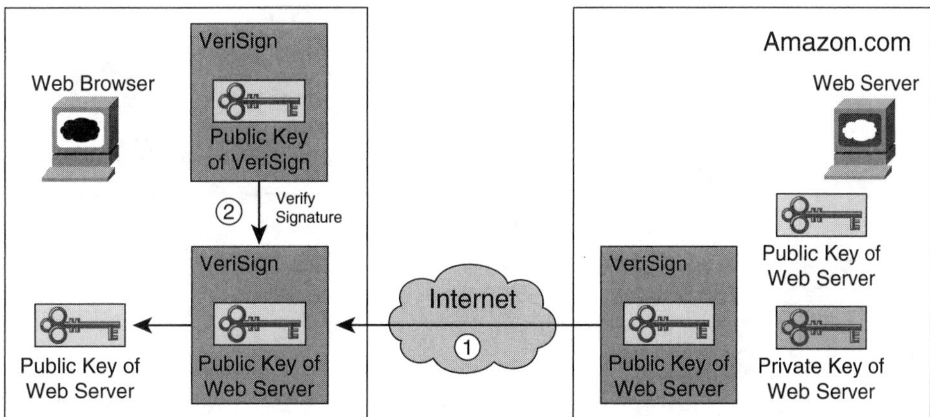

Authentication of the web server uses a challenge-response method, with which the server will prove that it possesses the private key of the desired server (www.amazon.com). However, to prove possession of the private key of the server, the browser needs the public key of the server first. Here is the sequence of events:

Step 1 When the client connects to the www.amazon.com web server, the web server first sends its certificate, signed by a well-known Internet CA to the client.

Step 2 The client uses one of the local root CA certificates (the issuer's certificate of the server certificate) to verify its validity, and optionally downloads the CRL to verify that the server certificate has not been revoked.

Step 3 If verification is successful, the client now knows that it has an authentic public key of the www.amazon.com server in its possession.

Next, the client challenges the web server to verify that the web server has the private key that belongs to the public key that the client received in the certificate of the web server. This private key should be known only to the www.amazon.com web server:

Step 1 The client generates random data, and sends it to the web server to be encrypted with the private key of the web server (challenge), as shown in Figure 25-9.

Figure 25-9 *Authenticating the Web Server*

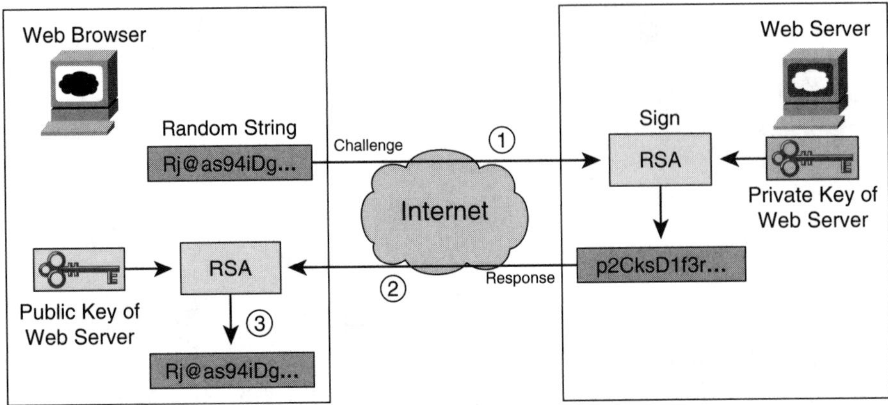

Step 2 The web server signs (RSA-encrypts) the random data using its private key and returns the signed random data to the client (response).

Step 3 The client verifies (RSA-decrypts) the signed random data using the public key of the server from the verified certificate and compares it against the random data that the client generated previously.

Step 4 If the signature is authentic, the web server really possesses the private key, corresponding to the public key in the certificate of the web server (www.amazon.com), and is, therefore, authentic.

NOTE In this example, the web server was authenticated by the client; the web server, however, has no idea about the identity of the client. Authentication of the client is optional in SSL and TLS and, if used, would use exactly the reverse procedure to authenticate the client, provided that the client also possesses a private and public RSA key pair and a certificate recognized by the web server. However, most servers choose to authenticate the client using a simple username/password mechanism over the secure SSL/TLS session because this method is easier to deploy than client-side certificates.

Using the authentic certificate of the web server, the client can now generate and send session keys, which are used by the symmetric encryption algorithm of SSL or TLS to communicate securely with the web server. As shown in Figure 25-10, the exchange of session keys is done in the following way:

Step 1 The client generates symmetric session keys for SSL or TLS Hash-based Message Authentication Code (HMAC) and encryption algorithms.

Step 2 The client encrypts these keys using the www.amazon.com public key of the web server and sends them to the server.

Step 3 The www.amazon.com web server (only) can decrypt the such-encrypted session keys using its private key.

Figure 25-10 *Exchanging Session Keys*

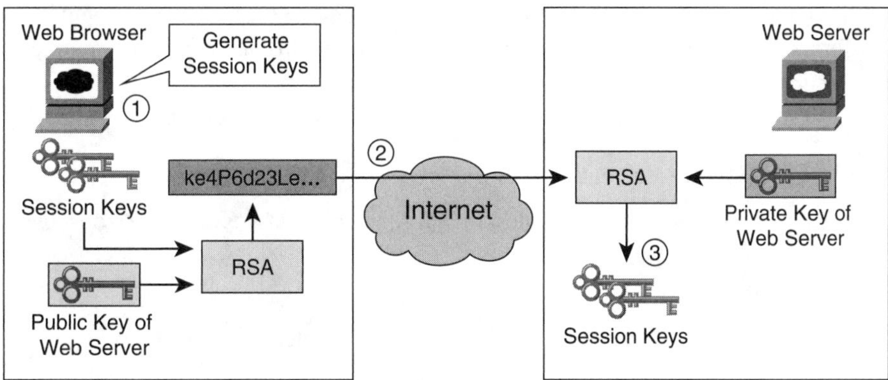

Now, after the client and the server have shared the secret session keys, they can use them to exchange authenticated (signed using the HMAC algorithm) and encrypted (using a symmetric encryption algorithm, such as Triple Data Encryption Standard [3DES], Advanced Encryption Standard [AES], or RC4) messages, as shown in Figure 25-11.

Figure 25-11 *Session Encryption*

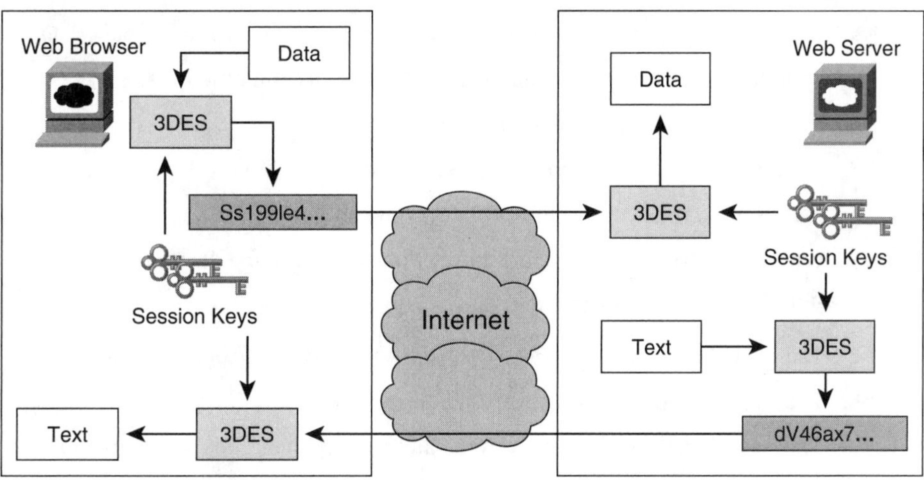

Summary

This chapter discussed the concepts behind the Public Key Infrastructure (PKI). PKI is needed for secure, scalable key exchange over larger corporate networks and public networks, such as the Internet. PKI uses the concept of a single "trusted introducer" to eliminate the need for any-to-any authentication. These trusted introducers are known in PKI as Certificate Authorities (CAs), which issue certificates, through a process known as enrollment, to its associated users. PKI revocation allows these certificates issued to the clients to be announced as invalid before the lifetime of the certificate has expired. This process is necessary when private keys become compromised and, therefore, cannot be trusted anymore. SSL, TLS, and S/MIME are common examples of PKI-enabled protocols.

Review Questions

You can find the solutions to these questions in Appendix A, "Answers to Review Questions."

1. What problem does PKI solve?
   a. The lack of a common encryption standard for Internet applications
   b. The problem that asymmetric encryption techniques do not work without a PKI
   c. The fact that Diffie-Hellman is not secure
   d. The problem of scalable, secure key exchange
   e. The problem of manually issuing bulk certificates
   f. The performance problem when using RSA
2. Which two statements about symmetric encryption are true?
   a. Symmetric encryption is a good choice for real-time encryption of bulk data.
   b. Symmetric encryption is commonly used to sign asymmetric keys.
   c. Symmetric encryption uses asymmetric keys.
   d. RSA is an example of a symmetric encryption algorithm.
   e. ASE is an example of a symmetric encryption algorithm.
   f. With symmetric encryption, the encryption key equals the decryption key.
3. Which two statements about trusted introducers are incorrect?
   a. The trusted introducer has to be trusted by all other members of the system.
   b. The trusted introducer has to trust all other members of the system.
   c. The trusted introducer guarantees the authenticity of entities it is introducing to others.
   d. Only the trusted introducer has to trust the root of the system.
   e. The trusted introducer is the root of a system.
   f. Any entity of the system can guarantee the authenticity of any other member.

4. Which statement about a certificate is true?

   a. A certificate includes the identity of the owner of the certificate and the symmetric key of the owner.

   b. A certificate includes the public key of the issuer.

   c. A certificate includes the identity of the owner of the certificate and the private key of the owner.

   d. A certificate includes the identity of the issuer of the certificate, the identity of the owner of the certificate, and the public key of the owner.

   e. A certificate does not include any keys in cleartext.

   f. A certificate includes an encrypted private key of the owner and a cleartext public key of the issuer.

5. Which of the following are the two valid options to secure enrollment in a PKI?

   a. Perform the enrollment from a trusted device only.

   b. Perform the enrollment in both directions.

   c. Perform the enrollment over a trusted network.

   d. Use self-signed certificates on all devices.

   e. Do not send the private key in the enrollment.

   f. Perform mutual out-of-band authentication between the PKI user and CA.

6. Which of the following is true about certificate revocation?

   a. Any entity of a PKI system that receives an untrusted certificate can request revocation of that certificate.

   b. The CA periodically revokes all expired certificates.

   c. Certificate revocation is needed when the public key has been transferred without a certificate.

   d. Certificate revocation is needed whenever the private key is not trustworthy anymore.

   e. Certificate revocation is needed whenever the public key is not trustworthy anymore.

   f. Certificate revocation is the process of adding a user to the PKI.

7. What is the certificate of a web server used for when you are using SSL?

   a. It is used to authenticate the client.

   b. The public key of the server is used by the client when encrypting the data sent to the server.

   c. The private key of the server is used by the client when encrypting the data sent to the server.

d. It is used to authenticate the server and to protect the challenge response traffic during client authentication.

e. It is used to authenticate the server and to encrypt the symmetric session keys used for the asymmetric encryption of the data stream.

f. It is used to authenticate the server and to encrypt the symmetric session keys used for the authentication and encryption of the data stream.

8. Which of the following is an asymmetric encryption algorithm?

   a. AES

   b. Diffie-Hellman

   c. DES

   d. Blowfish

9. When using asymmetric encryption, which key is transmitted from the sending to the receiving host?

   a. Public key

   b. Private key

   c. Shared secret key

   d. No keys are transmitted.

10. A nontrusted user has obtained the certificate of one of your public web servers. What should be done to ratify this situation? (Select all that apply.)

    a. Nothing

    b. The certificate should be immediately revoked and published to a CRL.

    c. The certificate should be immediately revoked. Clients can immediately find this revocation if they are using OCSP.

    d. The private key should be regenerated on the web server.

This chapter covers the following topics:

- Explaining how file manipulation, tampering with call-processing signaling, man-in-the-middle attacks, eavesdropping, and IP phone and server identity theft can compromise a Cisco CallManager system
- Explaining how the authentication and encryption mechanisms in a Cisco CallManager system protect against security threats
- Explaining the role of CAPF, external CAs, MIC and LSC, CTLs, and Cisco CTL client
- Explaining the PKI enrollment process in a Cisco IP telephony environment
- Explaining where keys and certificates are stored in a Cisco IP telephony environment
- Describing the processes of image authentication, device authentication, file authentication, and signaling authentication
- Describing the processes and protocols used for signaling encryption and media encryption

CHAPTER 26

Understanding Cisco IP Telephony Authentication and Encryption Fundamentals

Cisco IP telephony systems are subject to several threats, including eavesdropping, identity spoofing, and denial of service (DoS) attacks. In Cisco CallManager Release 4.0 and later, the Cisco IP telephony solution can be secured against these threats by enabling authentication and encryption features. This chapter explains how authentication and encryption can be applied in a Cisco IP telephony environment.

Threats Targeting the IP Telephony System

The main threats targeting the IP telephony system are as follows:

- **Loss of privacy**—If calls can be sniffed, conversations can be replayed or eavesdropped. Because of the open nature of IP networks and, especially, the low trust level in the Internet, privacy is a commonly raised concern when comparing IP telephony solutions against traditional telephony solutions.

- **Loss of integrity**—If voice call signaling or media messages can be intercepted, they can be modified. Although this issue might not arise for human conversations very often, do not forget that calls such as telebanking, e-mail or voice-mail access over a telephone, and similar applications using interactive voice response (IVR) might require secure communication.

- **Impersonation**—Identity spoofing is not limited to humans (for instance, the person behind a telephone) but can also extend to devices, such as Cisco CallManager, a voice gateway, or an IP phone.

- **Denial of Service (DoS)**—These attacks cause loss of functionality. They can be directed against IP telephony components, such as voice gateways, Cisco CallManager nodes, or IP phones, or against the underlying infrastructure. An example is replacing IP phone configuration files or images stored on a TFTP server with invalid files that cause the IP phone to malfunction.

How CallManager Protects Against Threats

Cisco designed Cisco CallManager 4.0 with security largely in mind. A Cisco IP telephony network can now be protected by using cryptographic services. These services are used to provide the following:

- **Secure signaling**—For authentication of devices and authentication and encryption of signaling messages. This precaution stops all kinds of signaling attacks.
- **Secure media transfer**—For authentication and encryption of media streams, preventing eavesdropping on conversations.
- **Authentication of phone images**—To stop attacks against phone images by ensuring the integrity of the image file.
- **Authentication of phone configuration files**—To stop attacks against phone configuration files, again by ensuring the integrity of the file.

Secure Signaling and Media Transfer

Secure signaling in Cisco IP telephony provides authentication and authorization of communicating devices (Cisco IP Phones and Cisco CallManager) and authentication of the signaling messages exchanged between them. It can also provide encryption of the signaling messages. Securing the call signaling is mandatory if you plan to secure the media transfer as well. The reason for this precaution is that the keys used for securing the media channels are exchanged inside signaling messages.

Secure signaling is achieved by using Transport Layer Security (TLS) and is based on the Cisco IP telephony Public Key Infrastructure (PKI) solution. The secure signaling encapsulates the Skinny Client Control Protocol (SCCP, or Skinny) messages in TLS. TLS provides transport-layer protection and is similar to Secure Sockets Layer (SSL), used for secure web browsing.

Secure media transfer in Cisco IP telephony provides confidentiality by encrypting the media stream. If a hacker captures the media streams, the hacker cannot interpret them or play them back. Secure media transfer also provides integrity and authenticity so that the packets cannot be altered while in transit. If an attacker modifies, removes, or adds Real-Time Transport Protocol (RTP) packets, the receiver detects this manipulation because of the missing or incorrect authentication data. Secure media transfer requires encrypted call signaling because the media encryption keys are exchanged over signaling channels. After you encrypt the media stream, the call is considered a Secure RTP (SRTP) session.

Figure 26-1 illustrates that for secure media transfer, SRTP is used instead of the insecure RTP to exchange voice packets between IP phones. Encapsulating the Skinny protocol inside of TLS encryption ensures secure communication between the IP phone and the CallManager. SRTP is a standard-based (RFC 3711, *The Secure Real-Time Transport Protocol*) and an application-layer encryption that performs inside-payload encryption where the protocol headers do not change. Because the headers in RTP and SRTP are the same, an attacker who sniffs the conversation does not know whether the RTP stream has been encrypted when examining the packet header only. Only when further analyzing the sniffed packets and trying to play them back can the attacker recognize that the audio has been encrypted.

Figure 26-1 *Secure Signaling and Media Transfer*

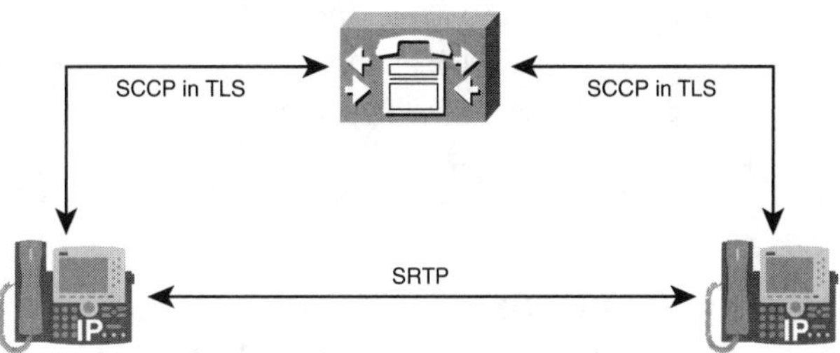

Authentication of Phone Images

To ensure the integrity of Cisco IP Phone images that are loaded from a TFTP server, authenticated images are used. Cisco IP Phones support image authentication on all Cisco IP Phone models. With image authentication, Cisco manufacturing signs the images (using a private key) and appends the signature to the actual firmware. This signature ensures the firmware is from Cisco Systems. Most modern Cisco IP Phones already include the Cisco Systems public key to verify that the signature is accurate, as shown in Figure 26-2. In addition, this feature also allows phones to check the image device type so that incorrect images (those for other phone models) are not loaded.

Figure 26-2 *Phone Image Verification*

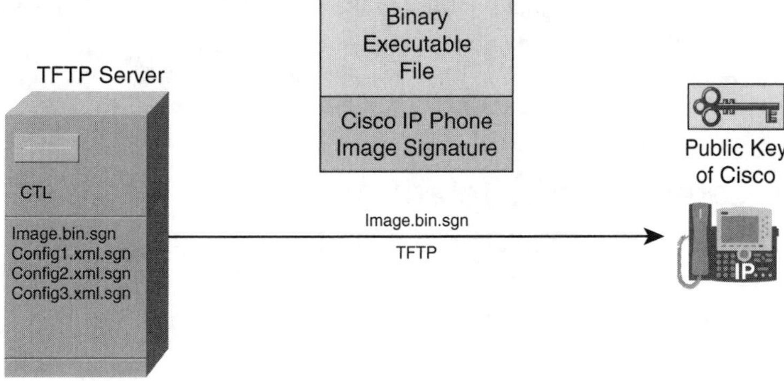

IP phone image authentication was introduced with Cisco CallManager Release 3.3(3). In this and later versions, phone images include the public key that corresponds to the private key used by Cisco manufacturing to sign phone images. In addition, the firmware accepts new images only if their signature is authentic.

IP phone image authentication does not need any additional configuration and is totally independent of the Cisco IP telephony PKI that is used for other features.

TIP If you need to downgrade to an IP phone image that does not yet support IP phone image authentication (earlier than Cisco CallManager Release 3.3(3)), a special "breakout" image can be obtained from the Cisco Technical Assistance Center (TAC). Simply trying to load an older image does not work because the current image will accept only signed images.

Authentication of Phone Configuration Files

In addition to IP phone images, IP phone configuration files can be signed as well. This eliminates man-in-the-middle attacks on the Cisco IP Phone configuration files, which would attempt to direct the IP phone to an alternate (rogue) CallManager server.

Signed IP phone configuration files are implemented differently from signed images. The configuration files are signed by the Cisco TFTP server (with its private key). An IP phone loading a new configuration verifies the configuration file before applying it. The IP phone needs the public key of the TFTP server to do so. Except for the Cisco development public key, the public key of the TFTP server is different for every installation and, therefore, cannot be embedded in the firmware of the IP phone. Therefore, verification must use the Cisco IP telephony PKI. Authenticated IP phone configuration files prevent tampering with the files on the TFTP server or in transit.

NOTE Because authenticated IP phone configuration files depend on the existence of a Cisco IP telephony PKI, the deployment of this feature is far more complex than signed IP phone images. On the other hand, when you enable your cluster for security, authentication of phone configuration files is automatic for all IP phones that are configured for secure operation.

PKI Topologies in Cisco IP Telephony

Unlike classic enterprise PKI deployments, the PKI topology in Cisco IP telephony is not a single PKI system. Instead of having a single Certificate Authority (CA) that issues all certificates, there are several instances issuing certificates:

- **Self-signed certificates**—Cisco CallManager and other servers issue their certificates on their own.

- **Certificates signed by the Cisco manufacturing CA**—Cisco IP Phone 7970 models (and later) have manufacturing installed certificates (MICs).
- **Certificates signed by Cisco CallManager Certificate Authority Proxy Function (CAPF) or by an external CA**—One of these two options is used to issue locally significant certificates (LSCs) to Cisco IP Phone models that support SRTP.

Self-Signed Certificates PKI Topology

Figure 26-3 illustrates several IP telephony services with self-signed certificates. This design requires each server (or server component) have its own self-signed certificate. In the example shown, the Cisco CallManager, TFTP, and CAPF servers all have created their own self-signed certificates. Each one of them act as their own PKI root (they establish their own authority).

Figure 26-3 *Self-Signed Certificate PKI Topology*

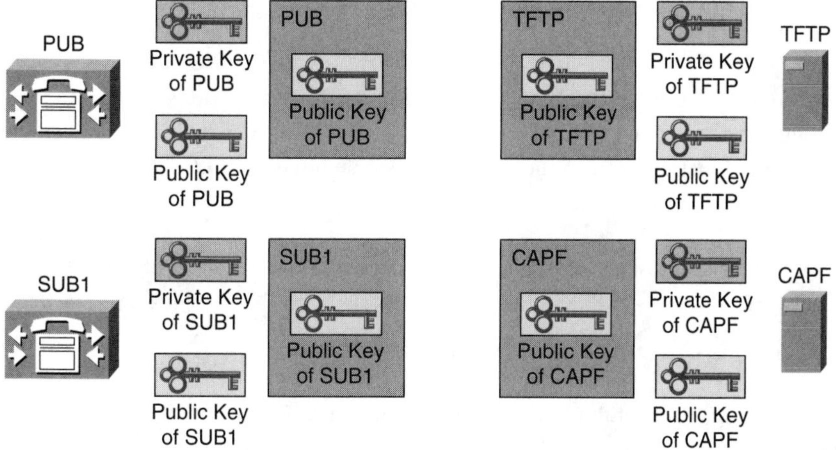

Manufacturing Installed Certificates PKI Topology

Currently, the Cisco 7911, 7941, 7961, 7970, and 7971 IP Phones have a certificate installed by Cisco in nonvolatile memory. This allows the IP phone to be capable of communicating securely with the CallManager out of the box. Cisco highly recommends that you replace these MICs with your own certificate as soon as possible. Figure 26-4 illustrates the keys used when an IP phone comes with an MIC preinstalled.

Figure 26-4 *MIC PKI Topology*

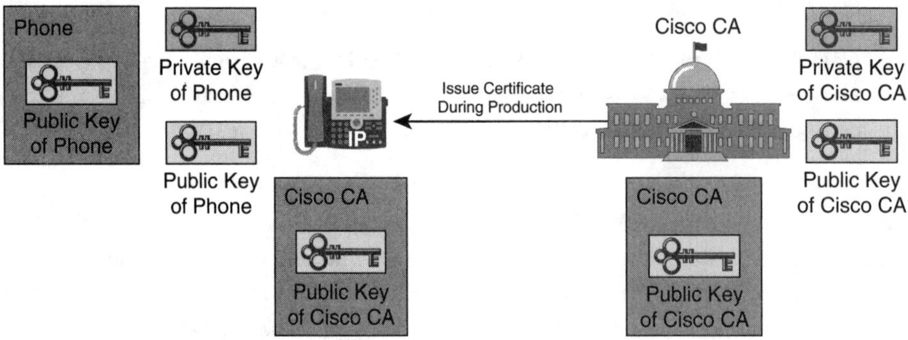

The IP phone with the MIC has its own public and private key pair and a Cisco manufacturing CA certificate installed. The certificate of the IP phone is signed by the Cisco manufacturing CA, which makes the Cisco manufacturing CA the PKI root for all MICs.

Locally Significant Certificates PKI Topology

LSCs are certificates that you install to the IP phone. These can be installed from the CAPF CallManager function or from another CA. When deploying the LSCs to the IP phones, you have a major choice to make:

- Deploy LSCs through a centralized, automated process to all IP phones attached to the network.
- Deploy LSCs manually on a phone-by-phone basis.

Of course, the factor that this decision hinges on is risk. By automatically deploying LSCs to the IP phones, you assume that all the phones that are currently plugged into the network are "friendly." The CallManager will automatically deploy LSCs to all phones. If a hacker has a phone plugged into the network, it will also get an LSC and become a trusted device. The alternate, manual method creates a huge amount of administrative overhead because you must visit each device and manually enter a sequence of digits provided by the CAPF. However, by following this method, you ensure that each IP phone be physically verified before it is considered a trusted device.

As shown in Figure 26-5, the CAPF can either generate LSCs itself, or it can act as a proxy between the IP phone and some other CA.

Figure 26-5 *LSC PKI Topology*

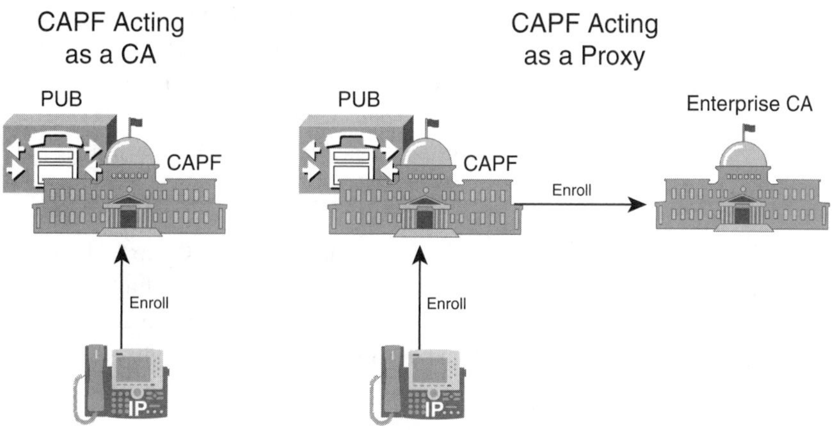

Independent, Separated PKI Topology

As illustrated in Figure 26-6, your IP telephony network might have several, coexisting PKI topologies. There is no single root; instead, there are multiple independent PKI topologies. So far, there is no trust relationship among these different PKIs. A trusted introducer is needed, bringing all the different PKI topologies together under one trusted source. The Certificate Trust List (CTL) client provides that function.

Figure 26-6 *Multiple PKI Topologies*

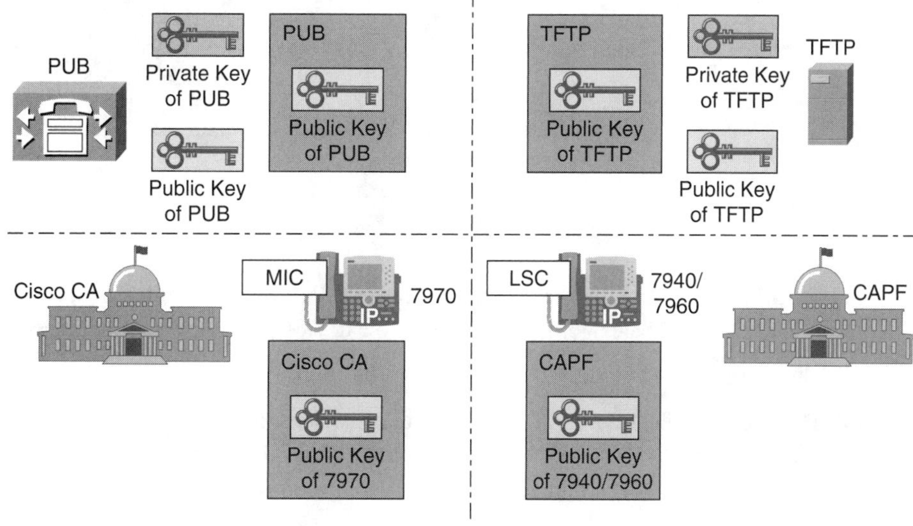

CTL Client

The Cisco CTL client itself has a certificate issued by the Cisco manufacturing CA. The goal of the Cisco CTL client is to obtain the certificates of all entities that issue certificates (self-signed certificates only or certificates for other devices). Then, the Cisco CTL client signs the list of these certificates, the CTL, using its private key. The public and private keys of the Cisco CTL client are stored on a smart token called a security token, which is just a USB key plugged into the PC running the CTL client.

Now there is a single, trusted introducer in the system again: The Cisco CTL client "introduces" trusted devices, not by signing their certificates, but by signing a list of trusted certificates signed by several PKI roots, as shown in Figure 26-7. The CTL can be compared to the root certificate store of Microsoft Internet Explorer. Both are a list of trusted certificate-issuing entities.

Figure 26-7 *CTL Client Creating a List of Trusted Certificates*

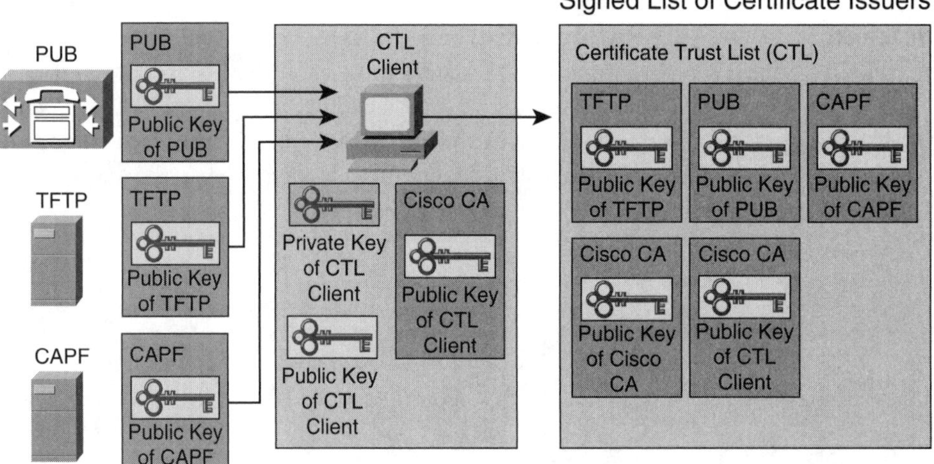

The CTL usually includes these certificates:

- **Cisco CallManager certificates**—Each Cisco CallManager has a self-signed certificate. It allows the Cisco CallManager to authenticate to a device (IP phone) during device registration.
- **TFTP server certificate**—The TFTP server that provides the IP phone with files, such as the IP phone image or the IP phone configuration file, is trusted by the IP phone only if the TFTP server is listed in the CTL of the IP phone.
- **CAPF certificate**—When you are using LSCs, the CAPF issues certificates to the IP phones. The certificate of the CAPF allows the CAPF to authenticate to an IP phone during the enrollment.

- **Cisco certificate**—MICs and the certificate of the security tokens (storing the keys used by the Cisco CTL client) are issued by Cisco manufacturing CA. To allow the phone to verify certificates issued by this Cisco CA, the phone needs the certificate of the Cisco manufacturing CA.
- **Cisco CTL client certificate**—The Cisco CTL client signs the CTL using one of the security tokens. The certificates of the Cisco CTL client (one per security token) have to be known to the IP phone to allow verification of the signature of the CTL.

As shown in Figure 26-8, When an IP phone boots, the CTL is downloaded from the TFTP server to the IP phone. It contains all certificates of the entities that issued self-signed certificates. By having this list, the IP phone knows which PKI roots to trust and can trust all certificates that have been issued by any PKI root contained in the CTL.

Figure 26-8 *Obtaining the CTL*

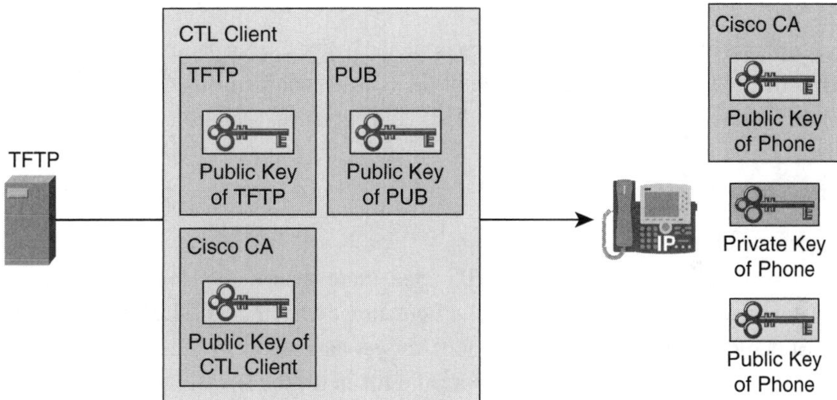

CTL Client Application

The Cisco CTL client software, available as a plug-in application on Cisco CallManager Administration, is used to create or update the CTL. When the list is accurate, the Cisco CTL client will ensure that the CTL is signed by the keys of the Cisco CTL client. These keys are stored on an external Universal Serial Bus (USB) device, which is called the security token. When the CTL needs to be signed, the Cisco CTL client passes the CTL to the security token, and the security token signs it and then returns the signed CTL to the Cisco CTL client application. The Cisco CTL client itself does not have access to the private key stored on the security token. Therefore, it is not the CTL client application that actually signs the CTL; the CTL client only interacts with the security token requesting the security token to create the signature. The public key of a security token is signed by the Cisco manufacturing CA during production, and the appropriate certificate is also stored on the security token itself.

The CTL file needs to be updated after configuration changes, such as changing or adding IP telephony servers or security tokens to the system.

The CTL also acts as an authorization list because it specifies which certificates belong to which IP telephony function. A TFTP server, for instance, is not allowed to sign a CTL, only IP phone configuration files. The CAPF, as another example, is allowed to sign the LSCs of other IP phones only but not the CTL or any TFTP files.

CTL Verification on the IP Phone

Every time that an IP phone receives a new CTL, the new CTL is verified. It is accepted by the IP phone only if it was signed by the Cisco CTL client using one of the administrator tokens. The phone can verify the signature using the public key (the certificate) of the Cisco CTL client (in fact, the certificate of the appropriate administrator token), which must be included in the currently installed ("old") CTL.

This certificate of the administrator token is signed by the Cisco manufacturing CA. This signature is also validated by using the certificate of the Cisco manufacturing CA, which also must be included in the currently installed CTL. This concept works well as long as the phone already has a CTL.

Initial Deployment Issue

For the first download of a CTL to an IP phone, there is an issue: How does an IP phone know which administrator tokens are trusted without already having a CTL? This problem occurs only at initial deployment, when the phone does not yet have a local CTL. In this case, any administrator token could pretend to be a valid token for the IP telephony system in question. An attacker could either replace the CTL file on the TFTP server with a falsified file or change the CTL file in the path between the IP phone and the TFTP server.

The problem can be solved by downloading the initial CTL over a trusted network to ensure that no falsified initial CTL is loaded to the phone. When the phone has a valid CTL, it will trust new CTLs only if they are signed using a security token that is already known to the IP phone. If the CTL file in the IP phone is erased, the same problem occurs. Again, you must ensure that the next CTL download is done over a trusted network path because the IP phone will blindly accept any CTL.

After the IP phone is deployed, it is usually difficult to trust the network path between the phone and Cisco CallManager. Therefore, a user should not be able to erase the initially installed CTL. There are two ways to remove a CTL from an IP phone: a factory reset or the IP phone Settings menu. A factory reset is not simple, but using the Settings menu is rather easy. To prevent users from using the Settings menu to remove the CTL, you should disable settings access at the phone.

When using authentication strings as the authentication method during CAPF phone certificate operations, you have to enable settings access during the enrollment. After successful enrollment, you should then disable settings access again.

PKI Enrollment in Cisco IP Telephony

To obtain a signed certificate, an IP phone needs to enroll with the entity that will issue (sign) the certificate. During enrollment, the phone will get the certificate of the issuer and then send its data to the issuer asking for a (signed) certificate. IP phone enrollment depends on the type of certificate.

With MICs, enrollment was already done by Cisco manufacturing during production. When the IP phone is shipped to the customer, it already has its public and private keys, a certificate issued by the Cisco manufacturing CA, and the certificate of the Cisco manufacturing CA installed. No other PKI provisioning tasks are required. MICs always remain on the phone, even if an LSC is added.

With LSCs, enrollment has to be done by the customer.

NOTE If the IP phone has both a MIC and an LSC, the LSC has priority.

CAPF Acting as a CA

To obtain an LSC from the CAPF acting as a CA, an IP phone has to enroll with the CAPF, as shown in Figure 26-9.

Figure 26-9 *CAPF Enrollment Process*

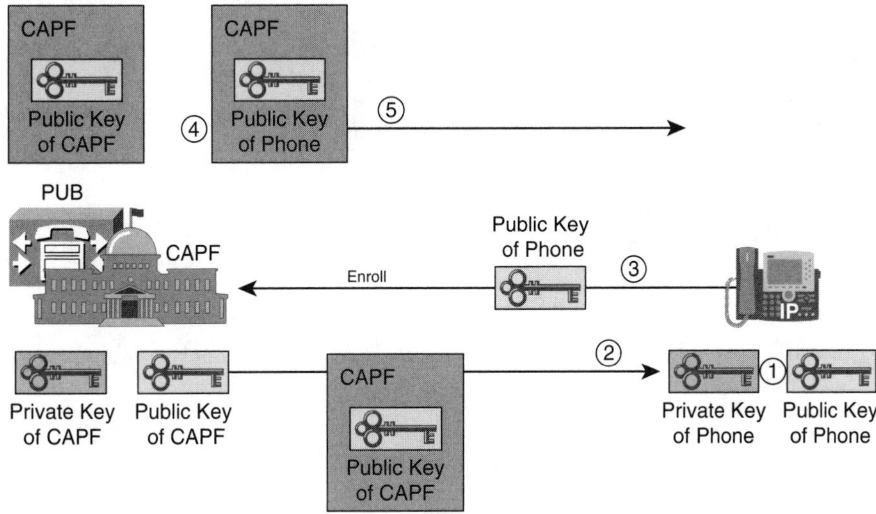

The CAPF enrollment process is as follows:

1. The IP phone generates its public and private key pairs.
2. The IP phone downloads the certificate of the CAPF and uses it to establish a TLS session with the CAPF.
3. The IP phone enrolls with the CAPF, sending its identity, its public key, and an optional authentication string.
4. The CAPF issues a certificate for the IP phone signed with its private key.
5. The CAPF sends the signed certificate to the IP phone.

CAPF Acting as a Proxy to an External CA

If an IP phone should obtain an LSC from an external CA using the CAPF as a proxy, the IP phone has to enroll with the external CA, as shown in Figure 26-10.

Figure 26-10 *CAPF External CA Enrollment Process*

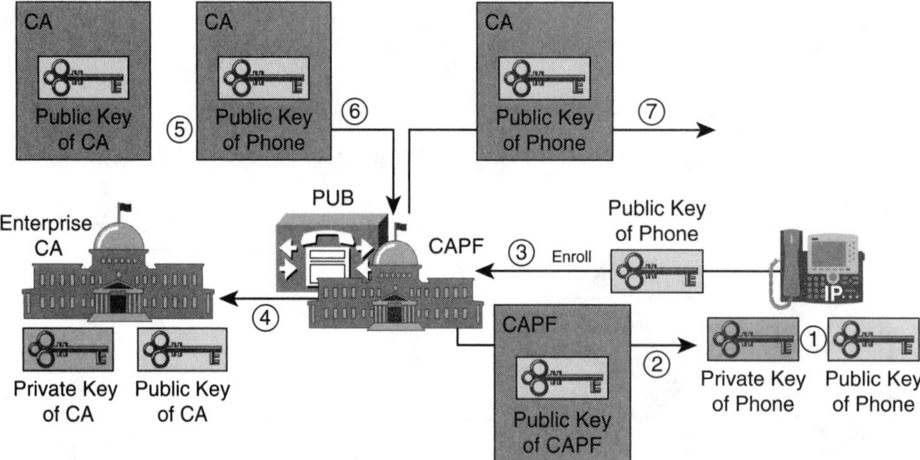

The external CA enrollment process occurs as follows:

1. The IP phone generates its public and private key pairs.
2. The IP phone downloads the certificate of the CAPF and uses it to establish a TLS session with the CAPF.
3. The IP phone sends an enrollment request to the CAPF, including its identity, its public key, and an optional authentication string.

4. The CAPF forwards the request to the external CA.
5. The external CA issues a certificate for the IP phone signed with the private key of the CA.
6. The external CA sends the signed IP phone certificate to the CAPF.
7. The CAPF sends the signed IP phone certificate to the phone.

Keys and Certificate Storage in Cisco IP Telephony

Key storage is a major part of key management because an improperly stored key can enable an attacker to compromise parts of the PKI or the whole PKI. The IP phone stores its public and private RSA keys and its certificate in its nonvolatile memory. This information is preserved across phone reboots and resets. The keys cannot be extracted from the IP phone unless the phone is taken apart and the nonvolatile memory is then physically analyzed.

The IP telephony servers (Cisco CallManager, CAPF, and TFTP server) store certificates on the local hard disk, in a special area called the Microsoft certificate store. The private key of the server is stored in the private-key storage. The private-key storage is protected by the periodically changed master key. The master key itself is encrypted with Triple Data Encryption Standard (3DES) using a key derived from the password of the user.

Microsoft Windows XP stores a certificate locally on the computer or device that requested it or, in the case of a user, on the computer or device that the user used to request it. The storage location is called the certificate store.

The Cisco CTL client stores its public and private RSA keys on the security tokens supplied by Cisco. The keys are embedded on the token during production, and the token is designed never to leak these keys from its memory.

Authentication and Integrity

Cisco CallManager allows authentication of calls. When you are configuring devices for authenticated calls, two services are provided:

- **Device authentication for the IP phone and the server**—Achieved by using device certificates and digital signatures
- **Authentication and integrity of signaling messages**—Achieved by using TLS Secure Hash Algorithm 1 (SHA-1) Hash-based Message Authentication Code (HMAC) (with symmetric keys)

Certificate Exchange in TLS

At the beginning of a TLS session, the Cisco CallManager server and the IP phone exchange certificates using the messages shown in Figure 26-11.

Figure 26-11 *Certificate Exchange Process*

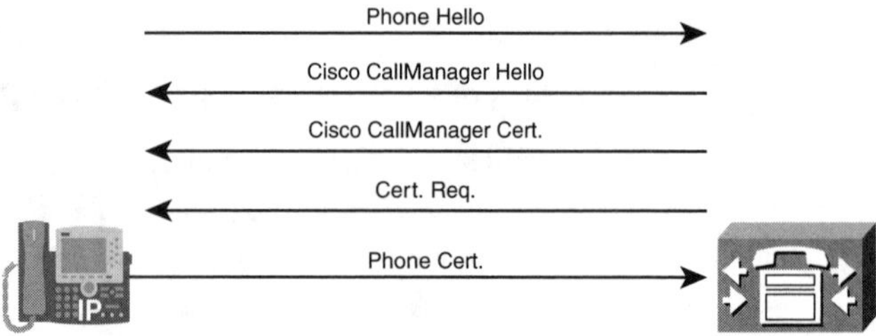

The certificate exchange process occurs as follows:

1. The IP phone and the Cisco CallManager server negotiate the cryptographic algorithms in the IP phone Hello and Cisco CallManager Hello messages.
2. The server sends its (self-signed) certificate to the IP phone.
3. The server requests a certificate from the IP phone.
4. The IP phone sends its certificate to the server.

At this point, both the IP phone and the server validate the certificates they just received over the network:

- The IP phone simply looks up the certificate of the server in its local certificate store. The received certificate must be found locally because it must have been sent in the CTL. If it is not included in the CTL, the session is dropped. If it is found, the public key of the server is extracted from the certificate.
- The server looks up the IP phone in the local device database to see if this IP phone is known and authorized to connect via TLS. Then, the certificate of the IP phone is validated using the locally available CAPF public key (from the CAPF certificate), and if valid, the public key of the IP phone is extracted from the IP phone certificate.

Server-to-Phone Authentication

The next stage of the TLS handshake is authentication of the server by the IP phone. A simplified version of the authentication steps is shown in Figure 26-12.

Figure 26-12 *Server-to-Phone Authentication*

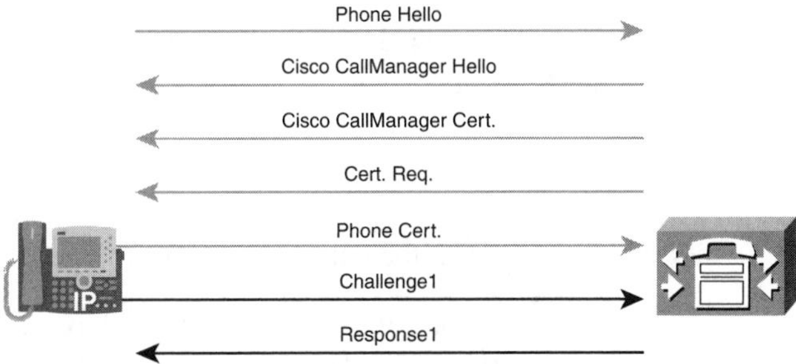

The CallManager-to-Phone authentication occurs as follows:

1. The IP phone generates a random challenge string and sends it to the server, requesting that the server sign it with the private RSA key of the server.
2. The server signs the message with its private RSA key and returns the result (response) to the IP phone.
3. The IP phone verifies the signature using the public key of the server.

Phone-to-Server Authentication

After the server has authenticated to the IP phone, the IP phone needs to authenticate to the server. A simplified version of the authentication steps is shown in Figure 26-13.

Figure 26-13 *Phone-to-Server Authentication*

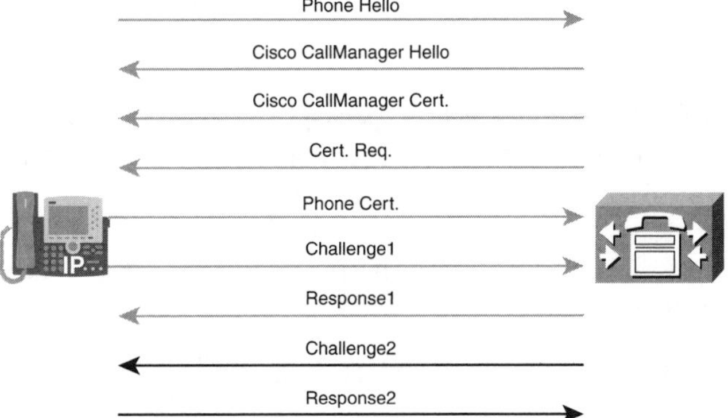

The Phone-to-CallManager authentication occurs as follows:

1. The server generates a random challenge string and sends it to the IP phone, requesting that the IP phone sign it with the private RSA key of the IP phone.
2. The IP phone signs the message with its private RSA key and returns the result (response) to the server.
3. The server verifies the signature with the public key of the IP phone.

NOTE In the certificate of the IP phone, the public key of the IP phone is tied to the identity of the IP phone. Because Cisco CallManager identifies an IP phone by MAC address and not by IP address or name, the MAC address of the phone is used as the identifier in the certificate of the IP phone.

TLS SHA-1 Session Key Exchange

After the bidirectional authentication, a SHA-1 session key is exchanged using these steps:

1. The IP phone generates a session key for SHA-1 hashing.
2. The IP phone encrypts it using the public RSA key of the server and sends it to the server.
3. The server decrypts the message and thus also knows which key to use for SHA-1 hashing of the TLS packets.

The IP phone and the server can now exchange signaling messages over authenticated TLS packets, ensuring the integrity and authenticity of each signaling message exchanged between the two.

Encryption

In addition to authentication and integrity, Cisco CallManager also provides confidentiality of calls by using encryption. When configuring devices for encrypted calls, signaling messages and media streams are encrypted as follows:

- Signaling messages are encrypted using TLS encryption with Advanced Encryption Standard (AES) 128-bit encryption.
- Media streams are encrypted using SRTP with AES 128-bit encryption.

To ensure the authenticity of encrypted packets, in Cisco CallManager, encryption is supported only if combined with authentication. This limitation applies to both protocols, TLS and SRTP.

> **TIP** It is a general rule in cryptography to always complement packet encryption with packet authentication. If encryption is used without authentication, the receiver of an encrypted packet has no guarantee that the packet comes from the expected source. Assuming that an attacker does not know the key to be used for the encryption, the attacker might not be able to send valid data but could send arbitrary data to keep the receiver busy with decrypting the packets. Because this decryption performed at the receiver can cause considerable processing overhead, an attacker could launch a DoS attack just by flooding a system with packets that will be decrypted by the receiver. In some situations, the attacker could even inject incorrect data into the application. This is possible when the sent data does not have any special format but when any bit patterns are considered to be valid data and are accepted by the receiver. An example is encrypted digitized voice samples. An example where the receiver can detect invalid data is the transfer of an encrypted Microsoft Word file. In this case, after decrypting the received arbitrary data (or a valid file that has been encrypted with an incorrect key), the receiver would not recognize the file as a valid Word document.

TLS AES Encryption

If an IP phone is configured for encryption, it will not only create a SHA-1 key but also an AES key after the two-way authentication in TLS. The IP phone encrypts both keys using the public RSA key of the server and then sends them to the server. The server decrypts the message so that the IP phone and the server can exchange signaling messages over authenticated and encrypted TLS packets. In Cisco IP telephony, TLS encryption requires TLS authentication so that the authenticity of the encrypted TLS packets is always guaranteed.

SRTP Media Encryption

Media streams are encrypted by using SRTP. Cisco CallManager generates the SRTP session keys (for media authentication and media encryption) and sends them to the IP phones inside signaling messages. If the signaling messages are not protected, an attacker could easily learn the SRTP keys just by sniffing the signaling messages. To ensure protection of the key distribution, encrypted signaling is mandatory in Cisco CallManager when media streams are encrypted.

As stated before, in Cisco CallManager, encrypted packets always have to be signed to ensure the authenticity of the source and the content of the packet.

To summarize, these rules apply to Cisco CallManager authentication and encryption:

- Signaling encryption requires signaling authentication.
- Media encryption requires media authentication and signaling encryption (hence also signaling authentication).
- Media authentication requires media encryption.
- Signaling encryption requires media encryption.

As a consequence of these rules, you can configure one of the following secure operation modes in Cisco CallManager:

- **Authenticated**—This mode provides authenticated signaling only (TLS SHA-1).
- **Encrypted**—This mode provides authenticated and encrypted signaling (TLS SHA-1 and TLS AES) and authenticated and encrypted media transfer (SRTP SHA-1 and SRTP AES).

SRTP Packet Format

As shown in Figure 26-14, the SRTP packet header does not differ from an RTP packet header. The RTP payload differs only in the sense that it is not clear text voice but encrypted voice. In addition to the encrypted payload, a 32-bit SHA-1 authentication tag is added to the packet. The authentication tag holds the first 32 bits of the 160-bit SHA-1 hash digest computed from the RTP header and the encrypted voice payload ("truncated fingerprint"). As you can see from the figure, the RTP packet header and the RTP payload (encrypted voice) are also authenticated. Therefore, RTP encryption is performed before RTP authentication. RTP Header Compression (cRTP) is supported in conjunction with SRTP.

Figure 26-14 *SRTP Packet Format*

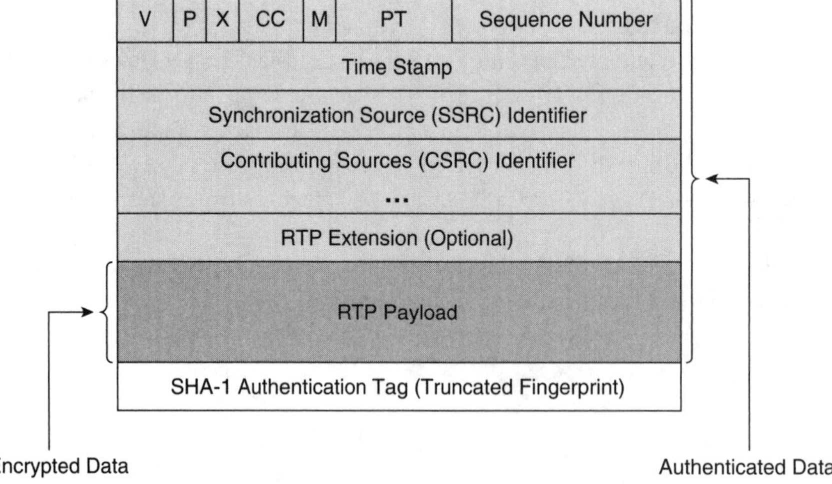

Secure Call Flow Summary

When a call is placed between two IP phones when encryption is enabled, the following sequence occurs:

1. The IP phones and Cisco CallManager exchange certificates.
2. The IP phones and Cisco CallManager authenticate each other by requesting some random data to be signed. When this process is finished, Cisco CallManager and the IP phones know that the other devices are authentic.
3. Each IP phone creates TLS session keys. One key will be used for TLS SHA-1 authentication; the other key will be used for TLS AES encryption.
4. Each IP phone encrypts the generated keys with the public key of the Cisco CallManager and sends the encrypted keys to Cisco CallManager.
5. Now each IP phone shares its session keys with Cisco CallManager. At this stage, each phone can exchange signaling messages with Cisco CallManager over an authenticated and encrypted TLS session.
6. When the call is established between the two IP phones, Cisco CallManager creates SRTP session keys. One key is used for SRTP SHA-1 authentication; the other key is used for SRTP AES encryption.
7. Cisco CallManager sends the generated SRTP session keys to both IP phones over the secured TLS session.
8. The IP phones now share the session keys for authenticating and encrypting their RTP packets. At this stage, the two IP phones can start secure media exchange.

Summary

This chapter discussed the concepts behind securing the IP telephony network. The threats targeting Cisco IP telephony include eavesdropping, IP phone image and configuration file tampering, and DoS attacks. To combat this, Cisco IP telephony uses authentication and encryption techniques. Because there is no single PKI topology in Cisco IP telephony, the CTL client acts as a trusted introducer for the different PKI systems. The IP phones can use preinstalled certificates from Cisco (called MICs) or use LSCs issued by the CallManager CAPF or a company CA.

Cisco CallManager stores all self-signed certificates in the operating system private key storage. The keys used by the CTL client are stored on security tokens, and the keys used with IP phones are stored in protected nonvolatile memory.

Cisco CallManager supports device authentication, authenticated signaling (using TLS SHA-1), and authenticated media (using SRTP SHA-1). It also supports encryption of signaling messages using TLS AES and encryption of media using SRTP AES.

Review Questions

You can find the solutions to these questions in Appendix A, "Answers to Review Questions."

1. Which of the following are not security threats to an IP telephony system? (Choose two.)
   a. Loss of privacy
   b. Impersonation
   c. Integrity
   d. Loss of integrity
   e. Loss of control
   f. DoS
2. Which of the following represent correct mappings of application—protocol—security features? (Choose two.)
   a. Secure signaling—SRTP—device authentication, integrity
   b. Secure signaling—TLS—device authentication, integrity, privacy
   c. Secure media—SRTP—privacy, confidentiality, security
   d. Secure media—TLS—privacy, confidentiality, security
   e. Secure media—TLS—privacy, integrity
   f. Secure media—SRTP—privacy, integrity
3. Which two statements about trusted introducing are incorrect?
   a. The trusted introducer has to be trusted by all other members of the system.
   b. The trusted introducer has to trust all other members of the system.
   c. The trusted introducer guarantees the authenticity of entities it is introducing to others.
   d. Only the trusted introducer has to trust the root of the system.
   e. The trusted introducer is the root of a system.
   f. Any entity of the system can guarantee the authenticity of any other member.

4. Which two statements about PKI topologies in Cisco IP telephony are true?
   a. MICs are self-signed by the IP phone.
   b. Cisco IP Phone 7940, 7960, and 7970 models can have MICs and LSCs.
   c. The CAPF has a self-signed certificate.
   d. Only Cisco IP Phone 7940, 7960, and 7970 (and subsequent) models can have LSCs.
   e. The CTL is signed by the Cisco manufacturing CA.
   f. MICs are signed by CAPF.
5. Which are the two valid options to secure enrollment in a PKI?
   a. Perform the enrollment from a trusted device only.
   b. Perform the enrollment in both directions.
   c. Perform the enrollment over a trusted network.
   d. Use self-signed certificates on all devices.
   e. Do not send the private key in the enrollment.
   f. Perform mutual out-of-band authentication between the PKI user and CA.
6. Which statement about enrollment in the IP telephony PKI is true?
   a. MICs are issued by CAPF itself or by an external CA.
   b. LSCs are issued by the Cisco CTL client or by CAPF.
   c. CAPF enrollment supports the use of authentication strings.
   d. CAPF itself has to enroll with the Cisco CTL client.
   e. Enrollment of IP phones occurs automatically if the cluster is in secure-only mode.
   f. LSCs can be issued by an external CA when using the CTL client as a proxy.
7. Which of the following entities uses a smart token for key storage?
   a. CTL
   b. CTL client
   c. CAPF in proxy mode
   d. CAPF in CA mode
   e. Cisco IP Phone 7940 and 7960
   f. Cisco IP Phone 7970

8. What are the authentication features of TLS in Cisco IP telephony?

   a. Two-way device authentication

   b. Two-way device authentication and signed media messages

   c. One-way device authentication and signed signaling message

   d. Two-way device authentication and signed signaling messages

   e. One-way device authentication and signed media messages

   f. Signed signaling messages

9. During an encrypted call between two IP phones, which two of the following does not happen?

   a. Mutual certificate exchange between Cisco CallManager and each IP phone

   b. Mutual certificate exchange between the IP phones

   c. SRTP packet authentication and encryption

   d. Encrypted transmission of SRTP session keys between the IP phones

   e. TLS packet authentication and encryption

   f. Encrypted transmission of TLS session keys between Cisco CallManager and the IP phones

10. Which is the most accurate list of tasks required to configure a Cisco CallManager cluster for security?

   a. Enable services, set cluster to mixed mode, create a signed CTL, and deploy certificates to the IP phones.

   b. Enable services, set cluster to secure-only mode, create a signed CTL, and deploy certificates to the IP phones.

   c. Enable extended services, set cluster to authenticated or encrypted mode, create a signed CTL, and deploy certificates to the IP phones.

   d. Disable extended services, set cluster to mixed mode, create a signed CTL, and deploy certificates to the IP phones.

   e. Enable services, set cluster to mixed mode, create a signed CTL, deploy certificates to the IP phones, and set the device security mode.

   f. Run the auto-secure feature.

This chapter covers the following topics:

- Identifying the steps to configure a Cisco CallManager system for authentication and encryption
- Activating the Cisco CTL Provider service and the CAPF service in Cisco CallManager Serviceability
- Installing the Cisco CTL client on a Windows 2000 server or workstation with a USB port
- Configuring the Cisco CTL client to create a CTL file and setting the cluster security mode
- Using the CAPF settings in the Phone Configuration window to install, upgrade, delete, and troubleshoot LSCs
- Configuring the default security mode for supported IP Phone models and the device security mode for a single device
- Generating a CAPF report in Cisco CallManager Administration to view authentication strings and authentication modes
- Finding IP Phones in the network that support authentication, support encryption, or use CAPF for LSC operations

CHAPTER 27

Configuring Cisco IP Telephony Authentication and Encryption

Cisco IP telephony systems are subject to several threats, including eavesdropping, identity spoofing, and denial of service (DoS) attacks. In Cisco CallManager Release 4.0 and later, you can secure the Cisco IP telephony solution against these threats by enabling authentication and encryption features. This chapter explains how to configure the authentication and encryption that you can apply in a Cisco IP telephony environment.

Authentication and Encryption Configuration Overview

Cisco CallManager Release 4.0 and later releases support authentication and encryption in a Cisco CallManager cluster. By using these features, you can secure the following communication methods:

- **Signaling messages between a supported Cisco IP Phone and Cisco CallManager**—Cisco IP Phone 7970, 7960, and 7940 models can be configured to use Transport Layer Security (TLS) for authenticated and encrypted signaling.
- **Media exchange between two supported IP Phones within a Cisco CallManager cluster**—Cisco IP Phone 7970, 7960, and 7940 models can be configured to use Secure Real-Time Transport Protocol (SRTP) for authenticated and encrypted media exchange. Secure media exchange was introduced for the 7970 in Cisco CallManager 4.0. Support for the additional IP Phones was added in CallManager 4.1.

NOTE Cisco CallManager-to-Cisco CallManager intercluster communication is not secured. If two Cisco IP Phones are configured to use SRTP and are registered to different Cisco CallManager servers within the cluster, there is a security risk because the SRTP session keys need to be exchanged between the Cisco CallManager nodes (in cleartext). Therefore, if the communication paths between Cisco CallManager nodes within a cluster are not trusted, the recommendation is to use IPsec between the Cisco CallManager nodes.

- **Media exchange between a supported Cisco IP Phone and a supported Media Gateway Control Protocol (MGCP) and H.323 gateways**—Cisco IP Phone 7970, 7960, and 7940 models and Cisco IOS MGCP gateways (running Cisco IOS Software Release 12.3(11)T2 or later) can be configured to use SRTP for authenticated and encrypted media exchange. H.323 support for SRTP was added in Cisco IOS Software Release 12.4(6T).

NOTE When using SRTP with an MGCP gateway, the SRTP session keys by default are exchanged in cleartext between Cisco CallManager and the MGCP gateway. Therefore, if the communication path between Cisco CallManager and the MGCP gateway is not trusted, the recommendation is to use IPsec between Cisco CallManager and the MGCP gateway.

- **Signaling messages between a supported IP Phone and a supported Cisco Survivable Remote Site Telephony (SRST) device**—Cisco IP Phone 7970, 7960, and 7940 models and Cisco IOS SRST Version 3.3 or later devices (running Cisco IOS Software Release 12.3(14)T or later) can be configured to use TLS for authenticated and encrypted signaling.

NOTE The Cisco SRST device can also provide SRTP session keys to the Cisco IP Phones so that the IP Phones that are in fallback mode can still use both signaling message and media exchange protection.

With the current release of Cisco CallManager, authenticated and encrypted calls are not possible in any other situation than listed, including the following:

- **Calls to other Cisco CallManager clusters using intercluster trunks**—Secure signaling and media exchange are supported only for calls within a Cisco CallManager cluster; intercluster trunk calls are not supported.
- **Calls that are connected to any media resources, such as conferences, transcoders, or music on hold (MoH)**—Secure media exchange is supported only between supported endpoints (Cisco IP Phones and Cisco IOS MGCP gateways); conference bridges, transcoders, or MOH servers are not supported endpoints.

To enable authentication and encryption support in your Cisco CallManager cluster, you need to complete these tasks:

Step 1 **Enable security services**—You need to enable the Cisco Certificate Trust List (CTL) Provider service and the Cisco Certificate Authority Proxy Function (CAPF) service.

Step 2 **Use the Cisco CTL client to activate security options**—You need to configure mixed mode and create a signed CTL.

Step 3 **Configure devices for security**—IP Phones need to have certificates (either manufacturing installed certificates [MICs] or locally significant certificates [LSCs]), they have to be configured for a security mode (authenticated or encrypted), and the CAPF parameters have to be set if LSCs are used.

Enabling Services Required for Security

When enabling security in your Cisco CallManager cluster, you have to activate these services:

- **Cisco CTL Provider**—This service has to be activated on all Cisco CallManager servers and Cisco TFTP servers of your cluster.
- **Cisco Certificate Authority Proxy Function**—This service has to be activated on the publisher server.

Activate Cisco CallManager services from the Cisco CallManager Serviceability Service Activation window, shown in Figure 27-1.

Figure 27-1 *Enabling Services Required for Security*

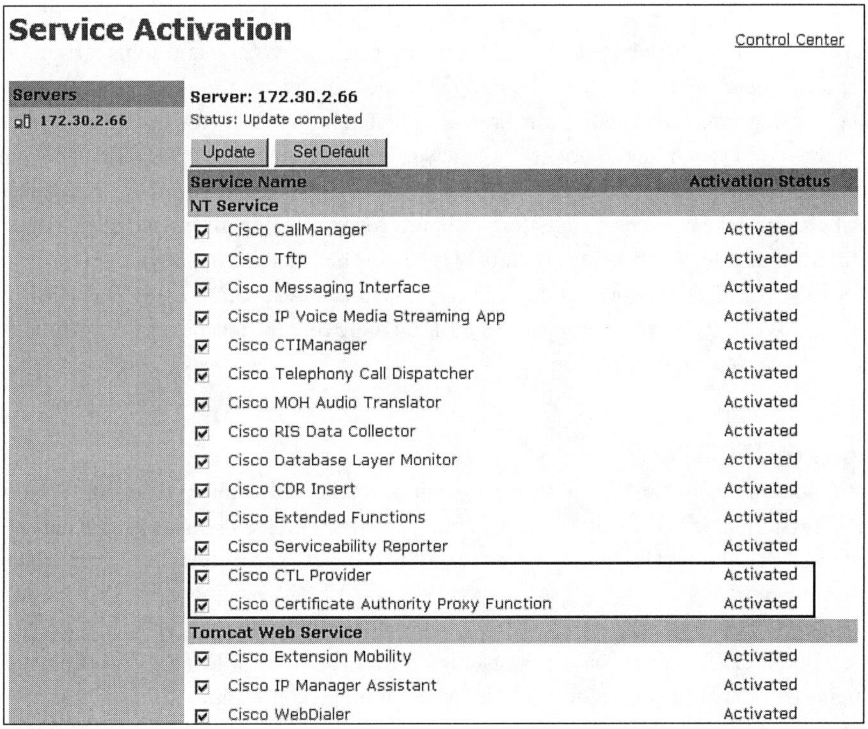

Using the CTL Client

The Cisco CTL client software, available as a plug-in application on Cisco CallManager Administration, is used to create or update the Certificate Trust List (CTL). The CTL is a list of the trusted certificates in the CallManager cluster. When the list is accurate, the Cisco CTL client will ensure that the CTL is signed by the keys of the Cisco CTL client. These keys are stored on an external Universal Serial Bus (USB) device—the security token. When the CTL needs to be signed, the Cisco CTL client passes the CTL to the security token, and the security token signs it and then returns the signed CTL to the Cisco CTL client application. The Cisco CTL client is needed in these situations:

- For the initial activation of security in your cluster
- For the deactivation or reactivation of security in your cluster
- After modifying Cisco CallManager or Cisco TFTP server configuration (which includes adding, removing, renaming, or restoring a server or changing the IP address or hostname of a server)
- After adding or removing a security token (due to theft or loss)
- After replacing or restoring a Cisco CallManager or Cisco TFTP server

In all the situations listed, the Cisco CTL client creates a new CTL and signs it by using a security token. The Cisco IP Phones load the new CTL and are then aware of the changes to the IP telephony system. Any changes that are not reflected in the CTL (for instance, if you change the IP address of a server but do not create a new CTL using the Cisco CTL client application) cause the Cisco IP Phones to treat the corresponding device as untrusted. From this perspective, the CTL can be seen as the certificate root store of your browser (listing all trusted certificate-issuing entities). If any device that was previously trusted is not trustworthy anymore (for instance, when a security token is lost), there is no need for a certificate revocation list (CRL). Instead, you will use the Cisco CTL client and update the CRL by removing the untrusted entry (for instance, a lost security token) from the list.

Installing the CTL Client

The Cisco CTL client application can be installed on any PC running Microsoft Windows 2000 or XP Workstation or Microsoft Windows 2000 or 2003 Server, as long as the PC has at least one Universal Serial Bus (USB) port. This device can be any Cisco CallManager server in your cluster or any client PC.

The Cisco CTL client application is installed from the Cisco CallManager Administration Install Plugins window. You can accomplish the installation just by walking through a simple wizard, as shown in Figure 27-2. During installation, you are prompted for the destination folder; you can set any directory of your choice or simply accept the default.

Figure 27-2 *Installing the CTL Client*

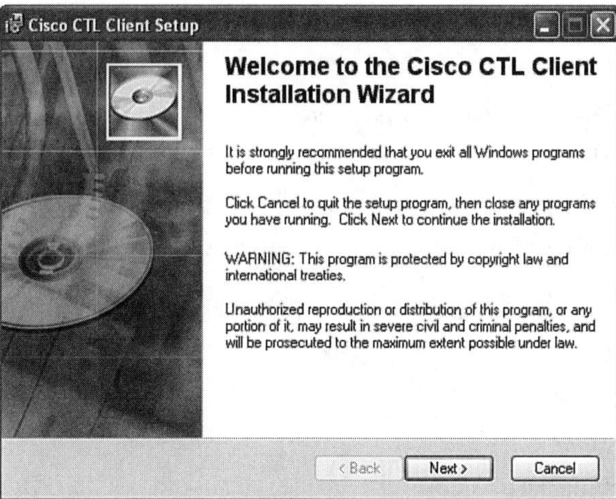

The Smart Card service has to be activated on the PC. To activate the Smart Card service under Microsoft Windows 2000, choose **Start > Settings > Control Panel > Administrative Tools > Services** to launch the Microsoft services administration tool. Then use the tool to verify the status of the Smart Card service. The service should have the startup type of Automatic and the Current Status should be Running.

After you have installed the CTL Client, you can access it from the icon automatically placed on your desktop. Initially, it will ask for the CallManager server information for the cluster, as shown in Figure 27-3.

Figure 27-3 *Configuring the CTL Client*

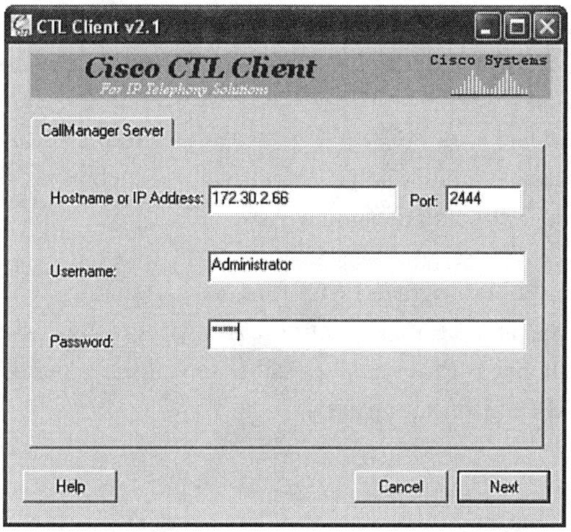

After entering the CallManager server information and successfully authenticating, you can either set the cluster security mode or update the CTL file. A Cisco CallManager cluster supports two security modes:

- **Mixed mode**—This mode allows secure calls between two security-enabled devices and allows nonsecure calls between devices where at least one of the devices is not security-enabled.
- **Nonsecure mode**—This is the default configuration, in which all calls are nonsecure.

NOTE There is no secure-only mode. This setting would prevent Cisco IP Phones without security enabled from placing calls. Many Cisco IP Phones do not support security features and would not be able to operate in a secure-only environment.

In addition to setting the cluster security mode, you use the Cisco CTL client to update the CTL file. This update is needed after adding or removing components, such as servers or security tokens. After changing the list of CTL entries, you need to sign the new CTL using a security token.

Working with Locally Significant Certificates

Cisco IP Phone 7940 and 7960 models do not have MICs; they only work with LSCs. The Cisco IP Phone 7970 can use either MICs or LSCs. If an LSC is installed in a Cisco IP Phone 7970, the LSC has higher priority than the MIC.

CallManager uses the CAPF to issue LSCs. CAPF can act as a Certificate Authority (CA) itself, signing the LSCs, or it can act as a proxy to an external CA, having the external CA signing the LSCs. You can configure the CAPF service at the CAPF service parameter web page shown in Figure 27-4. To access this page, choose **Cisco CallManager Administration > Service > Service Parameter > Cisco Certificate Authority Proxy Function**.

You can set the certificate issuer (CAPF itself or an external CA) and IP address of the external CA (if used). You can also modify some default values, such as the Rivest, Shamir, and Adleman (RSA) key size or the certificate lifetime.

When you want to install or upgrade LSCs for Cisco IP Phones that you are configuring, use the relevant CAPF settings at the Phone Configuration window by choosing **Cisco CallManager Administration > Device > Phone.** All possible settings are found in the Certificate Authority Proxy Function (CAPF) Information area.

Figure 27-4 *Working with Locally Significant Certificates*

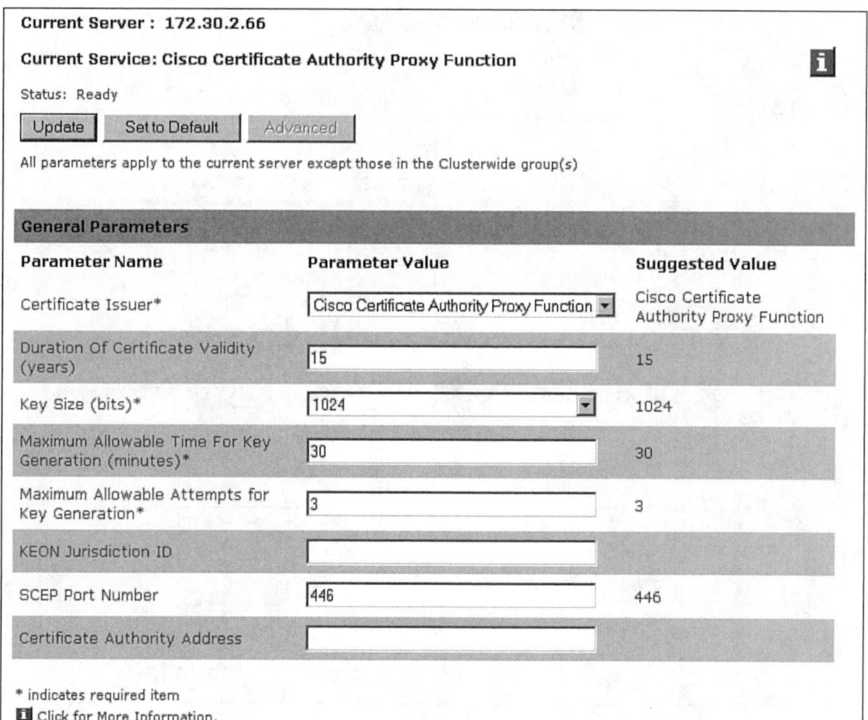

There are four operations options in the **Certificate Operation** field (as shown in Figure 27-5):

- **Install/Upgrade**—This operation allows the installation of an LSC (if the IP Phone does not already have an LSC) and the upgrade (replacement) of an existing LSC (if the IP Phone already has an LSC).
- **Delete**—This operation allows the removal of an existing LSC from a Cisco IP Phone.
- **Troubleshoot**—This operation retrieves all existing IP Phone certificates from the IP Phone and stores them in CAPF trace files. There are separate CAPF trace files for MICs and for LSCs. The CAPF trace files are located in C:\Program Files\Cisco\Trace\CAPF.
- **No Pending Operation**—This is the default value. You can also change back to this value when you want to cancel a previously configured operation that has not yet been executed.

Figure 27-5 *Selecting a Certificate Operation*

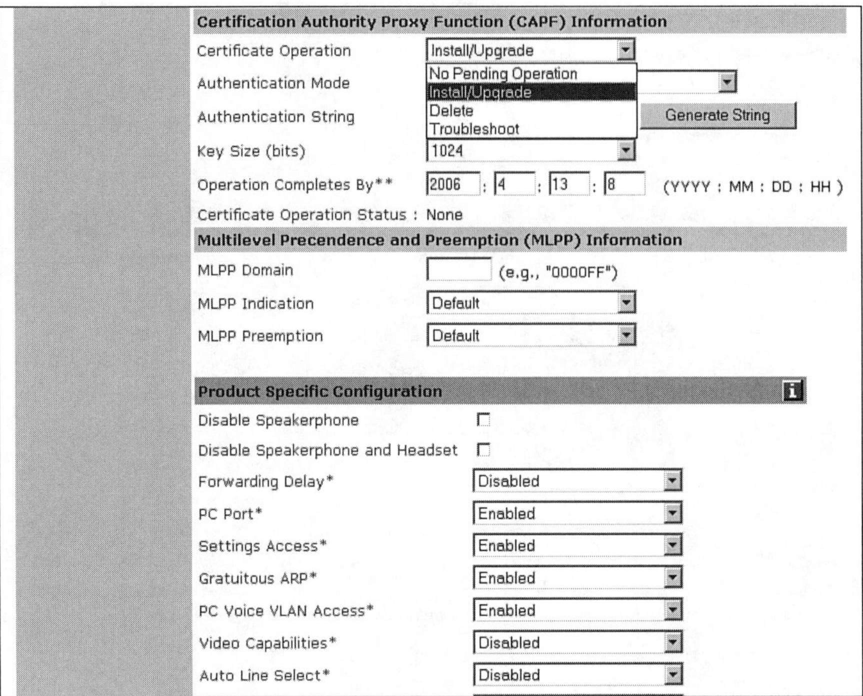

In the **Authentication Mode** field (as shown in Figure 27-6), you can choose one of four possible authentication modes:

- **By Authentication String**—This authentication mode is the default and requires the Cisco IP Phone user to manually initiate the installation of an LSC. The user must authenticate to Cisco CallManager by the authentication string that has been set by the administrator in the **Authentication String** field. To enable the user to enter the correct authentication string, the administrator has to communicate the configured authentication string to the user.

- **By Null String**—This authentication mode disables Cisco IP Phone authentication for the download of the IP Phone certificate (enrollment). The enrollment of the IP Phone should be done over a trusted network only when this setting is used. Because no user intervention is needed, the enrollment is done automatically the next time the Cisco IP Phone boots or is reset.

- **By Existing Certificate (Precedence to LSC)**—This authentication mode uses an existing certificate (with precedence to the LSC if both a MIC and an LSC are present in the IP Phone) for IP Phone authentication. Because no user intervention is needed, the enrollment is done automatically the next time that the IP Phone boots or is reset.

- **By Existing Certificate (Precedence to MIC)**—This authentication mode uses an existing certificate (with precedence to MIC if both a MIC and an LSC are present in the IP Phone) for IP Phone authentication. Because no user intervention is needed, the enrollment is done automatically the next time that the IP Phone boots or is reset.

Figure 27-6 *Selecting the IP Phone Authentication Method*

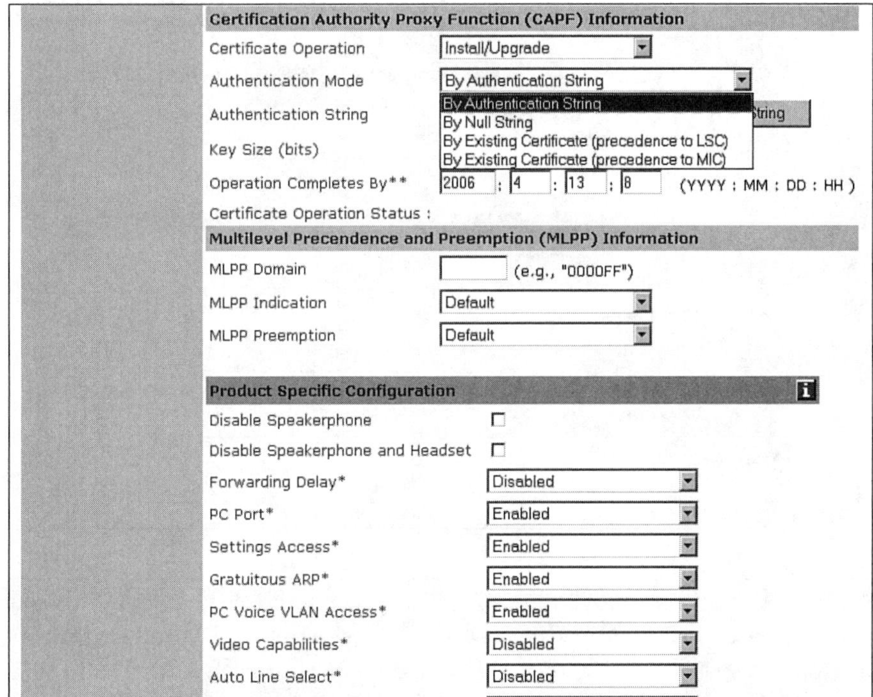

NOTE Some authentication options will only appear under specific phone models. For example, the "By Existing Certificate (Precedence to MIC)" option is unavailable on older Cisco IP Phones such as the 7940 and 7960.

Issuing a Phone Certificate Using an Authentication String

Figure 27-7 illustrates an example for a first-time installation of a certificate with a manually entered authentication string. For such a scenario, set the **Certificate Operation** field to Install/Upgrade and the Authentication Mode to By Authentication String. You can manually enter a string of four to ten digits, or click the **Generate String** button to create an authentication string (and populate the **Authentication String** field). After you click **Update** and reset the IP Phone, the IP Phone is ready for enrollment. However, enrollment is not automatically triggered; it has to be initiated by the user (from the Settings menu of the Cisco IP Phone).

Figure 27-7 *Issuing a Phone Certificate Using an Authentication String*

Certification Authority Proxy Function (CAPF) Information	
Certificate Operation	Install/Upgrade
Authentication Mode	By Authentication String
Authentication String	7310459212 [Generate String]
Key Size (bits)	1024
Operation Completes By**	2006 : 4 : 13 : 8 (YYYY : MM : DD : HH)
Certificate Operation Status : None	
Multilevel Precendence and Preemption (MLPP) Information	
MLPP Domain	(e.g., "0000FF")
MLPP Indication	Default
MLPP Preemption	Default
Product Specific Configuration	
Disable Speakerphone	☐
Disable Speakerphone and Headset	☐
Forwarding Delay*	Disabled
PC Port*	Enabled
Settings Access*	Enabled
Gratuitous ARP*	Enabled
PC Voice VLAN Access*	Enabled
Video Capabilities*	Disabled
Auto Line Select*	Disabled

NOTE The Settings menu can also be used to gain information about the IP telephony system or remove the CTL. Usually, you do not want IP Phone users to have access to such options, and, therefore, access to the settings on the IP Phone is often restricted or disabled. LSC enrollment with authentication by authentication string is not possible if settings access is not (fully) enabled. If access to settings is restricted or disabled, you have to enable it for the enrollment and then return it to its previous value.

When a user starts the enrollment procedure, the user has to enter the authentication string configured, and if the process is successful, the certificate is issued to the IP Phone.

On a Cisco IP Phone 7940, the user would complete these steps:

Step 1 Press the **Settings** button to access the Settings menu.

Step 2 Scroll to the Security Configuration option and press the **Select** softkey to display the Security Configuration menu.

Step 3 Press **# to unlock the IP Phone configuration.

Step 4 Scroll to LSC and press the **Update** softkey to start the enrollment.

Step 5 Enter the authentication string and press the **Submit** softkey to authenticate the IP Phone to the CAPF when prompted to do so.

Step 6 The IP Phone generates its RSA keys and requests a certificate signed by the CAPF. When the signed certificate is installed, the message "Success" appears at the lower-left corner of the Cisco IP Phone display.

Issuing a Phone Certificate Using the CAPF

You might use the CallManager CAPF for a certificate upgrade using an existing LSC to authenticate the communication. A reason for such an upgrade could be that an LSC will soon reach its expiration date. By issuing a new LSC shortly before the expiration of the existing LSC, the IP Phone can use the existing LSC for the upgrade (which avoids entering a manual authentication string at the IP Phone).

For such a scenario, set the **Certificate Operation** field to **Install/Upgrade** and the **Authentication Mode** to **By Existing Certificate (Precedence to LSC)**. After you click **Update** and reset the Cisco IP Phone, the IP Phone automatically contacts the CAPF for the download of the new certificate. The existing certificate is used to authenticate the new enrollment, and there is no need for a manually entered authentication string.

Configuring the Device Security Mode

After you have configured the Cisco CallManager for mixed mode using the CTL Client and the Cisco IP Phones have certificates, you must configure the IP Phones to support authenticated or encrypted calls. You can use the device security mode to configure a Cisco IP Phone for one of three security modes:

- **Non Secure**—The IP Phone will not support authenticated or encrypted calls.
- **Authenticated**—The IP Phone will support authenticated calls.
- **Encrypted**—The IP Phone will support encrypted calls.

The default device security mode is configured in the Cisco CallManager Enterprise Parameters window; choose **Cisco CallManager Administration > System > Enterprise Parameters**. The default mode is Non Secure.

In addition to setting the default value, you can configure each individual IP Phone with the device security mode. Choose **Cisco CallManager Administration > Device > Phone** to display the Phone Configuration window, as shown in Figure 27-8. The default mode is Use System Default.

Figure 27-8 *Configuring IP Phone Security Options*

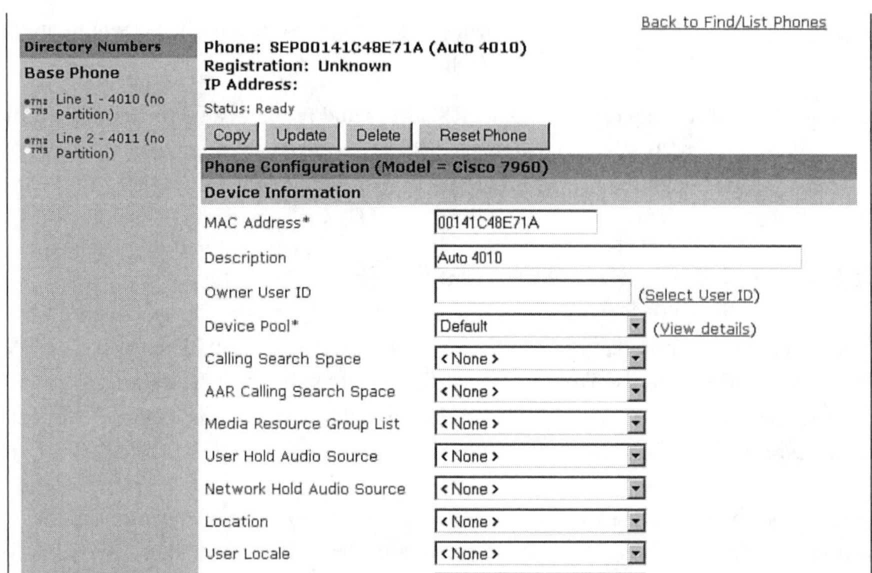

NOTE In several situations, you should not use cryptographic services for Cisco IP Phones at all. With some Cisco IP Contact Center (IPCC) applications, for instance, cleartext signaling messages or media packets have to be seen by other devices (for instance, attached PCs). Another example is the use of Network Address Translation (NAT) or Port Address Translation (PAT). Because the translating device has to see cleartext signaling messages to be able to dynamically allow the negotiated UDP ports that will be used for Real-Time Transport Protocol (RTP), encryption cannot be used.

Negotiating Device Security Mode

The actual security mode used for a call depends on the configuration of both IP Phones participating in the call. As shown in Figure 27-9, these rules apply:

- If either device in a conversation is set to Non Secure, a nonsecure call (that is, a call without authentication and without encryption) is placed.
- If both devices are set to Encrypted, an encrypted call (that is, a call with authentication and encryption) is placed.

- If one device is set to authenticated and the other phone is set to either authenticated or encrypted, the resulting call will be authenticated.

Figure 27-9 *Device Security Negotiation*

		Phone 2		
		Non Secure	Authenticated	Encrypted
Phone 1	Non Secure	Non Secure	Non Secure	Non Secure
	Authenticated	Non Secure	Authenticated	Authenticated
	Encrypted	Non Secure	Authenticated	Encrypted

Generating a CAPF Report

CAPF reports can be quite useful because you can use them to search for IP Phones matching selected CAPF criteria:

- Certificate Operation Status

NOTE The Certificate Operation Status displays the result of the last CAPF activity for each IP Phone. Possible values include None (typically shown on IP Phones with device security mode Non Secure), Operation Pending (when CAPF waits for a user to manually retrieve a [new] certificate), and result information (success, failure) after upgrade, delete, or troubleshooting operations.

- Device Security Mode
- Authentication Mode
- Authentication String

You can click entries from the results list to display the configuration window of the corresponding IP Phone. You can also save the results list of a search to a file in Comma-Separated Values (CSV) format.

You can create CAPF reports from Cisco CallManager Administration. Figure 27-10 shows a CAPF report where the administrator accessed the CAPF Report window by choosing Cisco **CallManager Administration > Device > Device Settings > CAPF Report** and started a report to search for all IP Phones where the authentication string matched a specific value. This allowed the administrator to quickly locate the status for a specific IP phone.

Figure 27-10 *Generating CAPF Reports*

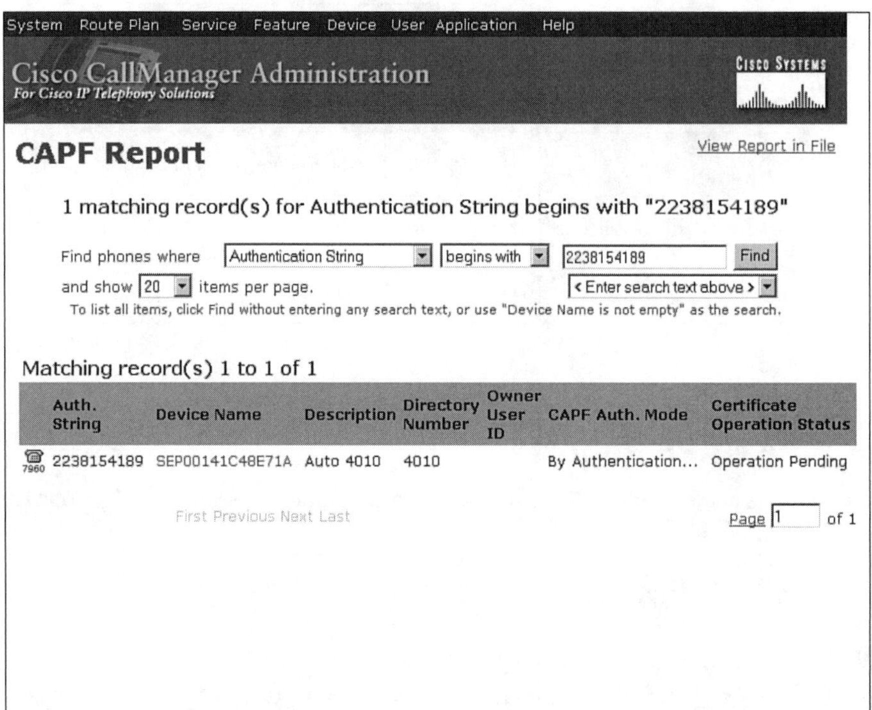

In addition to using CAPF reports to locate devices, you can use the Find and List Phones window to search on a variety of other criteria. For example, Figure 27-11 shows a query to search for IP Phones where the device security mode is Encrypted. Two IP Phones have been found matching the search criteria.

Figure 27-11 *Searching Using the Find and List Phones Query Tool*

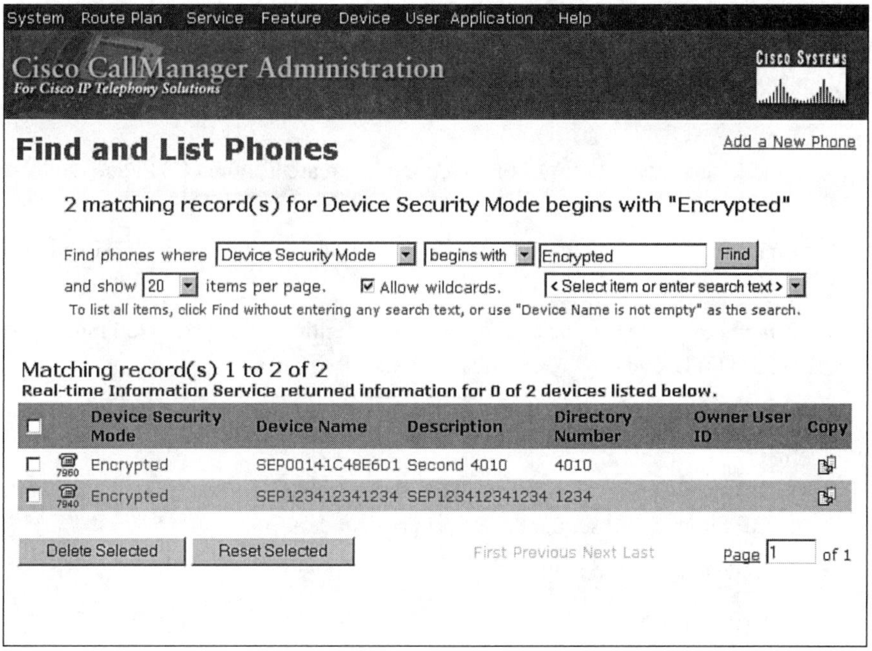

Summary

This chapter discussed the configuration of encryption and authentication in the Cisco IP telephony network. To enable either of these features, you must activate the Cisco CTL Provider and the Cisco CAPF services. From there, you must install the CTL Client on at least one machine in the cluster to sign the CTL using a security token, which is manually plugged in to the USB port of the machine. This CTL Client must be rerun each time the CTL entries change.

Cisco allows the use of LSCs on all security-enabled IP Phones. You can configure the Cisco IP Phones for nonsecure calls, authenticated calls only, or authenticated and encrypted calls. When the phones communicate, they will agree on a lowest-common-denominator security standard. You can locate the phones that have successfully enabled security functions using the CAPF report utility.

Review Questions

You can find the solutions to these questions in Appendix A, "Answers to Review Questions."

1. Which is the most accurate list of tasks required to configure a Cisco CallManager cluster for security?
   a. Enable services, set cluster to mixed mode, create a signed CTL, and deploy certificates to the IP Phones
   b. Enable services, set cluster to secure-only mode, create a signed CTL, and deploy certificates to the IP Phones
   c. Enable extended services, set cluster to authenticated or encrypted mode, create a signed CTL, and deploy certificates to the IP Phones
   d. Disable extended services, set cluster to mixed mode, create a signed CTL, and deploy certificates to the IP Phones
   e. Enable services, set cluster to mixed mode, create a signed CTL, deploy certificates to the IP Phones, and set the device security mode
   f. Run the auto-secure feature
2. Which two services must be enabled when configuring a Cisco CallManager cluster for security?
   a. Cisco CAPF
   b. Cisco Authority Provider Function
   c. Cisco CTL Provider
   d. Cisco CTL Proxy
   e. Cisco CTL Client Provider
   f. Cisco Extended Functions
3. What are the minimum needs for the PC when you are installing Cisco CTL Client?
   a. Windows 2000 or XP operating system, at least one USB port, Smart Card service enabled
   b. Windows XP operating system, at least two USB ports, Smart Card service enabled
   c. Windows 2000 operating system, at least two USB ports, Smart Card service disabled
   d. Installation on Cisco CallManager publisher server only, two available USB ports, Smart Card service enabled
   e. Windows 2000 operating system, PCMCIA slot, Smart Card service enabled
   f. Windows 2000 operating system, at least one USB port, Cisco VT Advantage camera, Smart Card service enabled

4. When is update of the configuration using the Cisco CTL client not needed?
   a. When an LSC of the IP Phone is upgraded
   b. When a security token is added to the system
   c. When a Cisco CallManager has been removed
   d. When an IP address of the Cisco TFTP server has been changed
5. Which two statements about LSCs are correct?
   a. On a Cisco IP Phone 7970, a MIC has priority over an LSC.
   b. On a Cisco IP Phone 7960, an LSC has priority over a MIC.
   c. The CAPF issues LSCs if used as a CA and MICs if used as a proxy.
   d. The certificate operation of the CAPF can be set to install, upgrade, or delete.
   e. The certificate operation of the CAPF can be set to install/upgrade, delete, or troubleshoot.
   f. CAPF authentication can be configured to be done by authentication string, null string, or existing certificates.
6. Which two combinations of device security modes and resulting call type are correct?
   a. Phone 1: Non Secure, phone 2: Authenticated; call: authenticated
   b. Phone 1: Non Secure, phone 2: Encrypted; call: authenticated
   c. Phone 1: Authenticated, phone 2: Non Secure; call: nonsecure
   d. Phone 1: Encrypted, phone 2: Authenticated; call: authenticated
   e. Phone 1: Authenticated, phone 2: Encrypted; call: encrypted
   f. Phone 1: Encrypted, phone 2: Non Secure; call: encrypted
7. Which two of the following options are not search criteria when you are creating a CAPF report?
   a. Authentication mode
   b. Certificate operation status
   c. Device name
   d. Certificate lifetime
   e. Authentication string
   f. Device security mode

8. Which two of the following options are not search criteria when you are searching for IP Phones using the Find and List Phones window?
   a. Authentication mode
   b. LSC status
   c. Device name
   d. Directory number
   e. Authentication string
   f. Device security mode
9. Which phone model does not support phone security options?
   a. Cisco 7920
   b. Cisco 7970
   c. Cisco 7961
   d. Cisco 7960
10. Which of the following types of communication cannot be encrypted? (Choose three.)
   a. Signaling messages between an IP Phone and an SRST gateway
   b. Calls to other clusters using intercluster trunks
   c. Calls communicating using a conference bridge
   d. Calls using a transcoder

Part VI: IP Video

This chapter covers the following topics:

- Classifying the functions and components of the Cisco IP video telephony solution
- Characterizing a video call in terms of the RTP stream types and codecs, and describing audio and video bandwidth requirements
- Comparing an H.323 video call in a Cisco CallManager environment with an SCCP video call
- Describing the two main factors that determine the bandwidth requirement for video calls and calculating bandwidth requirements
- Implementing call admission control within a cluster using the locations and regions of Cisco CallManager Administration
- Describing call admission control between clusters using a gatekeeper

CHAPTER 28

Introducing IP Video Telephony

Companies that want to enable video calls can install and use products from the Cisco enterprise video products portfolio. Video communication capabilities are integrated into Cisco CallManager Release 4.0. These capabilities extend several video features to benefit end users, network administrators, and enterprises as a whole. A common IP infrastructure for all communications not only provides an enterprise with reduced cost of ownership but with a faster return on investment (ROI) as users more readily and easily adapt to a system that can be deployed to the desktop. This chapter introduces the benefits, terms, and concepts of video telephony.

IP Video Telephony Solution Components

Cisco introduced its IP video telephony solution in Cisco CallManager Release 4.0. With this solution, video is fully integrated into Cisco CallManager, and new endpoints are available from Cisco and its strategic partners. Video is now just as easy to deploy, manage, and use as a Cisco IP Phone.

The Cisco IP video telephony solution consists of products and solutions:

- Cisco CallManager Release 4.0 or later. Cisco CallManager provides call routing and a centralized dial plan for voice and video devices.
- Cisco IP/VC 3500 Series Multipoint Control Units (MCUs) for both H.323 and Skinny Client Control Protocol (SCCP) videoconference calls. The MCUs are responsible for mixing the various video and voice streams in a videoconference. In a videoconference, all devices send their streams to the MCU; the MCU mixes these streams into a single picture and sends the mixed stream back to the endpoints.
- Cisco IP/VC 3500 Series H.320 gateways interconnect the IP world with the ISDN world. To interconnect the H.323 with the H.320 (ISDN) world, a video gateway is required. Unlike a voice gateway, a video gateway is able to bond bearer channels (B channels). An H.263 video call needs at least 128 kbps, at lowest quality, in each direction; the VT Advantage default for a video call is an H.263 384-kbps video call. For a 384-kbps call, the

video gateway needs to open six ISDN B channels at the same time. The IP/VC 3500 Series H.320 gateways support B-channel bonding. The IP/VC 3500 Series H.320 gateways require an H.323 gatekeeper to register.

- A Cisco IOS H.323 gatekeeper is required to register third-party H.323 devices and the 35XX MCU. The main tasks of an H.323 gatekeeper are endpoint registration, bandwidth management, and directory number (DN) resolution. Many video devices, such as H.323 MCUs or H.320 video gateways, require an H.323 gatekeeper for registration.

- Cisco Video Telephony (VT) Advantage is a video telephony solution comprising the Cisco VT Advantage software application and Cisco VT Camera, a video telephony Universal Serial Bus (USB) camera. With the Cisco VT Camera attached to a PC collocated with a Cisco IP Phone, users can place and receive video calls on the enterprise IP telephony network. Users make calls from Cisco IP Phones using familiar telephone interfaces, but calls are enhanced with video on a PC, without requiring any extra button-pushing or mouse-clicking.

- TANDBERG SCCP endpoints are developed by the videoconference equipment vendor TANDBERG under Cisco license.

- The existing range of H.323-compliant products from vendors such as Polycom, TANDBERG, Sony, VCON, and VTEL Products. (Most H.323 video devices require a gatekeeper to register.)

- The Cisco 7985 IP Phone is one of the newest IP Phones added to the Cisco fleet. The 7985 supports full videoconference capabilities out of the box.

- Cisco IP Communicator 2.0 and later allows you to integrate the VT Advantage solution with the on-screen IP Communicator softphone.

Cisco CallManager Release 4.0 and later adds support for video in both the SCCP and H.323 protocols. Cisco CallManager can now manage H.323 endpoints, MCUs, and gateways, providing the system administrator with PBX-style control over all call routing and bandwidth management for those devices.

The video telephony solution consists of end-user devices, infrastructure, and applications. The end-user devices include video phones, soft video phones for remote workers (such as Cisco IP Communicator 2.0), and desktop environments that incorporate existing telephones and desktop computers. Additionally, the existing H.323 endpoints that the customers already own will become part of the video telephony environment.

Cisco CallManager is the center of the IP telephony infrastructure and supports both voice and video telephony. Cisco CallManager provides a single dial plan for all endpoints; there is no need for an additional video dial plan. The same applications are still supported: voice mail, conferencing, and scheduling for audio and video resources are possible.

The video stream mixing is accomplished by the MCU. In a Cisco CallManager environment, the MCU can be SCCP or H.323 or SCCP- and H.323-controlled. The main difference is that the H.323-controlled MCU needs an H.323 gatekeeper to register.

To allow external H.320 parties to participate in a videoconference, a video gateway, such as the Cisco IP/VC 3521 BRI Videoconferencing Gateway or IP/VC 3526 PRI Videoconferencing Gateway, is required. The normal voice gateways used in the Cisco CallManager environment do not support ISDN B-channel bonding and cannot route video calls from and to the public switched telephone network (PSTN).

Video Call Concepts

Using video endpoints in the Cisco CallManager system is, from the perspective of a user, as easy as placing a telephone call. Video terminals can be either H.323- or SCCP-controlled and are able to communicate with each other regardless of the protocol controlling the device. All video devices use the same dial plan as all other devices in the Cisco CallManager system. For Cisco CallManager, video devices are treated like voice devices, with the same configuration options. For the Cisco VT Camera, the same DN as the associated IP Phone is used. There is no additional number to remember to be able to reach someone over the video system. The video signaling is transparent to the user, and the devices negotiate their video capabilities, such as codec, format, and bit rate used for the video call, with no additional user action.

Cisco CallManager Involvement in Video Calls

A video telephony call can be established between any two video-enabled endpoints. If one of the endpoints is not video-enabled, the call is set up as a normal voice call. When both endpoints are video-enabled, Cisco CallManager signals the voice and video capabilities to both endpoints, as shown in Figure 28-1, and the endpoints directly build two RTP streams, one for voice and one for video. Call control for video calls operates the same way as the call control that governs voice calls.

Figure 28-1 *CallManager Video Involvement*

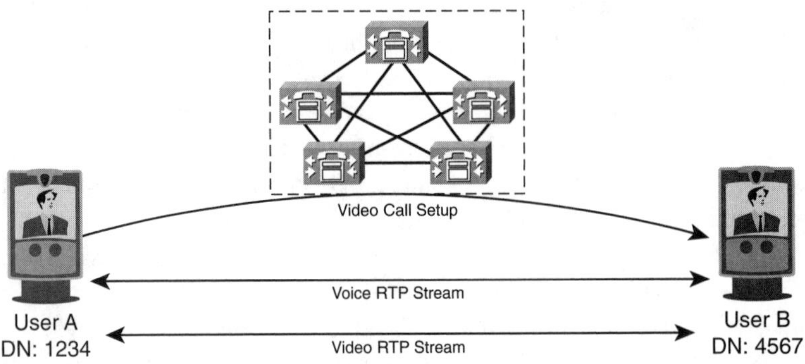

> **TIP** The term "video call" is sometimes confused with the term "videoconferencing." A videoconference is a video call with at least three participants.

For videoconferences in the Cisco CallManager system, extra hardware is required. The device that mixes the video streams is an MCU.

Video Call Flow

The typical video call includes two RTP streams in each direction. A basic video call includes two unidirectional RTP streams for voice and two unidirectional RTP streams for video. The call can include these stream types:

- **Audio**—These are the same codecs as used in audio-only calls, G.711 and G.729, plus additional codecs, G.722 and G.728. These additional codecs can be used when communicating to third-party equipment. Because Cisco IP Phones do not use these codecs, transcoding is necessary.
- **Video**—The video codecs used are H.261, H.263, H.264, and Cisco Wideband codecs. The video codec is a software module that enables the use of compression for digital video. There is a complex balance between the quality of the video, the video call bit rate, the complexity of the encoding and decoding algorithms, the robustness to data losses and errors, the ease of editing, the random access, the state of the art of compression algorithm design, the end-to-end delay, and a number of other factors.
- **Far-end camera control (FECC)**—FECC is used only for H.323 devices and is optional. FECC enables a user to control the camera of the far side during an active video call. This feature must be supported by both video-enabled H.323 devices. When FECC is used, two

more unidirectional RTP streams are sent between the video devices. The two additional RTP streams are used for the camera control parameters. This functionality is typically used for security cameras.

In the example shown in Figure 28-2, the video-enabled endpoints report their video and audio capabilities to Cisco CallManager. Cisco CallManager now treats the endpoints simply as video phone devices. When a call is placed or received between two video-enabled devices, Cisco CallManager signals for both audio and video streams. First the audio capabilities, such as audio codec information and audio bit rate, are signaled and negotiated, and then the audio stream is set up. After the audio stream is set up, the video capabilities, such as video codec information and video channel bit rate, are negotiated, and the devices exchange their video streams separately from the audio. In this example, the video call has four RTP streams—two unidirectional RTP streams for voice and two unidirectional RTP streams for video transmission.

Figure 28-2 *Video Call Flows*

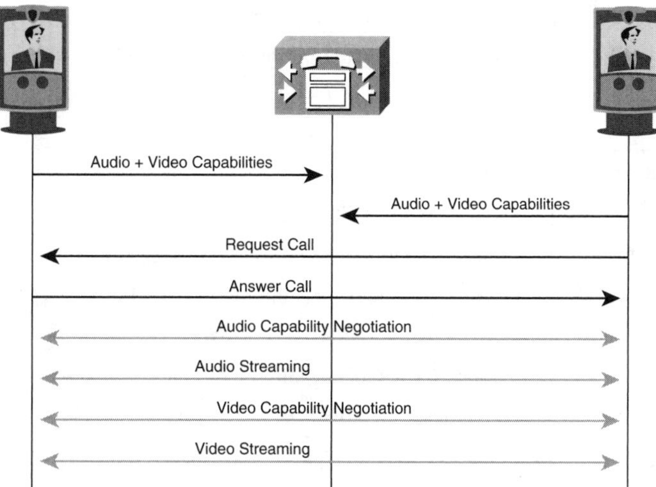

Video Codecs Supported by Cisco CallManager

Cisco CallManager supports several standard video codecs and a Cisco proprietary video codec. H.263 is a video codec specified by the International Telecommunication Union Telecommunication Standardization Sector (ITU-T) as a low-bit-rate encoding solution for videoconferencing. It was first designed to be used in H.324-based systems (PSTN and other circuit-switched network video environments) but has since found use in these other solutions as well:

- H.323 (IP-based videoconferencing)
- H.320 (ISDN-based videoconferencing)

- Real-Time Streaming Protocol (RTSP)
- Session Initiation Protocol (SIP)

H.263 was developed as an evolutionary improvement based on experience with H.261, the previous ITU-T standard for video compression, and the Moving Picture Experts Group-1 (MPEG-1) and Moving Picture Experts Group-2 (MPEG-2) standards. The first version of H.263 was completed in 1995, and it provided a suitable replacement for H.261 at all bit rates. H.263 was further enhanced in H.263 version 2 (H.263v2, also known as H.263+ or H.263 1998) and H.263 version 3 (H.263v3, also known as H.263++ or H.263 2000).

The next enhanced codec specified by the ITU-T after H.263 is the H.264 standard. Because H.264 provides a significant improvement in capability beyond H.263, the H.263 standard is now considered primarily a legacy design (although this is a recent development). Most new videoconferencing products include H.261, H.263, and H.264 capabilities.

The video codecs supported by Cisco CallManager Release 4.1 include H.261, H.263, and H.264. These codecs exhibit the parameters and typical values listed in Table 28-1.

Table 28-1 *Video Codec Parameters*

Parameter	Values
Video call speed	128 kbps, 384 kbps, 768 kbps, and 1.544 Mbps
Resolution	• Common Intermediate Format (CIF); resolution of 352 x 288 pixels • Quarter CIF (QCIF); resolution of 176 x 144 pixels • 4CIF; resolution of 704 x 576 pixels • Sub QCIF (SQCIF); resolution of 128 x 96 pixels • 16CIF; resolution of 1408 x 1152 pixels
Frame rate	15 frames per second (fps) 30 fps

The Cisco Wideband codec is a proprietary codec that is a fixed-bit-rate codec and runs on a PC that is linked to a phone. It enables the PC to associate with a call that the phone receives and can only be used by the Cisco VT Camera.

Video Protocols Supported in Cisco CallManager

Cisco CallManager Release 4.0 added support for video in both the SCCP and H.323 protocol. You can make calls between SCCP clients, between H.323 clients, and between SCCP and H.323 clients.

H.323 and SCCP endpoints have these characteristics:

- H.323 devices typically register with an H.323 gatekeeper (such as the Cisco IOS gatekeeper). The H.323 gatekeeper maintains the registration state of each endpoint, but it directs all call requests to Cisco CallManager. SCCP devices register directly with Cisco CallManager.
- H.323 devices send the complete dialed number all at once in their H.225 setup messages. SCCP devices send each dialed digit one-by-one as they are entered on the keypad. The difference is subtle but worth noting because it affects the experience of the user. Dialing on an H.323 device is much like dialing on a cell phone—the user enters the entire number and then presses the **Call** or **Dial** button to initiate the call. SCCP devices are more like a traditional telephone, in which the user goes off-hook, receives a dial tone from Cisco CallManager, and then starts dialing digits.
- H.323 devices are configured through the user interface of each endpoint. Changes to the configuration or software or firmware loads must be done locally on each endpoint (or, in some cases, through Simple Network Management Protocol [SNMP] or other vendor-specific management applications). SCCP devices are centrally controlled and configured in Cisco CallManager Administration. The configuration and software or firmware loads are then pushed to the endpoints via the TFTP. TANDBERG SCCP devices that receive their configurations via TFTP are the exception; however, software or firmware upgrades must be done manually (or through TANDBERG management applications).
- H.323 devices advertise their capabilities to Cisco CallManager on a call-by-call basis using H.245. SCCP devices advertise their capabilities when they register with Cisco CallManager and whenever their capabilities change. Cisco CallManager then decides, on a call-by-call basis, which types of media channels are negotiated between the endpoints.
- H.323 video devices offer basic call capabilities in interaction with Cisco CallManager. SCCP devices offer PBX-style features, such as hold, transfer, conference, park, pickup, and group pickup.
- For both types of endpoints, the signaling channels are routed through Cisco CallManager, but the media streams (audio and video channels) flow directly between the endpoints using RTP.
- H.323 and SCCP endpoints can call one another. Cisco CallManager provides the signaling translation between the two protocols and negotiates common media capabilities (common codecs).

- SCCP endpoints can invoke supplementary services, such as placing the call on hold, transferring the call, and conferencing with another party. H.323v2 devices support receiving Empty Capability Set (ECS) messages. ECS allows the devices to be the recipients of such features (that is, they can be placed on hold, transferred, or conferenced), but they cannot invoke those features.
- H.323-to-SCCP calls are not the only types of calls allowed by Cisco CallManager. Any device can call any other device, but video calls are supported only on SCCP and H.323 devices. Specifically, video is not supported in these protocols in Cisco CallManager Release 4.1:
  - Computer telephony integration (CTI) applications (Telephony Application Programming Interface [TAPI] and Java TAPI [JTAPI])
  - Media Gateway Control Protocol (MGCP)
  - SIP

Table 28-2 summarizes the key differences between H.323 and SCCP endpoints.

Table 28-2 *SCCP and H.323 Comparison*

SCCP Clients	H.323 Clients
Register with Cisco CallManager	Register with H.323 gatekeeper
Send dialed number digit-by-digit	Send entire dialed number at once
Are configured in Cisco CallManager Administration	Are configured through user interface
Advertise their capabilities when registering	Advertise their capabilities on a call-by-call basis
Offer PBX-style features	Offer basic call capabilities in interaction with Cisco CallManager

SCCP Video Call Characteristics

If a call is placed from an SCCP phone that reported video capabilities to Cisco CallManager and the other end supports video as well (another SCCP phone with video capabilities or an H.323 device), Cisco CallManager automatically signals the call as a video call. The amount of bandwidth the call can consume is determined by your region configuration. The system does not ask users for bit rate.

In Cisco CallManager Release 4.1, H.264 support was added for SCCP video devices. H.264 contains a number of features that allow it to compress video much more effectively than older codecs. This capability allows H.264 to deliver better video call quality over less bandwidth. Cisco CallManager supports the H.261 and H.263+ codecs as well. In addition, Cisco CallManager

Release 4.1 supports the audio codecs G.711, G.722, G.723.1, G.728, G.729, Cisco Wideband codec, and Global System for Mobile Communications (GSM). The wideband video codec of Cisco VT Camera reduces PC CPU utilization, unlike the resource-intensive H.263 and H.264 codecs. However, you will sacrifice a significant amount of bandwidth when using the wideband codec. For this reason, you will use this codec primarily in LANs, not over WAN links.

Cisco CallManager uses out-of-band H.245 alphanumeric dual-tone multifrequency (DTMF). DTMF might not work between SCCP and third-party H.323 devices because many H.323 devices pass DTMF in-band.

H.323 Video Call Characteristics

Call forwarding, dial plan, and other call routing–related features work with H.323 endpoints. During all this, the Cisco CallManager remains the central call-routing intelligence. In Cisco CallManager, H.323 endpoints can be configured as H.323 terminals, H.323 gateways, or H.323 trunks. Many H.323 devices request a gatekeeper for registration.

Some vendors implement call setup such that they cannot increase the bandwidth of a call when the call is transferred or redirected. In such cases, if the initial call is audio, users might not receive video when they are transferred to a video endpoint.

Video H.323 clients that use trunks to other Cisco CallManager systems or other H.323 systems can use the same features as audio-only H.323 clients. Currently, neither video media termination points (MTPs) nor video transcoders exist. If an audio transcoder or MTP is required for a call, that call will be audio only. H.323 video endpoints cannot initiate hold, resume, transfer, park, or offer other similar features. Only if an H.323 endpoint supports ECS can the endpoint be held, parked, and so on.

Dynamic H.323 addressing within Cisco CallManager provides a facility to register H.323 video terminals on Cisco CallManager when the video terminal receives its IP address through a Dynamic Host Configuration Protocol (DHCP) server. Endpoints are tracked based on their E.164 address registration with an adjacent video gatekeeper. The E.164 address is a static identifier that remains constant from the perspective of both gatekeeper and Cisco CallManager. The feature became available with Cisco CallManager Release 4.1. To move to a converged voice and video dial plan, it is highly desirable that Cisco CallManager become the entity that manages call routing and digit manipulation for both the voice and video endpoints, regardless of call-signaling protocol. Earlier releases of Cisco CallManager required that an H.323 video terminal be configured on Cisco CallManager based on static IP address information. As a support and mobility issue, this design could not facilitate a scalable method for endpoint management because configuration information was accurate only as long as the DHCP lease did not expire with the endpoint in question.

Cisco CallManager Release 4.1 supports H.261 and H.263 when using H.323-based video endpoints; H.264 is supported only for SCCP endpoints. H.323 video clients support the voice codecs G.711, G.722, G.723.1, G.728, and G.729. H.323 endpoints can also support far-end camera control (FECC). FECC enables a user to control the camera of the far side during an active video call. For FECC, two separate, unidirectional RTP streams are set up. This feature was introduced in H.323 version 5 (H.323v5) as Annex Q.

Cisco CallManager uses out-of-band H.245 alphanumeric DTMF. DTMF might not work because many H.323 devices pass DTMF in-band. If an H.323 device uses in-band DTMF signaling, Cisco CallManager will not convert it to out-of-band signaling, and the DTMF signaling will fail. Both sides need to use a common scheme; either both devices need to use out-of-band signaling or the H.323 device needs to support both methods and autodetect the method it should use.

SCCP and H.323 in Cisco CallManager

The call-related features of the Cisco IP video telephony integration strongly depend on the protocol in use. FECC, for example, is an H.323 feature supported only by H.323 devices and is not available on SCCP devices. Videoconferencing with three or more parties on a call requires an MCU. The Cisco IP/VC 3540 MCU supports both protocol stacks: H.323 and SCCP. This can be configured in the MCU Administration window.

The Cisco IP/VC 3521 and 3526 videoconferencing gateways bridge the gap between the installed base of ISDN videoconferencing group and room systems and IP-based H.323 systems. The gateways connect H.320 video systems on ISDN to H.323 systems on IP by translating calls initiated from the PSTN to their equivalent on the packet network, and vice versa. To enable SCCP to call H.320 endpoints, an H.323-based video gateway is necessary as well.

Beginning in Cisco CallManager Release 4.1, mid-call video is supported. Mid-call video allows an active voice call to become a video call if the video capabilities are added during the active call (for instance, if the Cisco VT Advantage software is turned on). Cisco VT Advantage will then associate with the phone and try to set up a video stream. If both parties are SCCP video endpoints, the call immediately becomes a video call. If the other party is an H.323 endpoint, the SCCP endpoint tries to request a video channel. If the H.323 endpoint rejects the incoming channel or does not open a channel, the call becomes either one-way video or audio only.

Bandwidth Management

Bandwidth management with Cisco CallManager call admission control enables you to control the audio and video quality of calls over a WAN link by limiting the number of calls that are allowed on that link simultaneously. In a packet-switched network, audio and video quality can begin to degrade when a link carries too many active calls and the bandwidth is oversubscribed. Call admission control regulates audio and video quality by limiting the number of calls that can be active on a particular link at the same time. Call admission control does not guarantee a particular level of audio or video quality on the link (this is the job of QoS), but it does allow you to regulate the amount of bandwidth that active calls on the link consume.

The actual bandwidth required is more than just the speed of the video call. The speed of the video call is just the payload, but the final packet also includes some amount of overhead for header information that encapsulates the payload into RTP segments, User Datagram Protocol (UDP) frames, IP packets, and finally a Layer 2 transport medium (such as Ethernet frames, ATM cells, or Frame Relay frames). References to the video call bandwidth should include the sum of the video call speed and all packetization overhead (RTP, UDP, IP, and Layer 2).

Video Call Bandwidth Requirement

A typical video call consists of two media channels: one for the video stream and one for the audio stream. These channels are referred to as logical channels in the H.323 protocol, and each logical channel is negotiated separately. For the call to succeed, Cisco CallManager checks that audio is successfully signaled; if video cannot be negotiated, the call will be an audio-only call. The audio channel consists of the actual audio bit rate. This bit rate is dictated by the audio codec in use. In the case of a G.711 codec, the bit rate is 64 kbps, whereas in the case of a G.729 codec, it is 8 kbps. For an audio channel, only the pure audio data is considered, not the packetization overhead.

The bit rate available for the video channel depends on the negotiated audio codec and the video call speed. The video channel bit rate is the speed of the video call minus the bit rate of the codec used for the audio channel. In the case of a 384-kbps video call with an audio channel that uses G.711, the bit rate left for the video channel is 320 kbps (384 kbps minus 64 kbps). In the case of an audio channel using the G.729 codec, the payload of the same video call (384 kbps) leaves 376 kbps. Table 28-3 lists possible video call speeds, their possible audio channel codecs, and the associated video channel bit rates.

Table 28-3 *Video Call Speeds and the Associated Audio and Video Codecs*

Video Call Speed	Audio Codec and Rate	Video Codec and Rate
128 kbps	G.711 at 64 kbps	H.261 or H.263 at 64 kbps
128 kbps	G.729 at 8 kbps	H.261 or H.263 at 120 kbps
128 kbps	G.728 at 16 kbps	H.261 or H.263 at 112 kbps
384 kbps	G.729 at 8 kbps	H.261 or H.263 at 376 kbps
384 kbps	G.711 at 64 kbps	H.261 or H.263 at 320 kbps
768 kbps	G.729 at 8 kbps	H.261 or H.263 at 760 kbps
768 kbps	G.711 at 64 kbps	H.261 or H.263 at 704 kbps
1.472 Mbps	G.729 at 8 kbps	H.261 or H.263 at 1.464 Mbps

continues

Table 28-3 *Video Call Speeds and the Associated Audio and Video Codecs (Continued)*

Video Call Speed	Audio Codec and Rate	Video Codec and Rate
1.472 Mbps	G.711 at 64 kbps	H.261 or H.263 at 1.408 Mbps
7 Mbps	G.729 at 8 kbps	Wideband at 7 Mbps (minus 8 kbps for the audio stream)
7 Mbps	G.711 at 64 kbps	Wideband at 7 Mbps (minus 64 kbps for the audio stream)

For example, as shown in Figure 28-3, a 384-kbps video call may be G.711 at 64 kbps (for audio) plus 320 kbps (for video). If the audio codec for a video call is G.729 (at 8 kbps), the video rate increases to maintain a total bandwidth of 384 kbps. If the call involves an H.323 endpoint, the H.323 endpoint might use less than the total video bandwidth that is available. An H.323 endpoint can always choose to send at less than the maximum bit rate for the call.

Figure 28-3 *Video Call Bandwidth Requirement Examples*

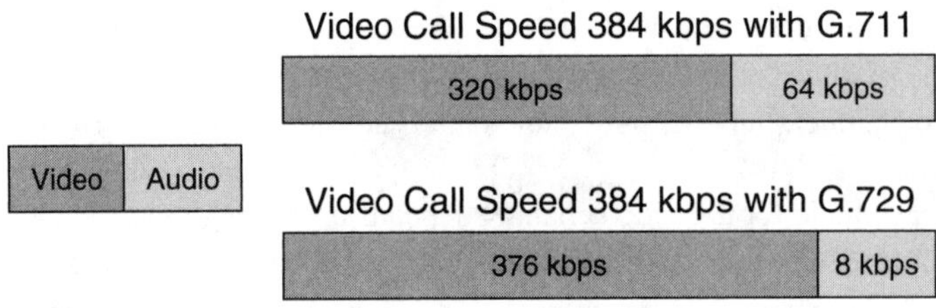

NOTE None of these values include packetization overhead.

Calculating the Total Bandwidth

The two main factors that influence bandwidth requirements for video calls are the media channels and the bandwidth used per call.

Actual Bandwidth Used Per Video Call

To calculate the exact overhead ratio for video, it is recommended that you add about 20 percent to the video call speed regardless of which type of Layer 2 medium the packets are traversing. The additional 20 percent gives plenty of headroom to allow for the differences among Ethernet, ATM, Frame Relay, PPP, High-Level Data Link Control (HDLC), and other transport protocols and also some cushion for the bursty nature of video traffic. Keep in mind that the amount of bandwidth consumed by the video correlates directly to the amount of movement on the video. Video streams with constant motion of the person speaking and the background (such as speaking in front of an ocean backdrop) can potentially double the amount of bandwidth required. The 20 percent rule is a general guide, but your actual results might vary.

Table 28-4 shows the recommended bandwidth values to use for some of the more popular video call speeds, incorporating this 20 percent margin.

Table 28-4 *Video Call Speeds and the Associated Audio and Video Codecs*

Video Call Speed Requested by Endpoint	Actual Bandwidth Required on the Link
128 kbps	153.6 kbps
256 kbps	307.2 kbps
384 kbps	460.8 kbps
512 kbps	614.4 kbps
768 kbps	921.6 kbps
1.5 Mbps	1.766 Mbps
7 Mbps	8.4 Mbps

Call Admission Control in Cisco CallManager

As shown in Figure 28-4, the location configuration settings for Cisco CallManager–based call admission control have also been enhanced, compared to earlier Cisco CallManager releases not supporting video, to provide for accounting of video bandwidth on a per-call and aggregate basis. The location setting for call admission control defines the overall bandwidth allowed for all video calls to a certain location. That is the video call speed for all video calls. To allow five video calls with a bandwidth of 384 kbps for each video call (defined in the Cisco CallManager regions), the value to enter in the Cisco CallManager location is 1920 kbps.

For video calls, the negotiated bandwidth for a video-enabled device typically includes both audio and video; for example, a 384-kbps video call comprises 64-kbps audio and 320-kbps video channels. For voice-only calls, the region uses the same setting that is used for the audio channel in video calls. The negotiated bandwidth for an IP telephony device includes the "real" audio bandwidth including IP overhead; for example, a G.711 64-kbps audio call uses 80 kbps, and this value has to be entered in the Cisco CallManager location configuration.

Figure 28-4 *Cisco CallManager Enhanced Location Configuration*

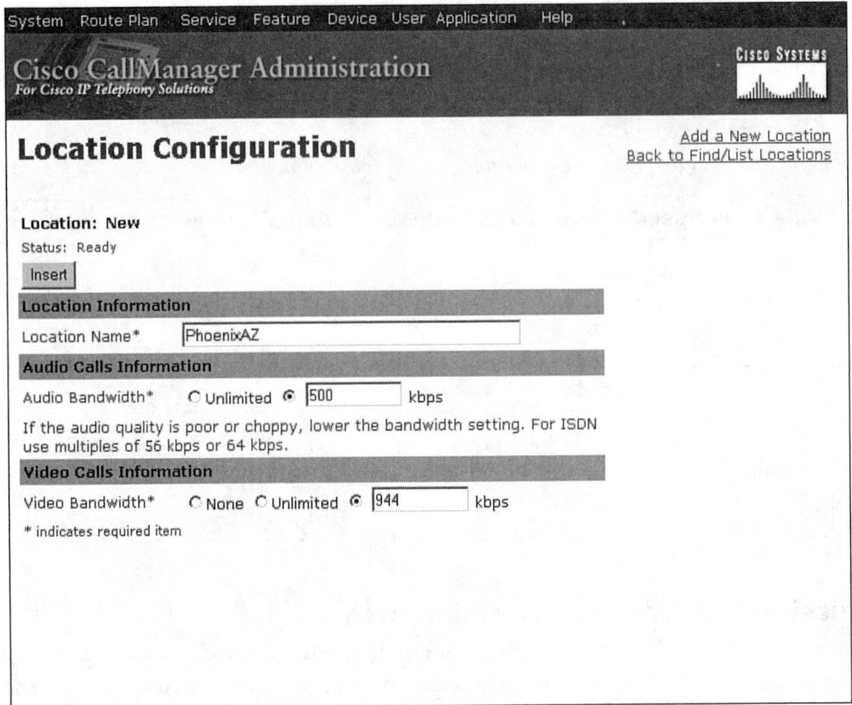

H.323 gatekeepers have slightly different bandwidth measurements. The H.323 specification dictates that the bandwidth values must be entered as twice the codec bit rate. For example, a 384-kbps video call would be entered as 768 kbps in the gatekeeper. A G.711 audio-only call would be entered as 128 kbps in the gatekeeper.

NOTE Call admission control behavior changed in Cisco CallManager Release 3.2(2)c and Cisco IOS Software Release 12.2(2)XA. Before that release, Cisco CallManager asked for bit rate plus Layer 3 overhead, and Cisco IOS gateways asked for 64 kbps, regardless of the type of call.

Call Admission Control Within a Cluster

Why do you need to configure call admission control for video calls? The answer to this question is quite simple. If you do not control the number of video and voice calls over your WAN links in a centralized deployment (shown in Figure 28-5), periodically you will see decreased video and voice throughout the whole system. With call admission control, you control the number of calls on the WAN link and ensure that all calls, video and audio-only, are processed throughout the network with acceptable quality.

Figure 28-5 *Typical Centralized Call Control Environment*

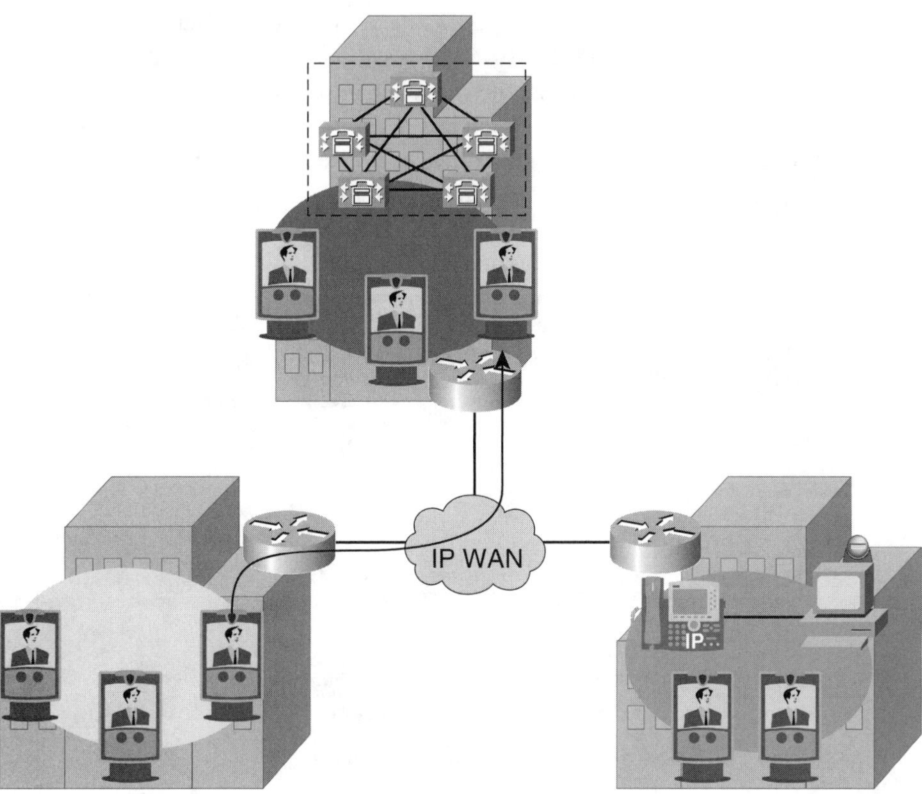

Cisco CallManager uses regions and locations to implement call admission control:

- Regions define the codec used and maximum video bandwidth allowed per call. This value is configurable for calls within each region and for calls between any pair of regions.
- Locations define the maximum bandwidth allowed for all calls to and from a location.

In Cisco CallManager, devices derive their region setting with the associated device pool configuration. You can assign locations on a per-device basis. If you assign locations at the device level, it overrides the setting inherited from the device pool.

Calls between devices at the same location do not need call admission control because the assumption is that these devices reside on the same LAN that has "unlimited" available bandwidth. However, for calls between devices at different locations, the assumption is that there is an IP WAN link in between that has limited available bandwidth.

Region Configuration

When you are configuring a region, you set two fields in Cisco CallManager Administration: the **Audio Codec** and the **Video Call Bandwidth** fields, as shown in Figure 28-6. Note that the audio setting specifies a codec type, whereas the video setting specifies the bandwidth that you want to allow. However, even though the notation is different, the **Audio Codec** and **Video Call Bandwidth** fields actually perform similar functions. The **Audio Codec** value defines the maximum bit rate allowed for audio-only calls and for the audio channel in video calls.

Figure 28-6 *Cisco CallManager Region Configuration*

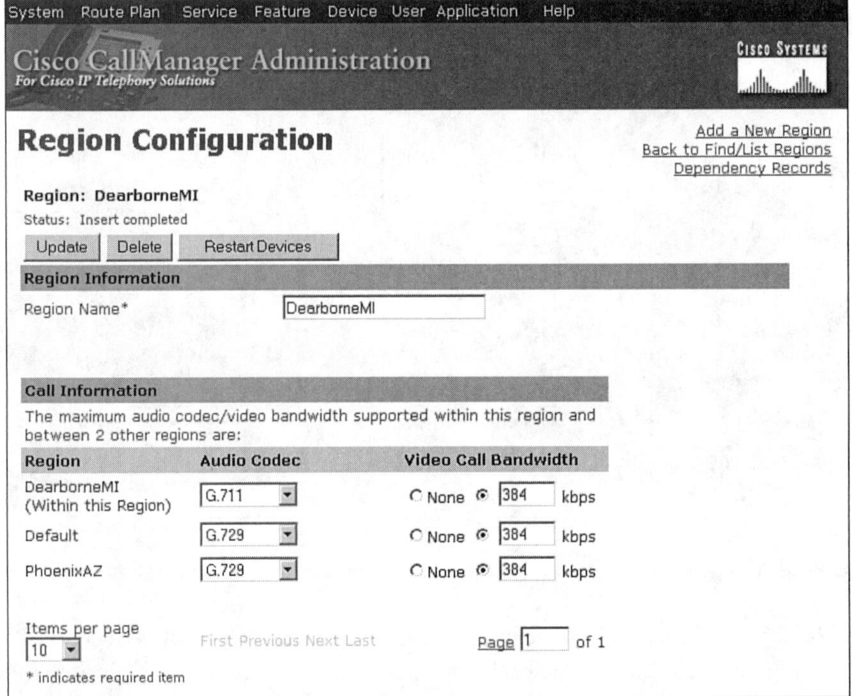

For instance, if you set the **Audio Codec** value for a region to **G.711**, Cisco CallManager allocates 64 kbps as the maximum bandwidth allowed for the audio channel for that region. In this case, Cisco CallManager permits calls using G.711, G.728, or G.729. However, if you set the **Audio Codec** value to **G.729**, Cisco CallManager allocates only 8 kbps as the maximum bandwidth allowed for the audio channel; in addition, Cisco CallManager permits calls using only G.729, because G.711, G.722, and G.728 all require more than 8 kbps.

The **Video Call Bandwidth** value defines the maximum bit rate for the video call, that is, the bit rate of the voice and video channels. For instance, if you want to allow video calls at a speed of 384 kbps using G.711 audio, you would set the **Video Call Bandwidth** value to **384** kbps and the **Audio Codec** value to **G.711**. The bit rate that would be used by the video channel thus would be 320 kbps. If the **Video Call Bandwidth** value is set to **None** for the region, Cisco CallManager either terminates the call or allows the call to pass as an audio-only call, depending on whether the calling device has the **Retry Video Call as Audio** option enabled.

In summary, the **Audio Codec** field defines the maximum bit rate used for the audio channel of audio-only calls and for the audio channel of video calls, whereas the **Video Call Bandwidth** field defines the maximum bit rate allowed for video calls and includes the audio portion of the video call.

NOTE Video endpoints typically support only G.711 and G.722, whereas audio-only endpoints typically support only G.711 and G.729. Because you cannot configure the audio codec for audio and video calls separately, often the only common audio codec for mixed environments (including third-party equipment) is G.711.

Location Configuration

When configuring locations, you also set two fields in Cisco CallManager Administration: the **Audio Bandwidth** and the **Video Bandwidth** values, shown in Figure 28-7. Unlike regions, however, audio bandwidth for locations applies only to audio-only calls, whereas video bandwidth again applies to the video call (that is, audio and video channels).

Figure 28-7 *Cisco CallManager Location Configuration*

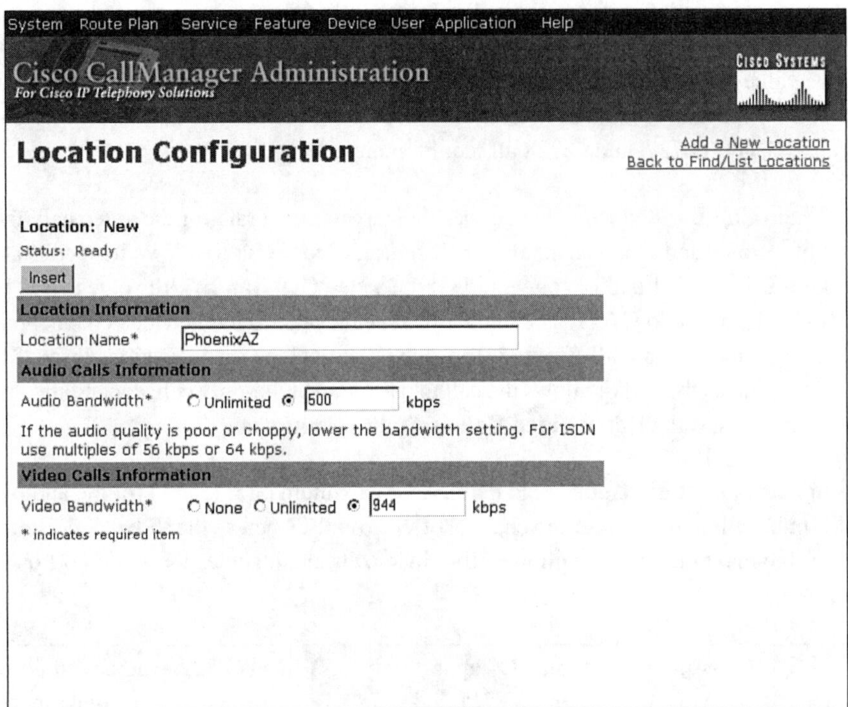

The audio and video bandwidth are kept separate because if both types of calls shared a single allocation of bandwidth, it is very likely that audio calls would take all of the available bandwidth and leave no room for any video calls, or vice versa.

Both the **Audio Bandwidth** and the **Video Bandwidth** fields offer three options: **None**, **Unlimited**, or a field that accepts numeric values. However, the values entered in these fields use two different calculation models:

- For the **Audio Bandwidth** field, the value entered has to include the Layer 3 and 4 overhead required for the call. For instance, if you want to permit a single G.729 call to or from a location, you would enter the value 24 kbps. For a G.711 call, you would enter the value 80 kbps. The payload of a G.711 voice call is 64 kbps; the 80-kbps value is the 64-kbps payload plus 16-kbps RPT plus UDP.

- The value in the **Video Bandwidth** field, by contrast, is entered without any overhead. For instance, for a 128-kbps call, enter the value 128 kbps; for a 384-kbps call, enter the value 384 kbps. As with the values used in the **Video Bandwidth** field for regions, it is recommended that you always use increments of 56 kbps or 64 kbps for the **Video Bandwidth** field for locations.

> **NOTE** The value **None** in the **Video Bandwidth** field indicates that video calls are not allowed between this location and other locations. Video calls can, however, be placed within this location.

Call Admission Control Example

Figure 28-8 illustrates an example of audio and video bandwidth requirements for a company with a three-site network. The San Francisco location has a 1.544-Mbps T1 circuit connecting it to the San Jose main campus. The system administrator wants to allow four G.729 voice calls and one 384-kbps video call to or from that location.

Figure 28-8 *Video Call Bandwidth Example*

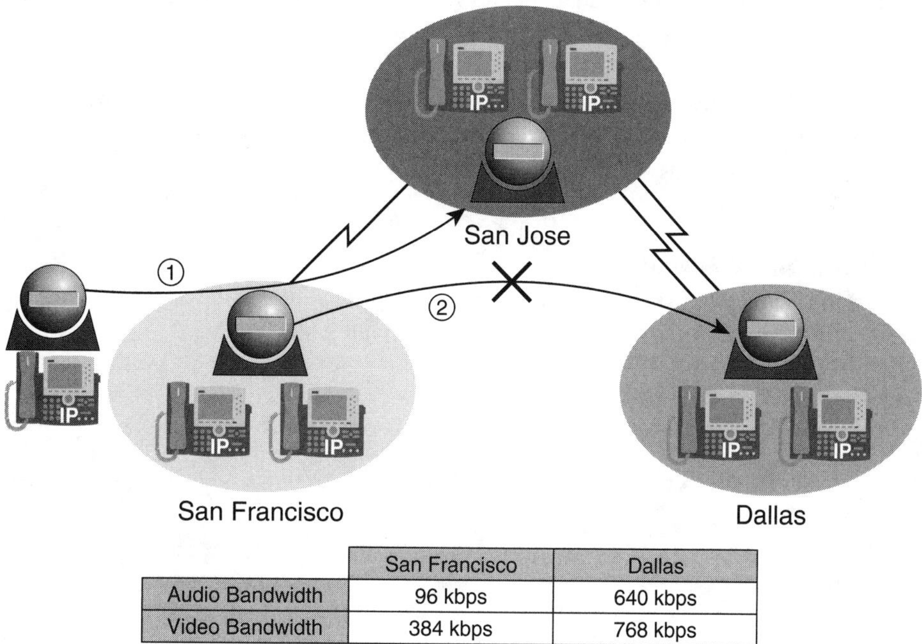

	San Francisco	Dallas
Audio Bandwidth	96 kbps	640 kbps
Video Bandwidth	384 kbps	768 kbps

The Dallas location has two 1.544-Mbps T1 circuits connecting it to the San Jose main campus, and the administrator wants to allow eight G.711 voice calls and two 384-kbps video calls to or from that location.

For this example, the administrator might set the San Francisco and Dallas locations to the values in Table 28-5.

Table 28-5 *Bandwidth Example*

Location	Number of Audio Calls Desired	Audio Bandwidth Field Value	Number of Video Calls Desired	Video Bandwidth Field Value
San Francisco	Four using G.729	96 kbps (4 * 24 kbps)	One at 384 kbps	384 kbps
Dallas	Eight using G.711	640 kbps (8 * 80 kbps)	Two at 384 kbps	768 kbps

First, a video device in San Francisco calls a video device in San Jose. Call admission control allows exactly one 384-kbps video call between San Francisco and any other location. The video call is active.

Next, another video device from San Francisco tries to set up a video call to a video device in Dallas. Call admission control does not allow a second video call from San Francisco to any other location and denies the video call.

If the call fails because of insufficient location bandwidth, it will not be retried with lower-bit-rate codecs. In this scenario, with no further configuration of the Cisco CallManager, the call (both audio and video portions) will be rejected.

Retry Video Call as Audio

The **Retry Video Call as Audio** setting appears as a check box in the IP Phone configuration in Cisco CallManager Administration, as shown in Figure 28-9.

Figure 28-9 *Configuring the Retry Video Call as Audio Setting*

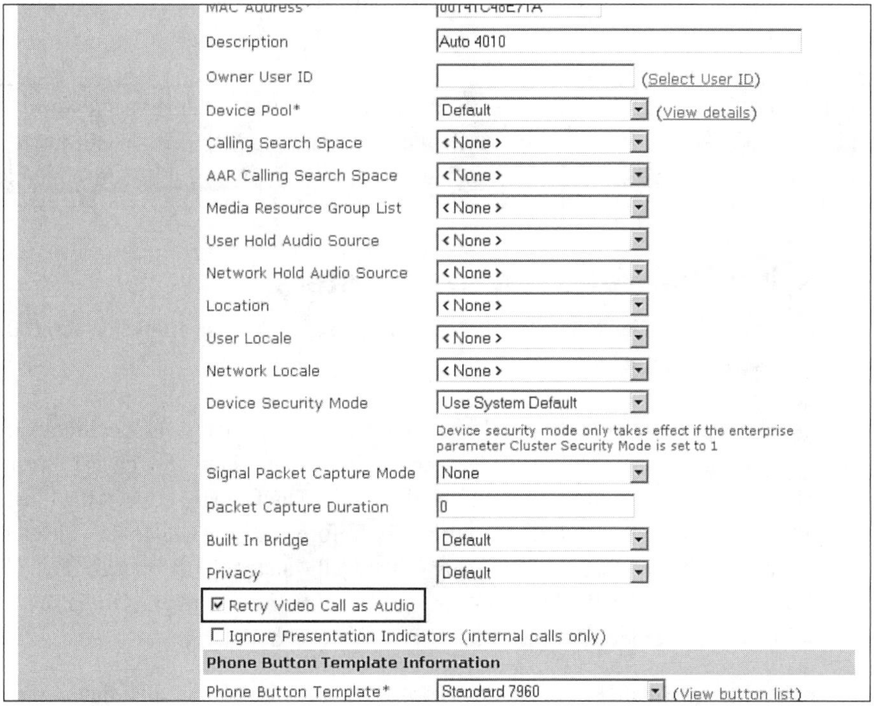

This setting is enabled by default on all device types and applies to these scenarios only:

- The region is configured not to allow video.
- The location is configured not to allow video, or the requested video speed exceeds the available video bandwidth for that location.
- The requested video speed exceeds the zone bandwidth limits of the gatekeeper.

When this option is activated (checked), if there is not enough bandwidth for a video call (for example, if the Cisco CallManager regions or locations do not allow video for that call), Cisco CallManager will retry the call as an audio-only call. When this option is deactivated (unchecked), Cisco CallManager will not retry the video call as audio only but will instead either reject the call or reroute the video call by whatever Automated Alternate Routing (AAR) path is configured.

The **Retry Video Call as Audio** option takes effect only on the terminating (called) device, allowing flexibility for the calling device to have different options (retry or AAR) for different destinations.

> **NOTE** The called device determines the result. In other words, when one device calls another and any of the discussed insufficient bandwidth conditions applies, Cisco CallManager looks at the destination device to see whether the **Retry Video Call as Audio** option is enabled.

Call Admission Control Between Clusters

Calls between Cisco CallManager clusters typically use intercluster trunks. Cisco CallManager Release 4.1 supports these types of trunks:

- **Nongatekeeper-controlled intercluster trunks**—This trunk type is specifically designed for communications between Cisco CallManager clusters and should not be used with other types of H.323 devices. The name implies that there is no gatekeeper between the clusters to regulate the bandwidth used between them. Therefore, the only way to provide call admission control for this type of trunk is by using Cisco CallManager locations. To have Cisco CallManager control call admission control, the intercluster trunk has to be in a separate Cisco CallManager location than the devices that use the intercluster trunk.
- **Gatekeeper-controlled intercluster trunks**—This trunk type is specifically designed for communications between Cisco CallManager clusters and should not be used to register other H.323 endpoints or devices. The name implies that there is a gatekeeper between the clusters to regulate the bandwidth used between them. To provide call admission control, you configure an H.323 zone in the gatekeeper for each of the Cisco CallManager clusters and assign zone bandwidth limits to each zone. If the gatekeeper-controlled intercluster trunk is not in the same location as the devices, the location settings need to be reconsidered. A device will need to get its call admission control permissions first from Cisco CallManager, because the device is in a different location than the trunk, and call admission control will be carried out at the gatekeeper.
- **H.225 gatekeeper-controlled trunks**—The H.225 gatekeeper-controlled trunk is designed for use with any H.323 device other than a Cisco CallManager cluster. In an H.225 gatekeeper-controlled trunk scenario, only the gatekeeper has control over call admission.
- **SIP trunks**—SIP trunks are designed for use with any SIP device, including other Cisco CallManager clusters, either directly or via a Cisco SIP proxy server.

> **NOTE** Because Cisco CallManager Release 4.1 does not support video over the SIP protocol, this chapter does not cover SIP trunks.

Gatekeeper Call Admission Control Options

H.323 gatekeepers are hierarchical in nature. A gatekeeper can have one or more local zones. Using multiple zones allows you to group the devices that use the gatekeeper and gives better call admission control options (intrazone and interzone limitations). Zones that are served by another gatekeeper are called *remote zones*, shown in Figure 28-10. These zones can be configured with different call admission control settings as well.

Figure 28-10 *Sample Gatekeeper Design*

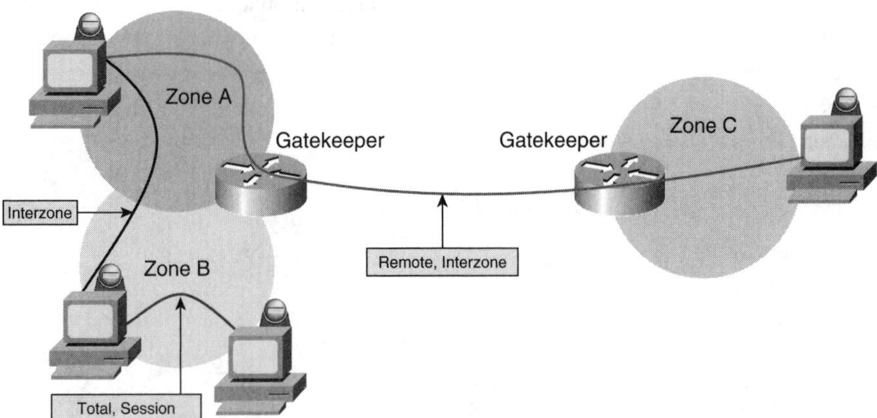

The Cisco gatekeeper might reject calls from an endpoint because of bandwidth limitations. Rejection can occur if the gatekeeper determines that the bandwidth available on the network is not sufficient to support the call. This function also operates during an active call when a terminal requests additional bandwidth or reports a change in bandwidth used for the call. The Cisco gatekeeper maintains a record of all active calls so that it can manage the bandwidth resources in its zones.

When an endpoint or gateway is configured to use an H.323 gatekeeper, it first sends an admission request (ARQ) to the gatekeeper. The gatekeeper checks whether there is bandwidth available. If the available bandwidth is sufficient for the call, an admission confirmation (ACF) is returned; otherwise an admission rejection (ARJ) is returned.

As of Cisco IOS Software Release 12.3(1), you can configure the following types of zone bandwidth limitations on the Cisco gatekeeper:

- **Interzone**—The maximum bandwidth of all calls from a local zone to all other zones (local or remote)
- **Total**—The maximum bandwidth of all calls within a local zone

- **Session**—The maximum bandwidth allowed for a single session within a local zone
- **Remote**—The maximum bandwidth for all calls from all local zones to all remote zones

The first three limitations can be configured individually for each local zone. However, you can also specify the default configuration for all local zones that are not configured explicitly.

Gatekeeper Call Admission Control Example

The intercluster trunk gatekeeper provides address resolution and bandwidth control between Cisco CallManager clusters. For example, suppose that your network has two Cisco CallManager clusters connected via a digital signal level 3 (DS-3) WAN link, as shown in Figure 28-11. Also assume that you want to allow a maximum of twenty G.711 audio calls and five 384-kbps video calls between the two clusters.

Figure 28-11 *Gatekeeper Call Admission Control Example*

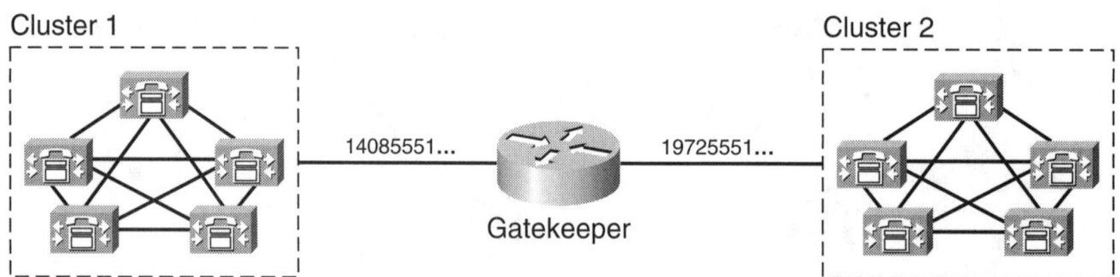

In this case, configure one zone per cluster using the **bandwidth interzone** command to restrict the bandwidth between the two zones to the total of twenty G.711 calls plus five 384-kbps video calls. If you want to set the maximum bandwidth per call in a local zone, use the **bandwidth session** command. The following is a partial H.323 gatekeeper code snippet:

```
zone local cluster-1 domain.com
zone local cluster-2 domain.com
zone prefix cluster-1 14085551...
zone prefix cluster-2 19725551...
bandwidth interzone cluster-1 6400
bandwidth session cluster-1 768
bandwidth interzone cluster-2 6400
bandwidth session cluster-2 768
```

Table 28-6 shows a sample scenario using this environment.

Table 28-6 *Example for Twenty G.711 Audio Calls and Five 384-kbps Video Calls*

Desired Calls	Gatekeeper Bandwidth Value
20 * G.711 audio calls	128 kbps * 20 = 2560 kbps
5 * 384-kbps video calls	768 kbps * 5 = 3840 kbps
20 * G.711 audio + 5 * 384-kbps video calls	2560 kbps + 3840 kbps = 6400 kbps

The bandwidth value that you have to enter is twice the bit rate of the call. For example, a G.711 audio call that uses 64 kbps is denoted as 128 kbps in the gatekeeper, and a 384-kbps video call is denoted as 768 kbps. Table 28-7 shows the bandwidth values for some of the more popular call speeds.

Table 28-7 *Bandwidth Values for Frequently Used Call Speeds*

Call Speed	Gatekeeper Bandwidth Value
G.711 audio call (64 kbps)	128 kbps
G.729 audio call (8 kbps)	16 kbps
128-kbps video call	256 kbps
384-kbps video call	768 kbps
512-kbps video call	1024 kbps
768-kbps video call	1536 kbps

NOTE You cannot avoid having more G.711 calls active than desired because the bandwidth for voice and video is not managed separately. It can happen that more G.711 calls are active than desired and that they consume the configured bandwidth actually reserved for video calls, leaving no bandwidth for video calls.

Summary

This chapter discussed the concepts behind a Cisco video telephony solution. Cisco video telephony supports SCCP and H.323 devices communicating in any combination. For videoconferences, an MCU is required. The typical video call includes two or three RTP streams in each direction. Using SCCP clients allows you to offer end users major PBX features, whereas using H.323 clients limits your end users to only supporting basic call functionality.

When determining bandwidth requirements for the audio and video calls, adding 20 percent to the payload bandwidth requirement for video calls provides plenty of buffer for overhead information. Bandwidth call admission control within a cluster is done using Cisco CallManager locations and regions. Between clusters, you must use H.323 gatekeeper control.

Review Questions

You can find the solutions to these questions in Appendix A, "Answers to Review Questions."

1. What is the video payload in a video call using 384 kbps and the G.711 codec?
   a. 300 kbps
   b. 320 kbps
   c. 376 kbps
   d. 384 kbps
2. To enable video calls with a requested speed of 256 kbps, what would the recommended bandwidth setting be on Cisco CallManager locations?
   a. 307.2 kbps
   b. 256 kbps
   c. 512 kbps
   d. 281.6 kbps
3. Which video codec will be used when an SCCP and H.323 device communicate?
   a. H.263
   b. H.264
   c. Cisco wideband codec
   d. H.261
4. How is call admission control performed between Cisco CallManager clusters with a nongatekeeper-controlled intercluster trunk?
   a. Gateway
   b. Cisco CallManager locations
   c. Gatekeeper
   d. MCU
   e. Intercluster trunk
5. Which device performs call admission control within a cluster?
   a. Gateway
   b. Cisco CallManager locations
   c. Gatekeeper
   d. MCU
   e. Intercluster trunk

6. Which device is needed to integrate H.320 into the Cisco video solution?
   a. MCU
   b. Video gateway
   c. MGCP gateway
   d. H.323 gatekeeper
7. Which of the following are required to support videoconferencing capabilities?
   a. Gateway
   b. Cisco CallManager locations
   c. Gatekeeper
   d. MCU
   e. SCCP Clients support videoconferencing natively.
8. Which of the following best defines FECC?
   a. The ability to negotiate audio codecs between H.323 and SCCP devices
   b. The ability to negotiate video codecs between H.323 and SCCP devices
   c. The ability to change the position of a remote camera
   d. Converting between the H.320 and H.263 video codecs
9. How much bandwidth is consumed by the Cisco proprietary wideband codec?
   a. 384 kbps
   b. 768 kbps
   c. 1.544 Mbps
   d. 7 Mbps
10. Which Cisco CallManager release first added video support?
   a. Cisco CallManager 3.2(3)
   b. Cisco CallManager 3.3(3c)
   c. Cisco CallManager 4.0(1)
   d. Cisco CallManager 4.1(1)

This chapter covers the following topics:

- Describing the features and functions of Cisco VT Advantage
- Explaining how placing and receiving calls works with Cisco VT Advantage
- Configuring Cisco CallManager for video
- Configuring feature settings in Cisco CallManager to support video on Cisco IP Phones
- Installing the Cisco VT Advantage application and identifying the hardware and software required to run it

CHAPTER 29

Configuring Cisco VT Advantage

Cisco Video Telephony (VT) Advantage is a video telephony solution comprising the Cisco VT Advantage software application and Cisco VT Camera, a video telephony Universal Serial Bus (USB) camera. With the Cisco VT Camera attached to a PC wired through a Cisco IP Phone, users can place and receive video calls on the enterprise IP telephony network. By using the VT Advantage solution, you can take full advantage of your existing IP network to deliver communications that extend voice and video to every user in the organization. This chapter discusses the concepts and configuration behind Cisco VT Advantage.

NOTE As with most products in the Cisco IP telephony line, the Cisco VT Advantage has recently been renamed to Cisco Unified Video Advantage. For brevity, we have decided to use the shorter VT Advantage name throughout this chapter.

Cisco VT Advantage Overview

Cisco VT Advantage brings video telephony functionality to the Cisco IP Phone 7940, 7960, and 7970 (and later) models. Cisco VT Advantage software coupled with the Cisco VT Camera (a USB camera) allows a PC connected to a Cisco IP Phone to add video to telephone calls without requiring any extra button-pushing or mouse-clicking. When registered to Cisco CallManager, the Cisco VT Advantage-enabled Cisco IP Phone has the features and functionality of a full-featured IP video phone. Supplementary services, such as call forward, transfer, hold, and mute, are also available for video calls and are all initiated through the Cisco IP Phone. Cisco VT Advantage is intended for desktop-to-desktop IP video telephony environments, not as a general-purpose videoconferencing solution for use in conference rooms.

Cisco VT Advantage Components

To deploy Cisco VT Advantage, the minimum requirement is Cisco CallManager Release 4.0(1) with Service Release 2 or higher. Currently, you can enable video on Cisco IP Phone 7940G, 7960G, and the 7970G (and later) models. The Cisco VT Camera is connected to a PC (via USB) where Cisco VT Advantage software is installed. Cisco VT Advantage software works only with the Cisco VT Camera.

NOTE Cisco VT Advantage and the Cisco IP Communicator (Softphone running on a PC) can run on the same PC; however, Cisco VT Advantage is not supported to interconnect with Cisco IP Communicator.

Cisco VT Advantage software provides the user with an easy-to-use graphical interface, with these options:

- **Receive Only Mode**—Users can choose to view incoming video only and not transmit video.
- **Video Check**—Users can check their video before calls are placed or received.
- **Mute Video on Audio Mute**—When users mute the audio on the IP phone, video is automatically paused until the audio on the IP phone is restored.
- **Video Signal Indicators**—The quality of the incoming and outgoing video is graphically displayed.
- **Connectivity Indicator**—Graphics are used to indicate the state of the connections from the PC to its associated Cisco IP Phone and Cisco VT Camera.

Users can operate the Cisco IP Phone as they normally do. The Cisco VT Advantage software is controlled from the PC connected directly to the access port labeled "PC" on the back of the Cisco IP Phone. The PC and the Cisco IP Phone that is registered in Cisco CallManager as a video-enabled device build an association. The voice Real-Time Transport Protocol (RTP) streams flow between the two IP phones, as in a normal voice call. The video streams flow between the two PCs where the Cisco VT Advantage software is installed.

Cisco VT Advantage Supported Standards

Cisco VT Advantage, like any other application that runs on a PC, has an impact on system performance that should be taken into consideration. Cisco VT Advantage supports two types of video codecs: H.263 and the Cisco VT Camera wideband video codec. Of these two types, the Cisco VT Camera wideband video codec places the least demand on the PC. Therefore, if your network has plenty of available bandwidth, you can use the Cisco VT Camera wideband video codec and save on PC CPU and memory resources.

When you are using a codec that performs compression, more CPU power is needed. The H.263 codec is more demanding of PC system resources, but it requires less bandwidth. Therefore, if you want to use H.263 compressed video to conserve bandwidth on the network, you should ensure that your PCs have enough CPU and memory resources available. The Cisco VT Advantage H.263 codec supports a range of speeds up to 1.5 Mbps.

Regardless of the video standard used, the VT Advantage supports video formats with up to 30 frames per second (fps) at the following resolutions:

- VGA (640x480)
- CIF (352 x 288)
- SIF (320 x 240)
- QCIF (176 x 144)
- QSIF (160 x 120)

Table 29-1 lists the video codecs that Cisco VT Advantage supports.

Table 29-1 *Video Codecs Supported by Cisco VT Advantage*

Codec	Parameters
H.263	• Bandwidth: 128 kbps to 1.5 Mbps • Native Resolution: Common Intermediate Format (CIF) and Quarter CIF (QCIF) • Frame rate: Up to 30 frames per second (fps)
Cisco VT Camera wideband video codec	• Bandwidth: 7 Mbps • Native Resolution: 320 x 240 • Frame rate: Up to 30 fps

Protocols Used by Cisco VT Advantage

Cisco VT Advantage supports several industry-standard and Cisco networking protocols required for video communication. Table 29-2 displays an overview of the supported networking protocols.

Table 29-2 *Overview of the Supported Networking Protocols*

Networking Protocol	Description	Usage Notes
Cisco Audio Session Tunnel	• Allows communication between the Cisco IP Phone and associated software, such as Cisco VT Advantage. • Uses source and destination port 4224. • Uses TCP. • Cisco proprietary protocol.	• Cisco Audio Session Tunnel is used between Cisco VT Advantage and the IP Phone — To build an association (after the PC discovers the IP phone using Cisco Discovery Protocol) — To send signaling information for video streams from the IP phone to Cisco VT Advantage (after the IP phone receives the signaling messages for both audio and video from Cisco CallManager) • Cisco Audio Session Tunnel signaling messages include these: — Call video stream start and stop — Call hold and resume
Cisco Discovery Protocol	• A device-discovery protocol that runs on all Cisco manufactured equipment. • A Layer 2 protocol. • Works only between directly connected neighbors. • Using Cisco Discovery Protocol, a device can advertise its existence to other devices and receive information about other devices in the network. • Cisco proprietary protocol.	• Cisco VT Advantage uses Cisco Discovery Protocol to communicate its capabilities to the Cisco IP Phone, and the Cisco IP Phone uses Cisco Discovery Protocol to communicate information, such as its IP address, to Cisco VT Advantage.
RTP	• A standard for using User Datagram Protocol (UDP) to transport real-time data, such as interactive voice and video, over data networks.	• The RTP protocol is used to encapsulate and stream the audio (between Cisco IP Phones) and video (between Cisco VT Advantage endpoints).
Skinny Client Control Protocol (SCCP, or Skinny)	• A Cisco protocol using low-bandwidth messages that allows the exchange of signaling messages between IP devices and the Cisco CallManager. • Works on TCP port 2000. • Cisco proprietary protocol.	• Cisco VT Advantage does not use SCCP itself. It uses Cisco Audio Session Tunnel to send signaling messages to the Cisco IP Phone, which acts as a proxy and passes the signaling messages to Cisco CallManager using SCCP.

How Calls Work with Cisco VT Advantage

When a Windows PC has Cisco VT Advantage installed, it should be connected to the secondary Ethernet port (that is, PC port) of a Cisco IP Phone 7940G, 7960G, or 7970G (or later) model. In most configurations, the PC will be in a different VLAN than the Cisco IP Phone (located in the voice or auxiliary VLAN). In such configurations, all IP-based communication between Cisco VT Advantage and the Cisco IP Phone has to be routed between the VLANs, and only Cisco Discovery Protocol is exchanged directly. The following list explains the call process shown in Figure 29-1:

1. Cisco Discovery Protocol exchange takes place so that Cisco VT Advantage and the Cisco IP Phone can discover one another. A Cisco Discovery Protocol driver is installed on the PC during the installation of Cisco VT Advantage. This allows the Cisco VT Advantage application to dynamically learn the IP address of the Cisco IP Phone during the Cisco Discovery Protocol exchange, and associate with it. This serves as both an ease-of-use feature for the end user and for security. The use of Cisco Discovery Protocol to facilitate the association process allows it to occur automatically, without the user having to configure the Cisco VT Advantage application. This allows for mobility of the application between different IP phones on the network. The user can plug into the PC port of any supported Cisco IP Phone on the network (if permitted by the administrator) and begin making video telephony calls. Cisco Discovery Protocol also provides a measure of security in that the IP phone will respond only to association messages from a Cisco VT Advantage client that matches the IP address of the device that is connected to its PC port (that is, its Cisco Discovery Protocol neighbor), minimizing the risk of someone else associating with your Cisco IP Phone over the network and receiving video when calls are placed on your IP phone. The Cisco IP Phone begins listening for Cisco Audio Session Tunnel messages on TCP port 4224.

2. After Cisco Discovery Protocol discovery, Cisco VT Advantage and the IP phone exchange Cisco Audio Session Tunnel protocol messages over TCP port 4224. Cisco VT Advantage sends a Cisco Audio Session Tunnel message to the IP phone, which is in a different IP network (VLAN). The packet first travels through the PC VLAN to the default gateway, where it is routed toward the IP phone (using the voice VLAN). The Cisco Audio Session Tunnel protocol allows Cisco VT Advantage to associate with the IP phone and receive event messages from the IP phone when calls are placed or received. After this association process occurs between the Cisco VT Advantage client and the IP phone, the IP phone updates its registration status with Cisco CallManager, advising Cisco CallManager of its video capabilities.

3. When the Cisco IP Phone receives signaling information for video calls, it acts as a proxy toward Cisco VT Advantage for the setup of the video streams. Only the signaling is proxied, but when the RTP endpoints (IP addresses and UDP RTP port numbers) are negotiated, the IP phone specifies the IP address of the PC for the video stream and its own IP address for the audio stream. When Cisco CallManager tells the Cisco IP Phone to open the video channel,

(communicating to the IP phone using the voice VLAN) the IP phone proxies those messages to Cisco VT Advantage using the Cisco Audio Session Tunnel protocol. These Cisco Audio Session Tunnel messages have to be routed between the voice and the PC VLAN again.

4. After the voice and video channels have been successfully set up, the audio stream is sent to the IP address of the IP phone (to the voice VLAN), whereas the video stream is sent directly to the PC IP address (to the PC VLAN).

Figure 29-1 *Cisco VT Advantage Call Process*

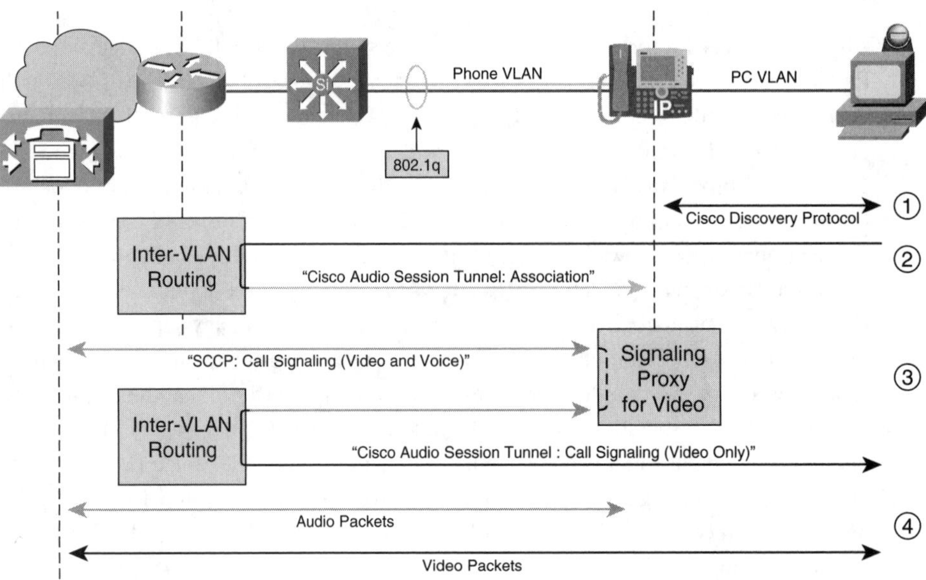

> **NOTE** Firewalls or access control lists (ACLs) must permit TCP port 4224 to allow the exchange of Cisco Audio Session Tunnel messages.

Cisco VT Advantage Video Modes

For privacy, the participants can switch to a mode called receive-only mode to prevent the camera from sending a picture to the other end of the call. Table 29-3 shows various scenarios of the calling or the called party activating or disabling receive-only mode.

Table 29-3 *Cisco VT Advantage Video Modes*

Cisco VT Advantage Mode on Your PC	Cisco VT Advantage Mode on the PC of the Other User	Result
Enabled	Enabled	When you place or answer a call, two video windows open on your PC—you will see yourself in the Local Video window and the other party in the Remote Video window.
Receive-only	Enabled	When you place or answer a call, you will see the other party in the Remote Video window. The Local Video window will not display. The other party will see a blank image in the Remote Video window.
Enabled	Receive-only	When you place or answer a call, you will see yourself in the Local Video window and a blank image in the Remote Video window. The other party will not see a Local Video window.
Receive-only	Receive-only	No one will see the other party; this mode is similar to a telephone call.

NOTE When Cisco VT Advantage is not running on your PC or on the PC of the remote peer, the call functions as a regular telephone call without video.

Configuring Cisco CallManager for Video

When you are setting up a video IP telephony environment, you first have to configure video in Cisco CallManager. Cisco VT Advantage requires Cisco CallManager to handle video call processing. Before enabling video on Cisco CallManager, you must update your locations and regions settings to adjust your bandwidth settings. Media Resource Group Lists (MRGLs) are used to control the access to multipoint control units (MCUs). Only devices that are allowed to use an MRGL are able to use the resources in the MRGL. Using this feature, you should restrict access to the video conference MCU resources to only the video-capable endpoints. Otherwise, the MCU resources could be depleted by managing audio conferences best handled by other hardware.

Further, you have to reconsider the call-routing configuration when using, for example, Automated Alternate Routing (AAR). Another important point that arises during the consideration of video is the Differentiated Services Code Point (DSCP) settings for quality of service (QoS).

In large Cisco CallManager environments, you have to consider whether it makes sense to use the Cisco VT Advantage Deployment Tool to make Cisco VT Advantage software available for download in Cisco CallManager.

Call-Routing Considerations

One of the advantages of using Cisco VT Advantage is that you can use the existing dial plan. If the bandwidth needed by an endpoint for a video call is not available, by default the call is retried as an audio call. To use route or hunt lists or AAR groups to try different paths for such video calls instead of retrying them as audio calls, uncheck the **Retry Video Call as Audio** check box in the configuration settings for the applicable gateways, trunks, and IP phones.

Video-enabled IP phones should have a separate MRGL with the videoconference bridge as the first choice. If the nonvideo-enabled IP phones use the videoconference bridge as a first choice, you run the risk of having no videoconference resources available for videoconference calls because all the videoconference resources are occupied by audio-only conferences. It is recommended that you create two separate MRGLs—one for video-enabled IP phones and one for nonvideo-enabled IP phones.

Video is as time-critical as voice. In a voice- and video-enabled network, you have to prioritize voice and video packets so that you do not experience quality issues. Both voice and video must be of higher priority than data, for example.

DSCP packet marking includes these characteristics:

- Audio streams in audio-only calls default to the Expedited Forwarding (EF) class.
- Video streams and associated audio streams in video calls default to Assured Forwarding, Class 4, with low drop precedence (AF41).

You can change these defaults using the Cisco CallManager Enterprise Parameters.

These service parameters affect DSCP packet marking:

- **DSCP for Audio Calls (for Media RTP Streams)**—This parameter specifies the DSCP value for audio calls.
- **DSCP for Video Calls (for Media RTP Streams)**—This parameter specifies the DSCP value for video calls.

VT Advantage Deployment Tool

For simplified and scalable deployment of Cisco VT Advantage client installation software, you can use the Cisco VT Advantage Deployment Tool. Administrators can use this tool to make the Cisco VT Advantage installer program available on a Cisco CallManager publisher server. The installer program will then reside in the CCMPluginsClient website that is mapped to the C:\CiscoPlugins\Client\CVTA directory. This website is set up with the correct permissions to allow anonymous access to the Cisco VT Advantage Installer executable file to facilitate installation for your technicians and users.

The Cisco VT Advantage Deployment Tool lets you set these options for the installation:

- **AutoUpdate**—Sets the AutoUpdate option so that users are notified automatically about updates to Cisco VT Advantage
- **Proxy**—Sets proxy server information for users needing to use a proxy server to reach the Cisco CallManager publisher server
- **Error Reporting Tool**—Sets the e-mail or FTP addresses where users send reports generated by the Error Reporting Tool

To publish Cisco VT Advantage to Cisco CallManager, the administrator must download the latest available Cisco VT Advantage Deployment Tool from Cisco.com. Run the DeployMan.exe file to set up Cisco VT Advantage for end users. The Cisco VT Advantage installer program is now stored in Cisco CallManager and a download link will be made available on Cisco CallManager user-accessible installation pages.

To install Cisco VT Advantage on a PC, users must complete these steps:

Step 1 Access the Cisco CallManager user installation page and download the Cisco VT Advantage software: https://<CCM Publisher Server name or IP address>/CCMUser. (This URL is found in the Services Help screen on Cisco IP Phone models that support Cisco VT Advantage.)

Step 2 Install Cisco VT Advantage software on the PC.

When you execute the DeployMan.exe file, the DeployMan window opens, as shown in Figure 29-2. When you click the **Use Defaults** button in the DeployMan main window, the Cisco VT Advantage Deployment Tool must be running on the Cisco CallManager publisher server. If this is not the case, change the path in the CVTAInstall.exe Destination field by referring to the C:\CiscoPlugins\Client\CVTA directory at the publisher via a network file share. The Choose Host Name dialog box opens. Enter the hostname (or IP address) of the Cisco CallManager publisher server. This value populates the Update URL field for the AutoUpdate feature.

Figure 29-2 *Using the VT Advantage Deployment Tool*

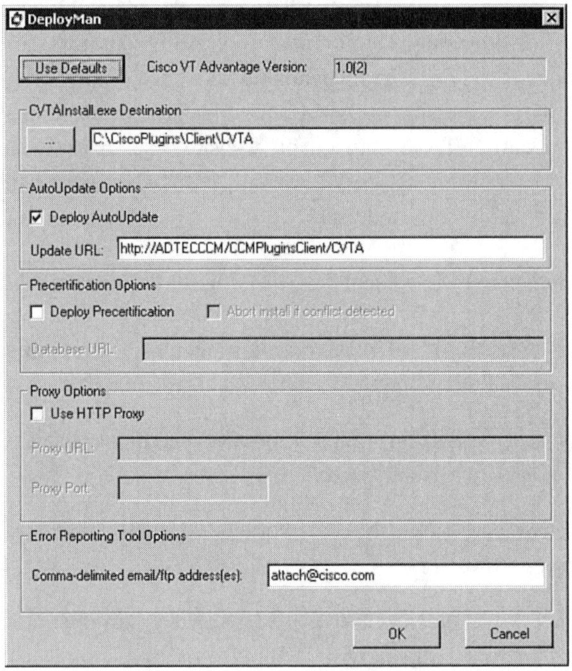

These fields are automatically populated with default values:

- Cisco VT Advantage Version
- CVTAInstall.exe Destination
- Update URL
- Comma-Delimited E-Mail/FTP Addresses

Make sure that the **Update URL** field in the AutoUpdate Options area contains the hostname (or IP address) of the Cisco CallManager publisher server. If you do not want to use AutoUpdate, uncheck the **Deploy AutoUpdate** check box. The Precertification Options area will be usable only in later versions of the deployment tool, even though it is shown in the GUI of the current version (2.0).

If users in the network need to use a proxy server to reach the Cisco CallManager publisher server, check the **Use HTTP Proxy** check box and fill in the **Proxy URL** and **Proxy Port** fields with the appropriate values.

In the **Comma-Delimited E-Mail/FTP Addresses** field of the Error Reporting Tool Options, enter the e-mail or FTP addresses to which error reports generated by users can be sent. You can enter multiple addresses separated by commas. The default e-mail address is attach@cisco.com. This e-mail address is used by the Cisco Technical Assistance Center (TAC) to pick up files sent by customers.

When you have filled in all necessary options, click **OK** to make the Cisco VT Advantage installation program available to users.

Configuring Cisco IP Phones for Cisco VT Advantage

In addition to the global Cisco CallManager parameters that are needed for a video-enabled IP telephony network, you have to configure the individual devices (IP phones) to support video calls. The Cisco IP Phone requires Cisco CallManager for call processing and the appropriate phone load to support video on the IP phone. When you are configuring IP phones for video in Cisco CallManager, you will need to ensure you have configured these settings:

- Make sure that a phone load that supports video is installed on each Cisco IP Phone that will be video-enabled.
- The port labeled "PC" on the back of the Cisco IP Phone connects a PC or a workstation to the IP phone so that they can share a single network connection. Make sure that this feature is enabled on Cisco IP Phones that operate with Cisco VT Advantage.
- The Cisco IP Phone has to be configured to support video calls.
- Check or uncheck the **Retry Video Call as Audio** check box. When the **Retry Video Call as Audio** check box is checked, a Cisco IP Phone that cannot obtain the bandwidth that it needs for a video call will retry the call as an audio call.
- Verify that the Cisco IP Phone is video-enabled after configuring the IP phone in Cisco CallManager configuration.

Verifying Phone Loads

As shown in Figure 29-3, CallManager assigns each device type a phone load that it will use from the TFTP server. Devices must use phone load 6.0(3) or later for the Cisco IP Phone 7940 and 7960 models to support the Cisco VT Advantage. For the Cisco IP Phone 7970, use the phone load 6.0(1) or later. To verify the phone loads, from the Cisco CallManager Administration, choose **System > Device Defaults**.

Figure 29-3 *Configuring Phone Load Defaults*

Cisco 30 SP+	P00103010100	Default	Standard 30 SP+
Cisco 30 VIP	P00203010100	Default	Standard 30 VIP
Cisco 7902	CP7902060000SCCP05012	Default	Standard 7902
Cisco 7905	CP7905060000SCCP05012	Default	Standard 7905
Cisco 7910	P00405000600	Default	Standard 7910
Cisco 7912	CP7912060000SCCP05012	Default	Standard 7912
Cisco 7920	cmterm_7920.4.0-01-08	Default	Standard 7920
Cisco 7935	P00503010900	Default	Standard 7935
Cisco 7936	cmterm_7936.3-3-7-0	Default	Standard 7936
Cisco 7940	P00307010200	Default	Standard 7940
Cisco 7960	P00307010200	Default	Standard 7960
Cisco 7970	TERM70.6-0-2SR1-0s	Default	Standard 7970
Cisco 7971	TERM70.6-0-2SR1-0s	Default	Standard 7971
Cisco ATA 186	ATA030101SCCP040610A	Default	Standard ATA 186
Cisco Conference Bridge (WS-SVC-CMM)	None	Default	None
Cisco IOS Conference Bridge (HDV2)	None	Default	None
Cisco IOS Media Termination Point (HDV2)	None	Default	None
Cisco IOS Software Media Termination Point (HDV2)	None	Default	None
Cisco IP Communicator		Default	Default IP Communicator Template
Cisco Media Termination Point (WS-SVC-CMM)	None	Default	None

NOTE You can always download the latest phone loads from Cisco.com.

Configuring IP Phones to Support Video

The IP phone configuration settings that are required for video support can be found in the IP Phone Configuration window (shown in Figure 29-4) of Cisco CallManager Administration.

Figure 29-4 *Configuring IP Phones to Support Video*

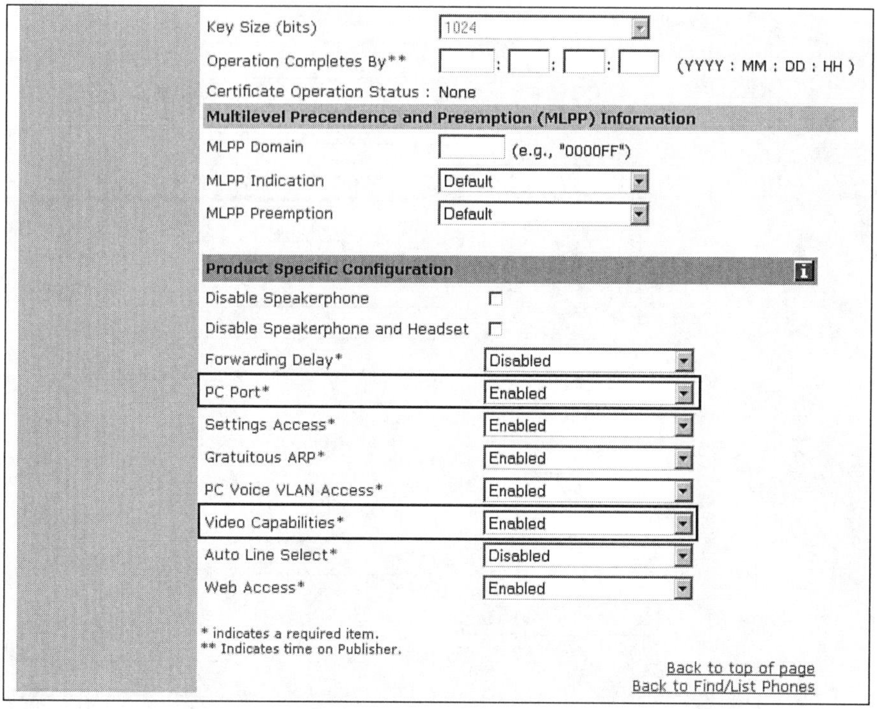

Key Size (bits) 1024
Operation Completes By** : : : (YYYY : MM : DD : HH)
Certificate Operation Status : None
Multilevel Precendence and Preemption (MLPP) Information
MLPP Domain (e.g., "0000FF")
MLPP Indication Default
MLPP Preemption Default
Product Specific Configuration
Disable Speakerphone
Disable Speakerphone and Headset
Forwarding Delay* Disabled
PC Port* Enabled
Settings Access* Enabled
Gratuitous ARP* Enabled
PC Voice VLAN Access* Enabled
Video Capabilities* Enabled
Auto Line Select* Disabled
Web Access* Enabled
* indicates a required item.
** Indicates time on Publisher.
Back to top of page
Back to Find/List Phones

TIP The IP phone settings need not be configured before Cisco VT Advantage can be loaded on the client PC. But the preferred sequence is to configure the IP phone first and then install the Cisco VT Advantage software.

Because the PC that has Cisco VT Advantage installed needs to be physically connected to a PC port of the IP phone, ensure that the PC port of the IP phone is not disabled in the Cisco CallManager IP phone configuration. By default, the PC port is enabled.

When the **Video Capabilities** field is set to **Enabled**, the phone will participate in video calls when connected to an appropriately equipped PC. Make sure that this feature is enabled on Cisco IP Phones that operate with Cisco VT Advantage. Video capability is disabled by default.

In addition, a video-enabled Cisco IP Phone can be configured to retry video calls as audio calls if the video call cannot be set up. The **Retry Video Call as Audio** check box is located in the Phone Configuration window, shown in Figure 29-5, and this feature is activated by default. To enable the Retry Video Call as Audio feature, choose **Cisco CallManager Administration > Device > Phone**.

Figure 29-5 *Enabling Retry Video Call as Audio*

MAC Address*	00141C48E6D1
Description	Second 4010
Owner User ID	(Select User ID)
Device Pool*	Default (View details)
Calling Search Space	< None >
AAR Calling Search Space	< None >
Media Resource Group List	< None >
User Hold Audio Source	< None >
Network Hold Audio Source	< None >
Location	< None >
User Locale	< None >
Network Locale	< None >
Device Security Mode	Encrypted Device security mode only takes effect if the enterprise parameter Cluster Security Mode is set to 1
Signal Packet Capture Mode	None
Packet Capture Duration	0
Built In Bridge	Default
Privacy	Default

☑ Retry Video Call as Audio

☐ Ignore Presentation Indicators (internal calls only)

Figure 29-6 *Verification of Phone Configuration*

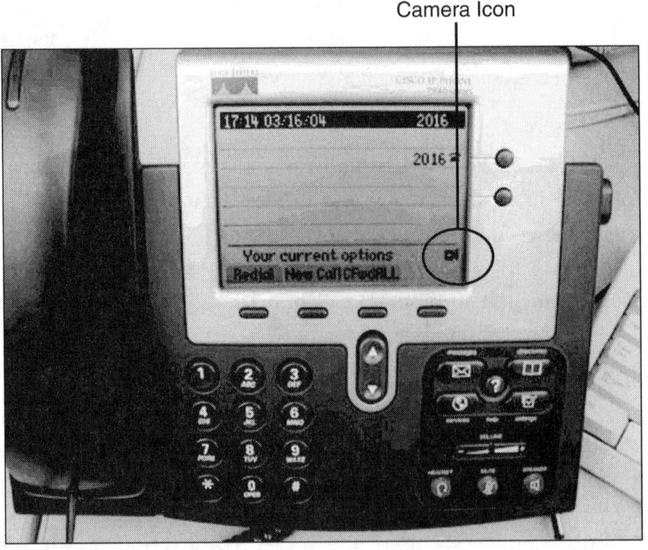

Verification of Phone Configuration

An IP phone enabled for video displays a video camera icon in the lower-right corner of its liquid crystal display (LCD) screen, as shown in Figure 29-6. A PC with Cisco VT Advantage installed does not have to be connected to the IP phone to produce the video camera icon. The camera icon is displayed as soon as video is enabled for the IP phone in Cisco CallManager configuration.

Installing Cisco VT Advantage on a Client

After configuring Cisco CallManager and the Cisco IP Phone, you need to install Cisco VT Advantage on the PC. When installing VT Advantage, use this setup procedure:

Step 1 Consider the hardware and software requirements to install Cisco VT Advantage.

Step 2 Verify the preparation checklist to ensure that all necessary preinstallation tasks have been completed successfully. After the verification, install the Cisco VT Advantage software and hardware.

Step 3 Verify the Cisco VT Advantage installation using Cisco VT Advantage tools.

Cisco VT Advantage Hardware and Software Requirements

To run the Cisco VT Advantage, you must be using one of the Cisco IP Phone 7940, 7960, or 7970 (or later) models. In addition, Table 29-4 describes the hardware requirements for the PC where the Cisco VT Advantage software is installed.

Table 29-4 *Cisco VT Advantage Hardware Requirements*

PC Feature	Minimum Requirements
CPU	1.0-GHz or higher Pentium III or compatible processor (Streaming Single Instruction Stream, Multiple Data Stream [SIMD] Extensions support required) 1.4-GHz or higher Pentium III or compatible processor recommended
System memory	256 MB minimum
Free disk space	40 MB
Universal Serial Bus (USB) port	At least one free USB (1.1 or 2.0 compliant) port
Video display	Video-capable graphics card at 800 x 600 x 16 bits or better
Network	10/100-Mbps Ethernet network interface card (NIC)

Of course, the Cisco VT Camera will be connected to the PC when prompted during the installation process of the Cisco VT Advantage software on the PC.

NOTE Cisco VT Advantage supports only the Cisco VT Camera, and the Cisco VT Camera works only with the Cisco VT Advantage software.

The PC must be using either Microsoft Windows 2000 Professional with Service Pack 3.0 or later or Windows XP Professional with Service Pack 1.0 or later.

The Cisco VT Advantage Software can be downloaded in two ways:

- From the Cisco CallManager publisher (if the administrator used the deployment tool):

  The default URL for the software download when Cisco VT Advantage is deployed with the deployment tool is https://<CCM Publisher Server name or IP address>/CCMUser.

- From Cisco.com:

  — To download the Cisco VT Advantage software from Cisco.com, users need a valid Cisco.com account with the necessary software download privileges.

  — Alternatively, the administrator can download the Cisco VT Advantage software and provide it to users via CD, file server, or any other means.

Cisco VT Advantage Installation Preparation Checklist

Check these points before installing Cisco VT Advantage software on a PC:

- Ensure that the Cisco IP Phone is properly connected to the corporate telephony network. You could do a short audio test call to ensure that the IP phone is working correctly.
- Ensure that the Cisco IP Phone is video-enabled. If the LCD screen on the Cisco IP Phone displays the video camera icon on the status line, the phone is video-enabled.
- Ensure that the Ethernet port of the PC is connected to the PC port of the IP phone because this connection is mandatory for Cisco VT Advantage.
- For the Cisco Audio Session Tunnel protocol to operate between Cisco VT Advantage and the IP phone, the PC must be capable of reaching the IP phone over TCP/IP. Typical IP telephony designs use separate voice and data VLANs, as well as ACLs or firewalls between those VLANs to secure the IP telephony network.

NOTE Do not forget to enable port 4224 on your firewall.

Installing Cisco VT Advantage

To install the Cisco VT Advantage software on a client PC, complete the following steps:

Step 1 Open your web browser, enter the Cisco VT Advantage download URL in the address field, and press **Enter**.

> **NOTE** The default URL, when Cisco VT Advantage is deployed with the deployment tool is https://<CCM Publisher Server name or IP address>/CCMUser.

Step 2 On the Cisco CallManager Client Install Plugins page, click the **Cisco VT Advantage Installer Plug-In** icon, shown in Figure 29-7. The camera should *not* be connected at this time.

Figure 29-7 *VT Advantage Plug-In Installation*

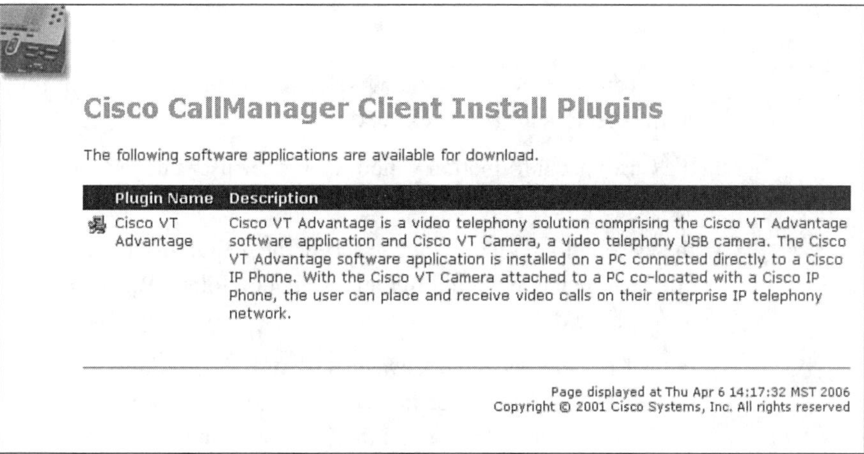

Step 3 Follow the instructions presented in the dialog boxes to complete the installation of Cisco VT Advantage:

- In the Welcome window shown in Figure 29-8, click **Next** to start the installation wizard.

Figure 29-8 *VT Advantage Installation Wizard*

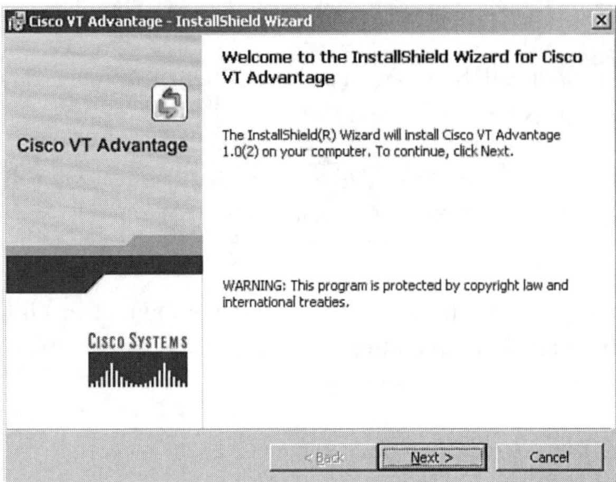

- In the License Agreement window, select **I Accept the Terms in the License Agreement**, and click **Next**.
- In the Customer Information window, enter the user information, select the desired option, and click **Next**.
- In the Destination Folder window, accept the default installation folder or click **Change** to enter a different installation folder. When you are done, click **Next**.

  — In the Ready to Install window, click **Install**. Depending on the setup of your PC, you might see messages for the installation of the Cisco Media Termination Driver and the Cisco VT Camera software that differ, based on the operating system of the PC:

  — **Windows 2000**—If a "Digital Signature Not Found" message appears, the driver software has no Microsoft digital signature that would affirm that the software has been tested with Windows and that the software has not been altered since it was tested. Click **Yes** to continue.

  — **Windows XP**—If a "Hardware Installation" message appears, the software that you are installing has not passed Windows Logo testing to verify its compatibility with Windows XP. To continue the installation, click **Continue Anyway**.

Step 4 Plug the Cisco VT Camera into an available USB port on the PC. As soon as you plug in the camera, the operating system finds it automatically. A window appears offering the creation of a shortcut to the application. Choose the desired option and then click **Next**.

Step 5 A window appears indicating that the installation has completed. Confirm the message by clicking **Finish**. If you are prompted to restart the PC, click **Yes** to restart the PC.

Cisco VT Advantage Installation Verification

When the Cisco VT Advantage application is started, verify its connectivity; if a connection to the Cisco IP Phone or to the Cisco VT Camera is not working, a red X is displayed over the corresponding connecting line, as shown in Figure 29-9. If the connections are functioning, the corresponding lines are shown without the red X and the lines themselves are green.

Figure 29-9 *Verifying VT Advantage Connections*

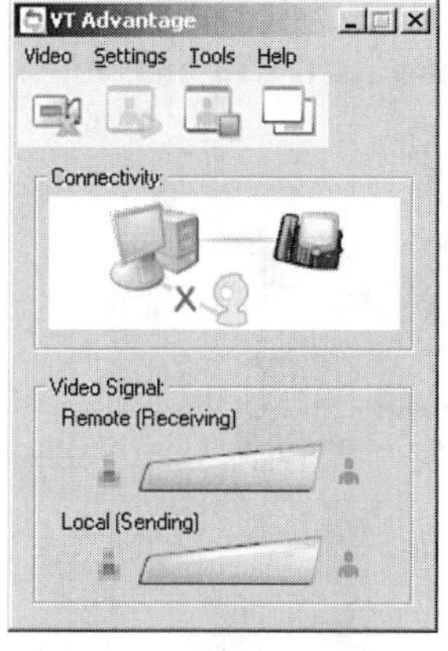

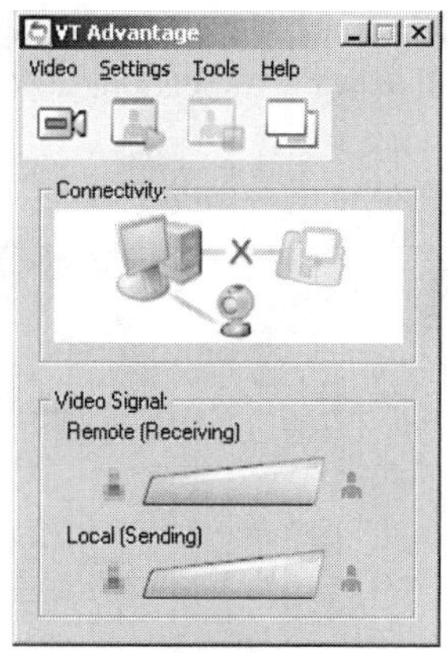

When you have ensured that the camera connection is functioning, you should run a video check. To start the video check, choose **Video > Start Video Check**. While the video check is being performed, two green bars are displayed (one for the sending video signal and the other for the receiving video signal) when the system is working. In addition, two popup windows show the local and remote views, as shown in Figure 29-10. During the video check, you will see the same image in both windows.

Figure 29-10 *Cisco VT Advantage Video Check*

After a successful video check, you should be able to place and receive calls. Place a test call to another IP phone with Cisco VT Advantage enabled, and verify the local and remote views. While in a call, you can launch the diagnostic tool, shown in Figure 29-11. The diagnostic tool provides some technical details about the current state of the Cisco VT Advantage software that is running on the PC, as well as some indications about the Cisco VT Camera frame rate and light level.

Figure 29-11 *Cisco VT Advantage Diagnostic Tool*

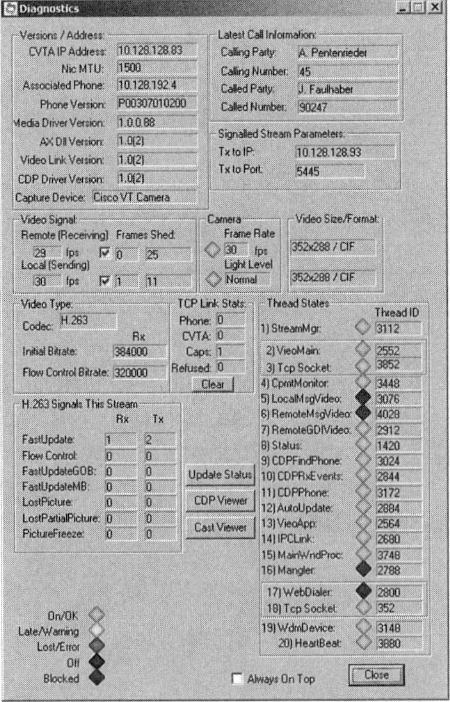

To use the diagnostic tool, open the Cisco VT Advantage main window and double-click the video signal quality bars. The Diagnostics window opens. When users report seeing a low signal quality bar, you can check the Cisco VT Camera frame rate and light level. Look near the center of the Diagnostics window for the Camera area. It contains two fields:

- **Frame Rate**—Indicates the frames per second reported by the camera. The values are **5**, **10**, **15**, **20**, **25**, or **30**. The LED colors correspond to the frame rate: Green is 30 fps, yellow is 5, 10, 15, 20, or 25 fps, and black is blank or off.
- **Light Level**—Indicates the lighting conditions reported by the camera. The values are **Off**, **Normal**, and **Low Light**. The LED colors correspond to the light levels: Black is off, green is normal, and red is low light. Increasing the lighting conditions near the camera should result in a higher frame rate and a normal light level. When you are troubleshooting some Cisco VT Advantage problems with the assistance of Cisco TAC representatives, they might ask you to provide them with the information displayed in the Diagnostics window.

A low frame rate can be caused by low light conditions. The Cisco VT Camera is normally set for automatic exposure. When the lighting is low, the camera has to expose each frame for a longer time, resulting in a lower frame rate. To test for this issue with the diagnostic tool, double-click the signal quality bars. The Diagnostics window opens. The Video Signal area at the middle left of the window contains fields showing the current number of frames per second being processed. At this point, all the data is coming from the camera, so if the value is less than 15 fps, the problem most likely is the lighting conditions. Improving the lighting near the camera should result in a higher frame rate and a normal light level.

Summary

This chapter discussed the concepts and configuration behind Cisco VT Advantage. This software associates with the Cisco IP Phone, which registers as a video-capable phone with Cisco CallManager. The IP phone then acts as a SCCP proxy between the Cisco VT Advantage software and Cisco CallManager.

To properly configure video telephony, you should first configure Cisco CallManager locations and regions to support video bandwidth levels. You should then configure the Cisco IP Phones for video using the CallManager Administration utility. Finally, you must install the VT Advantage software on the end-user PCs. Be sure to wait until the installation wizard prompts you to plug in the Cisco VT Camera.

Review Questions

You can find the solutions to these questions in Appendix A, "Answers to Review Questions."

1. What does the icon of a video camera on the Cisco IP Phone status line mean?
   a. The Cisco VT Camera is connected to the PC, and the PC is connected to the Cisco IP Phone.
   b. The Cisco IP Phone has web access.
   c. The Cisco IP Phone is configured with video capabilities.
   d. The Cisco IP Phone is receiving a video call.
2. Into which port should the PC with Cisco VT Advantage client software installed be plugged?
   a. Cisco Catalyst switch port
   b. Cisco IP Phone access port
   c. MCU port
   d. Videoconferencing port
3. Which protocols are supported by Cisco VT Advantage?
   a. Cisco Audio Session Tunnel
   b. FTP
   c. RTP
   d. SSH
   e. TFTP
4. Which SCCP Cisco endpoints are video-capable? (Choose three.)
   a. Cisco IP Phone 7902
   b. Cisco IP Phone 7910
   c. Cisco IP Phone 7912
   d. Cisco IP Phone 7920
   e. Cisco IP Phone 7940
   f. Cisco IP Phone 7960
   g. Cisco IP Phone 7970

5. Which of the following IP phone settings are enabled by default in Cisco CallManager? (Choose two.)
   a. Video capabilities
   b. PC port
   c. Retry Video Call as Audio
   d. Video calling search space
   e. AAR
6. Video calls using 384 kbps need to be supported across a gatekeeper-controlled trunk. What value should be entered into the gatekeeper to support this bandwidth?
   a. 192 kbps
   b. 384 kbps
   c. 512 kbps
   d. 768 kbps
7. Which of the following web camera(s) is VT Advantage compatible with? (Select all that apply.)
   a. Cisco VT Camera
   b. Logitech E905
   c. Creative Labs ClearStream
   d. Mindworks v11
8. How much bandwidth is consumed by the Cisco proprietary wideband codec?
   a. 384 kbps
   b. 768 kbps
   c. 1.544 Mbps
   d. 7 Mbps
9. The VT Advantage software can stream up to ______ fps.
   a. 10
   b. 15
   c. 20
   d. 30

Part VII: IPT Management

This chapter covers the following topics:

- Examining the database structure and replication status and reactivating broken database connections
- Identifying the purpose of the major services that Cisco CallManager Serviceability provides
- Explaining how to use the Control Center to start and stop services
- Explaining how to use the Service Activation window tools to enable and disable services
- Classifying the tools used to monitor Cisco CallManager by their function

CHAPTER 30

Introducing Database Tools and Cisco Unified CallManager Serviceability

Phone communication is one of the most critical services for businesses today. It is necessary to maintain and troubleshoot Cisco CallManager installations as fast as possible to reduce the risk of system outages. Administrators need tools to easily gather information about system behavior and troubleshoot database replication. This chapter introduces database tools that allow administrators to manage the Microsoft Structured Query Language (SQL) databases used by Cisco CallManager. It gives an overview of how to use Cisco CallManager Serviceability and other tools that you can use to maintain the Cisco CallManager system.

Database Management Tools

On Cisco CallManager systems, Microsoft SQL 2000 Enterprise databases are used to store system and device configuration as well as call detail records (CDRs). To maintain data consistency throughout the cluster, the publisher database server uses one-way, or unidirectional, replication to each subscriber. All information is stored on one server (the publisher server) and replicated to the other servers (subscriber servers) in the cluster. Replicating the SQL database is a core function inside Cisco CallManager clusters.

Configuration changes on Cisco CallManager systems are possible only while the publisher server is available. To make sure that CDRs are written even if the publisher server is offline, every server stores CDR information locally in flat files. Cisco CallManager writes information to the publisher database only if Cisco CallManager web components are installed or Cisco CallManager Administration is performed directly on the publisher server. All entries that are made using the Cisco CallManager Administration page of the subscriber are written to the database on the publisher server. If the publisher is down, no updates can be made in the Cisco CallManager Administration page of the subscriber server.

CDR records are *not* written into a database of the subscriber, but they are written locally in *transaction files* at the subscribers (but not directly in the CDR database). Those files are periodically processed and inserted in the Microsoft SQL Server 2000 database by the CDR Insert service on the publisher server. If the publisher server is down, transaction files reside on the subscriber server to be processed as soon as the publisher is available again. After CDRs are processed, they are replicated from the publisher to subscriber database.

When you are building a publisher server, Cisco CallManager software itself might or might not be installed. If the publisher server does not have Cisco CallManager installed (and only has the SQL database installed), Cisco refers to the server as a *glass house*. This configuration is the best solution in large clusters. The publisher (either running Cisco CallManager or not [glass house]) holds the only copy of the database that is allowed to be written to. All subscribers replicate with the database of the publisher only, so they are in read-only mode.

In addition, the publisher occasionally acts as a backup CallManager service for the configuration. This configuration is typically used only in smaller clusters.

Database Management Tools Overview

Two tools are used to maintain the Cisco CallManager database services and are based on Microsoft SQL Server 2000:

- **Microsoft SQL Server 2000 Enterprise Manager**—Provided by Microsoft and included in each Microsoft SQL Server 2000 installation
- **DBLHelper**—Provided by Cisco and needs to be requested from Cisco Technical Assistance Center (TAC) to resolve Cisco CallManager database issues

Both tools allow administrators to verify proper working of Cisco CallManager Microsoft SQL Server 2000 databases. You can use the Microsoft SQL Server 2000 Enterprise Manager and DBLHelper when administrators need to examine the database structure and replication. You can use these tools to reactivate broken database connections.

In many cases, the reason for a broken database connection is publisher downtime. For example, administrators might take the publisher off the network to perform a software upgrade and restore it later. After reloading a Cisco CallManager publisher server, verify the database connection. A broken connection would not cause any obvious problem in system activity. Usually, users become aware of a broken connection only if the publisher becomes unresponsive again and any system changes are lost. For example, call forwarding instructions that are months out of date are active or newly added phones are unavailable when they failover to a subscriber server. Failures of the Extension Mobility functionality might also point to a broken publisher connection.

When you are troubleshooting Cisco CallManager SQL databases, it is beneficial to use both tools together.

Microsoft SQL Server 2000 Enterprise Manager

Microsoft SQL Server 2000 Enterprise Manager is included with the Microsoft SQL Server 2000 Enterprise software. To access it, choose **Start > Programs > Microsoft SQL Server > Enterprise Manager**. This is the primary administrative tool for Microsoft SQL Server 2000 and provides a Microsoft Management Console (MMC)–compliant user interface, shown in Figure 30-1, which allows users to do the following:

- Define groups of servers running SQL Server.
- Register individual servers in a group.
- Configure all SQL Server options for each registered server.
- Create and administer all SQL Server databases, objects, logins, users, and permissions in each registered server.
- Define and execute all SQL Server administrative tasks on each registered server.
- Design and test SQL statements, batches, and scripts interactively by invoking SQL Query Analyzer.
- Invoke the various wizards defined for SQL Server.

Figure 30-1 *Microsoft SQL Server 2000 Enterprise Manager*

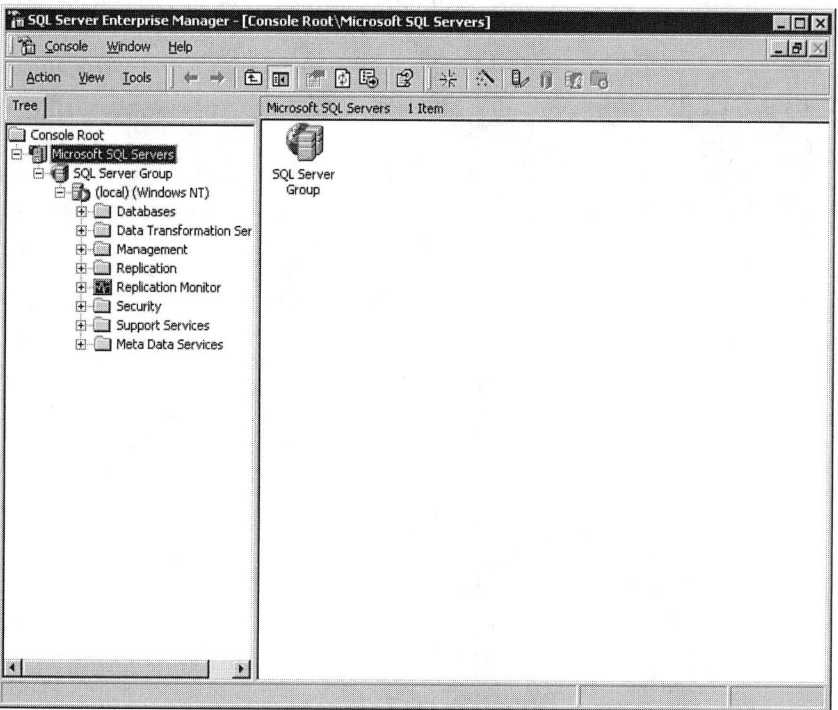

> **NOTE** Because the Cisco CallManager installation includes the database and database structure needed for Cisco CallManager servers, it is not necessary to create new databases.

> **CAUTION** Do not change the structure of the Cisco CallManager database. The Cisco CallManager will malfunction or, in the worst case, stop responding.

The Microsoft SQL database name of Cisco CallManager is CCM03*xx*, where *xx* starts at 00 and increases incrementally with each Cisco CallManager upgrade (for example, upgrading from release 4.0 to 4.1).

You can use Microsoft SQL Server 2000 Enterprise Manager to determine whether a server is the publisher or the subscriber. Expand the database hierarchy down to the database—Microsoft SQL Servers\SQL Server Group\<Server_Name>\Databases\CCM03xx, as shown in Figure 30-2:

- For a publisher, a Publications folder is displayed in the Database browse list.
- For a subscriber, a Pull Subscriptions folder is displayed in the Database browse list.

Figure 30-2 *Determining Publisher Server Function with SQL Server 2000 Enterprise Manager*

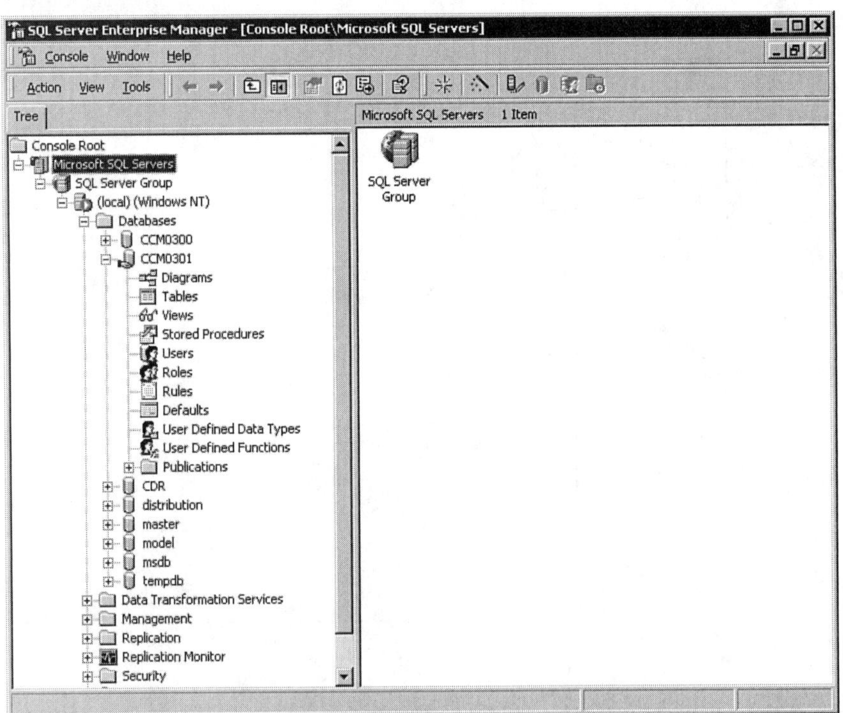

TIP The second way to determine whether the server is the publisher or subscriber is to check whether the Replication Monitor is present on the specific Microsoft SQL server. The Replication Monitor is present only on the publisher and monitors the status of database replication between the publisher and the subscribers.

DBLHelper

In the event that the subscriber stops replicating data from the publisher, you need to rebuild the relationships between the publisher and subscriber. The DBLHelper utility, a tool provided by Cisco, republishes or reinitializes a nonfunctioning subscription between the publisher and the subscriber databases. For DBLHelper to work, the SQL account password and administrative rights must be the same on the publisher and the subscriber. Because this tool is automated and nonintrusive, you might make a schedule of running it once per week to ensure the subscriber and publisher database links are active. If the link fails, you might not detect it for a considerable time because the symptoms are so subtle.

NOTE If you are upgrading from an earlier version of Cisco CallManager, DBLHelper.exe is usually located on the Cisco CallManager server in the C:\Program Files\Cisco Systems, Inc\Cisco CallManager Upgrade Assistant\DbReplCheck folder. Otherwise, contact Cisco TAC for the latest version of DBLHelper.

You can also use Microsoft SQL Server 2000 Enterprise Manager to re-create broken database connections between Cisco CallManager servers in the cluster, but this process is far more complex than using DBLHelper. The recommendation is to first try repairing the replication using DBLHelper. If DBLHelper cannot fix the problem, use the Microsoft SQL Server 2000 Enterprise Manager. For more information on how to use the Microsoft SQL Server 2000 Enterprise Manager to repair replications, search for "Reestablishing a Broken Cisco CallManager Cluster SQL Subscription" or "Broken SQL Replication" on Cisco.com. The documents for the 3.x version of Cisco CallManager also apply to the 4.x CallManager versions.

In Figure 30-3, DBLHelper shows two different states of Cisco CallManager Microsoft SQL Server 2000 databases. On the left, running DBLHelper.exe found that the replication was working. This status is depicted by the two green smiley face icons. On the right, a red (lower) sad face icon indicates that databases are out of synchronization. In this case, database connections need to be reestablished. Clicking the **Republish** button deletes the current subscription and re-creates it. Clicking the **Reinitialize** button reinitializes all subscriptions and starts the snapshot agent. It also begins an attempt to rebuild the subscription with the current database. To get more information about the current tab, click the **Help** button, which shows some additional information.

> **NOTE** If there is more than one subscriber and only one has a broken database connection, use the **Republish** button to republish only the broken connection. If you use the **Reinitialize** button, all subscriptions will be reinitialized, which could cause a long system outage.

Figure 30-3 *Using DBLHelper to Restore Broken Links*

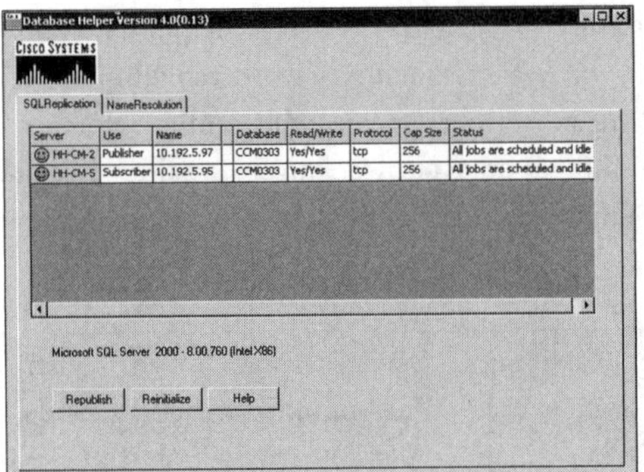

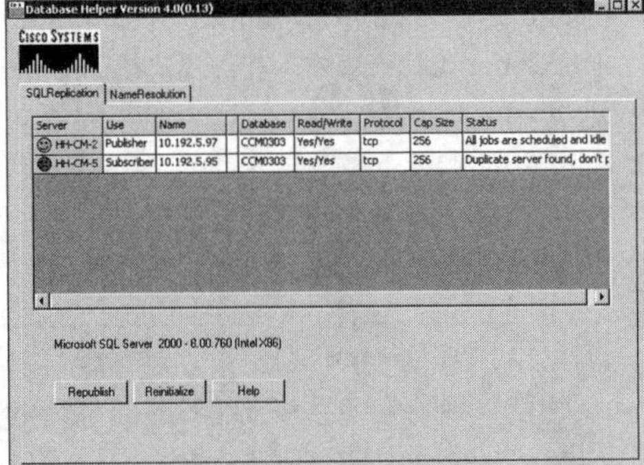

Cisco CallManager Serviceability Overview

The Cisco CallManager Serviceability tool is available on each Cisco CallManager. It is the main tool used by administrators to maintain the Cisco CallManager installation. To access the Cisco CallManager Serviceability tool, choose the **Application** menu in Cisco CallManager Administration, choose **Start > Programs > Cisco CallManager 4.1 > Cisco Service Configuration** from the Cisco CallManager system, or use a browser to go directly to **https://<CallManager_IP>/CCMService**.

Serviceability Components

Cisco CallManager Serviceability provides these menus, as shown in Figure 30-4:

- Alarm
- Trace
- Tools
- Application
- Help

Figure 30-4 *Cisco CallManager Serviceability Interface*

Cisco CallManager 4.1 Serviceability

Details

Copyright © 1999 - 2004 Cisco Systems, Inc.
All rights reserved.

This product contains cryptographic features and is subject to United States and local country laws governing import, export, transfer and use. Delivery of Cisco cryptographic products does not imply third-party authority to import, export, distribute or use encryption. Importers, exporters, distributors and users are responsible for compliance with U.S. and local country laws.
By using this product you agree to comply with applicable laws and regulations. If you are unable to comply with U.S. and local laws, return this product immediately.

A summary of U.S. laws governing Cisco cryptographic products may be found at:
http://www.cisco.com/wwl/export/crypto/tool/stqrg.html
If you require further assistance please contact us by sending email to export@cisco.com.

Alarm

The Alarm service stores information about Cisco CallManager service events for troubleshooting and provides alarm message definitions. Alarms can be forwarded to trace files, Microsoft Windows 2000 Event Viewer, and a Syslog server for further analysis:

- With the Configuration menu item shown in Figure 30-5, the Cisco CallManager Serviceability alarms allow configuration of Cisco CallManager to write an event to a trace file or the Windows 2000 Event Viewer when an incident occurs, such as the failure of a telephone to register. Alarms for Cisco CallManager servers can be configured in a cluster or for the services in each server.
- The Definitions application contains alarm definitions and the recommended actions in a Microsoft SQL Server 2000 database. The system administrator can search the database for the definitions of all alarms. Definitions include the alarm name, description, recommended action, severity, parameters, and monitors.

Figure 30-5 *Serviceability Alarm Menu*

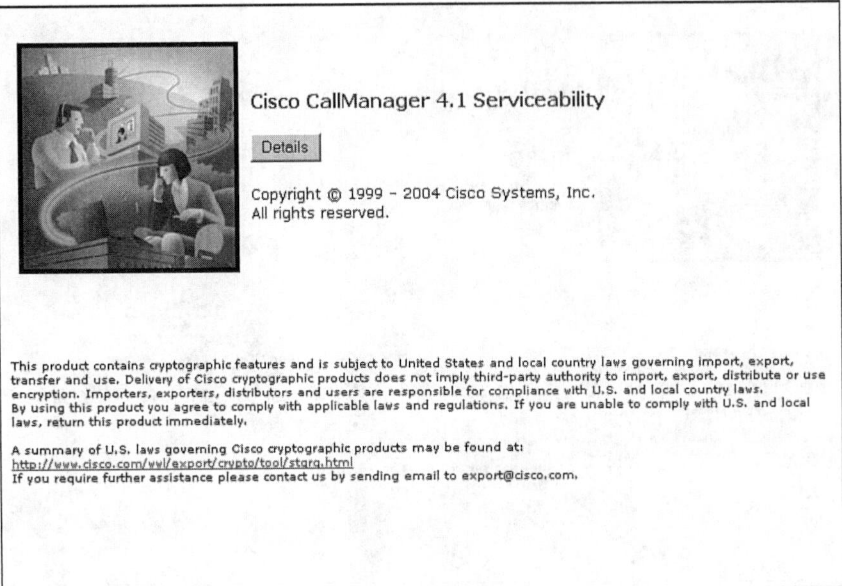
Cisco CallManager 4.1 Serviceability
Details
Copyright © 1999 - 2004 Cisco Systems, Inc.
All rights reserved.
This product contains cryptographic features and is subject to United States and local country laws governing import, export, transfer and use. Delivery of Cisco cryptographic products does not imply third-party authority to import, export, distribute or use encryption. Importers, exporters, distributors and users are responsible for compliance with U.S. and local country laws.
By using this product you agree to comply with applicable laws and regulations. If you are unable to comply with U.S. and local laws, return this product immediately.
A summary of U.S. laws governing Cisco cryptographic products may be found at:
http://www.cisco.com/wwl/export/crypto/tool/stqrg.html
If you require further assistance please contact us by sending email to export@cisco.com.

Trace

The Trace service allows you to save detailed logs of Cisco CallManager events for troubleshooting system problems. Trace data can be configured, collected, and analyzed using the menu options shown in Figure 30-6:

- Use the Configuration application to specify the trace parameters; for example, the Cisco CallManager server within the cluster, the Cisco CallManager service on the server, the debug level, and the specific trace fields.
- Use the Analysis application to provide greater trace detail on a signal distribution layer (SDL) trace, a system diagnostic interface (SDI) trace, a Cisco CallManager service type, or the time and date of a trace. You can choose a specific log file from the list and choose information from that log file, such as host address, IP address, trace type, and request a device name.
- The Q.931 Translator application filters incoming data from Cisco CallManager SDI logs and translates the data into Cisco IOS messages. The Q.931 Translator application displays the message in the message translator interface.

- Use the Troubleshooting Trace Settings application to choose the services in Cisco CallManager for which troubleshooting trace settings, which are predetermined in the alarms configuration, need to be set.

Figure 30-6 *Serviceability Trace Menu*

Cisco CallManager 4.1 Serviceability
Details
Copyright © 1999 - 2004 Cisco Systems, Inc.
All rights reserved.
This product contains cryptographic features and is subject to United States and local country laws governing import, export, transfer and use. Delivery of Cisco cryptographic products does not imply third-party authority to import, export, distribute or use encryption. Importers, exporters, distributors and users are responsible for compliance with U.S. and local country laws.
By using this product you agree to comply with applicable laws and regulations. If you are unable to comply with U.S. and local laws, return this product immediately.
A summary of U.S. laws governing Cisco cryptographic products may be found at:
http://www.cisco.com/wwl/export/crypto/tool/stqrg.html
If you require further assistance please contact us by sending email to export@cisco.com.

Tools

The Tools service offers these applications, shown in Figure 30-7:

- The CDR Analysis and Reporting (CAR) application supports analysis and reporting of CDRs. CAR generates reports for quality of service (QoS), traffic, and billing information.

> **NOTE** The CDR Analysis and Reporting menu item will only appear if you have installed the CAR plug-in for Cisco CallManager. It is not installed by default.

- The Service Activation application can activate and deactivate nearly all of the Cisco CallManager services for all Cisco CallManager servers.

- The Control Center application allows starting, stopping, restarting, and viewing the status of Cisco CallManager services.

- The Real-Time Monitoring Tool (RTMT) application monitors the real-time behavior of most components in a Cisco CallManager cluster and displays on-screen feedback through a Java-based application.

- The QRT Viewer application allows filtering, formatting, and viewing problem reports. Cisco IP Phones can be configured with a Quality Report Tool (**QRT**) softkey so that users can report problems with IP Phone calls (for example, poor quality). When users press the **QRT** softkey on the IP Phone, they are presented with a list of problem categories. Users can then choose the appropriate problem category, and the system logs the event in an Extensible Markup Language (XML) file.

- The Serviceability Reports Archive application generates five daily reports in Cisco CallManager Serviceability: Device Statistics, Server Statistics, Service Statistics, Call Activities, and Alerts. Each report provides a summary that consists of various charts that display the statistics for that particular report.

Figure 30-7 *Serviceability Tools Menu*

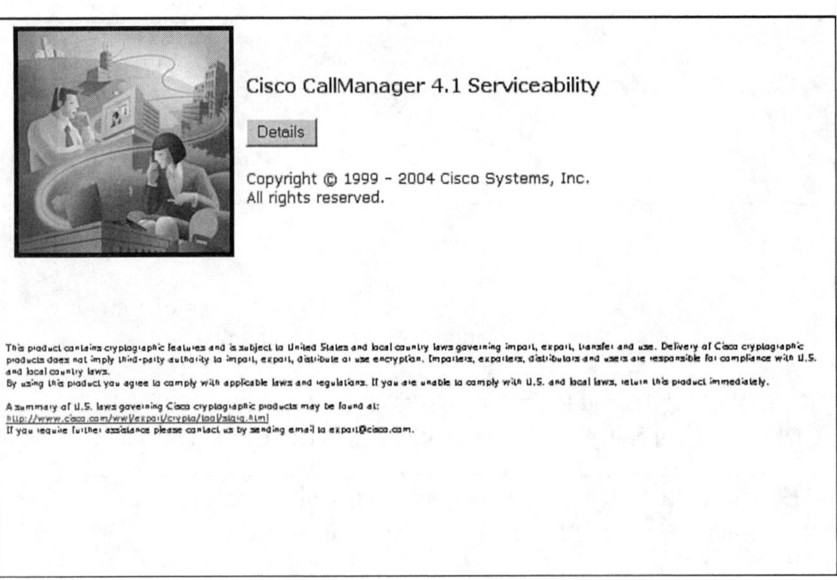

Application

The Application menu in Cisco CallManager Serviceability, shown in Figure 30-8, offers several applications:

- The Install Plugins application can help to extend the functionality of Cisco CallManager by providing links to software plug-ins that are either installed in Cisco CallManager itself or on a client PC.
- The Cisco CallManager Administration menu item provides a convenient, direct link to the Cisco CallManager Administration page.
- The Bulk Administration Tool (BAT) application adds multiple telephones and users to Cisco CallManager and performs bulk modifications.

> **NOTE** The Bulk Administration Tool (BAT) menu item will only appear if you have installed the BAT plug-in for Cisco CallManager. It is not installed by default.

Figure 30-8 *Serviceability Application Menu*

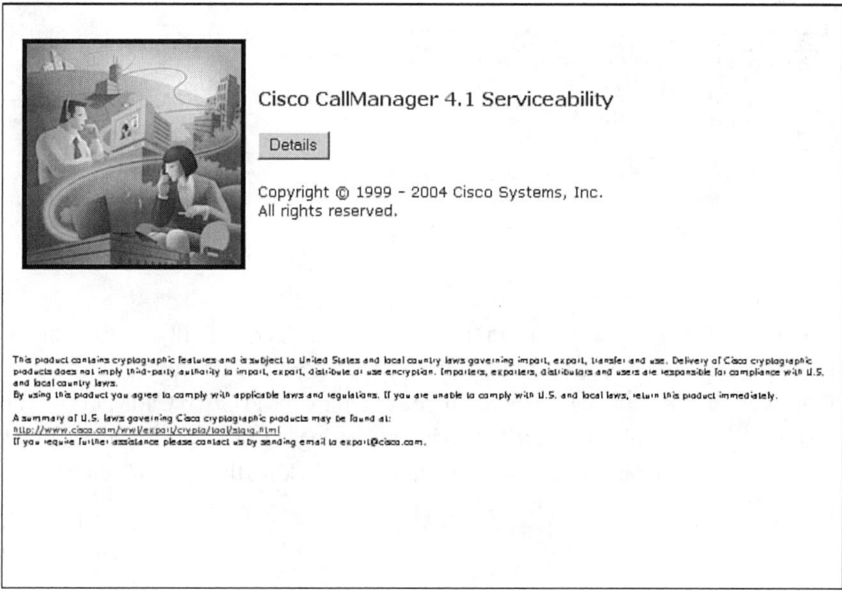
Cisco CallManager 4.1 Serviceability
Details
Copyright © 1999 - 2004 Cisco Systems, Inc.
All rights reserved.
This product contains cryptographic features and is subject to United States and local country laws governing import, export, transfer and use. Delivery of Cisco cryptographic products does not imply third-party authority to import, export, distribute or use encryption. Importers, exporters, distributors and users are responsible for compliance with U.S. and local country laws.
By using this product you agree to comply with applicable laws and regulations. If you are unable to comply with U.S. and local laws, return this product immediately.
A summary of U.S. laws governing Cisco cryptographic products may be found at:
http://www.cisco.com/wwl/export/crypto/tool/stqrg.html
If you require further assistance please contact us by sending email to export@cisco.com.

Help

The Help menu, shown in Figure 30-9, provides online assistance for every option in Cisco CallManager Serviceability. Moreover, it can be used to display the latest installed component version information for all Cisco CallManager servers in the cluster.

Figure 30-9 *Serviceability Help Menu*

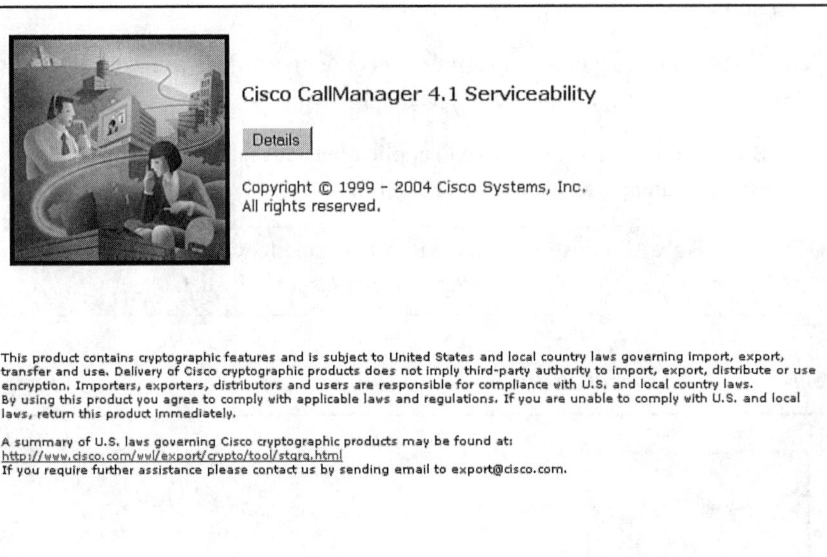
Cisco CallManager 4.1 Serviceability
Details
Copyright © 1999 - 2004 Cisco Systems, Inc.
All rights reserved.
This product contains cryptographic features and is subject to United States and local country laws governing import, export, transfer and use. Delivery of Cisco cryptographic products does not imply third-party authority to import, export, distribute or use encryption. Importers, exporters, distributors and users are responsible for compliance with U.S. and local country laws.
By using this product you agree to comply with applicable laws and regulations. If you are unable to comply with U.S. and local laws, return this product immediately.
A summary of U.S. laws governing Cisco cryptographic products may be found at:
http://www.cisco.com/wwl/export/crypto/tool/stqrg.html
If you require further assistance please contact us by sending email to export@cisco.com.

Control Center

On the Control Center, accessed from the CallManager Serviceability Tools menu, Cisco CallManager services can be started, stopped, or restarted. For example, restarting a Cisco CallManager service could be necessary if you change central Cisco CallManager functionalities, such as intercluster trunks or intersite bandwidth settings. To start, stop, or restart a service, first select the service and then start, stop, or restart it by clicking the appropriate button, as shown in Figure 30-10.

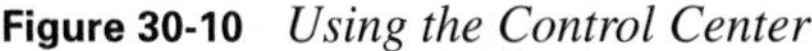

Figure 30-10 *Using the Control Center*

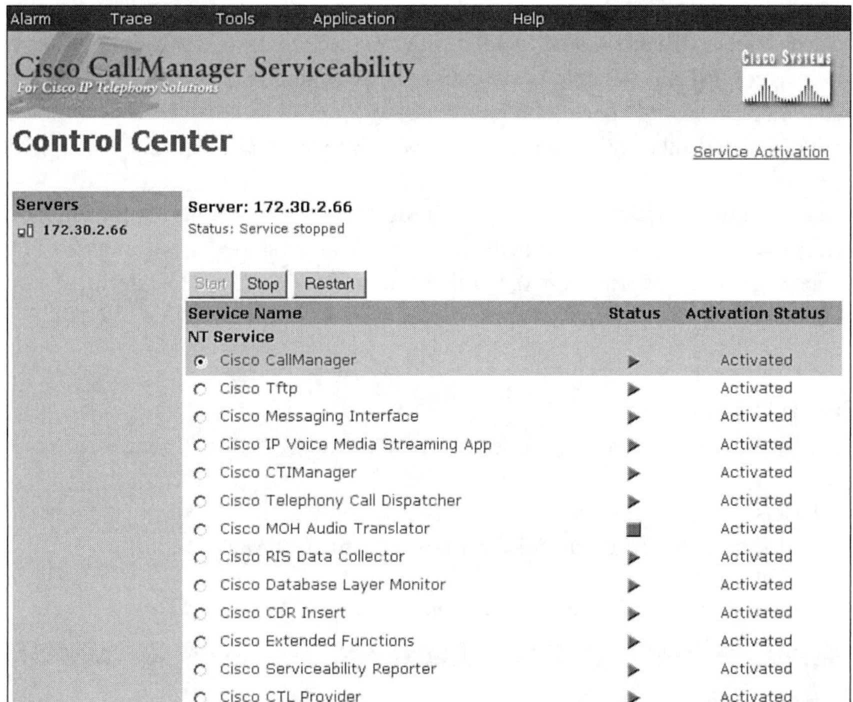

The Status column shows whether a service is started (a right arrow in the Status column) or stopped (a square in the Status column). In addition, the Activation Status column tells how the service is configured. A status of Activated or Deactivated indicates whether the service is configured to be started at Windows startup.

> **NOTE** Services with a status shown as Deactivated and Started are not activated in Service Activation but are still started at Windows startup.

You cannot start Cisco Tomcat web services using the Control Center. To start them, you could use the Microsoft Windows 2000 Server Services Management Console. In addition, with Cisco CallManager Release 4.0 or later, Cisco Tomcat Web Application Manager allows you to start, stop, or restart Tomcat services. To access Tomcat Web Application Manager, go to http://<CallManager_IP>/manager/list.

Starting and stopping the Cisco CallManager service causes all Cisco IP Phones and gateways that are currently registered to that Cisco CallManager service to failover to their secondary Cisco CallManager service. In addition, starting and stopping the Cisco CallManager service causes other installed applications (such as Conference Bridge or Cisco Messaging Interface) that are homed to that Cisco CallManager to start and stop as well. Stopping the Cisco CallManager service also stops call processing for all devices that are controlled by that service. When a Cisco CallManager service is stopped, active calls from an IP Phone to another IP Phone continue; calls in progress from an IP Phone to a Media Gateway Control Protocol (MGCP) gateway also continue, whereas other types of calls, such as calls to an H.323 gateway, are dropped.

If you are upgrading Cisco CallManager, all services are stopped during the upgrade process. Services that had been started before the upgrade began are started again afterward. Those that had not been started remain deactivated. Service configurations are not lost during the upgrade process.

Service Activation

Two tools allow you to manage services running on the Cisco CallManager system:

- The Cisco CallManager Serviceability Service Activation tool, shown in Figure 30-11, is used to activate or deactivate specific services on Cisco CallManager.

Figure 30-11 *Managing Services Using the CallManager Service Activation Tool*

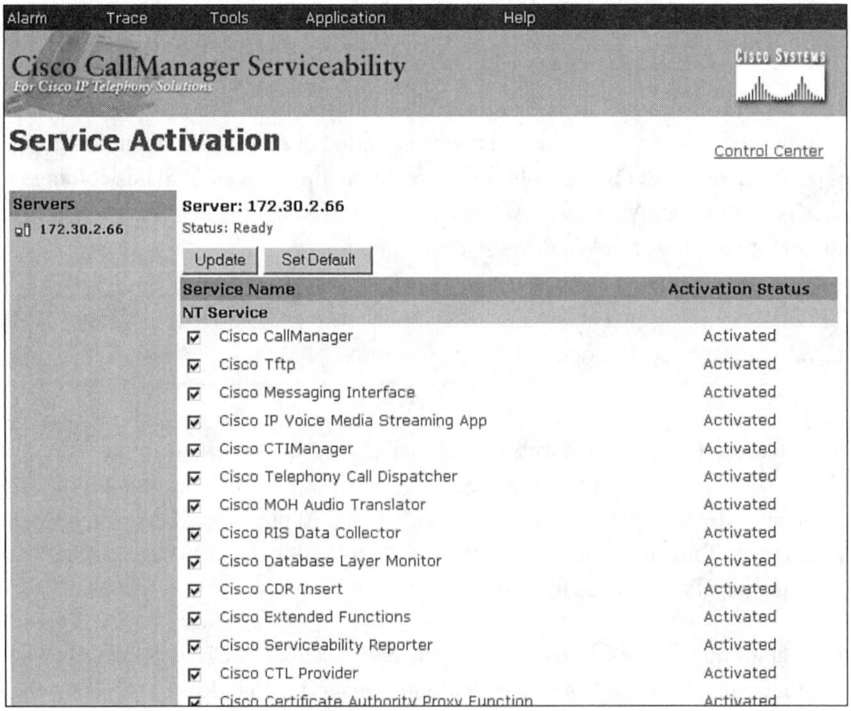

- The Services MMC, shown in Figure 30-12, is used to handle common Windows services. The Services MMC can be found at **Start** > **Settings** > **Control Panel** > **Administrative Tools** on the Cisco CallManager system.

Figure 30-12 *Managing Services Using the Windows 2000 Service Utility*

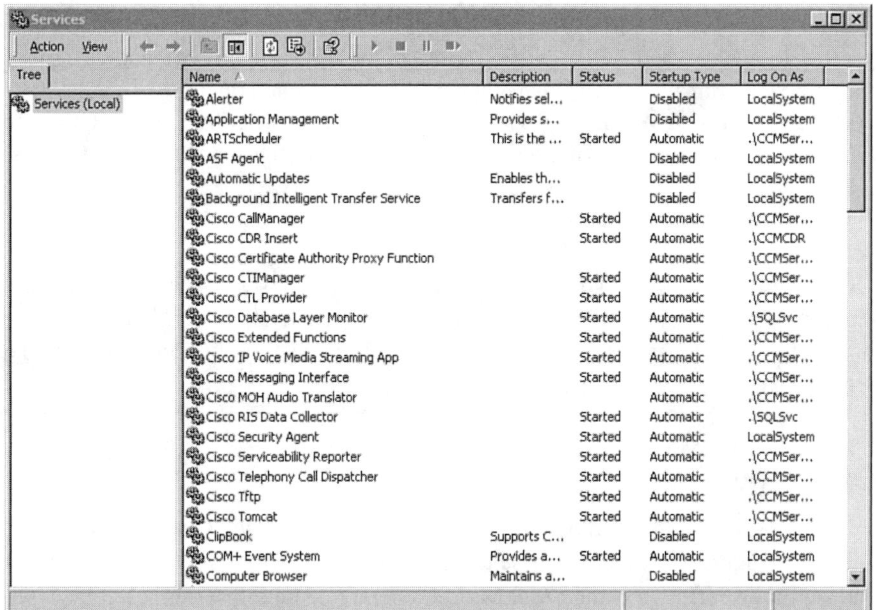

To optimize the performance of Cisco CallManager servers within a cluster, you can distribute services to servers across the cluster. For example, place the TFTP server service on one server, the Certificate Authority Proxy Function (CAPF) service on another server, and music on hold (MoH) services on a third server where no Cisco CallManager service is running, and so on.

Distribution of services can also be used for security purposes. Some services (such as those that provide IP Phone services with access to the Internet) must be exposed to the outside for proper operation, whereas others, such as the Cisco CallManager service, should not be exposed. If the exposed server is under attack, the attack would not have any impact on the other servers (for instance, the server routing calls that is running the Cisco CallManager service).

NOTE If the Cisco CallManager and Cisco CTIManager services are deactivated in the Service Activation window, the Cisco CallManager where the service was deactivated no longer exists in the database. This means that the Cisco CallManager cannot be chosen for configuration operations in Cisco CallManager Administration because it will not be displayed in the GUI.

If the services are then reactivated on the same Cisco CallManager, the database re-creates the Cisco CallManager and adds a "CM_" prefix to the server name or IP address; for example, if the Cisco CallManager or CTIManager service is reactivated on a server with an IP address of 10.192.5.97, then "CM_10.192.5.97" is displayed in Cisco CallManager Administration. The Cisco CallManager with the new "CM_" prefix can now be chosen in Cisco CallManager Administration.

CAUTION When you deactivate the Cisco CallManager service, the server is removed from Cisco CallManager groups but not added back after reactivation. So after activation or reactivation, you must add the server to Cisco CallManager groups, otherwise no devices will register to it.

Tools Overview

Several tools make administration easier when you are managing Cisco CallManager system status or configuration. Some of those tools are provided by Cisco Systems, whereas others are Microsoft tools included in the Windows 2000 Server operating system used by Cisco CallManager. Table 30-1 provides an overview of these tools.

Table 30-1 *CallManager Management Tools*

Management Tool	Function	Device
Microsoft SQL Server 2000 Enterprise Manager	Verify proper working of databases	Any Microsoft SQL Server 2000 server in the domain
DBLHelper	Verify proper replication between databases	Cisco CallManager publisher server
Services MMC	Manage services	Actual Windows 2000 server
Microsoft Event Viewer	Identify system-level events and errors	Actual Windows 2000 server
Microsoft Performance Monitor	Monitor system and device statistics	Actual Windows 2000 server
RTMT Client	Monitor Cisco CallManager system in real time	Any PC on the network
Password Changer Tool	Change the CCMAdministrator password	Cisco CallManager publisher server

Table 30-1 *CallManager Management Tools (Continued)*

Management Tool	Function	Device
CAR Tool	Analyze Cisco CallManager CDRs	Cisco CallManager Web page via browser
Dialed Number Analyzer	Analyze calls in a Cisco CallManager dial plan	Cisco CallManager web page via browser
QRT	Create quality problem reports	Cisco CallManager web page via browser

The following is a brief description of the purpose of each of these tools:

- Microsoft SQL Server 2000 Enterprise Manager can be used to verify the proper working of the databases and to evaluate the Microsoft SQL environment. This tool can be used on any Windows 2000 server in the domain to access the SQL database. By default, it is installed on every server that has Microsoft SQL Server 2000 installed.
- DBLHelper allows the verification and re-creation of the replication process between the Cisco CallManager publisher and subscriber databases. This tool needs to be run on the Cisco CallManager publisher server. Beginning with CallManager Release 4.0, this tool is available only from Cisco TAC.
- The Services MMC allows for management of services on Windows 2000 Server. Each Windows 2000 server has its own Services MMC preinstalled. Even though administrators can create their own MMC to manage services on any other system, it is recommended that you use the preinstalled MMC on each server locally. Otherwise, you risk confusion, because all the servers look the same.
- Microsoft Event Viewer allows identification of system-level events and errors. Each event and error of the Windows 2000 system is stored in Microsoft Event Viewer. Different kinds of messages are grouped into a system log, an application log (where most information related to Cisco CallManager is stored), and a security log. Because Event Viewer is also an MMC snap-in, an MMC that includes Event Viewer can be created on any system but it is not recommended to manage remote systems.
- Microsoft Performance Monitor shows system and application statistics and is available on every Microsoft Windows 2000 system. Although it is also an MMC snap-in for Microsoft Windows 2000 Server, it can be used only on the server itself because it uses an ActiveX control. To monitor performance statistics of remote systems, use the local snap-in as an alternative and include remote counters.

- The RTMT client allows you to monitor Cisco CallManager activities in real time. This Java-based tool can be installed on any Windows PC. It is available in the Install Plugins window of Cisco CallManager Serviceability.
- The Password Changer tool available on the Cisco CallManager server allows changing the administrator passwords on Cisco CallManager systems. This tool needs to be run on the Cisco CallManager publisher server.
- The CAR tool allows analysis of CDRs written on Cisco CallManager. CAR is available from Cisco CallManager Serviceability and can be accessed using the Microsoft Internet Explorer web browser on any PC on the network.
- Dialed Number Analyzer analyzes how inbound and outbound calls are handled in the Cisco CallManager call-routing configuration. It resides on the Cisco CallManager web server and can be accessed using Internet Explorer on any PC on the network.
- The QRT Viewer application allows you to filter, format, and view problem reports. It is located on the Cisco CallManager web server and can be accessed using Internet Explorer on any PC on the network.

NOTE Many of these applications are discussed in depth in Chapters 31 and 32, "Monitoring Performance" and "Configuring Alarms and Traces," respectively.

Summary

This chapter discussed the tools included with the Cisco CallManager software. You can use Microsoft SQL Server 2000 Enterprise Manager and DBLHelper to verify proper working of the SQL database and repair broken links, if necessary. You can use the tools in the Cisco CallManager Serviceability system to control and manage the CallManager system. You can use the Control Center to start, stop, or restart service related to the Cisco CallManager. The Service Activation and Services Windows 2000 MMC allow you to manage all services on Cisco CallManager. Many additional tools are provided by Cisco and Microsoft that allow management and troubleshooting of the Cisco CallManager server.

Review Questions

You can find the solutions to these questions in Appendix A, "Answers to Review Questions.""

1. Which two tools are available on Cisco CallManager systems to manage the SQL database?

   a. Microsoft SQL Server 2000 Enterprise Manager

   b. Cisco SQL Server 2000 Enterprise Manager

   c. SQL Server 2000 System Manager

   d. DBAHelper

   e. DBLHelper

2. Which of the following statements is true?

   a. Cisco CallManager Serviceability needs to be installed from the Cisco CallManager Install Plugins window.

   b. Cisco CallManager Serviceability provides a configuration interface to configure extension DNs.

   c. Cisco CallManager Serviceability allows you to start, stop, or restart all Microsoft Windows 2000 services.

   d. Cisco CallManager Serviceability provides services to monitor alarms, generate CARs, and collect and analyze traces.

3. Which two of the following services can be started, stopped, or restarted via the Cisco CallManager Control Center?

   a. Cisco CallManager

   b. Cisco DHCP

   c. Cisco TFTP

   d. Cisco Extension Mobility

   e. Cisco WebDialer

4. Where can Cisco CallManager Services be activated and deactivated? (Choose two.)

   a. In DBLHelper

   b. In Cisco CallManager Control Center

   c. In the Windows 2000 Services MMC

   d. In Microsoft Service Activation Tool

   e. In Cisco CallManager Service Activation

5. Where should DBLHelper be run?

   a. Only on the Cisco CallManager publisher server

   b. Only on the Cisco CallManager subscriber server

   c. On the Cisco CallManager publisher or subscriber server

   d. On any PC in the network

6. If the publisher server is down, where are configuration changes stored in the CallManager cluster?

   a. Configuration changes will be lost.

   b. Configuration changes are stored in the subscriber database file.

   c. Configuration changes are stored in the subscriber transaction files.

   d. The CallManager will prevent you from making configuration changes while the publisher is down.

7. If the publisher server is down, where are CDRs stored in the CallManager cluster?

   a. CDRs will be lost.

   b. CDRs are stored in the subscriber database file.

   c. CDRs are stored in the subscriber transaction files.

   d. The CallManager cluster will stop all calls while the publisher is down.

8. You are using SQL Server 2000 Enterprise Manager on one of your CallManager servers. Which two items should you see if this server is the cluster publisher?

   a. The existence of the Replication Monitor

   b. A publisher image at the top of the database

   c. A Publications folder under the database

   d. The title bar of the SQL Enterprise Manager will show "Publisher" next to the title

9. Which utility does Cisco highly recommend you use to repair SQL database replication issues?

   a. Windows 2000 Services

   b. DBLHelper

   c. SQL Server 2000 Enterprise Manager

   d. Serviceability Control Center

10. If replication has failed between a publisher and subscriber server, what does DBLHelper display?

a. A replication failed notice

b. A broken link

c. A red sad face

d. A yellow exclamation point

This chapter covers the following topics:

- Defining a performance object and counter and describing their interaction with Microsoft Performance Monitor and RTMT
- Using Microsoft Event Viewer to identify system-level events and errors
- Using Microsoft Performance Monitor to monitor system and device statistics
- Explaining the major monitoring categories that RTMT provides
- Using the default RTMT configuration and creating customized configuration profiles
- Identifying components of the RTMT window

CHAPTER 31

Monitoring Performance

Growing demands to the telephony systems increase hardware usage on the telephony system platform. If those demands rise too much, they could cause system overloads. Telephony systems are among those that most directly affect businesses, and overloads that lead to system outages could be extremely costly. Therefore, administrators must be able to monitor system performance. This chapter covers tools that are used to monitor Cisco CallManager systems. Further, this chapter describes Microsoft tools that are available on the Windows system, Real-Time Monitoring Tool (RTMT) from Cisco, and how they work together.

Performance Counters

Performance counters reflect the performance data of Cisco CallManager. A counter is a variable whose name is stored in the Registry. Each counter is related to a specific area of system functionality. Examples include busy time of the processor, memory usage, and the number of bytes received over a network connection. Each counter is uniquely identified through its name and its path or location. In the same way that a file path includes drives, directories, subdirectories, and filenames, a counter path consists of four elements: the machine, the object (for example, processor or IP), the object instance (type of counter value; for example, interrupt), and the counter name (special counter itself).

Performance counters are ideal for administrators for system maintenance, analysis, and troubleshooting tasks:

- An administrator needs to reset a voice gateway. With performance counters, it is possible to watch the system until the last call is disconnected and then reset the gateway.
- A user reports that using Cisco CallManager Extension Mobility to log in to the phone takes a very long time. In analyzing the statistics produced with performance counter data, the administrator discovers high processor usage and memory allocation due to problems with processes on the system.
- An administrator is dealing with a slow system. The system engineer has to decide whether system expansion is necessary or whether the current extensive system usage is only a one-time situation. To find out, the administrator should watch the system for a while.

> **NOTE** All performance counter values are based on system events and utilization information provided by the Microsoft Windows 2000 platform.

Performance Analysis

Microsoft Performance Monitor and Cisco Real-Time Monitoring Tool (RTMT) use Windows 2000 performance counters to monitor the system. Microsoft Performance Monitor, shown in Figure 31-1, reports both general and specific information in real time, whereas RTMT, shown in Figure 31-2, monitors focused Cisco CallManager performance by periodically polling Windows 2000 performance counter values.

Figure 31-1 *Microsoft Windows 2000 Performance Monitor*

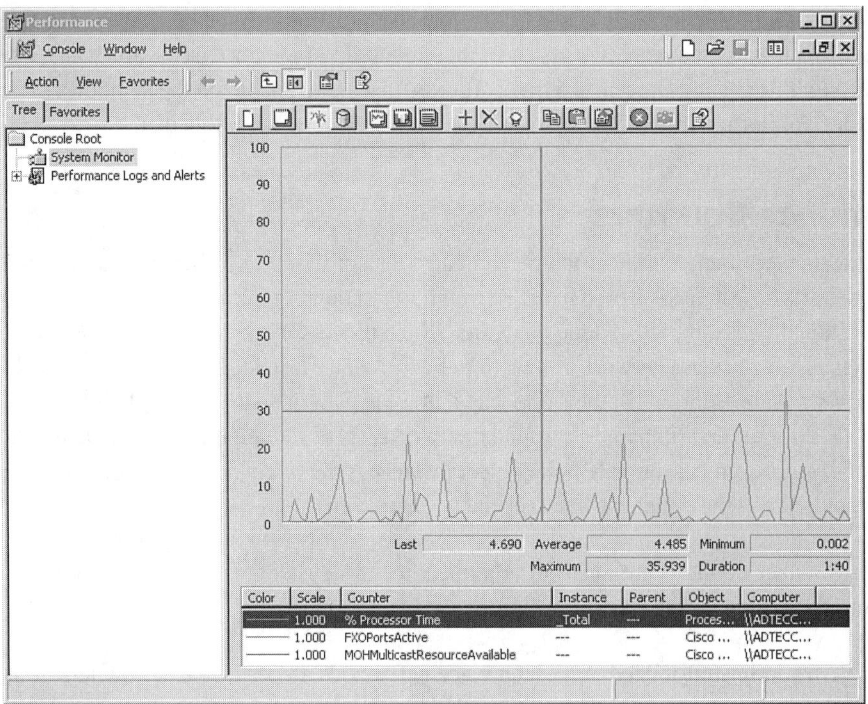

RTMT provides optimized monitoring of performance objects and devices related just to the Cisco CallManager. The device information includes device registration status, IP address, description, and model type. RTMT provides clusterwide information that is stored in eight tables. The tables include IP phones, gateway devices, media, H.323 devices, Session Initiation Protocol (SIP) trunks, hunt lists, computer telephony integration (CTI), and voice messaging. RTMT also displays object and counter information that is kept by each Cisco CallManager node in the cluster. RTMT directly monitors the performance objects and counters.

Figure 31-2 *Cisco Real-Time Monitoring Tool*

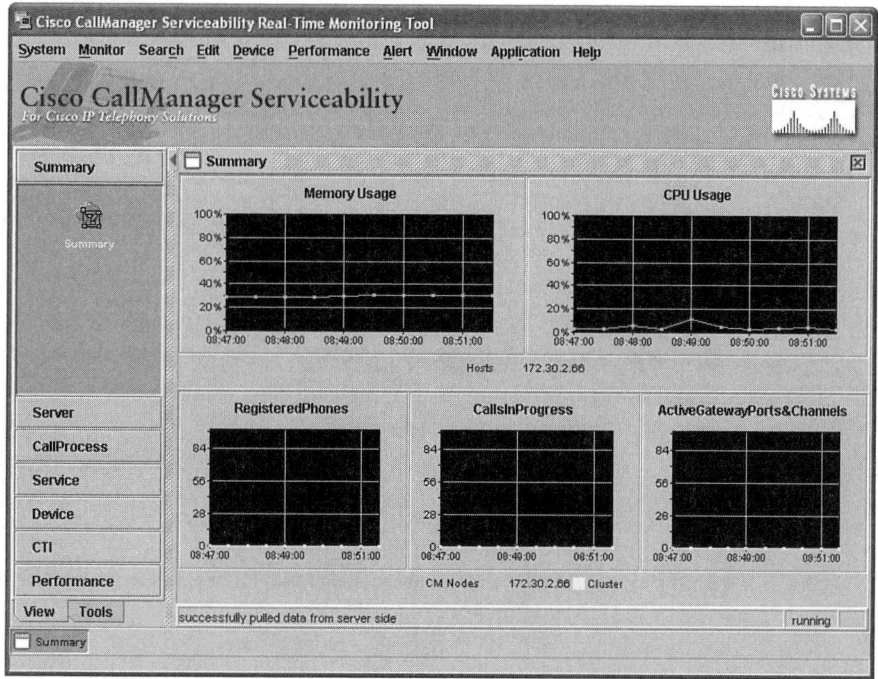

Microsoft Event Viewer

Microsoft Event Viewer is a Microsoft Windows system tool. It is available by default on every Windows NT-based system (Windows NT, Windows 2000, Windows XP, and Windows Server 2003). Beginning with the introduction of Windows 2000, Microsoft Event Viewer has been managed through the Microsoft Management Console (MMC). It is possible to create an MMC that includes the Event Viewer of each remote system. But keep in mind that using more than one Event Viewer on one system often leads to confusion and is normally not recommended.

Windows stores information related to an event or error in Event Viewer. Event Viewer can be used to gather, identify, and analyze Windows 2000 system events and information about hardware, software, and system problems. Because Cisco CallManager runs as a Windows service, information about Cisco CallManager events and errors can also be stored in Event Viewer.

Event Viewer, available at **Start > Settings > Control Panel > Administrative Tools > Event Viewer**, can help identify problems at the system level. For example, to pinpoint a problem, use Event Viewer to look for events involving Cisco CallManager Administration on the Internet Information Server (IIS) server.

As shown in Figure 31-3, Event Viewer uses log types to group different kinds of logs:

- **Application logs**—Contain events logged by applications or programs, such as Cisco CallManager.
- **System logs**—Report events logged by the Windows 2000 system components, such as the failure of an operating system component or driver.
- **Security logs**—Hold information records of security events. (Cisco CallManager does not report events in this log.)

Figure 31-3 *Microsoft Event Viewer*

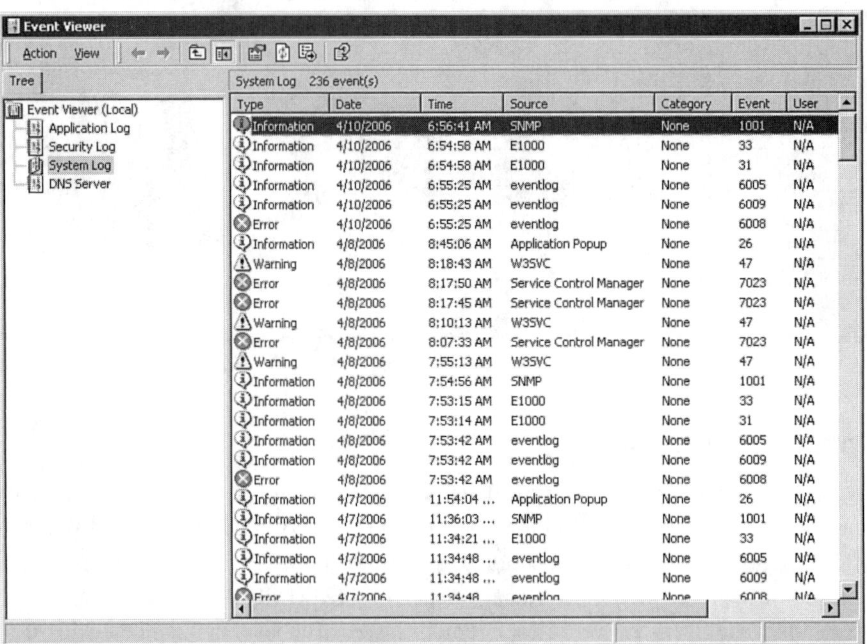

To classify events, Event Viewer provides three event types. Each is marked with its own icon. The Microsoft Event Viewer event types are as follows:

- **Error**—An indicator of a problem, such as the loss of data or failure to initialize properly; represented by a red "X"
- **Warning**—An event that might indicate a problem or a future problem, such as when a service is stopped or started, which is not necessarily an error; represented by a yellow exclamation point
- **Information**—System information messages that might include hostnames, the version of the database in use, or startup success; represented by a blue "i" symbol

Microsoft Performance Monitor

Microsoft Performance Monitor is a Windows 2000 Server application that uses Windows 2000 performance counters to create statistics. It displays the activities and status of the system. Performance Monitor reports both general and specific information in real time. You can use Performance Monitor to collect and display system and device statistics for any Cisco CallManager installation.

Performance Monitor, like the Cisco CallManager Serviceability tool, monitors and logs resource counters from the Cisco CallManager nodes in the network and displays the counters in real time. The update interval could be set to a period between 1 second and 45 days.

Performance Monitor can collect data from multiple systems at once and store it in a single log file. The monitor can then export this log file to a Tab-Separated Values (TSV) file or a Comma-Separated Values (CSV) file that you can view in most spreadsheet applications.

To access Performance Monitor, choose **Start > Settings > Control Panel > Administrative Tools** and choose **Performance**.

> **NOTE** Extensive monitoring (monitoring a very large number of counters and using short interval times) could cause rising processor usage. Therefore, it is recommended that you use Performance Monitor only for special situations and not as a network management tool.

Microsoft Performance Monitor Report View

Microsoft Performance Monitor needs to be customized for the parameters related to monitoring Cisco CallManager by choosing the objects, counters, and instances to include. As shown in Figure 31-4, Performance Monitor supports a very concise report view. Many administrators prefer this view because it gives exact figures rather than general estimates on a line chart.

Within Performance Monitor, alarms can be enabled to report certain value thresholds. For example, the number of telephone devices active on Cisco CallManager can be set to a particular level. If the number of devices exceeds that level, the monitor sends a network message alert to the administrator or the person in charge. To create such an alert threshold, right-click **Performance Logs and Alerts > Alerts** and choose **New Alert Settings**.

> **NOTE** Data collection must be enabled in Cisco CallManager for Performance Monitor to collect data. To verify that data collection is enabled, check the current settings in the Cisco Real-Time Information Server (RIS) Data Collector Service Parameters Configuration window in Cisco CallManager Administration. By default, the **Data Collection Enabled** parameter is set to **True**.

Figure 31-4 *Microsoft Performance Monitor Report View*

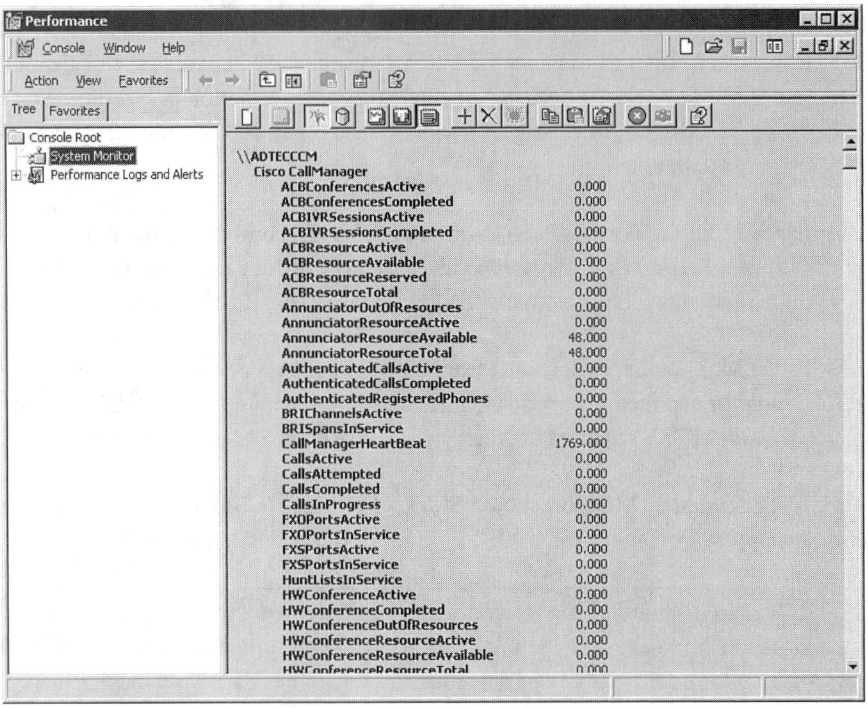

Microsoft Performance Monitor Graph and Histogram View

Microsoft Performance Monitor provides graph and histogram graphical views for a visual overview of how the system is currently in use and how it changes.

The graph view (shown in Figure 31-5) is ideal to see the current status of the counters and how they have changed over the most recent period. You can specify the period for status updates and include it in the graph. Using this tool is similar to using a heart-rate monitor. It displays the heartbeat of the monitored performance objects.

In contrast to graphs, the histogram view (shown in Figure 31-6) shows only the current status of the selected performance object counters. Because it uses only a single bar for each counter, the histogram view is ideal for monitoring many performance counters. To switch between the graph and histogram views, use the graph and histogram icons from the system monitor toolbar or press **Ctrl-G** (graph) and **Ctrl-B** (histogram) alternately.

Figure 31-5 *Microsoft Performance Monitor Graph View*

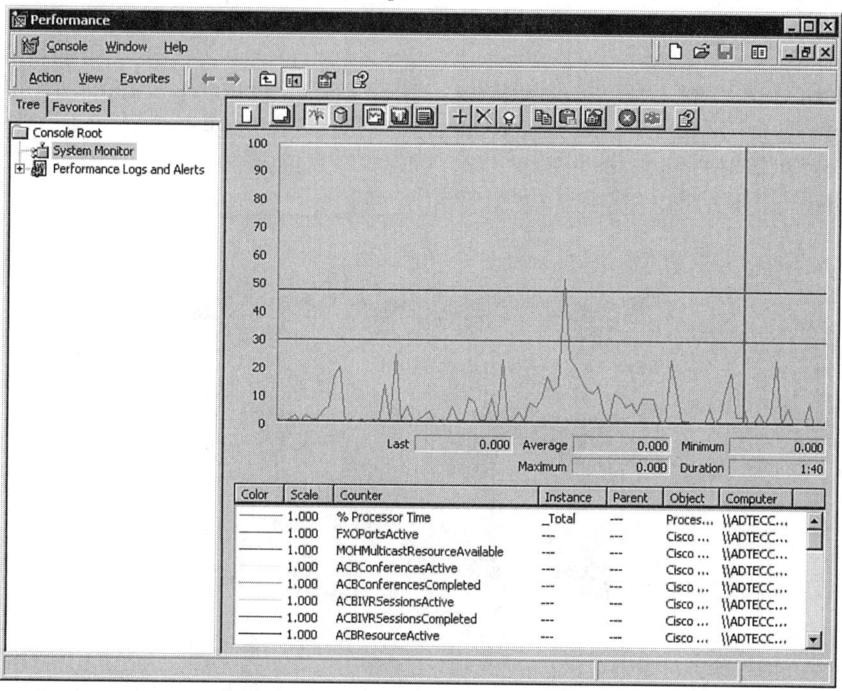

Figure 31-6 *Microsoft Performance Monitor Histogram View*

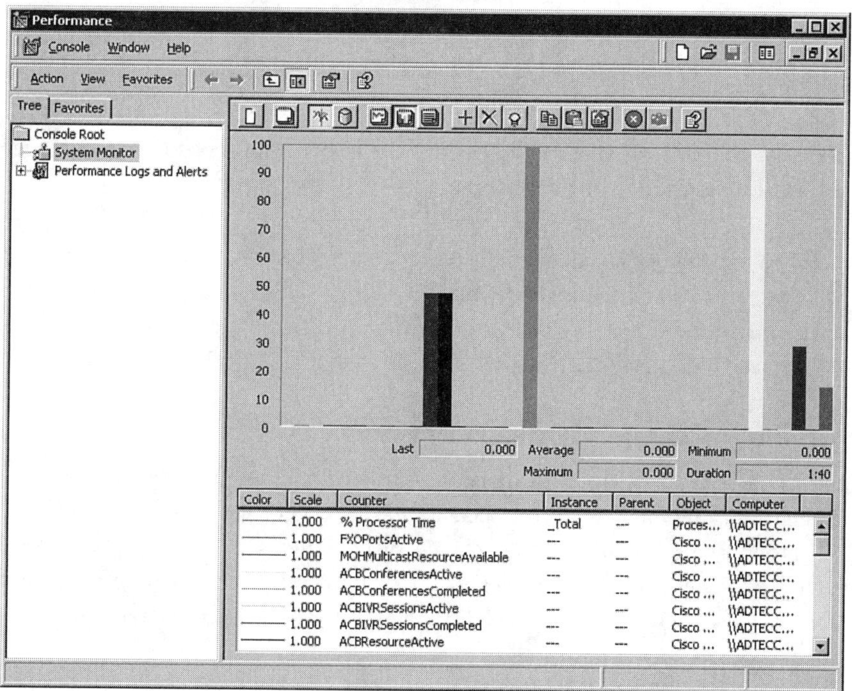

Microsoft Windows Task Manager

In addition to Microsoft Performance Monitor, you can use Windows Task Manager (shown in Figure 31-7) to get a fast view of the base performance values of CPU and memory usage. The **Performance** tab of Task Manager shows the CPU and memory usage of the system as a graph and histogram. Moreover, it provides some additional counter values, such as paged kernel memory in plain text. It is an ideal tool to get a quick impression of system health and activity, for example, if the system is working very slowly.

Figure 31-7 *Microsoft Windows Task Manager*

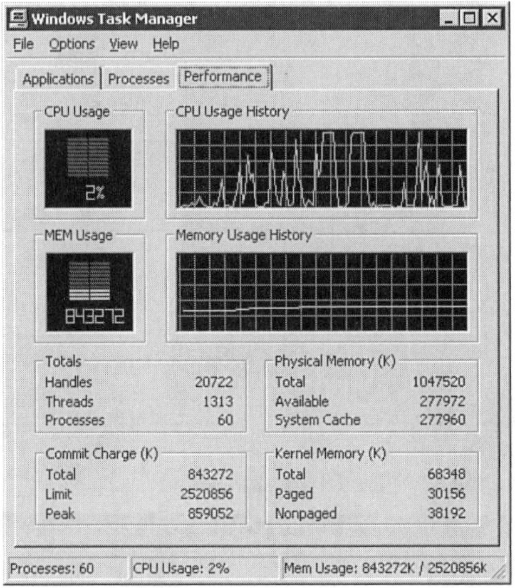

To access Windows Task Manager, right-click the taskbar and choose **Task Manager** from the menu or press the **Ctrl-Shift-Esc** shortcut.

> **NOTE** Windows Task Manager influences system performance because it also monitors all system processes and running programs. Therefore, it is recommended that you use it only to get a snapshot of the current situation and not for prolonged monitoring.

Real-Time Monitoring Tool Overview

With Cisco RTMT, the Cisco CallManager Serviceability tool provides a client-side, standalone Java plug-in that monitors real-time behavior of the components in a Cisco CallManager cluster. RTMT monitors a set of management objects by continuously polling the Windows 2000 performance counter values. It can generate various alerts in the form of e-mails for values that exceed or fail to reach user-configured thresholds. RTMT can also generate daily reports for these objects. The e-mail alerts work independently of the standalone Java front end. Therefore, it is not necessary to run the RTMT window all the time to generate e-mail notifications.

To download RTMT, choose **Cisco CallManager RTMT** from the Cisco CallManager Install Plugins page in the Application menu of Cisco CallManager Administration and Cisco CallManager Serviceability. After successful installation, you can launch RTMT by double-clicking the RTMT shortcut on the Windows desktop or by choosing **Start** > **Programs** > **Cisco CallManager Serviceability** > **RTMT**.

> **NOTE** To reduce the impact on the Cisco CallManager server, it is strongly recommended that you run RTMT on an administrator PC and not locally on the Cisco CallManager server. Moreover, RTMT should not run constantly.

As shown in Figure 31-8, The RTMT application is divided into four parts:

- **Menu bar**—The RTMT menu bar, located at the top of the RTMT window, uses drop-down menus that provide specific monitoring.
- **Controlling center pane**—The controlling center pane, located on the left side of the window, includes the **View** tab and the **Tools** tab. The **View** tab includes several different monitoring categories, whereas the **Tools** tab offers only the Alert category. On the **View** tab of the controlling pane, RTMT arranges the preconfigured monitoring objects into seven major categories:
  - **Summary**—The Summary category shows the activities of several predetermined monitoring objects in the Cisco CallManager cluster, such as memory and CPU usage, registered phones, calls in progress, and active gateway ports and channels.
  - **Device**—The Device category monitors phones, gateways, and media devices on each Cisco CallManager node and cluster. Monitored objects include the number of registered phones, gateways, and media resources for each Cisco CallManager node and cluster.
  - **CallProcess**—The CallProcess category monitors all call activity for each Cisco CallManager node and cluster. Monitored objects include CallsAttempted, CallsCompleted, and CallsInProgress for each Cisco CallManager node and cluster.
  - **Server**—The Server category monitors CPU usage, disk space usage, and critical services on each Cisco CallManager server. Monitored objects include CPU and memory usage on each server and the disk space usage for all logical drives on each server.

— **Service**—The Service category monitors CTIManager information for each CTIManager, Cisco TFTP server information, directory server information, and heartbeat rate information. Monitored objects include TotalTftpRequests and TotalTftpRequestsAborted.

— **CTI**—The CTI category provides CTI search and a CTIManager monitoring window that displays the number of open devices, lines, and CTI connections.

— **Performance**—The Performance category provides performance monitoring similar to Microsoft Performance Monitor.

- **Viewing pane**—In the viewing pane, located to the right of the controlling center pane and occupying most of the window area, RTMT displays the currently selected monitoring object.
- **Tab bar**—The tab bar, located at the bottom of the window, allows switching among all monitoring objects currently monitored in the viewing pane.

Figure 31-8 *Cisco Real-Time Monitoring Tool*

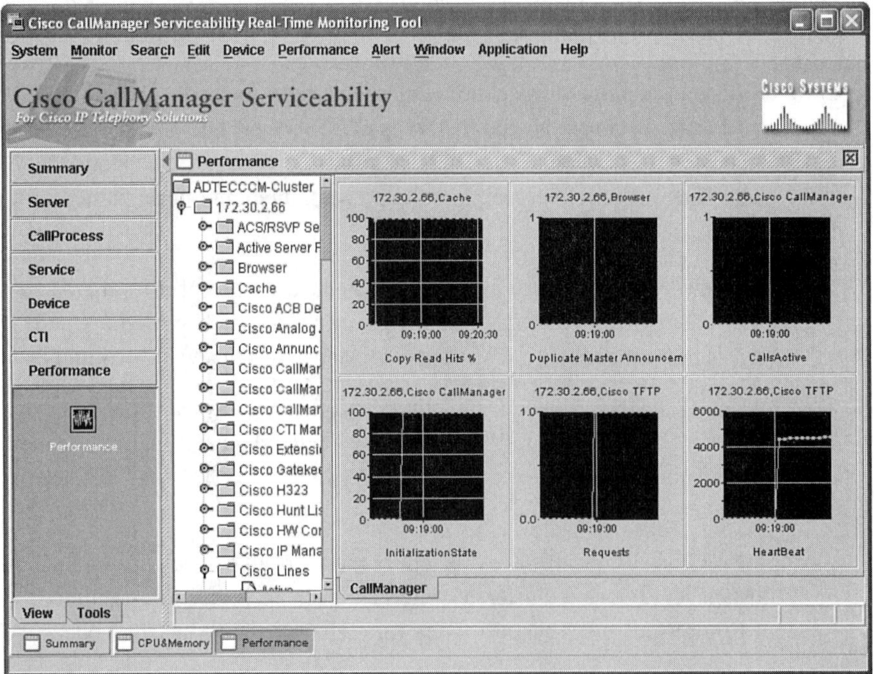

Real-Time Monitoring Tool Configuration Profiles

RTMT allows you to save monitoring configurations so that they do not need to be re-created every time you start RTMT. When you start RTMT, you can select the desired profile. The CM-Default profile is preconfigured. Its parameters include the number of registered phones, gateway status, CPU and memory usage, and the number of calls in progress.

To save the current monitoring configurations:

Step 1 Choose **System > Profile** (or press **Ctrl-Alt-P**) to open the Preferences window.

Step 2 In the Preferences Window, choose **Save**. The Save Current Configuration window opens.

Step 3 Enter a name and a meaningful description for the configuration, as shown in Figure 31-9, which will allow you to easily identify it later, and click **OK** to save your configuration.

Figure 31-9 *Configuring Real-Time Monitoring Tool Configuration Profiles*

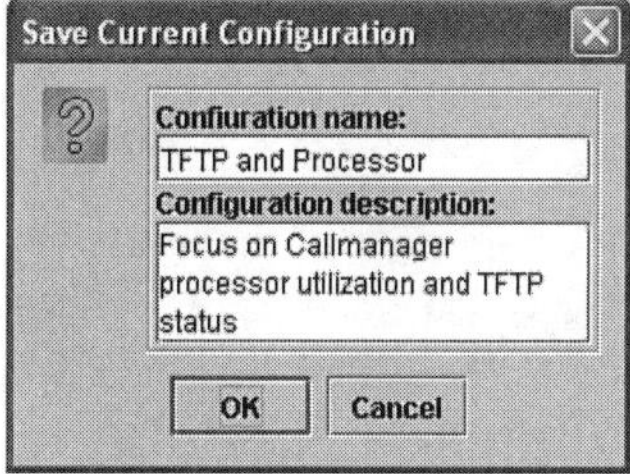

To make a copy of an existing configuration:

Step 1 Choose **System > Profile** (or press **Ctrl-Alt-P**) to open the Preferences window.

Step 2 Select the configuration that should be duplicated.

Step 3 Click **Restore** to load the configuration.

Step 4 Click **Save**, enter a name and description for the configuration, and click **OK**.

Using the Real-Time Monitoring Tool Effectively

The RTMT window monitors various aspects of Cisco CallManager performance by periodically polling Windows 2000 performance counter values. RTMT discovers devices regardless of their registration status, such as registered or failed, in the cluster. The tool searches by device name, device description, IP address, IP subnet, or directory number (DN) and monitors the status of discovered devices.

Some of the most useful monitoring objects on the RTMT window are these:

- **Summary**—Gives administrators a quick overview of their Cisco voice over IP (VoIP) system; this is the default view
- **Call Activity**—Shows active calls as well as attempted and completed calls
- **Device Search**—Allows administrators to define criteria for identifying which devices to display for analysis
- **Perfmon**—Allows system performance to be displayed within the RTMT window, which eliminates the need for a Microsoft Performance Monitor window to be running at the same time
- **Alert Central**—Displays current status and history of all the alerts in the Cisco CallManager cluster

Viewing Call Activity

As shown in Figure 31-10, the Call Activity window allows you to monitor call activity for each Cisco CallManager node in the cluster in real time. To display the Call Activity window, complete these tasks:

Step 1 In the controlling center pane at the left, click the **View** tab.

Step 2 Click **CallProcess**.

Step 3 Click the **Call Activity** icon.

Figure 31-10 *RTMT Call Activity*

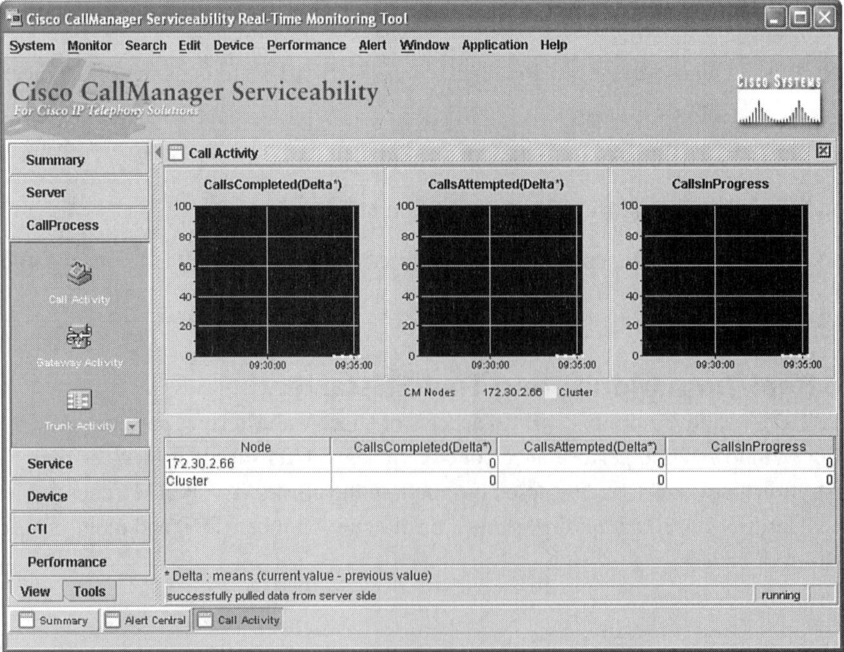

The Call Activity monitoring window displays the call activity for each Cisco CallManager node in the cluster and draws a history graph for the past few minutes.

Using Device Search

You can select the devices to monitor based on shared characteristics, such as a status of registered or rejected. RTMT device monitoring can be further refined to narrow the search characteristics to DNs or subnet. In addition, you can select the attributes to monitor, such as Node or StatusReason, and all others can be left out. Select only certain values to monitor because doing so saves time and eliminates unnecessary data in the monitor window. To access these configuration parameters, select the device for which you want to view monitoring information. The monitor then prompts you to enter the characteristics to narrow the search, as shown in Figure 31-11.

Figure 31-11 *RTMT Device Search Wizard*

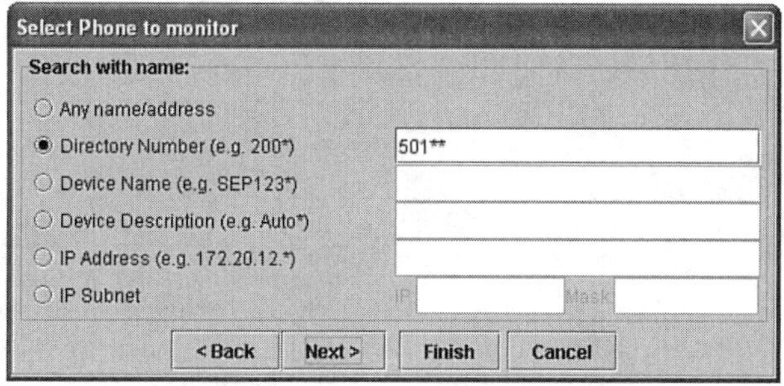

To create a search, complete these tasks:

Step 1 In the controlling center pane at the left, click the **Device** tab.

Step 2 Click **Device Search**.

Step 3 Double-click **Phone** in the white pane and follow the instructions.

Visiting Alert Central

In RTMT, you can configure alert notification for Perfmon counter value thresholds and schedule alert checks and status changes of devices (for example, a port is out of service). The **Tools** tab in the controlling center pane of the RTMT monitor includes the Alert Central category, as shown in Figure 31-12. Alert Central provides both the current status and the history of all the alerts in the Cisco CallManager cluster.

Figure 31-12 *RTMT Alert Central*

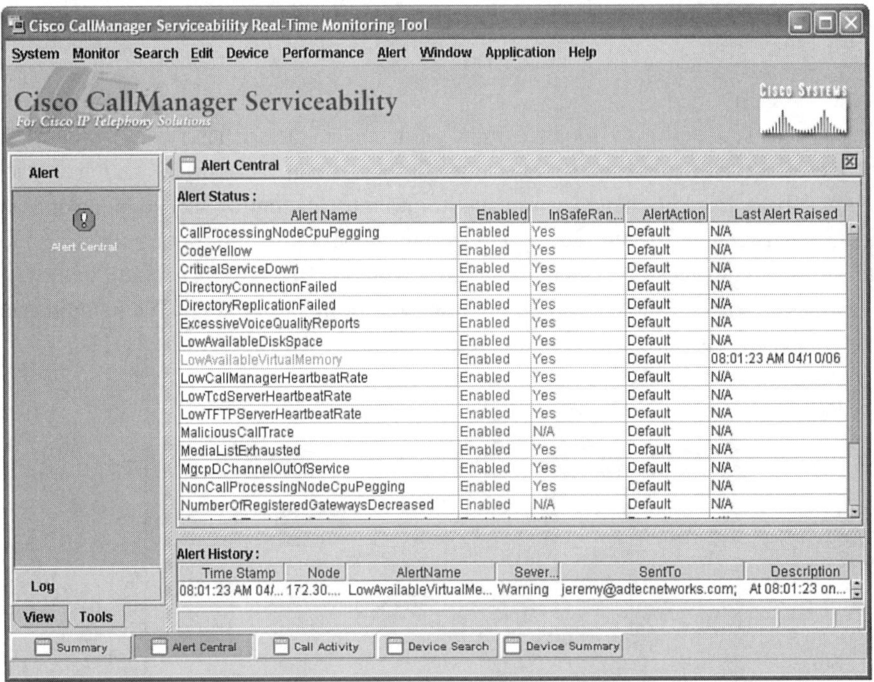

Figure 31-12 shows a sample alert for a system where the virtual memory of the system is currently too low. To allow administrators to qualify the message (to determine whether this is a one-time event because of a special situation or a continuing problem), RTMT also provides a time stamp of the most recent memory leak alert and a history of the most recent messages. In addition, you can configure the RTMT Alert to send e-mail alerts when the CallManager exceeds predefined thresholds. This configuration requires you to enter Simple Mail Transfer Protocol (SMTP) server information using the **Alert > Config Email Server** menu item.

Summary

This chapter discussed the concepts and configuration behind monitoring the Cisco CallManager cluster. Both Microsoft and Cisco include tools to monitor various aspects of each Cisco CallManager server or the cluster as a whole. The Microsoft Performance Monitor shows system parameters, including Cisco CallManager counters. The Microsoft Event Viewer can help you identify problems at the system level. The Event Viewer also records events generated from the Cisco CallManager software.

Cisco Real-Time Monitoring Tool (RTMT) is a standalone Java plug-in that provides information about Cisco CallManager from a remote workstation. You can save the RTMT configurations in configuration profiles to allow quick reference of preset counters. The RTMT window gives you the ability to monitor various aspects of Cisco CallManager performance and generate alerts, which the RTMT can send to you via e-mail whenever the CallManager reaches a predefined alert threshold.

Review Questions

You can find the solutions to these questions in Appendix A, "Answers to Review Questions."

1. Which two of the following statements about Microsoft Event Viewer are true? (Choose two.)
   a. Microsoft Event Viewer needs to be installed separately and is included in the Microsoft Windows 2000 support pack.
   b. Microsoft Event Viewer assists administrators in troubleshooting Cisco CallManager systems.
   c. Microsoft Event Viewer is limited to the most recent 100 events per log type.
   d. Microsoft Event Viewer stores system errors and warnings.
   e. There are four log types in Microsoft Event Viewer.
2. How can Microsoft Performance Monitor be used to maintain Cisco CallManager systems? (Choose three.)
   a. To monitor Microsoft Windows 2000 counters
   b. To monitor Cisco CallManager counters
   c. To monitor events in real time
   d. To analyze call flows
   e. To analyze CDRs
   f. To analyze trace files
   g. To analyze Cisco CallManager configuration
3. What can RTMT be used for? (Choose two.)
   a. Cisco CallManager performance monitoring
   b. Cisco CallManager configuration
   c. Cisco CallManager performance manipulation
   d. Alert e-mail generation
   e. Service activation

4. Which two of the following statements about the saving of configurations on RTMT are true?

   a. If administrators exit RTMT, the active configuration is stored automatically.
   b. Multiple configuration profiles can be stored.
   c. RTMT needs to be restarted to load a saved configuration.
   d. Configuration profiles can be identified by their number and date.
   e. Configuration profiles can be identified by their name and description.

5. Which of the following statements about the RTMT window is true? (Choose three.)

   a. The RTMT window supports tabs to allow many different elements to be viewed at one time.
   b. When switching between RTMT window tabs, real-time information graphs on inactive (hidden) tabs are stopped.
   c. The RTMT window provides performance monitoring similar to the Microsoft Performance Monitor.
   d. The RTMT window includes a link to start the Microsoft Performance Monitor MMC.
   e. E)The RTMT window includes an alert central.
   f. F)RTMT needs to be downloaded from Cisco.com.

6. Which area of the Microsoft Event Viewer would contain messages specific to Cisco CallManager?

   a. Error logs
   b. Application logs
   c. System logs
   d. Warning logs
   e. Security logs

7. What are the three views supported by Microsoft Performance Monitor? (Choose three.)

   a. Histogram
   b. Dynamic
   c. Active
   d. Alert
   e. Graph
   f. Report
   g. Tabbed

8. Which of the following utilities will allow you to see processor and memory utilization levels for a Cisco CallManager server? (Choose three.)

   a. Microsoft Performance Monitor
   b. CallManager Serviceability
   c. Cisco RTMT
   d. Windows Task Manager
   e. Event Viewer
   f. CallManager Control Center

This chapter covers the following topics:

- Identifying the functions of the Cisco CallManager Serviceability Alarm interface and its event levels and destinations
- Configuring alarms for Cisco CallManager services
- Identifying and configuring the trace functions of the Cisco CallManager Serviceability Trace tool and services
- Conducting a trace analysis and displaying trace records in XML format
- Collecting and compressing Cisco CallManager service trace files
- Explaining the features and functions of the Bulk Trace Analysis tool
- Identifying and explaining additional trace tools and describing when to use each of them

CHAPTER 32

Configuring Alarms and Traces

Administrators who install or maintain Cisco CallManager sometimes have to deal with technical or design issues on their systems. To troubleshoot and monitor those issues, Cisco CallManager provides alarms and traces similar to the functionality of the **show** and **debug** commands of Cisco IOS software. This chapter describes how to configure traces on the Cisco CallManager system and discusses tools that allow you to analyze those traces.

Alarm Overview

The **Cisco CallManager Serviceability Alarm** menu provides a web-based interface that has two main functions:

- To allow configuration of alarms and events
  - — Administrators can define what kind of information should be logged.
  - — Administrators can define where to store alarms and events.
- To provide alarm message definitions
  - — Administrators can evaluate what kind of information (such as parameter and kind of events) is included in which alarm.

Both functions assist you in troubleshooting and monitoring your Cisco CallManager system. You can configure alarms for services (for example, Cisco CallManager, Cisco TFTP, or Cisco CTIManager) for all Cisco CallManager servers in the cluster or for each server individually.

Alarms are used to provide the run-time status and state of the system and to take corrective action for problem resolution; for example, to determine whether phones are registered and working. Alarms contain information such as an explanation and recommended action. Alarm information includes the application name, machine name, and cluster name to help you troubleshoot problems that are not on the local Cisco CallManager.

You can configure the Alarm interface to send alarm information to multiple destinations, and each destination can have its own alarm event level (from debug to emergency). CallManager can direct alarms to the Microsoft Windows 2000 Event Log, a syslog server, system diagnostic interface (SDI) trace log files, or signal distribution layer (SDL) trace log files.

When a service issues an alarm, the Alarm interface sends the alarm to the chosen monitors. Each monitor forwards the alarm or writes it to its final destination (such as a log file). You can use this information for troubleshooting or to pass over to another person for assistance (for example, the Cisco Technical Assistance Center [TAC]).

You can turn on several alarm levels on Cisco CallManager. These alarm levels are equivalent to the widely used syslog severity levels. Table 32-1 shows all available levels and describes the kind of information that generates the alarm. As you can also see from the table, each level can be identified by its name (debug to emergency) or by its number (0 to 7).

Table 32-1 *Alarm Event Levels*

Level	Name	Description
7	Emergency	System unusable
6	Alert	Immediate action needed
5	Critical	Critical condition detected
4	Error	Error condition
3	Warning	Warning condition detected
2	Notice	Normal but significant condition
1	Informational	Information messages only

When the alarm event level is set to a certain value, it means that alarms that match the configured level and alarms that match more severe levels are generated. In other words, an alarm level of 0 (debug) means all alarms of 0 or higher, and an alarm level of 4 means all alarms of level 4 or higher. So if you configure an alarm level of 5, all critical, alert, and emergency alarms are logged.

Alarm Configuration

You can use the Alarm Configuration window in Cisco CallManager Serviceability to define where CallManager will store the alarms and which level of alarms CallManager should store. You can define the alarm level for each destination individually. Destinations for alarms are as follows:

- Locally on the Cisco CallManager system in Microsoft Windows Event Log
- Locally on the Cisco CallManager system in trace log files
- Remotely on any syslog server; for example, Kiwi Syslog Daemon, a third-party application that runs on Windows systems

Configuring Alarms

To configure alarms in Cisco CallManager, follow this procedure:

Step 1 From Cisco CallManager Serviceability, choose **Alarm > Configuration**.

Step 2 Choose the appropriate server, which will then be displayed under Servers on the left side of the window and at the top of the window. A box with available services for alarms appears.

Step 3 From the **Configured Services** drop-down list, choose the service for which you want to configure the alarm. The CallManager displays the chosen service at the top of the window in the Current Service area, along with the currently chosen server. A list of alarm monitors with event levels, similar to the one shown in Figure 32-1 (which shows the alarm configuration for the Cisco CallManager service), appears.

Figure 32-1 *CallManager Alarm Configuration*

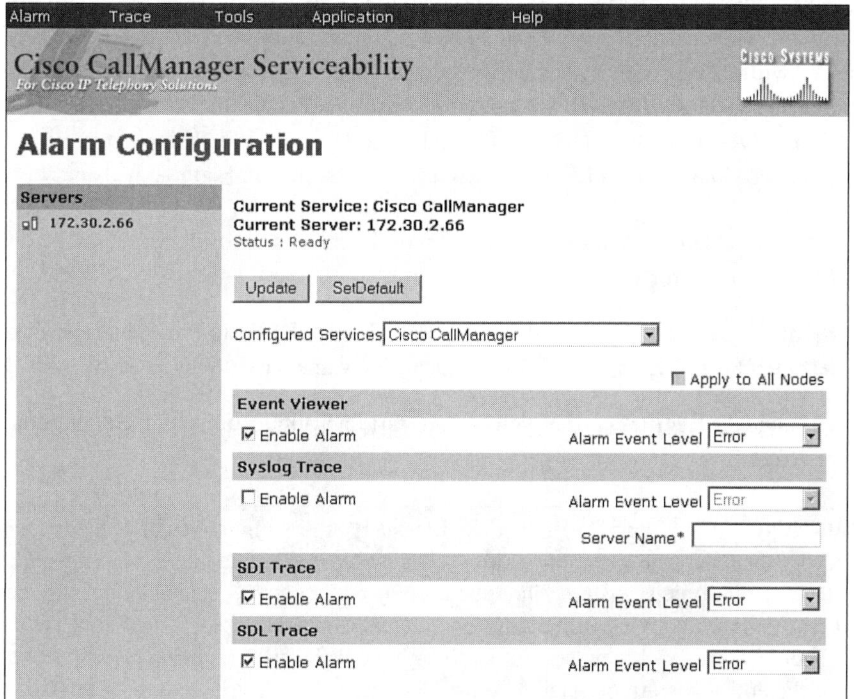

Step 4 Check the check box for each desired alarm destination.

> **NOTE** Only the Cisco CallManager and CTIManager services can use SDL Traces and only these services will have the check box for **Enable Alarm for SDL Trace** available.

Step 5 From the **Alarm Event Level** drop-down menu, choose the desired alarm event level for each of the available alarms.

Step 6 Save the configuration by clicking the **Update** button.

> **NOTE** To apply the current settings for selected services to all nodes in a cluster, check the **Apply to All Nodes** check box. To restore the default Cisco CallManager settings, click the **SetDefault** button and then the **Update** button.

Configuring Alarms for Java Applications

You cannot configure alarms for Java-based applications, such as Java Telephony Application Programming Interface (JTAPI) using the alarm configuration web pages. Use the Registry Editor provided with the operating system to view the alarm configuration and to change Registry entries. The Registry can be accessed by running the RegEdt32.exe or RegEdit.exe Registry Editors. Go to HKEY_LOCAL_MACHINE\SOFTWARE\Cisco Systems, Inc.\Cisco Java Applications\Monitors\Event Log in the Registry (as shown in Figure 32-2) and set these values:

- Set the Enabled key to a value of 0 to turn off Event Log or to 1 to turn it on (by default, Event Log is enabled for Java-based applications).
- Set the Severity key to a value between 0 and 7 to set the alarm event level (the default severity level for Java-based applications on Cisco CallManager systems is 6).

If you change the Registry entries, you must restart Java applications for the configuration changes to take effect.

> **CAUTION** It is recommended that you not change the Simple Network Management Protocol (SNMP) Trap and Catalog configurations. Those settings influence SNMP traps generated by the Cisco CallManager system. Those traps are used by network management applications, such as CiscoWorks. Changing the settings could cause malfunctioning of the entire network management system. Likewise, editing the Windows Registry is a dangerous process and can cause the entire operating system to crash. Be sure you exercise caution when making changes to the Windows Registry.

Figure 32-2 *CallManager Java Application Alarm Configuration*

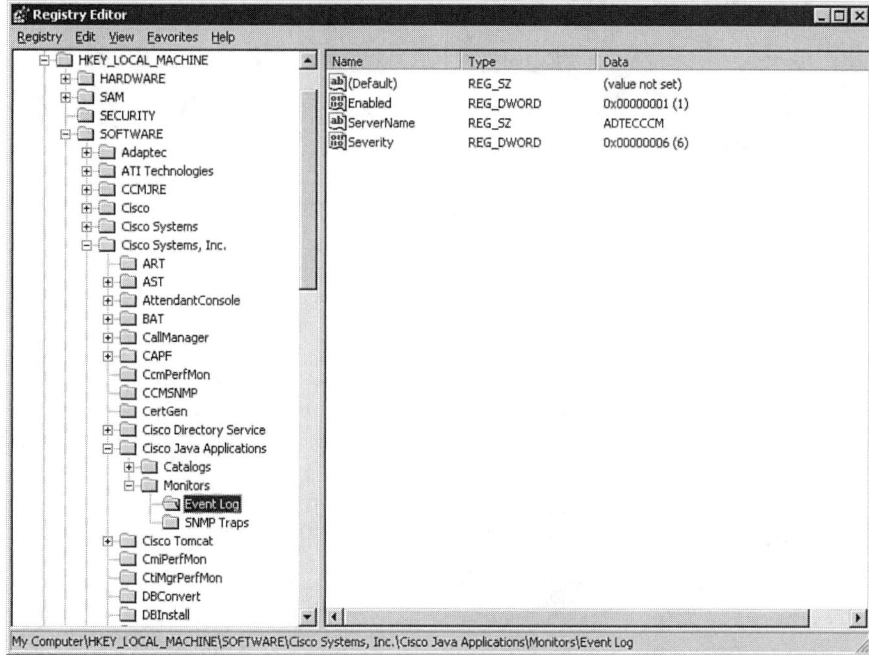

Alarm Details

Alarm definitions describe alarm messages. The definitions show what the alarms mean and how to recover from them.

To reach the alarm message definition details for an alarm, complete these steps:

Step 1 From Cisco CallManager Serviceability, choose **Alarm > Definition**.

Step 2 From the **Equals** drop-down menu, choose the service for which to check alarm definitions and click **Find**.

Step 3 From the window that opens (an example is shown in Figure 32-3), select the alarm to see details. Figure 32-4 illustrates the alarm details for the CallManagerFailure alarm.

Figure 32-3 *Listing of Available Alarm Definitions*

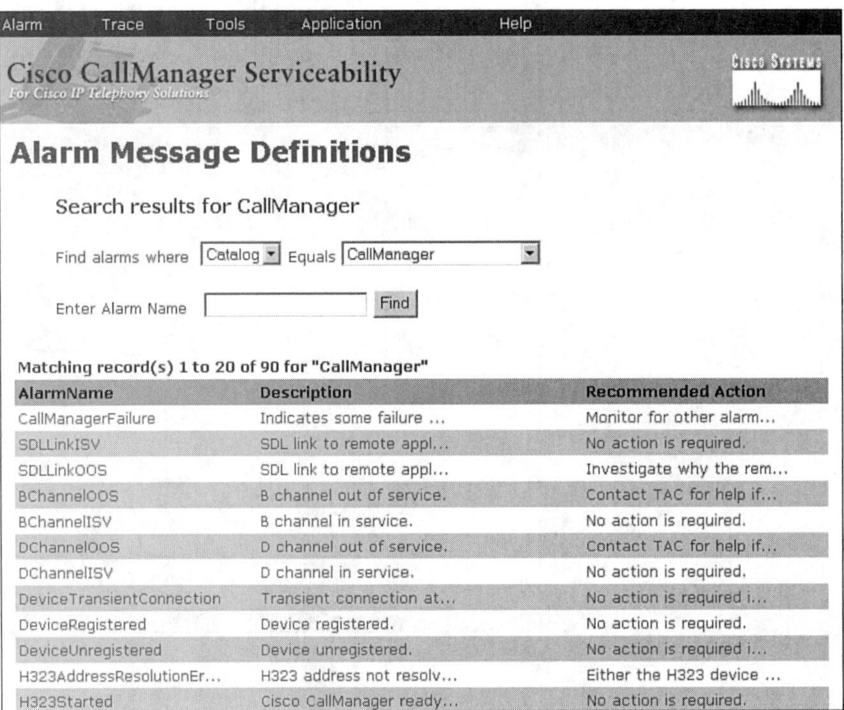

Cisco CallManager stores alarm definitions and recommended actions in a Structured Query Language (SQL) server database. You can search the database for definitions of all the alarms. The definition includes the alarm name, description, explanation, recommended action, severity, parameters, and monitors. This information aids you in troubleshooting problems that Cisco CallManager encounters.

> **NOTE** Administrators can add their own text to the alarm definition by simply entering information in the User Defined Text pane (not shown in Figure 32-4).

Figure 32-4 *Alarm Details for the CallManagerFailure Alarm*

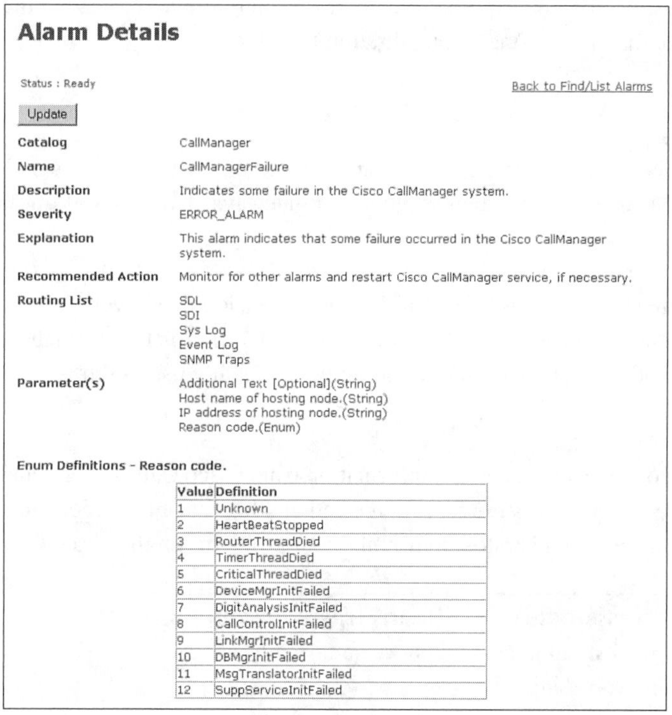

Alarm Details

Status : Ready

Back to Find/List Alarms

Update

Catalog	CallManager
Name	CallManagerFailure
Description	Indicates some failure in the Cisco CallManager system.
Severity	ERROR_ALARM
Explanation	This alarm indicates that some failure occurred in the Cisco CallManager system.
Recommended Action	Monitor for other alarms and restart Cisco CallManager service, if necessary.
Routing List	SDL SDI Sys Log Event Log SNMP Traps
Parameter(s)	Additional Text [Optional](String) Host name of hosting node.(String) IP address of hosting node.(String) Reason code.(Enum)

Enum Definitions - Reason code.

Value	Definition
1	Unknown
2	HeartBeatStopped
3	RouterThreadDied
4	TimerThreadDied
5	CriticalThreadDied
6	DeviceMgrInitFailed
7	DigitAnalysisInitFailed
8	CallControlInitFailed
9	LinkMgrInitFailed
10	DBMgrInitFailed
11	MsgTranslatorInitFailed
12	SuppServiceInitFailed

Trace Configuration

Cisco CallManager Serviceability provides a web-based trace tool to assist the system administrator and support personnel in troubleshooting Cisco CallManager problems. Cisco CallManager Serviceability Trace provides three main functions:

- **Configuration**—This function allows you to configure a variety of options when enabling traces. Options include the level of trace details and the trace file format (.xml or .txt).
- **Analysis and Q.931 Translator**—These functions allow you to analyze trace files.

NOTE The web-based Trace Analysis tool allows only analysis of Extensible Markup Language (XML) files; the Q.931 Translator analyzes both text and XML files. The XML format adds excessive overhead to the file, and causes the file to contain less information overall than saving the file in another format. For in-depth troubleshooting, Cisco recommends using formats other than XML.

- **Troubleshooting Trace Settings**—This function allows you to enable troubleshooting traces. With this feature, you can easily set up traces on multiple servers but there are fewer options available than in the Trace Configuration function.

Types of Traces

Traces for Cisco CallManager services can be based on debug levels, specific trace fields, and Cisco CallManager devices, such as phones or gateways. Two types of traces are available, SDI trace and SDL trace.

SDI traces are also known as Cisco CallManager trace log files. Every Cisco CallManager service includes a default trace log file. The system traces SDI information from the services and logs run-time events and traces to a log file. Programmers typically use SDI traces for development purposes.

SDL traces contain call-processing information from Cisco CallManager and Cisco CTIManager services. The system traces the SDL of the call and logs state transitions in a log file. This log information helps administrators to troubleshoot problems on the Cisco CallManager system.

TIP In most cases, extensive SDL traces will be gathered only when Cisco TAC requests it. SDL traces track communication between the CallManagers, whereas SDI traces track internal CallManager processing.

CAUTION Enabling traces decreases system performance; therefore, enable higher-level trace only for troubleshooting.

Trace Configuration and Analysis Overview

Figure 32-5 provides an overview of trace configuration and analysis options:

- **Troubleshooting trace settings**—Allows you to enable troubleshooting traces by server and by service for all servers from a single page.
- **Trace configuration**—Allows detailed trace configuration per server. The configuration options include the trace file format (.xml or .txt).
- **Analysis**—Allows you to analyze stored trace files (XML only).
- **XML or text editors**—Allows you to examine the content of the stored trace files.

Figure 32-5 *Trace Configuration and Analysis Overview*

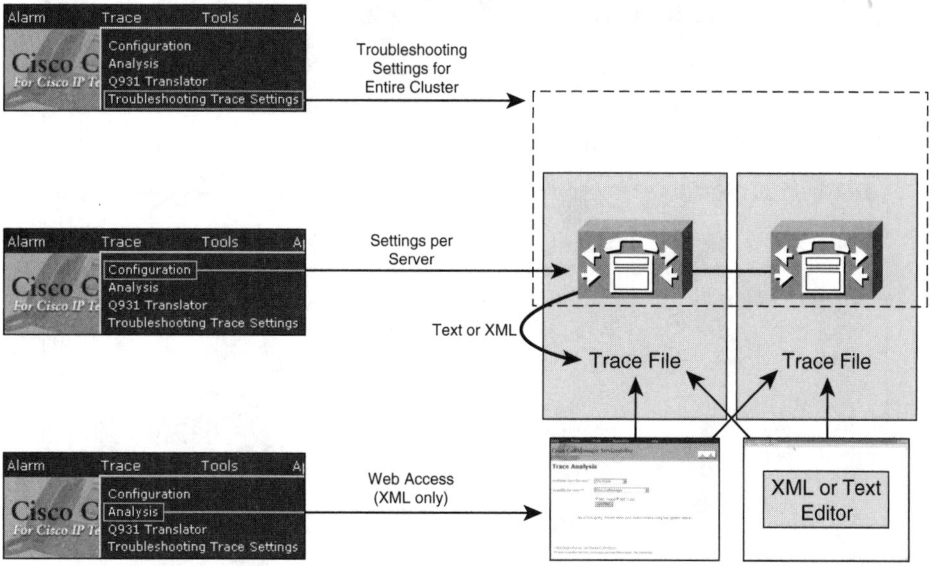

Trace Configuration

Cisco CallManager provides many services for tracing. You can enable tracing for each service individually for each server within the Cisco CallManager cluster. Perform these tasks in the Cisco CallManager Serviceability Trace Configuration window to configure custom settings for a trace:

Step 1 In Cisco CallManager Serviceability, choose **Trace > Configuration** and choose the server where you want to configure the trace settings.

Step 2 From the Configured Services list, choose the service to change the trace settings, as shown in Figure 32-6. The Trace Configuration window opens. Figure 32-7 displays a sample output of that window.

Figure 32-6 *Selecting a Service to Trace*

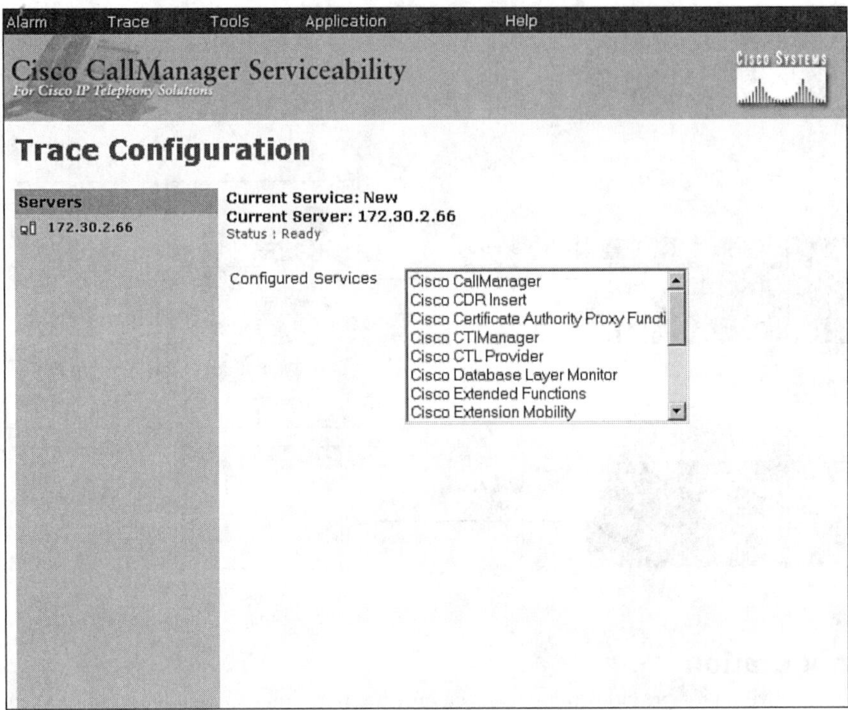

Step 3 To enable traces for the specified service, check the **Trace On** check box.

Step 4 Choose the desired debug level from the **Debug Trace Level** drop-down menu.

Step 5 Choose the trace fields to include in the trace files. This additional information is different for each service.

You can set the path and filename for the trace file. To allow creation of more than one file, Cisco CallManager uses the entered filename and adds an eight-digit string, starting with 00000000, that is incremented with each new file.

Figure 32-7 *Trace Configuration*

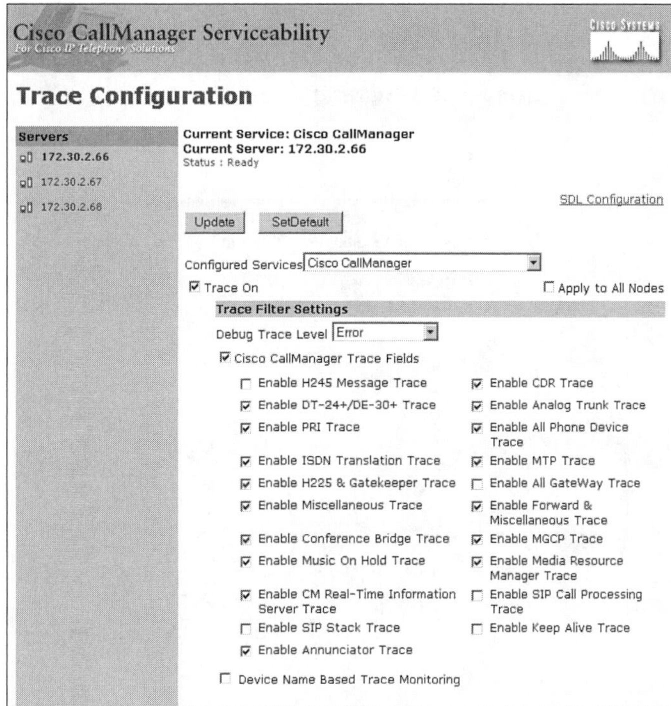

Enabling Clusterwide Trace Settings

The **Troubleshooting Trace Settings** menu item is misleading. This menu item allows you to enable or disable troubleshooting traces on different servers throughout the cluster, as shown in Figure 32-8. This window is usually used for troubleshooting when more than one server needs to be monitored. Each service can be selected or deselected individually for each server.

Figure 32-8 *Enabling Traces Clusterwide*

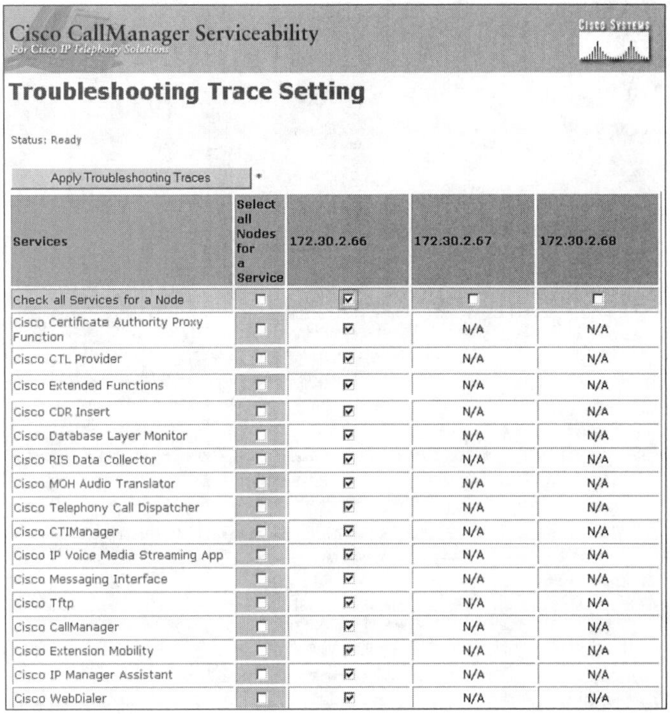

Cisco CallManager Serviceability
For Cisco IP Telephony Solutions
Cisco Systems

Troubleshooting Trace Setting

Status: Ready

Apply Troubleshooting Traces *

Services	Select all Nodes for a Service	172.30.2.66	172.30.2.67	172.30.2.68
Check all Services for a Node	☐	☑	☐	☐
Cisco Certificate Authority Proxy Function	☐	☑	N/A	N/A
Cisco CTL Provider	☐	☑	N/A	N/A
Cisco Extended Functions	☐	☑	N/A	N/A
Cisco CDR Insert	☐	☑	N/A	N/A
Cisco Database Layer Monitor	☐	☑	N/A	N/A
Cisco RIS Data Collector	☐	☑	N/A	N/A
Cisco MOH Audio Translator	☐	☑	N/A	N/A
Cisco Telephony Call Dispatcher	☐	☑	N/A	N/A
Cisco CTIManager	☐	☑	N/A	N/A
Cisco IP Voice Media Streaming App	☐	☑	N/A	N/A
Cisco Messaging Interface	☐	☑	N/A	N/A
Cisco Tftp	☐	☑	N/A	N/A
Cisco CallManager	☐	☑	N/A	N/A
Cisco Extension Mobility	☐	☑	N/A	N/A
Cisco IP Manager Assistant	☐	☑	N/A	N/A
Cisco WebDialer	☐	☑	N/A	N/A

NOTE Servers 172.30.2.67 and 172.30.2.68 shown in Figure 32-8 are currently offline, which is why the Troubleshooting Trace Setting window shows their services as N/A.

Table 32-2 describes the logging of each service that can be turned on or off in the Troubleshooting Trace Setting window.

Table 32-2 *Trace Settings for Multiple Servers*

Service	Logging
Cisco CallManager	Logs Cisco CallManager signaling information to trace files
Cisco Call Detail Records (CDRs) Insert	Logs information about writing of CDRs
Cisco Certificate Authority Proxy Function (CAPF)	Logs information about issues of Cisco CAPF
Cisco CTIManager	Logs information about issues on CTIManager of the Cisco CallManager

Table 32-2 *Trace Settings for Multiple Servers (Continued)*

Service	Logging
Cisco CallManager	Logs Cisco CallManager signaling information to trace files
Cisco Certificate Trust List (CTL) Provider	Logs information about issues of Cisco CTL Provider
Cisco Database Layer Monitor	Logs information about database usage of Cisco CallManager
Cisco Extended Functions	Logs information about issues referring to any of the Cisco CallManager extended functions, such as Quality Report Tool (QRT)
Cisco CallManager Extension Mobility	Logs information about issues of the Cisco CallManager Extension Mobility service and Extension Mobility application
Cisco IP Manager Assistant (IPMA)	Logs information about issues and usage of Cisco IPMA functionality on Cisco CallManager
Cisco IP Voice Media Streaming Application	Logs information about issues of the Cisco IP Voice Media Streaming Application in conjunction with every involved device
Cisco Messaging Interface	Logs information about issues of Cisco Messaging Interface
Cisco Music on Hold (MoH) Audio Translator	Logs information about issues with MoH on Cisco CallManager
Cisco Real-Time Information Server (RIS) Data Collector	Logs information about issues involving collecting real-time information on Cisco CallManager
Cisco Telephony Call Dispatcher (TCD)	Logs information about issues with attendant consoles and pilot points on Cisco CallManager
Cisco TFTP	Logs information about issues with the TFTP server service of Cisco CallManager
Cisco WebDialer	Logs information about issues with the click-to-dial functionality on Cisco CallManager systems

Trace Analysis

The Trace Analysis tool is a postprocessing tool that allows analyzing of XML trace files via a web GUI. The tool is available from the **Cisco CallManager Serviceability Trace** menu and provides trace details to help narrow your investigation of system problems.

When you are using the Trace Analysis tool, it is possible to specify what kind of information you need when analyzing the Cisco CallManager trace files. When troubleshooting, this makes it easier to go through the trace files and get the necessary information.

In the Trace Analysis window, choose what kind of information to analyze and from which trace file by following these steps:

Step 1 From the Cisco CallManager Serviceability window, select the **Trace > Analysis** menu item.

Step 2 Choose a Cisco CallManager server for which trace files should be analyzed.

Step 3 Choose the desired service, as shown in Figure 32-9.

Figure 32-9 *Choosing XML Trace Files Using the Trace Analysis Tool*

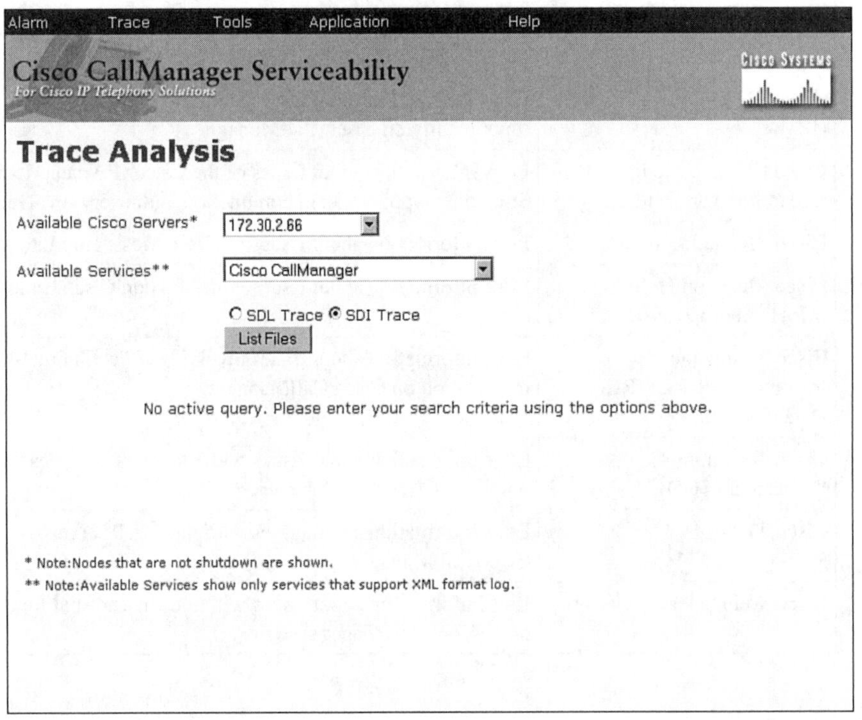

Step 4 Define whether to analyze SDI or SDL traces and click the **List Files** button to get the list of all available SDI or SDL files that meet the criteria.

Step 5 Choose the file to analyze.

Step 6 Open the Cisco CallManager Serviceability web GUI of the Trace Analysis tool. In the web GUI, define what information to list for the analysis.

Step 7 To process the records that meet your criteria, click **Display Records**.

> **NOTE** The Trace Analysis tool supports only trace files containing less than 2 MB of data.

From the selections that you made for trace analysis, Cisco CallManager creates a web page giving all the desired data. Figure 32-10 shows an example output.

Figure 32-10 *Analyzing XML Trace Files Using the Trace Analysis Tool*

e	1,100,119,1.4		Cisco CallManagerDeviceManager:initialized_DeviceStart Name=MTP_ADTECCCM Key={B5B92ED6-5973-415E-A840-A43659B2283D} RegisterDevice=1
e	1,100,119,1.4		Cisco CallManagerDeviceManager::insertDeviceInfo - Name=MTP_ADTECCCM Key={B5B92ED6-5973-415E-A840-A43659B2283D} Pid=(1,56,1)
			Cisco CallManagerDB search devName : MTP_ADTECCCM, boxPid 38 devPid 30 httpLvl 1
			Cisco CallManagercreateFile: File Global\CCMMEDIARESOURCETABLEMAPFILE0 already exist
			Cisco CallManager*--RISCMAccess::DeviceRegister(...)
e	0,0,0,0.0		Cisco CallManagerNew connection accepted. DeviceName=, TCPPid = [1.100.132.2], IPAddr=172.30.2.66, Port=0, Device Controller=[0,0,0]
e	0,0,0,0.0		Cisco CallManagerNew connection accepted. DeviceName=, TCPPid = [1.100.132.3], IPAddr=172.30.2.66, Port=0, Device Controller=[0,0,0]
e	1,100,119,1.5		Cisco CallManagerStationInit: (0000000) InboundStim - StationRegisterMessageId [Resource Device priority]:
e	1,100,119,1.6		Cisco CallManagerProcessing StationReg. regCount: 1 DeviceName=CFB_ADTECCCM, TCPPid = [1.100.132.2], IPAddr=172.30.2.66, Port=0, Device Controller=[1,126,1]
e	1,100,126,1.1		Cisco CallManagerUnicastBridgeControl - Started Request from TCPPid = [1.100.132.2]
e	1,100,119,1.6		Cisco CallManagerUnicastBridgeControl::StationRegister received from = CFB_ADTECCCM, TCPPid = [1.100.132.2]
e	1,100,119,1.6		Cisco CallManagerUnicastBridgeControl::StationRegister MaxStream=48, ActiveStream=0 CurrentStream=0
e	1,100,119,1.6		Cisco CallManagerUnicastBridgeControl - stationOutputRegisterAck KeepAliveInterval=30 TCPPid = [1.100.132.2]
e	1,100,119,1.6		Cisco CallManagerUnicastBridgeControl - stationOutputCapabilitiesReq TCPPid = [1.100.132.2]
e	1,100,119,1.7		Cisco CallManagerStationInit: (0000000) InboundStim - StationRegisterMessageId [Normal Device priority]:
e	1,100,119,1.8		Cisco CallManagerProcessing StationReg. regCount: 1 DeviceName=ANN_ADTECCCM, TCPPid = [1.100.132.3], IPAddr=172.30.2.66, Port=0, Device Controller=[1,12,1]
e	1,100,119,1.8		Cisco CallManagerAnnDControl - Started for device= ANN_ADTECCCM Type=126 -- Registration Request received
e	1,100,119,1.8		Cisco CallManagerAnnDControl - Tsp Received for device= ANN_ADTECCCM -- Capabilities Requested From Device
e	1,100,119,1.8		Cisco CallManagerAnnDControl - stationOutputRegisterAck KeepAliveInterval=30 TCPPid = [1.100.132.3]
e	1,100,119,1.8		Cisco CallManagerAnnDControl - stationOutputCapabilitiesReq tcpHandle=1
			Cisco CallManager--*RISCMAccess::DeviceRegister(...)

You can directly open trace files from the folders where they are stored (subdirectories under C:\Program Files\Cisco\Trace). You can use text editors (for XML and .txt files) or XML viewers or editors to view XML files. Trace files in .txt format cannot be analyzed by using the Trace Analysis tool. They can be analyzed by the Q.931 Translator tool; however, this tool interprets only Q.931 messages. To examine other messages from stored .txt trace files, you can use a text editor, as shown in Figure 32-11. Cisco TAC also provides other in-depth trace analysis tools such as Translator X, Triple Combo, and the Voice Log Translator (VLT).

Figure 32-11 *Analyzing TXT Trace Files*

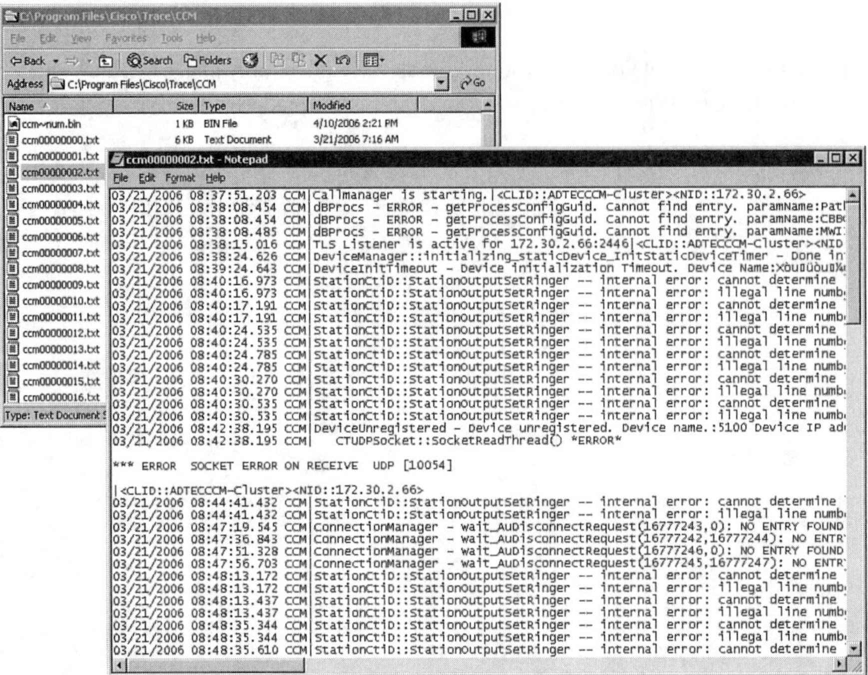

Trace Collection

To analyze trace files of a Cisco CallManager system locally on an administrator PC, it is necessary to collect trace files from the Cisco CallManager file system and copy them to the PC of the administrator. Instead of manually copying all trace files from all servers of the cluster, you can use the Trace Collection tool, which automates this process.

If you want to analyze trace files from multiple servers on your local PC, use the Trace Collection tool to transfer the trace files to your local PC, where they can then be analyzed by the Bulk Trace Analysis tool or a text editor. There are three steps involved, as illustrated in Figure 32-12:

Step 1 When traces are enabled, Cisco CallManager writes trace information to the local trace files.

Step 2 The Trace Collection tool can be used to download all trace files (including XML trace files) from all Cisco CallManager systems in the cluster.

Step 3 The Bulk Trace Analysis tool allows analysis of XML trace files at the administrator PC. You can view text files using a text editor.

Figure 32-12 *Remote Analysis of Trace Files*

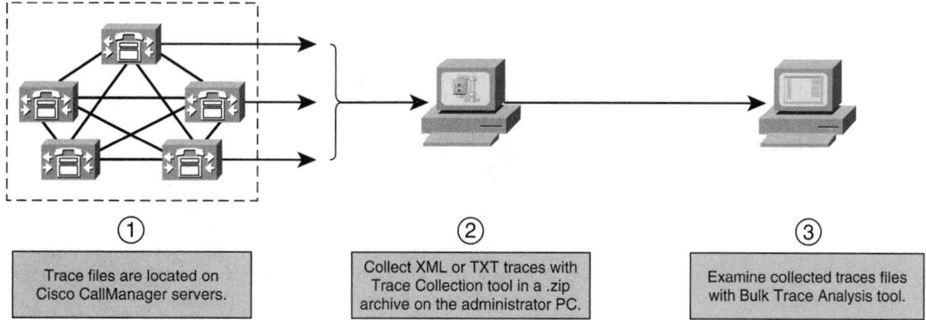

The Trace Collection Tool

The Trace Collection tool allows you to collect trace information for any Cisco CallManager service of any Cisco CallManager throughout the cluster, including the time and date of the trace for that service. You can run this tool on any PC on the network because it is available from the Cisco CallManager Install Plugins window.

After the Trace Collection tool is installed on the PC, enter the IP address, username, and password for Cisco CallManager. As soon as the connection to the server is established, the window shown in Figure 32-13 opens.

Figure 32-13 *Trace Collection Tool*

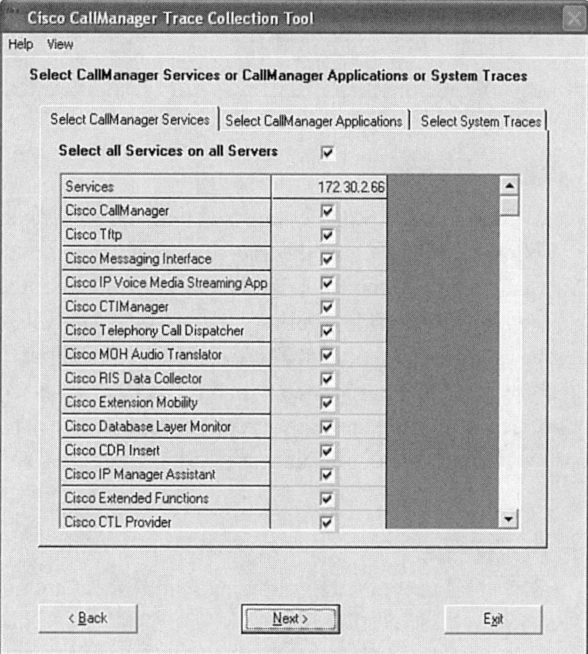

Three tabs are available in the Cisco CallManager Trace Collection Tool window. Each has its own function, as described in Table 32-3.

Table 32-3 *Tab Functions in the Cisco CallManager Trace Collection Tool Window*

Tab	Function
Select CallManager Services	Provides a grid of services for the Cisco CallManager nodes in the cluster. Choose all or some of the services for which traces should be collected by checking the appropriate check boxes.
Select CallManager Applications	Provides the list of Cisco CallManager applications for which traces can be collected. Choose all or some of the applications in this tab.
Select System Traces	Provides a list of all system logs from which data can be selected.

NOTE The **Back** and **Next** buttons shown in Figure 32-13 move you between the three tabs.

After selecting the desired system logs, define the date range for the data to be selected to help minimize the amount of data that needs to be collected. You can then click the **Collect Traces** button for the application to start downloading and compressing all files locally to the PC. All files are added to the system primary hard drive (C:\) to an archive named CiscoCallManagerTraceCollection.zip.

CAUTION Selecting all kinds of data from all Cisco CallManager servers on the system leads to extremely long download times, extensive file-compression processing, and large compressed files.

Bulk Trace Analysis

The Bulk Trace Analysis tool is a postprocessing tool that allows analyzing XML trace files on every PC locally. You must first download the trace files that you want to analyze using the Trace Collection tool. You can download the Bulk Trace Analysis tool from the Cisco CallManager Install Plugins window. This tool works similarly to the Trace Analysis web GUI on Cisco CallManager, but it has some extra features. These extra features allow the user of the Bulk Trace Analysis tool to analyze files more easily than with the Trace Analysis web GUI. This tool is ideal to analyze trace files received from external sources because you only need the trace files for the analysis and not access to the Cisco CallManager system where they were created.

Bulk Trace Analysis Features

The Bulk Trace Analysis tool supports the following features that are not provided within the Trace Analysis web GUI on Cisco CallManager:

- It creates reports of information that can be analyzed for troubleshooting, using multiple trace files as the input source data.
- It allows multiple views of a single report to compare and analyze multiple issues simultaneously and concentrate on essential fields.
- It allows users to customize report formats, sort trace information by type, and filter information by special trace tags as well as date and time.
- It allows saving and printing of reports for further analysis.
- It works without using Cisco CallManager processing power because it runs locally on a PC.
- You can use it to analyze large trace files (larger than 2 MB).

Using Bulk Trace Analysis

Figure 32-14 shows the analysis of an XML trace file using the Bulk Trace Analysis tool.

Figure 32-14 *Using Bulk Trace Analysis*

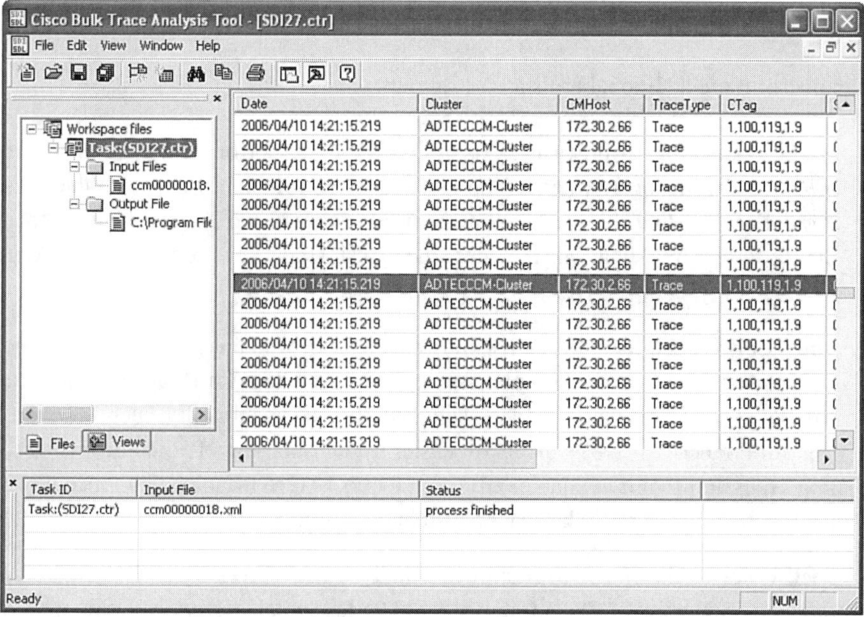

To generate this report, choose **File > New Report**. In the window that opens, choose whether to create an SDI or an SDL report and where the file for analysis is located. To add new views for the report, choose **View > New View**. In the window that opens, choose which kind of information should be included in the new view. To change the order of the columns or to add or remove columns, choose **View > Customize Header** and make the selections from the new window.

Additional Trace Tools

You can analyze the voice network using many additional trace tools provided by Cisco and other vendors. Table 32-4 summarizes the situations that might require you to use these tools.

Table 32-4 *Additional Trace Tools*

Tool	Use	Available From
Q.931 Translator	Analyzes Q.931 messages from Cisco CallManager logs	Cisco CallManager Serviceability
Voice Log Translator	Analyzes voice flows from Cisco CallManager logs	Cisco TAC or Cisco.com Voice Downloads page
Dick Tracy	Analyzes voice flow on T1/E1 and FXS ports on Cisco Catalyst 6500 systems	Cisco.com
Ethereal	Captures network traffic, which also allows you to analyze voice traffic on the network	Ethereal.com

Examples of those additional tools are as follows:

- **Q.931 Translator**—Allows analysis of Q.931 messages from text or XML log files created on Cisco CallManager systems. The tool shows the ISDN messages and their Cisco IOS translation. The Q.931 Translator can be used to save Cisco IOS translations to another log file for further investigation. To access the Q.931 Translator, from Cisco CallManager Serviceability, choose **Trace > Q931 Translator**.
- **Voice Log Translator**—Formerly known as X-Log, which is a standalone application that can be used to analyze the complete voice flow from Cisco CallManager log files. The tool is based on Q.931 Translator but adds some additional functionality, such as Skinny Client Control Protocol (SCCP) support for easier troubleshooting of voice flow issues. The Voice Log Translator tool is available only from Cisco TAC to troubleshoot voice flows on nonfunctioning Cisco CallManager systems.
- **Dick Tracy**—Allows you to capture and analyze voice flows on T1/E1 or Foreign Exchange Station (FXS) ports of Cisco Catalyst 6500 Series switch systems running the CatOS. To download the Dick Tracy tool from Cisco.com, you must hold a valid Cisco.com account. This tool is available to users with valid CCO account access at http://www.cisco.com/cgi-bin/tablebuild.pl/dctool.

- **Ethereal**—One of the most powerful, open-source network capture and analysis tools. It supports analysis of nearly all types of packets captured from the network. For voice analysis, it includes special features, such as painting graphs of voice over IP (VoIP) signaling flows or saving G.711 Real-Time Transport Protocol (RTP) streams as .au files for playback with media players. Ethereal is available for free at http://www.ethereal.com.

Summary

This chapter discussed the use of the alarm and trace features of Cisco CallManager. Eight alarm levels are available on Cisco CallManager, which map to the syslog levels used by Cisco routers and switches. The alarm configuration allows you to define where CallManager should save alarms and what level of information the server should include.

Administrators can define the type and format of information that CallManager writes to trace files. To analyze trace files, you can use the Serviceability Web interface, the Trace Analysis tool, or a simple text or XML editor. The Trace Collection tool allows you to download and compress CallManager trace files to a local PC. You can then analyze the trace files using the Bulk Trace Analysis tool. Additional trace tools provided by Cisco and other vendors allow administrators to further analyze their voice network.

Review Questions

You can find the solutions to these questions in Appendix A, "Answers to Review Questions."

1. What does Cisco CallManager Serviceability Alarm menu provide? (Choose two.)
   a. Configuration of alarms
   b. Alarm analysis
   c. Alarm message definitions
   d. Configuration of traces
   e. Alarm modification
2. When you are configuring alarms on Cisco CallManager Serviceability, which of the following statements is true?
   a. You can define an e-mail address to which you can send alerts.
   b. It is possible to define which fields should be included in written SDI and SDL trace files.
   c. More than one destination can be used to write alarm logs in parallel, and each of them can use its own alarm level.
   d. Alarm levels are predefined on Cisco CallManager and cannot be changed.

3. What is the difference between configuring alarms for Java applications and configuring alarms for other services on Cisco CallManager?

   a. Nothing; the alarms are both configured from CallManager Serviceability.

   b. Java applications are not able to be monitored using Cisco CallManager.

   c. Alarms for Java applications use system resources more heavily.

   d. You must enable Java application alarms through the Windows Registry.

4. Which three of the following statements about SDI and SDL traces are true?

   a. SDI traces log services and run-time events.

   b. SDL traces log services and run-time events.

   c. SDI traces log call-processing information.

   d. SDL traces log call-processing information.

   e. SDI and SDL traces can be written to plaintext and XML files.

   f. SDI and SDL traces can be written to plaintext files only.

   g. SDI and SDL traces can be written to XML files only.

5. What does the Trace Collection tool do?

   a. Collects traces from Cisco CallManager systems and writes them to remote hosts

   b. Allows you to configure the kind of information that should be collected and written to trace files

   c. Downloads and compresses trace files from Cisco CallManager systems to a computer

   d. Saves disk space on Cisco CallManager by deleting trace files after downloading them

6. What can you do with the web-based Trace Analysis tool in Cisco CallManager Serviceability? (Choose two.)

   a. Analyze plaintext-formatted SDI trace files.

   b. Analyze plaintext-formatted SDL trace files.

   c. Analyze XML-formatted SDI trace files.

   d. Analyze XML-formatted SDL trace files.

   e. Analyze files larger than 2 MB.

7. What is the difference between the Q.931 Translator and the Voice Log Translator?
   a. Q.931 Translator supports SCCP.
   b. Q.931 Translator supports MGCP.
   c. The Voice Log Translator can be used to analyze log files without access to the Cisco CallManager system.
   d. The Q.931 translator is provided for free, but to use Voice Log Translator, you must pay a special license fee.
8. Which services support SDL trace logging? (Choose two.)
   a. Cisco TFTP
   b. Cisco CallManager
   c. Database Layer Monitor
   d. CTIManager
   e. SDI Monitor
9. You receive an alarm level 5 message coming in from the Cisco CallManager service. What well-known name is this alarm level assigned?
   a. Emergency
   b. Error
   c. Critical
   d. Alert
10. Which of the following represent a valid CallManager alarm destination? (Choose three.)
   a. Microsoft Event Log
   b. Syslog Server
   c. SMTP Server
   d. Trace Log File

This chapter covers the following topics:

- Describing the uses, features, and operation of the CAR tool
- Explaining the contents of CDR and CMR
- Explaining the three levels of CAR users and the reporting capabilities of each
- Explaining the types of CAR reports and which user levels can generate them
- Configuring CAR system parameters
- Configuring the system schedule to schedule daily, weekly, and monthly reports
- Configuring CAR alerts when the database size exceeds a configured threshold
- Generating, viewing, or mailing user reports using CAR

CHAPTER 33

Configuring CAR

The Call Detail Record (CDR) Analysis and Reporting (CAR) tool is a powerful application that gives an overview of the call volume of users or departments. CAR can also generate reports for special route patterns and features such as Client Matter Codes (CMC) and Forced Authorization Codes (FAC). This chapter discusses the concepts and configuration behind CAR and the applications for a corporate IP telephony deployment.

CAR Overview

The Cisco CallManager Serviceability CAR tool, formerly known as Administrative Reporting Tool (ART), generates reports of information for quality of service (QoS), traffic, user call volume, billing, and gateways. The CAR tool generates reports in either Portable Document Format (PDF) or Comma-Separated Values (CSV) format. The PDF format limits the number of records in the CAR reports to 5000, and CSV format limits the number of records to 20,000. If the number of records exceeds these limits, a message warns that the results are truncated. To avoid truncating reports, reduce the date range and regenerate the reports.

> **NOTE** CAR is not installed during the standard Cisco CallManager installation and must be added separately.

If CAR is running on your system before you upgrade to a new version of Cisco CallManager, the upgrade process automatically upgrades CAR. If Cisco CallManager is being installed for the first time, CAR has to be installed manually from the Cisco CallManager Administration. You can install CAR from the standard plug-ins web page (**Application > Install Plugins**). You must install CAR on the Cisco CallManager publisher that hosts the CDR database. CAR uses the Cisco Tomcat service.

CDRs and CMRs

Call detail records (CDRs) and Call Management Records (CMRs) are both stored in the CDR database, accessible with the Microsoft SQL Server Enterprise Manager. Choose **Start > Programs > Microsoft SQL Server > Enterprise Manager** to open the Microsoft SQL Server Enterprise Manager on the Cisco CallManager publisher. Both types of records store information about a call. The CDR table stores details about the call itself, whereas the CMR table stores information about QoS parameters for the same call. The SQL database refers to the CDR and CMR tables as CallDetailRecord (for CDRs) and CallDetailRecordDiagnostic (for CMRs), as shown in Figure 33-1. For every CDR entry, CallManager also generates a CMR entry.

Figure 33-1 *CDR and CMR Tables in the SQL 2000 Database*

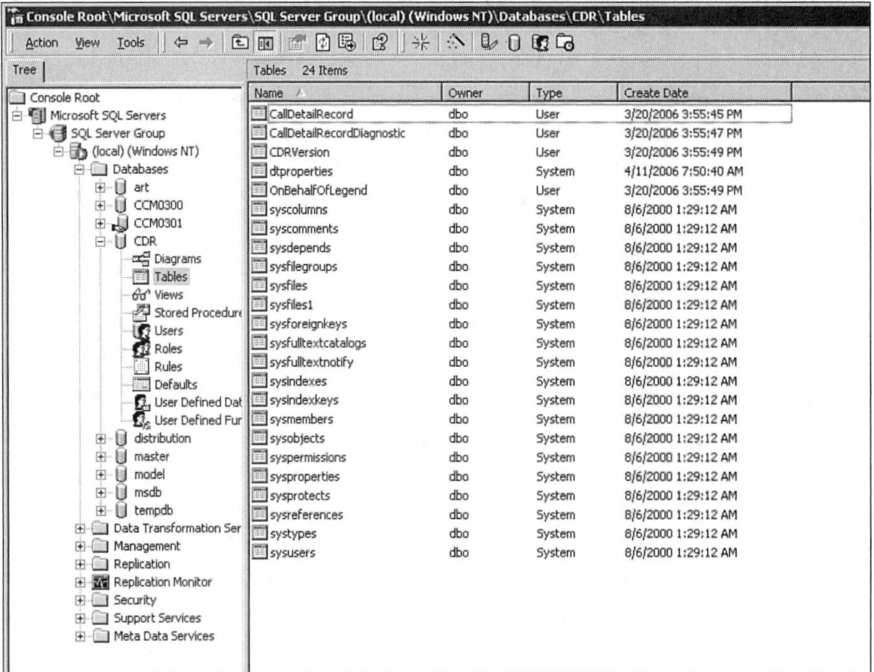

> **NOTE** When you purge a record in the CDR database, CallManager deletes the related entries for a call in both the CallDetailRecord and CallDetailRecordDiagnostic tables.

The CallDetailRecord table stores extensive information about a call. Each record has a unique identifier called the *pkid* that enables you to find and identify a single record. The CallDetailRecord table also contains information about the calling party, called party, duration of or information about call forwarding, CMC, and FAC, to name the most important fields of a record. In total, the CallDetailRecord table contains 68 information fields.

The number of columns for the CallDetailRecordDiagnostic table, in contrast to the CallDetailRecord table, is very small. It has only 18 information fields. A unique identifier (pkid) for every call is included in the CallDetailRecordDiagnostic table as well. The pkid for a call in the CallDetailRecordDiagnostic table is not the same as the pkid for the same call in the CallDetailRecord table. To reference a call in the tables, use the oriLegCallIdentifier and destLegIdentifier field information. Among other things, information about the packets sent and received, jitter, and latency are stored for QoS reports.

CAR Users

CAR has a distinct management interface from the Cisco CallManager Administration and Serviceability web pages, as shown in Figure 33-2. The available menus in CAR depend on the level of the user authenticating to the system. CAR provides reporting capabilities for three levels of users:

- **Administrators** can generate system reports for load balancing, system performance, and troubleshooting. The administrator can also grant administrator access to other users, configure the dial plan and gateway, and set the system preferences.
- **Managers** can generate reports for users, departments, and QoS. The reports provide information for budgeting or security purposes and for determining the voice quality of the calls in their department.
- **Individual users** can generate a billing report for their own calls.

Figure 33-2 *CDR Analysis and Reporting Administrative Interface*

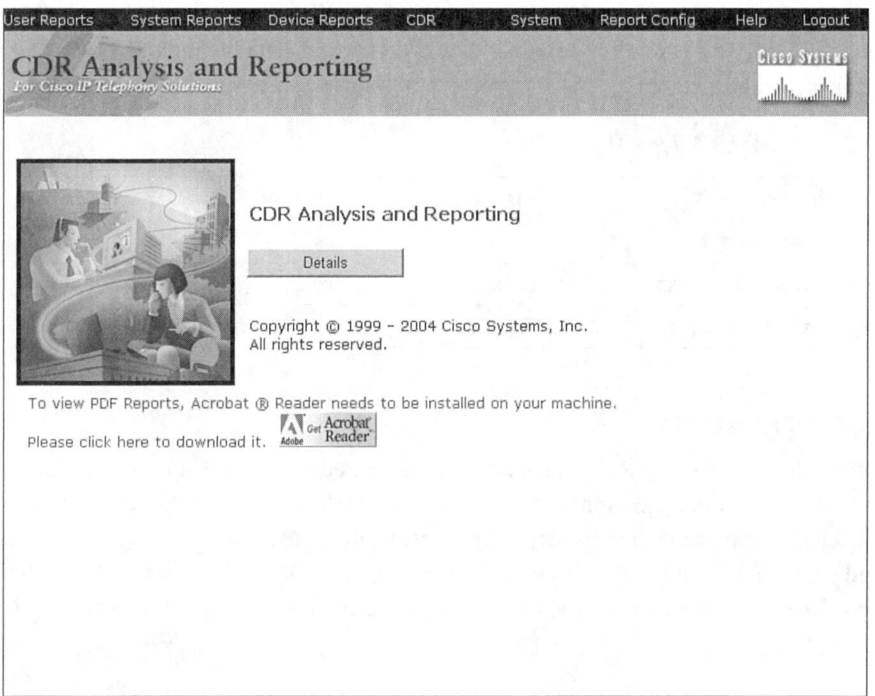

CAR Report Types and User Levels

There are three report types available in CAR:

- **User Reports**—Allows you to generate reports for bills, Top N users, Cisco IP Manager Assistant (IPMA), computer telephony integration (CTI), and phone services. Bills can be generated for individual users, groups of users, or all users. With the Top N report, it is easy to find, for example, the top five users with the highest cost, highest call duration, or highest number of calls.
- **System Reports**—Allows you to generate reports for QoS, traffic, and malicious calls. With these reports, it is possible to find part of the network where QoS does not work properly or where there is more traffic than planned in the design phase. Reports for Multilevel Precedence and Preemption (MLPP), CMC, and FAC are also available for information about the cost of projects or controlled long-distance calls with authorization codes.
- **Device Reports**—Generates information about the gateway, route plans, conferences, and voice messaging. These kinds of reports are useful for the administrator in optimizing the network.

The administrator can generate all types of reports: user reports, system reports, and device reports. Managers can generate only parts of the user and system reports, such as billing, Top N, and QoS reports, and only for employees who report directly or indirectly to the manager. Users can check only their own bills in general or in detail, and send the report by e-mail. Table 33-1 summarizes these rights.

Table 33-1 *Report and User Type Matrix*

Report	Administrator	Manager	User
User Reports	Full Access	Bills, Top N	Only their own bills
System Reports	Full Access	QoS	No Access
Device Reports	Full Access	No Access	No Access

CAR Configuration

The configuration of CAR is done through a web-based interface that uses the same look and feel as the Cisco CallManager Administration and Serviceability windows. After you have installed the CDR application on the publisher server, a new CDR Analysis and Reporting menu item appears under the **Tools** menu of the Cisco CallManager in a similar fashion to the Bulk Administration Tool. The following sections walk you through the configuration and use of the CAR utility.

Initial Configuration

You must initially access the CAR web interface through the CallManager Serviceability window by using the **Tools > CDR Analysis and Reporting** option. This menu option will only exist after you have installed the CDR application on the publisher server through the Install Plug-ins window. When initially accessing the CAR web interface, the authentication settings will be in a strange state. Even if you have enabled Multilevel Administration (MLA) for Cisco CallManager, you must use a default login to CAR of a username of admin and a password of admin.

> **NOTE** After you have initially configured the CAR utility, users (and managers) will be able to access the utility at https://<*Publisher IP Address*>/ART.

After you have authenticated, the only available option is the **Admin Rights** menu. Selecting this option takes you to the window illustrated in Figure 33-3.

Figure 33-3 *Initial CDR Admin Rights Window*

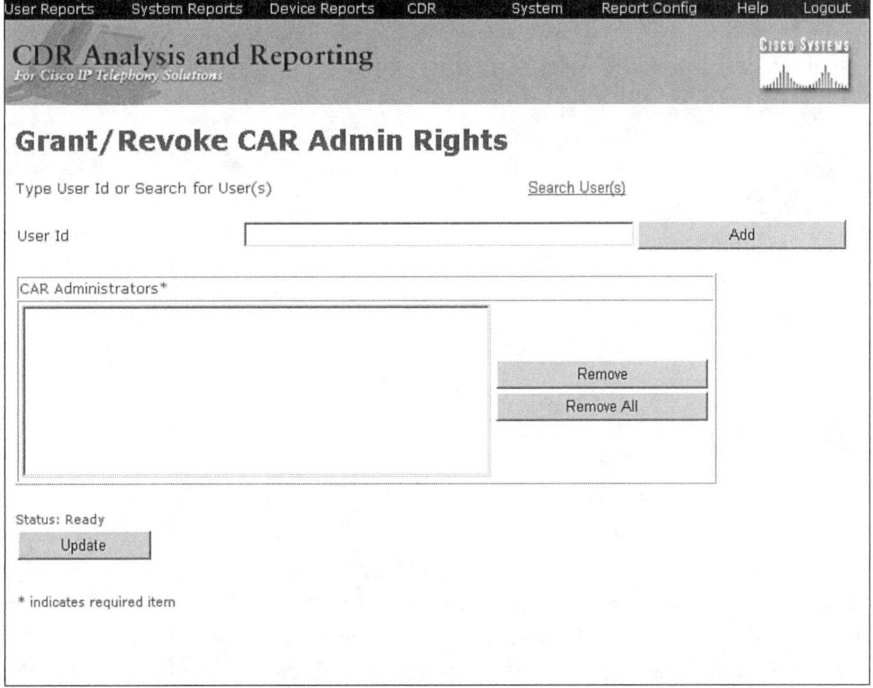

From here, you must add the initial CDR user from the CallManager database (or Windows database if you have not enabled MLA). CDR Analysis and Reporting immediately places this initial user into the CDR Administrators group, giving this user full administrative privileges to the web interface.

NOTE Following the addition of the first user, CallManager disables the default username and password of admin.

CAR System Parameter Menu Configuration

After you have added the initial administrator to the CAR system, you must log in as the new user. After a successful authentication, you will be able to see all CAR menu options. As part of the initial setup, most administrators will configure the **System > Service Parameters** menu option, shown in Figure 33-4.

Figure 33-4 *Configuring CDR Service Parameters*

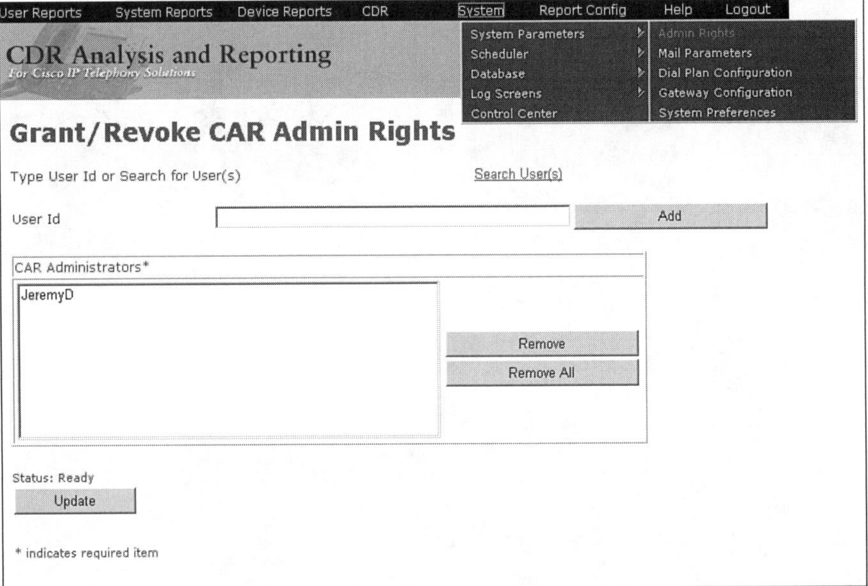

You can configure additional CAR administrators by using the CAR tool itself. Choose **System > System Parameters > Admin Rights** to assign administrative rights to any user in the Cisco CallManager user database. The manager and user levels are not configured in the CAR tool. These roles are based on the user configuration in the global directory. In Cisco CallManager Administration, choose **User > Global Directory** to edit users in the global directory. For each user, you can configure the user ID of the manager of the user in the **Manager User ID** field. CAR assigns users who you have configured as managers to the manager level in CAR. CAR assigns all other users to the user level in CAR.

You can configure the additional Service Parameters menu items as follows:

- The **Mail Parameters** option allows you to configure an SMTP server allowing the CDR Analysis and Reporting tool to send alarms and e-mails to administrators directly.
- Cisco has configured CAR to categorize calls using the North American Numbering Plan (NANP). If your organization uses additional dial plans (such as interoffice dialing), you can add them to CAR using the **Dial Plan Configuration** menu item. This gives CAR the ability to classify call types correctly on reports. CAR classifies external calls based on the outside number.
- In the **Gateway Configuration** menu item, you can provide the maximum number of ports information for each gateway to enable CAR to generate accurate utilization reports.
- Use the **System Preferences** menu item to specify generic parameters, such as the company name, that CAR will insert in every report.

These items are discussed further in the following sections.

Administration Rights and Mail Parameters

Choose **System Parameters > Admin Rights** to grant or revoke administrative rights to users from the Lightweight Directory Access Protocol (LDAP) directory. You can search for users in the LDAP directory or directly enter the user ID. As stated earlier, access rights for managers and users are not granted in the CAR tool but are derived from the roles configured in Cisco CallManager Administration.

CAR can send reports by e-mail. To enable this feature, choose **System Parameters > Mail Parameters** and configure the e-mail account information. Enter the mail ID and the password that CAR will use, as shown in Figure 33-5. This e-mail account must exist on the mail server. You also need to specify the mail domain and the mail server name. The mail domain is added automatically when a user enters only the name of the recipient without the mail domain. Every time a report is sent with the CAR tool, this account will be used.

Figure 33-5 *Configuring CDR Mail Parameters*

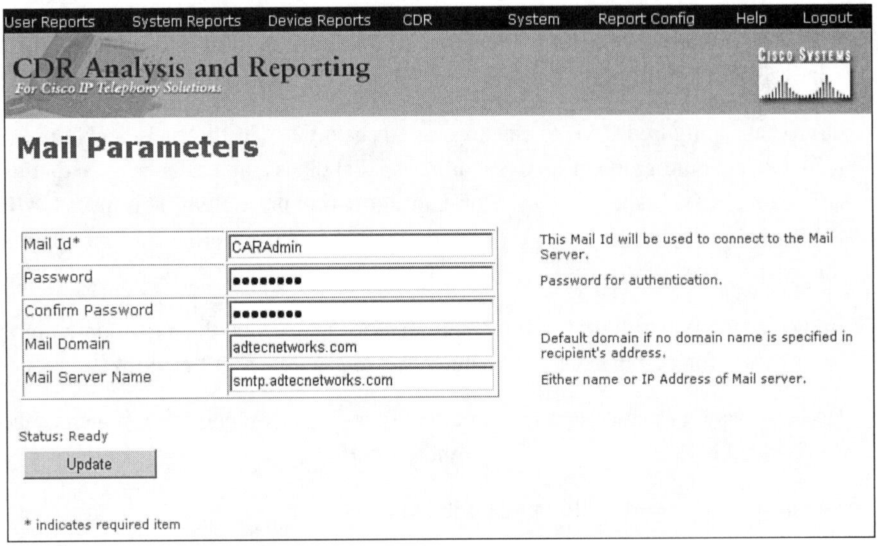

Dial Plan Configuration

The default dial plan in CAR specifies the NANP, as shown in Figure 33-6. To configure the dial plan, define the parameters for outgoing call classifications. Call classifications include International, Local, Long Distance, On Net, and Others. For example, if local calls in the area are six digits in length, specify a row in the dial plan as follows:

- **Condition— =**
- **No of Digits— 6**
- **Pattern— !**
- **Call Type— Local**

Figure 33-6 *Configuring CDR Dial Plan Parameters*

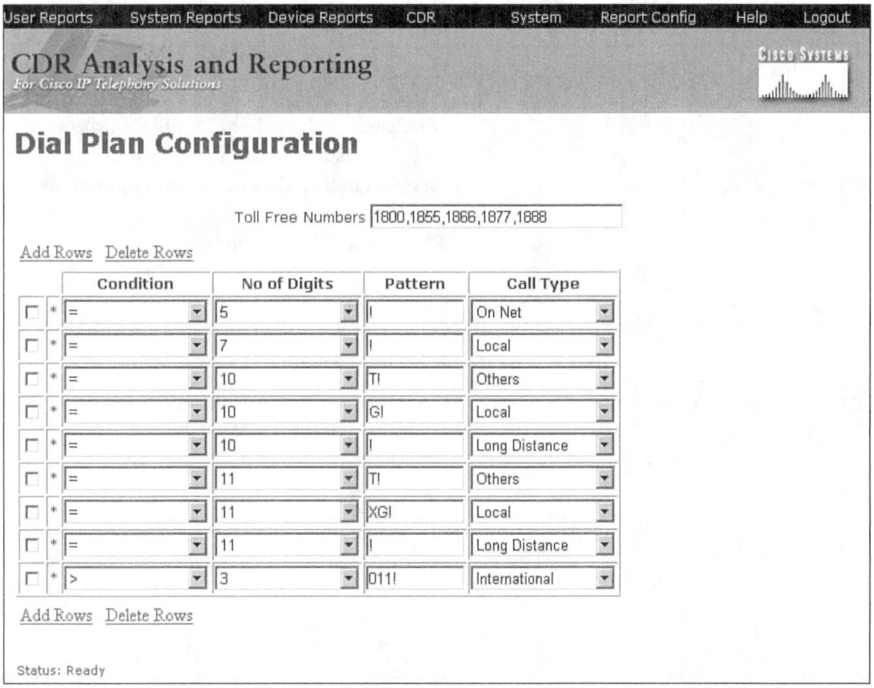

Table 33-2 describes the parameters in the Dial Plan Configuration window and lists their possible values.

Table 33-2 *Explanation of CAR Dial Plan Parameters*

Parameter	Possible Values	Description
Condition	> < =	Condition of the rule—greater than (>), less than (<), or equal to (=) the specified value in the **No of Digits** field.
No of Digits	NA A digit	Number of digits in the directory number (DN) to which this rule should be applied. If the number of digits does not affect the rule, specify **NA**.

continues

Table 33-2 *Explanation of CAR Dial Plan Parameters (Continued)*

Parameter	Possible Values	Description
Pattern	G T ! X	Used for the call classification: **G** means that the call is classified as specified in the rule (that is, G is a wildcard for the gateway area codes specified in the "Gateway Configuration" section). **T** retrieves toll-free numbers. **!** signifies multiple digits. **X** signifies a single-digit number.
Call Type	International Local Long Distance On Net Others	Choose this call type if the condition is satisfied.
Toll-free Numbers	Digits	Numbers in the dial plan that can be placed without a charge.

Gateway and System Preferences

Configure the gateways in CAR before using the CAR gateway reports, and update the gateway configuration every time you add a new gateway to the Cisco CallManager Administration. When you delete gateways in Cisco CallManager Administration, CAR automatically deletes them from its tracking. CAR uses the area code information, shown in Figure 33-7, to determine whether calls are local or long distance. Provide the maximum number of ports information for each gateway to enable CAR to generate the utilization reports. Remember, **G** is a wildcard for the gateway area codes used in dial plan configuration.

Figure 33-7 *Configuring CDR Gateway Parameters*

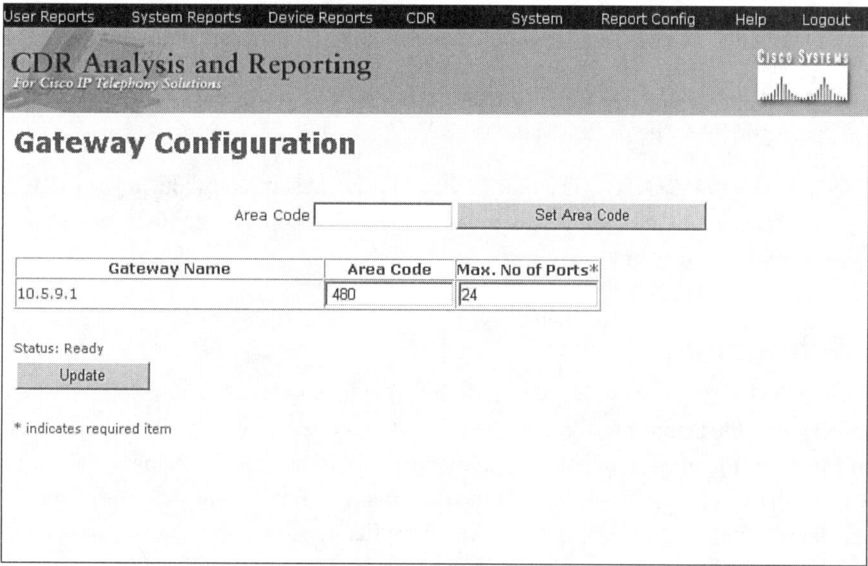

CAR uses the values you configured for the gateway when you added the gateway in Cisco CallManager Administration. Therefore, some gateways might already have an area code setting or have a maximum number of ports.

CAR provides default system preferences, shown in Figure 33-8.

Figure 33-8 *Configuring CDR System Preferences Parameters*

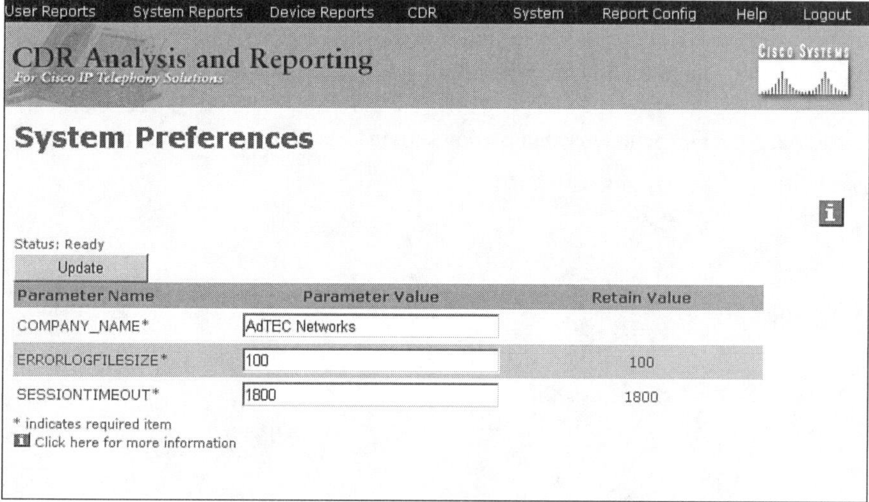

The following list provides a brief description of each of these fields:

- **COMPANY_NAME**—The company name is used as header information in reports.
- **ERRORLOGFILESIZE**—The maximum size of the error log file in kilobytes, with a range from 1 to 9999. The default value is 100.
- **SESSIONTIMEOUT**—The time in seconds that must pass without any activity before a user is logged out of CAR, with a range from 60 to 86,400 (1 minute to 24 hours). The default value is 1800 (30 minutes).

Report Scheduling

Every Cisco CallManager writes the CDR data first locally into flat files. A flat file is a temporary file without a file extension stored in the C:\Program Files\Cisco\CallDetail\ folder on Cisco CallManager. Flat files store call information to import the data on the publisher server into the CDR database. At a specified time, all the CallManager servers transfer the flat files to the Cisco CallManager publisher. Loading CDR data from flat files into the CDR database on the Cisco CallManager publisher can cause performance degradation on the Cisco CallManager server. Cisco recommends that you use the default loading time or schedule the loading to occur at a time when Cisco CallManager performance will be least affected. By default, CDR data loads every day from midnight to 5:00 a.m.

You can manage CDR loading through the **System** > **Scheduler** menu, as shown in Figure 33-9. These menu options are discussed fully in the upcoming sections. Disable CDR loading when you are installing or upgrading the system in the same off-hours during which CDR loading normally occurs. Because loading CDRs drains Cisco CallManager resources, you can suspend CDR loads until other operations complete. Of course, CallManager does not update the CDR data when CDR loading is disabled. Be sure to enable CDR loading again as soon as possible. The CAR tool does not affect CDR generation in Cisco CallManager.

In addition, the CDR Scheduler menu allows you to generate reports for these periods:

- Days
- Weeks
- Months

Figure 33-9 *Configuring CDR Scheduler Parameters*

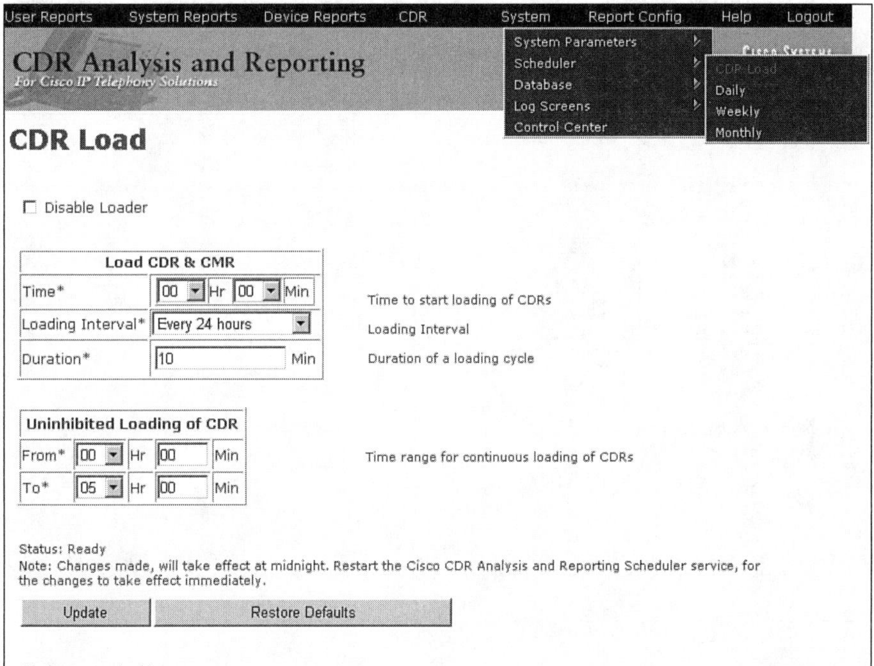

Managing the CDR Load

You can use the CDR Load menu to enable and disable the CDR load. Disable loading if you are upgrading the Cisco CallManager in the time specified for CDRs to load. Otherwise, the CDR load could consume critical system resources.

Configure the Load CDR & CMR area parameters as follows, shown in Figure 33-10:

- The **Time** field specifies time when the CAR tool should start to load CDR data from the local CDR files into the CAR database.
- The **Loading Interval** specifies how often CAR will load the CDR entries. The minimum interval is 15 minutes and the maximum is 24 hours.
- The Uninhibited Loading of CDR section allows you to define the duration of the loading interval defined to limit the loading time to a maximum length to minimize the impact on Cisco CallManager resources during business hours.

Figure 33-10 *Configuring CDR Load Parameters*

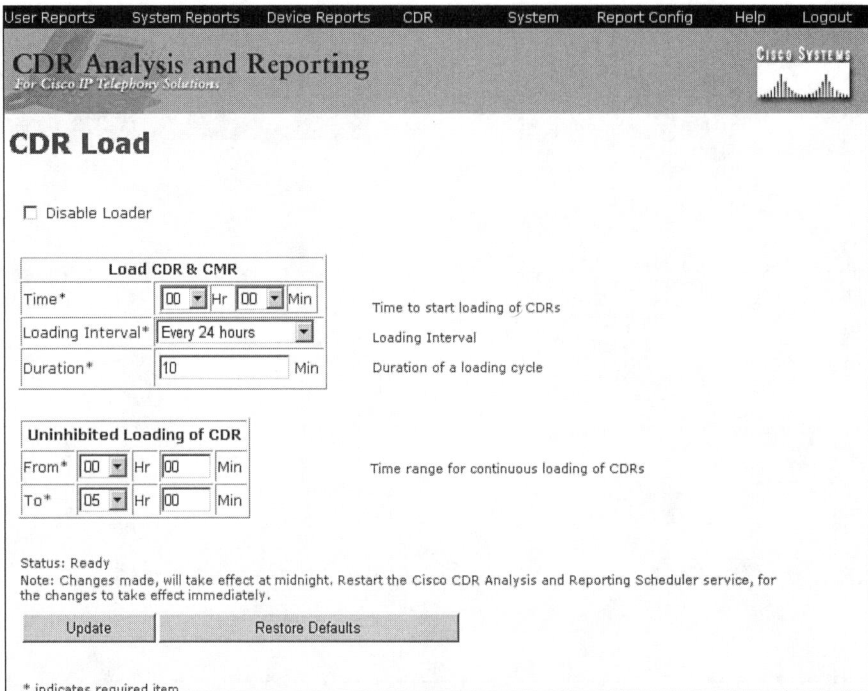

NOTE Depending on your configured loading interval, CAR might not update the CDR records for a full 24-hour period (which is the configured default). This minimizes the near-real-time monitoring of placed calls in the IP telephony network. You will need to balance the loading interval time cycle based on your available resources.

Configuring the Schedulers

You can configure schedulers to generate reports on a daily, weekly, and monthly basis. The schedulers are preconfigured as follows:

- CAR generates daily reports (shown in Figure 33-11) every day at 1:00 a.m.

Figure 33-11 *Configuring CDR Daily Reports*

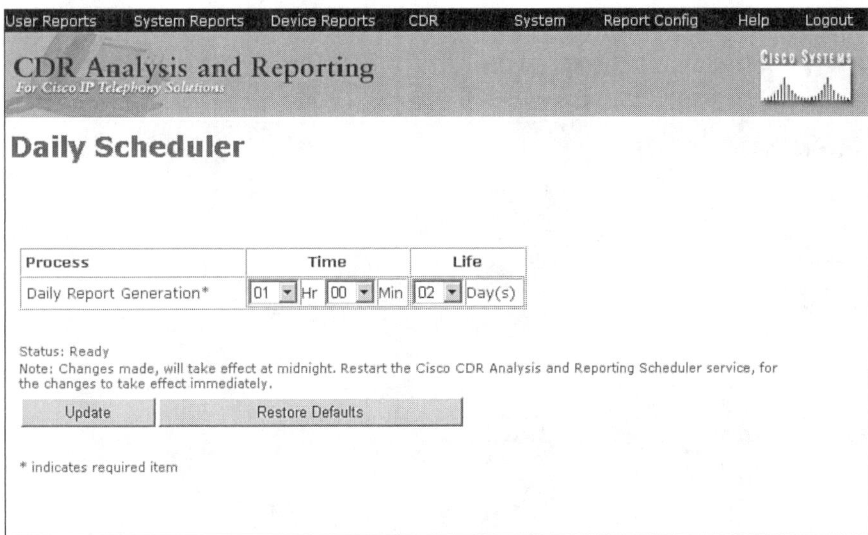

- CAR generates weekly reports (shown in Figure 33-12) every Sunday at 4:00 a.m.

Figure 33-12 *Configuring CDR Weekly Reports*

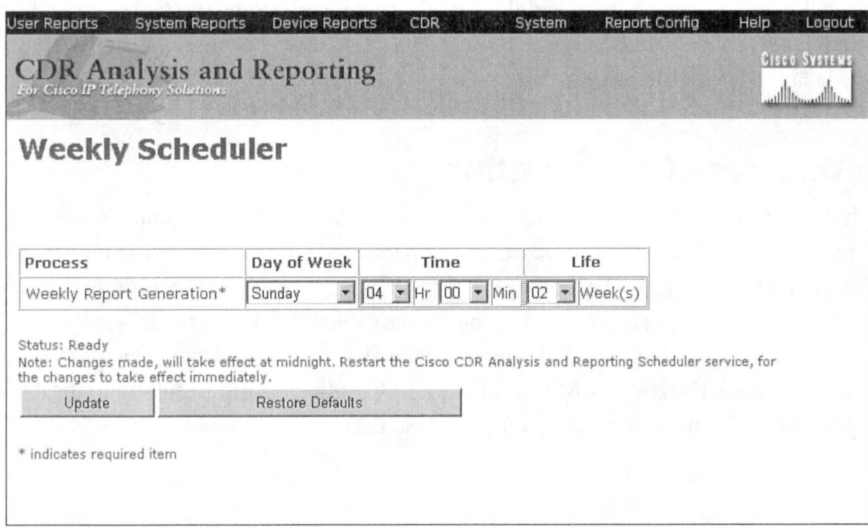

- CAR generates monthly bills (shown in Figure 33-13) on the first day in the month at 3:00 a.m., and other reports at 2:00 a.m.

Figure 33-13 *Configuring CDR Monthly Reports*

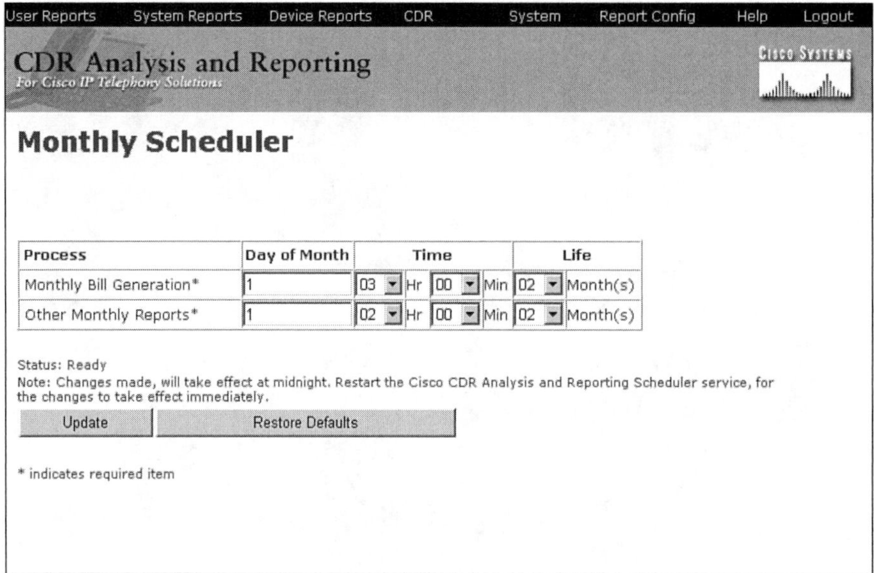

The **Life** field in the schedule configuration specifies the number of days, weeks, or months (depending on the type of the schedule) that the reports are stored on the system. Choose the desired value; for example, for weeks, from 0 to 12. After the configured lifetime has elapsed, CallManager deletes the reports.

System Database Configuration

In the **System > Database** menu, you can configure CAR to notify an administrator when the CAR database size or CDR database size exceeds a percentage of the maximum number of records, as shown in Figure 33-14. Set the message and the maximum number of records, and specify the alert percentage. CAR restricts you from editing the maximum number of records in the CDR database. Sometimes, it might be necessary to purge the database to reallocate the database space. You can use the **System > Database > Manual Purge** or **Configure Automatically** to disable database purging manually, or automatically purge the database.

Figure 33-14 *Configuring CAR Database Alerts*

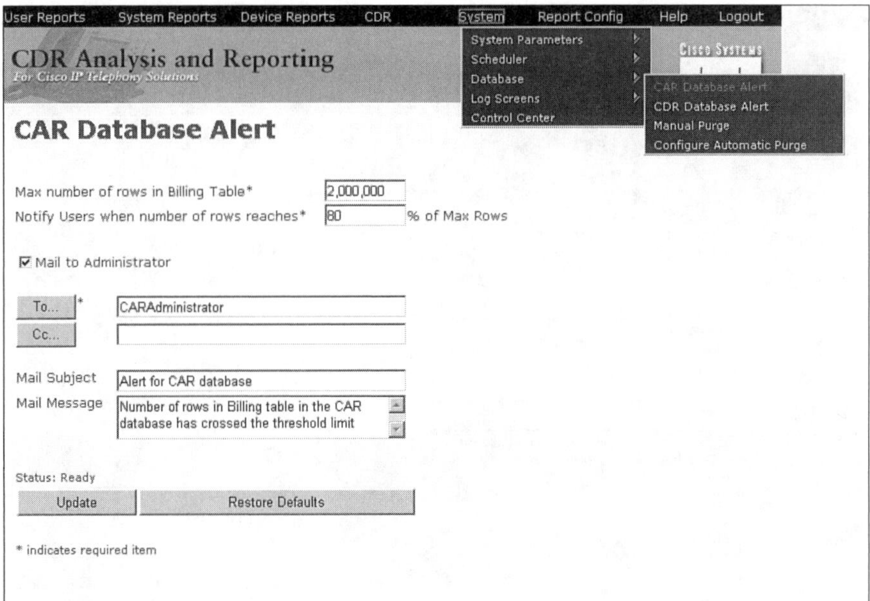

CDR and CAR Database Alerts

With the database alerts, CAR informs the administrator about predefined alert thresholds:

- For a CAR database alert (shown in Figure 33-14), the maximum number of rows in the billing table is 2,000,000 rows. A notification is sent when 80 percent of the rows are used. By default, the CAR administrator receives an e-mail, and the users specified in the **CC** field are also notified. The predefined e-mail subject is "Alert for CAR database." Also, the e-mail message is predefined as "Number of rows in Billing table in the CAR database has crossed the threshold limit."

- For a CDR database alert (shown in Figure 33-15), the alert mechanism works in the same way, and the threshold is predefined at 80 percent also. The difference is that the maximum number of rows is 1,500,000.

Figure 33-15 *Configuring CDR Database Alerts*

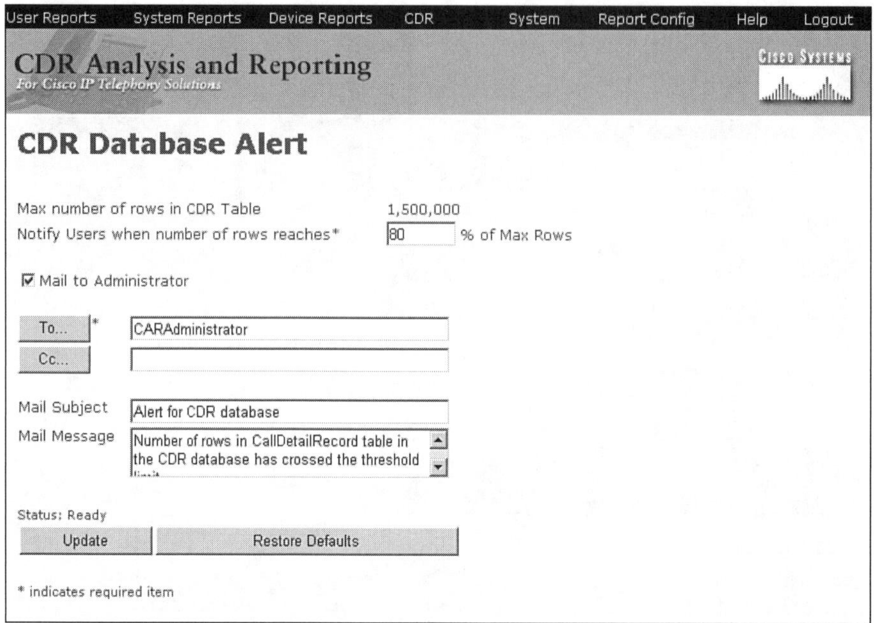

Database Purges

Storage in the database is limited, so you must purge the database from time to time. To do this operation manually in the Manual Database Purge configuration area, follow these steps:

Step 1 In CAR, choose **System > Database > Manual Purge**. The screen that appears is illustrated in Figure 33-16. Choose the database in the **Select Database** drop-down list. The two possible options are **CAR** and **CDR**.

Step 2 Choose the table to purge using the **Select Table** drop-down list. Possible values are the **CallDetailRecord**, **Tbl_Billing_Data**, **Tbl_Error_Log**, and **Tbl_Purge_History** tables. The **Table Information** button displays an overview of the number of records in each of the tables and shows when the first and last records were stored in the database.

Step 3 To delete records, use the **Delete Records** option. Database entries older than the date specified in the **Older Than** field or from the range of dates specified in the **Between** fields will be deleted.

Step 4 Click the **Purge** button.

Figure 33-16 *Manually Purging the CDR Database*

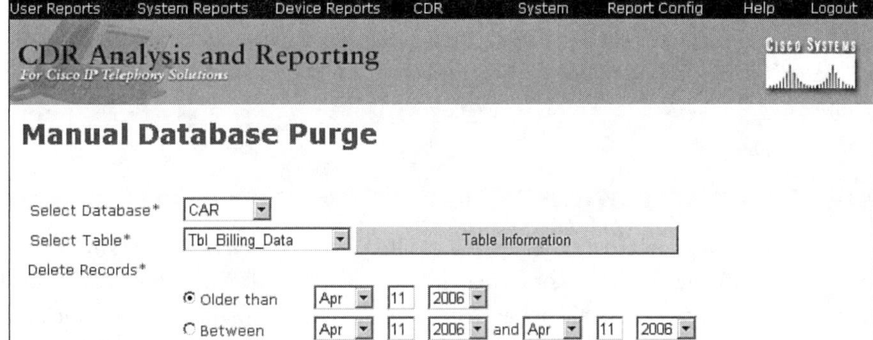

In addition to the manual purge option, CallManager can purge the databases automatically by configuring the parameters in the Configure Automatic Database Purge area. All data older than the specified number of days will be deleted from the CDR or CAR database. In the example illustrated in Figure 33-17, CallManager will automatically purge records in the database older than 100 days.

Figure 33-17 *Automatically Purging the CDR Database*

User Reports System Reports Device Reports CDR System Report Config Help Logout

CDR Analysis and Reporting
For Cisco IP Telephony Solutions

Cisco Systems

Configure Automatic Database Purge

CDR Purge
Disable CDR Purge
Delete CDR Records older than 100 Day(s)

CAR Purge
Disable CAR Purge
Delete CAR Records older than 100 Day(s)

Update Restore Defaults

Status: Ready

* indicates required item

In most cases, third-party products are used for billing. Make sure you do not purge the database before the billing system has replicated the data. Some billing products are also able to delete the data after a successful replication. Be aware that there is no way to restore the deleted database entries after the purge. Automatic purging of both the CDR and CAR databases is disabled by default.

User Report Configuration

Users can access the CAR tool by browsing to https://<*Publisher IP Address*>/ART and logging in with their username and password. A single user has limited access to the CDR database and can generate only a report for his or her own calls. This limitation helps ensure the privacy of the call data for users.

A user can generate an individual bill in a summary or detailed form. To generate a report, the user can use the **Bills > Individual** menu to access the screen shown in Figure 33-18. From here, they can choose either the CSV or PDF report format, set the time range, and click the **View Report** button. For a PDF report, Adobe Acrobat Reader must be installed on the PC from which the user is browsing to CAR. To send the report by e-mail, the user can click the **Send Report** button.

Figure 33-18 *Generating User Reports*

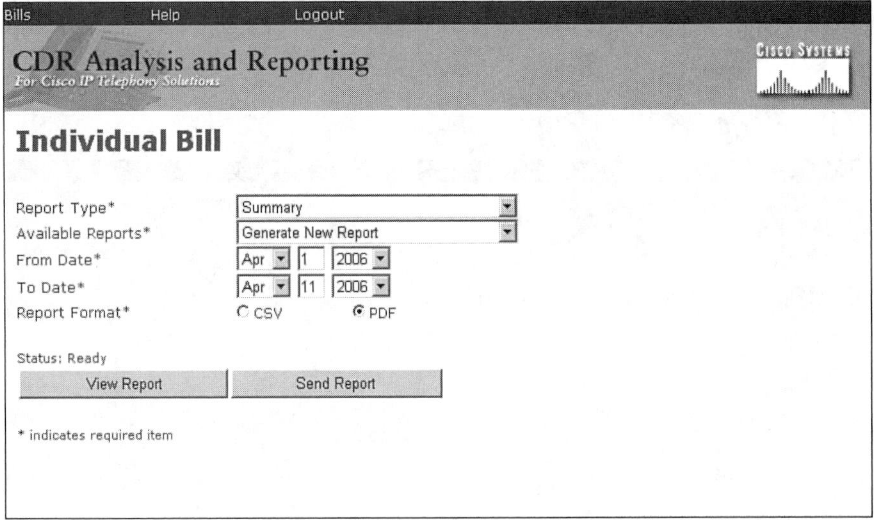

Viewing the Report

As shown in Figure 33-19, the user clicked the **View Report** button after specifying PDF format, and the individual bill was generated. As the figure shows, Sue Monk has no reported calls from the date range of April 1, 2006 through April 11, 2006.

Figure 33-19 *Viewing User Reports*

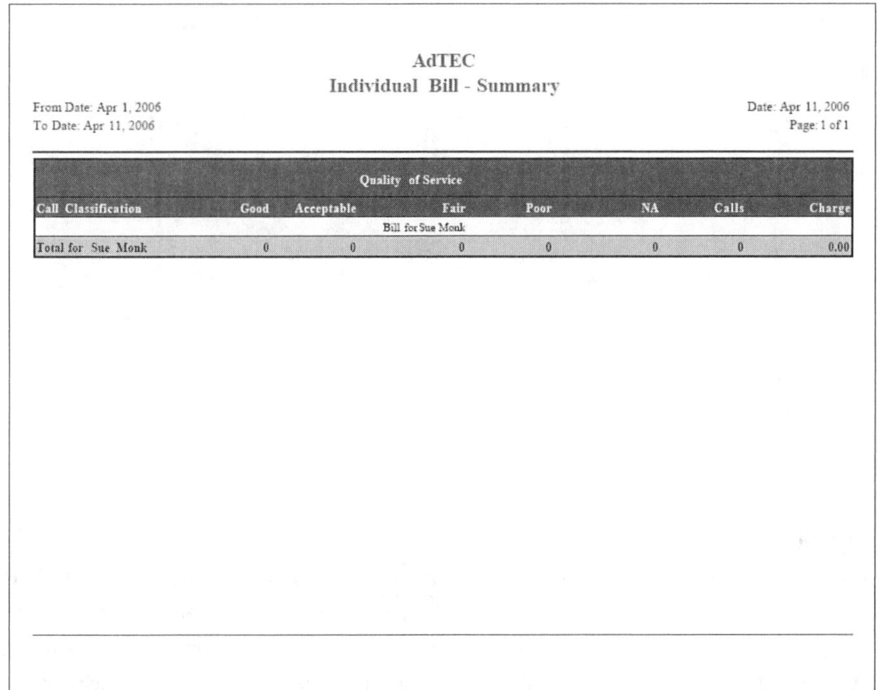

AdTEC
Individual Bill - Summary

From Date: Apr 1, 2006
To Date: Apr 11, 2006

Date: Apr 11, 2006
Page: 1 of 1

	Quality of Service						
Call Classification	Good	Acceptable	Fair	Poor	NA	Calls	Charge
Bill for Sue Monk							
Total for Sue Monk	0	0	0	0	0	0	0.00

Sending the Report

Alternatively, the user could click the **Send Report** button to display a window for sending an e-mail after the user specifies the recipients. As shown in Figure 33-20, the user could also send copies by specifying the relevant e-mail addresses in the **CC** field. The subject of the mail is predefined. Users can add information in the text field if necessary and click **Send** to e-mail this report to the specified recipients.

Figure 33-20 *E-Mailing User Reports*

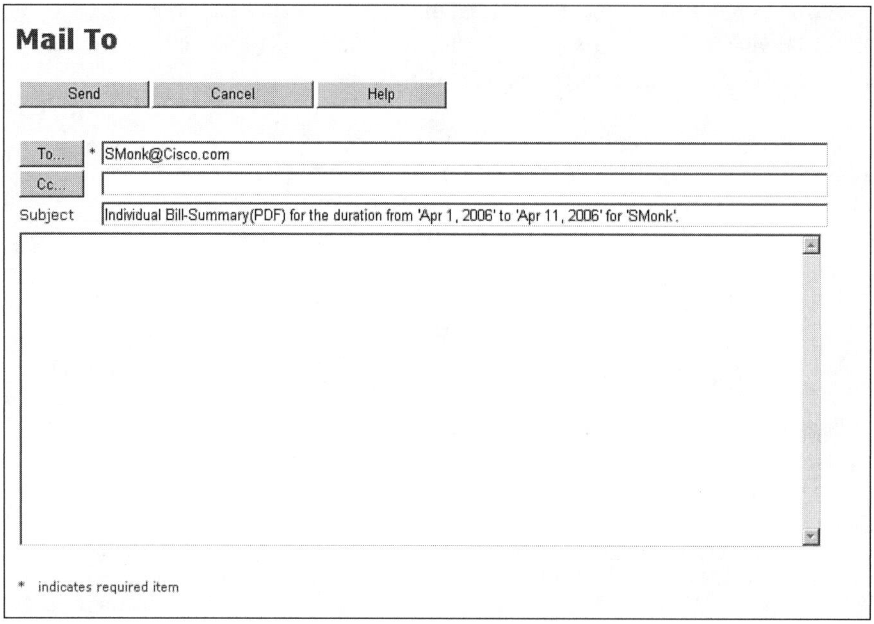

Mail To

Send | Cancel | Help

To... * SMonk@Cisco.com

Cc...

Subject Individual Bill-Summary(PDF) for the duration from 'Apr 1, 2006' to 'Apr 11, 2006' for 'SMonk'.

* indicates required item

Summary

This chapter discussed the use of the CDR Analysis and Reporting (CAR) utility. CAR was formerly known as the Administrative Reporting Tool (ART) and comes as an optional utility. To use it, you must install it on the publisher server from the plug-ins window. CallManager stores the CDRs in the CallDetailRecord SQL table and the CMRs in the CallDetailRecordDiagnostic SQL table.

Within the CAR utility, there are three levels of users: users, managers, and administrators. Likewise, there are three different reports that are available: user, system, and device reports. You should disable CDRs when you are upgrading Cisco CallManager because the resource utilization can be high during CDR replication. In addition, the CDR database can grow quickly in a thriving IP telephony network. You should purge the database regularly either manually or automatically.

Review Questions

You can find the solutions to these questions in Appendix A, "Answers to Review Questions."

1. Which three statements about the CAR tool are true?
   a. PDF reports are limited to 5000 records.
   b. PDF reports are limited to 10,000 records.
   c. CSV reports are limited to 20,000 records.
   d. CSV reports are limited to 25,000 records.
   e. CAR has to be installed on the publisher only.
   f. CAR does not have to be installed on the publisher.
2. Which statement about CMR and CDR is true?
   a. Both are stored permanently in flat files.
   b. CMR stores call details.
   c. CDR stores QoS parameters.
   d. They are related to each other.
3. Which username and password combination is used for the first login to CAR?
   a. cisco and cisco
   b. cisco and dipsy
   c. admin and admin
   d. admin and cisco
4. Which is a valid CAR report type?
   a. QoS reports
   b. CDR reports
   c. Database reports
   d. Device reports
5. What is the first thing to do after the first login to CAR?
   a. Grant access rights.
   b. Configure the mail server.
   c. Configure the dial plan.
   d. Adjust the system preferences.

6. When is the CDR data loaded by default?

   a. From midnight to 1:00 a.m.

   b. From midnight to 3:00 a.m.

   c. From midnight to 5:00 a.m.

   d. In real time

7. The CAR and CDR database alerts the CAR administrator by default when _____ percent of the maximum number of rows is reached.

   a. 70

   b. 75

   c. 80

   d. 85

   e. 90

8. Which call type is valid in individual bills?

   a. On Net

   b. Intersite

   c. MLPP

   d. Video

9. What two file formats are valid for report generation in CAR?

   a. TXT

   b. XLS

   c. PDF

   d. CSV

10. If the publisher server is unavailable in a CallManager cluster, what happens to CDRs?

    a. They are lost.

    b. CDRs are stored on the root of the subscriber hard drive.

    c. CDRs are stored in the memory of the subscriber server.

    d. They are stored on the subscriber in "flat files."

This chapter covers the following topics:

- Explaining the use of SNMP, syslog, and CiscoWorks ITEM in remotely managing and maintaining a Cisco CallManager system
- Explaining the use of dependency records, enabling them, and accessing them
- Using the Password Changer tool to change passwords
- Using the Cisco Dialed Number Analyzer to analyze inbound and outbound calls in a Cisco CallManager dial plan
- Configuring the QRT feature to display IP phone problem reports from users

CHAPTER 34

Using Additional Management and Monitoring Tools

Management and monitoring tools are available to help system administrators monitor, troubleshoot, and manage the health of an IP telephony network. This chapter explains Cisco CallManager tools such as dependency records, Password Changer tool, and Cisco Dialed Number Analyzer. The Quality Report Tool (QRT), a tool used by end users to report IP phone issues to administrators, is also covered.

Remote Management Tools

Network management software, such as CiscoWorks IP Telephony Environment Monitor (ITEM) or syslog servers, performs specific tasks to monitor and manage the health and availability of devices in a network. These tools are typically used in large-scale data networks (such as computer networks and telecommunication networks).

CiscoWorks ITEM Overview

CiscoWorks ITEM is a powerful suite of applications and tools that continuously evaluate and report on the operational health of the Cisco IP telephony implementation. CiscoWorks ITEM is used to manage Cisco IOS software-based IP telephony environments. CiscoWorks ITEM provides the following:

- Proactive health and fault monitoring of converged IP networks and IP telephony implementations
- Powerful tools to effectively manage the day-to-day customer care responsibilities of help-desk personnel
- The ability to capture performance and capacity management data

CiscoWorks ITEM consists of a product suite:

- **CiscoWorks IP Telephony Monitor (ITM)** —Monitors Cisco voice elements in the network to alert operations personnel to potential problems and to help minimize downtime. It also includes CiscoWorks Common Services, a common foundation for data storage, login, access privileges, and navigation and launch management for all CiscoWorks applications.

- **CiscoWorks IP Phone Information Utility (IPIU)** —Provides operational status and implementation details about an individual IP phone. It also provides security reports that document IP phone moves, adds, and changes, as well as information about the physical and logical connections of every Cisco IP Phone installed in a given network.
- **CiscoWorks IP Phone Help Desk Utility (IPHDU)** —Reports operational status and implementation details about individual IP phones. It works in conjunction with IPIU to make read-only access to Cisco IP Phone installation details available to help-desk personnel.
- **CiscoWorks ITEM Gateway Statistics Utility (GSU)** —Collects performance and behavior statistics about IP telephony gateways controlled by Cisco CallManager and Cisco IOS software, which can be processed by third-party software to produce utilization and capacity management reports.
- **CiscoWorks WAN Performance Utility (WPU)** —Measures the performance, latency, and availability of multiprotocol IP networks on an end-to-end and hop-by-hop (router-to-router) basis.

CiscoWorks ITEM also provides real-time fault detection and determination about the underlying Cisco IP fabric on which the IP telephony implementation executes. CiscoWorks ITEM reports faults that occur on Cisco network devices, often identifying problems before users of network services realize that a problem exists. CiscoWorks ITEM supports more than 200 types of the most popular Cisco routers, switches, access servers, and hubs. For each of these supported devices, CiscoWorks ITEM automatically looks for a broad spectrum of common problems at the device and VLAN level, all without ever requiring operations managers to write rules or set polling or threshold values. CiscoWorks ITEM can listen to traps or can send polls and pings to get information for devices. CiscoWorks ITEM can send alerts and events automatically to an e-mail client or a pager. To monitor the network, CiscoWorks ITEM can be accessed via a web-based interface or a CiscoWorks desktop client.

Network management systems (NMSs) use Simple Network Management Protocol (SNMP), an industry-standard interface, to exchange management information between network devices.

Simple Network Management Protocol

SNMP is an application-layer protocol, part of the TCP/IP protocol suite. SNMP enables administrators to remotely manage network performance, find and solve network problems, and plan for network growth. There are three versions of SNMP:

- SNMP Version 1 (SNMPv1)
- SNMP Version 2 (SNMPv2)
- SNMP Version 3 (SNMPv3)

SNMPv1 and SNMPv2 have a number of common features, but SNMPv2 offers enhancements, such as additional protocol operations. Standardization of SNMPv3 is pending.

SNMP Basics

An SNMP-managed network consists of three key components:

- **Managed devices**—A managed device designates a network node that contains an SNMP agent and resides on a managed network. Managed devices collect and store management information and make it available by using SNMP.
- **Agents**—An agent, as network management software, resides on a managed device. An agent contains local knowledge of management information and translates it into a form that is compatible with SNMP.
- **NMSs**—An NMS comprises an SNMP management application together with the computer on which it runs. An NMS executes applications that monitor and control managed devices. An NMS provides the bulk of the processing and memory resources that are required for network management. These NMSs share compatibility with Cisco CallManager:
  - — CiscoWorks2000
  - — HP OpenView
  - — Third-party applications that support SNMP and Cisco CallManager SNMP interfaces

This list specifies Cisco CallManager SNMP trap messages that are sent to an NMS that is specified as a trap receiver:

- Cisco CallManager failed
- Phone failed
- Phones status update
- Gateway failed
- Media resource list exhausted
- Route list exhausted
- Gateway Layer 2 change
- Quality report
- Malicious call

SNMP itself is a simple request-and-response protocol. NMSs can send multiple requests without receiving a response. Table 34-1 defines six SNMP operations.

Table 34-1 *SNMP Operations*

Operation	Definition
Get	Allows the NMS to retrieve an object instance from the agent.
GetNext	Allows the NMS to retrieve the next object instance from a table or list within an agent. In SNMPv1, when an NMS wants to retrieve all elements of a table from an agent, it initiates a Get operation, followed by a series of GetNext operations.
GetBulk	Makes it easier to acquire large amounts of related information without initiating repeated get-next operations. GetBulk (new in SNMPv2) was designed to virtually eliminate the need for GetNext operations.
Set	Allows the NMS to set values for object instances within an agent.
Trap	Allows the agent to asynchronously inform the NMS of some event.
Inform	Allows one NMS to send Trap information to another (new in SNMPv2).

SNMP Configuration on Cisco CallManager

Administrators have to enable SNMP for each device in the network that they want to monitor. For example, if you want to monitor Cisco CallManager with SNMP, on the Cisco CallManager server, click **Start > Programs > Administrative Tools > Services**. From the Service menu, search for the SNMP service and open the service to configure it. The SNMP Service Properties window shown in Figure 34-1 opens.

Figure 34-1 *CallManager SNMP Service Configuration*

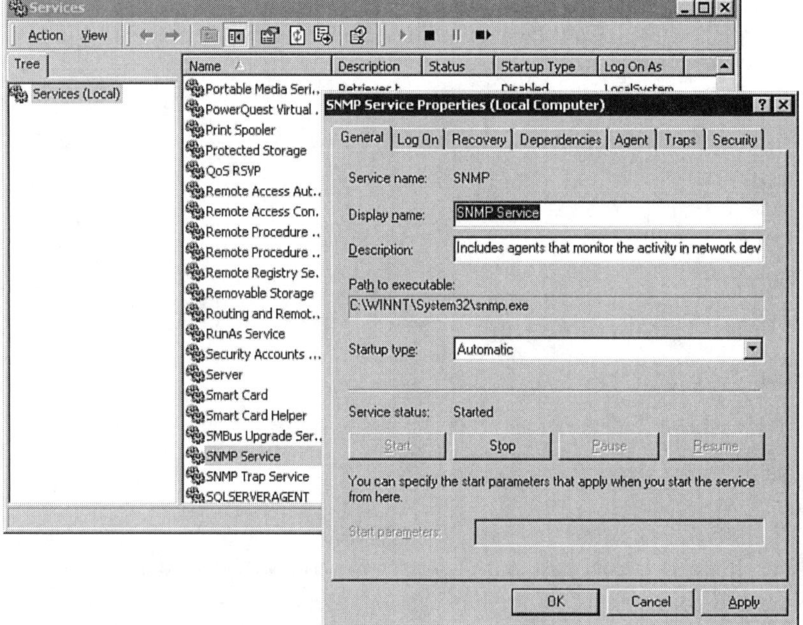

Cisco CallManager supports SNMPv1 and SNMPv2. SNMPv1 lacks authentication capabilities (SNMPv2 increases the security capabilities of SNMP, and SNMPv3 supports authentication and encryption), which results in vulnerability to a variety of security threats:

- Masquerading consists of an unauthorized entity attempting to perform management operations by assuming the identity of an authorized management entity.
- Modification of information involves an unauthorized entity attempting to alter a message generated by an authorized entity so that the message results in unauthorized accounting management or configuration management operations.
- Message sequence and timing modifications occur when an unauthorized entity reorders, delays, or copies and later replays a message generated by an authorized entity.
- Disclosure results when an unauthorized entity extracts values stored in managed objects, or learns of notifiable events by monitoring exchanges between managers and agents.

Because SNMPv1 does not implement authentication, many vendors do not implement Set operations, thus reducing SNMP to a monitoring facility.

The first thing you need to do to configure SNMP management is to enable SNMP access. Enable access by configuring community strings, which act somewhat like passwords. The difference is that there can be several community strings and that each of them can grant a different form of access.

A community string can be the following:

- **Read-only**—Gives read access to all objects in the MIB except the community strings but does not allow write access
- **Read-write**—Gives read and write access to all objects in the MIB but does not allow access to the community strings
- **Read-write-all**—Gives read and write access to all objects in the MIB, including the community strings

To define the SNMP read community string, complete these steps:

Step 1 Choose **Start > Programs > Administrative Tools > Services**.

Step 2 Choose the **SNMP** service, double-click the service name, and choose **Security**.

Step 3 In the Security window, define community strings and assign them read permission.

This would now be the read community string a remote system could use to view various attributes of the Cisco CallManager server. In the example shown in Figure 34-2, the community string is "item."

Figure 34-2 *CallManager SNMP Community String Configuration*

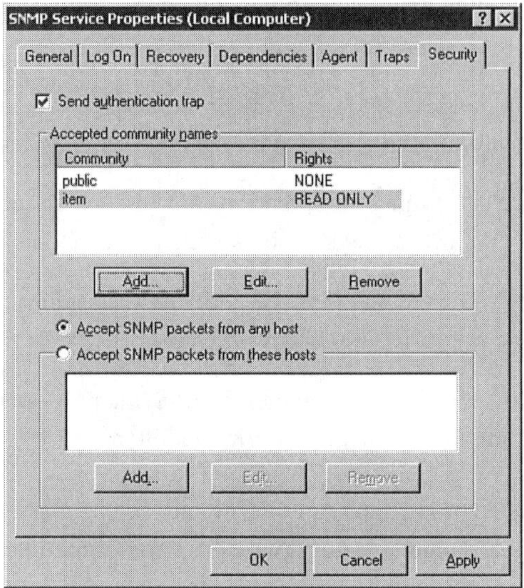

Cisco Systems supports numerous Management Information Bases (MIBs) that organize and distribute information for a variety of network management devices.

You can use the MIB table that supports Cisco CallManager to provide all of the management interfaces for monitoring and managing your Cisco CallManager network. This MIB table is periodically updated, reflecting the current status of your Cisco CallManager network:

- **CISCO-CCM-MIB**—To perform network management, you can use the CISCO-CCM-MIB to get provisioning and statistical information about Cisco CallManager, its associated devices (for example, IP phones and gateways), and its configuration.
- **CISCO-CDP-MIB**—You can use the Cisco CallManager SNMP agent to implement the Cisco Discovery Protocol MIB, CISCO-CDP-MIB. This MIB enables Cisco CallManager to advertise itself to other Cisco devices on the network, allowing discovery of other Cisco CallManager installations on the network.

NOTE To get more information about the MIB tables, go to Cisco.com and search for CISCO-CCM-MIB.

Syslog Overview

Syslog allows logging of events across the network to various destinations. It provides an orderly presentation of information that assists in the diagnosis and troubleshooting of system problems. Theses messages can be saved in a file or sent to, for example, a CiscoWorks server, a third-party syslog server (such as Kiwi Syslog Daemon), or the host itself.

> **TIP** Kiwi Syslog Daemon is a freeware Windows syslog server. It receives, logs, displays, and forwards syslog messages from hosts, such as routers, switches, UNIX hosts, and any other syslog-enabled device. For more information, go to http://www.kiwisyslog.com.

When the local host is used, Remote Syslog Analyzer Collector (RSAC) software must be installed. RSAC can be installed on a remote UNIX or Microsoft Windows 2000 or Windows NT machine to process syslog messages.

Syslog Configuration in Cisco CallManager

Cisco CallManager syslog messages are configured in Cisco CallManager Serviceability. To configure alarms, use the Cisco CallManager Serviceability web page and select **Alarm > Configuration**. After selecting your server and the CallManager service, the Alarm Configuration window shown in Figure 34-3 opens. To enable syslog messages, simply check the **Enable Alarm** check box under the Syslog Trace section and enter the IP address of your syslog server.

Figure 34-3 *CallManager Syslog Configuration*

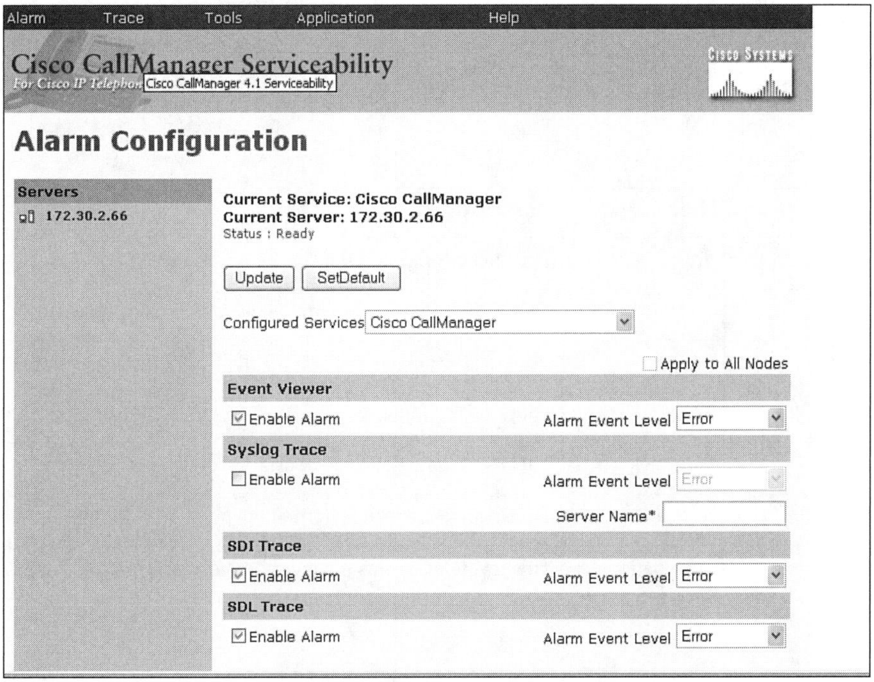

Table 34-2 lists alarm events that can be configured in the alarm trap.

Table 34-2 *Configurable Alarm Events*

Name	Destination Description
Enable Alarm for Event Viewer	Windows 2000 Event Viewer program. The program logs Cisco CallManager errors in the application logs within Event Viewer, and provides a description of the alarm and a recommended action.
Enable Alarm for Syslog	Cisco CallManager Syslog capabilities. Check the **Enable Alarm** check box in the Syslog Trace area of the Alarm Configuration window to enable the syslog messages and configure the syslog server name. If this destination is enabled and no server name is specified, Cisco CallManager sends syslog messages to the local host. Cisco CallManager stores alarm definitions and recommended actions in a Standard Query Language (SQL) server database. The system administrator can search the database for definitions of all the alarms. The definitions include the alarm name, description, explanation, recommended action, severity, parameters, and monitors. This box is unchecked by default.
Enable Alarm for System Diagnostic Interface (SDI) Trace	The SDI trace library. Ensure that this alarm destination is configured in Trace configuration of Cisco CallManager Serviceability.
Enable Alarm for Signal Distribution Layer (SDL)	The SDL trace library. This destination applies only to the Cisco CallManager and Cisco CTIManager services. Configure this alarm destination using Trace SDL configuration.

Table 34-3 lists alarm levels used by Cisco CallManager.

Alarm Event Levels

Level	Name	Description
7	Emergency	This level designates the system as unusable.
6	Alert	This level indicates that immediate action is needed.
5	Critical	Cisco CallManager detects a critical condition.
4	Error	This level signifies that an error condition exists.
3	Warning	This level indicates that a warning condition is detected.
2	Notice	This level designates a normal but significant condition.
1	Informational	This level designates information messages only.

The Cisco CallManager Serviceability Alarms window provides a web-based interface that has two main functions:

- To configure alarms and events
- To provide alarm message definitions

Both functions assist the system administrator and support personnel in troubleshooting Cisco CallManager problems. Alarms can be configured for Cisco CallManager servers in a cluster and for services for each server, such as Cisco CallManager, Cisco TFTP, and Cisco CTIManager.

Alarms can be forwarded to a Serviceability Trace file. The administrator configures alarms and trace parameters and provides the information to a Cisco TAC engineer. Administrators can direct alarms to the Windows 2000 Event Log, syslog, SDI trace log file, SDL trace log file (for Cisco CallManager and CTIManager only), or to all these destinations.

Dependency Records

In Cisco CallManager Administration, numerous configuration elements are referenced by other elements (for example, a route pattern refers to a route list, which refers to a route group, which refers to a gateway). In many cases, you cannot delete such elements if they are currently referenced elsewhere in the system. It can be difficult and time consuming to find out which configuration element is referencing the element that you are trying to delete. The mechanism that allows you to determine, delete, change, or modify a record in Cisco CallManager is called dependency records. Dependency records help you to determine which records in the Cisco CallManager database use other records. For example, which devices (such as computer telephony integration [CTI] route points or IP phones) use a particular calling search space?

To delete a record from Cisco CallManager, you can use dependency records to show which records are associated with the record that you want to delete. You can then reconfigure those records so that they are associated with a different record.

For example, the administrator tries to delete a device pool. A message is displayed that some devices still use this pool. The administrator clicks the dependency records link to find out which devices use this device pool.

Enabling Dependency Records

Because dependency records are disabled by default, they must be activated in the Cisco CallManager Administration Enterprise Parameters window if you want to use the feature. Set the **Enable Dependency Records** parameter to **True** to activate dependency records and display them as an option in Cisco CallManager Administration. To access this record, use the Cisco

CallManager Administration page and navigate to **System > Enterprise Parameters**. An illustration of this is shown in Figure 34-4.

Figure 34-4 *Enabling CallManager Dependency Records*

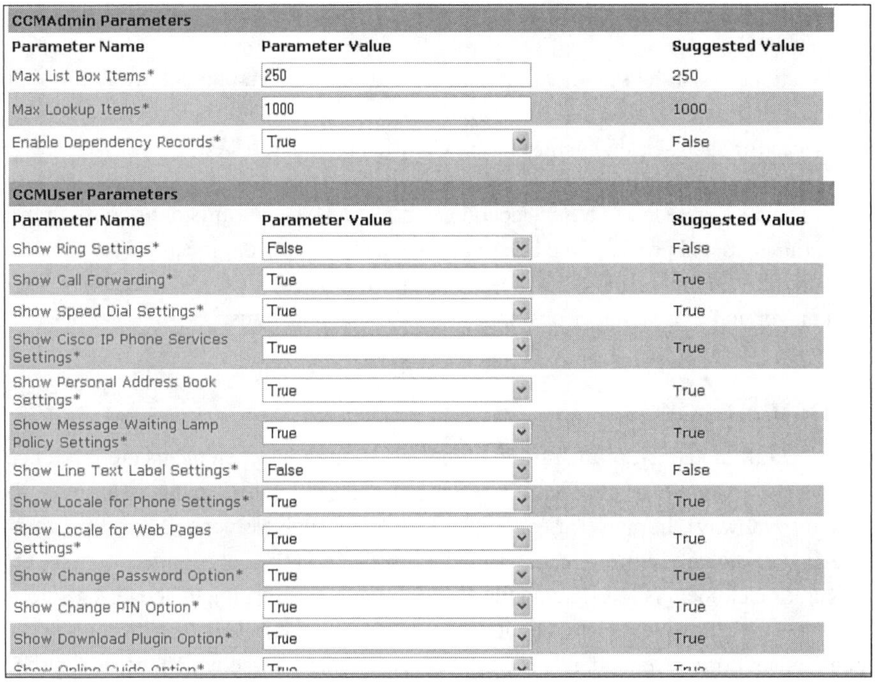

CCMAdmin Parameters		
Parameter Name	**Parameter Value**	**Suggested Value**
Max List Box Items*	250	250
Max Lookup Items*	1000	1000
Enable Dependency Records*	True	False

CCMUser Parameters		
Parameter Name	**Parameter Value**	**Suggested Value**
Show Ring Settings*	False	False
Show Call Forwarding*	True	True
Show Speed Dial Settings*	True	True
Show Cisco IP Phone Services Settings*	True	True
Show Personal Address Book Settings*	True	True
Show Message Waiting Lamp Policy Settings*	True	True
Show Line Text Label Settings*	False	False
Show Locale for Phone Settings*	True	True
Show Locale for Web Pages Settings*	True	True
Show Change Password Option*	True	True
Show Change PIN Option*	True	True
Show Download Plugin Option*	True	True
Show Online Guide Option*	True	True

CAUTION Displaying dependency records leads to high CPU usage and takes some time because it executes in a low-priority thread. If you are monitoring CPU usage, you might see high CPU usage alarms. To avoid possible performance issues, display dependency records only during off-peak hours or during the next maintenance window. Close and reopen the web browser for the parameter change to take effect.

Accessing Dependency Records

To access dependency records from a Cisco CallManager configuration window, click the **Dependency Records** link, as shown in Figure 34-5. The Dependency Records Summary window opens. This window displays the number and type of records that use the record that is shown in the Cisco CallManager configuration window.

Figure 34-5 *Accessing Dependency Records*

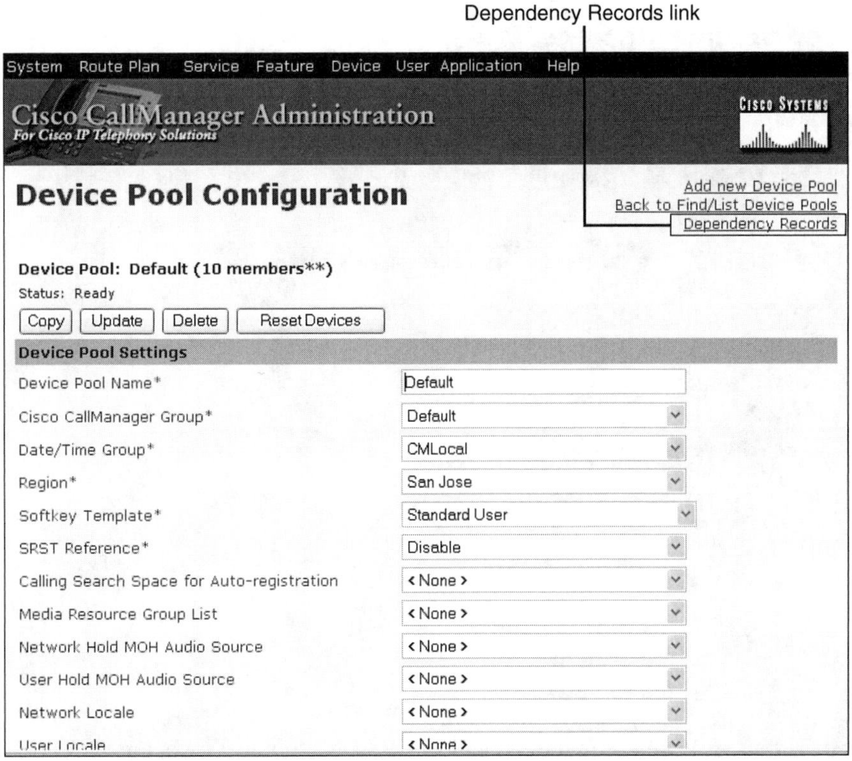

Dependency Records link

System Route Plan Service Feature Device User Application Help

Cisco CallManager Administration
For Cisco IP Telephony Solutions

CISCO SYSTEMS

Device Pool Configuration

Add new Device Pool
Back to Find/List Device Pools
Dependency Records

Device Pool: Default (10 members**)
Status: Ready

Copy | Update | Delete | Reset Devices

Device Pool Settings

Device Pool Name*	Default
Cisco CallManager Group*	Default
Date/Time Group*	CMLocal
Region*	San Jose
Softkey Template*	Standard User
SRST Reference*	Disable
Calling Search Space for Auto-registration	< None >
Media Resource Group List	< None >
Network Hold MOH Audio Source	< None >
User Hold MOH Audio Source	< None >
Network Locale	< None >
User Locale	< None >

NOTE If the dependency records are not enabled, the Dependency Records Summary window displays a message stating that the Dependency Record feature is disabled (and also tells the administrator how to enable this feature).

After you click the dependency records link in an administration window, you will see a list of all records that refer to the item that you selected, as shown in Figure 34-6. This list is in summary style and shows the depending records only by type and number. You can click an entry of the summary list to view the detailed list of dependent records. You can click a single device in the dependency records detail window to go to the configuration window of the device. To return to the original configuration window, click the **Back to <configuration window name>** link.

Figure 34-6 *Dependency Records Summary*

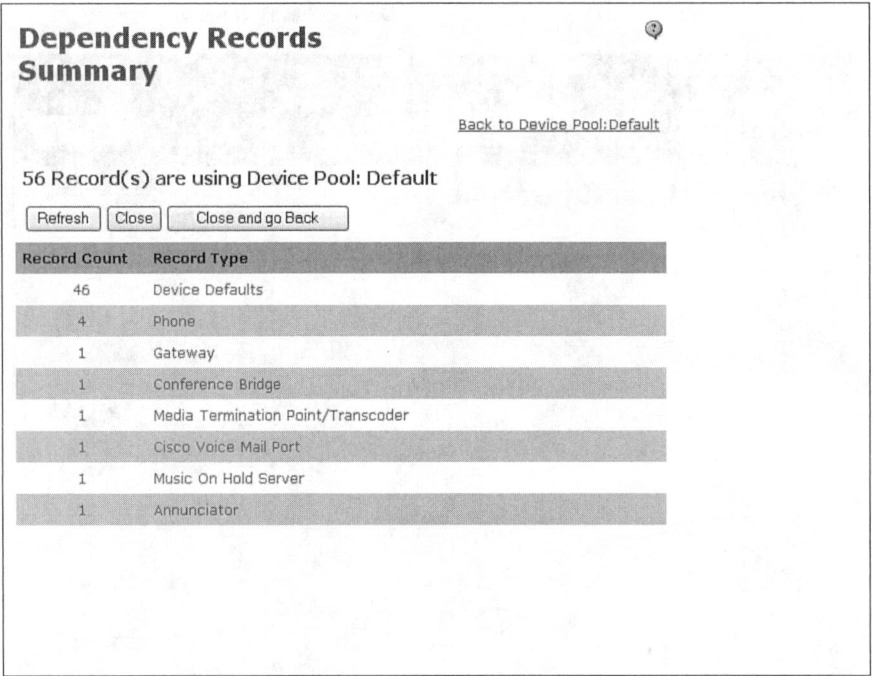

Three buttons are available in the Dependency Records Summary window:

- **Refresh**—Updates the window with the most up-to-date information.
- **Close**—Closes the window but does not return to the Cisco CallManager configuration window in which the user clicked the **Dependency Records** link.
- **Close and Go Back**—Closes the window and returns to the Cisco CallManager configuration window in which the user clicked the **Dependency Records** link.

Password Changer Tool

The Password Changer tool is used to change the CCMAdministrator, IPMASysUser, CCMSysUser, or the Directory Manager accounts. The Password Changer tool is stored by default on every Cisco CallManager server in the cluster. When you want to change the Directory Manager password, you must change it on every Cisco CallManager server in the cluster (publisher and subscriber). For the other accounts, the password must be changed only on one server in the cluster.

NOTE The CCMAdministrator account is used only when you are using MultiLevel Administration (MLA). The Microsoft Windows administrator account is used when MLA is not used. When you change the password for the Windows administrator account, you have to use the new password when you log in to Cisco CallManager Administration. The Windows administrator account cannot be changed with the Cisco Password Changer tool, whereas the passwords for users in the DC Directory of Cisco CallManager can. When Cisco CallManager is integrated in a Lightweight Directory Access Protocol (LDAP) directory, the users are changed directly in the corresponding LDAP directory.

These users can be changed with the Password Changer tool:

- **CCMAdministrator**—CCMAdministrator is used as the administrator account when you are using MLA.
- **CCMSysUser**—Cisco Extended Functions, Cisco Tomcat, and Cisco CallManager Extension Mobility services use a special user, cn=CCMSysUser and mail=CCMSysUser (Netscape) or SAMAccountName=CCMSysUser (Microsoft Active Directory), to authenticate with Cisco CallManager.
- **IPMASysUser**—IPMASysUser is used by Cisco IP Manager Assistant (IPMA) to authenticate with Cisco CallManager.
- **Directory Manager**—Directory Manager is the superuser account for the integrated LDAP database in Cisco IP telephony systems. In Cisco CallManager, it is the DC Directory.

Using the Password Changer Tool

To start the Password Changer tool, complete these steps:

Step 1 Choose **Start > Run > CCMPWDChanger** in Cisco CallManager.

Step 2 After some time, you will be able to enter the DC Directory administrator password (not the administrator password that is used to access the server). Click **Next**.

Step 3 Choose the user whose password you want to change, as shown in Figure 34-7.

Figure 34-7 *Selecting the User*

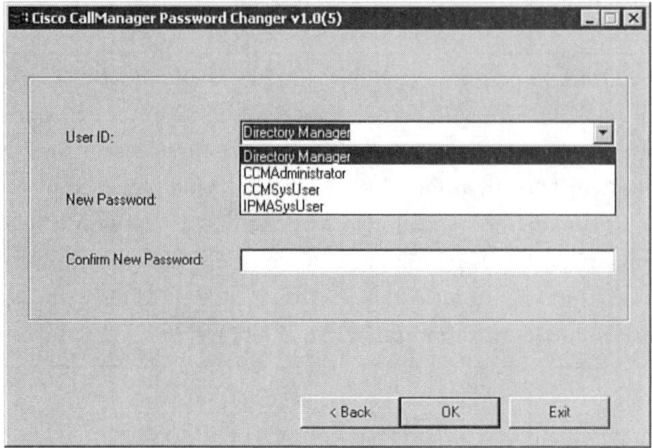

Step 4 Enter the new password twice.

Step 5 A message notifies you that the password for the user has been successfully changed. Click **OK** to close the window.

Step 6 After finishing all password changes, click **Exit** to leave the Password Changer tool. The next time that you log in to Cisco CallManager Administration, the new passwords take effect.

Cisco Dialed Number Analyzer

The Dialed Number Analyzer is installed as a plug-in for Cisco CallManager. The tool allows you to test a Cisco CallManager dial plan configuration prior to deploying it. The tool simulates internal-to-internal calls and internal-to-external calls. You can also use the tool to analyze dial plans after the dial plan is deployed.

A dial plan can be very complex, involving multiple devices, translation patterns, route patterns, route lists, route groups, calling- and called-party transformations, and device-level transformations. Because of this complexity, a dial plan can contain errors. You can use the Dialed Number Analyzer to test a dial plan by providing dialed digits as input. The tool analyzes the dialed digits and shows details of the calls. You can use these results to diagnose the dial plan, identify problems, if any, and tune the dial plan before it is deployed.

The Cisco Dialed Number Analyzer runs as a service that can be accessed from the server on which it is installed or from a remote PC. It runs as a low priority and does not affect Cisco CallManager performance. With the Cisco Dialed Number Analyzer tool, you can analyze various types of calls, such as IP phone-to-IP phone, gateway-to-IP phone, IP phone-to-gateway, and gateway-to-gateway calls. Furthermore, you can analyze calls to feature-specific patterns, such as CTI route points or pilot points.

Installing Cisco Dialed Number Analyzer

The Dialed Number Analyzer (DNA) includes a separate executable file that is available in the Cisco CallManager plug-ins window. You can install the Dialed Number Analyzer if Cisco CallManager Release 3.3(4) or later has been installed. You can install the Dialed Number Analyzer on any Cisco CallManager node in a cluster, either publisher or subscriber. Install the Dialed Number Analyzer preferably on the publisher to use the actual SQL database that is used by all Cisco CallManager servers. During the installation, you have to enter the Cisco CallManager cluster private password phrase you configured during the Cisco CallManager installation. When the Dialed Number Analyzer is installed, it installs as a service called Cisco Dialed Number Analyzer. You can start and log in to the Dialed Number Analyzer from the server on which it is installed or from a remote PC by using a web browser (Microsoft Internet Explorer 6.0 or later versions).

The Dialed Number Analyzer tool can be installed from the Cisco CallManager Plugins web page at **Application > Install Plugins > Cisco Dialed Number Analyzer**. After you have installed the tool, you can access it at https://<cmaddress>/dna, where <cmaddress> specifies the node name or IP address of the device on which the Dialed Number Analyzer is installed. In the **User Name** field, enter a valid user ID and a password (for the administrator account to get access to Cisco CallManager Administration). The Dialed Number Analyzer window shown in Figure 34-8 should appear.

> **NOTE** The Windows administrator account must be used to access the Cisco Dialed Number Analyzer even if you have the Cisco MultiLevel Administrator (MLA) installed with Cisco CallManager.

Figure 34-8 *Cisco Dialed Number Analyzer*

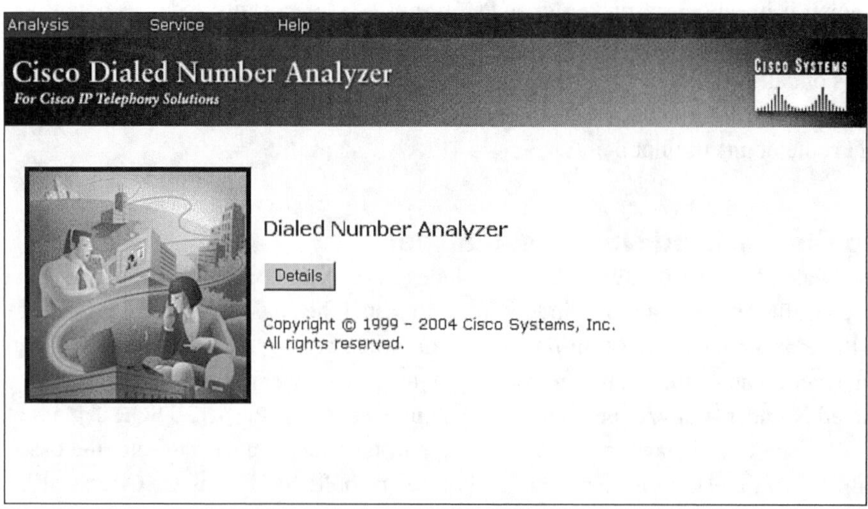

Using the Cisco Dialed Number Analyzer

The analysis involves entering calling-party and called-party digits in the Dialed Number Analyzer tool and choosing a calling search space for the analysis. The Dialed Number Analyzer uses this calling search space and analyzes the dialed digits. You need not choose specific devices or provide any other input. The Dialed Number Analyzer allows you to analyze a route pattern, translation pattern, directory number (DN), or CTI route point. Furthermore, beginning with Cisco CallManager Release 4.1, the Dialed Number Analyzer tool supports Call Coverage, H.323 FastStart, Hospitality, trunk-to-trunk transfer, Forced Authorization Codes (FAC) and Client Matter Codes (CMC), BRI, Multilevel Precedence and Preemption (MLPP), U.S. Department of Defense (DoD) requirements, Q signaling (QSIG), and time-of-day features.

As shown in Figure 34-9, a call between 4015 and 4010 with the calling search space IntLocCSS is analyzed. The Calling Party and the **Dialed Digits** fields are mandatory. When you want to test, for example, time-of-day routing, you can specify a time zone as well. After you have chosen all values, click the **Do Analysis** button to start the analysis.

The result of the analyzed call between 4015 and 4010 is displayed in a compact version, as shown in Figure 34-10. For complete information, click the **Expand All** button. The match result information is the first point to check. Is the call routed correctly or is it restricted? RouteThisPattern means that the call is routed correctly.

Figure 34-9 *Dialed Number Analyzer Example*

Figure 34-10 *Dialed Number Analyzer Results*

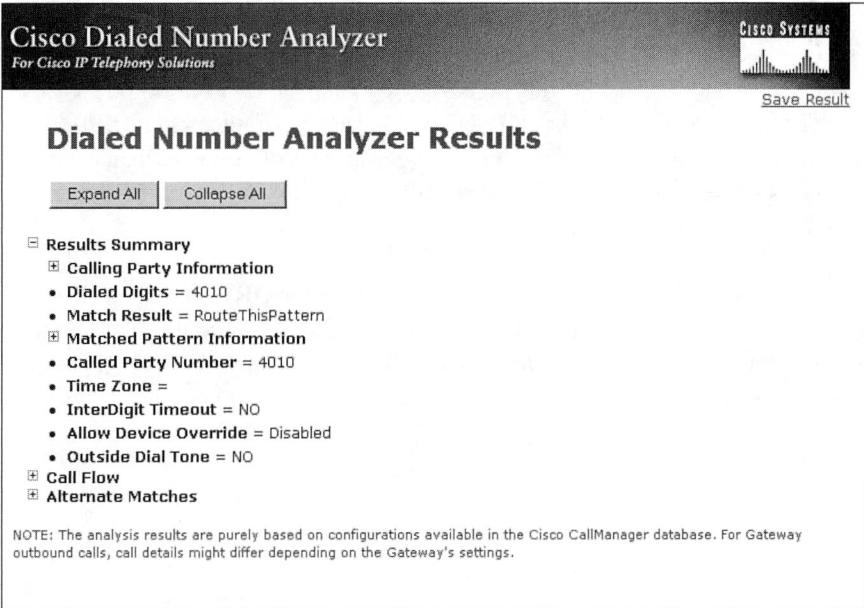

Quality Report Tool

QRT is a voice-quality and general problem-reporting tool for Cisco CallManager IP Phones. The Cisco Extended Functions service supports the QRT feature. The QRT Viewer, located in the Tools menu of Cisco CallManager Serviceability, allows administrators to filter, format, and view problem reports that are generated.

Administrators can configure Cisco IP Phones with QRT, which is installed as part of the Cisco CallManager installation, so that users can report problems with IP phone calls. Users report issues by using a Cisco IP Phone softkey that is labeled **QRT**. Any Cisco IP Phone that supports an HTTP web server also includes support for QRT. The IP phone must be in the Connected, Connected Conference, Connected Transfer, or On Hook state for the **QRT** softkey to be available.

QRT is a feature that extends to Cisco IP Phones as a Microsoft Windows NT service. Cisco Extended Functions, which supports the QRT feature, must be enabled in the Cisco CallManager service activation window. To enable Cisco Extended Functions, choose **Cisco CallManager Serviceability > Tools > Service Activation** and activate the service called Cisco Extended Functions.

When a user presses the **QRT** softkey, as shown in Figure 34-11, QRT displays a feedback window. It is possible that while the user is interacting with the QRT screen, another application, such as Cisco Call Back or Cisco IP Manager Assistant (IPMA), or function keys, such as settings, directories, messages, and so on, could overwrite the QRT screen. In this situation, QRT cannot send the feedback. To send feedback in such cases, the user has to press the **QRT** softkey again.

If a user presses the **QRT** softkey to generate a report and forgets to stop the logging process (the user must manually stop the logging process by pressing the **End** softkey on the Cisco IP Phone), the QRT tool periodically checks all IP phones that are generating reports and closes them. This action prevents the device from consuming large amounts of resources that, over time, could impact CTI performance. Currently, the default setting is to check every hour and to close devices that have remained open for more than an hour.

QRT records are written only when the end user presses the **QRT** softkey on the IP phone, selects a problem, and sends the report to the administrator. Otherwise, no records are written and the administrator cannot troubleshoot the problem. The figure shows the logging process of an audio call between two IP phones.

Figure 34-11 *QRT Submission Process*

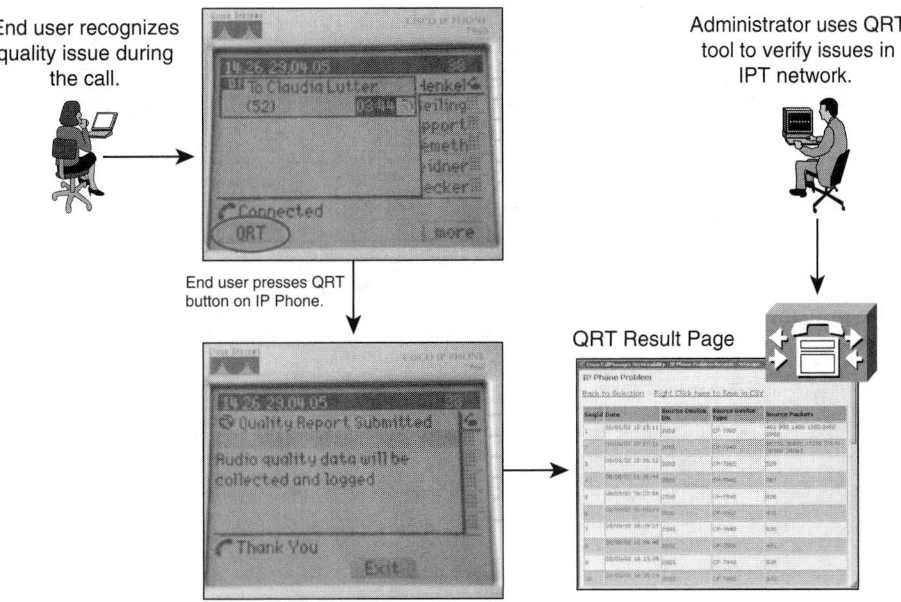

Depending on how the system administrator configured QRT for the Cisco IP Phone, users can use the **QRT** softkey in either of the two ways described in Table 34-4.

Table 34-4 *QRT Interaction*

Issue	What To Do
To quickly report an audio problem with a current call while on a call, press **More > QRT.**	Your IP phone system will collect and log call data for the current call and route this information to your system administrator.
To report a problem with your phone calls, press **More > QRT.**	Select the problem that you want to report from the list of problem categories. Some problem categories include a reason code that you can select to provide more details about the problem. Your IP phone system will store the information in a database or file and the administrator can run reports to diagnose the problem.

Activating the QRT Softkey

The system administrator can temporarily configure a Cisco IP Phone with QRT to troubleshoot problems with calls. Reconfigure the softkey layout for the IP phone (choose **Cisco CallManager Administration > Device > Device Settings > Softkey Template > softkey_template_name > Softkey Layout**) to activate the **QRT** softkey, as shown in Figure 34-12. Users can now report problems by using the **QRT** softkey during or after a call.

Figure 34-12 *Adding the* ***QRT*** *Softkey*

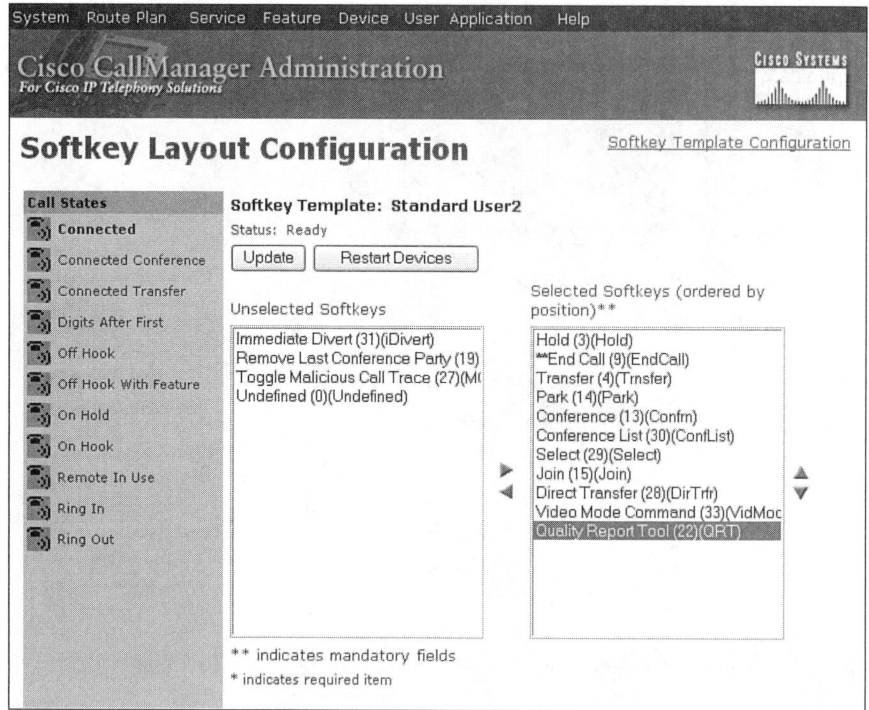

When the administrator modifies the softkey templates to activate the **QRT** softkey, the softkey should be added to the following call states:

- Connected
- Connected Conference
- Connected Transfer
- On Hook

Viewing QRT Logs

Administrators can view the IP phone problem reports that are generated by QRT by using QRT Viewer.

> **NOTE** QRT collects streaming data only once per call. Therefore, if user A calls user B and both submit reports for that call, only the first report includes streaming data (for example, delay, jitter, and ports being used).

Use the following steps to view the QRT logs:

Step 1 To open the IP phone Problem Reporting window, choose **Cisco CallManager Serviceability > Tools > QRT Viewer**.

Step 2 Choose the Cisco CallManager server for which you want to view a problem report. Enter a start and end date in the **Date** fields. In the **Time** fields, you can specify the time for those dates, if needed. An illustration of this is shown in Figure 34-13.

Figure 34-13 *Generating a QRT Query: Time and Date Fields*

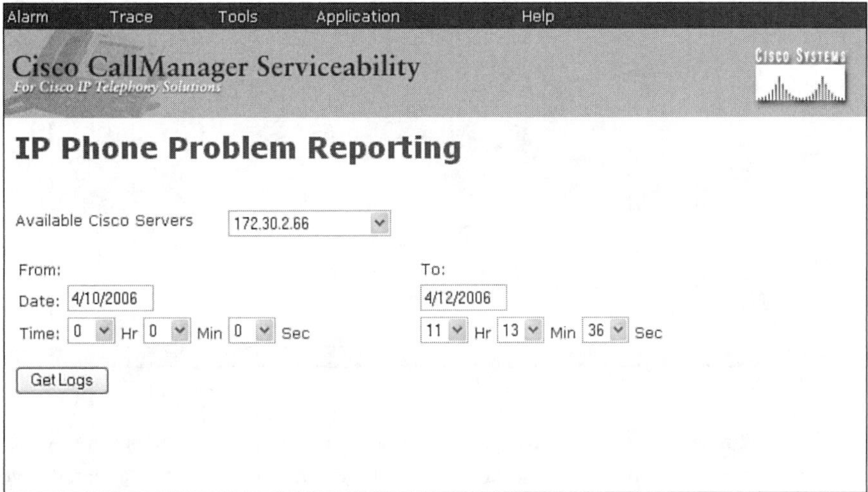

Step 3 Click the **Get Logs** button.

Step 4 From the **Extension Number**, **Device**, and **Category** drop-down menus, choose the extension numbers, the devices, and the problem categories that you want to include in the report, as shown in Figure 34-14.

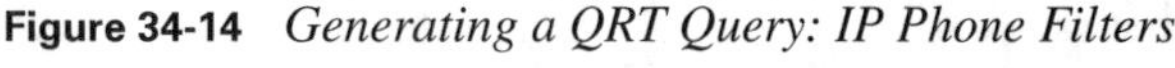

Figure 34-14 *Generating a QRT Query: IP Phone Filters*

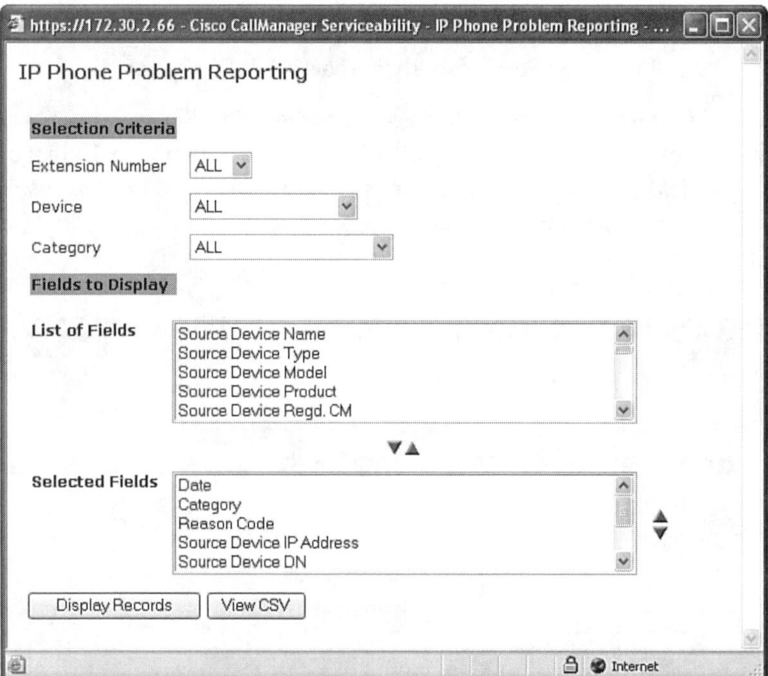

Step 5 From the **List of Fields** drop-down menu, select the fields that you want to include in the report and click the **down** arrow to move the selected fields to the Selected Fields pane.

The QRT output displays all IP phone problems for the specified time frame. For the filters set in the query, all issues within the time frame are displayed. In Figure 34-15, two QRT reports matched the submitted query. One of the QRT reports came from extension 4015 and the other from extension 4010.

When you choose **All** from the **Category** field, all problems are displayed. The Category and Reason Code columns are the areas that you should look at first. These two columns describe the problem and the reason. The output can be saved in a Comma-Separated Values (CSV) file.

> **NOTE** Because QRT reports are based only on entries in the QRT database and records are added to that database only if a user presses the **QRT** softkey, **QRT** cannot detect any problems on its own; it relies completely on user activity.

Figure 34-15 *QRT Report Sample*

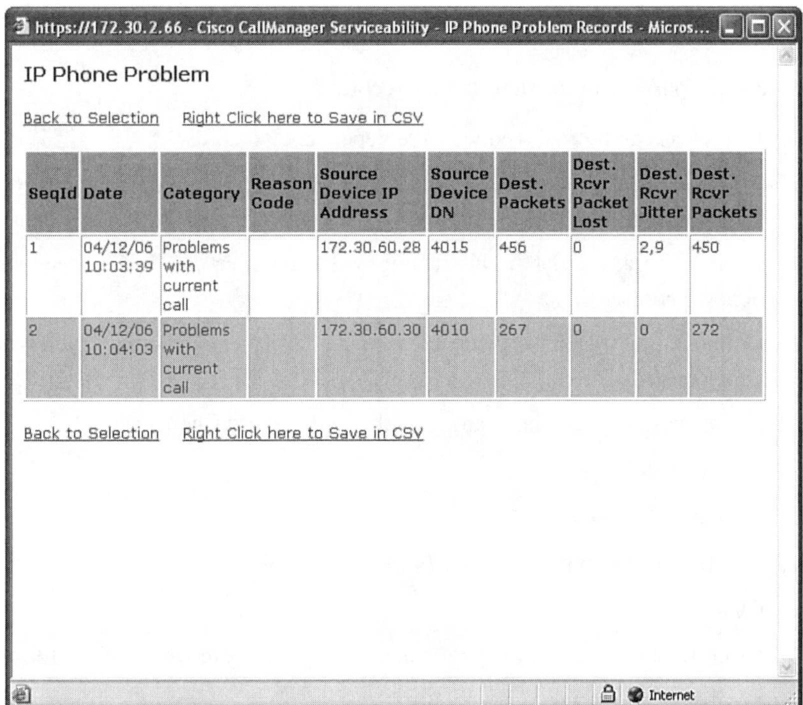

Summary

This chapter discussed the use of additional CallManager management tools, such as CiscoWorks ITEM, SNMP, and syslog. CiscoWorks ITEM is a suite of tools to monitor devices in an IP telephony network. SNMP and syslog are standards-based monitoring and alerting protocols used across nearly all Cisco platforms.

Cisco CallManager dependency records help in determining which devices are associated with other devices. The Password Changer tool can change passwords of CCMSysUser, CCMAdministrator, IPMASysUser, and Directory Manager with an easy-to-use interface. The Dialed Number Analyzer tool helps diagnose, tune, and trace dial plans. QRT helps administrators identify and resolve problems in an IP telephony network. End users can use QRT to send errors and call information to the administrator.

Review Questions

You can find the solutions to these questions in Appendix A, "Answers to Review Questions."

1. What is the purpose of the dependency records?
   a. Dial plans can be analyzed with the dependency records.
   b. It helps to find links between devices that keeps you from deleting a record in Cisco CallManager.
   c. Users and profiles that are interacting with each other can be displayed with the dependency records.
   d. Collaborating system services in Cisco CallManager can be displayed with the dependency records.
2. Which user password can be changed with the Password Changer tool?
   a. IPMAAdminUser
   b. CCMAdminUser
   c. CCMAdministrator
   d. CCMUser
3. The Cisco Dialed Number Analyzer can be used to analyze which of the following?
   a. Dial plans in an IP telephony environment
   b. Erlang b and Erlang c values
   c. CARs
   d. Dialed service numbers called by users
4. Complete the following sentence to make it true: When using QRT, reports are created __________.
   a. Automatically for all users
   b. In a round-robin fashion for all users
   c. When an administrator activates QRT Viewer
   d. When an end user presses the **QRT** button on the IP phone
5. Which SNMP version supports encryption and authentication?
   a. SNMP Version 1
   b. SNMP Version 2
   c. SNMP Version 3
   d. SNMP Version 5

6. What is the drawback of using CallManager dependency records?
   a. The dependency record function only shows devices that are directly related.
   b. Dependency records can lead to high CPU utilization.
   c. Dependency records require CDP to function.
   d. Dependency records only work with Cisco equipment.
7. When using the Password Changer tool, the passwords of the specified user accounts are changed _________.
   a. In the LDAP Directory of a single server
   b. In the LDAP Directory of all servers in the cluster
   c. In the Windows user database of a single server
   d. In the Active Directory for all servers in the cluster
8. How can you access the Password Changer tool?
   a. Using the **Serviceability Tools** menu
   b. Using the **CallManager Administration Tools** menu
   c. By typing **CCMPWDChanger** from a Windows Run prompt
   d. By selecting **CCMPWDChanger** from the Windows **Start** menu
9. You receive an alarm level 5 message coming in from the Cisco CallManager service. What well-known name is this alarm level assigned?
   a. Emergency
   b. Error
   c. Critical
   d. Alert
10. 10)Which of the following is the valid way to access Cisco DNA?
    a. Using a skin sample from John Chambers
    b. By using the **Application** menu in CallManager Serviceability
    c. By using the **Application** menu in CallManager Administration
    d. By entering the URL **https://<cm address>/DNA**

Part VIII: Appendix

APPENDIX **A**

Answers to Review Questions

Chapter 1

1. B

   The Cisco Unified Communications strategy focuses around designing network equipment equipped with the hardware resources and software features to handle a converged network environment.

2. B

   The Cisco CallManager is part of the call-processing layer. This layer is responsible for the call routing intelligence behind the IP telephony network.

3. A, B, and D

   The Cisco CallManager is responsible for call processing, signaling and device control, dial plan administration, phone feature administration, directory services, and a programming interface to external applications.

4. C

   The Cisco CallManager uses the proprietary Skinny signaling to communicate with the Cisco IP Phones.

5. A, B, and D

   The Cisco CallManager is responsible for handling all call-processing functions between Cisco IP Phones. The only communication element Cisco IP Phones are capable of handling alone is the streaming of RTP audio (spoken voice) between devices.

6. A and C

   Cisco CallManager runs using Windows 2000 and SQL 2000 as foundation operating system components. Windows 2000 provides base functionality, whereas SQL 2000 acts as the database store and replication agent for the information that drives the IP telephony network.

7. A

   Cisco includes a very simple user-management system called DC Directory to store user information for the IP telephony network.

8. C

The Cisco MCS 7825 can support a maximum of 1000 IP Phones. Because of its lack of redundant hardware, it is typically used in lab environments and small network deployments.

9. False

Cisco CallManager requires you to maintain a user directory primarily for advanced configuration features such as Extension Mobility and the IP SoftPhone.

10. B and C

By default, Cisco IP Phones use Skinny signaling to communicate with the Cisco CallManager server. Optionally, you can download a SIP image for the phone to allow it to operate under the Cisco SIP Proxy Server or with a third-party management system.

Chapter 2

1. A, B, C and D

All four of these are valid Cisco CallManager designs. E is incorrect because you need at least one call-processing agent in each cluster.

2. A

A 1:1 redundancy design offers maximum redundancy because each Cisco CallManager involved in call processing has a dedicated backup server. This model is often very cost prohibitive to most companies.

3. C and D

Although using a single cluster over WAN connections has very strict delay and bandwidth requirements, there are plenty of benefits. A common dial plan across all sites allows the network administrator to create a single dial plan, which replicates to all remote sites. In addition, if a Cisco CallManager fails, the IP Phones can failover to a Cisco CallManager server at another site, maintaining their full feature set.

4. B and C

Every Cisco CallManager cluster should have at least two servers, which allows call processing to continue should a single server fail. The data of the voice network is made redundant through the SQL database replication that occurs between servers in the cluster.

5. B

There can only be a single publisher server for the entire Cisco CallManager cluster. This is a SQL 2000 database restriction as the SQL publisher maintains the only writable copy of the database.

6. C

   A Cisco CallManager cluster supports a single SQL publisher and up to eight SQL subscriber servers.

7. B

   Survivable Remote Site Telephony (SRST) is absolutely necessary in a centralized Cisco CallManager design. SRST supports the remote IP Phones, providing PSTN calling access if the WAN connection fails.

8. True

   If the Cisco CallManager server at a location fails, the IP Phones can failover to another Cisco CallManager server at a remote site.

9. A and C

   The H.323 gatekeeper and SIP proxy server have the ability to be the centralized point of dial plan information. This keeps the network administrator from having to re-create the network dial plan at each of the sites.

10. E

    Cisco will support a maximum cluster size of 30,000 IP Phones in Cisco CallManager 4.0. This large cluster size was introduced in Cisco CallManager version 3.3 and was a tremendous increase from earlier Cisco CallManager versions.

Chapter 3

1. C

   Cisco CallManager installs using Windows 2000 as a foundation operating system.

2. D and E

   By default, all Subscriber servers install with the IIS web services enabled. This opens a point of access for a potential intruder. In addition, it consumes resources on the server that could be used for other mission-critical services that the Cisco CallManager provides.

3. B

   The Hardware Detection disk allows the installation program to determine which operating system software image is appropriate for your MCS platform. The Hardware Detection disk only recognizes Cisco-approved hardware.

4. C

To install multiple servers into a cluster, you must first configure hostname resolution. The most common method is through DNS; however, if DNS is unavailable, you can statically type a LMHOSTS file on each of the servers, which is nothing more than a text file mapping hostnames to IP addresses.

5. A, B, and E

The following services are not typically used on a production Cisco CallManager server platform:

— DHCP client

— Fax service

— FTP Publishing Service

— Smart Card

— Smart Card Helper

— Computer browser

— Distributed File System

— License Logging Service

6. C

The **Set Default** button activates the minimum services necessary to run the Cisco CallManager in a single-server configuration.

7. B

After the Cisco CallManager installation has completed, you should activate all services the Cisco CallManager will use. If you apply any configuration before you activate the services, unpredictable results can occur.

Chapter 4

1. A and D

Modern Cisco IP Phones support the G.711 (64 Kbps) and G.729 (8 Kbps) codecs. The old Cisco IP Phones acquired directly from Selsius supported the G.711 and G.723 (6.3 Kbps) codecs.

2. A and D

Because Cisco was one of the first companies to market with IP Phone technology, the Power over Ethernet (PoE) standard was not fully developed. Because of this, Cisco created its own, prestandard inline power. In modern times, the IEEE has solidified the 802.3af inline power standard. The Cisco IP Phone 7961G supports both of these inline power standards.

3. B, C, and E

The Cisco IP Phone 7905 and Cisco ATA 186 do not have built-in Ethernet switches; rather, they terminate a 10BASE-T Ethernet connection. The Cisco IP Phone 7912 is exactly the same as the 7905 but supplies the built-in 10/100 Ethernet switch. The same is true of the Cisco ATA 188.

4. C

The Cisco 7980 is the only IP Phone that provides built-in video-processing capabilities.

5. A, C, D, and B

When the IP Phone goes through the boot process, it initially obtains inline power using the Cisco prestandard or IEEE 802.3af. From there, it loads its built-in firmware image, which directs it to receive VLAN information through CDP. After it has a VLAN assignment, it broadcasts for a DHCP address, which also contains the TFTP server hostname or address. It then contacts the TFTP server to download its configuration file.

6. C

DHCP Option 150 is used to deliver the IP address of a TFTP server to a Cisco IP Phone. DHCP Option 66 is used to deliver the hostname of a TFTP server to a Cisco IP Phone.

7. A

Most Cisco IP Phones (all except the 7902G) support XML processing, which is an industry standard for storing data with processing and formatting options.

8. A and D

The Cisco IP Phone 7961 supports both the Cisco prestandard and 802.3af inline power, whereas the 7960 supports only the Cisco prestandard. In addition, the Cisco 7961 IP Phone adds support for Gigabit Ethernet connections.

9. C

The Cisco ATA 188 provides two Foreign Exchange Station (FXS) ports that allow you to convert up to two analog devices into VoIP devices.

10. A

The Cisco IP Phone 7902G is the most cost-effective, single-line IP Phone available from Cisco. It is the only IP Phone not equipped with a display screen, so the features are limited to that of a standard analog-style device.

Chapter 5

You can find the solutions to these questions in Appendix A, "Answers to Review Questions."

1. B, C, C, E, and F

Although a device pool can assign other settings, Cisco CallManager absolutely requires these elements to create a device pool.

2. B

A Cisco IP Phone 7960 only has a total of six line/speed dial buttons available, which immediately eliminates answers C and D. The IP Phone must have at least one line button assigned to it, which eliminates answer A. Answer B represents the default phone button template assigned to the Cisco IP Phone 7960.

3. B

To configure auto-registration, you must access the **System** > **Cisco CallManager** configuration screen and access the server for which you want to perform the auto-registration. Once there, you can define the range of extensions that the Cisco CallManager should assign to the Cisco IP Phones.

4. D

The Cisco CallManager ties configuration information to IP Phones through the MAC address. This is one of the most difficult aspects of adding Cisco IP Phones to the SQL database.

5. A

The Region configuration allows you to define the codec used to communicate within the IP Phone's region (typically a LAN environment) and with other regions (typically communicating over the WAN).

6. B

By changing the hostnames to IP addresses under the **System** > **Server** menu, the Cisco CallManager will automatically update the TFTP server configuration files to use IP addresses rather than hostnames. This eliminates an IP Phone's reliance on DNS.

7. D

The Cisco IP Phone uses a list of up to three redundant Cisco CallManagers for registration. This is known as its CallManager Group.

8. C

You cannot modify or delete the default CMLocal date/time group. IP Phones using this date/time group will use the same time and time zone the Cisco CallManager is using.

9. B

The softkey template governs the feature buttons available to the user on the bottom of their IP Phone display.

10. A, B, and C

All of these three methods allow you to obtain the MAC address of the Cisco IP Phone. Although the phone does also support a web interface where the MAC address can be found, it does not support Telnet capabilities.

Chapter 6

1. B

To access the user web pages, you can use the URL http://<*CCM IP Address*>/CCMUser/logon.asp. The most recent versions of CallManager also allow you to enable SSL support for the user web pages.

2. C

DC Directory is compatible with the Lightweight Directory Access Protocol (LDAP). This is a standard method for querying and modifying user database storage.

3. False

The IP telephony network will function correctly without the need for a user database. However, to gain advanced application support and to allow users to modify their own phone features through a web-based interface, you should add user database support to the network.

4. B, C, D, E, and H

These fields are all required when creating a user who is able to use a Cisco Softphone application. The "SoftPhone Support Enabled" is not a valid option on the user creation web page.

5. A and C

To configure a Cisco IP Phone through the CCMUser web pages, a user must have a valid user account created for them in the Cisco CallManager database and that account must be associated with at least one Cisco IP Phone.

6. D

   To use both the personal address book and fast dial features, the user must first subscribe to the appropriate XML services. These services will then be made available by pressing the **Services** button on the Cisco IP Phone.

7. A

   The default Message Waiting Lamp policy for the Cisco CallManager system configured on each Cisco IP Phone is to use the system policy. The system policy default setting is to always light the lamp and prompt the user.

8. False

   Cisco CallManager only ships with one language: English. You can download additional languages from Cisco as needed.

9. C

   After subscribing to the fast dial service, a user can configure their IP Phone with up to 99 fast dial codes associated to users in their personal address book.

10. A

    The CCMUser pages only provide the Call Forward All option to the user. Call Forward Busy and Call Forward No Answer are available from the CCMAdmin pages.

Chapter 7

1. C, D, and F

   You can use Cisco's BAT to insert IP Phones, users, device profiles, IPMA managers and assistants, Catalyst 6000 FXS ports, VG200 analog ports, client matter codes, forced authorization codes, Call Pickup groups, and phone certificates.

2. B

   Auto-registration is used to allow newly installed Cisco IP Phones to gain a temporary extension that the user or administrator can use to dial in to the TAPS extension to configure their IP Phone.

3. B and C

   To perform a successful device import using BAT, you must use a comma-separated value (CSV) text file to define unique device values and a valid device template specifying common device settings.

4. D

   This Excel spreadsheet eases the CSV file creation process and is always stored in the directory C:\CiscoWebs\BAT\ExcelTemplate.

5. A

   The Cisco BAT utility will only install on the Publisher server because it makes changes directly to the SQL database.

6. A

   The device template can define many line settings, but BAT will only configure the lines you have specified in the CSV file. The trouble occurs when you have more lines defined in the CSV file than exist in the device template. If this situation occurs, BAT will cut off the number of lines on the device to equal that of the device template.

7. C

   The Create Dummy MAC Address check box generates random MAC addresses for the IP Phones and saves them in the CallManager database. The administrator can then manually update the entries or use TAPS to automate the process.

8. B

   You can accomplish bulk updates using a query in the BAT utility. A query can match devices based on any number of criteria. You can then specify the setting you want to change on the matched devices (music on hold, in this case).

9. B

   TAPS relies on the Customer Response Application, which manages the automated prompt and update process for the user.

10. A and D

    CSV files are simply text files containing data separated by commas. Cisco has included the Microsoft Excel template to make the generation of these files easier. However, an administrator can define their own CSV format by manually creating a CSV file using a simple text editor, such as Microsoft Notepad.

Chapter 8

1. E

   The syntax to turn on PoE on a CatOS-based switch is **set port inline power** *mod/port* **auto**.

2. B, C, and D

   Cisco Catalyst switches have the ability to provide PoE (both 802.3af and the Cisco prestandard) and handle CoS tagging on incoming packets (both on the data and voice VLANs).

3. A, B, and D

   To support dual VLANs on a single port, you must configure the port with voice and access VLANs and use the trunk tagging mechanism (802.1Q) to mark the packets. Of course, the IP Phone must also have an internal switch to support an additional device (such as a PC) connection.

4. A, C, and E

   Cisco IP Phones can be powered through wall power (using an additional power brick sold separately from the IP Phone), Cisco prestandard PoE, or the Cisco Power Patch Panel (midspan power injection). All Cisco IP Phones do not yet support the IEEE 802.3af PoE standard. This support will be added as newer models are released.

5. D

   802.3af is the IEEE industry standard for PoE.

6. C

   The Catalyst 3750 uses the NativeIOS operating system. The set-based syntax only applies to the CatOS. In addition, there is no "on" mechanism for inline power, rather, only an auto-detect mechanism exists.

7. B and C

   Dual VLAN configurations can only be accomplished using the 802.1Q tagging mechanism. When deploying this configuration on a 6500 series switch running the CatOS, you must use the auxiliary VLAN configurations. Voice VLAN configurations apply to the NativeIOS.

8. D

   When you enable the auxiliary VLAN on a CatOS switch, the tagging mechanism handles the trunk configuration for you. No further configuration is needed.

9. C

   A Cisco IP Phone tags all voice traffic using a CoS marking of 5. This is the highest user-defined marking Cisco recommends.

10. B

    Attached devices are considered untrusted (by default) by a Cisco IP Phone. This means that the Cisco IP Phone will mark traffic with a CoS value of 0, unless otherwise specified by the administrator.

Chapter 9

1. A and D

   Foreign Exchange Station (FXS) ports connect to analog station endpoints (such as fax machines, modems, and telephones). Foreign Exchange Office (FXO) ports connect to the PSTN or act as PBX trunk connections. The third type of analog interface (E&M) is not listed in the question.

2. B and D

   Cisco Catalyst switches have the ability to provide PoE (both 802.3af and the Cisco prestandard) and handle CoS tagging on incoming packets (both on the data and voice VLANs).

3. B and C

   All Cisco IP Phones use Skinny signaling to communicate with the Cisco CallManager, but only the router-like device that uses Skinny is the VG200 series. This is because the VG200 series acts as a number of end devices with numerous FXS ports.

4. D

   The correct wildcard to use on voice gateway devices is the "." which matches any dialed digit. When configuring route patterns on the Cisco CallManager, you use the "X" wildcard to accomplish this same thing.

5. C

   The Call Classification feature gives you the ability to distinguish and monitor OnNet and OffNet calls through the gateway. Using this information, you can prevent toll-fraud techniques using conference calls and transfers.

6. B

   When configuring an MGCP router, you can use the syntax **mgcp call-agent** *ip_address* to designate the primary Cisco CallManager. You can use the **ccm-manager redundant-host** syntax to designate the secondary and tertiary Cisco CallManager servers. The tertiary CallManager in this syntax is 10.1.1.6.

7. A and B

   You can configure a switch running the NativeIOS using the same configuration as you would a standard voice gateway. Non-IOS MGCP is used if the 6500 Catalyst switch is running the CatOS operating system.

8. B

   Trunk configurations are logical links to other networks. They have the ability to determine the location of an endpoint, but do *not* carry voice traffic. Gateways also act as logical links to other networks, but the CallManager also uses them to route voice traffic.

9. B

Gatekeepers ease configuration of Intercluster Trunk connections by providing a central point of trunking. Without a gatekeeper, every CallManager cluster must have an Intercluster Trunk connection to every other cluster in a full-mesh relationship. Unfortunately, gatekeepers also introduce a single point of failure in the network, which is why you should consider additional failover mechanisms for this device.

10. C

CallManager uses the H.225 Registration, Admission, and Status (RAS) protocol to communicate with the gatekeeper. You can think of this as a conversation protocol that allows the CallManager to determine the location of an endpoint and the authority to send the call.

Chapter 10

1. D

CallManager route plans are always configured from the bottom-up. Devices/trunks come first, then route groups, route lists, and, finally, route patterns.

2. False

You can only configure digit manipulation to occur at the route list and route pattern levels. This is why you should group similar devices together in the same route group: All devices in the route group will have the same digit manipulation settings applied.

3. A

After a device has been assigned to a route group, it is made unavailable to any other configurations. If you want to use a device for multiple route patterns, associate its route group with multiple route lists. You can only associate devices directly with route patterns if you are not already using those devices in a route group.

4. C

Voice gateways are used to bridge VoIP networks to either non-VoIP networks (such as the PSTN) or to other VoIP networks.

5. A

Route groups contain a list of gateways to use in precedence order.

6. B, C, and D

The ! wildcard represents a variable-length string, the . wildcard represents a single digit, and the @ wildcard represents the entire NANP. The * is not a wildcard as it represents just the * digit on a telephone keypad.

7. C

Route lists contain an ordered list of route groups that CallManager should use when it matches a route pattern.

8. E

When digits are contained within braces, they match only a single digit in the extension. In this case, [45] could be read in plain English as, "Four or Five" (mentally insert a comma between the digits).

9. B

To stop the secondary dial tone, you need to remove the check from the **Provide Outside Dial-Tone** check box for the route pattern. It is checked by default when the route pattern is created.

10. C and D

The X wildcard matches any dialed digit, whereas the ! wildcard matches any variable-length dial string (zero digits or more). By placing the 7XX before the !, the CallManager expects to see at least three dialed digits followed by any number of digits.

Chapter 11

1. D

Translation patterns are defined to provide a "translation of last resort." CallManager processes them just before it routes a call. After the translation pattern has modified the dialed digits, CallManager sends the transformed digits through digit analysis again.

2. C

The DN 0111 passes through the right-justified X wildcards. The result is that the CallManager prepends the 972555 to the 0111 and sends 9725550111 as the CLID information.

3. B

The predot digit discard instructions remove all dialed digits before the period.

4. A

You must apply the route filter to either a route pattern or a translation pattern for it to take effect. After you have applied it to a route pattern, you must select either **Route This Pattern** or **Block This Pattern** to define the allow or deny action.

5. A

The 11D@10D digit discard instruction takes an 11-digit long-distance number and converts it to a 10-digit number. This is typically used for toll-bypass purposes.

6. D

Applying a calling-party transformation mask of 8 causes all caller ID information to be replaced and become just the digit 8. To prefix an 8 using a transformation mask, wildcard digits (X) would be necessary.

7. B

Called-party transformation masks always transform the dialed-number information.

8. D

The order of application of digit translation applies the transformation mask before the prefix digits, causing the resulting caller ID to display as 5555123.

9. D

In this case, you have created a routing loop within the CallManager. The route pattern prefixes an 8 to the 4xxx dialed numbers and the translation pattern strips the 8 and returns the digits to the CallManager for processing. The call will loop ten times through the CallManager route plan and then return a fast busy signal.

10. B

Calling-party transformations change caller ID information, whereas called-party transformations change dialed-number information.

Chapter 12

1. B

If you have checked the **Use Personal Preferences** check box in the Hunt Forward Settings section of the Hunt Pilot Configuration window, CallManager will check the Call Forward No Coverage settings for the original called number that forwarded the call to the hunt pilot. If you have not defined a number for this setting, the caller will receive a reorder tone when CallManager attempts to forward the call.

2. A

Using the top-down distribution algorithm causes the Cisco CallManager to distribute the incoming call to the first member of the line group and work down if the parties are unavailable. If you were using the circular distribution algorithm, the call would have been distributed to party 4 because party 3 received the last call.

3. B

The maximum hunt timer always overrides the RNA reversion timeout configured on the line group. In this case, the call would only hunt through the first three members of the group before the call reached the maximum timer of 15 seconds.

4. A, B, and C

To configure a hunt group, you must first configure a line group, which groups member DNs together. Then, you must set up a hunt list, which orders one or more line groups together. Finally, you must configure a hunt pilot pointing to the hunt list.

5. B

Available lines are serving an active call but can accept a new call. Idle lines are those categorized as not serving any calls at this time.

6. B

The broadcast distribution algorithm rings all members of the line group at the same time. The first one to retrieve the incoming call will receive it.

7. A

The **Stop Hunting** selection causes the CallManager to use just the first member DN in the line group and stop if the member is unavailable.

8. E

By checking the **Use Personal Preferences** check box, CallManager ignores any call forward settings defined under the hunt pilot. Instead, it looks to the Call Forward No Coverage section of the original called party that triggered the call to the hunt group.

9. A

Hunt groups are configured from the bottom up, just like the CallManager route plan. You must first add member DNs to the CallManager configuration, then group them into a line group, followed by the hunt list and hunt pilot.

10. B

By default, CallManager matches the hunt pilot DN and hunts through the members listed in all line groups defined in the hunt list. This could take a considerable amount of time if there are many members or line groups configured.

Chapter 13

1. C and E

   When configuring time-of-day routing, you must apply a time schedule to the partition containing the DNs you want to restrict by time of day. You must also configure the partition for the correct time zone (or choose to use the local time zone of the phone placing the call).

2. B

   You can apply time-of-day calling restrictions only to the calling party through a calling search space. Because of this, the time period should be configured to allow calls from 08:00 to 17:00 Monday to Friday and the time zone of user A.

3. B, D, and E

   Any DN-assigned item can be assigned to a partition. Phones and gateways are not assigned DNs; phone lines, route patterns, and translation patterns are assigned DNs (directory number is used synonymously with phone line).

4. A

   The correct order of Class of Service configuration is as follows: DNs are placed in partitions; partitions are placed in calling search spaces; and calling search spaces are assigned to the calling device.

5. A, B, and C

   If you have assigned a calling search space to both the IP Phone and its directory number, the calling search spaces are combined where the directory number takes precedence. Route patterns are not calling devices and cannot be assigned a calling search space.

6. B

   CallManager processes the call by looking through the partitions in the calling search space from the top of the list to the bottom. To save on processing time, you should place the more frequently used partitions at the top of the user list. You can also use the ordered processing feature to implement access-list-like calling restrictions.

7. D

   Time periods are created first and added to time schedules, which are then assigned to a partition.

8. A

   CallManager will allow you to create identical, duplicate route patterns provided you have assigned them to different partitions. Likewise, you can only assign a route pattern to one partition. In this example, you must create two sets of PSTN route patterns. One set should be added to the partition restricted by the 8:00 a.m. to 5:00 p.m. time schedule. The other set should be added to a partition not restricted by a time schedule. A calling search space containing the restricted partition is then assigned to the users limited to 8:00 a.m. to 5:00 p.m. PSTN calling and a calling search space containing the unrestricted partition is assigned to the users able to reach the PSTN anytime.

9. C

Time-of-day restrictions can only be applied to partitions. These partitions are then added to a user's calling search space, at which point the CallManager applies them.

10. D

Time periods allow you to configure recurring days by selecting either "Repeat Every Week From…" or "Repeat Every Year On…". In this case, we would choose to Repeat Every Year On December 25th.

Chapter 14

1. B

Configuring an IOS-based gatekeeper eliminates the need to configure a full-mesh Intercluster Trunk relationship between disparate Cisco CallManager clusters in your organization. Instead, all the clusters can trunk directly to the H.323 gatekeeper, which provides a centralized point of admission and bandwidth control.

2. B

Router-based QoS mechanisms are not designed to handle CAC. If the CallManager routes too many calls over the IP WAN, the voice quality for all calls will degrade.

3. B and D

In a distributed call-control environment, an independent device is needed to manage admission and bandwidth control. This responsibility falls on the H.323 gatekeeper device. The Cisco CallManager only manages these functions in a centralized call deployment.

4. C

The IP Phones are assigned to a device pool, which points to an SRST Reference. This SRST Reference contains the IP address of the gateway running SRST or points the IP Phone to its default gateway. This configuration is sent to the IP Phone when it first registers with the Cisco CallManager.

5. D

Cisco CallManager deducts 24 kbps for each call in a location-based CAC deployment. Using this calculation, you can find that five calls consume 120 kbps, fitting nicely over a 128-kbps connection.

6. A, B, and E

   When AAR reroutes a call over the PSTN, CallManager takes the original DN of the IP Phone and combines it with the external phone number mask. The resulting number is then prepended with whatever additional digits are specified under the AAR group and forwarded over the PSTN.

7. C

   To configure SRST, you first enter the command **call-manager-fallback** from global configuration mode. The router then places you in a subconfiguration mode where the additional settings can be specified.

8. B

   AAR will use the external phone number mask configured under Phone B's DN to complete the call. This mask prepends the necessary digits to the DN, at which point the AAR group prepends any additional digits that might be required to exit the PSTN gateway and CallManager routes the call across the PSTN.

9. D

   Before AAR configurations can take effect, the feature must be enabled clusterwide. This is accomplished from the **Service > Service Parameters > Cisco CallManager Configuration** window.

10. D

    AAR is meant to act as a call redirection mechanism for location-based bandwidth restrictions. It does not reroute calls during a WAN failure. Although any of these answers could cause AAR redirection to fail, answer D is the most likely explanation.

Chapter 15

1. C

   MRGLs are an ordered list of MRGs. The MRGs contain the media resources in the Cisco CallManager cluster. By assigning a MRGL to a device, you grant access to whatever resources are contained in the MRGs the MRGL contains.

2. B and C

   The Media Resource Manager (MRM) manages all resources in the CallManager cluster. The software-based resources are all grouped under the Voice Media Streaming Application, which is activated in a Cisco CallManager server. Transcoding is one example of a hardware-based resource.

3. A

   Hardware-based conference bridge resources are identified to the CallManager by their MAC address. Most of the configuration for these resources takes place on the resource itself.

4. B

   The Voice Media Streaming Application is a service that runs on the Cisco CallManager servers. It allows the CallManager server to participate in all media resource functionality, including conferencing, media termination point, music on hold, and annunciator.

5. B

   Network hold MoH is played anytime a person is placed on hold because of a network-related function. These functions include conference calls, transfers, and Call Park. User hold MoH sources are only played when the user literally presses the hold button on their IP Phone.

6. A

   The Cisco CallManager server creates individual unicast streams for IP Phone users. Multicast support must be configured on a per-server and per-audio source basis.

7. B

   When a MRGL is assigned at both the device pool and IP Phone level, the MRGL on the IP Phone takes precedence. The MGM will use the MTP resource listed first in the first MRG of the IP Phone MRGL.

8. B

   By default, the media resources are assigned to the default MRG, which cannot be modified or deleted. The MRM will use a round-robin load-balancing system for these resources.

9. E

   Because of the amount of processor resources consumed by session transcoding, this function is limited to hardware-based digital signal processor (DSP) resources.

10. C

   The fixed audio source is always assigned audio source ID 51. This audio source ID must be linked to a fixed sound device in the CallManager server before it becomes active.

Chapter 16

1. A and D

   After an administrator has configured IP phone Services to be made available to the users, the users can subscribe to them through the User Options pages (http://<ccm_server_ip>/ccmuser). After the user has subscribed to the services, they can access them by pressing the **Services** button on the IP phone.

2. B, C, and F

   You can assign softkey templates to an individual IP phone (at the device level), to a group of IP phones (at the device pool level), or to all auto-registered IP phones (at the device defaults level).

3. B

   The transfer functionality works just fine without administrator configuration, provided you have provisioned MTP resources for the cluster.

4. A

   When a user performs a direct transfer (**DirTrfr**), the user making the transfer stays out of the call. This uses minimal cluster resources to accomplish the task.

5. B

   Barge only functions when multiple users are using the same line (shared line appearance).

6. D

   Auto answer capabilities are configured on a per-DN basis. They allow a user to answer a ringing phone automatically using either a headset or speakerphone.

7. C

   Michael will hear a dial tone. The busy trigger configuration for a shared extension will restrict any additional incoming calls after the line usage has reached the defined number. Only the maximum calls parameter can restrict outbound calls.

8. B

   Because you cannot modify the built-in softkey templates in Cisco CallManager, the only solution is to create a new softkey template, add the **Call Back** softkey to the Ring Out and On Hook call states, and assign the softkey template to all users in your organization.

9. B

   Group Call Pickup allows users to pick up a ringing phone located within their own Call Pickup Group or another Call Pickup Group. Standard Call Pickup allows users to pick up a ringing phone located within their Call Pickup Group. Other Group Call Pickup allows users to pick up a ringing phone in their pickup group or another pickup group without dialing a group number. Call Park allows users to pick up a call on hold by dialing the appropriate extension.

10. C

    Conference Barge (cBarge) allows a user to barge in a call and use dedicated conference resources to maintain the call. Furthermore, the on-screen display shows the user entering a conference. The standard Barge feature uses the built-in conference capabilities of Cisco IP Phones and does not show the user as being in a conference call.

Chapter 17

1. D

   When configuring the Cisco CallManager Extension Mobility feature, you must create a device profile for all users who plan on using the Extension Mobility capabilities. This device profile is then associated with the user account.

2. A and C

   CallManager transmits the MCID messages over a PRI connection. These messages are sent to a MCID-Terminating (T) device on the PSTN from an MCID-Originating (O) device.

3. F

   If a user enters the incorrect CMC, the CallManager requires them to hang up and attempt the call again.

4. B, D, E, and G

   By permitting the Connected Name and Line information, User A will be able to see the information of the room they are calling. By restricting the Calling Name and Line information, the hotel guest will not be able to see the information for User A.

5. A

   The default behavior of the Extension Mobility service parameters prevents a user from multiple logins using Extension Mobility.

6. D

   Forced Authorization Codes (FAC) allows users to enter a PIN to obtain a specific authorization. You can then assign route patterns a minimum authorization level to keep nonessential personnel from dialing high-cost PSTN numbers.

7. C

   Malicious Call Identification (MCID) is triggered by pressing the **MCID** softkey assigned to the Softkey Template Connected call state.

8. D

   CallManager 4.1 added the Executive Override MLPP parameter. In earlier versions of CallManager, Flash Override was the highest assignable MLPP level.

9. D

   The Ignore Presentation Indicators (Internal Calls Only) configuration setting from the device configuration allows you to overrule caller ID restrictions for internal calls on a device-by-device basis.

10. C

You only need to create a single logged out device profile for the Cisco IP Phones in your organization. They will adopt this profile when you select the Use Current Device Settings for the Logged Out profile of the device.

Chapter 18

1. 1. D, 2. C, 3. E, 4. A, 5. B

2. B

By selecting one of the hunt group members as an "always-route member," the Cisco CallManager will route the call to the destination when the queue is full or the hold time has been reached. This destination is typically a voice mail or auto-attendant system.

3. C and E

The Cisco Telephony Call Dispatcher (TCD) must be active to dispatch calls to the active Attendant Console clients. The CTIManager must be active to integrate the CTI-based Attendant Console software with the CallManager system.

4. C

Only the longest-idle distribution algorithm can be configured from the Pilot Point Configuration window. All others must be configured either from the Hunt Group Configuration window or from the Attendant Console Configuration Tool.

5. C

A CallManager cluster can have a maximum of 32 hunt groups.

6. B

When you have configured Broadcast Hunting (using the Attendant Console Configuration Tool), the incoming calls to the pilot point will be immediately placed into a queue that the attendants can answer, using the Attendant Console client, as they become available.

7. B

The ac user must be created and associated with all Cisco IP Phones used by the Attendant Console clients. As a good security practice, this username and password should be changed using the Attendant Console Configuration Tool.

8. D

Accessing the Attendant Console Configuration Tool is a strange task indeed. You must first dig through the hard drive to find the batch file and execute it for the Java-based utility to appear.

9. A

An operator can revert a parked call in many ways. The easiest is to right-click on the parked call in the Attendant Console software and choose **Revert Park**.

10. D

Attendant Console users are not added through the user menu; rather, they are added through the **Service > Cisco CM Attendant Console > Cisco CM Attendant Console User** window. Users added through the normal User menu will not be available to select as Attendant Console users.

Chapter 19

1. B

IPMA managers only have the ability to change the divert target from the IPMA Manager Configuration page. This allows them to direct incoming calls to another attendant.

2. C

It's so obvious, the question is almost difficult. Configuring Cisco IPMA in shared-line mode requires lines to be shared DNs between the manager and assistant.

3. A

Shared-line mode is supported by the CallManager 4.x versions and enabled features not previously supported in the proxy-mode, such as Call Join, Privacy, and Direct Transfer.

4. B and C

The three flagship Cisco IP Phones support IPMA: The Cisco 7940, 7960, and 7970.

5. B

Shared-line mode supports a maximum of 10 assistants per manager.

6. B

Cisco used the Tomcat server (developed under Apache) applied as a Windows service to manage many of the additional services that previously required the Customer Response Solution (CRS) software add-on.

7. C

After changing the service parameters, the MA Servlet must be restarted through the Tomcat web server.

8. B

   From this list, the first thing you must configure is the IPMA manager. You can then add assistants and install the Assistant Console.

9. D

   The IPMA Assistant Console is installed from a custom IPMA page managed by the Tomcat web server. By accessing the URL http://<IPMA server>/ma/Install/IPMAConsoleInstall.jsp, an automated script runs and places shortcuts on the assistant's desktop and Start menu to run the application.

10. B

   The IPMA service communicates to all servers in a CallManager cluster by using the CTIManager. It only requires a single CTI connection for all users in a cluster.

Chapter 20

1. A

   All critical hot fixes and patches to the Cisco IP Telephony Operating System are posted on Cisco.com for download within 24 hours of the announcement from Microsoft. All noncritical hot fixes and patches are bundled for a consolidated, monthly release from Cisco.com.

2. B

   Heuristic scanning should not be allowed because this feature can prevent CallManager Administration web pages from operating correctly.

3. C

   A headless (standalone) version of the Cisco Security Agent (CSA) is provided by Cisco, free of charge, to protect Cisco CallManager against malicious applications.

4. C

   Password expiration policies should be disabled on all service accounts. If the service account password were to expire, it could prevent a variety of CallManager services from operating correctly.

5. C

   The IIS service comprises 80 percent of all attacks on Windows servers. Because of this, it is a best practice to stop the IIS service on all Cisco CallManager Subscribers.

6. C

   The Cisco CallManager server is not designed to handle nonapproved third-party utilities.

7. A

   The most automated process for installing security updates and hot fixes to the CallManager server is e-mail subscription to the Cisco CallManager Notification Tool. The updates must then be manually downloaded and installed.

8. A and C

   The first of these scripts focuses on securing the foundation Windows 2000 operating system with security settings recommended for Cisco CallManager servers only. The second of these scripts focuses on securing the SQL communication on the server.

9. D

   There is not even a product called WebX SecureServer.

10. A and B

   Only virus protection software can prevent a server against virus infection. In addition, only the managed CSA version provides firewall functionality. The standalone CSA version allows all inbound network connections.

Chapter 21

1. C

   The default CallManager installation without MLA uses the Windows 2000 Administrator account for both CallManager Administration and server administration. A sniffed username and password could mean the demise of both the CallManager Administration interface and the underlying Windows operating system.

2. B

   The URL to access the Cisco CallManager Administration interface remains the same. The only difference is using the HTTPS protocol rather than just HTTP.

3. C

   There is no read-write access in Cisco MLA. This setting would be the same as full access.

4. D

   After you enable MLA and restart the World Wide Web Service in Windows 2000, a new account "CCMAdministrator" is stored in the Windows 2000 Registry for full CallManager Administration access.

5. A

   There is no Standard Device functional group. Rather, MLA splits the device functions into the specific devices managed, such as Standard Phone or Standard Gateway.

6. B

There is no FullAccess group in the MLA user group defaults. The full access role is assigned to the SuperUserGroup.

7. B

Self-signed certificates raise an automatic red flag in any client web browser. This is because there is no trusted authority (a Certificate Authority) authenticating the web server.

8. A

The MLA user accounts are stored in an LDAP directory. By default, this is the DC Directory installed with the Cisco CallManager; however, you can change this directory storage to anther directory (such as Active Directory).

9. D

CallManager MLA stores the CCMAdminstrator account in the Windows Registry. This allows a "back door" into the CallManager Administration interface if the LDAP directory is unavailable.

10. A and C

By default, MLA is disabled for a clean CallManager install; however, it will remain enabled (with a new, random CCMAdministrator password) if upgrading from previous MLA (and Cisco CallManager) version that was enabled.

Chapter 22

1. B and C

Users can exploit the Call Forward All feature (which they can configure through a web interface) and transfer from voice-mail features to make toll calls using the corporate voice network.

2. A

To restrict external call transfers (which block OffNet-to-OffNet transfers), route patterns and gateways should be classified as OnNet or OffNet. Route patterns are typically used to restrict outbound calls, whereas gateways are used to restrict incoming calls.

3. A and D

By default, the ad hoc conference restrictions are set to **Never**, which opens the possibility of toll fraud. You can choose to set the restrictions to **When Conference Creator Drops Out** or **When No OnNet Parties Remain in the Conference** to restrict this toll fraud method.

4. A

By default, the ad hoc conference restrictions are set to **Never**, which opens the possibility of toll fraud. You can choose to set the restrictions to **When Conference Creator Drops Out** or **When No OnNet Parties Remain in the Conference** to restrict this toll fraud method.

5. C

Forced Authorization Codes (FACs) allow you to restrict call routing to destinations based on user codes. This is not only useful to prevent toll fraud, but also to determine which users or departments are making toll calls for billing purposes.

6. B

Commonly exploited countries have special area codes that look like area codes of the United States. Not all international numbers begin with the 011 identifier (in North America). Because of this, you should be especially careful to restrict international area codes using route patterns.

7. A

The most automated process for installing security updates and hot fixes to the CallManager server is e-mail subscription to the Cisco CallManager Notification Tool. The updates must then be manually downloaded and installed.

8. B

The correct configuration of time-of-day routing is as follows: create time periods, add the time periods to a time schedule, assign the time schedule to a partition, and assign the partition to a calling search space.

9. D

Client Matter Codes (CMCs) are typically used to track calls to a specific department or user. However, they do not give you the varying authorization levels of the FAC feature.

10. A, D, and E

By classifying the route patterns, trunks, and gateways as OnNet or OffNet, you can effectively curb OffNet-to-OffNet transfer toll fraud.

Chapter 23

1. A

The IP phone contains key information about the IP addresses of the Cisco CallManager, network gateway, TFTP server, and DNS servers. Obtaining this information allows a hacker to map out the location of key network resources.

2. A

Only Cisco's flagship phones, the 7940, 7960, and 7970, support configuration file authentication. The 7920 wireless handset does not support this feature.

3. B

You can find all the security settings for an IP phone under the Phone Configuration window in the Cisco CallManager administration utility.

4. A

To access the built-in web server of an IP phone, simply access the URL http://IP-Phone's-IP-address. There are no security options; you will be directed to a page giving all the information about the IP phone's network settings.

5. B

Gratuitous ARP attackers always operate from the local network. This is necessary due to the nature of ARP packets.

6. C

Even with authentication and encryption features enabled, SCCP maintains its signaling role. There are no currently known attacks against Skinny signaling, so there was no reason to secure it further.

7. D

An IP phone can provide all the preceding information with the exception of the intranet server address.

8. D

Cisco CallManager does not allow you to disable the PC port of the 7912 IP Phone. Filling the PC port of the phone with glue (or some similarly drastic step), or downgrading to the 7905 IP Phone is the best step for now.

9. B

Secure Sockets Layer (SSL) was the predecessor to Transport Layer Security (TLS). SSL was primarily applied to HTTPS connections, whereas TLS became more universally used.

10. A

Since Cisco CallManager 3.3(3), the signed firmware validation feature is already enabled. This prevents hackers from constructing their own, rogue firmware images for the Cisco IP Phones.

Chapter 24

1. E and F

   Cryptographic services include functions for authenticity, confidentiality, integrity, and nonrepudiation.

2. A and F

   Because of its speed, symmetric encryption is a good choice for real-time encryption of bulk data. This speed is achieved because the encryption key is the same as the decryption key.

3. D and F

   Asymmetric encryption is very powerful because it provides a public key (capable of handling encryption and decryption of data) and a private key (also capable of handling encryption and decryption of data). Asymmetric encryption is often used to create signatures and for key exchange only because of the high overhead associated with the algorithm.

4. B and F

   If a hacker obtains a hash of some data, the only method they can use to reverse engineer the data is to use a brute force attack, which is computationally difficult. Hash does work well for ensuring data does not change accidentally; however, it does not protect against man-in-the-middle attacks. Because of this, hashing is often combined with an encryption algorithm, such as AES. AES can use MD5 or SHA-1 for hashing data.

5. F

   Only F does not apply to digital signatures. Digital signatures are created by encrypting the result of a hashing process using a private key.

6. D

   SHA-1 is the modern standard for creating a 160-bit hash. MD5 is no longer recommended because it can run into problems with duplicate hashes on large amounts of data.

7. A

   Nonrepudiation methods prove to others that a certain source sent some data. This is very similar to authentication; however, authentication can only prove to YOU that a certain device sent the data rather than proving to OTHERS that a certain device sent the data.

8. B

   Rivest, Shamir, and Adleman (RSA) is the only asymmetric algorithm in this list.

9. A

Asymmetric algorithms use two keys: one public and one private. The public key can be used for encryption and decryption of data and is sent to any requesting host. The private key can be used for encryption and decryption of data and is kept strictly for the sending host.

10. D

With current mathematical algorithms, it is feasibly impossible to generate a private key from a public key.

Chapter 25

1. D

Symmetric keys provide the fast encryption standards needed by today's applications; however, these keys need a method for exchange over an unsecured network. PKI provides a solution to this challenge.

2. A and F

Because of its speed, symmetric encryption is a good choice for real-time encryption of bulk data. This speed is achieved because the encryption key is the same as the decryption key.

3. D and F

The trusted introducer *and its clients* must trust the root of a system. The root guarantees the identity of the trusted introducer. Only the trusted introducer can guarantee the authenticity of any member of the system.

4. D

A certificate includes the identity of the issuer of the certificate, the identity of the owner of the certificate, and the public key of the owner.

5. C and F

Securing enrollment through a PKI can be a sticky situation. The best method is to perform the enrollment over a trusted network (or significantly secured public network). Otherwise, you must manually perform mutual out-of-band authentication between the PKI user and CA.

6. D

Certificate revocation is needed whenever the private key is not trustworthy anymore. This can occur through a loss of the private key (from a system rebuild or replacement), or a malicious compromise of the private key (from an intruder).

7. F

The web server certificate is used to authenticate the server to the client and to encrypt the symmetric session keys used for the authentication and encryption of the data stream.

8. B

   The Diffie-Hellman algorithm is commonly used as an automated method to securely exchange symmetric keys over a public network.

9. A

   Asymmetric algorithms use two keys: one public and one private. The public key can be used for encryption and decryption of data and is sent to any requesting host. The private key can be used for encryption and decryption of data and is kept strictly for the sending host.

10. A

    Certificates are not secret information and do not need to be encrypted in any way. The idea is not to hide anything but to ensure the authenticity and integrity of the information contained in the certificate.

Chapter 26

1. C and E

   Integrity and loss of control are typically terms to describe one's personal life rather than IP telephony security.

2. B and F

   Secure signaling is accomplished through Transport Layer Security (TLS). This security is crucial because CallManager sends the keys for SRTP (which secures the media) through signaling to the IP phone.

3. D and F

   The trusted introducer *and its clients* must trust the root of a system. The root guarantees the identity of the trusted introducer. Only the trusted introducer can guarantee the authenticity of any member of the system.

4. C and D

   In Cisco IP telephony PKI infrastructures, the CAPF has a self-signed certificate because the IP phones refer to this as the CA of the PKI. Only the Cisco IP Phone 7940, 7960, and 7970 (and subsequent) models can have LSCs because these are the only models that support device security at this point.

5. C and F

   Securing enrollment through a PKI can be a sticky situation. The best method is to perform the enrollment over a trusted network (or significantly secured public network). Otherwise, you must manually perform mutual out-of-band authentication between the PKI user and CA.

6. C

   CAPF enrollment supports the use of authentication strings. This is known as the manual enrollment method, which requires the administrator to visit each IP phone he wants to enroll and enter the correct string from the CAPF.

7. B

   The CTL client uses a smart token for key storage. This smart token exists on a USB key attached to the server running the CTL client. The smart token never leaves the key, but, rather, acts as a separate authentication engine to validate the CTL.

8. D

   TLS allows both the server and the IP phone to authenticate each other through a signed certificate. This also allows them to authenticate the signaling message to ensure they came from the correct source.

9. B and D

   Certificates are only exchanged between the Cisco CallManager server and the IP phone. The IP phones themselves do not exchange certificates directly. Likewise, the encrypted transmission of SRTP session keys occurs between the IP phones and the Cisco CallManager rather than between the IP phones.

10. E

    The most accurate list of tasks is to enable services, set cluster to mixed mode, create a signed CTL, deploy certificates to the IP phones, and set the device security mode.

Chapter 27

1. E

   To configure a Cisco CallManager cluster for security, first enable services, then use the CTL Client to set cluster to mixed mode and create a signed CTL. Finally, deploy the certificates to the IP Phones and set the device security mode through the CallManager Administration.

2. A and C

   You must enable both the Cisco CAPF and CTL Provider when configuring a Cisco CallManager cluster for security.

3. A

   At a minimum, the Cisco CTL Client requires the Windows 2000 operating system, and at least one USB port, Smart Card service enabled. It does also function on the Windows XP operating system.

4. A

   Upgrading an LSC on a Cisco IP Phone can be done through the CallManager Administration utility without updating the CTL using the Cisco CTL Client.

5. A and F

   These answers show the valid security configuration options of the Cisco IP Phone through the CallManager Administration.

6. C and D

   When a phone configured for authentication calls a nonsecure phone, the resulting call will negotiate to the lowest-common-denominator, which is nonsecure. Likewise, when a phone configured for encryption calls a phone configured for authentication, the resulting call will negotiate to the lowest-common-denominator, which is authentication.

7. C and D

   You can generate a query using the device name through the Find and List Phones window. The certificate lifetime is not a searchable field.

8. A and E

   You can query based on both the authentication mode and device security mode from the Find and List Phones window.

9. A

   The Cisco 7920 Wireless IP Phone does not support the phone security features.

10. B, C, and D

    All of these communication types cannot be encrypted using phone security. In addition, calls streaming music on hold (MOH) cannot be secured.

Chapter 28

1. B

   The provisioned video bandwidth amounts always include room for the audio payload. The payload for G.711 uses 64 kbps of bandwidth, leaving 320 kbps for the video payload.

2. A

   Cisco recommends adding 20 percent to the requested video bandwidth amount to provide a safe buffer for overhead. 256 kbps * 1.20 = 307.2 kbps reservation.

3. A

   H.263 is the lowest-common-denominator video codec between an SCCP and H.323 device. If two SCCP devices communicate, they will attempt to use the newer (and more efficient) H.264 codec.

4. B

   When using the nongatekeeper-controlled intercluster trunks, the only choice you will have for call admission control is the CallManager Location feature. By placing the local IP Phones and intercluster trunk in different locations, you can control how much bandwidth CallManager allows over the trunk.

5. B

   Within a cluster, CallManager locations control the WAN bandwidth used. This is typically done in a centralized call-processing environment.

6. B

   The H.320 standard is used to stream video over an ISDN network. To communicate with this standard, you must employ a video gateway.

7. D

   Videoconferencing requires you use a multipoint control unit (MCU) to mix the signals. SCCP clients can handle a video call (two users), but cannot handle a conference (three users or more).

8. C

   Far-end camera control (FECC) is an H.323 capability allowing you to remotely control a variety of settings on a video camera.

9. D

   The Cisco proprietary wideband codec offers impeccable quality, but is considered a "LAN-only" protocol due to the whopping 7 Mbps it consumes.

10. C

    One of the major features supported by the Cisco CallManager 4.0 release was video (along with the new IP telephony security structure).

Chapter 29

1. C

   The icon of a video camera on the Cisco IP Phone status line means that the Cisco IP Phone is configured to support video. This occurs when the administrator enables video capabilities in the CallManager Administration utility.

2. B

   Cisco requires you to plug the PC with Cisco VT Advantage client software into the access port of the IP phone. This allows the IP phone to recognize the client PC (and installed software) and enable video capabilities for incoming and outgoing calls.

3. A and C

   The Cisco Audio Session Tunnel is a Cisco proprietary protocol used to signal between the VT Advantage software and IP phone. RTP is used to stream video.

4. E, F, and G

   Only the Cisco 7940, 7960, and 7970 IP Phones (and later) can support video.

5. B and C

   Both the PC port and Retry Video Call as Audio settings are enabled by default. You must enable the video capabilities of the IP phone to support VT Advantage.

6. D

   The gatekeeper always requests double the amount of bandwidth required by the codec to allow sufficient room for overhead.

7. A

   The only camera hardware supported by the VT Advantage software is the Cisco VT Camera.

8. D

   The Cisco proprietary wideband codec offers impeccable quality, but is considered a "LAN-only" protocol due to the whopping 7 Mbps it consumes.

9. D

   The VT Advantage software can stream up to 30 fps. This level produces extremely smooth (TV quality) video streams.

Chapter 30

1. A and E

   Microsoft SQL Server 2000 Enterprise Manager allows you to manipulate the SQL database in many ways. It can be a dangerous tool because it can corrupt the CallManager database structure quite easily. Cisco recommends using the DBLHelper utility, which can quickly verify the status of the database replication and make repairs, if necessary.

2. D

   Cisco CallManager Serviceability provides services to monitor alarms, generate CARs, and collect and analyze traces. All other statements are false.

3. A and C

   The only services that can be managed through the Control Center are those that relate directly to the Cisco CallManager. In this case, the Cisco CallManager and TFTP services are valid choices. There is no Cisco DHCP service, and the Extension Mobility function is controlled as a TomCat web service. Cisco WebDialer is a separate application install.

4. C and E

   The Cisco CallManager services can be activated and deactivated through either the Windows 2000 Services MMC or in Cisco CallManager Service Activation. Cisco recommends the latter of these.

5. A

   The DBLHelper application should only be run directly on the publisher server because this server holds the only writable copy of the SQL database.

6. D

   Because the publisher holds the only writable copy of the SQL database, all configuration changes are prevented until the publisher server is restored.

7. C

   CDRs are the "exception to the rule" of modifying the database while the publisher server is down. In actuality, the SQL database is not modified, rather, the subscribers will write CDRs to their SQL transaction file while the publisher is down and replicate the updates back to the publisher after connectivity is restored.

8. A and C

   Only the publisher server will have a Replication Monitor (which has an image that looks like a heartbeat monitor) utility and will have a Publications folder under the database you are examining.

9. B

   DBLHelper provides an extremely simple interface that holds little risk for damaging the SQL Server 2000 database structure when repairing replication issues. SQL Server 2000 Enterprise Manager should only be used if DBLHelper is unable to repair the replication.

10. C

    A green smiley face means replication is working okay, whereas a red sad face indicates a replication failure.

Chapter 31

1. B and D

   The Microsoft Event Viewer is a Windows 2000 utility that can assist administrators in troubleshooting Cisco CallManager systems. The Microsoft Event Viewer stores system errors and warnings as they occur on the CallManager system, which allows for a historical viewing of any issues that might have occurred on the CallManager.

2. A, B, and C

   Microsoft Performance Monitor does nothing but monitor, monitor, and more monitoring. You can use it to monitor Windows 2000 counters and CallManager counters alike. All events are monitored in real time through a graph, histogram, or report view.

3. A and D

   The Real-Time Monitoring Tool (RTMT) allows you to view the performance of a specific CallManager server, and is geared for CallManager-specific counters. It also offers the ability to send e-mail alerts when the CallManager exceeds specific thresholds.

4. B and E

   The RTMT allows you to save multiple configuration profiles, which allows you to open a predefined set of counters to quickly monitor specific areas of the CallManager cluster. RTMT identifies these profiles by their name and description.

5. A, C, and E

   Cisco designed the RTMT window to allow easy navigation through the various performance counters of a Cisco CallManager server. This includes the support of multiple tabs to allow many different elements to be viewed at one time. The RTMT does provide performance monitoring similar to the Microsoft Performance Monitor; however, it has many distinct differences that tune it to be more effective in monitoring CallManager servers. The Alert Central feature of RTMT offers the ability to send e-mail alerts when the CallManager exceeds specific thresholds.

6. B

   The Application logs of Event Viewer contain messages specific to Cisco CallManager. The System logs contain messages specific to the underlying Windows 2000 operating system.

7. A, E, and F

   The Histogram view provides a bar chart giving instantaneous performance levels for your selected counters. The Graph view provides a line chart showing a history of your selected counters over time. The Report view provides a numerical table with specific counter levels.

8. A, C, and D

The Microsoft Performance Monitor, Cisco RTMT, and Windows Task Manager all allow you to see processor and memory utilization levels for a Cisco CallManager server.

Chapter 32

1. A and C

The **CallManager Serviceability Alarm** menu has only two options: **Alarm** and **Alarm Definitions**. The first allows the configuration of alarms on individual servers and services. The latter allows you to get a full definition of each alarm (and add your own custom notes to the alarm, if necessary).

2. C

The only true statement is that more than one destination can be used to write alarm logs in parallel, and each of them can use its own alarm level. Cisco CallManager relies on the reporting destination to have the proper functionality if e-mail or any other notifications are necessary.

3. D

You can configure alarms for every Cisco CallManager service through the Serviceability pages; however, you must enable Java application alarms through the Windows Registry.

4. A, D, and E

SDI traces log services and run-time events, whereas SDL traces log call-processing information. Both of these traces can be written to plaintext and XML files based on your Cisco CallManager Serviceability configuration.

5. C

The Trace Collection tool alleviates much of the trace analysis function from the Cisco CallManager server. This helps save resources and makes for easier, offline analysis of the trace files. The Trace Collection tool downloads and compresses trace files from Cisco CallManager systems to a computer. You can then use a text editor or the Bulk Trace Analysis tool to analyze the files.

6. C and D

The Trace Analysis tool only has the ability to analyze trace files that are less than 2 MB in size and are in XML format.

7. C

You must access the Q.931 Translator through the web interface of the CallManager Serviceability pages. The Voice Log Translator can be used to analyze log files without access to the Cisco CallManager system.

8. B and D

The SDL trace logging focuses on call logs between IP telephony devices. Naturally, only the Cisco CallManager and CTIManager services will support these types of log files.

9. C

The CallManager alarm levels use the same mappings as the syslog messages. An alarm level 5 is assigned a name of "Critical." The only levels above this are Alert (level 6) and Emergency (level 7).

10. A, B, and D

Cisco CallManager does not support sending alarms directly to SMTP servers (e-mail addresses). It relies on the Real-Time Monitoring Tool (RTMT) to provide this functionality. Cisco also assumes that you will configure the Microsoft Event Log or syslog server to use an SMTP alerting function, if necessary.

Chapter 33

1. A, C, and E

When using CAR, PDF reports are limited to 5000 records and CSV reports are limited to 20,000 records. CAR does have to be installed on the publisher server to work correctly.

2. D

Based on these answers, the only thing CMRs and CDRs have in common is that they are related to each other. CMRs store QoS parameters for the call, whereas CDRs store call details. They are stored permanently in the SQL database and only temporarily in flat files.

3. C

By default, you must log in to CAR using a username and password of admin.

4. D

There are only three types of reports you can reference in CAR: User reports, System reports, and Device reports.

5. A

Actually, the ONLY thing you are able to do after initially authenticating to CAR is to grant administrative access rights to one of the users in the CallManager LDAP user database. All other options are restricted until this step is completed.

6. C

The default restrictions load CDR data only from midnight to 5:00 a.m. This keeps the CDR replication and processing from interfering with normal IP telephony network operations.

7. C

   The CAR and CDR database alerts the CAR administrator by default when 80 percent of the maximum number of rows is reached. At this point, the administrator should consider manually purging the database.

8. A

   The CAR tool allows you to log calls based on the NANP. This dial plan can be modified, and includes an "On Net" classification by default.

9. C and D

   CAR allows report generation in Adobe PDF or Comma Separated Values (CSV) files.

10. D

    Even if the publisher is online, the CDRs are stored on the subscriber server in flat files. These files are replicated to the publisher database during a scheduled interval.

Chapter 34

1. B

   The dependency record capability was developed as a response to quite a bit of administrative frustration in early CallManager versions. CallManager would restrict you from deleting an item because something else was using it, but it would never tell you what that something else was. Dependency records helps track which devices are associated with each other in CallManager.

2. C

   The CCMAdministrator, CCMSysUser, IPMASysUser, and Directory Manager passwords can all be changed using the Password Changer tool.

3. A

   Cisco DNA can be used to analyze and test dial plans in an IP telephony environment.

4. D

   This question uses tricky wording. The QRT reports are actually created when the user presses the **QRT** button. They are displayed when the administrator uses the QRT Viewer.

5. C

   SNMP Version 3 (which is still awaiting standardization) adds support for both authentication and encryption.

6. B

Dependency records are disabled by default on the Cisco CallManager because they can lead to high CPU utilization. To minimize the effect, you can enable them during the off-peak hours.

7. B

The Password Changer tool only functions if you are using Cisco MLA, which prevents the CallManager server from sharing the user database with Windows. The passwords of the specified user accounts are changed in the MLA LDAP directory of all servers in the cluster.

8. C

The Password Changer tool can be accessed from the Run prompt within Windows.

9. C

The CallManager alarm levels use the same mappings as the syslog messages. An alarm level 5 is assigned a name of "Critical." The only levels above this are Alert (level 6) and Emergency (level 7).

10. D

You can access the Dialed Number Analyzer by entering the URL manually or accessing the added icon in the **Start** menu or on the Windows desktop after you have installed it on a CallManager server.

Index

Numerics

A

B

C

D

G

H

I

J-K

L

N

O

P

Q

R

S

U

V

W

X-Z

Cisco Press

NETWORKING TECHNOLOGY GUIDES

MASTER THE NETWORK

Turn to Networking Technology Guides whenever you need **in-depth knowledge of complex networking technologies.** Written by leading networking authorities, these guides offer theoretical and practical knowledge for **real-world networking applications and solutions.**

Look for Networking Technology Guides at your favorite bookseller

Cisco CallManager Best Practices: A Cisco AVVID Solution
ISBN: 1-58705-139-7

Cisco IP Telephony: Planning, Design, Implementation, Operation, and Optimization
ISBN: 1-58705-157-5

Cisco PIX Firewall and ASA Handbook
ISBN: 1-58705-158-3

Cisco Wireless LAN Security
ISBN: 1-58705-154-0

End-to-End QoS Network Design: Quality of Service in LANs, WANs, and VPNs
ISBN: 1-58705-176-1

Network Security Architectures
ISBN: 1-58705-115-X

Optimal Routing Design
ISBN: 1-58705-187-7

Top-Down Network Design, Second Edition
ISBN: 1-58705-152-4

Visit **www.ciscopress.com/series** for details about Networking Technology Guides and a complete list of titles.

Learning is serious business.
Invest wisely.